THE SWEDISH SOCIAL DEMOCRATS

HERBERT TINGSTEN

THE SWEDISH SOCIAL DEMOCRATS

Their Ideological Development

TRANSLATED BY GRETA FRANKEL AND PATRICIA HOWARD-ROSEN

INTRODUCTION BY RICHARD TOMASSON

BEDMINSTER PRESS
1973

Vreeland Avenue, Totowa, New Jersey 07512

Library of Congress Catalogue Card No. 72–94562
SBN 87087–032–7

Published with aid from
The Swedish Council for Social Science Research

Manufactured in the United States of America

PUBLISHER'S NOTE

This treatise was first published in 1941 in Swedish by Tidens Forlag, Stockholm and entitled "Den Svenska Socialdemokratins Ideutveckling." The original text contains numerous footnotes to sources such as newspaper articles, pamphlets, conference minutes, legislation, speeches. This material is accessible only to readers who know Swedish and has been deleted from the English version of the work since the scholars who want to work with it might as well use the Swedish version of this book.

Greta Frankel has translated the entire volume except pages 166–245 for which Patricia Howard-Rosen is responsible.

Contents

Introduction
By Richard F. Tomasson

Every country has its own socialism. . . . Take Sweden for an instance. Like her art, her science, her politics, her social institutions and much besides, her socialism and her socialists owe their distinction not to any peculiar features of principle or intention, but to the stuff the Swedish nation is made of and to its exceptionally well-balanced social structure.

Joseph A. Schumpeter[1]

PROFESSOR TINGSTEN's study of the ideological transformation of the Swedish Social Democratic party from its radical beginnings in the 1880s and 1890s down to the Second World War is a brilliant account of the most successful—by almost any criteria—Social Democratic movement in Western Europe. It is not at all an analysis of the ideas of sophisticated Socialist theorists—Sweden has been particularly lacking in them—but of the changing ideas of the leadership and rank and file as the party became larger and assumed greater power. *The Swedish Social Democrats* is based on what seems to be an almost exhaustive study of the party press, records of the party congresses, proceedings of the Riksdag, speeches and writings of the party leaders, and other primary sources, published and unpublished. Since the work first appeared in 1941 it has been the uncontested authority on the origins and development of Swedish Social Democracy.[2] Now—a quarter of a century later—it is available in English.

Even in this day of increasingly greater emphasis on the comparative study of the modernization of societies, there are few studies in English which provide any kind of detailed account of the Swedish experience.[3] There are only the most summary accounts of the development of Swedish Social Democracy in English. As far as I know the most detailed is the discussion in the two large volumes of Landauer's *European Socialism* which devotes 33 pages (including footnotes) to the subject.[4]

The central theme of Tingsten's study is the dissolution of orthodox socialism of a predominantly Marxist kind which began almost at the time the party became a national organization in 1889. This evolution, together with corresponding developments in the other parties, resulted in an "end of ideology" in Swedish politics in the 1930s. This is a very clear demonstration of the process of "deideologization" which has only more recently come about in the other stable European democracies. By the 1930s the traditional ideologies of conservatism, liberalism, and socialism had become highly attenuated in Sweden and were replaced by a far-reaching consensus politics which accepted democracy as an absolute principle, the necessity of collaboration and compromise, and a predominantly empirical approach to issues. Substantively, there was general acceptance by all of the parties of the essentials of the modern social service state. In his conclusion Tingsten writes that the differences "among the major political orientations in Sweden lay essentially in that they place emphasis on different viewpoints, that each party with particular energy stresses certain of the less actively presented demands of the others parties."[5] This is probably the first articulation of the concept of the end of ideology.[6] And it was a reflection of the situation which had come to prevail in Sweden in the 1930s. It was at this time that Sweden first captured the attention of the world for the effectiveness of her democratic politics in general and, in particular, her comparatively astounding success in overcoming the depression.[7] Marquis Child's *Sweden: The Middle Way* became a best seller in the United States in 1936.[8] And from England in 1937 the New Fabian Research Bureau sent a delegation to Sweden to find out about Swedish politics and institutions of which so little was really known in the English speaking world.[9] Of the Swedish experience at this time Landauer has written:

> The history of socialism knows no more successful combination of pragmatism and pathfinding in economic theory, of caution and willing acceptance of the risk of error, of loyalty to the socialist tradition and realistic choice of the most promising political strategy than the policies of the Swedish Social Democrats during the 1930s.[10]

How stunning the new Social Democratic government's application of the "new economics" really was is reflected in the decline in unemployment from 139,000 in July 1933, to 21,000 in August 1936, and to 9,600 in August 1937.[11]

This end of ideology concept, however, must not be extended to mean the end of class politics. The Swedish political party system has continued to be based on class and occupation to a greater extent than that of most democracies, perhaps more than any other, but its reality has become more statistical than psychological.[12] Under conditions of political democracy and the general security provided by the welfare state, it is precisely economic and class interests which men are most willing to compromise about. Cleavages over religion, language, region, and ethnic group touch the core of men's existence in ways that these issues do not. While the former do not make consensus politics impossible, as the Low Countries and Switzerland show, they do lessen its scope and make it more difficult to achieve and maintain. Tensions caused by the language issue in Belgium or events that emphasize to Catholics the Protestant traditions of the House of Orange in the Netherlands make for a less robust and more sensitive kind of consensus than exists in Sweden.

The political heritage of nineteenth century to twentieth century Sweden was a stable and efficient centralized state bureaucracy which functioned with a high degree of autonomy, together with representative institutions which worked to compromise the interests of the major societal groups. Monarchial absolutism had been only sporadic in Sweden, and it was never as thoroughgoing as in most of continental Europe. Like England, political institutions developed slowly over a number of centuries without any major internal altercations along the way; also, like England, a certain measure of common rights had existed since medieval times. But unlike England and all of the continental countries representative institutions in which even the farmers were represented had existed for centuries, even if they were sometimes disregarded in practice. A particularly important inheritance was the system of standing committees which became well-developed in the nineteenth century for reconciling differences among the Four Estates (Nobility, Clergy, Burghers, and Farmers), a structure which was kept with the transformation to the present two chamber system in 1866. The strong traditional emphasis on achieving consensus within these committees has acted to counteract the divisive effects of the political parties in the modern period. Thus, a mechanism for compromising the interests of different societal groups, was well developed in Sweden even before the appearance of the Social Democrats.

This was a state governed by a small but responsible upper class who dominated the civil service and the Upper House of the Riksdag; the independent farmers were the major element in the Lower House, but they were differential to the civil service and the Upper House. It was a traditional authoritarian state in which parliamentarism was not recognized and only a quarter of the adult males had the right to vote. The monarch and civil service were seen as the legitimate and natural ruling power. Yet a high level of literacy and popular education existed for the time as did a high degree of freedom of expression and freedom of the press, even though they appear to have been little used until the last two decades of the century to criticize the existing social order. There was virtually no attempt by the state to hinder the organization, growth, and activities of the trade union or socialist movements as almost everywhere else in Europe outside of Scandinavia and Switzerland.[13] Tingsten has suggested that as late as the 1880s "no other people with a comparable level of education seem to have shown such a low degree of political interest; only a minority of those who had the franchise for Lower House elections even voted."[14] This can be interpreted as an indication of the relative tranquility that prevailed in Sweden and of the legitimacy of the social and political order. It also reflects her relative isolation through most of the nineteenth century and the lateness of the major disruptions of industrialization and urbanization. The fact that the size of the depressed classes in Sweden—the agricultural proletariat and small farm owners—increased rapidly in this century requires some qualification of this view, but they had an "out" in emigration to America, and caused little political disturbance. The opening chapter portrays the cultural environment and the nature of the ideological debate in the latter decades of the nineteenth century when Social Democracy appeared on the scene.

What is unique in Sweden is that in the course of a generation, from the 1890s to about 1920, we see the rapid and simultaneous development of organized liberalism and socialism, of parliamentarism and popular democracy, and the transformation to an industrial society. Tingsten shows how both Denmark and Norway were more developed than Sweden in the closing decades of the nineteenth century, but how the pace of development in Sweden proceeded more rapidly than in these other Scandinavian countries. I know of no fact that highlights the late development of Sweden more sharply than that there was no nationally organized Liberal party of the modern type until 1902. Perhaps nowhere in the world has the full transformation from a traditional society to an industrial democracy occurred more rapidly. Indeed, all of the criteria proposed by social scientists for successful modernization were present in Sweden in the highest degree. There was long term political unification with a high degree of loyalty to the state, political decision making on a rational and secular basis, a well-developed national administration, an emphasis on performance in the governmental bureaucracy, together with a high level of literacy in a single language.[15]

The central and sometimes bitter place of the battle for universal suffrage during this period with the Liberals largely representing the lower middle classes, urban intellectuals, and religious nonconformists and the Social Democrats the industrial working classes has shaped the traditions of both parties. The Swedish Liberals at this time were strongly influenced by social reformists, democratic, and rationalist ideals, above all those of John Stuart Mill, and rather little by *laissez faire*. The fact that the Liberals, too, were an underdog party enhanced their social reformist and equalitarian tendencies, an orientation which they have continued to maintain, unlike their counterparts in continental Europe.[16] For the Social Democrats the overriding importance of the suffrage issue forced them to concentrate on practical problems and to keep their Marxist ideology in the background. The victory of universal suffrage in Sweden, as in some other countries, was an achievement of the Liberals and Socialists together. The Swedish Conservatives never extended the vote to gain support against the Liberals as the Conservatives had done in England, Germany, and Belgium.[17] The successful cooperation with the Liberals at all levels in the battle for the vote helped to mute their orthodox socialism and enhance their pragmatism. Such cooperation of the Socialists with the Liberals in the years prior to the First World War appears to have been a necessary condition for the steady development of stable democracy and the diminution of class cleavages. It occurred in Sweden, Norway, Denmark, Britain, and the Low Countries. It did not occur in Germany, Austria, and Finland.

The growth and ideological transformation of the Swedish Social Democratic party was very rapid. In the 1880s and early 1890s the party was a numerically insignificant radical sect; after the election in the fall of 1914 it had become the largest political party in the country and relatively one of the largest Social Democratic parties in Europe. In the early years the party adhered to orthodox Marxist views of the fundamental division of society into the bourgeoisie and proletariat, the inevitability of class struggle, the increasing impoverishment of the workers, the increasing concentration of wealth, and the necessary disappearance of capitalism and its replacement by the socialist utopia. All social evils from drunkenness and prostitution to war and the inferior status of women were seen as consequences of capitalism. Tingsten points out how the early leaders of the party were largely influenced by radical international socialist theory primarily from Germany, and not by Swedish conditions, for industrialism had scarcely begun. Most of these early leaders had not read much more of Marx than *The Communist Manifesto.* Their thought was an amalgam of popular Marxism and Englihtenment rationalism. This early socialism must be seen as an ideology of protest of unattached young intellectuals and self-educated workers against the paternalistic and hierarchical social system in which they found themselves. It was late in the day for the existence of such a social order. Everywhere else in Western Europe—even Germany—had progressed farther in expanding the franchise. The young radicals from this early period who lived into the 1920s and 1930s—a number seem to have died young—went through the whole transformation from orthodox Marxism to nondoctrinaire moderation.

The party became nationally organized in 1889, though Social Democratic clubs and unions had already existed in a number of places. It was the first party in Sweden to organize outside of the Riksdag. During the decade of the 1880s radical socialist and liberal ideas gained in circulation and were spread by a number of writers; August Strindberg was the most famous of them. This was the decade when Sweden began to open the door wide to radical thought from Norway and Denmark, England and Germany—influences which quickly undermined the foundations of the old paternalistic order.

Almost from the start the orthodox Marxism of the Social Democrats began to crumble. At the first party congress in 1891 it was decided to support the Liberals in the new suffrage movement. In 1896 Hjalmar Branting was elected to the Riksdag with the aid of the Liberals as the first Social Democratic representative. From the beginning he allied himself with the Liberals and proved himself a good committee worker as did the other Social Democrats who joined him several years later. In 1897 the party adopted its first official program based on the Erfurt Program of 1891. But unlike its German counterpart, which echoes *The Communist Manifesto* in its preamble, it specifically speaks of socialism developing "by degrees." Many of the specific social reforms demanded in the Swedish program such as the eight hour day and a prohibition of child labor were also aims of the social reformist Liberals. That the Swedish party was not strongly adverse to a policy of governmental collaboration with nonsocialist parties was evident as early as 1904 when the Swedish representatives at the International Socialist Congress in Amsterdam abstained from voting for Kautsky's victorious proposal opposing socialist collaboration with bourgeois parties in coalition governments. Yet in the period up to the First World War the party was in terms of its programmatic ideology and its general stance outside of the Riksdag among the more Marxist of the Social Democratic parties, at least when compared with the moderate Belgian and Danish parties.

The period from 1895 through 1907—when universal suffrage in Lower House elections was first passed by the Riksdag—saw a rapid growth in electoral support, and party membership increased from 10,000 to 133,000. The central and overriding concern of the party in these years was the achievement of universal male suffrage in Lower House elections. But after this was accomplished there still remained the problem of equal suffrage in communal elections. In Sweden, county and municipal councils elect the members of the Upper House. Voting in these elections continued to be determined by sharp income and property qualifications which left power in the hands of the rich. Equal suffrage was first passed here in 1918 by a coalition of Liberals and Social Democrats who had entered the government in 1917 forming the first parliamentary government in Sweden to be generally recognized as such. The coalition fell apart in 1920, after which the Social Democrats formed the first wholly Social Democratic government in Western Europe.

The 1920s was a period of minority parliamentarism with the Social Democrats forming three governments totalling about four years. Yet, they made no attempt to realize any of the radical demands in the party's 1920 Program. The party increasingly functioned, inside and outside of the Riksdag, as one democratic party among others. Influences on the party from Germany had become much less at this time and were partially replaced by the influence of the more pragmatic and less ideological English variety of socialism. The party began its long period of political dominance after the Lower House elections of 1932 since which time it has been the only party in the government or the senior partner in a coalition government, with the unimportant exception of the summer of 1936 when the Agrarians took over.

The Swedish Social Democratic party is the only European socialist or labor party ever to get a majority of the popular vote in general elections which it did in the Lower House election of 1940, and the communal elections of 1938, 1942, and 1962. More compelling, however, is the observation that the three nonsocialist parties (Conservatives, Liberals, and Agrarians) have never succeeded in obtaining a majority of the mandates or of the popular vote in any national election since 1934 except in the Lower House elections of 1956 and 1958; the silent support of the Communists has provided the Social Democrats with a functional majority in the Lower House of the Riksdag most of the time when they lacked an actual majority. The Upper House, still indirectly elected, has had a Social Democratic majority since 1941. No European political party in this century has had such long-term governmental dominance as have the Swedish Social Democrats.

A necessary condition for the success of the Swedish Social Democrats has been the high degree of industrialization that came about in the first three decades of this century. By the 1930s the only European country with a substantially larger industrial working class was Britain. In the Scandinavian countries, and perhaps most of all in Sweden, there has always been a very high level of support in the working class for the socialist left. In recent elections for which survey data exist less than 20 per cent of industrial workers who vote support nonsocialist parties.[18] By contrast, for example, a third or more of British and West German workers vote for nonsocialist parties.[19] In Sweden there have never been any religious, ethnic, or regional parties to dampen the operation of class politics as everywhere in western Europe except Britain, Denmark, and Iceland.[19a] The presence of Christian parties throughout continental Europe which have competed with the socialists for the votes of the workers have greatly limited the potential strength of the Social Democrats. Outside of Britain and Scandinavia with their predominantly secular political systems, no western European socialist party other than the Austrian has ever succeeded in obtaining as much as 40 per cent of the vote and a similar percentage of the mandates in a national election.[20] The general pattern in Belgium and the Netherlands, West Germany and Austria is for the Christian party to be the largest party and for the Social Democrats to play second fiddle. Nor has there ever been a Conservative working class tradition as exists in Britain. When Swedish workers vote nonsocialist, they most frequently vote Liberal, barely 2 or 3 per cent vote Conservative. On the other side, the Communists and Left Socialists have never been strong enough to seriously dissipate the strength of the Social Democrats. There have been a number of eruptions from the Left through the 1930s—there have been none since—but they never had much appeal, and the dissidents generally returned to the Social Democratic fold.

The relations between the Social Democratic party and the trade union movement have always been close and supportive—another key to the strength of the Swedish Social Democrats. Most of the organizations which came together to form the Swedish Social Democratic party were trade unions, yet none of the official leadership of the party has come from the unions. There appears to be some correlation between the level of development of the political and trade union aspects of the labor movement.[21] In Scandinavia and Britain both have been highly developed, in France and Italy neither. In fact the rapid success of the Swedish Social Democrats in the years prior to the First World War was largely a result of the success of the solidly Social Democratic trade union movement in organizing and politicizing the workers. Robert Michels claimed that Sweden even at this early date had a higher percentage of its workers in the trade union movement than any other country.[22]

The trade union movement and the Social Democratic party grew up together, yet each has kept its own identity and organizational autonomy. There has been little overlapping leadership between the two, and none at the national level. Few trade union officials have served in the government. There is no union representation as such at the congresses of the Social Democratic party. The relations that exist between them at the national level are informal and nonofficial.[23] Since 1909 there has been no statement in the rules of LO (*Landsorganisation,* The Swedish Confederation of Trade Unions) about any cooperative relationship with the party. However, such cooperation clearly exists and always has from the top level down.

LO members are collectively enrolled as members of the Social Democratic local organization if the majority of the members in a local so vote. Prior to First World War about 80 per cent of the membership of the Social Democratic party was collectively joined to the party.[24] This declined to about 60 per cent in 1945 where it has remained. LO has provided financial support to the Social Democratic press, most of which has not been self-supporting, officially supported the party in its journals, and has actively campaigned for and financially supported the election of Social Democrats. At the top there is an informal council of the party and LO leaders which meets regularly. To symbolize this supporting relationship the present chairman of LO, Arne Geijer, sits as a Social Democratic representative in the Upper House.

LO remains the only major interest group in Swedish society which has not through the years come to adhere to an official policy of political neutrality. The cooperative movement, farm organizations, employer organizations, and white collar unions have all come to adopt such a policy, even if their policies sometimes parallel those of one of the political parties. This supporting relationship together with the institution of collective membership has been a surce of irritation to nonsocialists in Sweden as in Britain and Norway, the only other countries where it exists. Recently, however, there have been signs that there is some opposition within LO to the institution of union locals collectively joining Social Democratic party locals.[25]

Comparatively speaking one might say that the Swedish (and, to a somewhat lesser extent, the Norwegian) Social Democrats have had the benefits of a strong trade union movement without the disadvantages. The trade union movement brought the workers to a high level of support for the party. Yet the party has never suffered from the onus of the British Labour party that it was only the political arm of the trade union movement—which indeed the Labour party was during the early decades of its existence. And, on the other hand, it has never had the hostility or indifference of the trade union as was the case in Germany prior to the First World War. Nor has there ever been the independence between party and union that characterizes the United States and France.

While there is now great similarity in the moderate social reformism of all the Scandinavian Social Democratic parties, their ideological histories have been strikingly different. The Danish movement, even though it was Marxist, was gradualist and accommodating from the start.[26] Unlike in Sweden, craft unionism was well established before the advent of social democracy in the 1870s. The early leaders of the party were largely skilled workers who saw the political movement as a means of enhancing union power. The slow and steady growth of industrialism and urbanism in Denmark prevented the growth of the masses of uprooted workers which occurred in Sweden and

Norway. Rapid industrialization in agrarian societies and the cultural discontinuities it engenders seems to be conducive to radical politics.

Until about 1915 the Norwegian Labor party held to a moderate socialist line similar to that which prevailed in Denmark.[27] In fact the Socialists cooperated with the Liberals to such an extent that they functioned virtually as one party vis-à-vis the Conservatives. However, a rapid industrialization after 1905 resulted in a large number of displaced farm owners and workers. Sweden underwent a similar period of rapid growth in the years prior to the First World War, but the rootless laborers did not comprise such a large proportion of the workers and were not able to turn the party in a radical direction as in Norway. A strong radical opposition developed within the Norwegian Labor Party that was influenced by syndicalist thought and the activities of the I.W.W. in the United States. The Russian Revolution further strengthened this Left Wing—as it did everywhere—and at the 1918 Congress its leaders were elected to the top offices in the party. In 1919 the party accepted the severe conditions of the "Moscow theses" and joined the Comintern. By so doing the Norwegian Labor party had become the most radical socialist party in Western Europe. The moderates broke away in 1921 and formed the Social Democratic party. The Labor party left the Comintern in 1923, rejoined the Social Democrats in 1927, and began to move in the direction of moderation and compromise. The program adopted in 1933 still adhered to a Marxist line and manifested an ambivalence about democracy, but when the Social Democrats began their 30 years in the government in 1935, they behaved democratically and moderately.[28] Not until after the Second World War, however, did the party program eschew Marxism and speak of serving all groups within society. In the party program adopted in 1949 there is not a trace of discussion about class struggle, socialist transformation, and the like.

There are a number of factors which distinguish the development of Social Democracy in these Scandinavian countries from thir counterparts elsewhere, in spite of their different histories. In Sweden, Denmark, and Norway the labor movement developed in an environment of freedom to organize and agitate. The relations between the political and trade union movements have been close and mutually supportive. These countries have had particularly strong radical liberal elements which were democratic and with which Social Democracy was able to cooperate in the early years. In Sweden and Norway, but not in Denmark, the Social Democrats were also later able to establish supportive and cooperative relations with the Agrarians—in Sweden in the 1930s and 1950s and in Norway in the 1930s. Almost everywhere outside of Scandinavia this most culturally conservative of the major societal groups has merged its interests with urban conservatives. This is a fundamental structural difference between the Scandinavian party systems and those of Britain and continental Europe. The inability of the urban conservatives to fuse politically with agrarian interests explains the weakness of the conservative parties in all the Scandinavian countries.[29] In addition, it is only in these three countries where the Social Democratic parties have clearly become the dominant parties and have been so for a number of decades. I am prepared to argue that the value consensus that has come to prevail in Sweden and Scandinavia has been shaped by the double radical traditions of Social Democracy and social reformist liberalism to a greater extent than elsewhere. While the philosophical roots of the two movements are very different, both have been supportive of rationalist, equalitarian, secular, and empirical values. And it is the pervasiveness of these value orientations which have become so characteristic of Sweden in recent decades.

The case of the Finnish Social Democratic party presents a very different picture from those of the other Scandinavian countries.[30] The party did not become nationally organized until 1899, but grew even more rapidly than its Swedish counterpart. Like all of the Scandinavian parties it was very much shaped by German influences. The Russian general strike of 1905 included Finland and resulted in the passage of universal suffrage the following year. The party emerged after the 1907 elections with 80 of the 200 seats in the parliament making it all of a sudden the largest party in Finland and the strongest Social Democratic party in the world. This astounding success was due to the absence of a liberal party similar to those which existed in the other Scandinavian countries. The lack of a sympathetic bourgeois left did not provide the Finnish Social Democrats with an intermediary between them and conservative elements. They did not learn to compromise and to become good committee workers, and being the largest party in the parliament did not result in their shedding their Marxist ideology. Juhani Paasivirta has summarized the behavior of the Social Democratic parliamentary group in the years after their 1907 victory as follows:

> Most of the members regarded criticism of nonsocialist opinions as their most important task, which in many cases resulted in a purely one-sided negative position. The socialist parliamentary activity was marked, thus, by a radical line of class conflict characterized by opposition to all compromise solutions.[31]

Up to the First World War the Social Democrats held to a pure Marxist line with the nonsocialists seen as reactionaries opposed to all social progress. The Russian revolution stimulated the ideological Finnish workers to attempt to repeat the Russian experience which led to the disastrous Civil War of 1918. The Left broke away from the Social Democrats in 1920 and formed the Communist party. The Social Democrats then proceeded slowly toward an acceptance of democracy which cannot be said to have been achieved until the mid-1930s, about the same time as Norway. In Finland, however, it was largely in reaction to the nationalist and near-Nazi Lapua movement and not to their forming a government. The heritage of class conflict remains strong in Finland as evidenced by the persistence of a Communist party almost as large as the French and Italian.

The course of Social Democracy in Germany, the party which so influenced the Swedish party prior to the First World War, is a study of internal conflict resulting from the continued pariah status of the party in a state dominated by militaristic and nationalistic values.[32] It was not really until Bismarck began his repression of the Social Democrats that they turned to Marxism. In 1878 the antisocialist laws were promulgated and the leaders went into exile. Their exclusion encouraged them to turn to revolutionary doctrines. The transformation of the German Social Democrats is indicated by the contrast between the Gotha Program of 1875 and the Erfurt Program of 1891, adopted after the repeal of the antisocialist laws. The Gotha Program, which so stirred the ire of Marx, was a moderate program—it speaks of accomplishing its ends through legal means, advocated universal suffrage, complete civil liberties, and a number of demands for the improvement of working conditions. It was a program designed to bring unity to the labor movement for the purpose of achieving democratic aims.

The Erfurt Program, by contrast, is revolutionary in its first part while in its second part contains a number of short term demands for improving the condition of the workers within the existing order. The function of the program was to satisfy both the revolutionists and the revisionists. Bismarck's opposition increased the isolation of the German industrial working class from the state, and began the great schism between the radicals and revisionists over whether the party should retain its position of revolutionary isolation or cooperate with the middle class without having its most elemental demands for genuinely equal suffrage and political responsibility met. Whereas the Swedish Social Democrats developed in a society with strong traditions of civil liberty, underwent no persecution, and quickly assumed political responsibility, the German Social Democrats continued to be discriminated against by the state, deserted by the liberal bourgeoisie, and denied a place in the government, even after they had become the largest party in the country in the last decade and a half of the Empire. For the Swedish Social Democrats, by contrast, the shedding of socialist ideology was irresistible as they continued to cooperate with the Liberals, to accept more political responsibility, and saw the possibility of entering the government as imminent. The persistence of orthodox and revolutionary Marxism among the German Social Democrats before the First World War was a consequence of the party being denied political responsibility or any foreseeable opportunity of achieving it. This was not the environment to encourage the dissolution of the party's ritualized orthodox Marxism. That this radicalism was only skin-deep, however, is indicated by the unanimous vote of the party's reichstag delegation for the war credits in August 1914.

The German Social Democrats entered a coalition government after the revolution of 1918-19 and adopted its first revisionist program at Görlitz in 1921. By this the radicals had left the Social Democrats and had become the Independent Social Democrats (and later the Communist party). During the Weimar period the party continued its isolation, but was now subject to hostility from both right and left. It was not until the 1950s that the German Social Democrats really made a concerted effort to become "a party of the people" and to overcome the antagonism and suspicion of the Catholic Church and the bourgeoisie, a rapprochement which was clearly achieved in Sweden in the 1930s. This attempt is clearly manifested in the party program adopted at Bad Godesborg in 1959 which goes much farther than any Swedish Social Democratic program in accommodating itself to other groups in the society.[33] The program states that socialism is "rooted in Christian ethics, humanism and classical philospohy . . ." and, later, that socialism "is no substitute religion. The Social Democratic Party respects churches and religious societies." The program also states that the party "favors a free market whenever free competition really exists," and that private property "can claim protection by society. . . ." The much stronger and wholly legitimized Swedish party has never had to go so far to overcome a negative and suspicious image. Indeed, the Swedish party still has May Day parades and a republican clause in its program. That the tables have become turned and the German party has come to look to the Swedish party as a model is indicated by the approving statement in the program that in "several countries of Europe [obviously the Scandinavian countries] the foundations of a new society have been laid under Social Democratic governments."

What a different view of the relationship between the leadership and the rank and file one gets in Tingsten's account compared with the analysis of the German Social Democratic party contained in Robert Michel's *Political Parties* and corroborated by a number of other students of the party.[34] Tingsten shows how the membership forced the leadership to change position on basic issues and how they were a factor in driving the leadership in the direction of moderation. This is true in spite of the fact that Swedish Social Democracy—like German Social Democracy and Social Democratic parties in general—have leaders who hold their positions for decades. The decline in the antireligious line was dictated largely by the desire to increase membership and by the strength of the opposition to such a line within the party. At first the leadership took a wholly negative line toward the temperance movement, but after the workers continued to join the orders, the leadership changed its position. A similar transformation occurred in respect to the cooperative movement. At first the leadership was opposed or at least skeptical, after the workers continued to form cooperatives, the leadership made an about-face.

The Austrian Social Democratic party became the most celebrated socialist party in Europe in the 1920s, even though its accomplishments were limited to the city and state of Vienna.[35] The strong majority position of the Social Democrats in Vienna at this time enabled the party to carry out some municipal socialism, an eight year single track school system, municipal housing, child welfare programs, and other welfare legislation. But this was not consensus politics. There was great opposition to these equalitarian and secular policies from the conservative Christian Social party. After the party established its clerical-fascist dictationship in 1934 the despised party was suppressed. Similar legislation under the Swedish Social Democrats was frequently late in coming because of the slow operation of consensus politics. Take the school reform for example. Vienna had a predominantly secular eight year single track school system in the 1920s.[36] Sweden had a conventional European double track school system until well after the Second World War.[37] The Swedish Social Democrats for all their equalitarian values did not begin to apply them to education until the late 1940s. But when the radical reform of a nine year single track school system did come about in Sweden, unlike in Vienna, it was achieved with a high level of consensus, and little bitter opposition.

The development of the Belgian Social Democratic party was more like that of the Swedish party—after its early radical period—than was that of any other continental party.[38] From the 1890s there was intimate cooperation with the progressive wing of the Liberal party around the issue of universal suffrage which culminated in 1914 in the first popularly supported coalition government of Socialists with Liberals. Their solidarity was enhanced by agreement on questions of Church and State in opposition to the Catholics. The party has always been pragmatic, moderate, adept at compromise, and not very Marxist in its programs. Intellectuals have played almost no role in the development of the party. It was revisionist and nondoctrinaire from the start. An example of the low opinion of the orthodox Marxists for the Belgian party is a petulant remark of Karl Kautsky: "They have nothing to revise, for they have no theory."[39] An historian of Belgian Social Democracy has assessed the party as follows: "What characterizes the Belgian socialist movement is its inclination toward the tangible."[40] One basic difference, however, from the Swedish party was that the unions, at least in the pre-1914 period, were of secondary importance and were clearly the industrial arm of the party. This was true to an even greater extent than in Germany.[41] The same was the case with the important Social Democratic cooperative movement which did not adopt a policy of political neutrality at an early date as in Sweden.

The Dutch Social Democratic party has had a rather different development than the Belgian.[42] The movement in the Netherlands has always been one of the weakest in Western Europe. Prior to the Second World War it sporadically cooperated with the Liberals in and out of parliament. It is difficult to classify the party prior to the Second World War as either moderate or radical, pragmatic or ideological. As early as 1902 the party went on record as not opposing "in principle" the granting of subsidies to religious schools, yet in 1913 when the Social Democratic leaders in parliament were offered some seats in a Liberal government they refused because of opposition from the party congress. During the interwar years the party was isolated in parliament and did not enter any government coalition until 1939, later than in any other western European country. In the Netherlands, as everywhere, the party aided greatly in raising the cultural and political consciousness of the workers, but did for many decades also contribute to the strong ideological cleavages in Dutch society. In this regard the Dutch movement must be reckoned as closer to the German and Austrian than to the Swedish.

In a book recently published in Sweden on the decline of the role of ideology in the successful democracies, Tingsten has used as an illustration the programmatic development of the Social Democratic parties in a number of Western European countries.[43] They have all evolved into democratic parties among other democratic parties and have totally given up orthodox ideas of the transformation of society, the complete take over of the means of production, and the inevitability of class struggle. However, they have arrived at this similarity via very different ideological histories. The Swedish Social Democrats moved from radicalism in the latter part of the nineteenth century to consensus politics in the 1930s. The Norwegian party was a moderate party for the first quarter century of its existence, turned to radicalism, then back to moderation. The Belgian and Danish parties have been moderate from the time of their founding while the Finnish, German, and Austrian parties were strongly Marxist until at least the First World War; the Dutch party was somewhere in-between. While these differences have depended on a variety of historical, structural, and personality factors, the most immediate factor in transforming socialist parties from ideological radicalism into compromising parties of the moderate Left appears to have been cooperation with the bourgeois Left. They acted as an intermediary between the politically immature working class and the conservative elements in the society. Their solidarity against the conservatives most often centered around the battle for universal suffrage and agreement on questions of Church and State. However, all of the recent programs of these parties show an unambiguous commitment to democracy and a near complete disappearance of orthodox socialism.

There are some exceptions to Tingsten's recent suggestion that ideological radicalism is associated with small size and powerlessness, and that the larger and more powerful parties became transformed into parties of moderation the most quickly.[44] The Danish party was moderate even when it was very small, and the large and powerful Finnish party of 1907–1918 continued to be radical. Lipset's view that moderation (in his terminology "stable democracy") requires a party system in which different parties do not correspond "too closely to basic social divisions" seems to be based primarily on the German case and is not tenable cross-nationally.[45] Party and class have corresponded in Sweden as closely as anywhere. Nor can it be claimed with Michels and Lipset that an absence of upper class leaders encourages the hostility of the middle class for working class political parties and inhibits the development of a moderate line.[46] This is based on comparing the German Social Democratic party with the British Labour party. An upper class leadership seems to have been limited to the English Fabians.

In the quarter century since the original publication of *The Swedish Social Democrats* there has been a continuation of the general lines outlined here. In a 1955 article on how the enormous stability of Swedish democracy has led to a certain loss of vitality, Tingsten has proclaimed the disappearance of all the old ideologies and the "growth of the fund of common purpose and the shrinkage of the margin for conflicts, particularly fundamental conflicts." What has happened is that:

> The great controversies have . . . been liquidated in all instances. As a result the symbolic words and the stereotypes have changed or disappeared. All parties emphasize their patriotism, their feeling for democracy, their progressiveness and their striving for social reform. Liberalism in the old sense is dead, both among the Conservatives and in the Liberal Party; Social Democrat thinking has lost nearly all its traits of doctrinaire marxism, and the label of socialism on a specific proposal or a specific reform has hardly any other meaning than the fact that the proposal or reform in question is regarded as attractive. The actual words "socialism" or "liberalism" are tending to become mere honorifics, useful in connection with elections and political festivities.[47]

The loss of vitality is a result of the growth of consensus and of a consequent "movement from politics to administration, from principles to technique."[48]

This account of Swedish Social Democracy ends about 1940 just when the movement reached the peak of its popular support by electing 134 of the 230 mandates in the Lower House, a larger majority than has ever been achieved by any Social Democratic or labor party anywhere, and a majority that has never since been approached in Sweden. This was a combined effect of the stunning achievement of the Social Democratic government in the 1930s, the introduction of a coalition government of the four major parties under the Social Democrats in the previous year, and the marked worsening of the international situation with both Norway and Denmark occupied by the Nazis. The composition of the Lower House from the 1940 peak down to the mid-1960s is shown in the table below.

	1940	*1944*	*1948*	*1952*	*1956*	*1958**	*1960*	*1964*
Conservative	42	39	23	31	42	45	39	33
Agrarians (Center Party)	28	35	30	26	19	32	34	36**
Liberals	23	26	57	58	58	38	40	43
Social Democrats	134	115	112	110	106	111	114	113
Communists	3	15	8	5	6	5	5	8
Total	230	230	230	230	231	231	232	233

* An extra election held in April 1958 after the government resigned.
** One member elected by the Citizens League was refused admission to the Center Party's Parliamentary group.

The coalition government under the Social Democratic prime minister Per-Albin Hansson continued during the war years with power very much centralized in the cabinet. After peace was achieved in Europe, the wartime coalition was dissolved and the Socialists formed a new government. However, they governed with only half of the Lower House, though they had a majority in the Upper House.

The 1944 program of the Social Democrats was made more radical, and after the forming of the new Socialist government in 1945, the party took a turn to the left which expanded the cleavage with the nonsocialist parties. In Sweden as elsewhere, both world wars strengthened the left. The Second World War increased the prestige of the Soviet Union and Communism. Everywhere in western Europe the Communist vote jumped. In the communal elections of 1946 the Swedish Communists got 11.2 per cent of the vote, the highest ever, and the Social Democratic vote fell to 44.1 per cent, the lowest since 1934. In the 1948 general elections the Communist vote fell sharply and the Liberals more than doubled their number of seats in the Lower House, largely at the expense of the Conservatives. After this election the Social Democrats changed course and moved back to moderation and little has been said since about socialization. Yet at this time the position of the government was not as secure as it had been, though it could still rely on a declining majority in joint votes with the Upper House.

After the 1948 election the Social Democrats approached the Agrarians to enter the government to provide a secure majority in the Lower House. They were rebuffed, but did accept an invitation three years later. This second "red-green" coalition lasted until 1957 when the Agrarians stated they could no longer remain in the government resulting in the resignation of the whole coalition government, an extraordinary extra election, and the formation of a minority Socialist government. The immediate reason for the dissolution was the inability of the Agrarians to accept the government proposal for a universal and compulsory pension plan similar to that provided for Swedish civil servants. However, a continuing decrease in the proportion of farmers and workers in the society had resulted in declines in both the Agrarian and Social Democratic vote; the coalition was becoming restive.[49]

This is not the place to give an account of the role of the Social Democrats in engineering one of the most advanced pieces of welfare legislation anywhere, but it reversed the downward trend in the Social Democratic vote of the 1950s and broadened the appeal of the party.[50] The strategy of the Social Democrats was to appeal to the interests of employees—both white collar and manual workers. Their success resulted in a great reversal for the Liberals in the extra election of 1958. After the government proposal was passed in May 1959, however, the Liberals quickly came to its support—they are continually torn in their support for social welfare and their desire to maintain a united front with the Conservatives and Agrarians; the Conservatives and Agrarians reluctantly did so after the 1960 election. In this election the Social Democrats succeeded in clearly becoming the leading party among the white collar workers; in the 1964 election they obtained more votes from white collar workers than the Conservatives and Liberals combined.[51] But the hold of the party is tenuous here, yet more and more this is the group which will determine its future fortunes.

It might be worthwhile to outline briefly what have been the additional major issues and developments in Swedish politics over the past quarter century and where the Social Democrats have stood.

Neutrality and National Defense. There has been a high level of consensus in Sweden over the issue of neutrality which all of the parties accept.[52] Yet in the late 1940s Herbert Tingsten, as editor of *Dagens Nyheter*—the most influential newspaper in Sweden, was the most vocal and prominent of a small minority, mainly in the nonsocialist parties, who advocated Sweden's joining NATO. The official position of the Social Democratic government was the establishment of a Northern Defense Pact to expand Swedish neutrality to include Denmark and Norway. In 1949, however, both countries joined NATO leaving Sweden to continue her neutrality alone. Since this time there has been a high level of consensus on a policy of formal neutrality.

During the late 1950s the traditional stances of the parties emerged over the issue of whether Sweden should become a nuclear power. The Social Democrats, in line with their pacifist heritage, were united in their opposition to any involvement with nuclear weapons. The Conservatives, also true to their heritage of a strong emphasis on national defense, supported Sweden's becoming a nuclear power. The Agrarians, too, supported nuclear weapons, but with more qualifications than the Conservatives. The Liberals, as on so many issues, were divided. *Dagens Nyheter* and a few other Liberal newspapers opposed the noninvolvement policy of the government; other Liberal elements, however, supported the government. This had subsided as an issue by the middle 1960s.

The consequence of these policies of neutralism and noninvolvement with nuclear weapons has been to prevent the kind of eruption to the left that has occurred in the other small western European countries with the easing of the Cold War tensions in the late 1950s. In 1958 a Pacifist Socialist People's Party came into being in the Netherlands which has dissipated the strength of the Social Democrats. In Norway a Socialist People's party formed in 1961 elected two mandates and held the balance of power in the Storting until 1965. The 1965 defeat of the Labor government can be regarded as a direct consequence of the dissipation of 6 per cent of the total vote to this left wing party. In Denmark a similar party came into being, though it broke away from the Communist rather than the Social Democratic party, which has been very successful in appealing to Social Democrats and Radical Liberals and obtained 20 of the 175 seats in the Danish parliament in 1966. As long as the status quo continues on these issues, the Swedish Social Democrats seem to be well protected from this sort of factionalism on the left.

Taxation and Economic Policy. In Sweden not only is there consensus on the need to control inflation, the maintenance of full employment, and the government's role in stabilizing the business cycle, there is consensus on the specific techniques for achieving these goals. About half of Sweden's manufactured goods are exported, a substantial proportion of which are high priced quality goods. Any marked inflation would, thus, be particularly damaging to business and industrial interests providing a kind of restraint almost absent from the American economy and not quite so compelling for most other western economies. The government's success in maintaining full employment has made for a rational labor market policy which has strong support from both employers and from labor—a cooperation difficult to comprehend for visiting trade unionists from Britain.[53] The ingenious methods pioneered in Sweden for controlling the business cycle have been extraordinarily successful and are strongly supported by business and industry. The Swedish economist Erik Lundberg has demonstrated that the Swedish economy has been more stable in terms of variations in the rate of economic growth and in the level of unemployment than the economy of any other highly industrialized society from the early 1950s through the early 1960s.[54] This, together with the jealously preserved independence of collective bargaining from government interference, are areas in which the level of consensus is probably greater than anywhere else. For example, there is a more active consensus here than in either Denmark or Norway.

On issues of taxation there can hardly be said to be any such kind of consensus. Here the Agrarians join the Social Democrats in favoring an equalitarian taxation and the Liberals join the Conservatives in opposition to highly progressive taxation. Taxation in Sweden is more progressive than in Denmark, but less so than in Norway.

Welfare. There is a high level of consensus on the principle of the welfare state. The Liberals are virtually at one with the Social Democrats here. In a less uncertain way than the Conservatives and in a more universalistic way than the Agrarians they support expanding welfare legislation. However, legislation is so thoroughly worked out and compromised in committee that much of it is passed unanimously. The nonsocialist parties frequently oppose the government on the grounds that welfare legislation is inadequate for certain groups in the population such as farmers, part-time students, the handicapped, older people, and so forth. Even the Conservatives accept the great bulk of social legislation passed over the past third of a century. However, they have generally opposed the raising of the child allowances, have advocated the abolition of the allowance for the first child, opposed educational allowances for students over 21, and favored the repeal of rent control.

Education and Religion. One of the most thoroughgoing achievements in the past quarter century has been the radical transformation of the school system. This began with the establishment on a trial basis of the nine-year common school in the early 1950s, and continued with a restructuring of secondary education in the 1960s. Changes in the structure of higher education began in the 1950s, but will be the object of greater changes in the late 1960s and 1970s. Sweden has achieved what is structurally the most equalitarian school system in western Europe. Yet, except as it involves the question of religion, there is no mention in Tingsten's account of education at all as an issue in the fight of the working class for equality. This is because it did not become defined as an important issue until the 1940s.

The past quarter century has seen an increase in criticism of religion and the Church which had so declined in the 1930s that Tingsten emphasizes the mutual appreciation between the Church and the Social Democratic government. In 1951 the Religious Freedom Act was passed realizing old Social Democratic demands, which provided, among other items, for the right to leave the State Church without joining another congregation (which had long been favored by the Church, too), removal of religious tests for holding office, and the establishment of "objective" teaching of religion in the schools. There was also a tug of war between the government and the Church (and within the Church) over the question of the ordination of women.[55] The government won; women are now ordained. There was also a marked increase in criticism of the relation of Church and State which resulted in the appointment of a governmental committee to investigate the possibilities and desirability of changing it.

The temperance article remains in the most recent Social Democratic program and a not negligible minority of the party's delegates in the Riksdag continue to belong to temperance societies.[56] There has similarly been no change in the party's relation with the cooperative movement, the policy of political neutrality continues.

Tingsten's magnificent study can serve as a kind of model of the process of the dissolution of socialist ideology that has occurred in all of the successful European democracies. Perhaps no other study of a national socialist movement so concentrates on the ideological component and deals so thoroughly with the major issues that have confronted all of the European Social Democratic parties. The transformation of the Swedish socialist movement has undergone an exceptionally continuous, clear, and smooth development. But this must be seen as only an aspect of the tranquility of the whole process of modernization that has occurred in Sweden. For these reasons, in addition to its having been the most successful of all such movements, make this study a particularly important and unique addition to the literature of political parties in English.

Richard F. Tomasson

Notes

1. *Capitalism, Socialism, and Democracy,* New York: Harper Torchbook, 1962 (3rd ed. 1950), p. 325.

2. The original title was *Den svenska socialdemokratiens ideutveckling* published in two volumes, Stockholm: Tidens förlag, 1941.

3. Among the studies which deal with the political development of modern Sweden in English are Nils Herlitz, *Sweden: A Modern Democracy on Ancient Foundations,* Minneapolis: University of Minnesota Press, 1939; Dankwart A. Rustow, *The Politics of Compromise,* Princeton: Princeton University Press, 1955; Elis Hastad, *The Parliament of Sweden,* London: The Hansard Society for Parliamentary Government, 1957; Douglas V. Verney, *Parliamentary Reform in Sweden, 1866–1921,* Oxford: Clarendon Press, 1957; Nils Andrén, *Modern Swedish Government,* Stockholm: Almqvist & Wiksell, 1961; and Nils Stjernquist, "Sweden: Stability or Deadlock?," in Robert A. Dahl, ed., *Political Opposition in Western Democracies,* New Haven: Yale University Press, 1966. A volume which deals with all the Scandinavian countries, but has a great deal on political development is J. A. Lauwerys, ed., *Scandinavian Democracy,* Copenhagen: Universitets-Bogtrykkeri, 1958.

4. Carl Landauer, *European Socialism,* Berkeley and Los Angeles: University of California Press, 1959, pp. 437–444, 1537–1554. However, a detailed account of the organization of the Swedish Social Democratic party is available in French: Raymond Fusilier, *Le Parti socialiste suédois,* Paris: Les Editions Ouvrières, 1954. A recent 26 page bibliography on political parties—mostly of American authorship—contained only one item dealing specifically with the Swedish case (Rustow, *op. cit.*): see Joseph LaPalombara and Myron Weiner, eds., *Political Parties and Political Development,* Princeton: Princeton University Press, 1966, pp. 439–464.

5. p. .

6. As far as I know the first statement in English of the end of ideology concept was Raymond Aron's article "Nations and Ideologies," *Encounter,* Vol. IV, No. 1 (January 1955), pp. 24–33. See also Tingsten's article "Stability and Vitality in Swedish Democracy," *Political Quarterly,* Vol. XXVI, No. 2 (April–June 1955), pp. 140–151; Edward Shils, "The End of Ideology?," *Encounter,* Vol. V, No. 5 (November 1955), pp. 52–58; Otto Kirchheimer, "The Waning of Opposition in Parliamentary Regimes," *Social Research,* Vol. 24, No. 2 (Summer 1957), pp. 127–156; Daniel Bell, "The End of Ideology in the West: An Epilogue," in *The End of Ideology,* rev. ed., New York: Collier Books, 1961, pp. 393–402; and Seymour M. Lipset, *Political Man,* New York: Doubleday Anchor, 1963, pp. 439–456, original edition 1960. An analysis of four different meanings of the end of ideology concept partly inspired by Tingsten's writings on the subject is to be found in Ulf Himmelstrand, "A Theoretical and Empirical Approach to Depoliticization and Political Involvement," *Acta Sociologica,* Vol. 6, No. 1–2, pp. 83–110.

7. See Arthur Montgomery, *How Sweden Overcame the Depression, 1930–1933,* Stockholm: Bonniers, 1938; and "Social Problems and Policies in Sweden," *The Annals,* Vol. 197 (May 1938).

8. New Haven: Yale University Press, revised 1938, 1947, issued as a Yale paperbound in 1961. A similarly admiring book was published in France in 1935 and translated into English the following year: Serge de Chessin, *The Key to Sweden*, Stockholm: Fritzes, 1936.

9. Their findings were published under the editorship of Margaret Cole and Charles Smith as *Democratic Sweden*, London: George Routledge, 1938.

10. Landauer, *op. cit.*, p. 1553.

11. Gustav Möller, "The Unemployment Policy," in *The Annals, op. cit.*, p. 51.

12. A phrase borrowed from Robert A. Dahl in *Political Oppositions in Western Democracies, op. cit.*

13. See comparative discussion in Reinhard Bendix, *Nation-Building and Citizenship*, New York: Wiley, 1964, pp. 80–87.

14. p. .

15. See listing of criteria in Douglas H. Mendel, Jr., "Japan Today: Case Study of a Developing Nation," *Trans-action*, Vol. 3, No. 3 (March–April 1966), pp. 15–21.

16. In Italy, Belgium, West Germany, and elsewhere the Liberals have become largely a party of business interests and are more generally conservative than the Christian parties. Reformist, social welfare type liberal parties seem to be limited to the Scandinavian countries and Britain.

17. See Stein Rokkan, "The Comparative Study of Political Participation: Notes Toward a Perspective on Current Research," in Austin Ranney, ed., *Essays on the Behavioral Study of Politics*, Urbana: University of Illinois Press, 1962, pp. 72–80; and David Harris, "European Liberalism and the State," *American Historical Review*, Vol. LX, No. 3 (April 1955), pp. 501–526.

18. Bo Sarlvik, "Political Stability and Change in the Swedish Electorate," *Scandinavian Political Studies*, A Yearbook published by the Political Science Associations in Denmark, Finland, Norway, and Sweden, New York: Columbia University Press, Vol. I (1966), pp. 188–222. See also the election reports published by the Swedish Central Bureau of Statistics. Sweden has the most detailed election statistics of any country in the world.

19. For a discussion of class and voting in Britain, see J. Blondel, *Voters, Parties, and Leaders*, London: Penguin Books, 1963, pp. 56–68; for Germany, see Richard F. Hamilton, "Affluence and the Worker: The West German Case," *American Journal of Sociology*, Vol. LXXI, No. 2 (September 1965), pp. 144–152, esp. p. 151.

19a. Norway has a small Christian People's party, the only confessional party ever represented in a Scandinavian parliament. Finland has a Swedish People's party which is the party of most Swedish speaking Finns.

20. See election statistics in Sigmund Neumann, ed., *Modern Political Parties*, Chicago: University of Chicago Press, 1956, *passim;* Dahl, *op. cit.*, pp. 405–435; and the statistical yearbooks for the various European countries.

21. See Walter Galenson's short book, *Trade Union Democracy in Western Europe*, Berkeley and Los Angeles, University of California Press, 1961.

22. *Political Parties,* New York: Collier Books, 1962 (1915 edition), p. 322.

23. T. L. Johnson, *Collective Bargaining in Sweden,* London: George Allen & Unwin, pp. 23–44.

24. *Ibid.,* p. 28.

25. On April 11, 1965 *Stockholms Tidningen,* until its demise in April 1966 the most influential Social Democratic paper in Sweden, proposed in an editorial that collective membership of LO members to party locals be abolished.

26. See Walter Galenson's comparative discussion of the development of the labor movement in Denmark, Norway, and Sweden in Galenson, ed., "Scandinavia," *Comparative Labor Movements,* New York: Prentice-Hall, 1952; see also Galenson, *The Danish System of Labor Relations,* Cambridge: Harvard University Press, 1952, pp. 1–27.

27. There is probably more on Norwegian politics in English than on the politics of any of the other Scandinavian countries. See, for example, Henry Valen and Daniel Katz, *Political Parties in Norway,* Oslo: Universitetsforlaget, 1964, pp. 12–99; Walter Galenson, *Labor in Norway,* Cambridge: Harvard University Press, 1949, pp. 1–77; Stein Rokkan, "Norway: Numerical Democracy and Corporate Pluralism," in Dahl, ed., *Political Oppositions in Western Democracies, op. cit.,* pp. 70–115; and Harry Eckstein, *Division and Cohesion in Democracy, A Study of Norway,* Princeton: Princeton University Press, 1966.

28. Herbert Tingsten, *Fran idéer till idyll,* Stockholm: Norstedt, 1965, pp. 185–187.

29. Stein Rokkan has pointed this out in "Electoral Mobilization, Party Competition, and National Integration," in LaPalombara and Weiner, eds., *op. cit.,* pp. 241–265, esp. pp. 256–265. See also Seymour M. Lipset and Stein Rokkan, *Party Systems and Voter Alignments,* New York: Free Press, forthcoming.

30. Here I rely on Juhani Passivirta, *Arbetarrörelsen i Finland,* Stockholm: Tidens förlag, 1949.

31. *Ibid.,* p. 26.

32. Here I largely follow the interpretation of Carl E. Schorske's superb study, *German Social Democracy, 1905–1917: The Development of the Great Schism,* Cambridge: Harvard University Press, 1955. This book contains an extensive bibliography on German Social Democracy between 1905 and 1917. Landauer, *op. cit.,* deals more with the German than with any of the other social democratic parties. Three recent works on German Social Democracy are Guenther Roth, *The Social Democrats in Imperial Germany,* Totowa, N. J.: Bedminster Press, 1963; Richard N. Hunt, *German Social Democracy, 1918–1933,* New Haven: Yale University Press, 1964; and Douglas A. Chalmers, *The Social Democratic Party of Germany: From Working-Class Movement to Modern Political Party,* New Haven: Yale University Press, 1964.

33. An English translation can be found in William G. Andrews, ed., *European Political Institutions,* Princeton, N. J.: D. Van Nostrand, 1966, pp. 187–198.

34. Michels, *op. cit.*

35. On Austrian Social Democracy, see Kurt L. Shell, *The Transformation of Austrian Socialism,* New York: University Publishers, 1962; Charles A. Gulick, *Austria from Habsburg to Hitler,* Berkeley and Los Angeles: University of California Press, 1948; and Frederick C. Engelmann, "Austria: The Pooling of Opposition," in Dahl, ed., *Political Oppositions in Western Democracies, op. cit.,* pp. 260–283.

36. For an excellent account of the Austrian school reform, see Ernst Papanek, *The Austrian School Reform,* New York: Frederick Fell, 1962; see also Gulick, *Austria From Habsburg to Hitler, op. cit.,* pp. 544–582.

37. For an account of the Swedish school reform, see Richard F. Tomasson, "From Elitism to Egalitarianism in Swedish Education," *Sociology of Education,* Vol. 38, No. 3 (Spring 1965), pp. 203–223.

38. For a discussion of Belgian Social Democracy, see Landauer, *European Socialism, op. cit.,* pp. 450–481 and 1560–1570; and Val R. Lorwin, "Belgium: Religion, Class, and Language in National Politics," in Dahl, ed., *Political Oppositions in Western Democracies,* pp. 147–187.

39. Quoted by Lorwin, *ibid.,* p. 156.

40. Marc-Antoine Pierson, *Histoire du socialisme en Belgique,* 1953, p. 121, quoted by Landauer, *op. cit.,* p. 468.

41. Landauer, *op. cit.,* p. 458.

42. Hans Daalder, "The Netherlands: Opposition in a Segmented Society," in Dahl, ed., pp. 188–236, esp. pp. 207–220.

43. *Fran idéer till idyll, op. cit.*

44. *Ibid.,* p. 194.

45. Seymour Martin Lipset, *Political Man, op. cit.,* p. 12.

46. *Ibid.,* p. 13.

47. "Stability and Vitality in Swedish Democracy," *op. cit.,* p. 145

48. *Ibid.,* p. 147.

49. Manual workers declined from 58.2 per cent of the labor force in 1940 to 51.3 per cent in 1960.

50. Pensions will be provided at age 67 equivalent to two-thirds of one's income during his best 15 years with generous upper limits. See the English summary of Björn Molin's Gothenburg University dissertation on the politics of the pension question: Björn Molin, "Swedish Party Politics: A Case Study," in *Scandinavian Political Studies,* Vol. I, *op. cit.,* pp. 45–58.

51. See *Riksdagsmannavalen aren 1959–1960,* II, Stockholm: Statistiska Centralbyran, 1961, p. 56; and *Riksdagsmannavalen aren 1961–1964,* II, 1965, p. 93.

52. Herbert Tingsten, "Issues in Swedish Foreign Policy," *Foreign Affairs,* Vol. 37, No. 3 (April 1959), pp. 474–485.

53. Andrew Shonfield, *Modern Capitalism,* London: Oxford University Press, 1966, p. 199.

54. From a lecture by Erik Lundberg, University of Illinois, Chicago, October 1965.
55. See English summary in Carl Arvid Hessler, *Statskyrkodebatten*, Stockholm: Almqvist & Wiksell, 1964, pp. 433–451.
56. An English translation of the most current (1960) program of the Swedish Social Democratic party is available from the headquarters of the party in Stockholm.

The Ideological Debate in Sweden at the Time of the Appearance of The Social Democratic Party

Political and Social Background

THE PARLIAMENTARY REFORM of 1866, which replaced division of the legislature into four estates with a bicameral system, was connected with developments that had taken place in Swedish society subsequent to the adoption of the 1809 Constitution. The nobility's social prestige, its position in the bureaucracy, and its economic position had all been weakened. The importance of the clergy had diminished in conjunction with the advance of popular education, the recognition of religious freedom, and the emergence of nonconformist religious sects. Not all the economic groups that had appeared with the development of commerce and industry were represented by the burgher class; above all, the regulations governing representation did not reflect the true significance of the occupational groups. The urban population was still but an insignificant part of the total national population (13 percent in 1870), but during preceding decades it had grown both in size and in economic strength. Notable changes had occurred in the farming population. Although the size of the agricultural class as such had decreased only slightly (in the early 1800s it constituted over 80 percent and in 1866 approximately 75 percent of the labor force), the number of propertied farmers had declined considerably in relation to the number of unpropertied farmers. A growing agricultural proletariat had appeared; it was composed of crofters, cotters, *statare,** farmhands, and servants. At the time of the parliamentary reform it was estimated that the independent farmers constituted less than one third of the whole agricultural population. It was primarily the growing urban middle class and the independent farmers, who had become a kind of rural middle class with the growth of the agricultural proletariat, that pushed through the representative reform of the *Riksdag,* the Swedish parliament. This was thus an agrarian version of the semidemocratic middle class reforms that had been carried out through peaceful or violent means in a number of countries during the middle of the nineteenth century.

The parliamentary reform did not, however, represent an important step in

* A landless class of married farm laborers with annual contracts but no tenure or prospect of eventual possession of land. [Ed. note.]

the direction of popular government. In the beginning there was no change in law or practice in the relation between monarch and the Riksdag. The king did, it is true, consider the climate of opinion in the Riksdag when selecting his cabinet; on several occasions a parliamentary defeat resulted in the resignation of a cabinet, and there was a patent desire to form a cabinet that could work together with the legislature. But parliamentary practice based on recognized principles did not exist. As a rule the prime minister and several cabinet ministers were high government officials who were assigned to their posts primarily or exclusively by virtue of their administrative merits. The appointed prime minister did not have free choice of his colleagues, even though the monarch sought and often followed his counsel. The monarch claimed the right to personally decide on many important matters. As a rule the cabinet acceded to his wishes, although at times ministers did resign because of disagreement with the king. There was no recognition of joint responsibility for the government—which was not considered as a political unit. The resignation of a cabinet because of difficulties with the Riksdag was not interpreted as a recognition of the principle of parliamentarianism but simply as the consequence of a practical failure. The departing cabinet was often replaced by another of the same political—or apolitical—color. The monarch and his cabinet were primarily leaders of a bureaucracy. In the farming nation that Sweden was at the time, this bureaucracy appeared to be the real source of power of the state and the driving force even in those activities which required the cooperation of the Riksdag.

The two houses of the legislature represented the two leading classes in the society: the upper house represented the true upper class with its core of government officials and property owners, the lower house the independent farmers. The middle class, which had worked so hard for the 1866 reform, was represented in both houses, but was predominant in neither. The character of the composition of the upper house was determined by indirect municipal elections, by stringent eligibility requirements for membership, and by the allotment of votes in municipal elections according to income and property. Although the franchise in municipal elections was far broader than that for elections to the lower house, the upper house therefore became a stronghold for the highest social groups. In 1870, of the 126 members of the upper house, 51 were government officials and high-ranking civil servants (of whom 34 were party officials), 46 were property owners, 28 were manufacturers, merchants, or businessmen. This house had approximately the same aristocratic and plutocratic character as the upper houses in countries where inheritance or royal appointment decided membership. The income or property requirements for the franchise in elections to the lower house (among them a minimum income of 800 crowns) disqualified the great majority of citizens. In the beginning of the 1870s, 22–23 percent of men of voting age (6–7 percent of the population) had the franchise; by the early 1900s this figure had risen to about 30 percent. During the decades immediately following parliamentary reform this category comprised most of the independent and a few of the unpropertied farmers, and well-to-do urban dwellers, including a great many independent craftsmen. With increasing prosperity, other groups—primarily industrial workers in the highest paid occupations—joined this category. During the whole period, however, propertied farmers constituted the majority in the house. Yet even here the proportion of government officials was high. In 1876, of 198 members, there were 114 farmers (of whom 19 were property owners), 48 employed in government service (of whom the majority occupied typically upper-class positions), and 33 engaged in commerce or industry, usually as independent entrepreneurs. The professions and the true working class were practically without representation in the Riksdag until the beginning of the twentieth century.

There were no modern parliamentary parties of the kind that, supported by a national organization, strive to win the electorate to a particular view and act as spokesmen for this view within the legislature. Only in exceptional cases where particularly burning issues were at stake (for example, the tariff controversy in 1887) were elections attended by notable agitation. No other people of a comparable educational level exhibited such a lack of political interest at this period. Only a minority of those who could vote for representatives to the lower house used their franchise. Nor could the upper house boast of more solidly organized, stable parties. The majority, who for a while united to form the so-called Majority Party, was distinctly conservative: the demands for protective tariffs and the strengthening of national defense had stronger reverberations here than in the lower house. Any currents of parliamentary principle that existed here became all the weaker as government policy tended to correspond to majority opinion and a large number of cabinet ministers were selected from the chamber's many public officials and property owners.

During most of the period prior to the turn of the century, however, the lower house was ruled by a comparatively well-organized party, the Ruralist party (*lantmannapartiet*), which, between 1888 and 1895 was divided into the New and the Old Ruralist parties because of differences of opinion on the tariff controversy. This party adopted platforms and established the course for its work in the legislature, but made little impact at elections: without giving much consideration to political questions, the farmers voted for trusted men within their group to be their representatives, and it was only when these representatives reached parliament that they joined to form a party. The aim was to alleviate or eliminate the economic troubles of the farmers (the land tax and quartering of soldiers) and the party was suspicious of any proposals to increase national expenditures—whether they concerned expansion of the bureaucracy or improvements in national defense Certain representatives of the liberal intelligentsia (E. Key, S. A. Hedlund, V. Rydberb) joined the party for varying lengths of time. On the whole, however, the party was definitely conservative: social, cultural, and more far-reaching democratic demands were alien to this agrarian majority. Although the party often strongly opposed the government and at times proposed solutions of current problems, it made no claims to seize government power. This lack of parliamentary ambition was closely connected with the negative, defensive position that was characteristic of the party, but it was also in part due to the social schism that still separated public official and farmer. Characteristically, when the party leader Count Posse became prime minister in 1880, a number of nonpolitical officials were appointed to cabinet posts but not one party member, except for Posse himself. The farmers did not demand positions in the government and felt no solidarity with it; they followed their leader "to the door of the cabinet" but no further. Besides the Ruralist party the lower house included only some loosely organized factions. The democratic and social reformist new liberalism, which was consolidated with the founding of the Liberal party in 1900, had S. A. Hedin as its chief spokesman during the last decades of the nineteenth century.

The praise accorded this bureaucratic and essentially undemocratic regime in the public debate, especially in official quarters, as being distinguished by freedom and self-government can be explained in part by purely historical circumstances. In Sweden absolute monarchy had existed for only brief periods and had never attained the degree of development of several monarchies on the Continent. The system of representation was backed by an unusually long tradition, even if the role of the Riksdag in government had at times been negligible. Swedish farmers had never been as completely suppressed as those in some other countries. Therefore Sweden, like England, had long provided the people with some rights, which were continually cited even if they were not always respected. Further, after 1809 a measure of balance of power in the government and significant civil liberties had been maintained. Compared with the history of most European countries, the evolution of the Swedish Constitution had been characterized by stability and established constitutionalism. The July and February revolutions had not led to very serious conflicts and there had been no upheavals from democracy to dictatorship. Freedom of the press, which was protected by the sanctity of the constitution, was the foremost manifestation of the principle of tolerance toward the expression of political opinions. Local self-government, which had been established by statute before the parliamentary reform, was another expression of the idea of a firm division of rights. Through the spread of popular education, the abolition of legal differences between different societal groups, and the introduction of economic freedom the state had recognized the principle of "an open race to all who qualify." Only significant vestiges remained of the legal barriers between the four states.

The transformation of Swedish society, which was a prerequisite for the genesis and growth of radical and socialist movements, continued in the years following the parliamentary reform. Urbanization and industrialization were the most marked features of this transformation. In 1870, 13 percent of the population lived in cities; by 1900 this figure had risen to 21.5 percent and by 1935 to 35.6 percent. Corresponding figures for densely populated areas were 19.3 percent in 1880, 39.1 percent in 1910, and 51.3 percent in 1935. In 1870, 72.4 percent of the population was engaged in farming and subsidiary occupations; in 1900 the figure had decreased to 55.1 percent and in 1930 to 39.4 percent. Corresponding percentages for industry and the crafts are 14.6, 27.8, and 35.7, those for commerce and communications 5.2, 10.4, and 18.2 percent. In this context the rapid growth of the working class around the end of the nineteenth century should be particularly noted. In 1870 the number of workers employed in industry, mining, and the crafts was estimated at 96,000; by 1880 their number had risen to 137,000, by 1890 to 189,000, and by the first years of the twentieth century to approximately 400,000. The size of the factories grew at the same time, and each factory came to employ more and more workers. Along with the industrial working class a growing lower middle class appeared in the cities, which was primarily composed of those engaged in industry, trade, and commerce.

This development did not mean proletarianization in the sense of a decline in the standard of living. On the contrary, the unpropertied agricultural class, the main source of recruitment of factory workers, on the whole obtained a better economic situation. Yet here, as in other areas, industrialization brought with it the conditions for a socialist movement.

The differences in the political and cultural life in Sweden compared with that in Norway and Denmark during the last decades of the nineteenth century are striking. In Denmark, the Left—representing the radical urban intelligentsia, some industrial workers, and a great many farmers, except for the wealthiest—had succeeded in gaining a majority in the lower house (*folket-*

ing) as early as the end of the 1860s. When the Left demanded parliamentarianism, the conservative government, supported by the upper house (*landsting*) took refuge for a long time in a kind of dictatorship clause in order to preserve the *status quo*. When a parliamentary system was introduced in 1901, it had been demanded by a majority of the people for more than three decades. A Social Democratic party, which exercised a great deal of influence on Swedish developments, had gained a firm foothold in Denmark as early as the 1870s. Conditions in Norway were essentially the same as those in Denmark. The Norwegian Left, whose composition and goals were similar to those of the Danish Left, had predominated in the Norwegian parliament (*storting*) since the 1860s, and in 1884, after much strife with the Swedish-Norwegian monarch, it succeeded in gaining control of the government. An active socialist movement had appeared in Norway as early as the 1850s; after this movement had died out, a more stable labor party was founded in 1886. Political interest on the part of the people in Denmark and Norway was far greater than in Sweden. Participation in elections in Sweden ranged from 20–40 percent but from 40–70 percent in the other two Scandinavian countries. Insofar as cultural development is concerned, we need only be reminded that Danish and Norwegian realism and social criticism largely provided the inspiration for the cultural output in Sweden in the 1880s.

Above all, Denmark and Norway represented greater political activity and a more critical intellectualism than Sweden. In the first place, we should note that at a time when a generally conservative and socially and culturally disinterested Ruralist party controlled the lower house in Sweden, the Danish and Norwegian parliaments were controlled by parties whose views closely corresponded to those of the Swedish new liberalism, which did not become a political force until the beginning of the 1900s.

This situation can to some extent be ascribed to differences in the political institutions of the three countries. In Denmark, the franchise to the lower house was far broader than in Sweden, 14.6 percent of the Danish population enjoyed the franchise in 1861, 15.4 percent in 1881, and 16.4 percent in 1901. This explains to some degree the relative radicalism of the Danish electorate. Before the reform of 1884, the franchise in Norway was even more limited than in Sweden (5.2 percent of the population in 1882), but it was thereafter considerably broadened: in 1894 it included 13.9 percent of the population, and in 1900 19.7 percent. Norwegian nationalism, which grew under the pressure of Swedish rule, probably played an important part in uniting the groups that constituted the Left and in formulating the demand for parliamentarianism.

Of more importance in explaining the differences is the fact that urbanization and industrialization were more developed in Denmark and Norway than in Sweden. In 1870 nearly 25 percent and in 1880 28 percent of the Danish population lived in cities—that is, proportionately almost twice as many as in Sweden. Corresponding figures for Norway in 1875 were 18.3 percent and in 1890 23.7 percent—that is, approximately 25 percent more than in Sweden. The situation has changed with time. During recent decades the urban population in Denmark has been about 20 percent greater than that in Sweden, but Norway's urban population has been smaller than the Swedish. According to the censuses of 1870 (for Norway, of 1875), out of every 1000 inhabitants, 724 Swedes, 455 Danes, and 557 Norwegians in their respective countries belonged to the agricultural class. Corresponding figures for trade and commerce are 52, 68, and 122; for industry and the crafts, 146, 209, and 165. Sweden was thus the most agricultural of the three nations, Denmark was the most industrial, and Norway the most trade-oriented. An equalization has also taken place in these spheres. By the early 1900s Swedish industry was just about equal in importance to industry in the rest of Scandinavia, and disparities in trade and commerce had decreased significantly; according to a fairly recent census the industrial population of Sweden is proportionately greater than that in Norway or Denmark.

It is difficult to obtain precise data on the differentiation within the various occupational groups. It is obvious that the number of independent farmers in Sweden and Norway was proportionately much larger than in Denmark; the total number of independent farmers in 1870 was 202,000 for Sweden and 62,000 for Denmark; the Norwegian total for 1875 was 93,000. Denmark had many large property owners and much of the balance of the agricultural population was composed of those in their employ. The Norwegian agricultural population below the level of independent farmers was far smaller than its Swedish counterpart, but in Norway it was the extremely small, so-called dwarf farms, that predominated. Sweden thus occupied a middle position, with a large number of propertied but not wealthy farmers, and an agrarian lower class that was proportionately smaller than its Danish but larger than its Norwegian counterparts. These conditions can help explain the political differences between the countries concerned. Danish radicalism could have been provoked by the disparities between large property owners on the one hand and tenants and small farmers on the other; radicalism in Norway could have been fed by the uniform poverty among the small farmers. The Swedish agricultural class that was represented in parliament was composed almost exclusively of propertied farmers, a kind of agricultural middle class that was not activated by resentment of the large property owners and which adopted a conservative position in respect to industrial workers and the rural proletariat.

Conflicts within the upper classes have been of central importance for the course of political development in a number of countries, especially in the struggles over liberal and democratic principles. Conservative opinion has been represented by the aristocracy, including large property owners, together with the clergy, public officials, and the military. Democratic movements, on the other hand, have won support among members of the professions—journalists, lawyers, doctors—and within the educated middle class in general. Businessmen have often advocated a liberal line in opposition to those groups which, by dint of birth or public activity, had earlier ruled supreme. Once the wishes of this class of businessmen had been met through reforms, it joined in the defense of the *status quo* against radical social-reformist demands. Among teachers a division often existed between those with higher academic degrees and primary school teachers. These circumstances serve to further clarify conditions as they then existed in the Scandinavian countries.

Sweden lagged slightly behind Denmark and Norway in regard to higher education. The number of students attending universities at the end of the 1880s was estimated to be 66 per 100,000 population in Sweden, 76–78 in Denmark, and 80 in Norway. In Sweden a relatively large proportion of those with higher educations apparently entered government service. In 1880, the number of government officials and civil servants (including those employed at the local level and postal, telegraph, and railroad employees but excluding ministers and teachers) was about 350 per 100,000 inhabitants in Sweden, compared with 280–300 in Denmark and Norway. Denmark had relatively more ministers and military officers than Sweden, which, in turn, had many more than Norway. Comparative figures—the number per 100,000 inhabitants—for ministers in 1880 was 67 for Denmark, 58 for Sweden, and 34 for Norway in 1875; in 1890 the figures for the three countries were 71, 56, and 31. Corresponding figures for officers in 1880 (1875 for Norway) were 57, 52, and 35, and in 1890, 58, 50, and 40.

In regard to the professions, on the other hand, Sweden was far behind the other Scandinavian countries. There were no special requirements for the practice of law in Sweden; legal proceedings were, to a large extent, handled by government officials—a notorious state of affairs that was made possible by the great importance attached to written legal procedural forms. Denmark and Norway, on the other hand, had special associations for lawyers. In Norway, membership in this association totaled 359 in 1876, 495 in 1891, and 682 in 1910. According to the Danish official annals the number of lawyers was around 200 in 1875; the 1911 Census—the first to include this group—reported their number at 1215. In Sweden, lawyers were included for the first time in the 1910 Census, which reported their number to be 386. At the end of the nineteenth century, substantially more lawyers were to be found in Denmark and Norway than in Sweden, and this professional group played a prominent role in the political life of the first two countries, especially on the side of the Left. No source data are available regarding journalists, another significant professional group. Information on the number of persons employed in printing as a whole, however, indicates that the status of journalism and literary production generally was rather low in Sweden. The numbers thus employed per 100,000 inhabitants in 1880 was 44 in Sweden compared with 81 in Denmark; in 1890 the corresponding figures were 62 for Sweden, 125 for Denmark, and 77 for Norway. In 1900 the situation was still essentially the same. Since then, however, Sweden has passed both other countries in this regard, Norway in 1910 and Denmark in 1930. Even though the above statistics must be interpreted with a certain amount of reservation, they surely point to a general trend. The number of physicians in Sweden was and still is very low. In 1900 there were 24 physicians per 100,000 population in Sweden compared with 59 in Denmark and 39 in Norway.

Two additional circumstances should be noted. As already mentioned, the class of large property owners was most marked if not most numerous in Denmark. In contrast, the Swedish nobility, which still enjoyed considerable social prestige and acted partly as a rural aristocracy, partly as a factor in the bureaucratic machinery and officers' corps, was far more numerous than the Danish. In Norway there was no indigenous nobility. General data concerning the different branches of industry show that in Sweden the proportion of the upper and middle classes engaged in industry and commerce constituted a negligible part of the total employed in these occupations. We encounter special difficulties in trying to compare the number of teachers. Specific data for Sweden are available only for primary school teachers; in 1880 their number was about the same as in Norway. At the same time the total number of teachers was considerably higher in Denmark than in Norway: 388 per 100,000 population in Denmark in 1880 compared with 285 in Norway in 1875. It is therefore probable that there were fewer teachers at different levels in Sweden than in Denmark and that popular education was generally less developed in Sweden.

Even though these statistics may be incomplete and, in several cases, somewhat unreliable, they nonetheless provide some insight into the situation in Scandinavia at the time and even into the subsequent developments. Sweden was the most markedly agrarian nation. The upper classes were relatively well represented among government employees in relation to those engaged in the professions, especially journalism. On the whole, Sweden at the time represents an earlier stage of development. The character of Swedish society was reflected in the parliament, where one house was dominated by propertied farmers, the other by owners of large estates and by government officials. In the latter part of the nineteenth century and beginning of the twentieth, Sweden took the lead over the other Scandianvian countries. The pace of urbanization, industrialization, commercialization, and cultural development was faster in Sweden. When the Social Democratic party made its appearance in the 1880s, however, the conditions necessary for its rapid growth were as yet not present. Inspired by foreign—primarily Danish and German doctrines—this movement made its appearance in Sweden too early. It was not supported by a background of general democratic and cultural radicalism as were its counterparts in Denmark and Norway. Not until the consolidation of liberalism that occurred around 1900 did Sweden get a large party of the kind that had for decades represented the reformist spirit in the other Scandinavian countries. It drew to it representatives of the urban intelligentsia, certain workers' groups that were as yet nonsocialist, the growing middle class, and a large proportion of less well-situated farmers. Democratic, liberal, and social reformist ideas as well as the demands pressed by special popular movements—sectarianism and temperance—were the rallying points. The leaders—many of whom had been members of the Verdandi student group in the 1880s—were often lawyers or journalists.

But the new liberalism arrived late and its sway was short-lived. After only a few decades, once democracy had been realized through the cooperative efforts of New Liberals and Social Democrats, socialism took the leading role; although this socialism was ostensibly clearly opposed to liberalism on principle, it had lost some of its original radical bite during its climb to power. Thus Sweden, which advanced from an agrarian to an industrial stage within a relatively short period of time, had a shorter liberal transition than the other Scandinavian countries.

The Ideas Propagated by State Institutions

IN DETERMINING which general ideas entered into opinion formation during a certain period, the ideas disseminated by the organs of the state at public expense form a category of their own. Not that they are necessarily predominant or even greatly influential; in many instances ideas other than those fostered by state organs have been the most seminal among the people, and—to use French terminology—an antithesis has existed between "the legal community" and "the real community." But "official" ideas are of particular interest not only because they are upheld or at least avowed by certain ruling groups, but also because they are efficiently disseminated among the people, regardless of whether they evoke an enthusiastic or critical reaction.

Naturally, in the constitutional and liberal Sweden we are now dealing with, official attempts to sway opinion did not have the same character as those demonstrated in certain early or recent authoritarian regimes. The principles of freedom of thought and speech, of tolerance toward different opinions, were constantly invoked. The state did not deliberately and systematically conduct political and social propaganda. No officially proclaimed political ideology existed. A wide gulf separates this order from one where all authorities and all educational agencies must disseminate the ideas established by the rulers and where every facility to influence opinion is drawn into the state's sphere of power.

However, it is incontestable that certain institutions exercised or sought to exercise influence on the political opinions of the people. The schools and the universities, in principle dedicated to education and research, became to some extent agencies for the propagation of set value judgments. The church, whose true mission was the promulgation of religious doctrine, also became occupied with the molding of opinion in entirely different fields, albeit within comparatively narrow limits. The opinions advanced by the bureaucracy also carried weight. They will be dealt with in another context inasmuch as they were not directed toward the public in the same manner.

A report delivered in 1887 concerning textbooks for use in primary schools gives a clear and illuminating account of the viewpoints that determined the content of such books. In regard to readers, the report underscored as self-evident the understanding that the books contain no suggestions of outlooks that deviated from Christian ethics. Instruction in Swedish history should "give a comprehensive and fully objective picture of the process whereby our people under God's guidance have gradually developed within themselves and in their relation to other people." Knowledge thus gained "would tend to have an ennobling effect on will and character . . . to revive love of one's native land; to stir and nourish the proper spirit of citizenship; to sharpen the observation of an inner conformity to law, as also revealed in mankind's trend toward freedom, and consequently [the observation] that the history of a people does not merely comprise accidental events independent of one another, but that in and behind everything lies a deep, inner coherence and a higher order; and finally to direct the will toward that which is truly great and noble and good."

These statements may hardly seem remarkable, but they suggest elements that figured significantly in education and, in effect, imparted to it a generally conservative character. A review of primary school texts of the period clearly reveals this conservatism. The view of life according to Christian ethics did not merely pervade religious instruction, which occupied a tremendous part of the curriculum, but all school subjects. The readers contained mainly narrations with a moral, glorifying the virtues of self-denial, contentment, steadfastness against worldly temptations. All instruction was suffused with an idyllic, patriarchal sentiment suggestive of a political and social quietism. History books were nationally and religiously colored to instill reverence for the Swedish Lutheran State Church, appreciation of the genuine unity of the Swedish people and their national past as well as respect for the established order. In accordance with the predominant viewpoint of historical research, the course of events was described as imperative and morally precious and, in the last analysis, as ordained by God. Political history dominated; cultural and, to an even lesser extent, social trends received scant mention; nothing was said about the breach in the relations between the different social classes. A discriminating analysis of the differences between the education of that day and today would be difficult to make and cannot be undertaken here. But there is no doubt that a mainly conservative philosophy was well represented in the primary schools of the period.

The same remarks are largely applicable to the secondary schools (*'läroverk'*). Besides the customary readers, the textbooks commonly used in history, Christianity, and philosophy demonstrate this. Even though the history texts evince an effort to attain objectivity, they bear the stamp of the prevailing basically conservative, constitutional, and antidemocratic principles. Their treatment of the liberal period in Sweden (*frihetstiden*) and of the Enlightenment in Europe is somewhat disparaging. The *coup d'etat* of 1772 is represented as a necessary reaction by the royal power, the Constitution of 1809 as a happy middle road between extremes; the socialist attempts to revolt in France in 1848 and 1871 are, however, condemned. Little or no attention was given to contemporary social questions and modern popular movements. The short accounts of socialism and communism given in the most widely used textbook on modern history is obviously misleading. The teaching of history in the secondary schools was obviously by and large intended to stimulate Swedish nationalism and Lutheran distrust of Catholicism. However, whereas history texts did not give explicit political directives, these did occur in texts on Christianity. The text on church history used around 1890 discussed socialist theory, primarily that advanced by Owen. It held that a socialist society could not be realized, and, furthermore, that it would aim at supplying only material needs. "All higher desires in man will be suppressed and only the baser desires occupied with worldly things will be allowed to develop. . . . From this it would naturally follow that each individual would want to work as little as possible and enjoy himself as much as possible, which, in turn, must call forth discord and antagonism. . . . Mutual love . . . must evaporate in the socialist corporation built on selfishness." In another contemporary history of the church, socialism was denoted as "this grossly materialistic, equally socially subversive, anticlerical, and anti-Christian teaching." In an ethics text later in use, Christians were declared to be duty-bound to willingly obey the authorities under all conditions. Estates and classes were "like limbs in the social organism"; the influence of each class would correspond to its contribution. At this juncture a detailed polemic was leveled at socialism. Socialism wanted to overthrow all existing society, including the institutions of the family and matrimony. No true state power would exist. A socialist order "would lead to a war of each against all, to the most insufferable suppression of every individual freedom, to the annihilation of all higher interests in life, to the ruination of humanity in every respect. . . . Socialism has become a sort of religion, which its followers blindly believe in with an enthusiasm and fanaticism that does not shun any means, not even the most criminal and brutal. . . . Their horrible zeal and overwhelming energy apparently stem from the powers of darkness." Socialism was also described as "a scourge from God upon a terrified civilization, a sentence of punishment from the Lord upon a degenerate Christendom." "Religious-ethical regeneration" was the only remedy.

In regard to university teaching, certain inferences may be drawn from the works published by representatives of the social sciences, such as practical philosophy, political economics, history and political science. In general, it may be said that scientists in disciplines purported to establish certain rules for human communal life, that they evolved a dogmatic certainty that would appear preposterous to the researcher of today and would not even impress the general public. For one, there was no relativity of values; there was no attempt to distinguish between empirical inferences and value judgments. For another, the methods used lent themselves to the formulation of the most rigid assertions without any empirical bases. Philosophers, proceeding from metaphysical postulates, lectured on the inexorable duties of the state and the individual; economists spoke of natural laws that had to be followed; political scientists prescribed how royal power should be constituted and how suffrage should be weighed in relation to the constitution, which was founded on true insight. In this way science and politics converged. Subjectivity was regarded as far more natural and was far less inhibited than in a later period of more reflective and relativistic thought.

The philosophical "Boström school" that remained predominant in Sweden decades after the death of Boström (1868), has been characterized as an ideal philosophy of bureaucrats. Boström regarded the state as a personal entity, "an organ for higher, rational entities and, ultimately, for the absolutely highest—religion—that is, the divinity considered as the absolute, highest regent or Providence and savior of all rational beings." The goal of the state, to uphold justice, could only be attained in a monarchy; the "true" state "is monarchic, for otherwise the public (the law) would not be able to appear as independent in relation to the private." The state itself consisted of personal entities such as the estates and the family. In view of this an authentic representative body must be established. To Boström this meant a Riksdag based on the four estates. The bicameral system was not a truly representative system, for it was not based on genuine organizations within the estate but was "something purely empirical and irrational." The theory of the state as an organism also provided grounds for criticism of all parliamentary and democratic tendencies. These thoughts were amplified by Boström's disciples, such as Edfeldt Nyblaeus, Sahlin, and Aberg. Constitutional monarchy was designated as the only polity that was philosophically sound. Government through parties was condemned as implying "that the government itself is partial to a certain social class and uses its power for the differential promotion of its interests." The monarchy and the administration, it was stated, simply represented the interest of the state against special interests.

This constitutional conservatism, however, constituted no more than an interesting sidelight in the political attitude of the Boström school. It is more significant to note that because of its extreme idealism this school generally tended to veil social realities, thereby erecting a barrier against radical and reformist movements. There was discussion on the concept of the state, the concept of the estates, the concept of the family; but there was no attempt to find out which interests really found their expression in the state government or in the legislature, or to discover in what measure the family, under the prevalent conditions, corresponded to the ideal attributes assigned to it. Underlying the constantly asserted organism analogy was the notion of harmony between the various parts of society; the estates or classes were regarded as limbs of the social organism and as having definite functions and conditions vital to their existence. Whether, in reality, such harmony existed was a question of no philosophical interest. That which merely existed in reality and not as an idea was just "purely empirical and irrational." In this way the dominant philosophy was made into a coulisse of suggestive conceptions joined to form an elaborate pattern that concealed personal interests and social struggles.

Political science and political history of the time revealed the strong influence of the Bostöm school, though not a corresponding doctrinaire unity. The general conservative tendency is nevertheless plain. Characteristically, several well-known scientists in these fields, such as Alin, Blomberg, Boëthius, Fahlbeck, Hjärne and Kjellén, appeared at the turn of the century as militant representatives of an outlook that was fundamentally conservative, though tempered in some cases by social reformist and, to a certain extent, by democratic views. Of particular interest in this context is the fact that as a rule these authors clearly expressed their political convictions in works that apparently were regarded as strictly scientific. They believed they could prove scientifically, for example, the necessity of royal power, the fallacies in parliamentarianism and the party system, the propriety of restricted suffrage, or suffrage graded according to income and property, and the absurdity of socialist demands.

In the 1850s the study of political economics, which was relegated to a very modest position in the curriculum of Swedish universities at the time, was chiefly concerned with the subject of liberalism, primarily as expounded in French literature on economics. J. W. Arnberg, H. Forssell, G. A. Hamilton, and C. G. Hammarskjöld were among the foremost exponents of economic liberalism. Among its basic principles were belief in free competition and in its power to promote the common weal, belief in the value of free trade, even in international commerce, and a concomitant distrust of sociopolitical reforms that might restrict freedom of economic activity. In the following we shall return to the formulation of liberal ideas during the debates of the 1870s and 1880s. In the 1880s, certain economists, such as J. Leffler and P. Fahlbeck, influenced particularly by German official socialism and by the social policies of Bismarck began to adopt a different orientation; they advocated both protective tariffs, and social reformist measures that were conservative in spirit.

It may be assumed that the state institution whose activity exercised the greatest influence on popular ideology at the time of the emergence of the Social Democratic movement was the church. The great mass of citizens belonged to the state church even after they had been given the opportunity to leave it. It is true that church services and religious life had already lost some of their significance through industrialization and immigration to the cities. However, at this time the church still occupied a central place in society in a different way than it would later on. For this reason, and because of the intensely antichurch and antireligious stand of the emergent Social Democratic movement, it is important to examine the position of the church on questions political and social. The material for this study has been drawn from collections of sermons published 1867–1890 (numbering between 30 and 40), from clerical publications, from the paper *Väktaren* (*The Sentinel*), and from pastoral letters, the minutes of clerical meetings, etc.

The gospel directly promulgated by the church contained elements that tended to foster a conservative outlook. If life on this earth is regarded merely as a preparation for the next life, in which virtues overlooked on earth will be rewarded and the iniquity that has triumphed here will be punished, then the superficial circumstances of success and failure, wealth and poverty, will seem less important. The kingdom of heaven may serve the poor as a substitute for a political utopia. This is connected with another idea that was also constantly preached by the clergy. Even if individual freedom of will is accepted, temporal conditions are by and large ordered in accordance with God's will. Attacking the established order consequently implied criticism of God's work.

The clergy based its political propaganda on this train of thought. First of all, churchmen uniformly stressed the duty to be loyal and obedient to authority. A few representative examples must suffice to illustrate this political sermonizing. One of the most widely disseminated collections of sermons of the time declared that a good Christian was always a good citizen "who renders unto the powers that be that which is their due. . . . It is true that common sense tells us that the reasonable commands which stem from authority ought to be obeyed if this land is to be happy; yet the teaching of Jesus places this concern in a much clearer light, in that it commits us to this by virtue of God's own command, through which the laws of the authorities indirectly become the laws of God Himself." Christianity "is the surest fundament for both the faith of the rulers and the advancement and security of the subjects." Another collection proclaimed that "the establishment of the authority cannot be anything but good, for God cannot do anything that is not good. . . . Thus a person who says he is searching for the kingdom of God but will not humble himself to be obedient to the whole human order and to visible authority cannot be secretly humble toward the Spiritual Father either, and in the measure that disobedience and insubordination prevail against the human order [sanctioned] by God will he prevent God's Gentle Spirit from entering into his heart. Therefore, for him who seeks the kingdom of God it is a good and glorious practice to be submissive to the human order for the sake of Our Lord." Thus did the men of the cloak take a stand on constitutional and political problems in their fundamentally religious promulgation. The established regime, and the autonomous power of the throne in particular, were described as the works of God. The national state and nationalist aspirations were similarly endowed with the sanction of religion.

A similar structure of ideas prevailed in regard to social and economic questions. Human society with its class differences, its poverty and need, was the work of God. A fairly amply differentiated defense of the *status quo* was constructed on this premise. One of the basic ideas evolved was that social groups and private individuals constituted the limbs in an organism that was in accordance with nature and therefore sanctified by God. This idea was related to age-old conservative concepts that had been refined to the point of perfection by Catholic theorists during the Middle Ages.

The posthumously published sermons of Archbishop Reuterdahl refer time and again to arguments basic to this kind of thinking. God ordains the temporal conditions of human beings, and all men ought to be content for this reason alone. Further: man's external circumstances are of no value from a loftier, spiritual point of view—at times they may even be dangerous—and are of scant importance to temporal happiness as well. If this happiness can really be affected by social circumstances it is because man's sense of contentment diminishes with wealth and success.

> Many times even the most ardent endeavors on this earth cannot banish need and misery, which shows that even worldly goods are not determined by man alone but rest in the hands of God, and that it is from these hands that crumbs of [worldly goods], now larger, now smaller, devolve to the people. . . . Humbly the Christian submits to the conditions prescribed for him and assumes the lowly rather than the lofty lot in the worldly order. . . . *The Christian holds that the inequalities, the privileges, and the defects that occur in the world are not essential.* What does it matter if we eat a meagre piece of bread by the sweat of our brow or if we have acquired riches and plenty? Do you think that the one who is high and mighty lacks troubles and work? Then walk into his castle and look at him in his solitude and you will find anxiety in his eyes and cares in his heart and strivings and struggles in his life. Do you think that the lowly and poor have no joy or peace? Then look in on the lowly

> and poor, who know the sole high and mighty [one] in heaven and on earth, and you will find that the lowly hut is not lacking in joy nor the humble cottage in peace. Yes, even if one place should contain some more suffering, some more work, some more struggle than another, what of it? . . . It is not so easy to tell which duty is the heaviest, that of the superiors or that of the subordinates. The subordinates commonly think that they are the hardest pressed, the most distressed. . . . But if the subjects saw and understood all that weighs upon their righteous and earnest masters, if the beggar wandering with his staff saw and understood all that troubles the commander with his fasces, yes, carrying high a royal sceptre, then the former would not wish to change places with the latter. . . .

These lines of thought or variations thereof were expressed in more or less clear and vigorous terms in most of the instructional literature of the time. A clergyman wrote: "God has arranged it so that there shall be a difference in status among the people, higher and lower statuses, in the same way as He has ordained that there shall be both rich and poor in the world." Discontent with the wordly status was discontent with the decision of God. "A human sower tries to distribute the seed as evenly as possible on the field. God acts quite differently when He, by His hand, sows His temporal gifts on the field that is this earth, among them all worldly possessions. He sows these unevenly, thickly on some strips, sparsely on others. The enlightened eye recognizes both wisdom and love in this, whereas many men of the world are not only puzzled by the ways of God but also bitterly denounce them in their hearts." From the viewpoint of eternity a desirable worldly status involved constant temptation. Riches and success were traps that enticed man to overrate the importance of life on earth and thereby diminish the prospects of happiness in heaven. On the other hand, poverty, correctly understood, is beneficial to spiritual, religious development and thus furnishes great possibilities for salvation. "It is namely reasonable and confirmed by experience, as if grounded in the nature of things, that those who have emotions that are not smothered by life's pleasures and vain solicitudes would more willingly follow the invitation to seek treasures in another, eternal world, and that those so dissatisfied with the physical conditions of their lives would sooner feel and sincerely acknowledge the deficiencies of their inner life." When God "tests His children through some corporeal distress, this is done in order to preserve their true happiness and welfare. Because as He observes that their success and temporal joy would attract them into the world and its multitude of things, thereby injuring their spiritual life, perhaps even causing them to fall out of grace, then He imposes upon them a cross. They thereby become more and more liberated from the bonds that tie them to the earth and become schooled for heaven." Therefore those who are rich in a mundane sense are poor in a higher sense and those who are poor in a mundane sense are rich from the perspective of eternity. The distinction between riches and poverty in a false, or vulgar sense, and in a true, or metaphysical sense, was drawn throughout.

The views just outlined appeared to dominate clerical pronouncements on political and social conditions from the time of the reform of the legislature to about 1890. There is no doubt but that the promulgations of the clergy constituted a conservative force of the first order. This conservative influence was exerted indirectly in the teaching that the established order was a reflection of God's will and that earthly existence was of minor importance, and directly in exhortations to be content and in criticism of social-radical demands. This is not contradicted by the clerics' exhortations to the rich to be kind and charitable and their frequent initiatives in various kinds of relief measures. Nor is the total picture changed by the fact that some clergymen called for improvements in relief work and swayed their congregations to this view. We should note, however, that certain clerical statements of this period did depart from the general picture described. While most clergymen were content to sanction the *status quo* in conventional religious terms, some disclosed—without asserting or intimating radical opinions—a tragic sympathy with the difficulties of the social problem and a deep desire to find a solution that would both agree with the traditions of the church and with human compassion. In Rudin's sermons of the early 1870s, for example, the usual exhortations to the rich to provide for the poor reveal a pathos, a personal ardor that are not found in the sermons of many of his colleagues. Another case in point are the sermons of Wikner, which evince the same sentiments, although they also manifest scepticism about the prospects of in any way reducing the disparity between "earthly destitution and earthly happiness" that he saw everywhere.

In the foregoing we have touched upon clerical statements that were made prior to the appearance of socialism, or that, in any case, did not directly address themselves to the relation between Christianity and the labor movement. We shall now explore documents that are directly concerned with this relationship. In the main, these documents belong to a somewhat later period, the end of the 1880s and the beginning of the 1890s.

Two schools of thought distinguished the clerical discussion on socialism. On one hand, Social Democracy was attacked as revolutionary, atheistic, and materialistic, as well as inimical to social tenets sacred to Christianity, primarily the right of private ownership. On the other hand, socialism heightened the church's perception of social wrongs; churchmen placed more emphasis on the duties of the upper classes to the lower classes and called for public measures in addition to private charity. Frequently the two schools merged into a social-conservative outlook that, differentiating it from Social Democracy, is called Christian socialism. Influences from earlier French and English Christian socialism seem to have been nugatory in shaping these thoughts. On the other hand, the Christian Socialist movement in Germany at the end of the century made an obvious impression. Catholic social conservatism, sanctioned and stipulated in the encyclia of Leo XIII of 1891, also seems to have stimulated the social interest of Swedish Lutherans.

In 1875 a publication in Swedish written by the Danish Bishop Martensen, a famed theologian, appeared under the title "Socialism and Christianity." Here we encounter the Christian Socialist ideas that did not gain currency in the Swedish church until around 1890. Socialism in the usual sense was sharply criticized. Poverty was held to be the inevitable consequence of sin, and was thus in conformity with the decree of Providence. But in addition, Martensen advocated an "ethical socialism" of a conservative and antirevolutionary brand, designed to help the workers obtain a secure existence and to assimilate them gradually into the middle class. He recommended not only self-help, but also sociopolitical measures, such as a state-established minimum wage. Martensen's general views reverberated not infrequently in the Swedish debate.

Around 1880 we encounter a few tracts in Swedish, written by Swedish clerics, that dealt with the attitude of the church toward socialism. In an address delivered in the city of Karlskrona in 1878, a Reverend Wollin expounded opinions highly reminiscent of Martensen's. "Socialism is an interesting as well as a terrible phenomenon and deserves sympathy as well as disgust." It was valuable in "that it arouses and incites the worthy forces of society to recognize the misery and danger of pauperism and to work for its eradication." The foremost remedy would be the injection of a Christian spirit into the relationship between employer and employed. But certain social-political reforms were also conceivable, such as supervision of conditions in factories and workers' living quarters, and profit sharing. Another clergyman, the Reverend Kronblad, adopted a strictly negative line in a tract issued in 1881. Socialists were pictured as a horrible cosmopolitan gang that denied the existence of God, rejected religion and the fatherland. The bulwark against socialism was Christianity. "A Christian is the most faithful subject and summons all others to be loyal to authority." In this capacity Christianity should engender sympathy in all who wished to protect the existing order." Inasmuch as Christianity now is . . . the preservative element in society, without which the people would certainly ripen for socialism, it is incumbent upon all good citizens and patriots to feel preeminently called to contribute with all diligence and might toward the correct evaluation of this protection, toward its ever more widespread use and ever more forceful assertion in both private and public life." The subject of socialism was broached at a clerical meeting for the first time in 1884 when the Reverend (later Professor) S. L. Bring lectured in Lund on the question whether socialism could in any way be justified from a Christian point of view. Bring's answer was in the affirmative. He affirmed society's obligation to provide for the temporal necessities of the individual. It would not be possible to have the state as employer, or to have the workers share in profits, but social measures could make the workers more secure. Yet socialism was also at variance with Christianity because of its attacks on rights of private ownership and inheritance, the prerequisites of the family.

The paper *Väktaren,* published by and for the state church clergy until 1888, by and large represented the opinion of the church. Time after time it featured articles that attacked Social Democracy with extreme animosity and concurrently stressed in general terms the need for improved conditions for the workers. It is true, reads an article of 1885, that Christians ought not to deprive themselves of their property, but ought to let God determine its disposition. "Christianity is thoroughly socialistic; it strives to impart as much as possible of the common nature of heavenly treasures to worldly possessions. But it is a socialism that does not circumscribe freedom in the slightest. A little later the paper declared that one could not "shut one's eyes to the element of truth hidden within the terrible teachings of socialism, nihilism, and communism." *Väktaren*'s tone became progressively sharper. During the Stockholm strikes of 1886, it contended that the discontent of the workers was caused by agitation, and that urban labor was really often in a better economic position than educated groups. The government was called upon to take action against socialism. "Nothing more insane than socialism has ever appeared in the history of the world. Socialists preach the abolition of Christianity, of the moral law, the rights of private ownership and inheritance, of matrimony, the family, the government, and all other authority except brute force. . . . Socialism must therefore be seen as the mortal enemy of church and state, and of each and every peace-loving private citizen, [and] it ought to be combatted with all available means. Those who preach it ought to be handled by the state in the same way as those guilty of lese majesty or of murder and stealing. . . . The Social Question can only be solved in one way, and that is the way of love, patience, obedience, and mutual service." The clergy was urged to treat The Social Question in sermons in order to counteract socialism.

Around 1890, clerical discussion on socialism was exceedingly lively. There are several possible explanations for this, among them the formation of the

Social Democratic party and the increased urgency of certain demands for sociopolitical reforms. Antisocialism was the predominant feature of this discussion, but social reformist views were also asserted more vigorously than before.

Several articles in *Tidskrift för kristen tro och bildning* (*The Journal of Christian Faith and Education*) typified the moderate Christian Socialist view. In 1888, Stave (then a docent, subsequently a professor and dean) wrote on "The Importance of the Christian World View to The Social Question of Our Time." Social Democracy was thoroughly criticized as materialistic, atheistic, and inimical to the freedom that is a requisite of religion and morality. Christianity meant deliverance from both individualism and socialism. "Christianity sanctions the institutions of human society as divine orders which the individual should gratefully acknowledge and utilize as organs for his moral and religious development." In regard to economic matters, Stave maintained that free competition was by and large good from the viewpoint of freedom and production, but that it could not be applied without any restrictions, for this would result in a"proletariat that would be unworthy of human, let alone a Christian society." According to Christian teaching, all should enjoy the right of private property. Yet Christianity also recognized the propriety of economic inequalities. "Because of its concept of human beings as limbs of an organism, in which one limb has different functions from another, presupposing differences in endowment and means, [Christianity] must also recognize inequalities in worldly possessions, with the provision that this inequality not exceed that which Christian justice and mercy can countenance." The clear words of the Bible also showed that those who work and serve must "show obedience, humility, and contentment in their duties," must be submissive toward their masters "not only the good and gentle [ones] but also the iniquitous." Biblical exhortations to men to be submissive were all the more applicable at the present time since they had been made during a period when masters had been far more severe toward their subjects (the slaves) than was now the case. The article did, however, conclude with a call for greater social compassion and for the introduction of measures to make the workers' conditions more secure. The views advanced by Dean J. A. Englund in an article on "Christianity and Socialism," published in 1890, were mainly in the same vein. The subject was again treated in the journal in 1892 in articles by Lecturer J. Nyqvist and the then Pastor N. Söderblom. Nyqvist's views were Christian socialist in tone, but he declared that socialism represented a distorted image of early Christianity. Söderblom paid particular attention to the causes for the workers' distrust of religion.

One important cause, said Söderblom, was the "inappropriate idea *that religion and the church are willing tools in the hands of the upper class to suppress the workers*. . . . Unfortunately, in this connection, the workers have been confronted with a reality far more grievous than socialism and materialism taken together. We have in mind the numbers of educated people who personally feel that they long ago grew away from the church and religion but who willingly retain them for the battle against Social Democracy." However, Söderblom also denounced Social Democracy because of its materialistic tendencies.

Around this time a series of clerical meetings also treated the subject of Social Democracy. The social obligations of church and state were affirmed, but the meetings mainly impugned the socialist movement. The church appeared to be launching a general offensive against socialism.

The most authoritative statements were those delivered by Archbishop Sundberg at a clerical meeting in Uppsala in June 1891 in a lecture on "Modern Social Democracy and Its Relation to the Christian Community." The Social Democrats persisted, the archbishop said, in following the road indicated by the French Revolution.

> The temples would be torn down or rebuilt into hospitals and living quarters for the workers, established lawful order dissolved, private property transformed into communal property, whose proceeds are supposedly to be bestowed upon all through a distribution adjusted according to the work and need of each one, and thoughts of sin, moral responsibility, and eternity would be totally left out of all considerations. In short, we are confronted here with an outlook and a phenomenon which many regard as innocuous, because they appear absurd to any measure of critical thinking; yet no one can escape the feeling that all this is not merely a menacing specter but a menacing dark reality. Yes, there is no doubt but that of the multitude of intellectual currents present today the one mentioned here is the most dangerous.

Socialism, it is true, was not always hostile to religion; if the term were interpreted positively, in the noblest and most beautiful sense, Christ would be the greatest socialist beyond comparison. But modern Social Democracy had become antireligious as a consequence of its unmitigated communist standpoint. It viewed the origin of all evil in external, especially economic conditions, and wanted to create a society built entirely on a materialistic foundation. There was talk of freedom, brotherhood, and equality. But in what sense? Equality would be "purely economic and material, which, in turn, is impossible without totally destroying *freedom,* with all its unconditional rights, even in respect to the gains of labor, by the unbridled tyranny of the complicated machinery of society. . . . Scrutinize . . . more closely Social

Democratic . . . brotherhood, and you will soon find that it, if any, is thoroughly egoistic. It is namely not at all the brotherhood of love but solely a brotherhood of common economic interests. . . ." In fighting Social Democracy, the church should "present the little that is suitable and weed out the rest" of its teaching. A Christian social line should be followed. In so doing, the church, although unable to undertake the technical solution of economic problems, should remember "that for every form of the community life of her congregation . . . she has in her hand the divine directives and the responsibility to assert sound Christian principles in all areas. . . . Therefore one should not fear to let the word of truth be heard in the hotbeds of socialist agitation, nor, still less, neglect to give those outside the small circle that each one is entrusted with clear answers regarding the right, scriptural concept of worldly property, of the trusteeship of the rich, of the true interrelationships between social classes, and, above all, of the abnegation of worldly things and self-denial incumbent on every human being." All good forces must unite "to counteract a movement that threatens to destroy both church and state."

The archbishop's speech suffers from a certain ambiguity. Above all, it leaves one to wonder whether the battle to which he so fervently summoned the clergy would entail primarily the dissemination of Christian-social ideas or criticism of socialist doctrine. It is evident, however, that to Sundberg the Christian-social line was mainly a means to stave off socialism. The fact that his speech constituted a direct appeal for antisocialist propaganda is also indisputable, no matter what the interpretation given his remarks in this regard.

Similar views were advanced at clerical meetings in the cities of Strängnäs, Kalmar, Västerås and Karlstad. At the Strängnäs meeting in August 1891, Bishop Ullman opened a debate on The Social Question. The bishop attacked Social Democracy even more vehemently than Sundberg. He declared, for instance, that the socialists wanted "the abolition of all private property . . . the abolition of matrimony in its present meaning, the abolition of all family life, the rearing of children from early infancy in state institutions so that the little ones will be completely alienated from their parents. This future society they want to bring about through revolution. . . ." As in Germany, socialism should be checked through the improvement of the workers' circumstances and the formation of antisocialist workers' associations. Of most importance to this end, however, was the arousal of greater religiosity. Bishop G. Billing greeted a clerical meeting in Västerås in 1892 by stating that Social Democracy was the most dangerous form of want of faith, "not least because it does not present the denial of God in undiluted bitterness but imbeds it in a mixture that, when taken, tastes rather sweet. . . . Social Democracy knows well how to cajole discontent, suspicion, envy, and other dark tendencies in the hearts of men, and knows equally well how to lull and dupe consciences by persuading them that the demands of Social Democracy are also the demands of rightousness and love." Bishop Rundgren expressed his condemnation of socialism at the Karlstad clerical meeting of 1893 in even more astringent terms. "Our economic laws . . . give every honest man and woman the right to self-support and the opportunities for education are open to all. Under such circumstances, physical need cannot be so crying that it is liable to arouse discontent and bitterness among the people. But unfortunately, here, among us as everywhere, there is a lack of the humility and patience that overcome many vexations." Sermons and lectures delivered by several less representative spokesmen for the church during this period promulgated at one and the same time antisocialist and vaguely Christian-social views.

It should finally be noted that at a theological congress held in Stockholm in 1897, N. Söderblom asserted a view that was rather original at the time but which gradually gained a strong footing within the church. His lecture, "Religion and the Social Development," was partly concerned with current Christian-social thoughts, but above all it proclaimed that the church must not bind itself to any economic and social system; one must not "yoke religion with a social state of affairs now existing or already bygone." This viewpoint, which was principally justified by citing religion's special sphere of activity, actually contained a political program for the church that tended to ensure the continued existence of the church regardless of changes in regimes. By not committing itself, by demonstrating tolerance, the church ought to be able to preserve its position.

The church's stand on The Social Question and particularly on Social Democracy can thus be schematically characterized by referring to the quotations of the three archbishops, Reuterdahl, Sundberg, and Söderblom, cited in this chapter. Reuterdahl represented the unreflective social conservatism that was matter-of-course before the appearance of radical movements. The established social order and economic inequalities seemed self-evident; churchmen cited the negligible importance of life on this earth and the transient, deceptive nature of all temporal happiness. The pressure of social revolutionary and Marxian socialism brought about the dominance of an attitude that was both mildly social reformist and aggressively pro the *status quo*. This attitude was most authoritatively expressed in Sundberg's major attack on socialism of 1891. Söderblom, who became archbishop the same year that Social Democracy became Sweden's largest political party, had long since expressed a policy of tolerance. The value of this policy from the point of view of church politics became generally recognized as socialism came closer and closer to holding the executive power of state; it became practicable from a religious standpoint because of the increasing moderation that socialism manifested.

The Debate on The Social Question

PENETRATING STUDIES have been made of the constitutional-political discussion of the last decades of the nineteenth century. Research has also been concerned to a comparatively great extent with certain other aspects of the ideological development during this period, particularly as reflected in literature. On the other hand, although social legislation per se and economic conditions have been authoritatively treated, there is no full account of the ideological debate on The Social Question. We do not aspire to fill this void. We can only try to intimate the prevailing ideas and their evolution, which are indispensable to the background of the Social Democratic views from their emergence in the 1880s. The primary sources for this account are, on the one hand, Riksdag debates and committee reports—which have been systematically perused—and, on the other, selections from the newspapers, journals, books, and pamphlets of the period. Because of the limitations the data present and the difficulty or impossibility of judging their representativeness, our conclusions will suffer from a certain amount of uncertainty—which the author hereby states once and for all.

In comparison with the period subsequent to the turn of the century, the decades immediately following the legislative reform present particular difficulties to the student of ideological discourse because the party system was only partially developed at that time. Few were the programs, pamphlets, speeches, or newspapers that could be said with any certainty to represent a specific party or group. This was especially true in regard to The Social Question. The very first fact that deserves emphasis is that The Social Question long played a completely subordinate part in the debate. Besides the ordinance covering relief for the poor, there were few provisions in the nature of social welfare. The alignments of parties and factions in the Riksdag were determined by other issues, such as the land tax, tariffs, defense, and the franchise. Newspapers and journals relatively seldom touched upon the issues that can be comprised under the designation "the labor question." Before the advent of Social Democracy there was no party, no large organization—

possibly with the exception of the liberal labor movement during the 1880s—that was committed to forcing through a solution to this problem. Prior to the 1890s, no group active in the Riksdag had issued a programmatic declaration on the subject. Characteristically, the pamphlet, *Vad folket vänter av den nya representationen* (*What the People Expect of the New Legislature*), written by the chief voice of radical liberalism before the turn of the century, S. A. Hedin, and published in 1868, did not call for any real social reform besides the abolition of the forced labor imposed upon vagrants.

One facet of this situation was a certain amount of vacillation in the positions taken on demands for reform. There was no group in the Riksdag that systematically promoted such demands, nor was there any group that systematically rejected them. The lack of policy produced a certain receptivity to argument. By making proposals and speeches, a skillful, assiduous riksdagman could achieve results that may seem surprising in view of the feeble interest evinced in such questions in the beginning. It is reminiscent of the situation in England some decades earlier, when a handful of conservatives or liberals were able to force through important social reforms in a Commons where the majority was indifferent to these issues; the essential thing was to gain the cabinet support necessary to secure the time required for consideration of a question.

The interval between the legislative reform and the appearance of Social Democracy marked the culmination of early liberalism in Swedish politics. The principle of legal social equality had won its great victory through the Riksdag reform; economic liberty and free trade had already been realized. The general principles of economic and social liberalism were constantly cited in public debate as finally discovered, now definitely established scientific truths. The right of private ownership and free enterprise would create optimum prosperity; a fundamental harmony prevailed in the relationships between competing economic interests. It was assumed that all enjoyed or should enjoy basically the same opportunities; little attention was paid to the real infringements of this principle that the right of inheritance and the unequal distribution of income entailed.

Besides this liberalism, to which we shall return shortly, one continuously encounters an element of basic conservatism or traditionalism in the debate. It is the combination of these two lines, which are, strictly speaking, mutually incompatible, that gives the prevailing ideology its special complexion. On the one hand, competition, initiative, and ambition were praised and society declared open to competence, whatever its origin. On the other hand, economic inequalities and class divisions were justified from a traditional point of view as natural, given, static phenomena. The clearest expression of this line is the clerical message previously mentioned, but the same trend of thinking was also manifest in the legislature and press. Under the influence of the major reforms that had been introduced, liberalism viewed society as a mass of individuals in constant motion and competition, which was beneficial to the whole. While liberalism was not inclined to acknowledge the stability of social differentiation that was independent of the new laws and institutions, conservatism could more openly ascertain this stability inasmuch as it regarded it as inevitable and warranted. It would be only a slight exaggeration and schematization to state that in liberalism's view the workers ought to be dissatisfied and eager to improve their individual circumstances, and that in the conservative view they ought to be satisfied with their lot and aspire to collective improvement within reasonable bounds. It might be said that liberalism suited entrepreneurs and businessmen who moved in the world of individual competition, between individuals, but not the industrial workers, for whom the chances for personal advancement were extremely limited. It should be emphasized, however, that sociopolitical reforms did not necessarily *have to be* regarded as objectionable per se from either of these viewpoints. Such reforms could be fitted into a system that was largely liberal as well as justified from socially conservative premises.

Both the trends which have here been termed liberal and conservative for want of more pregnant expressions, entered into the organizational and associational ideology typical of the social debate during this period. Liberalism, which outweighed conservatism in this regard, and, in its early form had rejected all systems of economic organization as contrary to the principle of freedom, now believed free cooperation would be conducive to arriving at a solution of The Social Question. This idea was not novel. As early as the 1830s, Geijer had praised the principle of association: "Breaking-up the corporations, obdurate in their exclusive privileges, releases precisely the natural spirit of association. . . . It is the corporation that has become mobile with the mobility of labor, in which the advancing auxilliary troops of the new state begin to become noticeable." In his publication of 1852, *Om arbetareassociationer* (*On Workers' Associations*), S. A. Hedlund had declared himself in favor of the formation of production associations among the workers. During the 1860s, these ideas gained considerable momentum, in all likelihood partly as a result of a slump in the economy. Typical of this form of liberalism as well as of the moderate, authoritative social debate on the whole are two documents: the pamphlet *Om arbetsklassen och arbetareföreningar* (*On the Working Class and Workers' Organizations*) of 1865 written by Hamilton, Professor of Economics at Lund University, and the essay "Arbetarefrågan" ("The Labor Question") written by the economist Arnberg (later head of the Bank of Sweden) and published in *Svensk Tidskrift,* 1870. Let us briefly review these documents.

Hamilton, who was deeply influenced by the writings of Schultze-Delitzsch that had been issued some years previously, stressed the difficulties of the working class—craftsmen and industrial workers—in connection with the inevitable trend toward industrialism. In his opinion, legislation and other government measures would not be able to achieve any material improvement. He said "that immediate state intervention in these societal conditions is always perilous, seldom if ever truly beneficial." The remedy was self-help through various kinds of workers' associations, such as organizations to handle the purchase of craftsmen's raw materials and housing, consumers' and production associations. The latter two were central to Hamilton's exposition. Such associations would, indeed, have to contend with great difficulties due a lack of capital, but this problem could be overcome because of the direct interest of every active member in the success of the whole association. Enterprises owned and controlled by private individuals should be able to exist in competition with workers' associations, in this as in other spheres. By implementing the concept of associations that he outlined, Hamilton believed that The Social Question would be solved. In his conclusion he wrote "that differences between the estates and classes will hereby gradually be equalized at the same time as the importance of the individual will steadily increase by virtue of the many new duties that always place new demands on the varied aptitudes and abilities of the individual at a higher level of industrialization; that the common sense of justice will be heightened by virtue of the practice of solidarity and cooperation in more narrow spheres; and finally, that respect for one's self and for others will elicit from all an ever deeper and more vital insight into the duty of work and the honor of work."

Arnberg ascertained in his essay that the conflict between capital and labor had become more acute. "In vain has political economics gravely warned labor against any hostility toward its best ally, productive capital; in vain has it shown that their economic interests are harmonious and that the progress of both parties, as well as of the world, toward increased prosperity primarily depends on their peaceful collaboration toward their common goal. . . ." Arnberg, who ostensibly based his version of the situation more on foreign than domestic conditions, believed that one had to find an organization of labor and distribution of its profits that was more favorable to the working class—but without encroaching upon economic freedom and right of ownership. Certain social reform measures such as the regulation of child labor might therefore be considered. The trade unions might prove to be of value, and even the right to strike had to be acknowledged, since there already was freedom of bargaining. Arnberg further recommended a system of profit sharing. Such an arrangement should "however, be regarded solely as a transitional form to one that is even more complete, where the worker is his own employer, to the perfect association among workers." This goal was admittedly distant, but it should be attainable by an ever-increasing number of workers' groups by dint of frugality and unity. "For not until the worker has acquired a working fund through his own industry and frugality and has demonstrated that he can further increase this through orderliness and proficiency in his trade, only then, say we, will he willingly be offered the capital without which no industry can advance and which, in reality, has no greater wish than to enter confidently into the service of labor."

Especially during the years around 1870, the suggestions of both authors regarding cooperation, primarily associations of manufacturers, marshalled considerable support. The attempt of the so-called workers' associations to translate them into practice will be dealt with in the following. During the 1870s, however, the concept of production cooperatives receded into the background, while other forms of self-help for the workers were uniformly recommended. A characteristic of all the literature on the labor question during this period was the absence of any suggestion of state intervention of any significant magnitude. There was, for example, no suggestion of state subvention of cooperative enterprises. The strong recommendation given to such enterprises must be viewed in light of the supposition that they would coexist with strictly private businesses. One probably did not anticipate that cooperative movements would supplant private enterprise to any appreciable extent, for in this event the liberal system in the true sense would have been abolished. The social reform measures that were considered practicable were most limited in scope. There was no mention of a standard work day or of a system of social insurance. Some publications and statements evince far less understanding of the working class than that revealed by the authors we have discussed. Poverty was said to be self-inflicted and the poor were admonished above all to observe contentment, frugality, temperance, and moral rectitude.

Some of the Riksdag debates that took place around 1870 illuminate the liberal-conservative stand on The Social Question. This is particularly true of the 1869 debate on poor relief. Conditions of distress had brought about a considerable increase in the number of persons entitled to relief according to the regulations in force, and the Riksdag thus declared itself in favor of a sharp curtailment of relief obligations: relief would only be obligatory in the cases of parentless children and the mentally ill; the relief board would decide on all other cases. It was generally claimed that the laxity of relief legislation was the main reason for the prevalence of pauperism; little heed was paid to the role that crop failure might have played in contributing to pauperism. The provisional committee that made a preliminary investigation of the issue in the upper house reported that the basic flaw in the legislation was the obligatory character of relief. The committee considered that "in accordance with the nature of the thing all assistance is an act of love and must be founded on voluntarism, compassion, and Christian aid, and thus on the law of conscience, not on civil law." The right to obtain relief, the committee continued, "eliminates the necessity of thinking on one's own, of securing one's position through work, frugality, and sacrifice, in short, of relying on one's self; it easily leads to laziness, an idle life, and the receipt of help from others. . . ." Among the causes for pauperism named by the committee of the lower house was the disdain demonstrated toward manual laborers, which, in turn, weakened their sense of responsibility. The committee expressed its sympathy with the efforts "that have as their purpose the improvement and securing of the position of the impecunious classes on the basis of the principle of self-help," and hoped for "good results from that spirit of association which has increasingly begun to penetrate down into the deep strate of the population." In the course of the debate, particularly that which took place in the upper house, several speakers emphasized that relief was a form of charity and should thus be voluntary, and that, as a rule, poverty was self-inflicted. God had not created men without the ability to provide for themselves; the cause of an individual's inability to do this must therefore lie in the fact "that he did not learn from the first moment to sacrifice and save" (von Otter). The Christian sentiment of charity and compassion "is by its very nature like certain flowers that wilt if one touches them. They must develop freely of their own accord, or they will wither away" (Henning Hamilton). "If the present relief statute were to be totally abrogated and nothing inserted in its place, but all instead left to private charity, the situation would be much better . . . the beggar who comes with the law in his hand ought to be turned away" (Dickson). Some speakers in the lower house did, however, maintain that poverty was related to difficult economic conditions and to the societal organization (Rundbäck, Hedlund, W. Nilsson, J. Pehrsson). Yet views of the same vein as those asserted in the upper house were also emphatically affirmed on the floor of the lower (Ribbing, Ridderstad, P. A. Bergström, Liss Olof Larsson).

The relief legislation that was enacted two years later was not as restrictive as had been anticipated in 1869; once the crisis had abated, the mood in the cabinet and Riksdag changed. In the course of the attendant Riksdag debate, however, the cabinet bill, which implied a tightening of the qualifications for relief in relation to those provided in the 1853 statute, was described as a step in the direction of state socialism. In answer to this charge, Cabinet Minister Wennerberg stated that even "as wretched and with reason discredited a doctrine" as communism could contain a germ of truth; in this case, however, it was only a question of applying Christian principles. The ensuing debate contained many a sharp attack on communism. "The right of private ownership," said one speaker, "is, next to freedom of thought and the right to life and physical freedom, the most essential, the most sacred, and the most precious [thing] which society must secure and preserve through its organs."

At the Riksdag of 1868, the cabinet proposed an appropriation of one-half million crowns for public works "to provide wages for that population in certain parts of the nation (primarily in the province of Norrland) which is in need as a result of crop failure and the high cost of living." The Committee of Supply proposed an appropriation of 200,000 crowns, and the Riksdag followed this recommendation. However, the very principle behind a demand for state intervention in a case such as this met with criticism. "If logically extended and applied, it (the principle) would lead us right into communism," proclaimed the leading member of the Ruralist party, Emil Key. "Should we acknowledge the state's obligation to provide assistance, not to the worker for labor, but to labor for the worker, and [acknowledge] this under all conditions? Should we proclaim that anyone who is either unable, prohibited from, or unwilling to work has the right to live at the expense of the state without limitations?" Defenders of the committee proposal protested that it was only concerned with special measures that had been necessitated by an exceptional situation.

On the whole, no reforms of a truly social reformist nature were introduced during the 1860s and 1870s. The only question in this area that came up during the 1870s was the regulation of labor by minors. The regulations then in force, which had been enacted around 1850, prohibited the employment of children under 12 years of age in occupational work and the employment of minors between the ages of 12 and 18 in factory night work. The lack of observance of these regulations was notorious. It should be pointed out, however that the industrial use of child labor in Sweden had always been comparatively small in scope. Proposals for the introduction of new regulations were brought in the Riksdag in 1870, 1871, and 1875; these proposals based the demand for new legislation on the defects in the enforcement of the existing law and on the need for more restrictive regulations. The 1870 and 1871 Riksdags yielded no result. Opposition to the proposal was largely justified by citing basically liberal views. During the debate in the lower house in 1870, one speaker averred that the proposal—which would limit the working hours of minors under 18 to 10 hours—represented an "arbitrary restriction of the rights of the employer, parents, and guardians. . . ." The Riksdag of 1875, however, voted to petition the king for new rules governing child labor.

The cabinet accordingly appointed an investigative committee with Pehr Ehrenheim as chairman. Like so many other inquiries into social reform issues that followed it, the committee's report was a model of clarity and accuracy. The report began with a historical recapitulation. The advance of industrialism had erased, step by step, the previous form of regulation of the economy and labor conditions. "The prevailing economic views have greatly contributed to this: with the general and unrestricted introduction of economic freedom, entrepreneurs as well as workers are left to themselves, and in their reciprocal relationships they are not subjected to any law other than that which, according to the same views, alone rules the economic world: self-interest." The subject of the position of the working class in this situation brought out divergent views. Some were of the opinion that the interests of this class would be best served if the state left "industry to itself to develop its inherent beneficial forces and potential in free competition." Others feared that uncontrolled development would widen the gulf between capitalists and the unpropertied and believed it incumbent upon "the state to protect the best interests of the weak by transforming industrial conditions on the foundation of law and equality." The committee did not take any stand on this question of principle; it emphasized instead that the subject of labor legislation was an exceptional case. (Characteristically, by "labor legislation" it meant the labor of minors, for there was no question of any other legislation in this area.) The necessity of regulation for the welfare of the children was incontrovertible. Even the employers had begun to abandon their opposition to this, since they elected "to be forced to do the right thing instead of being forced to do the wrong thing." The committee's proposal essentially recommended the introduction of regulations of substantially greater severity and the establishment of an inspective office to oversee enforcement of the regulations. This proposal provided the basis for a new statute governing the labor of minors that was enacted in 1881. Among other provisions, it stipulated that minors between 12 and 14 years of age were prohibited from factory work in excess of 6 hours daily and limited the corresponding labor for minors between the ages of 14 and 18 to 10 hours. No provision was made for inspection. The statute met with bitter criticism from industrialists; its sphere of application was subsequently circumscribed by new regulations. Because of the lack of surveillance, the 1881 statute was also frequently violated. Nevertheless, child labor did decline in the 1880s, as a report issued in 1892 demonstrates.

Even though strikes were often designated as inappropriate and dangerous for the workers themselves, labor's right to strike was, as a rule, apparently acknowledged during the period discussed. On several occasions, however, the authorities intervened in strikes in a manner that suggested that the state was in league with the employer. There performance of Provincial Governor Treffenberg in the strike that took place in the city of Sundsvall in 1879 is the most well-known and widely discussed instance of such intervention. Faced with the threat of eviction or application of a law (*försvarslöshetsstadgan*) that allowed the authorities to treat persons without property or fixed income as vagrants and deport them to forced labor camps, labor was, with the aid of military strength, compelled to return to work. Treffenberg's measures was approved by the government and praised by many newspapers. In his official report he described the strike in terms that would lead one to believe he was referring to a revolutionary action. Yet another example of the official view on strikes was the message that Uppsala's provincial governor issued in 1879 to the workers of Skutskär sawmill after the settlement of a strike had been reached there. He declared that strikes were reprehensible because the wages that employers paid were determined by the law of supply and demand. "The worker thus has . . . no other recourse when wages are down than to try to live as cheaply as possible in order to pull himself through the difficult period. . . . As surely as winter follows summer and night follows day, good and bad times alternate in the nation's economy. . . . In all likelihood there is hardly one among you all who has experienced good times who can in good conscience say that he could not have lived more frugally then he did." The workers were exhorted to practice frugality and sobriety, and to be scrupulous in their work.

The written and verbal statements concerning socialism were uniformly critical in tone. Socialism, or communism—the terms were used interchangeably—was not infrequently held to be almost a criminal movement. It was generally presumed, however, that socialism would not make inroads in Sweden because of the lack of industrial development in the nation and because relations between Skeden's different social classes were comparatively good. The statements do not warrant our close scrutiny because of their ambiguous, varying usage of the terms socialism and communism. In the early 1870s the Commune of Paris was foremost in the official mind; at the end of the same decade the German Social Democratic movement was foremost. Typical of the prevailing opinion are the statements made by the organ of the Ruralist party in the summer of 1875 upon learning of the formation of a socialist union in the city of Malmö. "Although we see no really serious reasons to fear that the socialist weeds shall find suitable soil [in which to grow] in our country, on the other hand it would be inadvisable to dismiss as totally unimportant the fact that socialism has been introduced into our country and has built a following around its misleading doctrine. . . . Thus it is not enough to be on guard, but in his own city each and every one who understands the danger that threatens—not society, but the blind scapegoats among the workers—must strive to expose the specter in its right, despicable light through all available means—informational and educational."

The convergence of a patriarchal-conservative spirit and economic-liberal principles is particularly evident in some publications. Charles Dickson, a member of the wealthy Dickson family of Gothenburg, a philanthropist and a member of the upper house for a number of years, wrote an account of the status of the Swedish working class in his capacity as a member of the industrial jury at the exposition in Paris in 1867. He underscored the merits of the "Nordic" worker: "fear of God, a persevering yet compliant and tractable temperament." On the whole, said Dickson, the labor question did not present any problems once a free economy had been realized. In order to become "what he ought to be, the surest support of the state and of society," the worker only required "popular education and freedom to work." These were the worker's "only rightful claims. . . . If the state has discharged the duties that devolve upon it in these respects it can then safely allow things to develop naturally of their own course." Nevertheless, various types of free associations, such as production associations, were of considerable value. There is every reason to hope, said Dickson, that the production associations "will bear abundant fruits for their participants and serve as the inspiration and model for the founding of several similar associations." The possibility that such associations could serve to support important industries was slight. "For the community [of workers] must be more or less suspended in large factories, and it is to be feared that sooner or later the entire factory will be owned by a small number of its founders and that the other original participants will again descend to [the status of] mere common laborers."

The journals published by the employers for the workers were a singular feature of the press of that day. The most important of these periodicals around 1880 were *Arbetarens vän* (*The Worker's Friend*) and *Svenske arbetaren* (*The Swedish Worker*). The former, which carried the subtitle "The journal for sobriety, moral rectitude, and fear of God," was started and published by the Stockholm industrialist C. O. Berg, who also functioned for a few years as its copublisher. Berg was a wealthy wholesaler who had worked himself up from humble beginnings and who became known during the 1870s and 1880s as a philanthropist and socially interested conservative politician (as a member of the upper house). *Svenske arbetaren,* "The patriotic journal for all social classes," was published with the financial backing of a number of persons, some of whom, at least, were employers. Exact data on the origin of the journal are not available. It is significiant, however, that many of the subscribers to the journal, which was intended for the workers, belonged to an elite of the nation's aristocracy and big bourgeoisie. Many of the members of the upper house and the titled property owners and industrialists that were listed as faithful readers of the journal subscribed to a great many (sometimes about one hundred) copies. Their purpose was obviously to support the journal and perhaps also to distribute it to subordinates and workers in general.

Certain currents of thought in the ideological debate of the period attained consummate expression in these journals. Extreme economic liberalism that did encourage self-help though associations—but not production associations or trade unions in the true sense—was combined with a romantic outlook on labor and the glorification of the virtues deemed appropriate for the workers. Articles, stories, and poems described the genuine happiness that results from contentment, moral rectitude, sobriety, and fear of God, and even the outward success that sometimes rewards these virtues. The basic principles in the propaganda offered in the journals are evident in a series of articles written by Peter Wieselgren and published in *Arbetarens vän* in 1877. The series was entitled "On the Working Classes throughout History and Today" and had previously been published as a pamphlet. It held forth that the only remedy for social problems was "industry, frugality, and the fear of God." "Wage levels, like everything else along this line, ought to be determined solely by supply and demand." Wages rise and fall automatically according to whether the trend of the economy is down or up. "Should one try to force the employer, whether through legislation or other measures as, for example, work stoppages, to pay to his employees the same wages in the former as in the latter case, one would simply be attempting to deprive him unjustly of part of his property; in order not to be ruined, he would be compelled to raise the prices of his goods or services to a corresponding level, and the consumer, even the poorest one, even the worker himself, would thus have to indemnify him for the injustice that had been perpetrated, which would therefore render a benefit to the worker equal to zero." The root of the problems was primarily man's love of pleasure, and character improvements were therefore essential. Self-help through organizations could also help uplift the working class. But one had to understand first of all that the rich and the poor belonged together, that they were parts of the same social body. "Society is an organism of which all the parts work for one another and for the whole." The propaganda in *Svenske arbetaren* was more naive and sentimental than that in *Arbetarens vän*. It, too, preached the principle of free competition, together with the virtues of contentment and idyllic bliss, which were supposed to come naturally precisely to the little man in society. When discussing the Social Democratic movement, the journal availed itself of the characteristic line of criticism. "We believe that all right-thinking workers know how to defend themselves against the delusions of *socialism* without any guidance, whether in the form of the law or its keepers. Our workers—the better ones, we are not concerned here with any other kind—are altogether too enlightened and too honest to allow themselves to be seduced by evil-minded so-called social reformers or to be led by the nose according to their fancies."

The 1880s are commonly regarded as a period of breakthrough in Sweden's societal life. Various phenomena come to mind: "verdandism," the emergence of socialism and, above all, the starkly realistic trend of social criticism in Swedish literature that gave rise to the designation "of the eighties." Some schematization in forming classifications of this kind is necessary, and this one seems justifiable. Yet there was no sudden or sweeping change during these years. As a literary movement, "the eighties" was of central importance but a few years. Conservative tendencies within certain groups were reinforced by the reaction to this movement; in the opinion of that day, these groups—not those involved in "the eighties" movement—surely stood out as the cultural leaders. During this decade, Social Democracy was an insignificant movement that did not gain appreciable support even from the industrial working class. A perusal of the records of the Riksdag, newspapers, and pamphlets does not suggest that the beginning of this decade heralded a new orientation. Yet during the eighties, trends that entailed a break with essential aspects of economic liberalism gradually began to come to the fore.

We shall not concern ourselves here with the literary "eighties," but we should note in passing that the only representative for the movement who—for a brief period—characterized himself as a socialist was Strindberg. It is not clear exactly what Strindberg meant by this. There is no reason to suppose that Strindberg was really familiar with socialist theories; in addition, the term "socialism" was given the most varied connotations during the period in question. Strindberg was apparently deeply influenced by Quiding's book *Slutlikvid med Sveriges lag* (*The Final Settlement with Sweden's Law*), which was published in 1875. This work had not, however, played any part in the Social Democratic movement and had, on the whole, not made any lasting impression on the ideological debate—except, possibly, for the terms upper class and lower class. Strindberg's attacks on big industry and his praise of the farmers show that, in any case, the kind of socialism he had in mind bore little resemblance to Swedish Social Democracy. This relationship

—or the lack of it—has been obscured to some extent since some Social Democrats did embrace Strindberg, together with other writers of the eighties, because of their realism and social criticism. In reality, an interesting indication of the scant heed paid Social Democracy during the eighties is the fact that none of the writers of the period—who stressed the social side of the contemporary scene—appeared to take a stand in regard to Social Democracy.

The first proposal of a general social reformist purport was brought by E. Westin in the lower house in 1882. The proposal asked for an investigation regarding measures for the improvement of the position and general conditions of the workers, and of industrial workers, in particular. Westin stated that the discontent of the agricultural class could be expected to disappear through the solution of the taxation and defense questions, but that the problem of the workers had not received the same amount of attention. One had to think of the interests of the whole of society and "in so doing, in the first place . . . of the poor worker, who must often bear the heaviest lot in life and moreover lacks the opportunity to make himself heard." Westin mentioned protection against occupational hazards and compensation for accidents incurred at work as subjects for the investigation. "Sound development will be furthered by the prudent and appropriate regulation of the relation between employer and employee, between capital and labor, and the socialist currents that arouse warranted apprehension in other countries and necessitate stringent legislative measures should thereby prove avoidable." Westin thus used as his point of departure two viewpoints that would thereafter constantly recur in social reformist debates. On the one hand, improvements in the circumstances of the worker were desirable per se; on the other hand, such improvements would ensure peace in society. The provisional committee that prepared the question emphasized the complicated nature of the labor problem. "The question has arisen for us only in recent times and as yet no definite opinion appears to prevail in regard to the two fundamentally divergent views on this question that are in sharp conflict abroad, one of which firmly insists upon the right of the individual and rejects all state involvement in free argeements, and the other of which does not hesitate, at the expense of freedom, to ascribe to state authorities both the right and obligation to regulate relations between employer and employee in order to alleviate the situation of the workers." The committee did not take a definite stand on the principle in question but recommended that the proposal be rejected, stressing that state authorities should "intervene with definite ordinances . . . only in cases where they can be based on needs that are clearly perceived and generally recognized." The extensive debate on the proposal in the lower house brought out the main lines that would dominate nonsocialist discussions during the following decades. Count Sparre laid down the socially conservative pattern of thought. He moved that the proposal be rejected, but suggested that statistics be compiled to assist legislators in forming a judgment on the labor question. This question was a subject of controversy everywhere, said Sparre. "We know that at this moment Germany's great statesman is considering proposing a law regarding workers' accident insurance, and people have not neglected to hurl at him immediately the accusation [that he harbors] socialist tendencies. . . . Since we do not look after this [segment of the] population and in many respects display an extravagant luxury that must appear flagrant to these people, it is no wonder that many of them develop a sense of dejection, envy of and prejudice against the upper classes that often express themselves in violence, which can be expected to lead to the gravest of consequences." A rapprochement between the social classes was necessary; "this has taken place in America, and therefore the working people go there." Certain social reform measures, such as accident insurance on a local basis, might be considered. An extension of the franchise would, however, prove valueless, for this would not provide bread. Furthermore, this might enable the workers to "to get the upper hand in the legislature, which would be especially dangerous since they have no appreciative regard." On the other hand, Granlund, who was basically more liberal, believed that an amelioration of the conditions of the workers could only be achieved through "enlightenment, increased work proficiency, frugality, industry, and sobriety. Working conditions and wages did not lend themselves to legislation; strikes were harmful to the workers themselves. Another speaker, von der Lancken, put forth much the same view when he recommended legislation regarding voluntary saving. Baron Nordenskiöld spoke of the workers' own weapon, the strike, as "an essential instrument for the workers in order that they might fight to win a fair share of the profits that industry yields." Yet he also believed "that the first and most important measure that should be taken to improve the situation of the worker, to raise his self-esteem, and to provide a firm and practical foundation for legislation for the workers is the extension of the franchise in order that the workers may have their own voice in Sweden's Riksdag." In the end, the proposal was rejected without a vote.

At the 1884 Riksdag, S. A. Hedin proposed an investigation on the subject of accident and old-age insurance. This proposal is notable above all because of its basic criticism of economic liberalism. Hedin reminded his listeners that this doctrine had been developed in reaction to the state guardianship of a former day, but that it had since evolved into an abstract system without relation to real life. "Its proponents have been in the habit of dissociating the multifarious and interlocking relationships in societal life and of treating them—people, their prejudices, their passions, their conflicting interests—as mathematical exercises on the blackboard whose results, if correctly computed, supposedly check with the answer book. Who has not heard to the point of bordeom the theses, for example, regarding the unrestricted right of 'freedom of contract' and [the law of] 'supply and demand' [advanced] as the sole determinants of value, proclaimed as inexorable laws of nature?" Hedin also criticized the ambiguous usage of the term "socialism." "Definitions or descriptions of or accusations against socialism are probably just about as numerous as the number of persons using the term in a sense that is at least to some extent specific. Some have even—and this is not unusual—used the term only to designate some vague horror, a political specter, or to make a person seem suspicious or a matter detestable." In a sense, there was already a good deal of "socialism" in society—otherwise society would disintegrate and collapse. As examples, Hedin cited poor relief and subsidies granted to industries. In defense of his proposal he brought out the workers' need for security and the state's obligation to intervene in behalf of the less advanced classes. In addition, he cited a German statement, according to which "the surest guarantee of reformist, nonrevolutionary progress would be obtained if one could unite the great majority of the working people in the maintenance of the established state organization." The Committee of Supply, with only one dissenting opinion—that of Liss Olof Larsson—recommended that the measure called for in Hedin's proposal be brought in a petition to the king on the ground that the importance of the question required an investigation. Both houses voted in favor of a petition, and the upper house did so without a debate. In the lower house several speakers explained their reasons for supporting the proposal by referring to the need to alleviate the discontent among the workers. In other countries, Sparre argued, the labor movement had assumed "threatening and distressing dimensions"; Sweden had all the more reason to help solve the labor question within her own boundaries in view of the fact that the Swedish labor movement was "the finest, the noblest, the most attractive one imaginable." Some proferred state finances and generally liberal arguments as grounds for rejection of the proposal. Said Liss Olof Larsson: "it may be dangerous to instill the people in advance with the idea that it is not so important to provide for the future themselves and that it is that state that will care for them when they become old and feeble." In the end, however, the social reformist movement won its first great victory without encountering any appreciable opposition.

Two years later S. A. Hedlund introduced a still more radical proposal in connection with the tariff controversy. An investigation was to be undertaken into the legislation that would be necessary in order to provide security for workers in those industries protected by tariffs. Hedlund recommended a maximum nine-hour standard work day, the establishment of minimum wages through councils composed of representatives of both management and labor, and various measures to provide decent housing for the working class. Hedlund's proposal seemed so extremely radical that some speakers interpreted it as merely an antiprotectionist protest that was not to be taken seriously. The legislative committee called for rejection of the proposal; it held that intervention of this kind would have a "disastrous effect . . . not only on the economy as a whole and on the business of employers, but also on the condition of the workers themselves. . . ." Hedlund defended his proposal with general, humanitarian arguments, but he also reminded his listeners of "the great movement that is taking shape in our part of the world and which assumes the dangerous forms of socialism, communism, Marxism, nihilism, among others. The labor problem would have to be solved amicably "if its solution were not to be accompanied by danger and violence." The few speakers who sided with Hedlund tried to show that rejecting social reformist demands would tend to further damage relations between social classes. One should not be frightened by the term state socialism. Speaking in the lower house, R. Gustafsson declared "As surely as the bourgeois elements in the societies of Europe fought to win their rights and shed the oppression of the nobility at the close of the last century, the liberation of the fourth estate will not be long in coming. . . . Do we not already hear a kind of distant rumbling from the masses, who are assembling to march forward? Let us not place weapons in their hands—in the manner of this committee—by coldly saying to them: we dismiss all thoughts of helping you; we abandon your demands without any consideration! . . . It would surely be saner and wiser to attempt to disarm the discontented through good reforms, for reforms that are good for the workers are also good for society." The proposal was rejected without a vote in both houses.

The recorded debates demonstrate that appreciation of social reformist demands grew during this period and that the extent of the reforms demanded were gradually broadened. This tendency should be viewed in the light of the decline in the economy that occurred during the same period, but on the whole, the interest in social reform increased steadily independently of the business cycle. The debates reveal, on the one hand, an old liberal attitude—but one articulated in extreme formulations with increasing rarity—and on the other hand, a general social reformism—but one that has not yet attained the stamp of a solidly constructed philosophy. Two motives dominate the foreground: humanitarian views and the desire to keep peace in society by appeasing the discontented. Two tendencies are discernible in the formulation of the second argument one patriarchal and socially conservative, another that is more egalitarian and democratic and that stresses the demand for social and political equality as well as economic demands. It is difficult to ascertain to what extent apprehension about the rise of Social Democracy in Sweden lay behind the recurrent references to socialism and the new labor movement. Apparently, no direct mention of the emergence of a socialist movement in Sweden was ever made. The example of Social Democracy in Germany exerted a profound and ever-growing influence; through Bismarck, social welfare policies gained respectibility within conservative circles.

As we have already noted, the word "socialism" was liable to varied interpretations. At times, state socialism was equated with social welfare policies; at other times, every form of state support or intervention was designated as socialism. In the course of the debate on Hedlund's proposal in the lower house in 1884, a characteristically old-school liberal (von der Lancken) avowed that he was not intimidated by the word socialism "because socialism and an ordered state organization are interchangeable concepts." Yet it is evident that there was an undercurrent of thought associated with the word that was suggestive of socialism or communism as represented by the First International or other revolutionary movements. Because different connotations were given to the words, socialism could be described in disparaging or meritorious terms by persons sharing the same point of view. Therefore, the fact that one man might declare himself a socialist and another vehemently attack socialism did not per se define their philosophies. It was only after the breakthrough of Social Democracy in Sweden that the word gradually gained a certain uniformity of meaning through its association with this movement.

During the years around 1887 political debate centered on the tariff question. The victory of protectionism meant a depreciation of economic liberalism in that it overthrew the latter's classical principal stand. In all likelihood these circumstances helped weaken the fundamental opposition to social welfare policies. Once the basic principle of economic freedom and the absence of state action had been abandoned on a central issue it was difficult to defend its application to other issues.

The positions taken by the politically and culturally leading newspapers toward Social Democracy and the labor movement during the 1880s had several features in common. The so-called liberal labor movement, founded on workers' associations, was consistently described in sympathetic terms—except for occasional warnings in regard to its radical tendencies. Liberal papers, in particular, were also sympathetic and encouraging toward the trade union movement, which had made rapid advances during the decade and had not yet come under the influence of Social Democracy to any appreciable extent. In the beginning, Social Democracy agitation attracted little attention; when it did draw comments, these were often a mixture of criticism, irony, and indulgent benevolence. In its early years, the movement apparently aroused no anxiety. It was evidently expected that it would be inconsequential or else develop along moderate lines. *Göteborgs Handels- och Sjöfartstidning,* a paper that systematically advocated production associations, apparently entertained the hope that Social Democracy would follow this line; in view of Palm's early agitation, such an expectation was understandable. The conservative, protectionist paper *Nya Dagligt Allehanda* intimated that conservatives and socialists did share some points in common, but that old-school liberals did not understand the labor question; they advocated tariffs, but considered broadening of the franchise to be without value to the workers.

A few years later the mood was different. Both interest in and criticism of Social Democracy were heightened. Newspapers that had previously regarded Social Democracy as harmless and had even demonstrated a certain appreciation of the movement now reiterated that the movement's revolutionary tendencies threatened the social order; they declared that if the working class turned Social Democratic, it would forfeit the sympathy it once enjoyed. In April 1889, *Dagens Nyheter* stated that socialism had steered the Swedish labor movement onto an impractical course. "Instead of restricting itself to attainable reforms and to assembling all the forces that work toward progress [for these reforms], socialism is content with nothing less than the total transformation of the existent society, and it decries everything and everyone that does not directly aim toward this goal." In England the workers had behaved more sensibly and had therefore achieved greater success. In November 1886, *Svenska Dagbladet* underscored the revolutionary nature of Social Democracy and continued to editorialize: "It is as clear as day that if a large number of our Swedish workers join such a movement they will, on the one hand, become suspect in the eyes of all who wish to protect the foundations of our present society, and, on the other, lose the sympathy of many who are concerned with the workers' welfare and the improvement of their condition."

Statements of this kind, which recurred constantly during subsequent years, lend support to the supposition that during its initial phase Social Democracy actually smothered rather than fanned the spirit of reform. Obviously, no definitive judgment can be passed on this question. It is in any event clear that Social Democracy cannot be credited with forcing through social reform legislation at the close of the century. The apprehension created by the movement may have caused some to be more inclined to grant concessions, but may have cooled the sympathies of others and solidified the basic conservative outlook.

The investigative report called for by the Riksdag of 1884, pursuant to Hedin's proposal, caused the government to appoint a committee under the chairmanship of F. Hederstierna the same year. In 1888 and 1889 the committee delivered a series of reports that included, among other recommendations, proposals for protective workers' legislation accident insurance, an old age insurance. In its report concerning protective legislation and accident insurance, the committee emphasized the precarious position of the working class. As the tasks of the worker became more complex and he became subject to forces that he could not foresee or control, more effective legislation would be necessary to protect him.

> This does not permit of the objection that the interests of the parties concerned can best be served by leaving it up to them to decide among themselves with full and unrestricted freedom the conditions under which the work ought to be carried out. The socially and economically weak position of manual laborers in general produces [a situation] in which they are not infrequently forced to undertake work even under conditions highly unfavorable to them, to their lives, to their health. . . . As experience clearly shows, where such inequality prevails between the conditions of the parties, legislation aimed at furthering the welfare of all must particularly seek to safeguard the interests of the employees.

The report on old age insurance noted the argument that obligatory insurance supposedly entailed undue interference with individual freedom by depriving a person of the right to spend his earnings as he pleased. In answer to this charge the committee contended that societal life always entails curtailment of an individual's freedom in disposing of his own property and that "old age insurance for the benefit of the majority can only be attained through compulsory [means]. . . ." This statement, in turn, gave rise to objections on the part of the committee chairman, among others. Hederstirna protested that the state had no right "to interfere in the actions or utterances of a responsible adult with the claim that it is doing so for his own good," and that most people would consider compulsory insurance detestable.

Official comments made in response to the committee's last mentioned proposal were predominantly negative, but in the main they were not based on the theories of economic liberalism. The provincial governor of Örebro county, A. Bergström, stated that the proposal amounted to a kind of state socialism and noted that social legislation in Germany had proved instrumental in removing the causes of socialism. Measures of the kind indicated in the proposal were per se justified. "If the disparities between the classes of manual laborers on the one hand and the well-to-do, educated social classes on the other appear in such a glaring light that the former not only become irreconcilable but indeed give cause for us to fear an outbreak of social strife between the two classes—yes, a revolution—then it would seem that the moment had arrived to move toward legislation that can effect a reconciliation and smother the expected outbreaks of flaming class hatred." The provincial governor in Kopparberg county, Treffenberg, made a pathetic appeal for a position that was both humanitarian and also fundamentally conservative. It was the duty of the state to work toward the betterment of the conditions of the working class, and such efforts would coincidentally make social peace possible. Treffenberg concluded his remarks with a recommendation for broader social measures. "If this comes to pass and the labor movement nevertheless threatens to gain ascendancy that disturbs social peace and summons all good citizens to the protection of that peace, then and not until then, can these citizens allow themselves the consolation of a clear conscience, in which spirit Bismarck recommended his program of old age insurance to the German Reichstag with the exclamation 'If we must fight, let us be able to do so with a clear conscience.'" The report of the committee on worker insurance was partly revised by a new committee, which subsequently issued a report that agreed in principle with that put forth by the first committee.

Even a summary account of the many debates on social reform that took place in the Riksdag in the course of the decade following the presentation of the recommendations of the committee on workers' insurance would lead us too far afield. The majority of these debates did not produce any positive result. Discussions of insurance matters in particular were largely concerned with technicalities and without ideological relevance. However, the principles of old liberalism and social reformism continued to be at variance. In 1880 workers' protection legislation was passed on government initiative. At the time of its enactment several speakers protested that state interference was unnecessary and inadvisable, that the legislation made the state play the role of a custodian, and that the government's action was really prompted by a desire to gain popularity among the workers. In contrast, the minister of civil affairs asserted that "the theory of freedom of contract, according to which government authorities would not act in respect to such circumstances" was untenable; "closing one's eyes to the fact we also have a labor problem is playing hide-and-seek with time." The law was described as a necessary means to quiet labor unrest. (One speaker even declared "the law will prove an obstacle to socialism.") Employers, too, acknowledged the practical necessity of the legislation. Among the proponents of social reformist views in subsequent debates were not only the radical S. A. Hedin but also Bishop Billing and Provincial Governor Treffenberg, whose basic conservatism was indisputable. Speaking in the 1891 debate on accident insurance, Billing said:

> Just as the worker does not sense and cannot grasp his employer's problems, so we, who are more well situated, cannot grasp the workers' problems—their bread-and-butter problem—their unremitting anxiety about their daily bread in the literal sense of the word. Since they are weighed down by this worry each and every day it is not surprising that they lend a willing ear and mind to words that appeal to the basest elements of their inner selves, words aimed at teaching them to say "it is we who do the work and another who reaps the profits." . . . This requires an antidote, and a strong one. . . . There is and always has been but one way to silence those who speak evil, and that is through good deeds.

In the 1895 debate on workers' pensions, Treffenberg criticized the objection raised by the Committee of Supply, which held that the consequence of pension plans might be that the worker would "cease to rely on his own ability and foresight." Countered Treffenberg: "The experience of almost nineteen centuries ought to have taught the author [of the committee report] that it has been precisely the hopelessness of the struggle of the working class, including the gravest [struggle], that of protection against need in old age, that has necessarily and totally suffocated their feeling of responsibility, a feeling that can be cultivated and strengthened only when and if the conditions of society provide that each worker with the right outlook can secure a tolerable livelihood in old age." One of the main champions of classical—if a somewhat modified—liberalism was Hans Forssell. In the 1891 debate he advanced a recurrent theme of the opponents of social welfare in his statement that state socialism "had not encouraged caution, care, and reflection, but had augmented carelessness and recklessness."

By and large the predominant line on social legislation remained negative. This line was based in part on general liberal arguments and in part on arguments related to fiscal policy and on criticism of details of the proposals put forward. The proposals for social legislation advanced during the 1890s embraced just about all issues that would be subjects of debate for the next thirty years—issues such as working hours and housing, together with the measures already mentioned. These proposals did not, however, yield any material result at the time. Of note is the fact that the Riksdag rejected several bills, including bills for accident insurance and old age pensions. On numerous occasions the upper house demonstrated a more markedly conservative tendency than the lower, even though its membership did include some of the most able representatives of social reformism. Yet the 1890s can more justily be called the breakthrough period for social legislation than the 1880s. The number of proposals for social legislation advanced during the '90s was incomparably greater than during the previous decade, and the debates on the issues were penetrating and afforded considerable clarification. In addition, within the legislature there gradually emerged a social reformist ideology that was fundamentally opposed to old-fashioned liberalism and which obviously gained an ever-increasing number of supporters in spite of the defeats it suffered. Around this time, too, the question of social reformism began to make an imprint on party programs. The subject was treated, albeit in vague terms, in the 1893 elections platforms of both ruralist parties; the more progressive of the two declared that it wished to lend "vigorous assistance to the cautious implementation of the demands of others as well, [demands] which are called for by the times and which could contribute to the peaceful development of the nation and to the people's happiness and prosperity." "The People's party" (*folkpartiet*), organized in 1896, represented the "new liberalism" that would later form the core of the Liberal party. *Folkpartiet* declared that it wished to strive for "effective measures for the protection of the lives and health of the workers, for facilitating the settlement of conflicts between workers and employers, and for the provision for workers of an economically secure existence in the event of privation or incapacity to work."

A social reformist ideology was developed in a series of publications that were part of the discussion on the subject outside of the chambers of the Riksdag. Swedish writers were influenced by Bismarck's social policies, the so-called official socialism, and by Christian socialism as proclaimed primarily in the papal encyclical of 1891. The most thorough, comprehensive exposition was that written by Fahlbeck in his work *Estates and Classes,* published in 1892. This work combined distinct social reformism with incisive criticism of Social Democracy and disaffection toward democracy. Fahlbeck wrote that the proletarian in modern society "cannot bless poverty in the manner of St. Francis of Assisi or even calmly acquiesce in it when he sees his legal equals wallowing in all the splendours of riches. In a society that has established equality as a fundamental principle, social misery acquires a sting that it did not possess under a different social order." The right of private ownership and initiative were essential to progress, but the public ought to be able to exert substantial influence on working conditions. The goal was that each person attain a standard of living corresponding to his contribution of work, and that no one own capital without working. Among other measures, Fahlbeck recommended protective legislation, workers' insurance of different kinds, and profit-sharing for workers.

There is no doubt that, by and large, there was a considerable difference between the social reformist programs advanced within and outside of the Riksdag by bourgeois groups that were influential, if not yet pace-setters, and the social welfare demands espoused by Social Democrats. As a rule the bourgeois groups called for changes that were considerably less far-reaching. But this difference was not at the core of the dichotomy between bourgeois and Social Democratic ideology that prevailed at this time. The main reason for the schism was that the Marxist-oriented Social Democrats viewed social welfare measures as a gain of limited value or as a means to attain the one objective that overshadowed all others: the social revolution. In 1897 Branting wrote that although state socialism was conservative in principle, the party could, in certain cases, help bring about state socialist measures "while we strive for a complete revolution." Danielsson expressed the same thought in harsher terms: the bourgeois proposals for reform were intended to "patch up the gaps or prevent additional damage to the structure of established bourgeois society." Social Democracy, on the other hand, sought "reform action according to certain determined methods that will pave the way for and facilitate a social revolution."

As the foregoing indicates, bourgeois social reformism was combined with a definite repudiation of Social Democracy. This became most apparent in 1889 when the government proposed a so-called socialist law that provided punitive action against persons agitating for measures "that imply a threat to the societal order or a danger to its existence." This provision was striken by a ruling of the lower house, but the debates on the law are indicative of the vehemence with which all groups reacted to the revolutionary aspirations of Social Democrats. A series of proposals to curtail the right to strike, which were put forth (and generally rejected) during the 1890s, can only be interpreted as attacks on the Social Democratic workers' movement.

Before concluding we should note the ideological trends within certain popular movements. These movements were wholly or principally rooted in the working class, and in considering their views we must turn to other kinds of data than those used in the previous discussion.

Before the breakthrough of the socialist-colored trade union movement in the 1890s and the early 1900s, there was no organization or movement that could authoritatively claim to represent the viewpoint of the working class.

In the years immediately following the Riksdag reform, only the so-called liberal labor movement really acted as the voice of labor. The extent to which this movement truly represented the class it claimed to speak for defies accurate judgment. There are no exact data on the number of labor associations; organizations from between 40 and 50 localities were represented at workers' meetings held 1879-1890, but organizations existed in other localities as well. Sundry figures provide the only records of membership size in the various associations. In 1874 the Stockholm association reported approximately 3500 members; in 1868 membership in the Malmö association was 2400, and membership in the Gothenburg association in the same year—the year of the largest membership—was 3450. In addition, persons who were not craftsmen or laborers were, as a rule, accepted by the associations. (The city of Norrköping was one exception to this.) Leaders of the associations were not infrequently persons with distinctly "bourgeois" professions—factory owners, journalists, and teachers, for example. This catagory of member constituted about half of all the representatives at workers' meetings, a statistic that can probably be explained by the fact that the most prominent, well-situated members were the ones to be chosen as delegates. Of the members who could be counted as working class, craftsmen apparently constituted a majority. These observations notwithstanding, the radical demands that the workers' associations at times expressed indicate that the associations cannot, contrary to some assumptions, be viewed as upper-class organizations acting in the name of labor.

The liberal labor movement associated itself with ideas that had been sporadically advanced in other periods and with early forms of workers' organizations. It can, nevertheless, with some justification be characterized as an independent movement that emerged in the middle of the 1860s. Two publications that appeared in 1865 were of particular moment to the development of the movement. The first was the previously mentioned work by Hamilton, *On the Working Class and Workers' Associations,* the other a pamphlet, *On the System of Associations in Foreign Countries with Special Reference to the Schultze-Delitzschska Credit Associations.* Ljungberg, the author of the latter, called for different kinds of workers' associations: housing and credit associations, associations for the purchase of raw materials for craftsmen, consumers' associations, and producton or manufacturing associations. In 1866 Ljungberg formed "a society for the promotion of workers' associations." A substantial number of workers' associations arose in the course of the next few years as well as several organizations along cooperative lines. The cooperatives, however, proved to be of transient significance, for within a few years most of them failed. Not until the end of the century would a more stable and comprehensive cooperative movement make its appearance. (This movement had no relation to the liberal workers' associations and shall be treated in a subsequent section.) The only exception was a peculiar type of cooperative, the Smith "ring movement," organized in 1883 by a distiller called L. O. Smith. Within a few months it gained many members, particularly among Stockholm's workers; it subsequently died a sudden death, however, and probably left only a legacy of suspicion of all cooperative movements among large groups of workers.

In the beginning, workers' associations were evidently totally under the sway of the liberal ideology of self-help. They did not call for public support of the cooperative activity they recommended; instead, they reiterated that state and local governments should not interfere in the economy. Socialist movements in other nations were frequently described as dangerous and unrealistic. Workers' associations could "peacefully and sensibly . . . accomplish many times more than the large international workers' associations of England, France, and Germany accomplish with all their noise and commotion and their fierce and frequently illegal demonstrations. . . ." Social equality was a recurrent theme: citizens should not be evaluated and treated according to their wealth, birth, or position. Another recurrent demand was improvement of the education of workers: this would lead to the realization of the idea of equality and generally raise the status of workers. The associations did serve as educational agencies by holding lectures and discussions. Other means advanced to improve the lot of labor were sobriety, frugality, and proper moral conduct. The associations adhered to traditional principles in regard to religion and nationalism. Some examples of slogans that are indicative of the associations' programs typify the general ideological posture. "Help yourself and God will help you" proclaimed a heading in *The Paper for Stockholm's Workers' Associations* (which began publishing in June 1870, changed its name to *The People's Paper* in October of the same year, and ceased publication in March 1871). Its counterpart in Malmo, *The Bee Hive,* carried the slogans "Pray and work, Well-being, Education, and Contentment, Unity is strength." The first issue of the paper of the Gothenburg association explained that the workers' associations would bring about social equality "by energetic dissemination of the ennobling fruits of enlightenment among their members, by providing them with easier access to work, by furthering their material wealth, by enhancing moral purity through example and the supervisory censure that is part of the association system, by teaching members Christian mutual aid through prudent arrangements in the hour of need, by teaching them frugality and to live within one's means." One radical demand was attached to this typically liberal-conservative line: universal suffrage. The first issue of *The Paper for Stockholm's Workers'*

Associations carried a programmatic demand for "equal civil rights for all who fulfill their obligations to state and local governments." In 1871 the workers' associations petitioned the king for a proposal favoring "political franchise for all self-supporting citizens over 21 who enjoy civic confidence." In the beginning this demand was apparently overshadowed by plans for cooperatives, but it was subsequently put forth with ever-increasing ardor. On the whole, the liberal workers' movement became increasingly oriented toward political and social reform, and thus became a precursor of the democratic and social reformist New Liberalism of the 1900s.

The general trend of development can be illustrated by reviewing the proceedings at workers' conventions, where representatives of the various associations gathered. The first meeting of this type took place in 1870 and included representatives of Norwegian and Danish associations as well. The subject of cooperatives dominated the foreground, and the convention passed a number of resolutions recommending various kinds of cooperative associations. It also adopted general statements favoring education, sobriety, and proper moral conduct. Some discussion on the franchise followed the introduction of this subject by a speaker, but the convention did not adopt a resolution on this issue, on the ground that the franchise question was not germane to a forum comprising representatives of different nations with different domestic conditions. The question "can work stoppages benefit workers and the national economy?" was answered in the negative. The writings of representatives of the liberal workers' movement of the time manifest the same attitude.

Subsequent conventions were attended only by Swedes. The first in this category was held in 1879. This time scant attention was paid to the cooperative question. A resolution calling for universal suffrage was adopted, although a powerful minority wanted the franchise limited to tax payers. A resolution on children proclaimed "that the Swedish worker should raise his children with loving earnestness, with a true fear of God, willing obedience to the law, respect for parents, teachers, and authority, a clear outlook, and industry." The resolution also called for minor educational reforms and certain restrictions or ameliorations in respect to child labor. Debates within separate workers' associations suggest the existence of doubts concerning the advisability of general legislation of the work of children and minors. The convention attested to the workers' willingness to defend their country, but demanded the adjustment of some inequalities in military training. After Anton Nyström had spoken on the strike question, the convention passed a resolution to the effect that "peaceful work stoppages or strikes cannot be considered unjustifiable or unlawful, but unless they are especially well prepared and arranged, they usually turn out to be far more detrimental than beneficial to the workers." Proposals to protest against the behavior of the authorities during the Sundsvall strike were rejected, but most of the speakers in the attendant debate apparently considered the treatment of the strikers to be unjust. The convention further declared that "at present we appear to have nothing either to fear or hope for in political or social respects within Sweden . . . from the socialist, communist, or nihilistic movements in other countries." The national, religious, democratic, and liberal ideology embraced by the delegates was expressed in various contexts. The second workers' convention, held in 1882, advanced in the main the same demands as the first. Of note is the fact that the second convention espoused separation of church and state, declared its approval of the 1881 ruling regarding the labor of minors in factories and the crafts, and proclaimed its opposition to an increase in defense expenditures.

The third convention, held in 1886, adopted a program for the workers' associations that signified a definite step in a radical direction. The program articles included the following points: "Complete freedom of religion. Equality of suffrage at all political and local elections for all upright citizens who have reached their majority and have fulfilled their obligations to state and municipality. . . . Improved, tuition-free education, with a public school serving as an elementary school from which one can directly graduate to schools of higher learning. —The complete separation of education in the schools from the church. . . . The introduction of direct, progressive income and inheritance taxes. . . . The establishment of a standard work day of a maximum of 10 hours. . . . National accident and old age insurance with state contributions." The convention was attended by some Social Democrats —among them, Branting. The agenda included the question "can workers really benefit by joining the Social Democratic movement?" The delegates voted, by a bare majority, not to "enter into closer relationships with bodies whose intentions may be honorable but whose ways of reaching their goal can be subject to doubt." The minority voted for a proposal declaring that the question had not been sufficiently explored. The fourth and last convention was held in 1890. A few Social Democrats also participated on this occasion, and helped introduce some program amendments of a radical orientation. The convention approved in principle the demand for a standard 8-hour work day; the pertinent program article read as follows: "a legislated work day of 10 hours, which shall successively be reduced to 8 hours."

The convention demonstrated little interest in holding additional gatherings of this kind. The liberal workers' movement, which was built upon the workers' associations, did, in effect, come to an end with the 1890 convention.

The foremost organizational form *sans pareil* of the working class was the trade union movement, which was moving more and more under socialist influence. Workers' associations that were not connected to a political party survived. Some became purely educational organizations; others put forward political demands and arranged demonstrations for special causes. In many cases Liberals and Social Democrats worked together within the associations, which can therefore be said to have played a role in furthering collaboration between the two parties. The workers' associations have not, however, been of political significance as an independent movement since 1890.

As this account indicates, the movement gradually adopted a series of radical political, social, economic, and cultural demands. The content of the program of the liberal workers' movement was essentially the same as that of the Social Democrats' contemporary operational program. The main difference between the two was the underlying ideologies of the programs. It was Marxism, and its concomitant constellation of concepts that was the hallmark of Social Democracy.

The nonconformist religious movements, which rapidly increased in significance during the 1870s and 1880s, represented in part the same views on The Social Question as the Swedish state church. The traditional Christian social doctrine that different social classes were parts of a divinely sanctioned, harmonious whole was also expressed in sectarian preaching and provided the basis for exhortations urging loyalty and contentment. The right of private ownership was regarded as decreed by God and as necessary to society. Socialist theories were renounced as immoral and materialistic. In addition, however, the nonconformist movement contained ideas that led to a disposition favoring liberalism and democracy. Work was idealized as ordained by God and as an external sign of true piety. Worldly success resulting from industry and thrift became suffused with religious sanctity in the eyes of believers; wealth acquired a spiritual value, as long as it was not employed for temporal pleasures. It has been said that the Methodist Church did not arise from the middle class, but that it was well suited to create a middle class. The same applies in varying degrees to the nonconformist churches in general. Their relationship to economic liberalism is patent here. Because of their feeling for individualism and freedom, nonconformist movements would also form ties with the political and social aspects of liberalism. Liberal arguments were advanced to support a reduction of state coercion, including the religious coercion implied by the state church. Both conservatism and socialism were branded as doctrines that were hostile to freedom. Democracy, primarily universal suffrage, became a means of realizing religious and political freedom.

This description applies mainly to the Methodist and Baptist movements. During the 1870s and 1880s the main organs of these movements (*The Little Messenger,* later to become *The Swedish Messenger,* and *The Weekly Post,* respectively) often published articles which, in basic accord with economic liberalism, urged tolerance in relations between the classes and advocated contentment as a virtue for the poor. Such articles also editorialized regarding the elevation of the working class through sobriety, thrift, and moral propriety. Socialism was condemned on the grounds that it was inimical to freedom, was materialistic, and revolutionary. Nevertheless, the over-all impression conveyed by the nonconformist groups suggests a greater understanding of social needs than that evinced by the state church. Some articles from nonconformist papers published in 1885, when the Methodist and Baptist organs treated related questions with relative frequency, illustrate this difference. On one occasion *The Swedish Messenger* pointed out that employers did not seem to care whether their workers gained a decent livelihood or not, and that it would not be surprising if workers resorted to strikes under such conditions. Another article decried the existing great economic disparities and remarked that it was strange that the harder one worked the lower the wages one received. Such conditions "testify to selfishness on the part of those in power rather than to charity toward the needy." When, pursuant to these remarks, an employer questioned whether the paper had become socialist, the editorial reply was that the paper stood for order and the right of private ownership. "With these views, we naturally cannot approve of socialism's violent revolutionary plans . . . but there is surely a Christian socialism, to which we wish every success." The paper also attacked the opinion vented in several publications issued by the state church, which held that poverty would necessarily always exist since Jesus had spoken of poverty without disapproval. The paper contended that Jesus had not meant to sanction poverty thereby, but had simply postulated a real, existent, miserable state of affairs. The chief Baptist paper expressed similar views. History showed that class differences could be narrowed, and Christianity ought to participate in developments in this direction. It was intimated that socialist agitation was dictated by a thirst for personal gain and power and that it constituted an attack on Christianity.

The Waldenström movement, which evidently attracted members of somewhat higher social standing than those who joined the Methodist and Baptist churches, represented—at least during the period concerned—a distinctly more conservative approach than the other two movements. It showed comparatively little interest in politics or social questions; when these subjects were mentioned, it was in a tone distinctly reminiscent of that adopted by the state church. Waldenström's own sermons and edifying writings were markedly conservative, with elements of typical nonconformist old-fashioned liberalism. The powers that be are God's will and must receive unconditional obedience. An authority that is good is so by the grace of God to the people, a bad authority represents God's judgment on the people. Obedience to authority, whatever its character, does not curtail individual freedom. "He who willingly and with all his heart obeys his God and, even in the face of the most grievous misfortune, reverses the expressions of God's good and merciful will, he is free even in the gravest of external circumstances." Class differences are also ordained by God. "Life is such that some must be relatively rich, others, on the other hand, relatively poor. This is not determined by chance or by aggression by one party, but is part of God's order. All attempts to change this are in vain." If the rich employers were to lose their property, the workers employed by them would suffer the most. Work is a duty, and the acquisition of riches through work is natural. But neither rich man nor poor man ought to give his heart to winning wealth or property. The poor man has much greater reason to be content, since riches do not really bring happiness. "Perhaps none lead such an empty, restless, and anxious life as the rich. On the other hand, no one can describe the riches and happiness of the man who eats his daily God-given bread, earned through honorable work, in the fear of God and with a contented soul, and who lives and dies trusting for himself and those dearest to him in God's paternal grace." The press of the Missionary Federation (*Missionsförbundet*) frequently leveled sharp attacks on socialism; general statements on The Social Question tended to devolve into exhortations for contentment and "faith in little things." Yet the liberal-democratic line was without doubt more apparent in this press than in Waldenström's own religious and political sermonizing.

When, around the turn of the century, nonconformist religious movements became more politically activated as a cadre within the new Liberal party, the demand for democracy held the foreground. Among the political objectives one wanted to reach through democracy were the abolition or limitation of the system of the state church, legislation to promote national temperance, and a reduction of the defense system. Collaboration with the Social Democrats proved feasible to a certain extent on each of these points. Possibilities for such collaboration now existed within the sphere of social policies as well, for the nonconformists had increasingly come to accept the social reformist line and had abandoned the old-fashioned liberalism to which they had adhered earlier.

Another organization that deserves mention in this context is the Salvation Army. It had succeeded in making inroads in Sweden during the 1880s, and represented a pathos demonstrated by charitable deeds and social works that was not bound to any ideas of political action or governmental reform. As Thörnberg said, the movement thus became "a temporary stronghold of conservatism for us within the broad strata of the masses"; the army was not infrequently depicted as a dangerous rival to Social Democracy.

The modern temperance movement made its appearance at about the same time as Social Democracy, and its early course of development was often marked by competition with the latter. The political position of this movement will therefore be treated in a separate chapter dealing with the Social Democratic stand on the temperance issue. We shall therefore only point out here that, in the main, the temperance cause underwent the same type of development as the other movements discussed. It became more and more adament in its demands for not only individual sobriety but for political and social legislation against abusive use of alcohol as well; in the process, it also became committed to the realization of universal suffrage and other democratic reforms as means by which it could reach its goals.

This exposition has primarily dealt with the discussion that can be described as directly concerned with The Social Question. Only in passing have we noted the recognized fact that the force of democratic and cultural trends made itself felt ever more keenly toward the end of the nineteenth century. The demand for universal suffrage was pressed partly for basic democratic reasons and partly because of its potential use as a tool for social reformist, religious-liberal, sectarian, and temperance movements. The prerequisites for the formation of the Liberal party, which would represent a victorious middle road in Swedish politics in the early 1900s, were thereby given. Opposition to this party came from the Right, Although not fettered by the views of old-fashioned liberalism, the Right represented a larger measure of conservatism in social reform than did the New Liberalism, and it clearly disassociated itself from the latter by its distrust of consummate democracy and its rigid adherence to certain traditional institutions; in time, strengthening national defense appeared to become the paramount positive mission of this party. Counter to both bourgeois parties, Social Democracy aimed at a total reconfiguration of society. In comparison with this goal, Social Democrats viewed mundane reforms relevant only to the politics of the day as being of subordinate importance, and they regarded democracy primarily as a means of accomplishing their ultimate objective. The next few decades may be meaningfully interpreted as a successive attenuation of the fundamental antagonisms between the parties. Liberals and Social Democrats joined forces in the fight for popular government. This collaboration served to whet the Liberals' desire for social reform on the one hand, and to mollify the revolutionary demands of the Social Democrats on the other. Once democracy was a reality, it gradually came to provide a basis for accommodation and for a concerted political life that was born of concord and included all the major parties.

Marx and Modern Social Democracy

The Principal Features of Marxian Theory

IN ESSENTIAL RESPECTS the socialist theories that grew in prominence in political debates after the French Revolution postulated the same value judgments and objectives as liberalism and its precursory philosophies of enlightenment. They believed that human reason, freed from prejudice and the shackles of tradition, could attain the happiness and intellectual development of the individual that was their goal. Political, social, and religious doctrines and institutions were regarded as the causes of problems and wrongs in society. Insofar as these theories presupposed that under certain conditions human beings could coexist and interact in freedom and peace on both an international and national scale they also presupposed a natural goodness in mankind. Liberalism's principles of social equality, political self-government, and civil liberty were accepted. Progress, that is, the realization of the established goals, was considered by many to be a kind of natural law, at once inevitable and worth striving for.

While pursuing liberal criticism of ideas that had once held sway, socialism also attacked the economic doctrines underlying contemporary liberal policy. It was not alone in this. Ideologists who could commonly be classified as adherents of conservative or liberal schools of thought put forth acid criticism of liberal thinking, criticism that would prove significant to the development of socialism. However, writers who could really be designated as socialists, called for far more thoroughgoing changes than other theorists. They wrote of a new society, a new system, a new organization of economic life, not of reforms or improvements within the contours of society as it existed. Moreover, socialism came to act ever more emphatically as the representative of the industrial working class. In the socialist view, while this class was steadily growing in importance, its conditions were progressively deteriorating, or were, in any case, not undergoing the same kind of improvements as those of other groups. In opposition to the nobility, to the clergy, to the landowner—in general to the conservatism or traditionalism of the classes that had ruled uncontested prior to the revolution and to the liberalism of entrepreneurs and businessmen—stood the socialism of the industrial workers, their demand for economic security and a higher standard of living through planned, collectivist production.

Early socialists employed different approaches and therefore cannot, as frequently occurs, be grouped under a common label such as "Utopian" or "rationalist." Certain writers, such as Saint-Simon and Fourier, wove their views into a historical-philosophical fabric, a common practice at that time. According to these schemas, the history of mankind was divided into a series of epochs; the author commonly thought of himself as writing just at the dawn of a new epoch, or even of a final, definitive stage of development. Others, such as Owen, tried primarily to win support for their aims by appealing to discontent and compassion: socialism was considered a consequence of certain value judgments, and little heed was paid to historical points of view. Some appealed mainly to the upper classes in the belief that they could thus acquire a sympathetic understanding of the idea of a social revolution; others counted on the workers' own efforts and concentrated their agitation within this class. There were those who believed in a violent takeover of power and in a dictatorship, as well as those who trusted in gradual change through legal forms, using democratic institutions. Similar contradictions, particularly on the issue of tactics, manifested themselves in the workers' movement, which was functioning on a practical level but did not enjoy the direct participation of many of socialism's leading theorists. The Chartist movement in England, the strongest organized movement within the working class during the first half of the nineteenth century, produced examples of divergent opinions on the question of tactics; and competing lines of thought that correspond to Social Democracy and syndicalism in recent times.

A brief review of the main themes in the foremost early socialist theories will illustrate the similarities and differences between them. Saint-Simon anticipated Marxian socialism on important points. Throughout history, a certain social class had exploited the labor of others; in the present society industrial workers were the most exploited group. The task at hand now was to substitute "exploitation of the land by men in compact" in place of "exploitation of men by men." The right of private control of the means of production leads to desultory acts and waste. Production should therefore be organized and led by the state, which would cause an increase in production conducive to general prosperity. The right of inheritance ought to be abolished in order that all might proceed from the same starting point. Full equality would nevertheless not prevail, for outstanding ability must be rewarded. An elite formed as a natural consequence of free competition between individuals would conduct the affairs of their states. Progress toward the state of the future would be slow and peaceful, for all would be convinced of the wisdom of the transformation to take place. Fourier wanted to build up voluntary production unions of a special kind, consisting of a relatively small number of persons (ca. 1500), which would operate within delimited geographic areas. Class differences would not be totally eliminated; members of the "phalansteries" would receive different incomes according to their ability, work input, and the capital they invested. All would, however, be entitled to minimum necessities. A detailed work schedule would provide considerable variety in job assignments. These small production units would be part of larger production combinations, and, in the final analysis, all of humanity would form a just economic entity. Owen stressed the educational viewpoint above all others. Like Fourier, he aspired to the formation of small, self-governing communities. In his last work, *The Revolution in the Mind and Practice of the Human Race,* published in 1849, he put forth a complete constitution for such "townships." The principles and methods used by society in raising children would, within a short space of time, bring about a human community in which each person would think rationally, with the furthering of the common weal as his prime motivation. Total equality would prevail. Owen, too, foresaw a peaceful development of the order of the future. The French socialists who succeeded Saint-Simon and Fourier, on the other hand, evinced revolutionary trends of thought. Proudhon was the first to utilize a Hegelian method in support of his socialist theories, particularly in his work of 1840 on the right of ownership, in which the main theme is "property is theft." His later works display varying lines of thought, both in regard to political tactics and the organization of the new society, and can be cited by anarchists as well as by pure socialists. Louis Blanc wished to carry out collectivism by organizing state factories, which would progressively gain control of all industrial production.

Around the middle of the nineteenth century it was common to designate as "socialism" these and other currents of thought that called for collective ownership of the means of production, or at least for collective management of production, and that linked these demands with the idea of abolishing poverty and attaining a more equitable distribution of wealth. The term "social democracy" was used to designate a brand of socialism whose adherents aspired to achieve their goals within a democratic framework. Sometimes the word communism was used as synonymous with socialism. At one time a distinction was drawn between the two concepts: communism was interpreted to entail common ownership of necessities other than the means of production. This delineation subsequently fell into disuse, and toward the end of the century the designation "communism" itself fell into obscurity.

The term would not be revived again until after the Russian October Revolution of 1917, when it was returned to currency in a modified sense.

Marx's theories were worked out in collaboration with his friend, Friedrich Engels, who later added to and refined them. They represent to a large extent a systematization according to Hegelian method and use Hegelian concepts previously featured in socialist debates. We shall not attempt here to closely examine the various influences on Marx or try to determine which aspects of his ideas were original. We shall, instead, confine ourselves to a consideration of the essential ingredients in his theory. In order to understand Marxian doctrine and the various interpretations of it we must bear in mind that Marx, like Hegel, applied different perspectives. The two most important of these are known as his major and minor perspectives. Marx fashioned his most important generalizations from his major perspective. In using this perspective he sought to give an overview of the central themes in the development of mankind and, at the same time, to analyze in particular the factors he believed would lead to an early social revolution. In this respect he wore the mantle of a philosopher-historian. In other contexts, he concerned himself with more specific, concrete events and conditions. In his second role, that of a political writer and journalist, he attempted to fix the central themes to a contemporary period and deliver prophecies of a future that was close at hand.

His grand design of human development was not suitable for such considerations. When he wished to capture proximate political and social realities, Marx was forced to impart a different meaning to the terms he used and generally made statements that are incompatible with the basic ideas in his major perspective. The doctrine that can be constructed from the ideas expounded in this, Marx's minor perspective, deviates in substantial respects from general historical-philosophical teaching. A number of basic concepts—for example, classes, revolution, the dictatorship of the proletariat—lend themselves to varying definitions and therefore to varying factual interpretations, all of which can be supported by citing Marx. Differences in interpretation of Marx are largely occasioned by such extrapolations.

We shall not endeavor a complete analysis of Marx's works in accordance with this apparently basic point of view. We shall only summarize the central features of both perspectives—which are naturally not mutually exclusive. This account will be based on Marx's later works, particularly those that have been of significance in the Social Democratic debate. The works of his youth, which are directly derived from Hegel or directly criticize Hegel's doctrine, will be omitted. Since our purpose is to present Marx as the theorist of socialism, not to examine the evolution of his thinking, our review will make no attempt to clarify Marx's views at different periods.

According to Marx, the history of mankind passes through three epochs. This postulate was presented in *Deutsche Ideologie,* written in collaboration with Engels, 1845–1846. The prehistoric epoch, which was treated briefly, corresponded to the state of nature depicted by the ideologists of the Enlightenment. Mankind lived in a kind of primitive communism, without divisions of labor, class differences, or government. Freedom prevailed in the sense that societal coercive power was absent, but not in the sense in which Hegel conceived of it, which entailed the existence of opportunities for full individual development. Man had not yet learned to utilize nature's resources and therefore lived in poverty and ignorance. During the second epoch man fashioned instruments that enabled him to make more effective use of natural resources. Division of labor and social differentiation arose. Class stratification led to the establishment of a coercive order, the state, which defended existent conditions, particularly the successively emergent right of ownership. In the course of this epoch the system of production underwent repeated change: new classes that possess more modern production techniques come to power. Finally, when production potentials have reached a certain peak and a universal exchange of goods has been established, the third epoch is ushered in. Mankind has now won a complete victory over nature and no longer encounters any difficulties in meeting material needs. Class stratification and with it, the state, which had been a necessity during former times of scarcity, have now disappeared. Man is liberated from state coercion, and he is also freed in the sense that he now has the prerequisites for unrestricted intellectual and material development.

This classification into epochs is the background for Marx's studies, which are primarily concerned with conditions during the second epoch and the transition from this to the third epoch. The second epoch goes through several stages of disintegration. A new mode of production leads to a new division of labor, the rise of a new ruling class, and a new structure of society. Marx believed that he was living in the end of the last stage of the second epoch. According to his prediction, the death of this stage meant that mankind would would pass from the second to the third epoch, which would herald a higher, more genuine life for all humanity.

"The history of all societies that have existed up to this time is the history of class struggle." So begins *The Communist Manifesto*. The statement refers to the second epoch of mankind's development, but it does not mean to imply that all events stem from social conflicts, an assertion that would seem absurd according to common parlance. Marx's intent is that the decisive stages of development in the epoch concerned are determined by change in the relations of production, which results in the emergence of a new mode of production and a new ruling class. By "ruling class" Marx meant that social group which, in each stage, owns the means of production characteristic of that stage and in this capacity exploits and oppresses other groups. The best examples of a ruling class were the feudal nobility of the Middle Ages and the beginning of modern history, and the bourgeoisie (the entrepreneurs) of the period after the French Revolution. According to some of Marx's statements, only the ruling class can be described as a class in the true sense; the others, the oppressed groups, do constitute a class vis-à-vis the rulers, but they are not united by a spirit of solidarity that would cause them to form a class "of themselves." In each stage an antagonism eventually develops between existing social relations and the forces of production; the latter have developed to such an extent that a new mode of production and a new social order have become necessary. Now the oppressed groups, who will sustain the new order, band together to constitute a class, and there begins a class struggle, which is by its very nature always a political struggle, a struggle for supremacy in the state. The class struggle turns into a revolution, after which a new ruling class assumes leadership. The example of such a transformation most frequently cited by Marx is the seizure of power by the bourgeoisie, symbolized by the French Revolution.

We must bear in mind that Marx conceived of the class struggle as beginning only when a certain order of production and the class that sustains it have finished playing their roles, that is, are no longer able to utilize the forces of production in a rational manner. "Each societal form must do its best, so to speak, before the attempt to revolutionize society is able to make progress through the organization of a revolutionary class"; thus Hagerström interprets Marx's thinking. When a revolutionary class arises it acts not only in its own interest but in the interests of the whole of society, for its victory means an increase in production and a more rational utilization of the forces of production. In its struggle against the ruling class, a revolutionary class thus acquires support even from groups over which it will, in turn, emerge ascendant. A corollary to Marx's view is that the predominant ideas of each stage are rational from a special point of view. "The ruling ideas of each age have ever been but the ideas of its ruling class," writes Marx in the *Communist Manifesto.* Even though they may contain absurd or contradictory notions, the ideologies are basically a correct expression of the interest of the ruling class, and thereby of the interest of society as a whole; they are "nothing but the idealistic expression of the prevailing material relations." The appearance of revolutionary ideas indicates that a revolutionary class is in the process of formation and that revolution is imminent. Thus are Marx's theories supposed to demonstrate their own validity: since Marx was able to predict a social revolution, such a revolution must be impending.

According to Marx, social classes thus become the social instruments by which progress is brought about. The advent of each new ruling class brings with it a new, improved order of production. In Marx's theory, classes fulfill the same function as nations in Hegel's theory inasmuch as they represent stages in the evolution toward perfection. Yet according to Marx's major perspective, not all social groups can be regarded in this manner. Farmers, for example, never have and never will be the vehicles of progress. It follows that they can never constitute a class in the true sense. An analogous line of thought runs through Hegel's thinking: most collective bodies, referred to as states or peoples in common parlance, do not play any role in the development of the Universal Consciousness or Spirit and therefore are not states or people in the special Hegelian sense. In order that Marx's scheme be sustained, a class must be regarded as a natural unit, as a kind of organism. This does not preclude intraclass conflicts, but it does mean that a class constitutes a delimited entity in relation to other social groups. The acts, interests, and aims of a class are described as if it were human. This is essentially what is new in Marx's class theory. As Marx himself said, many writers before him had discussed the concept of class and had emphasized the importance of class struggles; Marx's innovation was that he fit the classes into his Hegelian schema as if they were superindividual personalities operative in history. This was the thought underlying the idea that the liberation of the working class "must be its own doing."

It may seem strange that Marx gave no definition of the class concept in his statements based on the major perspective. This seeming omission is obviously connected with his way of treating the contributions of the classes. A class is first of all a symbol for a specific order of production, which determines its nature. However, there have been many attempts to establish the Marxian class concept in a formula. These endeavors have not always paid sufficient heed to the fact that Marx imparted different connotations to the word "class"—as we shall see in the following. The class concept just considered is fundamental to the major perspective and for the doctrine of class struggle in the true sense. According to this concept, there is normally but one class in a society; only during revolutionary periods does an additional class arise, the ruling class of the future, and a class struggle ensues. In other contexts Marx speaks of classes in a totally different manner that is closer to common usage; we shall return to this point.

The social revolution Marx considered imminent would be of a fundamentally different character than previous revolutions. Proceeding from Marx's premises, the reasons for this can be established in various ways. The productive forces reach such a high level that the division of society into rulers and subjects, exploiters and exploited no longer needs to be maintained because the struggle over the means of production, and thereby over the products, underlying this division is no longer necessary. The class, the proletariat or industrial workers, which will carry out the coming revolution, has no other classes beneath it; it will not in turn become the oppressor of others in the manner of previous victorious classes. "All previous movements have been movements of minorities or in the interests of minorities," writes Marx in *The Communist Manifesto*. The proletarian movement is an independent movement of the great majority, in the interest of the great majority. The proletariat, the lowest stratum in present society, cannot rise, cannot raise itself up without blowing apart the entire superstructure of strata that constitutes official society." After the victory of the proletariat all class differences will therefore be overcome and thus the official power itself, the state, whose existence has been contingent upon class differences, will be superfluous. In *The Communist Manifesto* Marx describes the final phase of the development he predicted in this manner:

When, in the course of development, class distinctions have disappeared, and all production has been concentrated in the hands of a vast association of the whole nation, the public power will lose its political character. Political power, properly so called, is merely the organized power of one class for oppressing another. If the proletariat during its contest with the bourgeoisie is compelled, by the force of circumstances, to organize itself as a class, if, by means of a revolution, it makes itself the ruling class, and, as such, sweeps away by force the old conditions of production, then it will, along with these conditions, have swept away the conditions for the existence of class antagonisms and of classes generally, and will thereby have abolished its own supremacy as a class.

In place of the old bourgeois society, with its classes and class antagonisms, we shall have an association in which the free development of each is the condition for the free development of all.*

Marx conceived of this ultimate revolution as universal in scope, although it did not necessarily have to occur simultaneously in all nations. A general tendency toward similarity in mode of production prevails, and with it, similarity in the division of society and the concomitant requisites for a social rev-

* From *The Communist Manifesto,* translated by Samuel Moore, edited by Joseph Katz. The Washington Square Press, Inc., New York, 1964, pp. 94–95.

olution. The proletariat, in particular, acquires the same interests everywhere and progressively forms an international class—even though the work for its liberation must primarily be accomplished within each separate nation. Marx wrote in *German Ideology* that industrialism "has by and large created identical relations between social classes everywhere and has thereby destroyed the uniqueness of the several nations. And further, while the bourgeois class in each nation still preserves special national interests, big industry has shaped a class that has the same interests in all nations and whose nationality has already been destroyed." *The Communist Manifesto* declares:

> The workingmen have no country. We cannot take from them what they have not got. Since the proletariat must first of all acquire political supremacy, must rise to be the leading class of the nation, must constitute itself *the* nation, it is, so far, itself national, though not in the bourgeois sense of the word.

National differences and antagonisms between peoples are daily vanishing, owing to the development of the bourgeoisie, to freedom of commerce, to the world market, to uniformity in the mode of production and in the conditions of life corresponding thereto.

The supremacy of the proletariat will cause them to vanish still faster. United action, of the leading civilized countries at least, is one of the first conditions for the emancipation of the proletariat.

In proportion as the exploitation of one individual by another is put to an end, the exploitation of one nation by another will also be put to an end. In proportion as the antagonism between classes within the nation vanishes, the hostility of one nation to another will come to an end.

Why exactly must capitalist society be succeeded by a classless socialist society? Marx tried to explain this by analyzing the nature of the existing order and its developmental tendencies. His theory of value was based on the classical political economic concept of labor as the source of value. The value of a commodity was determined by the socially necessary labor expended upon it. "Socially necessary labor" meant labor-time, using the standard technical facilities of the period in question. The value of labor itself was determined by the costs entailed in producing and reproducing labor that were necessary at a certain point in time. Proceeding from this proposition it was self-evident that the disparity between the price a product commanded and the wages paid for its manufacture constituted a "surplus value" that the capitalist expropriated without doing anything to gain it. (Marx did not follow the liberal economists in trying to justify return on capital as compensation for the entrepreneur's efforts or sacrifices.) As a rule, a worker spent a certain number of hours of his working day in meeting his own requirement, that is, in producing the value proportionate to his labor, and certain hours in producing surplus value for the employer. It was in the employer's interest to obtain as much surplus value as possible, which could be accomplished partly by raising prices, partly by reducing his labor requirements (through the introduction of machines and rationalization of operations), and partly by depressing the workers' standard of living.

The foregoing account of the labor theory of value has been presented as briefly and schematically as possible. In fact, Marx presented it in varying ways in different contexts. We cannot here go into the modifications, contradictions, and ambiguities that this resulted in. We need only note that in some cases Marx used the word value to mean price, in other cases to mean something independent of price. The main point is that Marx represented the employer's profit as dependent upon exploitation of the workers—a departure from earlier theories of value, which attempted to show that profit was both natural and necessary. Ultimately, Marx's theory implied a moral condemnation of capital returns. His adversaries, on the other hand, tried to demonstrate the value of capital returns. The doctrine that labor was the sole creator of value was a basic premise of both Marx and the writers he contested. This theory was, however, subsequently abandoned, even by Social Democratic theorists. The basic thought in this theory has nevertheless proved to be of significance insofar as the idea of the impoverishment and exploitation of wage earners has added an important ingredient to socialist doctrine.

When the massive volume of production that characterizes a capitalist society can no longer be disposed of domestically because of the existing economic order, capitalists are continuously forced to seek new markets, and the exchange of goods becomes ever more international in character. Despite the new markets, economic crises of ever-greater severity occur with increasing frequency because the commodities produced cannot be disposed of. The combination of the right of private ownership of the means of production and the steady augmentation of production facilities leads to the results that Marx depicts in the *Manifesto:*

Modern bourgeois society with its relations of production, of exchange and of property, a society that has conjured up such gigantic means of production and of exchange, is like the sorcerer, who is no longer able to control the powers of the subterranean world which he has called up by his spells. For many decades now the history of industry and commerce has been but the history of the revolt of modern productive forces against modern conditions of production, against the property relations that are the conditions for the existence of the bourgeoisie and of its rule. It is enough to mention the commercial crises that by their periodical return put on trial, each time more threateningly, the existence of the entire bourgeois society. In these crises a great part not only of the existing products, but also of the previously created productive forces, are periodically destroyed. In these crises there breaks out an epidemic that, in all earlier epochs, would have seemed an absurdity—the epidemic of over-production. Society suddenly finds itself put back into a state of momentary barbarism; it appears as if a famine, a universal war of devastation had cut off the supply of every means of subsistence; industry and commerce seem to be destroyed; and why? Because there is too much civilization, too much means of subsistence, too much industry, too much commerce. The productive forces at the disposal of society no longer tend to further the development of the conditions of bourgeois property; on the contrary, they have become too powerful for these conditions, by which they are fettered, and so soon as they overcome these fetters, they bring disorder into the whole of bourgeois society, endanger the existence of bourgeois property. The conditions of bourgeois society are too narrow to comprise the wealth created by them. And how does the bourgeoisie get over these crises? On the one hand by enforced destruction of a mass of productive forces; on the other, by the conquest of new markets, and by the more thorough exploitation of the old ones. That is to say, by paving the way for more extensive and more destructive crises, and by diminishing the means whereby crises are prevented.

Marx's predictions regarding the development of social classes is linked with his economic theory. Through the exploitation of workers and competition between capitalists, which begets the formation of monopolies, the wealth accumulated by individuals grows and becomes concentrated in ever fewer hands. The number of capitalists decreases in proportion as the amount of capital owned increases. These theories of the accumulation and concentration of capital are complemented by the theories of the downfall of the middle classes and the impoverishment of the proletariat. Declares the *Manifesto:* "The present lower strata of the middle class—the small entrepreneurs, merchants and rentiers, craftsmen and peasants—all these classes will sink down into the proletariat, partly because their diminutive capital is insufficient to carry on big industrial operations and is drowned in competition with bigger capital, partly because their professional skill is rendered worthless by new methods of production." The proletarianization of these social groups sharpens and simplifies the antagonism between capitalists and proletarians. The lot of the proletariat deteriorates. "The modern laborer . . . does not advance with industrial progress, but sinks deeper and deeper below the conditions of existence of his own class. The worker becomes a pauper, and poverty develops more rapidly than population and wealth," continues the *Manifesto.* "The accumulation at one pole thus also means the accumulation of misery, onerous toil, slavery, ignorance, brutalization, and moral degredation at the opposite pole, that is to say, for the class that produces capital by its own labor." Because of difficulties in disposing of commodities and related economic crises, there arises a "reserve army" of unemployed that depresses the wage level. "The greater the wealth of society, the active capital, the extent and force of its growth, that is to say, the absolute size of the proletariat and the productive force of its work, the greater the relative extent of overpopulation or the size of the industrial reserve army. The available labor force develops for the same reasons as the expansive potential of capital. Thus the relative size of the industrial army grows in proportion to the potency of wealth. But the larger the reserve in relation to the active worker army, the more immense the size of the constant surplus population, whose misery is in inverse proportion to its burden of toil."

In *Capital* Marx provides an exposition of the fall of capitalist society through the expropriation of the expropriators which so well illustrates his theory as a whole that the principal points of his presentation merit citation.

This expropriation is brought about by the operation of the immanent laws of capitalist production, by the centralization of capital. One capitalist lays a number of his fellow capitalists low. Hand-in-hand with such centralization, concomitantly with the expropriation of many capitalists by a few, the cooperative form of the labor process develops to an ever increasing degree; therewith we find a growing tendency towards the purposive application of science to the improvement of technique; the land is more methodically cultivated; the instruments of labor tend to assume forms which are only utilizable by combined effort; the means of production are economized through being turned to account only by joint, by social labor. All the peoples of the world are enmeshed in the net of the world market, and therefore the capitalist regime tends more and more to assume an international character. While there is thus a progressive diminution in the number of the capitalist magnates (who usurp and monopolize all the advantages of this transformative process), there occurs a corresponding increase in the mass of poverty, oppression, enslavement, degeneration, and exploitation; but at the same time there is a steady intensification of the wrath of the working class—a class which grows ever more numerous, and is disciplined, unified, and organized by the very mechanism of the capitalist method of production. Capitalist monopoly becomes a fetter upon the method of production which has flourished with it and under it. The centralization of the means of production and the socialization of labor reach a point where they prove incompatible with their capitalist husk. This bursts asunder. The knell of capitalist private property sounds. The expropriators are expropriated.

The capitalist method of appropriation proceeding out of the capitalist method of production, and consequently capitalist private property, is the first negation of individual private property based upon individual labor. But, with the inexorability of a law of nature, capitalist production begets its own negation. It is a negation of a negation. This second negation does not reestablish private property, but it does reestablish individual property upon the basis of the acquisitions of the capitalist era; i.e. on cooperation and the common ownership of the land and of the means of production (which labor itself produces).

The transformation of scattered private property based upon individual labor into capitalist property is, of course, a far more protracted process, a far more violent and difficult process, than the transformation of capitalist private property (already, in actual fact, based upon a social method of production) into social property. In the former case we are concerned with the expropriation of the mass of the people by a few usurpers; in the latter case we are concerned with the expropriation of a few usurpers by the mass of the people.

Marx consistently focuses his attention on the two classes that are most significant in modern society according to his theory: the bourgeoisie and the proletariat. More or less in passing he also asserts that developments in agriculture will take the same course as those in industry. Large-scale production will become the rule, land will be accumulated in ever fewer hands, small farmers will be transformed into farm laborers. In this area, too, socialization will be brought about as a consequence of the antagonism between collective production and the right of private ownership.

According to the statements made by Marx cited in this text and others, the capitalist period will supposedly end with the breakdown of the prevailing order of production; capitalism will suddenly turn into its very antithesis. This line of thinking has become known as the "theory of catastrophe," although Marx himself never used this expression. It need hardly be emphasized that this theory contains a very peculiar notion: while capital is being accumulated by a few, the masses become impoverished; a change in this situation will occur only when, to paraphrase one of Branting's expressions, a few millionaires and the starving millions confront each other. This idea has played an exceptional role in socialist debate as a kind of theoretical basis for faith in the victory of socialism.

The theories and predictions in Marx's major perspective must be viewed in the light of his philosophical view of history. Like Hegel and many other interpreters of history of the same period, Marx was convinced that he had found the central theme in human development; he saw history as a successive realization of definite purposes. The insight Marx believed he possessed made it possible to predict with certainty the important events of the future. To Marx, socialism was not something that ought to be carried out, but something that would of necessity come to pass. According to Marx and the Marxists, the inevitability of the realization of socialism was the original contribution of Marx's teaching. His doctrine therefore came to be called "scientific socialism," in contrast to Utopian socialism, which purportedly regarded the value placed on socialist society as the decisive factor in bringing it about. Marx constantly emphasized that wishes and hopes were of no importance in his exposition. "Communism," he once wrote, "is to us not a condition to be brought about, not an ideal to which reality should conform. We call communism the *real* movement that eradicates present conditions." Twenty years later, with reference to the Paris Commune of 1871, he wrote that the working class "has no ideals to realize; it need only liberate those elements of the new society that have already developed in the bosom of the disintegrating bourgeoisie. Fully conscious of its historic mission and with heroic determination to act in a manner worthy of that mission, the working class can laugh at the coarse contumely of the lackeys of the press. . . ." Here and elsewhere, Marx shows not only that he hopes for that which he considers inevitable but also that he holds in contempt that which his theory marks as doomed. All Marxist propaganda has come to be stamped by this antinomy. Marx regarded free trade as part of the capitalist system, yet he pleaded ardently for free trade as a requisite of the development he had predicted. The class struggle is designated as a historical necessity, yet Marx constantly incited class struggle. Like other "deterministic" movements, Marxism has been unwilling to recognize determinism as an excuse for its opponents. According to Marx's over-all schema, the sway of the bourgeois class must certainly be regarded as rational and necessary as long as it persists, but this has not prevented Marx and his disciples from subjecting this class to the most fierce attacks.

The method Marx considered fundamental to his analyses and predictions has since become known as the materialist conception of history. Marx never gave a full account of this conception. The following passage from Marx's *A Contribution to the Critique of Political Economy,* published in 1859, is commonly given as the most lucid expression of its content.

"In the social production of their life, men enter into definite relations of production which correspond to a definite stage of development of their material productive forces. The sum total of these relations of production constitutes the economic structure of society, the real foundation, on which rises a legal and political superstructure and to which correspond definite forms of social consciousness. The mode of production of material life conditions (*bedingt*) the social, political, and intellectual life process in general. It is not the consciousness of men that determines (*bestimmt*) their being, but, on the contrary, their social being that determines their consciousness. At a certain stage of their development, the material productive forces of society come in conflict with the existing relations of production, or—what is but a legal expression for the same thing—with the property relations within which they have been at work hitherto. From forms of development of the productive forces these relations turn into their fetters. Then begins an epoch of social revolution. With the change of the economic foundation the entire immense superstructure is more or less rapidly transformed. In considering such transformations a distinction should always be made between the material transformation of the economic conditions of production, which can be determined with the precision of natural science, and the legal, political, religious, esthetic or philosophic—in short, ideological forms in which men become conscious of this conflict and fight it out. Just as our opinion of an individual is not based on what he thinks of himself, so can we not judge of such a period of transformation by its own consciousness; on the contrary, this consciousness must be explained rather from the contradictions of material life, from the existing conflict between the social productive forces and the relations of production. No social order ever perishes before all the productive forces for which there is room in it have developed; and new, higher relations of production never appear before the material conditions of their existence have matured in the womb of the old society itself. Therefore mankind always sets itself only such tasks as it can solve; since, looking at the matter more closely, it will always be found that the task itself arises only when the material conditions for its solution already exist or are at least in the process of formation. In broad outlines Asiatic, ancient, feudal, and modern bourgeois modes of production can be designated as progressive epochs in the economic formation of society. The bourgeois relations of production are the last antagonistic form of the social process of production—antagonistic not in the sense of individual antagonism, but of one arising from the social conditions of life of the individuals; at the same time the productive forces developing in the womb of bourgeois society create the material conditions for the solution of that antagonism. This social formation brings, therefore, the prehistory of human society to a close. . . ." *

* From Sidney Hook, *Marx and the Marxists, the Ambiguous Legacy,* D. Van Nostrand Company, Inc., New York, copyright © 1955 by Sidney Hook, pp. 140–142.

Renditions of the materialist conception of history based on these and other statements made by Marx generally stem from two lines of thought. According to one line, among the innumerable factors that enter into the development of society, one definite limited factor, the productive forces, is the really decisive one. This factor becomes the "ultimate cause" of everything; it is equivalent to God in a religious world view. The paradoxical nature of this line of thought is obvious: a certain something is supposed to be the cause of everything—of both a given situation and its antithesis. If one argues that this something itself undergoes change, that the productive forces develop, we are faced with the question of how this comes to pass, a question that has no solution in terms of Marxist theory. The other line of thought softens the argumentation in one of the following ways. Productive forces may be defined so loosely that they in effect include all factors that could conceivably be of significance. Or the productive forces or economic relations or the like may be described as not operating alone. In both cases the reasoning used is pure tautology. One arrives, not at a paradox, but at something that is self-evident: everything causes everything.

In order to clarify the lines in this discussion, we should first examine the varied interpretation of the concept "productive forces." Some have thought that this concept comprised only the technical means of production. Changes in mode of production, in the form of society, in ideologies, etc., would therefore be determined by technological development. Several of Marx's statements, however, indicate that at least in some contexts he used the term "productive force" in a much broader sense; for example, he referred to the revolutionary class as the mightiest of all productive forces. One has therefore been able to contend that the sciences, religions, and political ideologies are productive forces as well. A productive force thus becomes anything and everything that can conceivably affect developments, whatever the viewpoint. The tautological reasoning is thereby complete: productive forces determine events because everything that determines events is a productive force. Certain writers arrive at a similar result by posing the question of how productive forces change and answering it by saying that this occurs through human intervention. When intervening, human beings must be caught up by ideas of the value of the change and how it is to come about; thus one arrives at the conclusion that the materialist conception of a history implies that men's thoughts are decisive—a standpoint that is bewilderingly similar to that which was once called the idealistic conception of history. The same process has been unfolded when a theorist has chosen as his premise not productive forces but "the economic basis" or "the material foundation," or other expressions that Marx or Engels used in this context.

The theory has also been attenuated in another way. Economic or technological conditions are said to be of the "greatest" significance to developments, but they alone are not described as decisive. After the death of Marx, Engels stressed in a number of statements that the materialist conception of history ought to be interpreted to mean that economics was decisive "ultimately" or "in the last analysis." Engels has thus been cited as the authority in support of a view that assigns economics only a special importance side by side with other factors. It is this diluted version of the materialist conception of history that has subsequently been advanced most frequently. This version has been put forth with the very general assertion that special note should be paid to economic factors, that they are fundamental in a specific way, etc. As we have observed, many interpretations of the materialist conception of history would thus have it mean only "that economic factors have played a far greater role in history than historians that predate Marx realized."

We shall not attempt here to interpret Marx's own idea, but a few points that may aid in an understanding of that idea merit our attention. It is quite evident that Marx formulated his viewpoint in reaction to Hegel's idealistic conception of history, which he had once embraced. Both the materialist and the idealistic conceptions share common roots in Hegelian metaphysics. When Marx referred to the connection between material and intellectual factors in the section quoted, we should note that he evidently had in mind the momentous periods of historical development, the material he worked with in constructing his system. If one wishes to give his words a simple, reasonable interpretation, they can be construed to mean the establishment of the existence of a relationship between material and intellectual development; they would then mean, for example, that concepts of justice, forms of government, and political ideas in a highly developed industrial state are different from those among a primitive agricultural people. Observations in this vein were not novel; they can be found in the works of Aristotle. Yet Marx imparted to them a semblance of originality by virtue of the exaggeration and accentuation that attended dialectical reasoning.

Marx's works evince a continuous effort to show the derivation of judicial and political relations and ideological concepts from economic facts. This endeavor was plainly related to the materialist conception of history, but it can, of course, be explained independently of that conception. Typical of Marx's outlook was his view of religion as a reflection of the economic structure of a society. "The religious world," he wrote, "is but a reflection of the real world. For a society composed of producers of goods whose general societal relations of production consist in treating their products as commodities, as things of value, and in adjudging their individual work for one another in this factual form as equivalent to human labor [for such a society], Christianity with its abstract cult of human beings is the most fitting form of religion, particularly in its bourgeois forms such as protestantism, deism, and the like."

Yet we should also note that in his treatment of questions related to contemporary politics, Marx stresses time and again the importance of ideologies as inhibiting factors. An ideology that has evolved in response to a certain economic order could continue to exist after this order had become obsolete and thus obstruct rational development. In writing on the *coup d'état* carried out by Napoleon III, Marx even tried to demonstrate that the peasantry had been dedicated to Napoleon III because the ideas of his uncle, Napoleon I, had been congruous with the interests of the peasantry at the time. In some contexts he appears to regard religion as an instrument deliberately employed to suppress the lower class and refers to it as "the opiate of the people." Such statements were obviously incompatible with the thought that ideas always mirrored real interests.

The materialist conception of history has been of significance to socialism's ideological development in two respects. First, it has appeared as the method by which the necessity of socialism may be demonstrated and has thus represented a guarantee of victory. Second, it has tinged the discussion of particular political and social problems; the idea that economic factors are the fundamental ones and others concomitant phenomena has always influenced the positions taken on various questions—or has at least been cited as a ground for such positions.

The foregoing account has included what may be considered the principal theories in Marx's major perspective. It is primarily this perspective that made Marx the father of a trend within Social Democracy that was long predominant in the movement, and the creator of that which his disciples call scientific socialism. However, when Marx treated more concrete, immediate historical and political question, he was unable to confine himself to the application of the schema of the major perspective. He could not, for example, assume the existence of only two classes when a power contest obviously involved a number of competing or collaborating social groups; nor could he make the sweeping statement that the ultimate victory of the proletariat was inevitable when the question at hand was whether or not a specific revolutionary movement in a specific country and at a specific time would prove successful. As a result, many of Marx's most well-known works and statements contain an odd mixture of elements from the major perspective and lines of thought basically irreconcilable with this over-all view. As we have observed, this dualism is one of the main reasons why quotations from Marx on certain subjects lend themselves to interpretations that are basically incongruous.

Even when reasoning from a short-term point of view, Marx tried to underscore the historical determinism that permeated his overview of human history: he believed he could employ the "laws" he had formulated governing the long-range unfolding of events to predict the outcome of specific cases as well. His teleological approach prevented him from acknowledging or understanding that, viewed from the broad outline he had drawn, specific political events might appear to be sheer accidents, caused by circumstances that had not been considered at all in his formulation of the major perspective. In other words, such events might appear to fall into the same category as events that occurred during ancient times, which could not be considered "historical" in the Marxian sense. Throughout his life Marx therefore repeatedly, and with much certainty, made predictions that were soon thereafter negated by reality. Conclusive class struggles, crises, and revolutions were said to be just around the corner; it was later evident that, according to Marx's perspective, only "accidental" and unimportant events had taken place. His various comments on developments in France at the time are particularly rich in examples of prognostications that proved incorrect.

Marx's fallibility as a prophet is per se of secondary importance in this discussion. The important thing is that Marx frequently—particularly when writing on contemporary politics—made statements that were incompatible with his major perspective. We have already mentioned his modifications of the materialist conception of history. The word "class" was given different connotations in different contexts. In his exposition dealing with "the classes" in *Capital,* Marx departed from his general schema and differentiated between three classes: those who owned only the power of their own labor, those who owned capital, and those who owned land. This particular chapter was never completed, and the full reasons for this standpoint were therefore never given. On several occasions when writing on contemporary history Marx spoke of a great number of classes, such as the landed aristocracy and the financial aristocracy, big tradesmen and little tradesmen, big farmers and small farmers, unpropertied farmers and industrial workers. In *The Eighteenth Brumaire of Louis Bonaparte* he defined a class as a group of persons whose living conditions, interests, traditions, and culture distinguish them from other groups. Here, and in other works, he presupposes that proletarians should and can work jointly with other classes to accomplish the social revolution. The rigid classification into bourgeoisie and proletariat that characterized the major perspective is absent. There is therefore reason to assume that Marx actually required that the proletariat systematically cooperate with others in order to force through their common demands. Pertinent quotations from Marx can sustain on the one hand the idea of the necessity of an inexorable class struggle to be waged by the workers, and on the other, the view that only through collaboration with other classes will the workers emerge victorious.

According to Marx's major perspective, social welfare measures, trade union movements, and other endeavors to raise the economic status of the workers are largely in vain. The theories of catastrophe and impoverishment cannot be reconciled with the speculation that workers can gain definite benefits within the existent caitalist society. Nonetheless, in several instances Marx stressed the value of Social reforms as well as the possibility that the cooperative and trade union movements could be of significant assistance in improving the lot of the workers. In *Capital,* in particular, he underscored the value of English legislation regulating working hours, which he described as an expression of the "political economics of the working class," that is, of a kind of socialism. Side by side with the theory of catastrophe we thus find remarks that can be cited in support of social reformism. As has frequently been the case in respect to this and other points, one can, of course, attempt to remove such apparent incongruities: one can view predictions such as the theories of catastrophe and impoverishment simply as diagrammatic presentations of tendencies or trends that may be counteracted by other tendencies and are therefore not necessarily peremptory. But this reasoning obviously disavows the central themes in the major perspective, which is supposed to give a picture of inevitable developments.

The passages cited from the *Manifesto* in regard to the relation of the working classes to their native lands tend to convey the impression that national solidarity is valueless to the workers. Moreover, the whole theory of class struggle points to the same conclusion. These and related statements have perpetually been cited as proof that Marxism cannot accept the value of the national community and must be opposed to national defense in a capitalist society. Yet other statements made by Marx show that within certain limits he did recognize the national principle—although he followed Hegel's pattern of differentiating between "valuable" and "valueless" peoples. They further indicate that he considered some wars justifiable and that he himself took impassioned stands on the armed conflicts of his time. It is true that Marx often justified his stand on a current conflict on the ground that a certain outcome of the war would benefit the social revolution. However, it must be acknowledged that he did take a position against the basic "defense nihilism" that frequently and adamantly asserted that its views were supported by Marx's general statements on the essential character of classes and the obsolescence of the concept of national unity.

How did Marx envision the actual manner by which the proletariat would seize power and the consequent developments? This question has in recent times been a crucial point in the Marxist debate, particularly in relation to the communist revolution in Russia. The author believes that a definite, unequivocal answer is impossible. On this more than on any other point, Marx's statements, formulated according to different perspectives and at different periods in time, are in direct collision with one another.

The passages quoted from *Capital* in which Marx speaks of "the expropriation of the expropriators" unavoidably convey the impression that the proletariat's seizure of power will take the form of a sudden, violent revolution; because of its total dependence on external, economic conditions, this revolution can most closely be likened to a natural catastrophe. It hardly seems possible that the description of the social revolution given here could be reconciled with the idea of a successive evolution from a capitalist to a socialist society through democratic forms. It further seems obvious that, in this instance, Marx considered that the victory of socialism would be possible only after the capitalist system had become predominant and had thereby developed to a point where the internal contradictions Marx considered inherent in the system had also become fully developed. The latter line of argumentation in particular has played a central role in socialist debate. It has frequently been postulated that capitalism must be "ripe," that the mass of the population must be transformed into proletarians before the socialist revolution can materialize. The revolution itself has been regarded mainly as a result of the interplay of economic factors.

Other statements made by Marx give an entirely different picture of his ideas. Some statements exhorted the workers to try to push through social reforms within an essentially capitalist framework; others advocated social revolutions in nations that could not conceivably be considered to have reached the degree of capitalist development Marx spoke of in *Capital*. Pursuant to the revolutionary endeavors of 1848, he hoped for a power takeover by the workers in collaboration with other groups, after which the workers, as the leading class in the victorious majority, would realize its aims. He often seemed to assume that bourgeois democrats and socialists would fight for democracy together, whether by peaceful or violent methods; in the democracy thus achieved, the socialists would win a majority and launch socialization. The *Manifesto* declares that "the first step in the workers' revolution is the elevation of the proletariat to the ruling class, the winning of democracy." Thus, strangely enough, Marx believed that the proletariat would gain hegemony through the implementation of democracy. (Marx apparently used the term proletariat here in a different sense than in other contexts.) The proletariat would use its power "to gradually take away all capital from the bourgeoisie, to centralize all means of production in the state, that is, in hands of the proletariat, organized onto the ruling class, and to increase the volume of productive forces as quickly as possible." Here, too, Marx must have meant that the right of private ownership of essential means of production would persist for a while despite the rule of the proletariat. He did not call for immediate expropriation of all means of production, only for successive expansion of collective activity. In some instances Marx explicitly declared that in some democracies the proletariat should be able to carry out socialization without violence, that is, without revolution in the proper sense. In other instances, however, Marx (and, to a greater extent, Engels) put forth statements suggesting that even after democracy had been established a violent conflict would have to precede the elevation of the proletariat to the ruling class; in such contexts the democratic form of government was referred to with disdain. In some instances "the dictatorship of the proletariat" undoubtedly meant a democracy in which power was vested in the proletariat. In other contexts, the term can be interpreted to denote a true dictatorship. Social Democratic and communist writers have presented diametrically opposed interpretations of the tenor of Marx and Engels' statements in this regard, particularly when analyzing Marx's description of the Paris Commune of 1871.

In general, it may be said that, like the Marxian system as a whole, the statements made by Marx and Engels on this and related questions intended to convey the impression that the socialists' seizure of power must be total. Either the bourgeoisie or the proletariat rules; a state is either capitalist or is on its way to becoming socialist through the leadership of the proletariat. It is this doctrine, begot by the dialectical method, that has consistently influenced socialist movements. It is otherwise possible to derive the most disparate ideas from Marx's works. The seizure of power can take place only when the time is "ripe," when the economic process has reached a certain point of development. Yet the power takeover may also occur in underdeveloped nations, where special economic relations may propel the socipalist movement forward. In the latter case socialism will, so to speak, complete the development of the forces of production that is ascribed as the work of capitalism in the first perspective. Victory can be won in two stages: the first stage would be democracy, attained through violent or peaceful means; the second would be socialism, which could also be attained through violent or peaceful means. Yet victory may also be won in one stroke through a combined political and social revolution. The dictatorship of the proletariat may be understood to mean rule by a socialist majority, but it may also be construed to mean a dictatorship in the usual sense, whether by majority or minority rule. Democracy may mean bourgeois class rule or a proletarian dictatorship; revolution may mean a violent upheaval or a peaceful evolution. By combining these thoughts and modes of expression in different ways one can designate almost any view in this area as Marxist. It would be difficult to conceive of any standpoint on the problem "socialism and democracy" that could not be embellished with pertinent quotations from Marx.

As we have noted, Marx predicted that the second epoch in human history would end with the abolition of the state. Society, by which Marx meant a free union of individuals in contrast to the coercive order of the state, would form the human community. The notion may seem strange. How could the total economic planning Marx wanted to substitute in place of the haphazard economics of capitalism be achieved without an organization of the kind known as a state? This idea was essential to Marx's schema of concepts, albeit basically tautological. The state was described as organized class oppression; once classes had been eliminated, the state, too, would disappear. In reality, Marx must have postulated that some form of order that common usage would describe as a state would persist. It is typical of Marx's mode of thinking that he differentiated between the organizational form represented by the Paris Commune and the state in the usual sense of the word. Despite the strong concentration of power it manifested, the Commune was apparently not considered a "true" state. Nor does the idea of the abolition of the state seem to have occupied a central position in Marx's vision of the future; it almost seems to become a formally necessary appendix to his ideology of the class struggle. Engels, on the other hand, ardently pursued this idea; his statements on the subject are of fundamental importance to the communist doctrine that justifies dictatorship as a long-range plan to abolish the coercive order of the state.

Marx refused to provide specifics regarding the organization of socialist society. He considered forecasts of this kind unscientific. The absence of such a prognostication, which has been of paramount importance in socialist debate, must be seen according to the broad lines of the major perspective, according to the angle that viewed the victory of socialism basically as a passive result of the inevitable collapse of capitalism. At one point Marx treated this question in a relatively detailed fashion. He then asserted that during the first stage of the new society wages or compensation for labor would be proportionate to work output; equality would prevail insofar as the same yardstick would be applied to the labor performed by each man. "In a higher phase of communist society, when the slavish subordination of individuals by the division of labor and the concomitant division between intellectual and physical labor have disappeared, when work has become not just a means to a livelihood but the foremost drive in life, when the many facets of individuals have been developed and with them even the forces of production, and the springs of common wealth flow more abundant—only then can the boundaries of bourgeois rights be transgressed and society inscribe on its banners: To each according to his ability, to each according to his need."

One of the forerunners of modern Social Democracy was Ferdinant Lassalle. During the period between 1863 and 1864, when he was the leader of the burgeoning workers' movement in Germany, he advanced ideas that departed from Marxism in essential respects. Like Marx, he was deeply influenced by Hegel, but he was also profoundly swayed by Marx's reorganization of Hegel's schema. Like Marx and Hegel, he viewed history as a series of stages progressing toward perfection. Like Marx, he stressed the importance of material phenomena and considered the rule of the bourgeoisie a necessary stage on the road to the socialist society, in which production would be collective. His deviations from strict Marxism may be explained by the direct influence that Hegel and other pre-Marxian theorists exercised on him and by the fact that he directed his political activities toward achieving immediate, practical results.

As the leader of "The National German Workers' Association," Germany's first Social Democratic party, Lassalle endeavored to take advantage of the acute friction between Bismarck's conservative supporters and the progressive Liberal party that prevailed in Prussia at the time. The Liberal labor program, which recommended the establishment of associations through which workers might save and provide mutual assistance to one another, was declared to be of little significance in improving the lot of the working class. The same was said to apply to cooperative associations. Lassalle based his arguments for this negative position on "the iron law of wages" formulated by Malthus and Ricardo. This law "which determines wages under present conditions when supply and demand are decisive to labor, means that the average wage is always limited to a level that is absolutely necessary to sustain life, that is, to that which the mode of living of a people requires for existence and reproduction." If wages were to rise, the birth rate and, consequently, the number of workers would also rise, and wages would therefore be forced down to their previous level. If wages were to fall, the birth rate would decline, workers would emigrate, and their numbers thus be reduced by necessity; the law of supply and demand would then operate to raise wages. The only way to really raise wages was to transform the workers into entrepreneurs by founding production associations. The state should subsidize the establishment of such associations and regulate their activity. Wrote Lassalle, "The free, individual association among workers . . . made possible by the state's supportive and promotive intervention—this is the only way out of the desert where the workers' estate now dwells." In order to achieve this goal, the workers would have to obtain power in the state—and their means of accomplishing this was universal suffrage. Lassalle expected that the conservative Prussian government would be willing to grant the franchise to the workers and that it might even aid in the establishment of production associations. He thus directed his agitation almost exclusively against the progressive party in the hope that he might thereby win conservative support. In the final analysis Lassalle did not, of course, believe that The Social Question could be resolved through the franchise or production associations; his ultimate goal was socialization of production. Nevertheless, these immediate demands were the only ones he emphatically pleaded in his political speeches and publications.

A certain concept of the state that was related to Hegel's theory of the state came to be joined with this program. The state was held to be the chief means through which an individual could attain culture and liberty. Although Lassalle's position did not differ significantly from Marxism in regard to social goals, Lassalle did not harbor the fundamental animosity toward the state that Marx adopted as a consequence of his rearrangement of Hegel's schema. "The only salvation for the workers thus leads," wrote Lassalle, "through that institution in which they are still recognized as human beings: through the state, but through a state that undertakes as its duty the realization of that which in the long run is inevitable." In another context he described the state as "the great association of the poor classes." He thereby disclosed an affinity with the conservative standpoint even from an ideological point of view. Lassalle's view of the state was related to his rejection of the doctrine of class struggle—at least as demonstrated during his brief period of real political activity. Speaking to the workers, he declared that he did not wish to instigate a conflict between the propertied and the unpropertied. "It would be a splendid moment in civilization, it would be a triumph for the German name and the German nation, if the initiative in regard to The Social Question in Germany originated with the propertied, if the solution were reached through science and [brotherly] love, not through an explosion of hatred and wild revolutionary rage"; this would mean "a magnificent reconciliation between the classes." This quotation also suggests that Marxist criticism of national values was alien to Lassalle.

Lassalle's views were of decisive influence in the German workers' movement for only a brief period. His idea of state-supported production associations flickered in socialist debates in various countries but was never of great moment. Because of his interpretation of the state and his commitment to short-range reforms, Lassalle nonetheless influenced groups within the Social Democratic movement that wanted to prosecute policies which were more "reformist" than those Marx supposedly advocated. It has been said that the Social Democracy of more recent times, which has been engaged in practical activity has done so more in the spirit of Lassale than in that of Marx.

Anarchism first appeared as a faction within Social Democracy; it later became the enemy and rival of Social Democracy. Anarchism also contained several orientations. We shall not explore here the so-called individual anarchism formulated by the Hegelian Max Stirner in his extraordinary *Der Einzige und sein Eigentum* (*The Individual and His Property*), published in 1845. It is true that Stirner's theory that the individual would realize his individuality by liberating himself from all ideological concepts (including moral and political principles) was sometimes cited by political anarchists, but it was of little importance to the actual development of anarchism. As a political doctrine, anarchism means above all the abolition of the state's coercive order, which is to be superseded by free associations; this is to be achieved without the use of political measures in the usual sense. The anarchist and the Marxist goals may thus be said to be identical up to a point. (Marx may, indeed, have been influenced by anarchist ideas in this respect.) In contrast to Marx, however, the anarchists repudiate all forms of political and parliamentary activity. The Russian anarchist-nihilist Bakunin was profoundly influenced by Hegel; spurred by the ideas of Proudhon and others, he became anarchism's foremost spokesman during the 1860s. He wrote "We reject all privileged, patented, official, and legal legislation, authority, and influence, even if it emanates from universal suffrage, and we do so in the conviction that it always serves only a ruling, exploiting minority, not the vast, enslaved majority." Contrary to the "authoritarian communists"—as Bakunin called the Marxists—the end was not to be reached through political organizations but solely "through the development and organization of the power of the urban and rural working masses, which is not political but social, and therefore antipolitical." Through a revolutionary action, usually described as "spontaneous," the workers would crush the apparatus of the state and thereafter live in free associations or communes. The state and its institutions would thus not be used at all in the revolution; any contact with the state involved the risk of contamination. An anarchist congress in St. Irwin adopted a resolution stating "1) that the first duty of the proletariat is the destruction of all political power; 2) any establishment of so-called provisional, revolutionary political power in order to accomplish this destruction would be only further betrayal and would involve the same dangers to the proletariat that all present established governments represent."

The anarchists' descriptions of the organization of the new society were usually as vague as those given by Marx and his disciples. They frequently contended that annihilation of all existing institutions was the only goal that could be set up and that it would be unscientific to try to prophesize the nature of the future society that would then be constructed. It would under no circumstances include any coercive agency. The communal organizations, like the larger associations in which they would be included, would be based on the right of individuals to free self-determination. On one occasion, however, Bakunin did draft a plan of organization for the new society. According to this rough plan, the state and all institutions connected with it—courts, administrative agencies, standing army and police—would disappear, but Bakunin did presuppose the existence of a kind of governing body chosen by the people. Every person would be able to live as he pleased; he could be "lazy or industrious, immoral or moral." Yet the society could not be completely defenseless "against parasitic, malicious, and harmful persons." Any person who did not fulfill the obligations he had voluntarily assumed or committed an offense against the person or property of another would be liable to be judged and penalized. Bakunin did not consider this a departure from his basic principles, for the offender could instead declare himself willing to leave the society. In this case, any member of the society could kill him with impunity!

One of the notions that anarchism spawned was the idea that the downfall of the prevailing society could be accelerated through acts of violence directed against individual representatives of the system. In time, this became the most significant, or at least the most notorious form of anarchism. Toward the end of the 1880s, the term anarchism stood almost exclusively for this kind of violence. By this time, anarchism had lost all significance as a socialist faction, but some of its ideas had been adopted by syndicalism.

The International prior to World War I

In 1864, socialist-influenced organizations that declared themselves representative of the workers' interests joined to form The International Workingmen's Association, commonly called the First International. From its inception, Marx played an important, and at times decisive role in this International; many of its proclamations were steeped in Marxist thinking. However, not long after its formation the International began to show evidence of deep dissension between different theoretical orientations, and the programmatic resolutions it passed were frequently nebulous in wording and appeared to be products of compromise. If the early 1870s, ideological disputes and other factors brought on a conflict between the Marxists and the Bakunin-led anarchists. In 1872 Marx succeeded in forcing through a resolution expelling Bakunin and his cohorts from the organization. During the next few years the First International accomplished little of consequence, and was finally dissolved in 1876.

This initial attempt at building an international socialist organization was made before the appearance of any socialist party of significance. The 1870s and 1880s marked a breakthrough for socialism inasmuch as parties with socialist programs and growing memberships were formed in numerous countries. In the vanguard was the German Social Democratic party, founded in 1875 through a fusion of two rival workers' organizations, one predicated on Marx's thinking, the other on Lassalle's. Its first program, the Gotha Program, combined ideas derived from both Marx and Lassalle; thereafter, however, Marxian doctrine became predominant. Despite Bismarck's attempts to suppress it between 1878 and 1890 through his so-called socialist law, the party continued to grow. In 1891 it adopted a new program, the Erfurt Program, which uniformly followed Marxian doctrine and would greatly influence the development of party programs in other nations. Marxism seemed particularly well-suited to German conditions. Faced with the monarchic, aristocratic, and bureaucratic Prussian regime of the period, the party could not hope to share in or influence the government and the temptation to pursue a policy of compromise was therefore negligible. The bourgeois parties that supported the established order controlled such a large majority for so long that the Social Democrats could conduct systematic opposition without disrupting legislative activity. The existence of universal suffrage in Germany, together with the relatively good living conditions attending the empire's rapid industrial expansion and the social reforms that had been passed as measures indirectly aimed at preserving the *status quo*—all these factors were favorable to a movement that rejected revolutionary coups and expected that victory would eventually result from the natural, undisturbed course of events. More than any other Social Democratic movement, the German party based its thinking on the view, that, after a period of organization and tranquil progress, it would advance to a total power takeover through peaceful means. The politicians and theorists who personified these ideas—primarily Bebel and Kautsky—were long the undisputed leaders of the party. Social Democratic parties in most small nations in northern and central Europe were greatly influenced by the debate in Germany. Politically revolutionary and anarchist groups were long of comparative significance in many Latin countries, but even here Marxist parties took root. The French workers' movement evinced deep schisms arising primarily from disagreement on the advisability of collaboration with radical bourgeois groups—a problem that would soon become a burning issue in republican and parliamentary France. Marxian doctrine was, it is true, accepted by the leading socialist groups and by the United Socialist party formed in 1904. However, the idea expounded by Guesde, who held that a socialist victory could ultimately be won only through armed action—and that political and trade union activities were essentially preparatory steps for such action—was long in competition with the basically reformist stand represented by Jaurès.

Marxism never became of major significance in Anglo-Saxon countries The socialist parties formed in the United States did not gain much support from the working class. The trade unions, the workers' chief form of organization, mainly tried to realize short-range demands for reform through the established major political parties. A patently Marxist organization, the Social Democratic Federation, was formed in England in 1883, but it did not exert decisive influence on the socialist labour party that evolved in various stages around the turn of the century. The strong trade union movement, which had appeared before the spread of Marxist ideas, aimed at raising the workers' standard of living and at prosecuting social reforms. Its counterpart in radical intellectual circles was the "Fabian Society," whose members included S. Webb, Shaw, and Wallas. To be sure, the Fabians did establish collective production as their goal, but they systematically focused their attention on immediate problems and explicitly repudiated the Marxian system. While socialists on the Continent embroidered upon Marx's general themes, English socialists carried out concrete historical and sociological studies. The young Labour party did not immediately adopt a specific program, but its actions spoke for it. It rejected the Marxist program proposals put forth by the Social Democratic Federation, and, in 1901, ruled that the party's representatives in Parliament should "be prepared to cooperate with any party which on a given occasion strives to promote legislation that is in the direct interest of the working class. . . ." In 1908 the party resolved to lay down its socialist objectives; its goal was "socialization of all means of production, distribution, and extension of credit; these should be administered by the democratic state in the interest of society as a whole. . . ." On the same occasion the party rejected by an overwhelming majority a proposal that would have formulated the demand for socialization in a Marxist vein.

The cooperation between socialist parties that began with the international congress in Paris in 1889 and was subsequently pursued through congresses held at regular intervals and through an international socialist bureau is known as the Second International. From the outset the New International was embedded in Marxist ground. The debarment of anarchists was a rule that was underscored in several resolutions. In all likelihood, this International, which was most frequently under German leadership, helped to spread and consolidate Marxian doctrine. The German interpretation came more and more to stand for the authoritative "official" socialism. The resolutions passed by the International had considerable bearing on the policies of the several socialist parties in different nations and were constantly cited in their intramural debates.

A series of declarations adopted at the various congresses clarified the International's Marxian principles, but a real program was never formalized. In accordance with a previous decision, the congress of 1900 held in Paris invited as participants "1) all associations that support the fundamental principles of socialism: the socialization of the means of production and exchange; the organization of and action by the workers on an international scale; socialist seizure of government power through the proletariat, organized as a class party; 2) all other assemblies which, although they may not directly participate in a political movement, take the class struggle as their basis and declare their recognition of the necessity of political, i.e., legislative and parliamentary action." A resolution adopted at this congress further specified the theory of class struggle, following Marx's model. The proletariat was said to be the inevitable product of the capitalist mode of production, which had brought about "the political and economic expropriation of labor by capital." In order to emancipate itself the proletariat must "act as a militant class"; "socialism, which has assumed the mission of organizing the proletariat into an army in this class struggle, has above all the duty to . . . unite it [the proletariat] in a realization of its interests and its strength. . . ." Indicative of the central importance of the idea of class struggle is the manner in which the English Labour party was admitted into the International. The party was admitted in 1908 in response to its request to join on the ground that "the English Labour party ought to be admitted to the international socialist congress because, although it does not explicitly recognize the class struggle, it does in fact carry on such a struggle, and because the organization of the Labour party is independent of bourgeois parties and is thus founded on the class struggle."

As several resolutions adopted by the International indicate, it considered that the regular mode of waging the class struggle and seizing political power was action within the compass of bourgeois democracy itself. A ruling passed at the 1889 congress declared that proletarians in all countries where they enjoyed the franchise should join the socialist party and "strive to gain political power within the existing government administration . . . through their ballots." However, the resolution did not preclude revolutionary methods if universal suffrage did not exist and was not about to be granted; it stated that the franchise should be acquired "through all available means." Yet several subsequent congresses made statements espousing universal suffrage without giving any hint of the course of action that should be adopted if the franchise were not granted. Many members of parties that were part of the International undoubtedly considered a violent revolution imperative for the realization of socialism, but this view was not forcefully advanced in the International's debates.

As suggested in the foregoing account of Marxian doctrine, the application of Marx's major political perspective to short-range policies was bound to lead to difficulties. The shortcomings of the long-range view manifest themselves in the modifications of the major perspective that Marx was forced to make when considering day-to-day political issues. Certain features of the international socialist debate during the decades prior to World War I will further illustrate this point.

These difficulties were most salient when the major perspective was to be applied to the question of political tactics. Should the Social Democratic parties collaborate with bourgeois parties, whether in elections, in the legislature, or in government? According to Marx's major perspective and Engels' rendition of it, such collaboration was precluded. All bourgeois groups were basically concerned with maintaining the capitalist system; as long as this system prevailed, any government was basically nothing but an administrative committee of the bourgeois class. The conclusion must be, as Guesde worded it in a debate at one of the French congresses, that "from the point of view of state government, the workers are nothing as long as they are not everything," i.e., only total power was worth striving for.

The question was brought before the International primarily in regard to the subject of cabinet socialism. Could Social Democrats enter into a coalition government with bourgeois parties? Could they rightly even accept government commissions in a bourgeois society—that is, without the intention of immediately beginning to transform the society into a socialist one? During the early phases of Social Democracy, this idea was inconceivable. The German Social Democratic party was the leading group in the International; the very notion that it would be invited to partake in the German imperial government was naturally preposterous. Yet cabinet socialism did unexpectedly become an urgent question in 1899. Pursuant to the exacerbation of political conflicts evoked by the Dreyfus affair, a socialist, Millerand, was included in a democratic coalition government under Waldeck-Rousseau. The French Social Democrats split on the propriety of Millerand's participation in the government. A joint congress of socialist parties passed conflicting resolutions on the issue. Juarès was among those who believed that collaboration in a bourgeois cabinet was permissible in exceptional cases where the issues at stake concerned the protection of the people's political rights or the enactment of a reform of value to the working class.

The following year the question was broached at the congress of the International in Paris. The congress passed a resolution stating that "the class struggle prohibits any kind of alliance with any line within the capitalist class." Temporary coalitions, however, were conceivable. Another ruling decreed that the inclusion of a socialist in a bourgeois government could not be regarded "as the regular prelude to the seizure of political power, but only as an exceptional, temporary measure dictated by necessity." The ruling was adopted by a vote of 29 to 9; the minority voted for a proposal that would exclude socialists from any share in executive power until the party had won a majority in the legislature. The Swedish delegates were among the majority. In the attendant debate Juarès represented one line of argumentation which held that the socialist parties ought to have the tactical latitude to take advantage of opportunities afforded them in the legislature. The opposing camp, represented by Guesde and Ferri, contended that no one could serve two classes at the same time and that a cabinet post would necessarily attenuate the holder's social revolutionary spirit.

The majority resolution had been formulated by Kautsky. It was designed to serve as a platform for the groups that opposed cabinet socialism on principle but did not wish to reject totally the French experiment. At the 1903 German party congress in Dresden, Kautsky forced through a resolution that was more extreme in its repudiation of collaboration with other political lines than the Paris ruling. The resolution contained the equivocal statement that, in comformity with the Paris ruling, Social Democrats could not "strive for a share in government power within a bourgeois society." As the debate revealed, the import of the statement was that Social Democrats should not participate in a bourgeois government; "strive for" (*erstreben* in the German) was used in a sense approximately equivalent to "accept." The Dresden resolution was later presented at the international congress in Amsterdam in 1904, which adopted it by a vote of 25 to 5; 12 delegates, including Swedes, abstained. According to the French text, the statement on cabinet socialism distinctly proclaimed that Social Democrats could not accept government posts in a bourgeois society (*"ne saurait accepter aucune participation au gouvernement dans la societé bourgeoise"*). This established the precept that Social Democrats could only assume executive power when they had a possibility of carrying out socialism, that is, when society was no longer "bourgeois"; it renounced not only a coalition government but even a pure Social Democratic government in a "bourgeois society." The only logical inference was that Social Democrats had to obtain a majority in the legislature in order to form a government.

Dissension at the congress was in reality even more acute than the voting indicated. After adopting the resolution cited, the delegates rejected, 21 to 21, a proposal that was less far-reaching; the question of cabinet socialism was dealt with simply by referring to the Paris ruling. The congressional debate, which largely took the form of a duel between Juarès and Bebel, was indeed vitriolic. Jaurès argued that in certain cases collaboration with radical elements had proved most advantageous to French socialism. Among other things, it had abetted the successful conduct of the struggle for civilization. He further held that the position of the German Social Democrats on the question at hand was influenced by their total lack of opportunity to pursue practical policies in their homeland with any degree of success. Said Jaurès: "The adoption of the Dresden resolution by this international congress means that international socialism . . . identifies itself with the temporary but total impotence, with the passing but compulsory passivity that distinguishes the German democracy." Engels had believed that the revolution was not far off; "therefore socialists have lived in this illusion; they have believed that in an extraordinary situation of crisis they would be able to capture total power without having contributed to the work of reform." Bebel in turn protested that both the bourgeois republic and the bourgeois monarchy were class regimes whose basic concern was the maintenance of the capitalist order. He quoted an earlier statement made by Jaurès: "Socialism cannot accept a share in power, it must wait until it obtains total power. . . . If it has only a share, it has nothing."

As the debates and developments in various countries testified, the position demanded by the Amsterdam resolution presented enormous problems. Once Social Democracy had attained a certain strength, collaboration with other parties—possibly in the executive branch—was bound to follow as a consequence of parliamentarianism and, above all, as a vital means of introducing reforms that would benefit the working class. A conference of Social Democratic parliamentarians held in conjunction with the international Stuttgart congress of 1907 explored the problem objectively—in sharp contrast to the sweeping generalizations expounded in the large congressional debates. Troelstra, leader of the Dutch Social Democrats, gave a clarifying talk on the subject "The Political System of Social Democracy." Troelstra observed that as long as a Social Democratic party remained small it would encounter no difficulties on the question of tactics for the simple reason that it could not accomplish anything of note. When the party has grown large, however, the workers demand direct benefits from parliamentary activity. If nothing is done, discontent results. Yet if Social Democrats participate in the executive branch of government, they are considered to bear responsibility for the bourgeois political system as a whole. Social Democrats have not really clarified their position; they have just hesitatingly drifted into parliamentary work. They wish to participate in bringing about reforms and, at the same time, advance revolutionary demands. A Social Democrat is obliged to reap as many benefits as possible for the workers from his parliamentary work; otherwise the workers will be driven into the camp of bourgeois radicals. He is therefore also obliged to support bourgeois radicalism against reactionary parties, for the former wishes to help the workers. "One may set up revolutionary demands, but when it comes to a final decision one is forced to be satisfied with halfway reforms or quarterway reforms which flow from the parliamentary crucible. Parliamentarianism has its own laws, and no party that wishes to use this system may absolve itself of them." Under the bourgeois system "every Social Democratic action necessarily clashes more or less with our principles and bears more or less the stamp of opportunism." As a whole, Troelstra's address plainly demonstrated how equivocal and unrealistic much of the previous debate had been. Although he did not actually put it into words, Troelstra showed that cabinet socialism was an inevitable consequence of parliamentary tactics. However, no proposal regarding the Social Democratic position on this question was put forth either in Stuttgart or at subsequent congresses held prior to the war. The Amsterdam resolution thus prevailed.

A necessary premise of Marx's major perspective was that social measures to ameliorate the lot of the workers would not materialize, or that if they did, that such measures would not be effective. Otherwise the theory of impoverishment was untenable. As we have noted, however, in other contexts Marx spoke of social reform and of the value of social welfare policies in positive terms. He stressed, for example, significance of English legislation that established the 10-hour work day.

The annals of Social Democracy consistently reveal evidence of the contradictions that existed on this point. Of course the Social Democrats called for social reforms. A party that worked for the good of the working class could not disassociate itself from measures to improve the workers' lot within the framework of the existent society; it could not assert an extreme liberal line against bourgeois social reformists in order to provide for the realization of the Marxian prognosis. Still, proposals for social reform initiated by the bourgeoisie were viewed with suspicion and were readily rejected on the ground that they did not go far enough. Social Democrats constantly stressed that no social reforms could suffice to alleviate the class struggle and that they rather served as fuel to kindle the militancy of the working class. It was often maintained that all social reform was of subordinate importance. The first congress of the Second International, held in Paris in 1889, passed a resolution that called for a series of measures for the workers' protection. One of these was the 8-hour work day, which would later become the demand of the highest priority and a symbol of the cause of social reform. Other measures included in the resolution were prohibition of night work, special restrictions on the working conditions of women and children, public employment agencies, and the inspection of factories. Several similar rulings were adopted at later congresses; these demanded, among other things, measures to counter unemployment—even though unemployment was also designated as an inevitable consequence of the capitalist system and, according to Marx's major perspective, was evidence of the imminent downfall of capitalism. Still, the 1889 congress passed yet another resolution favoring social reforms, declaring them to be a means "of arousing the workers' class consciousness, which is a necessary condition for the liberation of the working class through its own efforts." The idea that reforms were desirable mainly because they reinforced solidarity and the spirit of class struggle rather than because of their ameliorative value was a recurrent theme. "Reforms are more shell than kernel" wrote the Norwegian Social Democrat Oscar Nissen in 1895. "If Social Democracy participates in reform efforts, it does so more for practice than to win." In a debate with Clemenceau Guesde made a remark that is typical of innumerable statements in the same vein: "Give us reforms, give us as many reforms as you can—you will never give us as much as we require. The result will be: either you give us reforms, and in so doing whet the craving and appetite of the working class and increase its demands, or else you refuse them, and then we shall nail you fast as bankrupts. So, whether you grant us reforms or refuse them, you will fan the fighting spirit of the working class." Thus it was ideologically possible to combine social reformism with the theory of class struggle; even representatives of the revolutionary wing of the party could lend their support to short-term demands. However, with the growing power of the Social Democrats and the successful social measures that were enacted within the bourgeois state, party opinion underwent a successive change. Problems that were close at hand seemed to grow in importance as the idea of revolution paled. This was the beginning of the dissolution of the original doctrinaire Marxism.

Marxian doctrine led to two particular difficulties on the question of defense. According to the pure theory of class struggle the proletariat must regard the bourgeois-ruled state as its true enemy. From this point of view participation in defense, in the protection of the capitalist society, would be absurd. Yet refusal to defend the state might produce undesirable effects. Democratic states in which socialism had the possibility of asserting itself or in which socialism may already have amassed some strength, might be vanquished by more reactionary states. Another danger was that the very principle of national self-determination that socialism recognized might be jeopordized. And so on. According to Marxism, capitalism was the cause of war; as long as capitalism prevailed, so must war also prevail. In conformity with this viewpoint, socialism scorned bourgeois peace movements as Utopian. Peace could be won only through socialism. Rigid adherence to this idea would necessarily entail repudiation of all peace efforts within the contours of the existent system. Yet keeping the peace seemed to be a self-evident interest to the working class. Thus Social Democrats were faced with the same problem as that presented by the question of participation in social reform. Could they disassociate themselves from all efforts toward improvements in the existing system because they expected that it would be superseded by another? This web of internal contradictions would leave its mark on the entire Social Democratic debate on the defense issue.

A resolution on military matters adopted at the International's Congress in Paris in 1889 indirectly expresses the ideological ambiguity of socialism on this point. The congress declared that "war, the sad product of the existing economic relations, will not disappear until the capitalist mode of production has yielded to the emancipation of labor and the international triumph of socialism." But the congress also proclaimed that it regarded "peace to be the principal and unavoidable condition for the emancipation of the workers." Thus—peace could not be achieved before the emancipation of the workers, but this emancipation could be won only in peacetime. The congress criticized the system of maintaining standing armies and called for a militia system patterned according to the Swiss model. The congress thereby took a stand espousing a certain type of defense organization within the established state. The next two congresses, held in Brussels in 1891 and in Zurich in 1893, rejected proposals put forth by semianarchist factions demanding that, in the event of an outbreak of war, socialists should effect general work stoppage in the countries engaged in hostilities and thus prevent the war. The arguments against such proposals held that they were both impracticable and would tend to weaken the very countries in which socialists were strong. In 1893 the Zurich congress adopted a resolution proclaiming that socialist legislators were duty-bound to vote against all military appropriations and to strive for universal disarmament. The socialist parties were also to support all organizations that worked for world peace. In conformity with this resolution, French and German socialists voted against all defense appropriations for a number of years thereafter. The same general attitude toward defense marked subsequent congresses. In 1896 socialists spoke of replacing standing armies with a militia system, of international courts of arbitration, and of referendums to vote on questions of war and peace.

The ideological dilemma was even more flagrant in the debates that took place within the several Social Democratic parties. Participants in these debates could hardly address themselves to a united world proletariat, but rather had to focus concern more closely on concrete domestic conditions. Conflicts between prodefense and antidefense factions were constantly in evidence. The so-called "defense nihilists," who were simply opposed to all defense under any conditions, usually cited Marx's major perspective to support their stand. Those favorably disposed toward defense viewed the question at closer range. At times this group advanced patently nationalist arguments, but it also emphasized that defense against aggression was a duty irrespective of nationalist attitudes and that defense of democracy and socialism against reactionism might be necessary even on an international scale. In Germany Bebel declared that it was even more in the interest of Social Democrats than of the ruling classes to repel Russian aggression. His statements indicate that he really considered German defense imperative, even though he and his party systematically voted against all military appropriations—with the certainty that they would be approved anyway. Speaking in the Reichstag,

Noske asserted that if Germany were attacked, German Social Democrats would close ranks with the bourgeoisie. The French, on the other hand, were preoccupied with the German threat. At the 1907 party congress, Jaurès contended that if defense nihilism were to prevail among socialists, the most aggressive and chauvinistic nations would be able to suppress other nations. Social Democratic refusal to vote military appropriations would be futile, for the party constituted a minority; if the party gained a majority it, too, would demand such appropriations. Jaurès held that the primary objective should be the creation of a militia that would be impregnable as a defensive force but could not be used as a weapon of offense; this militia would be *"l'armée nouvelle,"* as he referred to it in a speech of 1911. The idea of the invincibility of a popular rally to arms was inspired by the experiences of the great French Revolution. Guesde based his prodefense attitude on the ground that an army that had victoriously repulsed enemy aggression would thereafter bring about the social revolution. Views and sentiments latently at variance with the resolutions passed by the International cropped up in all Social Democratic circles.

The last international congresses to be held before World War I addressed themselves mainly to the question of how such a conflict might be prevented. Deep dissention between different viewpoints developed in Stuttgart in 1907. Hervè, the most militant representative of defense nihilism within the French party, called for a proclamation that it made no difference to the proletariat whichever national label were affixed to capitalist exploitation. Socialists should resort to arms only to accomplish socialism or to defend it once it had been achieved. All declarations of war, whatever their source, should be answered by antimilitary strikes and insurrections. This proposal thus embodied the extreme consequences of the stringent doctrine of class struggle. A majority of French Social Democrats, led by Jaurès, proposed a resolution stating that an outbreak of war should be prevented by all available means, possibly even through general strikes and uprisings; however, this resolution also emphasized the duty to defend one's country against attack. The Germans, in turn, maintained that the measures referred to could not possibly be employed in Germany and that an unsuccessful attempt to resort to such measures would be extremely hazardous to the workers' movement. The resolution the congress finally adopted most nearly approximated the German position. The working class should attempt to forestall war through all suitable methods; if war did break out, it (the working class) should work for an early peace and strive to use the war to achieve a socialist transformation of society. The congress held in Copenhagen in 1910 resolved to adopt a statement of much the same import. In response to the increase in international tension, an extra congress was convoked in Basel in 1912 to review the international situation and peace efforts. This congress adopted a comprehensive resolution exhorting the several socialist parties to work for an international *détente*. Social Democrats had high hopes that their party would be able to influence the course of events. The resolution pronounced that "the dread among the ruling classes of a proletarian revolution as an aftermath of a world war has shown itself to be an important guaranty of peace."

The Marxist line that dominated the International was subjected to attack from various quarters. The so-called revisionist opposition was the form of criticism that was most important to the ideological development of Social Democracy. As early as the 1890s a movement had appeared in Germany which took exception to significant aspects of Marxist doctrine and demanded a new orientation of the political activity of the German Social Democratic party. The German socialist Edward Bernstein, who had been influenced by the labor movement in England during his long stay in that country, gave a concise summation of the views of this movement. His important work *The Premises of Socialism and the Task of Social Democracy* was published in 1899. After criticizing various parts of the materialist conception of history in its most acuminated form as well as the dialectical method itself, Bernstein examined Marx's economic theory and social prognoses. Having presented a basic analysis of the theory of surplus value, Bernstein noted that this theory did not provide a gauge of the "sweating" of workers. He wrote that it was obvious that, according to this theory, the well-paid workers employed in successful businesses were the ones who were most exploited; the workers who were paid the least were subject to little exploitation. Bernstein penned an exhaustive criticism of Marxian social theories. The theory of concentration had been invalidated inasmuch as the corporate form of business permits large enterprises to be founded with capital owned by many shareholders. The predictions regarding the disappearance of the middle class and the impoverishment of the working class had not come true. Statistics from various nations indicated that the number of small businesses had increased—albeit not in proportion to the increase of large enterprises—and wages had also risen. Economic crises were less acute and less widespread than previously; terrible crises would not result from economic developments, but they might result from political conditions. Bernstein concluded that a socialist victory of the kind predicted by Marx was not to be expected; Social Democratic parties ought to work for social reform within the framework of democracy and ought to abandon their extreme positions on national defense and national values. He placed great importance on the cooperative movement. In the main, ideology had to be fitted to action. The movement's "influence would be far greater than it is at present if Social Democracy had the courage to liberate itself from a phraseology that has, in fact, outlived itself, and to manifest itself as what it already is in reality: a democratic-socialist reform party." Day-to-day efforts and successive reforms should be the party's real objectives, not a Utopian goal. "That which is generally called the ultimate goal of socialism is nothing to me, the movement everything."

Orthodox Marxists leveled sharp criticism at Bernstein. Indicative of this criticism is Kautsky's assertion that acceptance of Bernstein's view meant a denial of the potential of Social Democracy: if Marx's prognoses were not by and large valid, the movement would lose its theoretical foundation. Bernstein's critics contended that he had based his generalizations on a relatively short period of international calm and prosperity. The German party congress that was held shortly after the publication of Bernstein's work adopted a resolution repudiating revisionism; the resolution was, however, worded in such a way that many who were basically in agreement with Bernstein could vote for it. Similar declarations, affirming a desire to adhere to well-tried tactics, were made at subsequent German and international congresses. Yet revisionism continued to grow in importance, and gradually permeated Social Democratic parties in several countries, even in Germany. The gist of revisionism was that it unconditionally accepted democratic institutions as its vehicles of action, that it concentrated its activities more and more on immediate political and social reforms, and that it did not accept Marxist social theories as absolutely valid.

The leavening of these theories in the debates around the turn of the century has not been accorded the complete study that it warrants. As an example of the method of reasoning used in these debates, let us consider the treatment of the Marxian prediction that was perhaps most widely discussed and propagated—the theory of impoverishment. Following the thinking of earlier writers, Bernstein had asserted that no absolute exacerbation of the misery of the working class could be ascertained. This assertion gradually came to be acknowledged under the overwhelming weight of statistical evidence. However, new versions of the theory of impoverishment were put forth, most of which purported to plumb Marx's real intentions. The following theories of impoverishment were constructed: 1) The workers were relatively worse off, namely, in relation to the capitalists (the relative theory of impoverishment in the true sense); 2) The real wages of the workers had declined in relation to the increase in the intensity and productivity of labor; 3) The number of workers had grown, and, consequently, "the aggregate of misery had grown"; 4) The number of unemployed had increased and, consequently, the working class as a whole was worse off; 5) Women had become engaged in labor to an ever greater extent, with a consequent increase in total proletarianization; 6) The sense of poverty had become more acute, among other reasons because differences in education had been reduced but not the differences between the classes (the theory of psychological impoverishment); 7) The standard of the working class in Western nations had risen, but in view of the exploitation of colonial peoples, the misery of the working class could be said to have increased; 8) The situation of the working class had improved, but it would sharply deteriorate with the approach of the dissolution of the capitalist system. A similar flora of interpretations grew up around other tenets of Marxian doctrine. When dealing with more complex problems, such as the materialist conception of history and the "dictatorship of the proletariat," this kind of profundity could revel in even greater triumphs of theoretical gymnastics.

Social Democracy, which prevailed in the International, was also criticized from points of view that were diametrically opposed to revisionism. The most important of the opposing views around the turn of the century was that represented by the syndicalist movement. This had appeared in its modern form in France in the 1890s, and had subsequently won considerable support, primarily in Latin countries. Syndicalism, which was obviously related to anarchism, rejected political activity on the ground that it would not lead to the desired end but would rather weaken the spirit of class struggle and demoralize the workers and their leaders. Nor was revolutionary action in the usual sense considered feasible. The way to socialism would be laid through trade union activity; the ultimate victory of socialism would be won through a general strike, after which control of production would be transferred to associations composed of the workers in the respective business concerns. The idea of a general strike was the most salient feature of syndicalism. In 1892 a trade union congress passed a resolution declaring "that, among the peaceful and legal means inadvertently granted to the workers in order that they may carry their just struggle to victory is one that ought to be able to accelerate the economic transformation and, without risk of reaction, safeguard victory for the fourth estate; that this means is the general and simultaneous suspension of productive labor, that is, the general strike, which, even if limited to a relatively short period of time, will unfailingly bring the labor party to the realization of the demands laid down in its program. . . ." In the beginning, several prominent Social Democrats, among them Jaurès and Briand, endorsed the idea of a general strike. After some years Jaurès joined the ranks of the opponents of syndicalism; Briand gradually became estranged from Social Democracy; in 1910, as premier of France, he broke up a great railroad strike by conscripting the strikers into military service. Conflict over the issue developed at the international congresses of 1896, 1900, and 1904. A substantial majority of delegates rejected proposals calling for a revolutionary general strike. National strikes were thought appropriate for the purpose of forcing through definite economic demands and even for forcing concessions on constitutional matters. But it was asserted that a general strike to overthrow capitalism would be impossible to carry out and furthermore, that such a strike was at variance with the principle that the triumph of socialism would come about only after the capitalist society had attained a certain level of development. Syndicalism was accused of being a modernized version of anarchism.

In the ensuing years, syndicalism did not gain ground within social democratic parties; champions of the movement operated within the trade unions, in accordance with their programmatic declarations. Indices of the difference between the French and German labor movements are the 1905 declaration of the German trade unions that explicitly renounced the revolutionary general strike and the 1906 declaration by the French federation of trade unions, which just as definitively supported the general strike. Led by original thinkers, primarily Georges Sorel, a remarkable syndicalist ideology developed in Latin countries. With its antiintellectualism and pragmatism, its emphasis on the value and independent significance of forming ideals, its doctrine of the moral elite and its faith in the stimulating, purifying force of struggle, this ideology would help mold modern fascism.

True syndicalism did gain appreciable momentum in England, even though some trade union leaders were influenced by the summons to direct action issued by the French syndicalists. Traces of syndicalist notions may, however, be detected in the unique socialist movement, "guild socialism," whose tidings were proclaimed in the 1910s by a group of young English intellectuals. The theories of intensified class struggle and of a revolutionary general strike which characterized syndicalism were alien to guild socialism. However, the idea of occupational organizations as the carriers that would bring in the new society was common to both movements. According to guild socialism, all persons working within a certain branch of industry would form a guild, and would do so even under the established order. These guilds, reminiscent of both the medieval guilds and the production associations advocated by early socialists, would constitute independent units endowed with a large measure of self-government. Leadership within the guilds would be in the hands of representatives of those engaged in the specific industry, together with representatives of other interests (the state, the consumer). All production would gradually fall under guild management. As a rule, an uppermost right of ownership of the means of production was apparently assigned to the state. Local and national representative bodies would be formed in conformity with the principle of special interests; these bodies would thus particularly represent consumers and producers, but would also represent groups related to the guilds in other respects. The theorists of guild socialism are notorious for their ambiguity of expression; they never developed a unified, even passably specific theoretical structure. After a few years all the propaganda of the guild socialists died out. In postwar years the movement was of almost no significance at all in England, but it did affect certain social democratic parties in other nations. For a brief period around 1920 the demand for industrial self-government with a body representative "of interests" as the chief organ in society became one of the lines in socialist debate.

Socialism after World War I

THE INTERNATIONAL disintegrated as a result of the world war. With the exception of certain groups, the social democratic parties of different countries aligned themselves solidly with the sentiments in their respective nations. After the war an international social democratic union was again gradually established. It regarded itself as the successor of the prewar International, but it did not become the sole representative of the socialist labor movement; its rival and enemy became the Third, the Communist International.

We need only briefly review a few aspects of communist ideology as it was shaped in conjunction with the communist takeover in Russia. Its adherents believe that communism is rooted in Marxian premises. In respect to many of the theoretical points of contention between Social Democrats and communists it is actually impossible to determine definitely that one or the other is correct in its interpretation of Marx; Marx made enough vague or contradictory statements to furnish both combatant doctrines with arguments—most of which have been based on the contradictions between Marx's major and minor perspectives. We can only state with certainty that neither Social Democrats nor communists can be said to have acted in accordance with Marx's major perspective, which is of no use as a guideline for any political movement.

The basic idea behind communism is that socialist seizure of power is not contingent upon the "consummation" of the capitalist order in a nation. The capitalist order is regarded as a whole throughout the world; the objective of socialism is to capture power in any country where conditions are favorable to such a takeover, in other words to concentrate on breaking "capitalism's weakest link." Once socialism has security victory in a nation, industrial development can be continued and activated under socialist leadership. In agreement with certain statements made by Marx, Social Democrats have tended to think that industrialization must necessarily be accomplished in the main under capitalist management. Communists, on the other hand, make a sharp distinction between industrialism and capitalism. The latter, characterized by the right of private ownership of the means of production, can be overthrown before it has reached an advanced stage of industrialization, the process of industrialization can then continue under socialism. Once socialists had won in one country, the work of furthering socialist revolutions in other nations could be pursued with greater prospects of success. The degree to which a communist movement that had emerged victorious in a nation should directly aim at a "world revolution" has become one of the moot points in communist debates.

Directly connected with this view are the communist theories of revolution and the "dictatorship of the proletariat." If the seizure of power is to take place in a country without a fully developed industrial capitalism it cannot expect the support of a majority of socialist proletarians. Communists add, however, that socialism can under no conditions win power through peaceful means. In a bourgeois democracy, capitalism can use propaganda and pressure to corrupt labor leaders and to prevent the workers themselves from gaining insight into their own best interests or from acting in accordance with their interests. If, contrary to all expectations, a true socialist group should win a majority, the bourgeois class would resort to violent means to safeguard its rule. Bourgeois democracy is therefore really bourgeois dictatorship. To capture power, socialism must therefore use truly revolutionary methods. These methods must be wielded by the class-conscious proletariat, that is, by the segment of the proletariat that is aware of the real interests of its own class. This group, which in practice becomes synonymous with the Communist party, shall retain leadership even after victory has been won in order to carry out the socialist program. The dictatorship of the proletariat means proletariat rule over the surviving bourgeois class, and it also implies dictatorship within or over the proletariat by the class-conscious—the communists. Once socialization has been achieved, once the prejudices against a socialist order inculcated during the bourgeois period have been eradicated and production has reached a sufficiently high level, the entire system of state coercion will be successively liquidated, and the transition from the first stage of revolution, socialism, to its second stage, communism, will take place.

This schema was worked out primarily with reference to conditions in Russia. The despotism in Russia, which was hardly even veiled, precluded the growth of a democratic labor movement following the Western pattern. Here were the requisites for a successful revolutionary movement, even though—or, perhaps, just because—capitalism in the sense of industrial capitalism was relatively underdeveloped. However, in conjunction with the Russian revolution, communist parties sprang up in a series of countries, and in some cases these parties posed a grave threat to the hegemony of Social Democracy among the working classes. Through the machinations of Russian Communist leadership, the communist International manifested considerable ideological uniformity, even though the opinions it put forth were frequently modified in essential respects.

The differences between the ideologies and tactics of the various parties within the social democratic labor movement grew in importance after World War I. This can apparently be explained by two closely interrelated circumstances. On the one hand, Marxism became more flexible, revisionism gained in significance, and therefore accommodation to the conditions existing in a state gained theoretical sanction. On the other hand, Social Democracy, which was almost uniformly a sheer opposition party before the war, obtained a position of power in one country after another that was conducive to collaboration in the formation of governments or, in any event, to assuming a share of political responsibility. When the party's immediate concern in a nation was the molding of a constructive program of action, and not simply criticism of the established order, definitive consideration had to be political and social traditions and environmental factors.

As a consequence, the Social Democratic International came to play an even more modest role than before. Schematically speaking, it can even be said that this International tended to become a kind of depository for broad ideological perspectives, now abandoned or at least not completely accepted or found practicable by the member parties, as well as for ardent proclamations and protests that could not easily be voiced in certain countries. Some members of the International can be ascribed a certain degree of irresponsibility in that they formulated Marxian prognoses and addressed themselves aggressively to current issues at the same time as they acted realistically and opportunistically in domestic politics. An account of the resolutions adopted by the Social Democratic International, which became increasingly numerous and comprehensive in inverse ratio to the attention they received, is therefore not warranted in this text.

The International still clung to the premise of class struggle. The 1923 statutes pronounced that it consisted of "united socialist workers' parties that see their goal to be the replacement of the capitalist mode of production by the socialist mode, and the means of liberating the working class in the class struggle, that expresses itself in political and economic action." It was generally presumed that within a democracy the class struggle would be waged through democratic channels, and that revolutionary methods would be employed only in dictatorships. The value of democracy was brought out even more incisively than before, and the dictatorship—the antidemocratic form of government of the age—was condemned.

Yet modification in interpretation of the theory of class struggle was manifested in the change in attitude toward cabinet socialism and collaboration with other parties. After the democratic revolution in Germany, the German Social Democratic party viewed the tactics it had previously laid down in a succession of resolutions as no longer tenable; the parties in other countries underwent similar shifts in opinion. Social Democrats could not refuse to cooperate with other groups in maintaining the popular governments that had been formed largely through social democratic efforts. Pure social democratic rule was not feasible; despite universal suffrage, the party had not yet attained a majority. The International did not pass a new resolution on this point, but the chairman at the 1925 congress emphasized that the question of forming governments and collaborating in governments was merely contingent upon the appropriateness of such action; the 1931 congress refused to consider a proposal for a resolution declaring coalitions with bourgeois parties unsuitable.

The defense issue revealed a similar shift in opinion. Time and again the International discussed the possibilities of preventing war. It consistently called for international disarmament and for greater effectiveness in the use of the League of Nations as an instrument of peace. Social Democrats even recommended the use of a general strike and revolutionary pressure tactics in states that declined to submit conflicts to international arbitration. But social democratic parties were not enjoined to vote against military appropriations, and all proposals prescribing such injunctions were rejected.

Within the several social democratic parties, efforts to preserve and extend democracy came more and more to the fore, partly as a result of reaction to communist and national dictatorships. This was accompanied by a *rapprochement* with other parties that were based on democratic principles, and by a general reinforcement of the sense of national solidarity. As one country after another was taken over by dictatorial movements that suppressed Social Democracy, these tendencies grew stronger in the remaining countries where Social Democacy was still able to function freely.

Yet distinct differences of opinion on the tactics to be used within parliamentary democracies persisted in social democratic parties. Some groups completely accepted parliamentary rules and considered Social Democracy to be in the same position as other democratic parties in respect to forming coalitions and governments. Among other groups the idea of a seizure of total power persisted, even if in attenuated form, and prevented or complicated their unconditional support of the principles of parliamentarianism. As late as 1936 French Social Democrats refused to participate in the executive branch of the national government. They often asserted that the party should take over executive power only if it could realize its socialist program; to this end, power would be lodged in the government for a specific time and by virtue of a broad mandate. Similar currents of thought were advanced in England following the socialists' unsuccessful attempts at leading the government in 1924 and 1929–1931. If a new social democratic government were to be formed, it would introduce a socialization program with the support of an act of Parliament giving the government full authority. Adherence to parliamentary convention was naturally most unconditional in nations where complete democracy had first been realized in conjunction with World War I; in such countries Social Democrats stood out as those who were primarily responsible for the establishment of popular government, and their cooperation was essential to the preservation of this form of government.

The triumph of revisionism has broadened the scope of social democratic discussion. The schema that decreed that at a certain stage the means of production would be transferred from the hands of a few to the whole of society has had to give way to more discriminating currents of thought. To many the question of the ownership of the means of production has seemed to be of secondary importance. Socialism was thought to mean above all the organization of production, economic planning designed to secure the most effective utilization of the means of production. At times even a comprehensive program of social measures, combined with a certain amount of state control over the economy, has been designated as socialism. The cooperative movement has gained ever wider recognition as an important part of the socialist process of reconstruction. At various times proposals related to industrial democracy that would give the workers some say in the management of business, whether socialized or not, have been vigorously advocated as a kind of preparation or substitute for true socialization. The arguments advanced in support of measures described as socialist have to an ever lesser extent drawn upon Marx's economic theories and social prognoses. On the one hand it has been asserted that the waste in labor and means of production entailed in the competition and lack of planning inherent in the capitalist order would disappear with the introduction of socialization or economic planning. On the other hand equalization has been put forth as the essential view; as uniform distribution as possible according to the utilitarian pattern has per se been regarded as the way to create the greatest possible amount of satisfaction. In what is perhaps the most well-known social democratic work published after World War I, de Man's *The Psychology of Socialism,* Marxian theory has been completely replaced by ideas based on certain modern philosophical and social-psychological theories. In this work socialism is represented essentially as a method of freeing the workers from a sense of social malaise and inferiority, which implies a threat to all of society.

We shall not undertake an examination of the international discussion that has taken place since World War I. It is too extensive and contains altogether too many fluctuations in lines of thought to lend itself to a summary here. The results of this discussion will, however, be noted in subsequent chapters to the extent that they have had a bearing on the ideological development in Sweden.

Socialism and Society

Marxian Ideology and the Beginning of Its Dissolution

A DOCUMENT that Palm published in his newspaper *The Peoples Will* (*Folkviljan*) in November 1882 is often characterized as the first Swedish social democratic program. It was said to have been adopted by a small organization known as "The Swedish Social Democratic Workers' Federation," which Palm had founded in Malmö. In reality, the program was an almost uniform translation of the Danish Gimle Program adopted in 1876, which was, in turn, derived from the German Gotha Program of 1875. Palm's translation was poor, in some instances inaccurate; the various details in its formulation cannot be interpreted as expressions of specific ideas. This summary will not consider words or phrases that are obviously products of ignorance or misunderstanding.

The following sentence introduced the program: "Labor is the true source of all wealth and culture, and all the returns thereof should accrue to him who performs the labor." The tools of labor are the monopoly of capitalists; the surplus produced by labor should revert to the workers. Salaried labor should be abolished. Production unions should be established through state subsidies to lay the groundwork for the solution of The Social Question. These unions should be so organized "that the socialist organization can develop through collective work." The program set up a series of demands that were to be implemented even "under the present capitalist rule": progressive inheritance taxes, abolition of indirect taxation, which weighed heavily upon the masses, abrogation of the ordinance regarding the treatment of vagrants and the defenseless, the establishment of a standard working day, prohibition of the use of child labor in factories, which jeopardized the children's health, regulation of sanitary standards in workers' housing, factories, and other places of work, the workers' right to administer "without government intervention" funds for sickness and relief benefits, state care for the ailing, the aged, and for those disabled through accidents at place of work.

In the autumn of 1885 the Social Democratic Union in Stockholm worked out a program that was subsequently published in *Social-Demokraten* in February 1886. The introductory statements of principle in this program deserve to be rendered verbatim:

> Work is the source of all wealth and all culture, and the entire returns thereof should thus accrue to those who work.
>
> In the present society the tools of labor are the monopoly of a certain class, of the capitalists. That the working class is kept dependent on these is the ultimate cause of misery and all forms of oppression. The goal of the Social Democratic Workers' party is therefore to abolish the existing mode of production (the wage system) and to allow the means of labor the present private capital, to be converted into the common property of society, [which is] the only way of guaranteeing the worker full compensation for his work. As a first step in this direction the party calls for the formation of state subsidized production unions, [to be] under the active control of the workers and on a sufficiently large scale so that they may successfully compete with the production of big capital.
>
> Socialism's ultimate goal can by no means be realized in one stroke. Yet socialism should not only be a theory, a speculation as to the probable organization of the society of the future, but it should be a living reality, it should concern itself with the real endeavors of the working class, with its present needs, its daily struggles with those who have monopolized the capital of society and thereby also the social and political power in society.
>
> The fight for the liberation of the working class from its present position, which is beneath a free people, is not a fight for new class privileges and prerogatives but for equal rights and equal obligations for all and for the abolition of all class rule.

The program also incorporated "demands that can and ought to be realized as speedily as possible even in the existing society." These demands included the abolition of indirect taxes, which would be replaced by a single direct progressive income and inheritance tax, the establishment of a maximum work day in industry of 10 hours, "to begin with," curtailment of working hours for women, proscription of the labor of children under 14 years of age, protective legislation governing the health and lives of workers, inspection of the sanitary conditions in workers' living and working quarters, state care "of workers in case of sickness or accident and in old age."

In the autumn of 1886 it was decided that a few program items should be inserted in *Social-Demokraten*. The paper printed the first item in the statement of principles cited above, which designated labor as the source of all wealth and culture, together with its corollary, which dictated that all benefits accrue to the one who performs the labor. The sociopolitical demands advanced were "a standard eight-hour work day," protective legislation, the obligation of the state to lend succor in cases of illness, old age, and accident. The last program item listed by *Social-Demokraten* was worded as follows: "The state shall take over production, that is, the land, and all other means of production shall be the common property of all." This proclamation remained on the front page of *Social-Demokraten* until 1907, when it was replaced by a new, more fundamental exposition of the party's aims.

Among the many programs issued by various organizations before the formation of the Social Democratic party in 1889 was that prepared by Axel Danielsson. This program was adopted at the first workers' congress of southern Sweden in January 1888. It was introduced by this declaration of principles:

> The bourgeois society in Sweden gradually emerged out of the old warrior state in which the feudal class had ruled socially, politically, and spiritually through a series of violent acts stemming from the bourgeois-minded sovereign royal power (the expropriation of the property of the nobility by Charles X and Charles XI, Gustav III's systematic curtailment of the power of the nobility, among others), and because of the development of modern industry and the influence the burgher class thereby acquired on legislation, which has long been exclusively in its hands.
>
> Through violent or other means, a minority, the burgher class, has come into possession of all the means of production in this society (machines, tools, and factories) without which the society's industrial production cannot be carried on. According to the laws of society, this possession entitles this class to appropriate the entire proceeds of production, less a deduction for the so-called wages of labor, which, at best, constitute a subsistence minimum. This is the primary source of poverty, unemployment, slavery, and of all forms of oppression.
>
> But since the entire proceeds of labor should rightly accrue to those who labor, and since this cannot transpire until the instruments of labor are expropriated from the ruling class, the Congress sets forth the ultimate objective of the workers' movement to be *the socialization of capital,* or the conversion of means of industrial production into societal (common) property.
>
> Further, since even the land, together with all the working tools necessary to its modern cultivation, is in the hands of the minority, and since the formerly so populous farming class is becoming ever more debt-ridden and is disintegrating or being transformed into a class of wage earners for big capital, and finally, since landed property should be considered a means of production that yields no produce without human labor.
>
> The Congress rules that the class-conscious workers' movement must also aim for *the socialization of land,* or for its conversion into common property, whereby the dependence of the masses on the landholding class will come to an end for all time.

This presentation was coupled with a political program that was obviously designed for realization within the contours of the existing society. Here we encounter the usual demands: progressive income and inheritance taxes, "a standard work day, at present 8 hours, that corresponds to the needs of society," prohibition of child labor, and protective legislation for workers, among others.

Those parts of the programs which are of particular interest will be further considered. At this juncture we should note, however, that Danielsson's program included a singular line of reasoning which does not seem to have any counterpart. Danielsson referred to the power struggle between several

Swedish kings and the nobility as one of the causes of the origin of bourgeois society in Sweden; he even implied that the throne was of a bourgeois disposition. He obviously gave the word "bourgeois" a different connotation here than when he subsequently used the word to describe the position of the middle class in the existing society. In the first instance he used the word solely to designate the opposite of the nobility; in the second instance he made the word synonymous with capitalism.

The first constituent party congress did not adopt any particular program, but it was generally assumed for some time thereafter that the German Gotha program would be applicable to the Swedish party. We shall therefore quote the most fundamental and, in this context, most pertinent points in the Gotha Program:

> I. Labor is the source of all wealth and of all culture, and since labor that is of service to the general public is feasible only in and through society, the aggregate product of work belongs to society, that is to say, to all its members, each of which has the obligation to work and the equal right to satisfy his reasonable needs.
>
> In the present society the instruments of labor are the monopoly of the capitalist class; the dependence of the working class that this entails is the cause of misery and oppression in all its forms.
>
> The emancipation of labor requires that the instruments of labor be turned to use for the common good of society and that society regulate collective labor with equitable division of the proceeds of labor and their utilization for the commonweal.
>
> II. With these principles as a point of departure, Germany's Socialist Workers' party strives with all lawful means for the free state and the socialist society, strives to shatter the iron law of wages through the abrogation of the system of salaried work, the abolition of every form of exploitation, the removal of all social and political inequalities.
>
> In order to pave the way for the solution of The Social Question, Germany's Socialist Workers' party calls for the establishment with state aid of socialist production unions under the democratic control of the working people. The production unions formed in industry and agriculture should be so encompassing that they will give rise to the socialist organization of collective labor.

It was not before the fourth party congress in 1897 that the Swedish party got its own program, designed by Danielsson. This program was derived from the Erfurt Program of 1891, but it contained some formulations of its own. It has since been amended, but it has not been replaced by an entirely new program. Approximately half of the program was devoted to an account of the party's ideology, "General Principles." With the exception of the last paragraph, which concerns the party's internationalism, these principles are rendered below:

> Social Democracy differs from other political parties in that it aspires to completely transform the economic organization of bourgeois society and bring about the social

liberation of the working class to secure and develop intellectual and material culture.

The primary cause of the vices in today's civilization is the private capitalist system of production, which has dissolved the old petty bourgeois societal conditions, has collected wealth in the hands of a few, and has divided society into workers and capitalists, with intervening strata composed in part of vanishing early societal classes—small farmers, craftsmen, and small merchants—and in part of new emerging [classes]. In former times the right of private ownership of the means of production was a natural condition for production inasmuch as it guaranteed the producer his product. But to the extent that large-scale manufacturing displaces the craftsman, the machine the tool, and world-wide trade and mass production break down all market barriers, the true producers are transformed into a class of wage earners that incorporates the sinking dregs of the old middle class and has as its distinguishing social characteristic of propertyless condition and consequent dependence and oppression.

The extraordinary technical development of the work process, the fabulous increase in productivity of human labor, the continuous opening of new fields of production, all this, through which the nation's wealth has multiplied, is attended only by an unnatural accumulation of wealth on the one hand and a colossal growth of the working class on the other.

But at the same time these conditions and this disastrous tendency in the development of society force the workers to form a countermovement. They organize themselves as a class in order to seize as much as possible of the product of work in the form of wages. Thus arise trade unions and the continuous struggle in the national and international labor market between workers and work-buyers, a struggle that is assuming ever vaster proportions and which shall never end until the working class ceases to be a class of wage earners.

This, in turn, can only come about through the abolition of the monopoly of private capital on the means of production and their transformation into the common property of all society, together with the replacement of the planless production of commodities by a socialist production that meets the real needs of society.

Social Democracy therefore wishes to bring about the political organization of the working class as well, to take possession of public power, and gradually convert the means of production—transportation, forests, mines, mills, machines, factories, the land—into community property.

As with the program as a whole, these tenets were subject to only the briefest discussion at the congress. The only change made in Danielsson's proposal was the substitution of the words "completely transform" in place of "intervene with the purpose of changing."

The general statement of principles was followed by a "political program" obviously intended to comprise the demands that could presumably be satisfied within the contour of the existing capitalist society. The last six clauses in this section (VI–XI) read as follows:

VI. Gradated (progressive) income and property tax together with an inheritance tax. Repeal of all indirect taxes, which principally weigh upon the productive classes.

Vigorous development of the activities of the state and municipalities as the producers and leaders in exchange and distribution in order to meet national budget requirements.

Individual filing of tax statements and legal responsibility for assessment.

VII. State organization of public credit. Direct state control of farmers' credit. Laws which, while including guarantees for scientific farming, will prevent the expropriation of the small farmer without compensation of right of usage.

VIII. Effective legislation for workers' protection, principally: a) A standard working day of a maximum of 8 hours; b) Prohibition of the employment in industry of children under 14 years of age; c) Prohibition of night work in all cases except where necessitated by the technical nature of the work process or by the general welfare; d) Prohibition of the truck system.

IX. Supervision by a modern works superintendency of all branches of trade and industrial work.

X. The responsibility of society to care for all its members in a humanitarian way in case of accident or sickness and in old age.

XI. Legal equality between industrial workers, agricultural workers, seamen, and servants through repeal of the hiring law and revision of nautical law, among other measures.

Constitutional guarantee of full rights of organization, assembly, press, and speech.

Careful comparison of this program with the Erfurt Program shows that several clauses in the statement of principles of the Swedish program are less precisely worded and that the program is generally reformist in character. The German program alleged that capitalism created an ever-increasing number of unemployed, ever-increasing impoverishment among the workers, and ever more devastating crises; there are no counterparts to these allegations in the Swedish program. The Swedish program contains new formulations or thoughts: in the definition of the goal of socialism in the first paragraph, in the reference to the emerging new middle classes in the second paragraph, in the sentences regarding the "countermovement" and the importance of trade unions in the fifth paragraph, in the mention of "gradual" socialization in the seventh paragraph. We shall return to these clauses. Taken together, they lend the Swedish program a certain amount of originality. On the other hand, the special demands listed in the second part of the program are almost uniformly taken—often verbatim—from the Erfurt Program. Several of them had also been advanced by bourgeois elements in Sweden. Of the sections quoted, the third paragraph in Article VI (regarding societal production for budgetary needs) and Article VII (regarding agriculture) contain no new points in comparison with the Erfurt Program.

To understand the ideological development within the young Social Democratic party one must be familiar with the chief traits of the movement. First and foremost: for a long time the movement lacked quantitative significance. Membership at the time of the party's formation in 1889 was estimated to be slightly over 3000. During the next few years membership increased slowly: in 1892 it was slightly over 5600, and in 1895, over 10,000. The big jump forward began around the turn of the century through the growth of the trade union movement and the inclusion of the unions in the party. The party was represented in the Riksdag for the first time in 1897, then Branting was its sole spokesman. Six years would elapse before Branting would be joined in the legislature by other Social Democrats. During the last years of the nineteenth century and the first years of the twentieth the party was transformed from a movement that comprised but a fraction of the nation's workers and craftsmen into a party of significance that could justly claim to represent most of the rapidly growing working class.

It is safe to presume that those who joined the party during its early years represented a definite set of personality traits and personal circumstances. They had to have a special combination of discontent with existing conditions and optimism about the future in order to join the Social Democratic party which, despite its insignificant status, had great pretensions and expectations. In this respect Social Democracy was similar to other germinating, more or less revolutionary movements. Its members were certainly motivated by idealism to a relatively great extent, if idealism is taken to mean the capacity to enthusiastically embrace distant objectives that would seem unattainable to those of less robust faith. They were certainly also emotional individuals inasmuch as they became more incensed by the distress and injustice they saw about them than the majority. But their personal reasons for this reaction could vary: a great feeling of compassion, dogmatic belief in certain Marxian predictions, a naive faith in the future, bitterness due to personal failure.

We can also assume that the ranks of membership changed rapidly during those early years. Workers who were active in the party were often subjected to pressure and harassment by their employers and many of them probably left the movement for this reason. Accounts of the emigration of party members were common. Many probably left the party because of discontent arising from intraparty strife. As we shall soon see, representation at party congresses was highly variable. Although it cannot be proved, it seems probable that the party, far from being a group that was solidly welded together, largely consisted of persons who joined it for only limited periods. One can venture the assumption that, as a rule, a heterogeneous and shifting membership is distinctive of minor movements whose grand, optimistic plans attract emotional, unstable persons and that have not yet succeeded in gaining a social foothold to lend them stability. Small parties whose membership recruitment is largely based on psychological factors and whose members are not united by a desire to retain a position of power consistently manifest division and defections.

This explains certain features of the Social Democratic ideological debate of the period. Utopian, far-reaching visions were highly in evidence since there were no opportunities for concrete action. The Social Democrats' ideological frame of reference consisted of faith in the victory of the working class and in a future of free cooperation between equal citizens. Yet this frame could encompass widely divergent motives, arguments, and tactical policies. An opinion could quickly gain considerable influence, only to vanish from the debate with equal speed. The prime example of this are the short-lived successes of the anarchic line in the beginning of the 1890s. As Branting's stand on defense in 1900 shows, a change in the opinion of one of the leaders could decide the party's position. Stabilization of ideology and lines of action developed with the party's growth.

The party's real organ was the party congress: the first party administration did not come into existence until 1894. Changes in the delegations at the congresses is one of the most characteristic features of the party's early history. At the 1889 congress the number of delegates was 48; at the 1891 congress the number had increased to 52, at the 1894 congress to 61, at the 1897 congress to 92. Twelve delegates participated in more than two congresses and three participated in all four congresses. The lack of continuity was thus striking. Only a few belonged to the leading clique for an appreciable length of time. The three delegates who participated in all four congresses were Branting, Sterky, and Thorsson. Danielsson and Palm were among those who attended three congresses; the former was in jail at the time of the 1889 congress and the latter was not chosen a delegate in 1894. Branting and Thorsson were the only ones at the congress of 1900 who had participated in all the congresses held up to that point.

Most of the delegates were workers and craftsmen. During the first decades craftsmen were particularly well represented. On the whole they appear to have constituted a proportinately larger part of the party's membership than industrial workers. Both at the congresses and in the sphere of party activity, the group that theorized, discussed, and was ideologically dominant was largely composed of intellectuals, that is, of persons who had taken their matriculation examination (*studentexamen*) or had otherwise pursued an organized course of study and were engaged in journalism or other literary work. At the head of this group were Branting, Danielsson, and Sterky. The theoretical debate within Social Democracy during this period is, in fact, decidedly linked to their names. For a long time they were the editors of the chief party newspapers: Branting, of *Social-Demokraten* in Stockholm (from 1887 on, with the exception of the period 1892–1896), Danielsson of *Arbetet* in Malmö (1887–1899), and Sterky of *Ny Tid* in Gothenburg (1892–1898). This group also included C. N. Carleson, who was on the *Social-Demokraten* staff for many years and editor from 1892 to 1896, Hinke Bergegren, the foremost representative of the anarchic line, A. Wermelin, who published a couple of socialistic pamphlets but emigrated to the United States in 1887, A. F. Åkerberg, who was extremely active in the movement until the beginning of the 1890s. The following are some of the working-class members who occupied prominent positions in the party during this period: August Palm, who introduced Social Democracy in Sweden and was publisher of *Folkviljan* during various periods; K. J. Gabrielsson, editor of *Folkbladet* 1894–1901; Pehr Eriksson, editor of *Folkets Röst* 1887–1889; J. M. Engström, publisher of *Nya Samhället* 1886; G. A. Rydgren, who published *Proletären* for a while; A. C. Lindblad, who succeeded Sterky as chief of *Ny Tid;* Axel Rylander, and F. V. Thorsson.

Of particular note in this context is the fact that the ideological debate was almost uniformly conducted by young men who had not conducted penetrating studies of either social problems or sociological theory. Branting had been studying astronomy at Uppsala University when he became a journalist and agitator at some twenty-odd years of age; Danielsson had no academic training before he became a member of the *Social-Demokraten* staff and subsequently, at twenty-four years of age, editor of *Arbetet;* Sterky began his party work at approximately the same age. These and other representatives of the theoretical views of the party were captured entirely by the socialist teachings they gleaned from a number of foreign works, German works in particular. None displayed distinct theoretical independence. For all, socialist doctrine became the gospel, sufficient to fill their need for a philosophy of life. Once they had acquired peremptory certainty of belief they paid little heed to public criticism: attacks on socialism were a priori regarded as unwarranted and malicious. Their political philosophy had a religious quality; even though they subsequently abandoned certain tenets and, in effect, greatly modified their standpoints, they retained a kind of basic, intense insistence on the truth of a credo, a passionate faith in something indeterminate that was constantly referred to as scientific socialism. This explains the paradoxical views of socialist leaders: although they professed to represent hard realism and cold historical analysis and to scorn metaphysics and romanticism, they displayed little interest in exploring conditions in their own country. Almost no social democratic literature of this period offers a thorough economic or political investigation of these conditions. The study of a few foreign works was the substitute for the collection and analysis of factual data. The discussion largely centered around concepts shaped by Marx, which were components in his closed system.

There has been some discussion as to whether Marx or Lassalle had the greatest influence on early Social Democracy in Sweden. A systematic review of the available material leaves no doubt about the answer. The concepts of Marx provided the main theoretical foundation of the movement. One might even say that the more integrated expositions of the leading Swedish theorists most accurately represent paraphrases of and commentaries to the underlying ideas in *The Communist Manifesto.* Marx's major perspective was the basis of all attempts at an analysis of any appreciable scope.

This dependence has been somewhat obscured by two circumstances. First, Palm's early views showed the influence of his acquaintance—however superficial—with Lassalle's teachings. In effect, however, Palm never developed a complete doctrine; only a few of his phrases reveal more than general indignation at social inequalities and the political system then in force. A few years later Palm evidently became acquainted with Marx, directly or indirectly, and began to employ characteristically Marxian ideas. Palm himself apparently was not sufficiently reflective to carry out this modification in his standpoint consciously, or even to be aware of the change. Second, at an early stage Social Democracy in Sweden revealed a strong interest in bringing about social reforms within the contours of the existing state. This may to some extent have been a result of Lassalle's influence. However, in view of the generally Marxian character of the debate it seems more reasonable to regard this posture first and foremost as an accommodation to the political situation, and second, as a product of the gradual adoption of Marx's minor perspective, which foresaw important gains for the working class in social reforms within the capitalist society. It would thus be incorrect to consider every valuation of social reformism and of the role of the state as a political instrument as evidence of Lassalle's influence. There were two main differences between Marx and Lassalle: from a short-range viewpoint, the former rejected and the latter recommended state-supported production unions as a step toward socialism; from a long-range viewpoint, the former considered the abolition of the state the ultimate objective and the latter referred to the socialist society as the consummate state.

The best springboard for a presentation of Social Democratic debate of the time is Branting's address, "Why the Workers' Movement Must Be Socialist," given in Gävle October 24, 1886. As Höglund commented, this address can "be said to constitute the declaration of independence of the Swedish workers' movement and the first written platform of Swedish socialism." No other exposition made during this period presents the lines of thinking basic to the philosophy of the movement with anywhere near the same degree of cogency.

Branting wrote that mass production, made possible by developments in technological aids, had given rise to the labor problem in its modern form. The ideological counterpart of the prevalent system of production was the teaching of the Manchester School in regard to free competition. A loftier principle was now breaking through to victory, "the ordered, collective production of society, which is just as suitable for large-scale manufacture of goods as free competition but does not have the latter's irremediable shortcomings in regard to the distribution of the profits of labor."

Branting thereafter entered into a detailed examination of the effects of the system of free competition. Under this system one tries to make manufacturing costs and therefore also wages as low as possible. "The wages of the workers . . . strive to remain at the lowest level capable of sustaining life and breeding the next generation of wage slaves. . . ." The crafts labor are more costly than mass production and are therefore gradually being replaced by it. In large businesses the workers are divided into groups that have no personal contact with the employers. The egoistic class interests of the employers appears undisguised in the light of day. Thereby "However, the modern worker quickens to the emotion that will one day be his emancipation, his *class consciousness.*" Mass production intensified class conflict and class consciousness in another, more important way: it increased the inequalities in the distribution of wealth.

Branting gave a theoretical illustration to prove his point. In a city with twenty home bakeries, one single, modern and efficiently organized big bakery is established. The newcomer employs a smaller labor force to produce the same quantity of bread as the home bakeries, and is able to sell bread at a lower price. The results are "a real monopoly of the big bakery magnate of the bread sales of almost the entire city, through which he can more thoroughly fleece the public; the entire profits of the business go into one pocket instead of into twenty; some members of the city's solid middle class are forced down to the level of the proletariat and the position of others is considerably undermined; and finally, a number of workers become unemployed and thereby increase competition for the few remaining jobs, which the employers can therefore fill at lower wages than they paid before." In support of the thesis regarding the disappearance of the middle class that he incorporated into this example, Branting cited some German statistics indicative of such a trend. On the other hand, he added a kind of qualification to the proposition regarding the impoverishment of the working class: a slight rise in the standard of living was not proof that the gulf between rich and poor was not widened.

The conclusion drawn from this historical presentation was that socialism was in line with the future course of developments. "Doesn't one understand, then, that *if* the preceding arguments are valid, *if* economic developments propel us closer and closer to the future goal I just mentioned, when the last remains of the middle class have disappeared and the millionaires stand alone against the starving masses—that in this case no emergency legislation as in Germany, no mass executions as in France after the Commune can arrest the course of progress?" In effect the realization of socialism will be simple in comparison with the destruction of small crafts and their replacement by big industry. For the difficulties diminish in proportion to the number of people interested in maintaining the old system. "To transform what a few millionaires call 'their' property into the property of all of society must encounter far less resistance than the expropriation of a populous and mighty societal class, such as the petty bourgeois of a former time." Socialism actually demands nothing more "than that we open our eyes to the special process that is going on around us and that once we have become convinced of the direction in which it is leading, that we accommodate our social institutions accordingly and not let them remain as they were when the internal structure of society was completely different."

Using the bakery illustration, Branting then tried to demonstrate the rational nature of socialism. Should the society take over the big bakery, its owner would lose his unearned profit but all others would benefit. The price of bread would be reduced and the workers would receive higher wages and shorter working hours. The private capitalist is an unnecessary and harmful outgrowth of the system of production. "In his hands, in the form of private property, capital only serves to make him destroy himself in wild, criminal luxury, but if in society's possession, it would be used to alleviate the necessary burden of labor of *everyone* and thus make life happier for the great mass of people." The victory of socialism meant the breakdown of class dominion, the elimination of class conflicts, and the rule of true equality.

Branting continued by stating that it was the "great historic mission" of the modern working class to prepare for the transition to the socialist society. The workers' movement must rest on the recognition of the pre-emption of mass production—"thereby its position is also given in respect to all reactionary crooked attempts to try to turn back progress to the crafts and small-scale production with consequent tariff barriers and the like." It must understand that the only way out is "to expropriate the capital of the millionaires, to turn capital by civil law into what it already has become economically, the common property of society." The ideal of the future would be

> a society of equality in which all sources of class differences have been torn up by the roots, in which labor not only is the foundation of both material and intellectual culture, but is also recognized as such, in which ordered, collective work for both the individual and the general good has replaced ruthless, murderous competition between human beings, in which the struggle for survival is waged jointly by all of society against the natural obstacles that stand in the way of its happiness, not between private individuals within the society—this is the new, the coming kingdom that to us free thinkers and materialists has appeared as a certain, demonstrable prospect in place of the fairy tale about a heaven on the other side of the grave, which still represents to so many of the wretched the last refuge from life's storms.

This objective could not be reached within the lifetime of the current generation. Yet one should work toward it both through trade unions and a political party. The unions, which were to guard the interests of the working class on the labor market, would embrace all workers irrespective of their political beliefs. (Branting would soon change his mind in this respect.) The goal of the political party would be "to capture political power in the society for the workers and, until this had been completely accomplished, to try to achieve as favorable legislation as possible for the good of the workers."

Branting then addressed himself to the question of whether this power should be won through revolution or reform; his views on this will be given in another context (Cf. Part II). Finally, he leveled criticism at liberalism and especially at the liberal workers' movement. Even if the liberal program, including universal suffrage, the demand for a republic, and direct taxation, were realized and supplemented by social reforms such as a standard working day and state insurance coverage for all, it would still be insufficient. The central issue, the unequal distribution of wealth, would remain; mass poverty and unemployment would persist. Liberalism would lead to formal but not to true freedom for the workers. Branting concluded by saying that the Swedish worker could "by supporting Social Democracy with enthusiasm and perseverance . . . first prove himself worthy of the great task that the course of developments has given to him: to become the executioner of the class society and the founder of the society of equality."

It need scarcely be pointed out that the essential parts of this address were based on Marxism. The concept of class struggle pervades the exposition. The materialist conception of history may not be defined, but it is the obvious point of departure. The same can be said of Marx's theory of value. The Marxian theories that Branting most ardently espoused were the concentration of capital and the impoverishment of the working class, together with the related concept of the ruin of the middle class. Socialization is regarded primarily as a result of economic developments, not as a demand for justice. The working class must become aware of its historic mission; it is a question of insight, not evaluation—even though value concepts are clearly manifest.

Branting did not adopt certain elements of Marxian theory in his address, or only in passing. Yet he gave these elements strong emphasis on other occasions as, for example, in his article "Socialism," which appeared in the first edition of *Nordisk familjebok* in 1890 and was marked by clarity and conciseness. This article deals with unemployment and crises in capitalist society:

> The machines, which are constantly being improved, cause increasing numbers of workers to be unemployed and thereby create a reserve labor army that is not only plunged into misery itself but also forces down the wages of those who still have work. The lack of planning and enormous increase in production, without a comparable rise in the purchasing power of the broad strata of the populace, creates that strange phenomenon which was unknown in previous stages of development: *the crisis due to overproduction* (n.b. relative to purchasing power). Whereas they previously recurred roughly at ten-year intervals, the crises recently seem to tend to become chronic inasmuch as the demand for a product is scarcely created before it is instantly satisfied and more than satisfied. At the same time economic development continues; businesses expand into mammoth dimensions; entire armies of workers produce surplus value for a few multimillionaires; the whole production process assumes such proportions that it becomes evident that the bourgeoisie is no longer able to lead the forces that have grown under its protection and that the antagonism between social production and anarchist distribution must not be permitted to continue.

Later in the article Branting states that when the time is ripe the proletariat shall expropriate the property of the capitalists and take over leadership of production. Thus will "the social revolution be fulfilled." It is the course of economic developments itself that will force through a socialist organization of society. We can only "try to learn to know the laws of the evolution in progress and then use our knowledge to try to lessen the birth pangs of the new society that it is gestating."

Branting's article and address contain the main ingredients of the ideology of the Social Democratic movement. The next part of our discussion will be devoted to an account of the debate on the chief elements of that ideology. But we should note that in a way that was remarkable even from an international point of view, Branting placed Marx's major and minor perspectives in opposition to one another; he thereby revealed—but did not identify as such—two of the basic problems of Marxism, both of which have the same origin. In his general argumentation Branting assumed that economic developments would necessarily bring about socialism. By a certain time, which would be determined by the state of the productive forces or technology, society must be socialist. At the same time he urged the workers to build a Social Democratic party and even to work in the Social Democratic cause "with enthusiasm and perseverance." What was the point of fighting passionately for something that was inevitable at a certain stage? In a historical-sociological review, Branting asserted that capitalism would create a concentration of riches on the one hand and impoverishment on the other. The millionaires would stand alone against the starving masses. It was precisely because of this that socialism would be easy to accomplish. Later, however, using the perspective he had unfolded, Branting urged the workers to join a party which he held could be ascertained with scientific accuracy to be the party of the future, and to gradually improve their lot through this party. How could the truth of the sweeping prediction be verified if the exhortation to pursue political activity were followed and such activity proved successful?

The Marxian interpretation of history and its complement, the materialist conception of history, formed the climate of thought of Social Democratic theorists. They believed they held the key to an understanding of the dynamics of historical processes in the Marxian interpretation of history and that they could thus forecast the main trends in future developments. It was socialism's claim to be scientific, to make predictions, that persuaded many that it was superior to other currents of thought. Time and again, as in Branting's Gävle address, the idea that events followed a course independent of human volition was combined with the notion that the working class should enthusiastically embrace socialism. Sterky wrote that it was impossible either to arrest or to accelerate the march of developments. "Life . . . goes its majestic way without regard to the wishes of some individuals to hasten developments. . . . This knowledge shall . . . effectively aid in the formation of a workers' party. . . . ." The worker's passion would be incited by the thought of working in the service of the tide of history, of life itself.

The import of the materialist conception of history was presented in close correlation with the teachings of Marx and Engels. Wrote Branting: Marx has taught us to regard history as the history of class struggles and to search for the economic substance underlying political or religious forms. He (Marx) has pointed out "how the very key to the rise, culmination, and downfall of these different classes is ultimately to be found in the changes that are continuously going on in the relations of production and exchange in society. The *economic* revolutions are the decisive ones; with and from them follow—accompanied, of course, by constant interaction between the ideological superstructures and the material foundations of the societal organism—all other transformations in the aspect of society." However, as indicated in this quotation, Branting also stressed, that the economic outlook had to be complemented by other viewpoints; his statements therefore sometimes approached the obvious or meaningless, in similarity with Engel's well-known definitions made in his later years. On one occasion Branting wrote that not all the answers to questions regarding the internal conflicts of states could be found in economic developments. Political, religious, material, and scientific traditions also played a part, albeit as secondary factors whose "strength is broken when they operate in a direction diametrically opposed to [that of] the economic impulses." As usual, Danielsson expressed himself in more extreme terms. Under the influence of Engels, he declared that the system of production in the first place and the form of the family unit in the second were "the primary sources of the mentality of a society. The entire political, literary, and scientific superstructure revolves on this axle and it is only from it that it receives durable impulses toward progress and development. This is the materialist conception of history."

The general view that developments were moving in the direction of socialism, as laid down in Branting's Gävle speech, recurred continuously in representative Social Democratic expositions. A steadily growing conflict of interests existed between the two classes that represented the present order and the future order, the bourgeoisie and the proletariat. The class struggle thus had an objective basis in real conditions; yet socialism must awaken and accentuate the class consciousness of the proletariat by providing insight into the developments brought about through changes in the productive forces and the mode of production. The proletariat will fight for its own interests, but in so doing it will be fighting in the interests of the whole of society. When production has truly become societal the means of production must be socialized. In this way the class conflicts that have prevailed throughout history will disappear once and for all, the class society will be abolished, and free and equal men will continue their endeavors to master nature and fully exploit her wealth.

This historical-evolutionary view was often combined with ideas of a completely different kind. As in the case of Marx and other theorists, we encounter a stream of thinking reminiscent of the concept of natural rights. This line of thought was primarily based on the idea that value is solely the product of labor and that capitalist profits constitute an exploitation, robbery of the workers. "Socialism wishes to provide the great masses, rendered propertyless by monopoly, with the property right that is due them in accordance with the laws of nature," wrote Palm. Free competition is described not only as irrational at a certain stage of development but also as destructive from a moral point of view. Although capitalism is basically regarded as a necessary transitional phase and the individual is said to be conditioned by the class to which he belongs, class hatred was proclaimed as well as class struggle. In his pamphlet *The Flies and the Spiders* (*Flugorna och spindlarna*) of 1889, Danielsson described the class struggle as a contest between villainy and innocence. "The spiders, they are the masters, the rich moneybags, the exploiters, the speculators, the capitalists, the corrupters. . . . The spiders are all who live at our, at the people's expense, who trample us under their feet and sneeringly mock our suffering and our fruitless striving." The value-charged terms "the impoverishers" and "the impoverished," "the exploiters" and "the exploited" are constantly used.

The act that will bring about socialism is described as a social revolution. This term was not necessarily intended to mean a violent or even a quick revolution. (Cf. Vol. II.) It was customarily thought that the social revolution would be a peaceful, gradual transformation, an evolution. This interpretation became official with the adoption of the 1897 program: "Social Democracy wishes . . . to achieve the political organization of the working class as well, to take possession of official power and *by degrees* convert all means of production into the property of society. . . ." Note that at this time —as in this quotation—the social revolution was always understood to mean systematic, deliberate socialization under the leadership of the Social Democratic working class. This revolution was thus understood to begin with a power takeover by the working class. The influence the workers might exert on the nonsocialist state while on the road to power was not considered a social revolution. The central idea was the winning of total power and its utilization for socialist purposes. As did Marx in *The Communist Manifesto,* one foresaw, more or less definitely, a transitional period during which the workers would control all political power, before the economic and social reconfiguration would be accomplished. The first line of action thus became the struggle for power and, thereby, the struggle for universal suffrage.

There was little discussion about how and in what order socialization would be effected once the power takeover had been accomplished. Conforming with Marxian principles, one avoided drawing up detailed plans. The important thing was to be in line with "developments." Nevertheless, banking, mining, forestry, transportation, and those branches of industry where mass production was most pronounced were sometimes cited as suitable objects for early socialization measures.

Nor did Social Democratic theorists treat in detail the organization of the future socialist society. Only one description of this society was offered. It was Danielsson's *The Stranger* (*Främlingen*), published in 1891 and written in the style of the Utopian novel with obvious overtones of Bellamy. But there was agreement on the distinguishing features of the society and on the aims it would achieve. According to the 1897 program, Social Democracy wished to transform the economic organization of bourgeois society and realize the social emancipation of the working class "with the end of securing and developing the intellectual and material culture." Planless capitalist production would be replaced "by a socialist production that corresponds to the true needs of society." These general evaluations and goals were further developed in Social Democratic literature and in the party press. Classes would disappear and class struggles would be succeeded by social harmony. Socialism would usher in "the republic of labor, in which there will be toil and suffering, which have always existed since life began . . . but in which no artificial social conditions, no class rule or political power will allow one man to enjoy the fruits of the travail of others. . . ." Mankind would be liberated from the dependency that bourgeois society causes through its division into classes and its right of private ownership of the means of production. Equality would rule, for no one would have better opportunities than anyone else because of his initial economic and social vantage point. There was no mention of whether equality implied absolute economic equality, but a levelling process was considered self-evident. This problem was, however, of secondary interest, for socialism would result in a tremendous increase in production. Said *Social-Demokraten,* "There is no reason to suppose that the socialist society of the future would not be capable of producing the necessities of life and goods for the enjoyment for all . . . for through the harmony that must necessarily emerge in both production and distribution, both requisite goods and those for [man's] enjoyment will become as available as air and water are today." This wording is extreme, but the underlying thought was a recurrent theme; strife over the yield of production was therefore considered inconceivable in a socialist order. Side by side with the increase in production would be a reduction of the working day to five or six hours. In answer to Pontus Fahlbeck's allegation in his work *Estates and Classes* (*Stånd och klasser*) that dividing the national income would result in small incomes for all, Danielsson declared that the realization of socialism would lead to an unprecedented rise in national income and to the satisfaction of the needs of all; "even though natural resources and the labor force may not suffice to provide a life of sumptuous luxury for all, each one shall be guaranteed prosperity and comfort in accordance with reasonable demands." For mass production would expand further with the advent of socialism, while unproductive work would be curtailed and the unproductive class would disappear. In addition, Social Democrats believed that increased material well-being and freedom would be attended by undreamed of cultural development.

This kind of reasoning often did not include the consideration that, according to the Marxist schema, socialism would be possible and desirable only when industrialization had reached a high level of development. For example, in the statements just cited Danielsson presupposed that socialism would bring about a great increase in production even if it were realized under existent conditions. One overlooked the fact that, according to Marx, Sweden had just entered the phase that could be described as capitalist, in which capitalism was regarded as the most appropriate form of production.

The foregoing has presented the principal features of the viewpoint that was characteristic of the social democratic party during this period. We shall now examine in slightly more detail the currents of thought included in this viewpoint and the changes they underwent.

In what sense were the recurrent expressions *bourgeoisie* and *proletariat,* which were key terms in the ideological propaganda, used in the Social Democratic debate? In order to understand the basic ambiguity that existed in connection with these terms we must bear in mind the system of dividing society into classes that Marx postulated in his major perspective. According to Marx's schema, class struggles arose when the development of the forces of production gave rise to a new order of production. The classes were determined by their position in the order of production, which would be liquidated by the ensuing class struggle. In the bourgeois society that would be superseded by socialism, the ruling class consisted of the owners of the means of production and the suppressed revolutionary class consisted of those who worked in production for the profit of its owners. According to Marx's social prognosis, which we shall consider further in the following, groups that were not included in either of these classes were doomed to extinction. Marx postulated the existence on the one hand, of true capitalists who lived on exploitation without working and, on the other, of workers who produced surplus value for the rich in return for payment that corresponded to their minimum needs. Those with a negligible capital income and those with a high income from labor were excluded from the equation because of the theory of the dissolution of the middle classes. The victory of socialism and the proletariat would mean a gain for the great majority, or, to put it more simply, for the people as a whole.

As with the debate in other countries, the debate in Sweden continuously mixed together that which actually existed with that which lay in the future according to Marx's theories. Most expositions used the term proletariat to mean industrial workers, that is, the workers in the capitalist system of production in the true sense. Sometimes agricultural workers were also included in this category, but as a rule, this inclusion was not firmly established. According to this usage then, the proletariat would comprehend a very small proportion, or in any case a minority of the total population. Yet Social Democrats persistently asserted that they represented the majority, even the overwhelming mass of the people. In this way they anticipated the conditions that would ensue in conformity with Marx's prognosis. However, because those groups which could not be classified as either bourgeoisie or proletariat really constituted the largest segment of the population, the use of this terminology must have been attended by considerable difficulties. In various ways one attempted to impart to these terms a meaning that was reasonable in relation to the existing state of affairs. It was thus asserted that the bourgeoisie or the well-to-do burghers constituted but a small part, only 10 or 15 percent of the people. (This estimate included the generally well-to-do.) One then drew the conclusion from this estimate that the workers and the unpropertied, who would profit by the victory of socialism, represented the majority. By avoiding the use of the word proletariat, which could not readily be said to include farmers and craftsmen, for example, and by focusing attention on the more well-to-do, it was possible to present Social Democracy—which, in other contexts was held to represent the proletarians—as representative of the great party of the people. Sometimes the proletariat itself was said to include all who had no source of income other than their labor; accordingly, there was said to be, for example, a proletariat of civil servants and a proletariat of teachers, as well as an industrial proletariat. In accordance with this reasoning, which proceeded from Marx's system of class division and developed this *in absurdum,* it would be possible to classify, for example, bankers, cabinet ministers, and professors with high incomes but without property as belonging to the proletariat. On the other hand, poor farmers and small craftsmen would be excluded from the proletariat class.

The interpretations given to this point also colored the debates on tactics. If one thought that under existing conditions Social Democracy already corresponded to the interests of the majority, to its innermost desires, or even that the majority of the people constituted a proletariat predetermined to embrace a socialist view, it would be natural to refuse collaboration with other parties and to regard systematic propaganda, or rather, a systematic program of enlightenment, as the only essential task. In this case, the primary goal would be to make the mass of the people understand what was best for them. The radical stand on tactics that Danielsson and Sterky in particular adopted for a while, was thus motivated by the opinion that the party claimed a potential majority in Sweden at that time.

Danielsson and Branting debated the question in the autumn of 1889. In an article in *Sozialdemokratische Monatsschrift,* Kautsky had contended that one had to distinguish between the concepts "the people" and "the proletariat." With the exception of England, the true proletariat comprehended only a minority of the population, perhaps 30 percent. The middle classes could not be included in the proletariat but, with the development of capitalism, they would gradually become proletarians; then the party would be a people's party or a majority party. Danielsson contested this view. Said he, the proletariat must include the whole of the unpropertied mass—he particularly mentioned agricultural workers, miners, and the unemployed,—as well as industrial workers; this represented a majority of the people. If it were true that the proletariat constituted but a minority, then one could try to work for a betterment of conditions for that minority, but one could not justly call for a social revolution. Kautsky's view was a convenient excuse for a policy of compromise and collaboration. "In contrast to him, we consider it to be a fact *that* the proletariat is the majority in society, *that* in our times the social revolution is more a matter of propaganda than 'a matter of developments,' and that the dissensions within the ruling class really do not concern the working class. . . . Finally, we believe . . . that every one of us would abandon the *revolutionary* stand if he became convinced that after a duration of 300–400 years the capitalist society had been able to displace only about three-tenths of the wage earners." Branting took a kind of middle road. Small farmers and burghers, who constituted a large proportion of the populace, could be called neither capitalists nor proletarians. It did not matter much whether the real proletariat represented a minority or a majority. The important thing was that 95 percent of the people were indigent and that from this point of view a socialist order could be considered to be in the interest of all the people. Another matter was how large a proportion of the 95 percent must be driven to socialism "by the force of circumstances," but this was not decisive to the legitimacy of the social revolution.

> Even if in a society there are only 30 percent whose direct class interest makes them the vehicle of socialism, we hold that one day precisely these 30 percent will nonetheless take the leadership of society into their own hands in order to reconstruct it for the true good of all. Why? Simply because these are sustained by the tide of developments, while the remaining 65 percent of the lower class dissipates its best forces in vain attempts to resist society's forward economic movement. . . . Behind the modern working class, whether it constitute more or less than half of the members of society, stand the forces of change, which compound its strength; the workers form the core of the modern lower class, and while other lower class elements may strain in different directions, this core, guided by socialist principles, should proceed without deviating from its course toward the goal of the definitive abolition of all class rule through its takeover of the means of production in behalf of society.

These quotations are good examples of the ambiguity that characterized the more concrete debates that were concerned with specifics. One suddenly seemed to forget the Marxist idea which was otherwise always advanced, according to which socialism was necessitated by the structure of modern society, by the concentration of capital, the vanishing of the middle class, and the growth and increased misery of the proletariat. Socialism was justified on the ground that only a few lived in plenty; socialism could have been justified in like manner under feudalism or under any period whatever. Danielsson called the mass of the population proletarians in the sense of the unpropertied, even though according to Marx the proletariat is distinctive of modern society and is a designation for precisely the particular lower class that arises in this society. Branting's idiom calls to mind the communist theory of the dictatorship of the proletariat, the theory that a minority of the people understand the true interest of the majority and shall therefore become the leaders. This does not seem to have implied a downgrading of democracy. The minority was said to be borne by the tide of developments, which would compound its strength, and would therefore emerge victorious—as if propelled by a divine or a mystic power. Note that Branting could not have used the term "developments" in this context to mean social change that would turn the proletariat into the majority, for he presupposed that a minority would capture power in the interests of the majority.

These peculiarities appear to some extent to be psychologically natural consequences of the attempt to apply Marxist thinking to a society like the one in Sweden at that time. How could socialism—which was declared to be the societal form of the proletariat—be promulgated as an urgent concern when the proletariat obviously constituted a minority? If one accepted the given premise the logical procedure would have been to declare socialism a necessity only at some future date when industrialization would have placed the proletariat in the position Marx predicted. But how could one construct political propaganda on the mere prediction that something would occur in fifty or one hundred years? The combination of long-range historical philosophy and immediate political action must give birth to strange intellectual products.

A more realistic view gradually made inroads. Marx's social prognoses were not accepted as unconditionally as before; the complicated nature of the structure of society was acknowledged; the fixation on the struggle between the bourgeoisie and the proletariat became less marked. We shall return to the new currents of thought that thereby emerged.

It is obvious that Marx's comparatively complex purely *economic theories* were of subordinate importance in the ideological propaganda. This was particularly true of the *theory of value* in its true sense. Moreover, a successive relaxation of the initially dogmatic stand on this theory can be detected. As a rule the programs adopted during the 1880s state that labor is the source of all wealth and culture. The Danielsson-formulated program of 1888 stated a bit more cautiously that value was produced by labor alone. Earlier Social Democratic documents had accepted Marx's theory of value without any reservations. Danielsson offered a relatively detailed presentation of this theory in a pamphlet issued in 1889 with the significant title *The Cornerstone of Socialism, A Historical and Theoretical Exposition of the Theory of Value.* The theory was also treated in Swedish translations and adaptations of other works. Judging by his Gävle speech, Branting at first apparently accepted Marx's theory of value as his point of departure.

Criticism of Marx's theory of value soon became the focus of considerable attention within Social Democratic circles. In his pamphlet on socialism published in 1892, Branting gave an account of Marx's theory that the value of a commodity is determined by the socially necessary labor-time required to produce it. However, he also called attention to the attacks leveled at this theory and did not try to deny the possibility that they might be warranted. Citing Engels, Branting stated that the entire controversy on the theory of value was not at all decisive to the question of private capitalism versus socialism. The main question pro or con scientific socialism was the truth or falsity of Marx's views on the general tendencies of societal development. The party program of 1897 that Danielsson drew up omitted not only the Gotha Program's tenet of labor as the source of all wealth and culture but also all contentions that labor was the real creator of value.

Strangely enough, the latter program did not refer to surplus value or even to impoverishment, a word that recurred throughout the Erfurt Progam. Nevertheless, it can be asserted without doubt that the idea of a surplus value produced by the workers over and beyond their wages—which was then expropriated by the capitalist exploiters—was sustained even after its basic premise, Marx's labor theory of value, had been abandoned or was in any case no longer generally accepted. Branting's reasoning in a speech given in 1900 on revisionism and other new currents in Social Democracy was evidently often advanced. In this speech Branting cited Bernstein's critique of Marx's theory of value and Kautsky's counter-critique, and then made the following pronouncement:

> Pursuant to this, however, it should be noted that socialism fortunately by no means stands or falls with Marx's theory of value, which is so sharply criticized in many quarters. For [the contention] that the propertied classes in the present society, are oriented *as a whole* to the labor of others is no theory but a *statistically demonstrable*

> fact, and no matter how the theory of value may be revised in the future, one can not get around this fact of society, and it will drive the class that now wrongfully receives too little to strive for a reformation that will give it *its due right* that is, for a socialist organization of society.

Here Branting justifies socialism on the basis of a natural rights idea, which holds true only if Marx's theory of value is acknowledged, at the same time as he declares that his view is independent of this theory. Similar general pronouncements on the impoverishment and exploitation of the proletariat and on the wealth acquired by the bourgeoisie at the expense of the workers occurred almost uniformly in Social Democratic publications.

The theory of the regularly recurring, ever-worsening *crises* in capitalist society was apparently generally accepted by Social Democratic theorists. However, this theory was also given a subordinate role in the debate, which can partly be explained by the fact that during this period Sweden did not suffer crises nearly as severe as those which provided the factual background of Marx's theory. The same can be said of the theory of *the industrial reserve army*. This concept was generally acknowledged but was seldom asserted. *The catastrophe theory,* which was directly related to the crises doctrine, was sometimes recollected as part of the background of Social Democratic discussion, but it was infrequently advanced as a material, essential viewpoint. Had this theory been accepted in its entirety, all endeavors directed toward tangible goals would have been meaningless. Even the idea of gradual socialization would then have become absurd. The party leaders were apparently able to acknowledge theories that were actually closely allied with the catastrophe theory without taking this theory completely seriously; it was too emphatically at variance with the ideas that led to practical political activity to be incorporated in Social Democratic agitation. It was nonetheless quite frequently stressed that by virtue of its inherent tendency capitalist society was moving toward a catastrophic crisis, but that this crisis could be averted through successive socialization.

That part of Marx's closed system that dealt with *the future of the social classes* was incomparably more important to the ideology of Swedish Social Democracy.

As indicated in the previous chapter, Marx's predictions regarding social developments in the interval between the bourgeois and the socialist revolutions can be divided into four main theories: *the theories of the concentration and accumulation of capital* (*which can be combined into one theory of the concentration of capital*), *the theory of the disappearance of the middle class,* and *the theory of impoverishment.* In Marx's writings and in early Social Democratic discussion these theories appeared together to form a whole insofar as each theory postulated the others. Capital concentration would be made possible by and proceed side by side with the downfall of the middle class and the increasing misery of the growing proletariat.

This line of thought does not appear in the Gotha Program, which is probably the reason why it was never inserted in the Swedish programs. The Erfurt Program of 1891 is, on the other hand, patently Marxist on this point. By the time Swedish Social Democrats adopted their first independent program in 1897, Marx's theories had already been discredited to some extent even within socialist circles, and the 1897 program therefore includes only intimations of these theories.

Yet the lack of mention of Marx's social predictions in the programs cannot be interpreted as a sign that they were unimportant in Swedish Social Democracy. To the contrary. One can state without hesitation that they occupied a position of central importance in the early phases of Social Democratic debate. A firm belief in the legitimacy of Marx's prognoses was the foundation on which Social Democratic theorists constructed their argumentation. The bitter criticism of the liberal workers' movement and everything connected with it can only be understood from this point of view. Discussion of the manner in which socialism was to be implemented was, as already emphasized, intimately connected with the social perspective.

Newspapers and pamphlets from the 1880s forever return to the thought that social development in the form prescribed by Marx would of itself lead to socialism. Declared *Social-Demokraten* early in 1886: "That which will drive developments forward in this direction (toward socialization) is, on the one hand, the ever-awakening self-consciousness and ever-increasing solidarity and unity of the working class, and, on the other, the gradual disappearance of the middle classes, the craftsmen, the small farmers, small merchants and small capitalists, together with the amassing of capital in fewer and fewer hands with a consequent decline in consumer power in society coextensively with a rise in production, which finally leads to an impasse where capital becomes valueless to its owners." According to this view, although socialization may basically be a catastrophic revolution, it really becomes more of a technical measure that does not involve any appreciable difficulties. A few capitalists who have accumulated all the means of production but who can no longer find consumers among the starving masses will disappear, thereby leaving a legacy of surplus for these masses. Carleson, writing in the same paper ten years later, could still put forth exactly the same line of thought: socialism would be a consequence of "the antagonism between *steadily progressing mass impoverishment and increased production of wealth through highly developed mechanical technology.*" Less sophisticated writers carried the doctrine to the point of the ridiculous. A *Proletären* article of 1888 held forth that the workers had only to organize in order to be prepared for the power takeover. "The allegations of great thinkers that the most adamant defenders and pillars of support of our modern, big industrial societies act in the same way as our clergymen when they strive to preserve the decadent church is obviously entirely correct. The more energetically the liberals work on, the faster *we* will arrive at the goal that, if not before, shall come to pass when all land, all machines, and all capital shall be amassed in the hands of a few. To attain power the proletarians then have only to lock up their tyrants and take possession of the property taken from them and their forefathers."

This outlook, which pervaded all of the early debate in more or less subtle formulations, obviously entails one special difficulty: at the same time as their degree of misery and dependency increases the workers are supposed to become increasingly self-conscious and better organized. Great self-consciousness and organization must logically lead to successful activities even within the existing framework of society. Connected with this internal contradiction was the fact that, on the basis of the predictions made, one sometimes contemplated a great upheaval, a catastrophe (the expropriators shall be expropriated), and at other times theorized that through its political activity the working class would prevent the complete realization of the prognosis, that at a certain point in time the working class would check the developmental tendencies in capitalist society.

We can not here enter into a close analysis of the validity of Marxist theories, but we should bear in mind a few points. The theories of concentration and accumulation can be said to have been verified, at least for a time and to a certain extent, inasmuch as big industries have tended to grow in size and significance. The nascent trust complex that was particularly prevalent in the United States in the late 1880s is often cited as evidence of this. Yet this development was not as marked as one might imagine, and, above all, it did not result in the dissolution of the middle class or the impoverishment of the proletariat as Marx had predicted. It became obvious that Marx had arbitrarily generalized and schematized a certain period in the history of English industrialism. One could and still can discuss whether and to what extent the middle class or middle classes have become weaker—the answer is contingent upon the definitions of these terms; yet it soon became apparent that, in any case, Marx's prognosis was so exaggerated that it could not be used in the manner of early theorists. For example, even if one could interpret the statistics of various nations as meaning that in the course of a decade the number of craftsmen had diminished by a few percentiles, this would not suffice to support general statements about the dissolution of the middle class. The middle classes—the small merchants, small farmers, and craftsmen—were paid particular attention by Marx, who made the relation to the means of production the basis for his class system. It was also apparent that even if these classes declined in importance other groups would wax significant, groups that popular usage would term typically middle class, such as members of the professions—teachers, civil servants, and business employees. Still more important was the fact that the theory of impoverishment proved untenable. As a natural result of industrialism, the workers of many nations had grown in number but they had not been proletarianized. To the contrary: irrefutable investigations revealed that real wages had risen. The theory of impoverishment, which had been regarded as the principal proof that workers would rally to socialism, therefore had to be given a new content. Instead of absolute pauperization, which was without doubt what Marx referred to in the *Communist Manifesto,* one began to speak of a relative decline in the standard of living; as already observed, various other formulas were also used to camouflage the retreat.

As early as the 1890s a modulation or revision of Marxist theories had begun in Sweden. Domestic experiences probably played some part in bringing about this change, but in all likelihood the effects of the German debate were more decisive. Swedish Social Democrats had uncritically accepted pure Marxism, but they quickly assimilated the criticism of Marx put forth in other countries. It should be noted that this criticism had appeared long before Bernstein specified and systematized its content in 1899.

The change in the opinions of Danielsson and Branting is striking. In the late 1880s, Danielsson had expounded Marxist principles in a series of vague utterances. Increased concentration of capital and growing poverty attended the advance of industrialism; socialism alone could eliminate this antithesis. Data from other nations made it seem probable that this process also resulted in the proletarianization of the middle class. Danielsson claimed it could be established that even in Sweden the crafts were in decline while mass production was on the increase and the number of big producers was growing. "Our multiplied 'national wealth'—as the aggregate wealth of the upper class is called—is matched by a multiplied working class that now comprises the majority in the nation and will soon have absorbed all that our people possess in the way of spiritual and physical strength, of a sense of liberty and hope for the future." In the course of the following years Danielsson's view became more modulated on this and other points. Although he did not directly deal with the theories of concentration and impoverishment, this change is revealed by his statements on the interrelationships of the social classes, on the value of social welfare policies and allied subjects. The best proof of Danielsson's modification of opinion is the party program that he drew up and which was adopted in 1897.

This program is of particular interest because of its declarations on the social consequences of capitalism. It touches upon all of Marx's theories without completely accepting any of them. The theory of concentration was acknowledged in that the program stated that private capital "had amassed wealth in the hands of a minority" and had brought about "an unnatural accumulation of riches." The theory of impoverishment resounded less distinctly. The true producers were being transformed into a class of wage earners whose "distinctive social feature is a state of propertylessness with consequent dependence and oppression." The program also stressed the colossal growth of the working class. However, the program contained no intimations about impoverishment in the true sense, or of the growing misery of the workers. It rather stated that the disastrous tendency in society's development had led the workers to form "a countermovement." The problem of the middle class was dealt with in equally vague terms. Petty bourgeois societal relations had disintegrated. Society is divided into workers and capitalists, declared the program, but immediately thereafter it negated this statement by the addition "with intermediate strata [composed] partly of disappearing old social classes—small farmers, craftsmen, and small merchants—and partly of emergent new ones." These last words, which Danielsson probably intended to refer to those employed in businesses and factories outside of the working class per se, left open the question of whether the middle class was, in fact, regressing. Compared with these words, subsequent mention that the salaried working class "incorporates the sinking residue of the old middle class" is of little importance.

A detailed comparison of this program with the Erfurt Program, with its extreme Marxist terminology, would lead us too far afield. Yet it behooves us to note that the latter program, with its fantastic but logically developed ideas, is an integrated whole in contrast to the 1897 program, which conveys the impression of an ideology that has begun to crumble. Ambitious beginnings end in qualifications and emendations; the total picture is one of general indecisiveness. It seems pointless or in any case contradictory to speak first of the division of society into workers and capitalists and immediately thereafter to acknowledge the rise of new middle classes, or to contrast the accumulation of wealth with the growth of the working class—without stating that the workers' circumstances have deteriorated or remain unchanged. The program availed itself of Marx's terminology but did not follow up the ideas behind it.

Branting's Gävle speech shows that in the beginning he believed verbatim in Marx's prophesies and gave them a pivotal place in socialist doctrine. The millionaires would stand alone against the starving masses—the theories of concentration and impoverishment could not be carried any further than this. To be sure, in respect to impoverishment Branting added that even if there were to be a negligible rise in the standard of living of the masses, the gulf between the rich and the poor might nevertheless widen if the wealth of the rich grew more rapidly than general improvements in the satisfaction of the needs of the masses. However, this qualification was added as a safeguard against criticism. Branting himself presupposed that the misery of the workers would become more acute. The same premise recurs in an article published in 1888. Wrote Branting, "All false statistics on trends [compiled] in the interest of the upper class cannot belie the fact that *misery* has increased in pace with [the growth of] national wealth." He added that investigations revealed that the circumstances of the working class had deteriorated since the rise of capitalism in the sixteenth and seventeenth centuries. Even if this finding should prove false, the proposition that the gulf between the classes had widened would remain valid. "The increase in wealth of developed capitalism is so colossal in our day that even a comparatively significant, speedy, and sure improvement in the circumstances of the workers would be compatible with the confiscation of by far the greater part of society's wealth by the parasitic class." In the previously cited article in *Nordisk familjebok* of 1890, Branting seems to adhere to the theory of impoverishment in its true sense. An article published in 1893 shows that at this date he was still trying to provide unqualified proof of the thesis of the dissolution of the middle class.

Some years later, however, we can detect a change. In a series of newspaper articles published in 1895 Branting qualified certain parts of Marx's prognosis. By dint of the growing power of the working class one had in some instances succeeded in "checking the unrestrained activity of the destructive forces that capitalism nourishes" and protective social legislation made it possible to "preclude to a far greater degree the worst forms of mass misery that Marx demonstrated would logically ensue from the societal mechanism of capitalism itself." However, this did not prove that the father of socialism had viewed capitalism too darkly, but that this order was no longer predominant. "There is already a whiff of morning air from the dawn of the day of the working class in our old societies!" Thus Social Democracy had already managed to modify capitalism and the theory of impoverishment had lost its validity. Some years later Branting wrote that the expression "the rich grow richer, the poor poorer" was "close enough to the truth to motivate a total reorganization of the foundations of society, to the end that one class may no longer live on the work of another." Yet he added that higher taxes for the rich and various social welfare measures could ameliorate the state of the working class. This was, however, no reason to suppose that socialism would not be implemented. "It would be strange indeed if a somewhat better situated working class that clearly sees the relationships in the social machinery would remain forever [in the stage of] private capitalism, tempered as much as possible by social legislation, instead of going to the root of the disastrous system and transferring those branches of national industry that gradually attain the maturity necessary for such an arrangement to the ownership and management of all of society." In a speech on "New Directions within Social Democracy" Branting adopted several of Bernstein's criticisms of Marx. In an essay dealing with the 1897 program and written a few years after its adoption, Branting averred that one of the greatest merits of the program was "the absence of view of the growing misery of the masses that hovers everywhere else." Branting now appeared to consider it obvious that this theory, in the absolute sense in which it was originally interpreted, was invalid. He held that the theory had been reinterpreted and was only relatively valid, that is, insofar as the position of the bourgeoisie had improved to a greater extent than that of the masses and the gulf between the classes had therefore widened. Yet Branting apparently even had doubts about this interpretation. He moreover viewed the program's cautious statements about the middle classes as a great step forward; it was evident "that one could not fit such a complex phenomenon as the changes in the intermediate strata of modern society into a single simplistic formula." With this statement Branting completely abandoned substantive aspects of his early views.

Around the turn of the century Swedish Social Democracy had thus arrived at a standpoint that was at sharp variance with the principles it had unconditionally accepted ten or fifteen years earlier. The theory of concentration was still, in the main, considered valid; the increase of big business in Sweden was also incontrovertible, a natural result of progressive industrialization. But the theory of the disappearance of the middle class was not sustained; the absolute version of the theory of the growth of mass impoverishment had been abandoned, its relative version questioned. The vast importance of this to the general attitude of Social Democrats is obvious. The idea of a social catastrophe vanished; collaboration with other groups became a natural course once one no longer expected that they would soon disappear; social reformism became a central precept instead of a palliative of scant importance; the idea of socialization lost some of its driving force.

A comparison of Branting's statements in the first and second editions of his Verdandi pamphlet *Socialism* (issued in 1892 and 1906, respectively) illustrates the changes in the Social Democratic view. In the first edition Branting cited Marx's tenet "about the increasing accumulation of wealth at one pole of society and the ever greater need among the growing proletariat" and followed this with the comment "here, in effect, lies [the core of] the great struggle between the scientific socialists and their orthodox-liberal or social reformist antagonists." Some socialists were willing to concede that the position of the middle class had definitely improved during the past fifty years, but "they affirm on the other hand, for one, the now chronic unemployment and generally greater uncertainty of [the workers'] position, and, for the other, that the share of the working class in the national product has hardly kept pace with the substantial increase of this product itself. . . ." Branting concluded by saying that he wished to leave it up to the reader, in view of this account, to answer the question "whether, retaining the basic conditions of the present society, the need of the masses will be succeeded without too much delay by general prosperity, forced unemployment disappear, and a speedy equalization of existing social antagonisms be accomplished, or whether this goal requires, as socialism prophesies, that the means of production become the property of society and that production be regulated by society." In the second edition Branting gave the same account of theories of concentration and impoverishment as before. But now he added that if these theories, and the second in particular, were valid "we would inexorably move toward that social catastrophe which the anarchists wish to accelerate but which the entire constructive work of Social Democracy strives to render superfluous." Branting then continued mainly in the same vein as in the first edition, but he concluded his exposition in such a manner that the answer to the question of the necessity of socialism was no longer contingent upon the validity or falsity of the theory of impoverishment.

In summary. In 1892 Branting believed that "the great struggle" concerned these Marxist theories; he presupposed that all who attacked them were "orthodox-liberals" or social reformists; one's position toward them determined whether or not one was a socialist. In 1906 Branting postulated that the theories gave support to anarchism and that a Social Democrat could not accept the theory of impoverishment. That which was considered orthodox-liberal in 1892 was in 1906 designated as a Social Democratic view; that which was considered socialist in 1892 was represented as an anarchist theme in 1906. Even though Branting may have expressed himself in hyperbole that did not entirely correspond to his real opinions, a comparison of his statements in the two editions reveals a remarkable general change in opinion.

The *iron law of wages* was presented side by side with the theory of impoverishment during the early years of Social Democracy. This doctrine was mentioned in the Gotha Program, which spoke of the nullification of the law as a consequence of the abolition of the system of wages. There is also a hint of it in Danielsson's program of 1888 in the statement that wages "at best constitute a minimum for existence." In his Gävle speech Branting disputed the belief in the value of thrift and sobriety for the working class by arguing that wages tend to fall to the lowest possible level, to a subsistence minimum. Danielsson attempted to give a more precise explanation of the meaning of the law. He wrote that the worker is not paid for the value of his labor but only for the value of his labor power, "that is, the value of the absolutely essential provisions for existence." This is so because the working class is an oppressed class. The law "operates independently of both workers' organizations and capitalist circles. It is also called the *iron-clad wage law* and the wages themselves a subsistence minimum or—starvation wages." Danielsson offered this "law," which he and other Social Democrats evidently regarded as an incontestable scientific truth, as an argument against investing inordinate hopes in the possible effectiveness of trade unions and particularly of strikes. Wermelin, like Branting, used the doctrine of the iron law of wages as an argument against working-class frugality. If the workers were to practice thrift "the never-dormant iron law of wages would begin to operate. However far down the masses might succeed in lowering the limit for the bare necessities of life, the wage level would steadily fall until the two coincided."

This concept, which was primarily inspired by Lassalle, evidently did not readily agree with the original version of the theory of impoverishment: if the workers lived at subsistence level, further impoverishment was impossible. On the other hand, the wage law was a good weapon against the liberal workers' movement and against its belief in the importance of self-help. Although this hardly occurred, the theory could be used as an argument against all social welfare policies in a capitalist society: if the workers received some benefits from the state, the employers could reduce their wages. Soon, however, Social Democratic leaders discovered that Marx had not accepted the iron law of wages and that it had actually been abandoned generally. As early as the beginning of the 1890s, Danielsson asserted that the iron law of wages had, indeed, been valid at one time but that it had now been replaced by what he called the cultural law of wages. Proceeding from Marx to some extent but not completely, he now alleged that wages were determined by the production costs of labor power, that is, by the average needs of the workers. He apparently believed in the main that the workers could raise their wages to a certain extent by increasing their needs, that is, their expenditures. In the course of the following years the theory of a wage law did not enter into the debate; it was not touched upon at all in the 1897 program. The abandonment of this theory opened new possibilities for the Social Democrats to adopt ideas that had previously characterized the liberal labor movement, above all, the temperance cause.

What was the position of early Social Democracy on *reforms and measures that did not entail or aim at socialization of the means of production?*

The question of establishing *produce associations* (*produktions-föreningar*) *with state aid* has a unique position in this context. Lassalle had propounded this idea so forcefully that it had come to be viewed as an independent socialist doctrine: socialization would be brought about successively through such associations. But producer cooperatives can also appear as one among many methods of improving the workers' position; in this case the supposition is that, like consumer cooperatives, this form of cooperative would be coextensive with private economic enterprise in the true sense. Lassalle's line was accepted on this point in the Gotha Program insofar as it recommended the establishment of production associations with state aid as an initial step in the socialist organization of labor. This recommendation recurred in Palm's program of 1882, and it was also included in somewhat modified form in the 1885 program of the Social Democratic Union. Subsequent programs, however, contain no mention whatsoever of produce associations and refer only to society's takeover of the means of production.

In view of the fact that the subject was included in many early Social Democratic programs one might expect that it would also play an important role in Social Democratic debates during the first years. This was not the case. In all probability, this point in the Gotha Program was translated or adapted and adopted without attaching much significance to it. Not even Palm, who was relatively heavily influenced by Lassalle, paid the matter much attention. To be sure, in his first speech Palm did mention on the one hand the state's takeover of production and on the other state loans to workers' associations as means of eliminating free competition. Yet although he subsequently often urged the realization of the first alternative, he did not again refer to the second, or, in any case, only in passing. On the whole we can find only isolated examples of the pursuance of this standpoint in the Social Democratic press and pamphlet literature. It soon was confirmed that the idea of production associations as a solution to The Social Question was a concept that had been superseded. "Nowadays no one believes in the possibility of reaching the new society along this route," wrote Danielsson in 1891. In a subsequent exposition he declared that the workers did not have to turn to the state to ask for aid for produce associations, for, by capturing political power, they would take possession of the entire machinery of production. He then added a strange reflection: "Had Lassalle succeeded in realizing his plan, a murderous competition would have arisen between the associations and the remaining private producers and the capital concentration necessary to a socialist society would thereby have been delayed." Even after the Social Democratic leaders had converted from criticism to an appreciation of consumer cooperatives (which we shall treat in a later chapter), they long retained their attitude of rejection or indifference to producer cooperatives. The subject was not brought up at any party congresses held during this period.

Social Democracy predicted the existing society would fall because of the aggravation of class conflicts. Pursuant to this it regarded socialism as an inevitable necessity, but it nonetheless called for *reforms for the benefit of the working class within the framework of capitalism.* The programs adopted or acknowledged during the 1880s presented in the main two groups of socio-economic demands: reform of the system of taxation (abolition of indirect taxes, the introduction of progressive income, property, and inheritance taxes), and sociopolitical legislative measures (establishment of the standard work day, prohibition of child labor, protective legislation, state care of the sick and aged). Beginning in the late 1880s, the principle of the eight-hour work day was in the foreground of Social Democratic agitation.

These sociopolitical demands entailed obvious problems. It was hoped that their implementation would improve the position of the workers. This immediately implied a potential rejection of the theory of impoverishment. In all events one had to take it for granted that such improvements would not be so extensive that they would satisfy the workers, for otherwise the class struggle itself would have to be abandoned. Here, as in other instances, we detect an element of duplicity in Social Democratic argumentation. Reforms were demanded with great ardor, by citing social evils and appealing to a universal spirit of justice. At the same time, however, one referred to reforms with a considerable lack of appreciation and, not infrequently, with a tinge of irony. It is your self-evident obligation to grant this to us, but do not believe that this will satisfy us; in a little while we shall crush you and inherit your rule—such was the spirit in which the movement addressed itself to the bourgeois holders of power. It was in great contrast to the mood of the liberal labor movement, which entertained more modest demands and promised gratitude and contentment if they were fulfilled.

The constituent congress of 1889 adopted a resolution that clarified the party's fundamental position on social welfare policies and also included a comprehensive program of reform. The resolution was an answer to the report of the Riksdag committee on workers' insurance and the 1889 Riksdag ruling on protective legislation. It read as follows:

The Congress considers that even the fraudulent protective legislation that is beginning to be offered to the workers has principally been adopted with the calculation that the property-holding classes thereby will be able to convince the workers of their good intentions and answer the growing discontent of the proletariat. An important contributing factor is their desire to throw, to the greatest extent possible, the growing burden of relief for the poor onto the workers themselves. Workers' insurance, however, does not touch upon the very heart of the social problem at all. An institution that at best would give the proletarian who is unable to work meager alms that he had paid for dearly himself does not deserve the name "social reform." *Genuine* [social reform] must directly intervene in the position of the working worker and have as its objective the abolition of the systematic despoliation of the working class. But anything along this line can only be the doing of those who are now being despoiled.

As long as the capitalist system of production endures, the consequences of the system of despoliation can, however, be confined to some extent by genuine, honest, protective legislation forcefully implemented. It is obvious that such [measures] would widely differ from the parody of protective legislation and its regulation that has recently been passed by the Riksdag. Effective protective legislation must at least include the following:

1) A maximum work day of 8 hours.
2) Minimum wages, established according to local conditions, that would guarantee at least a tolerable existence for those who produce everything in society.
3) Prohibition of work at night and on Sundays except in special exceptional cases established by law.
4) Prohibition of all work by children under 14 years of age.
5) Extension of the protective legislation to include the crafts and so-called cottage industries.
6) Prison sentences for violations by employers of the protective legislation.
7) Election of inspectors by the workers themselves through their organizations.
8) Places of work that are healthy and under control and, finally, an item the necessity of which recent events have demonstrated:
9) Constitutional recognition of the workers' rights of organization and assembly.

In addition, the Congress declares itself in favor of the international development of protective legislation.

This resolution typifies much of the debate on social welfare policies. The reforms that the regime in power was willing to implement were described as totally inadequate, as pseudoreforms intended to trick the workers to accept the *status quo*. One demanded radical social legislation, but even such reforms were designated as half-way measures; *real* reform must be concentrated on the realization of socialization.

This and subsequent congresses also adopted other sociopolitical resolutions. Particularly notable is the ruling of the 1894 congress on measures to combat unemployment. The prevailing planless conditions of production were said to cause a steady rise in unemployment. It was the task of the working class "to awaken insight among the rulers into the humanitarian duty to provide resources for the institution of useful work." But it was also emphasized that this directive contained a proviso: the measures called for would be required "until the working class assumes its natural mission to organize by itself the production of society."

Thus we see that the idea of socialization occupied the foreground in early debates, and that the social reforms that were demanded were often said to be of comparatively little immediate value. This outlook was especially pronounced in the viewpoint of Danielsson, who constantly affirmed that the social revolution was the only matter of consequence. (Cf. the following chapter.) As long as the workers were debarred from the means of production, said Danielsson before the Congress of Southern Sweden of 1888, the existing wrongs would persist. "The death struggle of bourgeois society is only prolonged by minor reforms." Branting was far more oriented toward social reforms, but he regarded them primarily as a preparation for socialism. "It is precisely the best-situated workers," wrote Branting in 1886, "those who have gradually obtained a standard work day, protective legislation, a minimum wage, who would be the first to demand the fulfillment of the complete liberation that can only be won by the abolition of the wage system itself and the realization of the principles of socialism." In an article in *Social-Demokraten* from 1889 on "state socialism," this term was treated as if it were synonymous with social welfare policies. The underlying idea of state socialism was "that the class state, in order to retain the wage system in the interests of the propertied class, in order that the rulers might thus cash in on the difference between the value of the worker's labor and his labor power, which later appears in his wages, elects to forego some of its profits in order to preclude some of the most troublesome consequences of the system. . . ."

A gradual shift in argumentation can be detected after a while. Support of sociopolitical demands becomes more deliberate and more rooted in principle —with the exception of the anarchic movement, which we shall consider later in this chapter. In the early 1890s Danielsson became increasingly interested in social reform. On one occasion he wrote "Social Democrats should disdain nothing that is of practical benefit to the workers and that is not unworthy of their basic principles as a fighting lower class, no practical efforts that are designed to mitigate need or make poverty more tolerable." At times social welfare measures, principally the standard work day, were justified on the grounds that they were in the interest of the employers as well as in the interest of the workers—an argument that seems strange indeed in view of the movement's ideological premises. At the same time, however, one can detect a note of concern that welfare measures will dissipate the striking force of Social Democracy. Would the bourgeois, with their conservative-inspired reforms, succeed in subduing the workers' discontent and thereby weaken

Social Democracy? Would socialism, by encouraging social reformism among the rulers undermine its own potential? Questions of this kind had long been raised in Germany, and the debate in that country exercised an influence on the debate in Sweden.

In agreement with Branting's declaration of 1886 cited in the foregoing, Swedish Social Democracy mainly responded to these questions with the assertion that social welfare policies would tend to strengthen, not weaken the movement—provided the idea of the class struggle were continuously thrust into the foreground. This response contained various shades of interpretation. Sterky in particular, one of the movement's most radical leaders in the early 1890s, regarded social welfare policies mainly as a means of strengthening the workers' power and of persuading them of the value of the contributions of Social Democracy. In an article published in 1892, he wrote that there was a certain danger "that the working class would attach too much weight to a number of small improvements so that when it did attain power, it would be incapable of using it in order to achieve a completely socialist society with all possible speed." One therefore had to take care that acrimony of the class conflict was not blunted in the pursuit of minor improvements and not place too great a value on the direct economic advantages that these provided. The workers still had too much faith in state authorities and did not comprehend that their enactment of reforms was always done in the interest of the ruling class. The same current of thought appears in *Social-Demokraten* from time to time. One article pointed out that The Great Social Question must not be allowed to disintegrate into a number of small questions with the result "that one goes into such detail that one completely loses sight of the common, connective viewpoints. . . ." Yet one must not spurn "this finicky [occupation] with small bits of The Social Question"; all that could be won through legislation would help "to strengthen the working class' militant readiness for a new move forward." On the whole, during this period Branting and Danielsson seemed to give more emphasis to the immediate value of social reforms than did Sterky. In addition, they sought to show that, if viewed from the right perspective, social welfare policies would stir the workers to new efforts. On this point Branting used the same mode of reasoning as when he asserted that socialism was imperative even if the theory of impoverishment should prove untenable. A working class that had been elevated through social reforms would have the strength to carry out socialism. The social reformists who believed they could disarm Social Democracy by making some concessions did not understand the essence of the movement, proclaimed Branting on one occasion. "Even if one succeeded in accomplishing all these social reforms, which are moreover beneficial and necessary, the class conflict would nevertheless persist as long as private ownership of the means of production remained unshaken. And one believes that one can erase this peremptory antagonism from the minds of men through accommodations in a fundamental class society!" Danielsson declared that according to Marx the proletariat would seize power "after first becoming politically educated and physically strengthened by rigorous workers' protection legislation."

A necessary corollary to this view was the repudiation or depreciation of reforms that could allegedly more rapidly achieve a social levelling and peace in society without socialism. In 1894, pursuant to an article in a foreign publication, Branting attacked with extreme vehemence the idea of granting the workers a share in business profits. This was an "artful way to squeeze out as much profit as can in any manner be drawn from the workers in exchange for the promise of a small tip"; one thereby hoped to constrain the workers' independence and split the working class. In responding to proposals for the establishment of arbitration in labor disputes, Branting put forth not only detailed objections but also a fundamental criticism. In some cases arbitration was a suitable institution, but one could not expect to reach peace in society along this course. "Let us . . . not lull ourselves into hopes of an impossible class peace in a capitalist society that becomes more humanitarian and is perpetuated through courts of arbitration or similar institutions!" Danielsson pointed out the irony in the thought that a progressive inheritance tax would lead to social levelling.

What stand should Social Democracy then take on proposals that aimed at socialization but not socialism, that is, at socialization measures recommended by nonsocialist groups that obviously did not have as their object what socialists called the abolition of the class society? Marx's major perspective had evidently not anticipated such measures. According to this perspective, the bourgeois state was the coercive agency of capitalists; would this state then obstruct or restrict private capitalism? How could Marx's social predictions be verified if the most important means of production were nationalized, if private competition were limited to include only a part of the economy and a large proportion of the proletariat were transformed into employees of the state? On the other hand: how could Social Democracy refuse to participate in individual socialization measures when it demanded socialization?

German Social Democracy had already been confronted with this dilemma in the early 1880s, when Bismarck had advanced a proposal regarding monopoly in the tobacco industry. The party had then voted against the proposal on the ground that the prevailing regime should not receive additional instruments of power. Ten years later the question became the subject of a lively debate pursuant to a pamphlet written by Vollmar. Vollmar contended that state socialism meant, in a limited sense, state management, and in a wider sense, social welfare policies as well. To be sure, under existing conditions state socialism did not involve anything truly socialistic, but proposals connected with it ought to be appraised from case to case because state socialist measures could mean direct economic benefits and also prepare the way for the general socialization that would follow the Social Democratic takeover of power. Vollmar's statements were bitterly attacked, especially by Liebnecht. All the same, the German party congress of 1892 adopted a resolution, with the aegis of Vollmar, which—without repudiating all forms of state socialism—stamped the principle itself as conservative. The resolution stated that the bourgeois were trying to alienate the workers from Social Democracy by offering minor concessions and thus paralyze the movement.

State socialism was discussed on principle in Sweden, partly in connection with the party strife in Germany and partly in connection with Pontus Fahlbeck's work *Estates and Classes*. This book, published in 1892, presented—in the face of Social Democratic criticism—a program of reform including, among others, the demand for state management in certain spheres of the economy. One year before Danielsson had discussed (in contradiction to some statements he had made a few months previously) what he termed monarchic state socialism—in contrast to democratic socialism. He thereby took a clear stand in favor of extending the functions of the bourgeois state. Even in the role of the opposition, Social Democracy ought to force the state to pursue a policy in the right direction "even if it is only a makeshift expedient to buoy up the ruling class a little while longer. . . . As soon as one branch of industry, one transport enterprise, or one municipal function has grown over the heads of the private entrepreneurs of its own accord, the Social Democratic party will call for *state* intervention. It aspires to the concentration in the hands of the state of the largest possible proportion of work, for this will facilitate the movements of society and simplify the social strife between labor and capital." Following the German debate on the subject, Danielsson reiterated these viewpoints and aligned himself with Vollmar. Branting on the other hand, adopted a middle way in a series of articles published during the summer of 1892. He wrote that state socialism wishes to extend the economic power of the existing state, the class state, the state of the impoverishers. Social Democracy wishes to entrust corresponding duties only to the coming classless society, to the fully democratized workers' society. State socialism had copied its form from genuine socialism, but it did not try to fit that form to the needs of the entire society, only to the needs of the ruling class. It was basically a caricature of socialism. It was not necessary to take a general stand for or against state socialism. In each separate case one had to pose the question whether a proposal for reform would tend to benefit the development and independence of the working class or not. "In reaching such a decision one side of the scale carries the advantage of the introduction of the socialist form: societal order instead of internal strife between individuals over a piece of bread; and also, not to be forgotten, the *psychological* reaction [produced] by every such step, preparing the minds [of the people] to an even broader socialist order. But on the other side of the scale weighs the danger of strengthening our enemy, the upper-class state, this tool of the ruling classes, and perhaps of making large groups of workers even more directly dependent, thus hampering the activities necessary for their liberation."

Some weeks after the appearance of Branting and Danielsson's articles the subject was broached at the Scandinavian Workers' Congress. This congress passed a resolution akin to Branting's stand: "The Congress considers that, for the time being, state socialism denotes a most variegated sociopolitical activity on the part of the present state and it [the Congress] sees in it a step forward for socialist principles only to the extent that in these political experiments of theirs the ruling classes recognize society's right to intervene in the private capitalist anarchy of production, and [the Congress] enjoins the workers' parties of various countries to carefully examine each concession offered under the label of state socialism before accepting it." This resolution evidently used the term state socialism in a broader sense than that applied in the German and Swedish debates of 1892.

During the next few years the question of the assumption of functions in production by the bourgeois state does not seem to have been discussed in the Social Democratic press. However, in drawing up the new program of 1897, Danielsson inserted a statement that can only be interpreted as a general demand for state socialist intervention in the sense intended by Vollmar. The third paragraph of Article VI read as follows: "Vigorous development of the activity of the state and local governments as producers and leaders in exchange and distribution to meet national budget requirements." This only mentions state management as a means of meeting budgetary requirements, but every expansion of state activity could evidently be justified on this ground. As an example of the evasiveness that characterized the Social Democratic debate of this period, this new demand was not even mentioned in newspaper commentaries on the program.

Some of Branting's utterances in the Riksdag during the late 1890s provide the first sign of the change that Social Democracy would and had to undergo as a party devoted to parliamentary activity. In a debate of 1897 on the rights of the crown and private individuals in regard to the exploitation of mines, Branting aligned himself exclusively with the state. His comments reveal not a trace of doubt concerning the suitability of the right of state ownership under the existing social system, no intimation of the problems that had been current during the debate of 1892. To the contrary. Branting tried to demonstrate—without using the term socialization—that societal control in various areas of the economy was readily in agreement with Swedish tradition. He called attention to the fact that fellow party members in France considered such control particularly warranted in regard to banking, communications and transportation, and mines. In respect to banking in Sweden, the case for making the national bank (*Riksbank*) into a central bank that would dominate the financial market had already been presented, above all in the lower house. A substantial part of the transportation system—the railroads—was already in the hands of the state. The crown was acknowledged to have traditional, far-reaching rights even in respect to mining. Branting indicated that Swedish custom in these areas of the economy should be established and further developed.

At the 1898 Riksdag Branting commented on the government bill on old-age and disability pensions. He supported the bill, but noted that he found it inadequate on several points. The basic views he put forth in the introduction are the most interesting part of his address. Branting recalled that when the same question had come up in Germany, Social Democrats had maintained that, contrary to the hopes of the proposal's sponsors, social discontent could not be eased by such a reform. The same was true in Sweden. Said Branting, insurance legislation could not "serve the purpose of effecting a social levelling unless it were complemented by measures that operate more directly and generally to the advantage and in the best [interests] of the working class." As examples of such measures he named the establishment of a standard work day and thorough-going protective legislation, together with guarantees of the workers' right to organize. The remarkable thing is that Branting spoke of these comparatively limited sociopolitical measures as ways of attaining a social levelling. He did not follow the line he maintained in his newspaper and insist that the class struggle could only be settled by the victory of the working class or that social welfare policies could only serve to reinforce the workers' commitment to carry out socialization. It was obvious to riksdagman Branting that he would be influencing the legislature in a direction that was directly contrary to the one desired if he were to dispute the value of social welfare policies that lay within the realm of possibility from the point of view of their contribution to peace in society. If he wanted to achieve a direct, positive result, he had to proceed from the same basis as his opponents and thus could not use Marxist ideology as his point of departure.

The Social Democratic stand on *tariffs* is indicated by the demand entered in various party programs that all indirect taxes—or at least those that weighed upon the broad strata of the population—be abolished. As a policy for the future this demand was held to be above all debate. Tariff barriers between peoples seemed inconceivable in the socialist society of the future that would be characterized by international brotherhood. Yet the principle of free trade was also asserted as material, partly from a general, internationalist point of view and partly because tariff duties, and duties on foodstuffs in particular, were believed to have the most adverse effect on the poor consumer.

The issue was, however, subject to little debate during this period. It is interesting that even in regard to this issue we can detect a shift from long-range ideological views to an emphasis on short-range practical policies. Some of the early articles on tariffs followed the line that the entire issue was of scant importance to the working class in the existing society. In 1887 Danielsson wrote that the manufacturers, wholesalers, and large landholders composed "a class of despoilers that exists by squeezing the vitality out of the majority in the nation." Within this class there was a battle over the spoils. This battle was of no interest to the workers unless one of the contestants were to promise extensive political rights to the working class. "Be the rich plunderer a large property owner or a capitalist, he belongs to *the upper class,* the band that stands with its feet on the chest of the nation, that exploits the labor force and smothers all attempts at insurrection against the coercive laws of the class society. . . . If, within a certain span of time, the worker produces goods with a value [equivalent to] two loaves of bread but the laws that govern wages in this society permit him to keep only one loaf, then it is all the same to him if the manufacturer and property owner fight over the division of the stolen loaf. What the worker has to do is to take possession of the entire product of his work." *Social-Demokraten* proffered the same line of reasoning: "The tariff controversy is a struggle between two classes, landholders and the industrial bourgeoisie, both of which are inimical to the proletariat and have as their class interests the preservation of private ownership of land and the tools of labor, together with the prevention of a social revolution." Just one year later this view had changed—probably as a result of worker reaction to the rise in the price of bread. The party's two main newspapers inveighed with extreme virulence against "starvation tariffs," stressing that the workers' circumstances had deteriorated and demanding political representation for the working class as a way to preclude further impoverishment under the protection of the state. In subsequent years the principle of free trade was adopted as the relevant precept whenever the subject of tariffs was at issue.

We shall not enter into a detailed discussion of the Social Democratic attitude toward *trade unions,* but there are a few points that we should take note of. Branting's attitude toward trade unions as presented in his Gävle speech, which held that they should be apolitical, was soon generally abandoned. The Social Democrats sought to make the trade union movement socialist, and they succeeded. Between 1898 and 1900, party membership was even a qualification for acceptance into the Swedish Confederation of Trade Unions. Together with the party itself, the trade unions were regarded as weapons in the power struggle, but also as agencies for the improvement of the circumstances of the working class within the existing society. The 1897 program presented the trade unions as evidence of the countermovement in society to which the working class had been driven by the developmental trends induced by capitalism. They were the organs of the workers "in the continuous struggle between labor and management in [both] the national and international labor market, a struggle that is assuming ever more prodigious dimensions, a struggle that shall never cease until the working class ceases to be a class of wage earners."

Social Democratic treatment of the *agricultural question* evinces important distinctions. Marxist theory was essentially based on industrial development. Marx's analysis was primarily directed at trends within this development; the classes included in his major perspective were the capitalist-entrepreneurs and the proletariat-industrial workers. Industrialism and the consequences it would entail completely dominated the Swedish debate as well. The pamphlets that were most representative of the movement did not even allude to the existence of agricultural workers. The fact that Branting's Gävle speech was solely devoted to a consideration of industry is typical; although farmers composed two thirds of Sweden's population, their problems were ignored. On the whole, in agrarian Sweden twenty articles in the Social Democratic press were concerned with industry; one single article was devoted to farming. In Marx's schema, agriculture was regarded as a kind of appendage to a society whose most salient feature was regarded to be the antithesis between mass production and the right of private ownership.

In agreement with the Marxist pattern, Sweden's Social Democrats as a rule automatically transferred to agriculture the ideas that had been developed in relation to industry. Party programs referred to the socialization of land together with the other means of production. Danielsson's program of 1888 supported this demand with special arguments. The program alleged that the agricultural class was running into increasing debt and that it was in a state of disintegration or transformation into a class of wage earners. Land must be socialized in order to put an end to the masses' dependence on the class of large landholders. The program of 1897 also contained a demand for conversion of land into communal property.

Party theorists initially tried to apply the same schema to both industry and agriculture. Particularly illuminating in this regard is a long essay by Branting on "An Undermined Position of Power" published in 1886. Branting attempted to demonstrate that the political power of the Swedish farming class did not correspond to its economic strength but was a vestige from a previous era, that is, it was a part of tradition of a kind that could persist for a while without any foundation in the economic order. (Branting may here have been directly influenced by Marx's exposition in *The Eighteenth Brumaire of Louis Bonaparte.*) The position of the farmers was, in reality, being undermined, not by any temporary difficulties (i.e. the agricultural crisis of the period), but by changes in the relations of production. As long as the farmers had been producing solely for the domestic market, small-scale production without pronounced growth trends appeared to be the natural form of agriculture. The opening of world markets changed all this: it called for the production of large quantities at low prices which, in turn, required large-scale production with an effective division of labor and modern technical resources. The farmer had no place in this new era. "His method of working is obsolete, his economic resources will inevitably always be inadequate, his very right of private disposition of the land is at variance with that which is required for the realization of the new system. . . . The relation between farmer and agriculturalist corresponds completely to that between *craftsman* and industrialist. Both [farmer and craftsman] have the same origin as products of medieval society, and, because they represent *small* capital, both are but ghosts in a developed big capitalist society, such as that which the modern civilized world is steadily approaching." Branting used statistics from Sweden and other nations to show that tendencies toward concentration and impoverishment also appeared in agriculture. The small independent farm was doomed; to attempt to save it would be an attempt to turn back developments. The farmer "is driven down into the proletariat class; he can either remain on the land as a worker in large-scale farming or migrate to the city and reinforce the ranks of the industrial proletariat. Thus agriculture displays the very same division between a capitalist class and an unpropertied working class that modern industry is in the process of producing in its field." The conclusion drawn was that the question of the farmers was basically a part of the question of the workers; the other classes were related to bygone historical epochs, to their needs and forms of production, "but the working class alone belongs to the future."

These views—though seldom so clearly expressed—recurred in the whole Social Democratic press. In an article published in 1889, Danielsson, partly due to the influence of Henry George's theories, speculated that socialization might proceed in two stages, the first of which would concern land, the second, other means of production. He nevertheless thought it probable that the land question would only be solved in connection with general socialization. He pointed to the depopulation of rural areas and the immigration to cities as evidence of the difficulties agriculture was encountering. He held that the land passed into the ownership of large property holders and large farmers while small farmers were transformed into an industrial proletariat. "What is this if not the capital-produced *mobilization* of the nation's populace into the service of the impending revolution." Danielsson concluded with the assertion that social reformation of agriculture was unavoidable—a reformation "that will return to the people their land by abolishing its character of private property." Several articles that appeared in *Arbetet* around 1890 returned to this thought. At the Scandinavian Workers' Congess of 1890 Danielsson forced through a resolution stated "that all attempts to preserve the class of small farmers—whether through loans on good terms or land reapportionment or leasing of the state's land—are condemnable from a social viewpoint because these efforts, if they do not fail completely, only help prolong the existence of the middle class that clings to the right of private ownership with the utmost tenacity and prejudice and has therefore become the vehicle of reaction to the revolutionary workers' movement." The resolution was passed, 44 to 14, with 36 abstentions; almost all the Swedish delegates (among them Danielsson and Sterky—Branting did not participate in the congress) cast their votes for the resolution.

Social Democratic agitation within the agricultural class during this period was evidently almost exclusively directed at farm laborers and concentrated on the demand for shorter working hours and other sociopolitical reforms. This was in full agreement with the party's radical ideology. Large property holders and large-scale farmers were considered the obvious antagonists; small farmers could not be expected to understand the principle of socialization and it was presumed that they, like craftsmen and other segments of the middle class, were on the way to extinction as a social group.

Little by little the Social Democrats perceived their error on this point, as they also did in regard to industry. They had regarded the class of farmers to be in a state of disintegration not, or at least not primarily, on the basis of their observations of conditions in Sweden, but because Marx had declared this disintegration to be inevitable. A schema that was untenable even in regard to the relatively industrialized nations on which it was based could not in the long run be applicable in Sweden, which was still predominantly an agricultural nation in which most of the land was divided into small farms. It was impossible to pretend that the independent farmers, who far outnumbered industrial workers, were scarcely existent or would, in any case, not exist in the near future. A real revision of Social Democratic ideology on this point was not initiated until the beginning of the twentieth century, but we can detect a mitigating trend in the middle 1890s. This trend originated in Germany, where party congresses held in 1894 and 1895 had discussed the advisability of retaining an unmitigated line of socialization in regard to agriculture. Bebel held to the old line, but Vollmar believed that one had to consider the farmers' sentiments favoring the right of private ownership. In Sweden, Danielsson changed from one extreme stand to another on this matter, as he did on many other issues. In 1894 he aligned himself with Vollmar's opinion that small plots of land be exempted from the contemplated farm expropriation. This programmatic change would win over the small farmers to the Social Democratic camp. The "clarity" of Social Democracy, that is, its certainty that the large properties would quickly devour the small farms "is in danger of becoming beclouded, not by compromises with the farmers, but by developments themselves. Under such conditions the speed of our party's progress is dependent upon [the dissemination of] sensible and intelligible propaganda among the small farmers. . . ." One would promise the small farmers that they could keep their land if they, in turn, assisted the Social Democrats in their common struggle against capitalism. Branting was more cautious. Capitalism was, in effect, in the process of expropriating the farming class, and Social Democrats could scarcely do anything about it except to try to alleviate the suffering. The bulk of the farmers were firmly bound to the conservative camp. Branting further held that it would be dangerous to make Social Democracy into a mixed farmers' and workers' party at the expense of clarity. Yet even *Social-Demokraten* contained an unsigned editorial affirming that the party wished to protect the small farmers against capitalism and was not eager to abolish their right of ownership; it contended that socialism was not opposed to private property per se but to the exploitation of human labor. "But in making this statement we are by no means trying to conceal our opinion as to the best form of production. We say to the small farmers: Be assured that you shall one day find it to your advantage to eliminate your boundaries and cultivate the land in collective farms. By pooling your forces you can avail yourselves of the technical resources of large-scale farming. One day you shall have everything to gain by allowing the *socialization* of your property, which, in this case, is *not* synonymous with expropriation, that is, with the deprivation of unjustly seized property, but is synonymous with the remolding of property in and for the more functional use of this means of production—the land. . . ." The German party congress of 1895 passed a resolution that repudiated the idea of elevating the farmers' class within the contours of the private capitalist society on the ground that reinforcing the rights of this class would also strengthen the capitalist state. Branting criticized this resolution and stressed that Social Democracy ought to try to help both farmers and workers within the framework of the state as it was. One could not omit to fight unemployment, even if it was connected with capitalism. In like manner it was natural that one should contemplate measures that would help the farmers, even if such measures temporarily strengthened the existing state. However, Branting still seemed to be of the opinion that the small farmers would agree to socialization in their own interests. In an article written somewhat later, Branting noted that the farmer occupied a kind of intermediate position as both employer and manual laborer. The small farmers were predominantly workers, and one hoped that they would be enlisted in the Social Democratic cause.

It is surprising that after the debate that took place in connection with the German congresses of 1894 and 1895, the Swedish party congress of 1897 adopted without controversy a program that took up the demand for land socialization. This demand was, however, complemented significantly by Article VII, which required both direct state control of farmers' credit and a law with guarantees for modern, scientific farming that nonetheless prevented the expropriation of small farms without compensation or right of use. This article was evidently intended to protect small farms against what was termed private expropriation, in other words, against large property holders, business, and banks. The formulation of the article was peculiar, for one could not directly state in the program of immediate action that one assigned some value to the right of private ownership of land when the over-all policy declaration generally referred to the socialization of land. Yet the purport of the article is clear. In this case, Social Democracy sided with one of the middle classes whose elimination had previously been held as a prerequisite for the movement's victory. The aim was to reinforce, at least provisionally, the right of private ownership of the means of production in one area and, at the same time, call for general socialization in the future. The new line thereby adopted was later enlarged upon and made more specific, particularly through the program revision of 1911. The Social Democratic press contained no comments on this part of the program. As far as is known, the agricultural question was not a subject of basic discussion in the course of the next few years, and it was not brought up at the congress of 1900.

Side by side with the general evolution of Social Democratic ideology just described ran a semi*anarchistic movement* that asserted itself briefly in the early 1890s, then receded completely into the background for approximately a decade. Foremost representative of this movement was Hinke Bergegren, who unfolded its views in the weekly *Under a Red Flag* (*Under röd flagg,* March-June 1891), and in a series of meetings that took place 1890–1891. The substance of the semianarchists' message was largely the demand for a change in party tactics, and it is in respect to this demand that the movement will be discussed here. In agreement with the radical tactical line, the movement also criticized party endeavors to bring about sociopolitical reforms: such reforms were said to be valueless in the established society and detrimental to party strength. At times stealing was held to be morally permissible in the capitalist state. In regard to the goals of party activity, the movement contended that production ought to be handled through free associations, which would also regulate consumption. There was to be no real societal power.

Social Democratic leaders stringently opposed the new faction; the main issue of the conflict was the question of tactics. The 1891 congress was the scene of general dissension between the two lines. Bergegren and others criticized the party's compromise-oriented activity and elaborated on the necessity of eliminating all state coercion and reaching the greatest possible degree of freedom. Bergegren attempted to demonstrate that Social Democrats and anarchists were basically striving for the same goal. Danielsson, backed by Branting and Sterky, violently assailed anarchism—evidently without realizing that Marx's objective could be purported to coincide with that of the anarchist line, as commonly interpreted. Danielsson contended that insofar as the anarchists wished to turn production over into the hands of free associations, they, in effect, wished to preserve the prevailing economic anarchy and thus had the same ideal as the liberals. Social Democrats, on the other hand, wanted planned production under society's leadership and a judicious restriction of freedom. Socialism and anarchism thus represented two contrary world views.

After the debate the congress passed a resolution that read as follows:

> The Social Democratic Workers' party derives its idealistic strength from a scientific knowledge of the laws governing the origin, development, and fall of the capitalist

society. The concentration of capital and the increasingly disastrous anarchy in production, together with the successive development of big industry, are the factors that necessitate a social revolution in the direction of the organization of the work of society in accordance with the principles of socialism, which have as their aim the common usufruct of the means of production and societal control of production.

In view of the fact that these fundamental, international ideas of socialism are absolutely irreconcilable with the obscure currents of thought and attempts at the formation of factions that have appeared under the name of anarchism and have played a transitory, obstreperous part in the practical agitation in most countries, aimed at sacrificing the socialist organization of labor for the absolute or preposterously exaggerated right of individual free action, the Party Congress declares this anarchistic social theory to be antidemocratic. It is no more than a one-sided development of the basic tenets of bourgeois liberalism, even though its criticism of the present social order may proceed from socialist viewpoints. Above all, it is irreconcilable with socialism's demand that the means of production pass into the hands of society as a whole and that society regulate production, and it runs into an insolvable contradiction if production is not to regress to the dwarflike standard of the small crafts.

Because of this fundamental difference between Social Democracy and anarchism the Congress rules that the Social Democratic Workers' party should definitively repudiate the anarchistic factions and objectively answer the anarchic theories when suitable occasions present themselves.

The voting on the resolution showed that the anarchic line had gained an appreciable amount of strength within a short period of time. The resolution was passed, 28 to 11; 12 declared themselves neutral, and one member was not present for the vote. The minority voted for this proposal: "Inasmuch as the goal of socialism is the abolition of the class society and the wage system, the Congress considers that all persons who sincerely have the same immediate objective should be regarded as good allies, whether they be called anarchists or anything else."

The Congress also had to consider a question posed by the Social Democratic Union of Stockholm on Bergegren's initiative: "Are thefts and other acts that conflict with the laws of the class society morally right when provoked by need or other social causes? And should not the party organs acknowledge the moral propriety of these acts?" The congress answered: "In view of the present class society, both stealing and some frauds should be morally sanctioned since one class has the moral right to steal from and fleece the other. But from a Social Democratic viewpoint, such acts are absolutely reprehensible, so much the more so because the party's mission is to abolish the present society and build a new one where the concept of theft will be unknown."

The anarchists were not expelled from the party in spite of the patent variance. However, the party conflict of 1891 on this issue would prove to be an episode of little significance to the party's development as a whole.

During the fifteen-year span between the commencement of the theoretical debate around 1885 and the turn of the century, Social Democratic ideology as expressed in party programs, the press, pamphlets, and speeches, underwent a remarkable transformation. The original formulas were modified or rejected on one point after another; dogmatic statements were replaced by indefinite observations or by assumptions circumscribed by important qualifications; questions that had been regarded as simple and unimportant in the major perspective became complicated and full of moment. It is almost impossible to select one important point of theory on which the two most prominent Social Democrats, Branting and Danielsson, did not change their opinions during this period. The interpretation of the meaning of the class struggle, the theory of value, the theories of the development of social structure, the iron law of wages, the attitude toward social welfare policies and the agricultural question—the picture is uniformly one of abandoned or modified points of view. The goal and the ideas surrounding it were not altered, but the entire conceptual system of which the goal was a part had changed gradually, almost imperceptibly.

Many factors contributed to this change. The contradictions and paradoxes inherent in Marxist ideology necessitated the adoption of new viewpoints, whether expressed in a conscious revision of thinking or in rewordings and distortions of Marxism. In the long run it was impossible to adhere to the amalgam of grand metaphysics and matter-of-fact instructions, which were the substance of Marx's statements as formulated in different stages. When in their early twenties the Social Democratic leaders had been captivated by Marx's most imposing theses and they always remained loyal to Marx insofar as they continued to cite him. By the time these leaders were in their forties, however, continued study and practical experience made it impossible for them to adhere to the undiscriminating, complete acceptance of Marx that they had maintained in their youth. The criticism of Marx advanced by both bourgeois and Social Democratic writers in other countries gradually exerted an influence on the debate in Sweden as well. Practical participation in politics altered the Social Democrats' point of view, revealed difficulties in the accepted system, and imparted a different content and meaning to the problems they dealt with. The insignificant party expanded into a great popular movement; the workers' groups that joined it demanded solutions to concrete, immediate problems. The large theoretical perspective grew more distant and less important when universal suffrage became the party's rallying point.

Although it often seems that the Social Democratic leaders were unaware of their own shifts in opinion on various issues, statements they made around the turn of the century indicate that they were definitely conscious of a general change within the party. In a speech delivered in 1900 Branting emphasized that new viewpoints had become decisive with the party's growth: "As long as the party is composed of only a few persons who lack the opportunity to exercise any real political influence, it is in the nature of things that their principles will be abstract in form and that the main emphasis will be on future goals. On the other hand, should the working class begin to take a hand in the machinery of society, certain immediate goals to improve its position will appear so attractive and occupy so much time and interest that the more distant ones will, relatively speaking, be shunted aside." In an article published in 1897, Danielsson recalled that Social Democrats had abandoned a series of dogmas that they had previously defended with fanatic zeal. This was proof of the movement's viability. In terms reminiscent of the antiintellectual vitalism of today, Danielsson extolled the capacity of Social Democratic theory to change and adjust. The theory "is distinguished by great elasticity and demonstrates its truth and practical fecundity in that it does not exhaust its forces in vain attempts to do violence to reality but allies itself naturally and voluntarily with all fluid popular movements in various countries for the purpose of leading the working classes on to a higher cultural level and a freer social position along navigable roads that have been opened by history."

The Socialist Debate at the Beginning of the 19th Century and the Bringing up to Date of the Question of Socialisation after World War I

THE PERIOD between the end of the 1890s and the World War was the period in which the Social Democratic party made its great breakthrough. The number of party members rose from 10,000 in 1895 to 67,000 in 1905, and 86,000 in 1915. Between the two latter-mentioned years there was a period of expansion, 1906–1908, and a period of decline directly following. However, this is not significant from the point of view of the development of the party's political strength. The number of the affiliated labour-communes (i.e. local body of the Swedish Social Democratic Party) rose steadily, from 22 in 1895 to 137 in 1905 and 784 in 1915. In the lower house, the party won 4 places in 1902, 13 in 1905, 34 in 1908 and 64 in 1911. In the spring election of 1914 they won 73 places, and 87 in the autumn election of the same year. By this latter election they became the biggest party in the country, and since then they have maintained this position. The political victories depended partly on the fact that the party gained steadily rising support, and partly on the constitutional reform of 1907–1909, which gave the franchise to a large section of the working class.

These victories meant that Social Democracy came to represent the mass of the industrial working class and also a growing (though in terms of actual percent insignificant) number of the poor farmers. A much firmer support was given to the party by the rapidly developing trade union movement, which in 1899 became the Swedish Federation of Trade Unions. Gradually the party leadership became stabilised. For a long period largely the same people are to be found on the party executive, in the parliamentary groups and at party congresses. Moreover, the leading group became very much a group of functionaries, and included those actively serving in organisations and concerns connected with the party, or those carrying out tasks connected with the party—trade union delegates, members of the party staff and members of parliament. The existing state of affairs was devoted to increasing the power of the party leadership, and creating stability and unity in proclamation and action. However it was during a later period, that this tendency was to show more manifest results. The period with which we are now dealing was characterised by many striking contrasts. In the first place the potentially anarchist young-socialist opposition asserted itself though it disappeared from the party when its leaders were expelled (1905, definitely 1908). Moreover, the Social Democratic Youth Organistion, founded in 1903, formed a fighting radical phalanx which, on certain issues, had a definite policy all of its own. It was in 1917 that the group having this orientation finally left the party, and in that year the Left-Socialist party was organised.

Due to the rapid growth of the party, youth, during this period, occupied an unusually prominent place within Social Democracy, in particular as far as debates of a more ideological nature were concerned. Naturally the older workers who joined the party were unable to assert themselves. Apart from Branting and Carleson, practically none of those who earlier were active within the party were theoretically interested and trained. Steffan and Lindhagen, members of the same generation, first came into the party about 1910. Considering the general age level within the party these men, born between 1860 and 1865 were part of the old order. A mid-way position, having been born around 1870, was held by both of the party's leading cultural and literary critics, Lidforss and Hedén, and also by Fabian Månsson, the self-educated worker. Then follows a line of young men who joined the party at the beginning of the 19th century and who quickly won for themselves a place in debates: Rydén, Palmstierna, Sandler, Örne, Hallén, Vennerström, Wigforss, P.A. and Sigfrid Hansson, Möller, Ström, Höglund, Nerman, Kilbom, Norling, Åkerberg. Of these men the first two were born 1878 and 1877 respectively, the rest between 1880 and 1885. Around 1915 many of the party's debators who were active in questions regarding the party programme and ideas were in their thirties. To a great extent generational differences brought with them political antagonism. Regarding the education of the young leaders, it should be pointed out that most of them had a grammar school education and that at some point many of them had undertaken academic studies. Others, such as the brothers Hansson and Möller, after some years as workers had achieved positions within the party and, through self-education, at an early stage had acquired political knowledge. Gradually the opportunities for gifted workers to acquire knowledge and intellectual training improved. In this respect the Peoples' College (Folkhögskola) in Brunnsvik was of especial importance. Both verbally and in the press the general level of debate shows a steady incline

In this period questions of Social Democratic principles took a relatively insignificant place in party debates. It can even be said that social and economic questions on the whole were relegated to the background. The external work of the party was largely concerned with the accomplishing of democracy; questions of defence and tactics dominated the internal controversies. In the fight between the leading groups in the party on the one hand, and young socialism and the Social Democratic Youth Organisation on the other, social and economic questions played a remarkably modest part. The youth movements were not interested in these issues. It is significant that at the 5 congresses of the Social Democratic Youth Organisation, 1905–1914, there was no single large debate on such issues. On no occasion were problems of socialisation and related questions dealt with. Neither did the party congresses exhibit any great interest in those issues central to Social Democracy, though at one of the congresses prior to 1920 the party's economic policy was discussed more thoroughly. This was in 1911, when there was a thorough revision of the basic principles and programme regarding the land question. Questions which, from the point of view of socialism in general, must be considered secondary—questions of religion, the republic, temperance—were given greater space in congress protocol than questions of social policy and socialisation. Partly this can be explained by the fact that due to the existing power conditions, the social revolution at which the party aimed had to be relegated to the future. Other more readily attainable goals became current and temporarily dominant. Above all democracy had to be achieved, as a foundation for future activity. The defence issue, amongst others, forced itself to the forefront of Swedish internal politics, offering a tempting field for a propaganda aimed at fanning discontent with the prevailing situation. It is possible that the Marxist perspective, which still characterised the party's ideology, also helped to create a sort of fatalism in the face of development as a whole, thereby helping to reduce interest in questions concerning the construction of a socialist society. Socialism would come when the time was ripe: it was already clear to everybody that the ripening process was taking rather longer than originally expected. Marx himself had refused to give more specific intimations regarding the realisation of socialisation and therefore it was often said that planning for the future involved an unscientific Utopianism. Menger's "Neue Staatslehre," 1903, was the outstanding attempt of that period to plan along similar lines. He was strongly criticised and accused of dilettantism, though he was one of the few professional scientists proceeding from Marx's ideas. It should also be observed that problems connected with socialisation presented incomparably greater difficulties than, for instance, the issues of the constitution or defence. No qualified economist joined the party who was able to lead or stimulate a debate on these problems. This also helps to explain why no work of any importance was written about the realisation of socialism and the socialist society, and why these questions were only peripherally dealt with in the press, in pamphlet literature, and at party meetings and congresses. To the extent that a debate more concerned with socialist principles took place, it mainly reflected differences of opinion abroad, particularly in Germany.

In relation to the general development traced by Marx, the watering down of the political viewpoints sketched above largely continued. However, adherence to Marx's principles was maintained, and Marxism was always considered to be the basis of the activity of the party. In this sense the young men who began to assert themselves within the party during the first decade of the 19th century were just as faithful to Marx as were the older generation. In internal conflicts, for example in the question of defence, both sides attempted to find support in Marx. To be a socialist but not a Marxist was still seen as practically an impossibility in the party's theoretical debates. Nevertheless, Marxism increasingly lost its importance as the party's guide. In a general sense one believed in Marx, but found it difficult to determine in detail just what exactly this belief consisted of. Gradually, Marxism became more a symbol than a doctrine.

Two important aspects of Marx's theory were emphasised with great energy; the concept of historical materialism and economic determinism, and the doctrine of class struggle. "Either one denies the idea of historical materialism and believes that a new society can be constructed at will, in the same way that a new house is built, or one is convinced of the truth of the idea, knowing that one must keep the economic maturity of society under the careful custody of the socialist tendencies within the society before entering the revolutionary struggle." This is a typical statement which could certainly be accepted by all the party's theoreticians. But with regard to the historical concept it was stressed that ideas could play an important part along with the conditions of production. One finally arrived at such statements as the one previously mentioned, by which productive forces "ultimately" or "in the last analysis" were decisive. The formation of an ideal was explained as being necessary if the goal of a socialist society was to be achieved, whether or not this ideal was considered definitely a consequence of economic change, or whether it was thought that such an idea could be produced from a degree of reflection unrelated to the economy.

This lack of clarity was expressed, for example, in Branting's statement that "the historical inevitability of socialism . . . should never be seen as fatalistic to the extent that we forget that work towards a socialist ideal is a necessary part of the realisation of this inevitability." In an article which attracted much attention, Wigforrs, one of the party's foremost young theoreticians, tried to show that the feeling of the working class that they are the bearer of a morally higher ideal of society was an important aspect in the success of socialism. "If the conviction could really take root within the working class that it is mainly due to their strivings that the future of the modern society depends, then this would mean an intensifying of the feeling of responsibility and of moral feelings as a whole such as only certain religious forms, in their early periods, were able to command." Nevertheless, Wigforrs believed himself to proceed from the materialist concept of history. At times it was thought that the certainty of a victory dependent on the autonomous development of the economy was a necessary pre-requisite for the formation of the socialist ideal, at times the formation of this ideal was seen as a pre-requisite for victory. At times it was asserted, in close connection to certain passages in Marx, that the formation of an ideal was superfluous, scientific certainty regarding the path of developing being sufficient. We need not look any closer at statements concerned with this question, in which words are given such varied and obscure meanings that an analysis takes a great deal of space without yielding results of any great interest. The important thing is to point out that the materialist concept of history was continually cited, and that it was thought to involve both the more general fact that economic factors were "basic" or "decisive," and also, more specifically, that sooner or later the development must result in socialism.

The principle of class struggle was still of central interest in the debates. With regard to this point it is hardly possible to see a tendency to "watering down," nor to the budding of the ideology of a "Peoples' Home." It was maintained that the social reforms which had been carried out could not lead to Social harmony, as this could be achieved only through socialism. In the propaganda, emphasis was placed on references to economic and social differences, and on appeals to dissatisfaction amongst those in the least favourably placed positions in society. In 1911 a summary of the arguments used in this propaganda was given in Sandler's text "Society As It Is," in which the differences in the distribution of income and fortunes was drastically exposed. In a simplified form pamphlet was intended to give the impression that an equal distribution of income would mean a considerable rise in general affluence. As earlier, there was a certain insecurity regarding the question of the participants in the class struggle, which in other connections was said to be unavoidable, able only to be established by the party itself. Generally, proletarians and capitalists were mentioned, though it was often asserted that the real struggle was between a few exploiters and the majority of the exploited. General affluence and social harmony would go hand in hand with the victory of socialism.

Several contributions to a debate held on the 7th February, 1908 in Stockholm on the subject of "The Foundations of Socialism" (later published in pamphlet form) illustrated the position adopted by social democracy during this period in relation to Marxism, and in particular to Marxist social theories. This debate grew as a result of a criticism of socialism made by the then Docent Eli Heckscher, and was initiated by Heckscher and Carleson. Strangely enough, to the best of our knowledge it is the only detailed, public and fully-reported exchange of opinion regarding the basis of the theory of socialism that has taken place in our country. It should also be stressed that no similar debate has ever taken place in the parliament. One theme in Heckscher's statement was intended to establish the thesis that the inevitability of socialism was built upon Marx's predictions regarding social development, and that these predictions—except as far as the tendency to concentration in industry is concerned—have been shown to be erroneous. As a rule the Social Democratic speakers, whilst continuing to support the criticised thesis, admitted that in some respects Marx's prognosis had not been proved to be correct. Carleson took up these questions only in passing, being more interested in defending the theory of surplus value (in this he seems to have stood practically alone in the party), and the concept of historical materialism. He ended by saying that socialism was: "in its purpose, economically motivated, in its nobility and justice, morally motivated and in its role of the bearer and promoter of culture, intellectually motivated." Branting explained that the theories that the capitalists would become fewer (not merely that capital would be concentrated), and that the middle-class would disappear had shown themselves to be untenable. But he added, refering here to Bernstein, that "in fact this is no advantage for the great mass of workers, who in consequence have to support not only a few millionaires, but the whole social pyramid which takes its additional income from the peoples' labour." It was of no importance if one or another formula changed. The important thing was "that the working class are more and more gathering around the ideals of socialism, which they are able to do with full confidence in development and in the justice and greatness of these ideals, (and) that the working class joins together and consciously strives to achieve such a social order as does not allow a tiny fraction of the nation to reap the lion's share of the fruit of all labour." One should note that this does not imply that Branting accepted Marx's theories of value and surplus value. On the contrary, in other contexts he has stated that these theories cannot be accepted. Höglund said that the theories of exploitation and crisis were untenable. However, this did not hinder the fact that "the working classes are still exploited by the owners of the means of production, and that this exploitation will not end until the means of production have become the property of society." Christiernson, on the other hand, considered that it was not proved that either the theory of exploitation or the theory of crisis were erroneous. Finally E. Söderberg, the only Social Democrat trade unionist to participate in the debate, explained that it was true that in Sweden Marx was appreciated as a pioneer, but that socialism was not dependent upon Marxism. "I am quite convinced that most of us are of the opinion that even if Marx's theories collapse, socialism presumably will not!"

In many respects this debate is typical. Marx's social predictions were discussed one by one, as if they were isolated from each other. This or that theory was considered to be correct, whilst others were untenable. There were differences of opinion regarding which theories could still be accepted, and the extent to which they could be realised. In some situations it seemed that Branting was quite willing to reject the theory of exploitation. In other situations, affected by a newly published paper, he asserted that the theory was correct and that the living standard of the proletariat had become worse relative to other social classes. Differences of opinion as to other social theories also emerged. This is of slight interest. What is important is that in this debate social theories were given an entirely different content from that attributed to them by Marx. In Marx's view it was a question of tremendous tendencies which would transform the whole culture of society, whilst those commenting on Marx discussed the ideas of equality at work, and the distribution of incomes, the importance of which could be judged in various ways, depending on the statistical methods employed.

Above all, the social prognoses were not seen as various aspects of a unified theory of the development of society, although it was due to his total picture of the future that Marx believed himself to be able to predict the victory of socialism. This means, to take just one example, that it is unreasonable to maintain that a certain concentration of enterprises, inseparably connected to industrialisation, was a confirmation of Marx's theories. Long before Marx's time it was very clear that such concentration went hand in hand with industrialisation.

Despite critical or reserved opinions regarding certain of Marx's theories, the party theoreticians maintained that socialism is a necessary consequence of development. In this respect, too, the debate of 1908 is characteristic. The evidence for this was not accepted, but the conclusions were seen as binding. The idea that socialism was scientific, that is that the victory of socialism could be proved scientifically, was energetically upheld. Most people still seemed to consider this characteristic of socialism. Other political opinions, unlike socialism, were said to be built only upon class interests and class prejudice, or on subjective ethical ideas.

But still another tendency began to appear. This can be seen in Söderberg's contribution to the debate mentioned previously. Socialism could be regarded as being independent of Marx, and independent of scientific inevitability. It could be justified from an ethical point of view, starting from the principle of equality and utilitarianism as a means of raising both production and general affluence. It is likely that such arguments, in particular the weak but constantly stated idea of injustice of the present society, had more effect on the working class than the so-called scientific socialism. Even among the intellectual elite of the party some hesitant voices were heard to take exception to the idea of the sole authority of Marxist doctrine. Quite naturally the first contributions of this type to the debate came from those who, in their middle age, had joined the Social Democrats largely because their own practical political aims were in accordance with those of the party. Mayor Carl Lindhagen, a former liberal radical who joined the Social Democrats in 1909, wrote an essay in the 1910 publication of "Tiden" entitled "Heresies" in which he asserted, with clear though mild reservations regarding Marxism, what he referred to as the importance of reason and a sense of justice, which idea was presented and discussed at the party congress held the following year. At the same time Gustaf Steffen, a professor of sociology who joined the party in 1910, wrote an article in "Tiden" entitled "My attitude to Social Democracy," with the intention of clarifying the motives which lay behind the position he adopted with regard to the party. He declared himself to hold ideas deviating from Marx, and criticised what he called a radical socialism which either exclusively or mainly was interested in a future total socialisation. Such a utopian idea implied a certain indifference to short-term reforms. It was Steffen's opinion that the most important aspect was the elimination of mass poverty, and the democratising of both the social spirit and the social institutions. He was not convinced of the value of total socialisation. "Social-economic radicalism," as Steffen labelled his own way of thinking "expressed negatively is a total war against poverty, and expressed positively, is the conscious and planned striving of the nation, from the very bottom of society upwards, step by step to improve its own physical and spiritual quality . . ." It was also necessary to precisely formulate and consciously strive towards definite goals. He believed that "social and cultural developmental fatalism" was untenable, and in this he was in agreement with Lindhagen. However, as has already been sufficiently stressed, the basic perspective of Marxism, what Steffen called "developmental fatalism," was predominant.

Before entering into the development of the party programme, and other ideologically important points in the parliamentary policy of the party, we shall pause to consider certain questions which are important from the point of view of the general social perspective, and which entered a somewhat new phase at the beginning of the 19th century.

It was first at the end of the 18th century that the special forms of industrial and commercial concentration known as trusts and kartells became important. In Sweden the first large monopolistic association occurred at the beginning of the 19th century (sugar, spirits, tobacco and certain foodstuffs). In socialist debates there was an inclination to greet these trusts (to use a comprehensive term) as evidence of the correctness of Marx's theories. The trusts heralded the enormous concentration that would precede and make possible socialisation. At the international socialist congresses in Paris in 1900 and Amsterdam in 1904 unanimous resolutions were taken along these lines.

It was stated in the Amsterdam resolution that the trusts involved rationalisation, even if under present circumstances this was only to the advantage of a few capitalists. Legislation against the trusts was pointless, as their appearance was "the unavoidable consequence of competition." Therefore, the congress stated that "the socialist parties in all countries should abstain from cooperating in all attempts to hinder the formation of trusts and limit their development." As member of this congress Branting agreed with this, and there is no doubt at all that it was the official position of Swedish Social Democracy, even if this was not established in any point of the programme or in any authoritatine resolution. Real homage was paid to the concept of trusts. In 1908 Sandler wrote that Social Democracy should "promote the concentration of industrial capital, and thereby promote productivity. Away with the naive and foolish cries about the victories of big capital. Those who enter into trusts, for example our saw-mill industry, almost deserve a statue to be raised in their honour in socialism's Sweden." At the same time P. A. Hansson, referring to the idea of trusts in America, wrote that "the amassing of fortunes . . . the fleecing and impoverishing of the masses and the proletarianising of the middle-classes are clearly aimed at considerably reducing opposition to (socialist) expropriation." But just as capitalism was denounced, despite the fact that it was considered to be a necessary stage of development, so were the trusts denounced with great energy as an apparatus for the perfection of exploitation.

On the whole the idea of joint stock companies occupied a more and more important place in the economy around the turn of the century. It is sufficient to remind the reader that between 1881 and 1908 the amount of share capital paid in rose from 455 to 2034 millions, and that that part of industry owned by share companies rose from 24% to 35% between 1896 and 1905. Bank share companies were particularly prominent. In 1881 the capital of these companies was 23 million. In 1908 it was 260 million. These circumstances, and the tendency toward trusts, indicate that Social Democratic ideas regarding capitalism increasingly came to be directed towards financial and industrial association, whilst earlier, in accordance with Marx, the talk had preferably been of capitalism as supported by the "entrepreneur," that is a limited class of private individuals.

However, in this period, land issues were of greater immediate importance in the development of Social Democratic ideas. Above all it became steadily clearer that the victory of large-scale production and concentration (which had been expected in the 1880's partly due to Marx's influence, and partly to the crisis in Swedish farming) was not going to take place. On the whole Swedish farming remained in the hands of the independent small farmers. Within the farming class, the number of independent farmers remained stationary in relation to dependent farmers and farm hands.

A number of other issues became of current interest. In certain parts of the country—Norrland (Northern Sweden) and Dalarna—the acquisition of land by corporations, particularly for lumbering, was increasingly seen as constituting a danger to the class of independent farmers, and also to the full exploitation of the land. According to the report of the "Norrland Committee" in 1904, in 1900 various corporations had acquired over a third of the privately owned land in Norrland. In Sweden as a whole the value of corporation properties rose threefold between 1890 and 1905. This does not imply concentration in Marx's sense, because the corporations did not replace small-scale management with large-scale management, but rather allowed land to lie waste, or rented it out in small allotments. Because of this the so called "Norrland question" became a burning issue. In parliament Lindhagen was foremost amongst those taking the initiative to reforms. For certain of his ideas he won support from all the political parties, though mainly from the Left. A large-scale inquiry was initiated in 1901, and in the years 1906–1909 a series of laws were made curtailing the opportunities of corporations to acquire real estate. In addition the terms of land lease were improved, and regulations introduced concerning neglect and regulating the dividing up of property in favour of farmers' self-support. Further, the question of how surplus population in the countryside (amongst others, an indicator of this was the still considerable emigration) could be absorbed into the economy (made possible through a state-loan) was taken up. A project for the forming of new, smaller farms, "owned homes," and legislation which in various ways strengthened the positions of farmers cultivating state land, were important in this connection. Other problems drawing attention to themselves and leading to state intervention were the increased debts within farming and the consequent dependence of land owners on the banks, and also the attempts within farming to cooperate with regard to the obtaining of machinery and the sale of products.

All this forced Social Democracy to continue its revision of the party's ideology with regard to farming discussed earlier. It became more difficult to continue to assert a general tendency towards large-scale production. It is true that a certain concentration could be said to have occurred—partly because of the acquisition of land by the corporations, partly because of the increased debts of the farmers—but this did not mean the success of the idea of large-scale production, not even a general tendency to accumulation in the question of land ownership. It was entirely unthinkable to consider the predatory exploitation of land by the corporations in the forest areas of the north as a rationalising of farming in accordance with Marx's scheme. This cultivation of land by the corporations was often combined with neglect, and with a reduction of acreage. It should be added that for a politically influential party, representative of the poorer groups of the population, it was difficult to support or accept even a "genuine" concentration within farming, i.e. a concentration of right of ownership of the land associated with large-scale production. To a certain extent a tolerant or benevolent attitude towards concentration was possible within industry quite simply because contrary to Marx's belief concentration did not bring with it either the proletarianising of the middle class, or the exploitation of the working class. What was called concentration meant, above all, the growth of new enterprises, new branches of industry, whose activity led to a general rise in affluence. Industrialisation could be seen as absorbing or destroying smaller concerns only to a very insignificant extent. On the other hand, Marx's type of concentration within farming must mean the absorption of smaller enterprises by larger enterprises, particularly in a country possessing large uncultivated areas of land. In this area, in which Marx's predictions regarding concentration never got a firm grip it was, from the point of view of principles, quite reasonable. Had a "genuine" concentration taken place within farming, would Social Democracy have approved of and encouraged this? That is to say, would they have taken the side of the corporations and the large owners against the small-holders?

The situation being as it was, the development of Social Democratic ideas could continue in much the same way, independent of Marxism. Clearly Marx's scheme was not applicable. In the main, the arguments for this put forward in debates were the question of immediate advantages to the poor farmers, and the need to win political support from this class. It appeared impossible that the party could gain the majority, without the cooperation of a large proportion of farmers. However, the change of opinion which took place, largely did so under the guse of Marxist terminology, and had a definite connection with certain statements made by Marx.

The ideology regarding the farming issue, which predominated at the beginning of the 19th century (though was connected with tendencies that appeared as early as the 1890s) to a very great extent meant that reforms were accepted that were proposed by bourgeois-radicals, although to a certain extent the demand for socialisation remained. It was admitted that development was not going in the direction of large-scale production, and that small-scale production was the most rational form of production for large areas of farming. Therefore it was necessary to protect and strengthen the class of small owners by limiting the power of the corporations, by regulating purchasing and leasing, by granting the use of the land on satisfactory terms, by equalising land distribution and by organising state credit for the farmers. Those lands in common ownership were to be utilised in the most suitable way, this to be decided for each individual case. Certain of the advantages connected with large-scale production were to be gained through cooperation. At times it was even thought that farming as a whole should be cooperative, and in that sense be socialised. (Örne). A proposal regarding land-value tax of the Georgian type was also put forward, but failed to win general support.

An article written by Branting in 1907 is representative of the prevailing opinion. This article was written after a conservative newspaper had reminded the public of Branting's predictions regarding the destruction of farming, made in "An undermined position of power" twenty years earlier. Strangely enough, Branting was surprised that the ideas he had put forward in 1886 had been confirmed by experience to such a great extent. However, he said that he was unable to endorse all the statements he had made earlier. Development had not confirmed all of Marx's generalisations: "therefore several current socialist authors see, in small-scale farming with its chances of intensive culture, a form of production with a great future." However, Branting proceeded from the fact that in the future small-scale farmers would have an entirely different position and an entirely different view of society than they had held earlier. "The new class of small farmers will be important not as possessors of the land, but as workers on the land. Their position can be organised to their complete satisfaction, with recognition of society's predominant right to the land, and cooperation with all its consequences, is of great help in creating a very different type of society from that of the old independent farmer." The class of small farmers should therefore feel solidarity with the workers, and with them work to "reorganise society so that it no longer serves the interests of those few who possess the capital, but rather that it becomes an organised planned system of producing and consuming groups, cooperating with each other." As did many others in the earlier stages of the land debate, Branting proceeded from the idea that the land should not be an object of private ownership in the real meaning of the term. What he termed "super-ownership" should belong to the society or the state. By means of expressions such as these a sort of formal compromise was reached between the recognition of independent farmers and the demand for socialisation.

Later this distinction was dispensed with, however, and the principle accepted that small farmers who were independent were to remain in this position. It was pointed out with great energy that Marx never said that small holdings should be taken over by the state. Naturally enough, as he predicted that they would be absorbed by large scale owners and capitalists!

The changed line in the land issue was not accepted without opposition, which fact is illustrated in particular by the debate at the congress in 1911. Certain elements in the party maintained a belief in Marx's prediction that large-scale production was inevitable. The young socialists considered the acceptance of the right to own land as a betrayal of socialism.

During that period the land issue occupied a foremost place amongst social-economic questions.

At the party congress in 1905, and in connection with motions which had been introduced regarding statements in the question on land, the party executive suggested that point VIII of the programme (due to changes in another connection, which corresponded to the previous point VII) should be formulated as follows:

"General credit to be organised through the state."

The direct regulation of farming credit through the state.

Stringent measures to be taken for the recovery of forest lands, mines and ore-fields, and for the retention by the state of waterfalls. Also for the protection of workers and small farmers against corporation domination. The state to extend its farming domains, support the efforts for improved farming amongst the small farmers, in particular cooperation, and also lease out its own land under guarantee that farming will be rational, and with security as to the independence and right to use the land of those holding such a lease."

The suggestion was accepted by the party congress after a single debate, which seems to have been rather short and which hardly receives a mention in the protocol of the congress. This new paragraph is mainly interesting because it means that the demand for steps leading to socialisation in several areas was now a part of the political programme. That it occurred as it did was clearly due to the reaction against the possessions and activities of the corporations in Northern Sweden. The congress seems to have been unanimous in the demand for state intervention. However, one speaker mentioned that two factions were apparent in the proletariat of the north. One of these wanted to "Let the corporations do as they please—it will only mean that the farmers of the north will be proletarianised even quicker." The other faction advocated opposing the recklessness of the corporations. One congress member (Lindley) proposed that a demand should be made that the state take over banks and insurance companies. This was rejected by 67 votes against 42. Opposing this proposal A. C. Lindblad said that it was unsuitable that "state capital should have too great a power under present conditions and that this would occur if the state took over economic institutions." In this connection the thought was expressed that, in a bourgeois society, socialisation would imply a danger for socialism.

The new formulation of the guide-lines for farming policy is hardly stringent. It shows, however, that there was no longer any thought of general socialisation of the land, but at the most only of protecting the small farmers from the corporations. Lindblad, the reporter for the party executive, alleged that "farming is tending in the direction of small scale production, and therefore we must see that these small farmers do not become the slaves of the large owners."

At the 1908 congress several motions regarding the land issue were proposed. Amongst these were two suggestions from labour municipalities in the north (Söderhamn and Sundsvall) which were directed particularly at the "Norrland question." The motion proposed by the Söderhamn municipality required that land should not be allowed to be purchased, sold or inherited, and that at the death of the owner all land should go to the state without payment. This is an example of the strange and extreme demands which came to light! However, the party executive proposed that the point in the programme regarding farming should be maintained unchanged. In accordance with a proposal made by a special drafting committee it was decided, on purely formal grounds, to substitute the word "småbönderna" (small-scale farmer) in the third paragraph with the word "småbrukarna" (smallholders). Yet again the debate on farming questions was of slight interest. From many quarters it was emphasised that the party was being accused by the Conservatives and Liberals of wanting to dispossess the farmers of the land, and that it was necessary to repudiate this accusation. It was maintained that on the one hand all talk of doing away with the right to land ownership should be avoided, and on the other hand that the farmers must be informed that right of ownership on the part of the state meant greater security than that offered by the prevailing conditions, under which the farmers were the slaves of the corporations. Social democracy must seek to win over the small-holders and agricultural workers by promoting their interests. This was especially important in view of the extension of the franchise which had been decided upon. There was a lack of clarity regarding the more detailed shaping of the party's farming policy. But it was agreed that the small-holders, particularly in the north, were in need of legislation which would hinder the acquisition of land by the corporations and guarantee a more secure right of tenure. A special resolution was passed with regard to the question of agricultural workers: "The congress expresses its warmest sympathy with the striving of agricultural workers for social freedom, and promises them the strongest possible support from the Social Democratic party." It was further decided that the party executive would undertake investigations in connection with farming.

There was a general feeling in the party that the modifications to the programme made at the congresses of 1905 and 1908 were insufficient. In particular the then liberals Lindhagen and Palmstierna worked for a more systematic and thorough treatment of the land issue. An extensive revision both of general principles and of the land programme took place at the party congress of 1911. The main starting point for this was a suggestion that there should be alterations in the basic principles and in the land programme, and that these should be made by a land committee appointed by the party executive. This suggestion was basically the work of Lindhagen, who had joined the party two years earlier and who served as chairman of the committee. Further, a motion was proposed regarding changes in general principles. This motion had been drawn up by Lindhagen and accepted in principle by the labour municipality of Stockholm.

In his proposal and his introductory speech Lindhagen represented a way of thinking that at this congress, and even later, came to play an important part in debates. He labelled his ideas as humanistic, and in them elements of Marxist thought were of practically no significance.

Socialism was regarded as the contemporary attempt to realise the ethical principles that were a part of humanism. In Lindhagen's view the "common human starting points" for the building of socialism had not been stressed sufficiently. He wrote that they were regarded as being so self-evident that no one spoke of them. However, these starting points should be strongly emphasised, as they were the real source of strength of socialism and they and they alone could gather together the mass of the people. A few clauses from the proposal just referred to can illustrate what was meant. Amongst other things Lindhagen wrote in his motion:

"The chances of socialism realising its innermost thoughts depends on its capacity to be true to these thoughts. Thus, it should never be forgotten that socialism is only the current term for the age-old struggle for the eternally human—humanism. Further, we should not lose sight of the fact that it does not concern only the liberation struggle of the working class. Rather, it concerns a struggle for the rights of all of us—'the final struggle.' Once and for all we wish to get to the bottom of that evil that has mainly been responsible for setting man against man—the struggle for property. *Doctrine and theory.* Humanism desires to ensure real spiritual and economic freedom to all people. As a consequence of this it desires to do away with poverty, because it knows that this is unjust and believes that that which is just can be realised . . . *Method.* Humanism desires to do everything for the present generation, to enable them to arrange things both big and small as well as is possible under present conditions. But in the work towards the goals that simultaneously takes place humanism is not interested in small reforms but only in structural changes. *Current programme.* Humanism wants to tear down the system of private privileges and give the fruits of society to all. In particular it desires to do away with the insoluble conflict between the highest profit and the highest wages and at the same time to build up mutual understanding between labour and the means of production. Therefore it aims at combining these factors, and this should now occur, in that society, that is, everyone, by means of their organisations take over the fruits of society, or those means of production that at present are in hands other than those of labour or also, and what is perhaps the key to the future, apportion to everyone his legitimate share of the means of production on a larger scale than previously as already is the case regarding small holders and craftsmen. Consequently it desires to get rid of the various wealthy classes and instead create a single middle class, in which every member feels that he works on behalf of both himself and of others. By means of these and other changes it desires to begin to increase the creative forces of the individual in order to achieve bread, freedom and self-responsibility."

These ideas were partly incorporated in the proposal of the Committee for the land programme. Several of this committee's statements of principle in the land question are typical of Lindhagen's opinions. For example, the basic thesis: "In the question of land, as in everything else, what is necessary from the humanitarian point of view is right for our times and for our country. This programme, based on such consideration, is socialist, because the task of socialism is to realise the rational."

This way of thinking was very clearly opposed to the general Marxist ideology of the party. Lindhagen argued from certain values, which he named, and which were considered to have objective validity, not from a historical interpretation of the predictions connected to them. The idea of class conflict was not central to his argument. In his presentation of the goals of socialism, in the reported motion there was a hint of sympathies for which the Marxists called a petit-bourgeois system of production.

Humanism came to be combined with the land question due to Lindhagen's position as farming expert, and initiator of reforms in land legislation. However, congress' decisions meant that Lindhagen's proposals regarding the land issue were largely accepted, even though the programme text which was drawn up by him as chairman of the committee for the land programme was somewhat changed. One the other hand, those proposals, based on a very special humanist point of view, were only accepted in certain details. Behind the decision lay a report of the special land committee, appointed by the party executive and congress.

Apart from the final paragraph regarding the international aims of the party, the basic principles were worded as follows (changes and important additions are in italics):

Social Democracy is distinguished from other political parties in that it desires to transform completely the economic organisation of the bourgeois society and bring about the social liberation of the *oppressed classes* to the satisfaction and development of the spiritual and material culture. The main cause of the deformity that in part characterises the present civilisation is the mode of production of private capital, which has dissolved the old petit-bourgeois society, amassed fortunes in the hands of a few and *made the conflict between the workers and the capitalists into the most characteristic aspect of the society of today.*

In earlier times private ownership of the means of production was a natural condition for production in that it assured the producer of his product. But to the extent that large scale manufacture supersedes craft, the machine, the tool, world trade and mass production breaks down all limits, to that extent the real producers are transformed into a class of wage earners, who in themselves include numerous elements of the middle-classes oppressed during the period of the development of capitalism, and who are socially characterised by their lack of possessions and their *insecurity,* and its consequent dependence and oppression.

Capitalism does not only require the submission of the wage earners. Even when it allows the old middle classes—small farmers, craftsmen, small tradesmen—formally to exist it undermines their independence. As far as farming is concerned small farmers feel their debt to private capital very strongly, and the dependent small farmer is hardly less oppressed than the dispossessed agricultural worker working on other peoples land.

The extraordinary technical achievements in the labour process, the enormously increased productivity of human labour, the continuous opening up of new production areas, the whole of the capitalist development in which national fortunes have been multiplied brings with it on the one hand an unnatural amassing of wealth, on the other hand a colossal growth of the working class.

But at the same time, these conditions and this disastrous tendency in society's development force the workers into a countermovement. As a class they organise themselves into *trade unions* in order to gain for themselves as much as possible of the products of labour in the form of wages, and also *by consumer cooperation bring about a reduction in the cost of living.*

In the same way the struggle between the workers and those who purchase their labour on the national and international market continues and assumes still more intense forms. On the commodity market a similar struggle between the various interest groups begins to appear. This class struggle will never cease until society is so organised that the fruits of labour are given to those who labour.

This demand is fulfilled when the means of production and labour are joined together (independent small farming or small scale craft). But over and above that it must be demanded that in modern production, dominated by large scale production, the monopoly of private capital must be transferred into state control and ownership, so that the present unplanned production can be replaced by a production planned according to the real needs of society, so that the means of production are utilised in the economically most advantageous manner.

This goal can only be realised through the organisation and political struggle of the working class and other groups in society who suffer from capitalist exploitation. Therefore Social Democracy, whose task is to clarify the goal and the means for achieving this goal and to unite the mass of the people, tries to win political power in order to bring about the socialist organisation of society, in the direction in which the development itself points.

Therefore Social Democracy wishes to do away with class power and create a firm base for the economic and spiritual freedom of all the people. It wishes to do away with poverty and introduce a type of society which allows everybody free access to bread, freedom and individual responsibility.

No further account of the changes will be given here. We will return to certain important points in our presentation of the programme revision of 1920 which in part meant the realisation of some of the tendencies which appeared in the text of 1911. In this context a reminder of the most important new points is sufficient.

Regarding the question of the goals of Social Democracy one point in the programme was directly connected to Lindhagen's motion. Apart from the old explanation of goals in the first paragraph, in the last quoted paragraph there was a statement according to which Social Democracy wanted to "do away with poverty and introduce a type of society which allows everybody free access to bread, freedom and individual responsibility."

The programme shows a tendency to rank in the same category as the working class the middle classes—small farmers, craftsmen and small merchants. In the first paragraph the "working class" is no longer mentioned. Now the social liberation of "the oppressed classes" is spoken of. In the second paragraph those words have been omitted which describe society as divided between workers and capitalists, and which describe other classes as occupying a "mid-position."

In the new fourth paragraph, which clearly goes against the logical line of the rest, it is said that capitalism undermines the independence of the middle classes. This way of thinking appears to be a consequence of one of the basic ideas lying at the root of the programme revision, namely that the right of ownership of the small holders was legitimate. This is proved by characterising the small holders as oppressed by capitalism and by quite definitely transferring them to the proletariat class. If the Marxist starting point was in any way to be retained the only thing to do was to establish that at one and the same time an individual could be both owner and oppressed. If the small holders did not belong to the oppressed classes, then they must be opposed. Some years previously Wicksell had written that Social Democracy was doubtful as to whether it should see the small holders "as exploiters or exploited," whether or not they should "threaten them as the capitalists, or confront them as the proletariat." This doubt was now settled.

But of necessity the small holders brought with them craftsmen and small merchants. If the former belonged to the oppressed classes, then the latter must also do so. The slide which had already begun continued in 1920 and led to a remarkable ideological reorganisation of the main line of thought of the programme.

Changes in the sixth paragraph were intended partly to establish cooperation in the development scheme. Furthermore, the final sentence in this paragraph was changed, with reference to the new characteristics of the middle classes. The terms under which the class struggle would cease were no longer that "the working class ceased to be a class of wage earners," but that "society is so organised that the fruits of labour go to those who labour."

According to the seventh paragraph this latter demand is fulfilled (and thereby the new position in regard to the middle classes justified) when "the means of production are united (independent small farming or small scale craft). This hints that the means of production owned by the small holders and the craftsmen are not to be socialised. Private ownership on a small scale and small scale production are accepted. In what follows it is only the fact that private capital monopoly in large scale production shall be transferred to society that is mentioned.

In the eight paragraph political action must take the consequences of the presentation of socio-economic development previously given. The political struggle is not to be fought by the working class alone but also by "other groups in society who suffer from capitalist exploitation." This is the only time that the word "exploitation" is used in this paragraph, despite the fact that it was a concept that was to be at the heart of the principles as they were shaped in 1920.

Taken as a whole, the programme revision of 1911 meant that ideologically the Social Democratic party ceased to appear as a labour party in the customary meaning of the term. Practically without debate, and apparently without reflection, and with a general emphasis on belief in Marx, an idea was rejected that was absolutely basic to Marxism, and which earlier had dominated Swedish socialist debate.

The debate on basic principles was confined to an exchange of opinions between Branting and Lindhagen. First Branting stressed the importance of the suggested revision of the programme. Socialism had never opposed non-capitalist small ownership, but was concerned only with fighting oppressing and exploiting private capital. By now this had been clearly expressed in the programme. However, Branting considered that small scale production would not come to be a large part of the total production. The socialised sector would quite definitely be of the greatest importance. The main part of Branting's speech consisted of a criticism of Lindhagen, whose humanism he considered to be reactionary, a return to utopian ways of thinking. Basic to modern socialism were the fundamental achievement won by Marx and Engels.

One "saw socialism as a link in a continuous development, prepared and created by capitalism itself. Therefore, the most natural transmitters of socialism are the members of the working class, whose class interests force it forward in the direction of socialism, and whose liberation means the liberation of the whole of mankind." Talking of justice and reason was not equivalent to setting forth sign-posts for development. An institution such as slavery, for example, had disintegrated due to economic development, not because it was considered to be unjust. Nevertheless, the party executive considered that certain good points contained in Lindhagen's proposal should be taken up. Amongst other things Lindhagen replied that whilst the economic interests were certainly of great importance as sources of power, man's ability to think independently should not be forgotten. One may not, as Branting recommended, "wait resignedly, which is better named reactionary and in every case is orthodox." It was necessary to set up a goal and idealise concepts. "Mankind longs for the economic liberation of the oppressed, but even more he longs for the spiritual freedom of all people, the inner freedom. This latter is by no means unimportant. Perhaps it is the real banner, the final aim that must inflame us all."

The point regarding the land question (XII) was worded as follows:

The soil and its riches, as all other important means of production, should be in the hands of the people. However, as within farming small-scale production at present exists and develops side by side with large scale production, and because in that field capitalism is in part taking other forms than it takes in industry, the fight against exploitation must to some extent follow different lines. Small-holders and crofters form the largest proportion of Swedish farming. For the small holders, the soil is not a means of gaining the fruits of others' labour, but only a means of obtaining the bare necessities of life for himself and his family. Just as the wage earners, they belong to the exploited classes. A land policy aimed at benefiting these people should consequently aim at increasing the produce of the land. It should stop the land being a victim of capitalist monopoly and speculation and instead assure those who work the land of the fruits of their labour. Society should insure that all who wish to work on the land can have suitable land on reasonable terms and under conditions of security.

In accordance with this, the party requires:

Private monopoly of natural riches, large forests, mines, waterfalls and large peat-bogs, to be transferred to the state. The system of concessions as a transition to socialisation. When reasonable land donations made by the crown to be returned to the state. Important waterways for timber floating to be taken over by the state. The state and municipalities to increase their land possessions. Depending on circumstances the farming domains to be given over either to large-scale production—through leasing out to cooperative production, or, until the time is ripe for this, to private persons, but with satisfactory guarantees for the workers—or to small-scale production under terms which ensure its existence and the right of the farmers. Plots of land to be replaced by leaseholdership rights, priority rights with regard to purchasing, and right of repurchase.

The right of industrial and forestry workers to unite themselves into organisations to be maintained. Professional inspection to be extended to the larger land and forest concerns and include domestic inspection. The secure possession of suitable land to be given over to agricultural workers and others who desire to be small holders, or to form cooperatives. In the last analysis this can be acquired by forcibly taking over large possessions (corporation domains, manors).

Crofters, those leasing from the companies, or leasing plots on other peoples' land can be dispossessed if necessary by force. Those farming other peoples' land to be safeguarded by effective legislation in the question of leases.

Independent small farmers and small-holders to be supported against all types of corporation and big ownership power.

Cooperation between farmers, and all other means by which small holders can gain the advantages of large scale production to be strongly promoted. Training in farming to be promoted. Rational forestry.

Credit for use in farming and accommodation, particularly for those with less means, to be directly regulated by society (state and municipality). Cooperative credit funds to be encouraged.

The first paragraph of this point has the character of an statement of principles and its justification and from this point of view belongs amongst general principles. No other point in the political programme begins with a similar declaration. Almost certainly this paragraph, as indeed the whole point regarding the land question, was first edited (this was also hinted at by Branting) and later the required changes made in the general basic principles. Most important in this paragraph is that the incomparably biggest part of the farming population is said to belong to the exploited classes. Therefore land policy should aim at increasing the products of the land, preventing capitalist monopoly and speculation and assuring the farm workers of the fruits of their labour.

From these very vague statements it is possible to arrive at a concrete demand, which was a mixture of socialisation and of safeguards for small scale production. Private monopoly of special natural riches should be transferred to the society. The state and municipalities should increase their land possessions. The latter proposition should be interpreted to mean that this increase should only take place at the cost of the corporations and large-scale owners.

However the socially owned land should not be given over to the state: rather it should be given to cooperative organisations or to private persons. The right of ownership on a small scale should be respected. Independent small holders should be supported against "all types of corporations and large-scale ownership power" and it was not anticipated that the state's right of ownership would enter into the question. Farmers who were not independent should be secured of their rights of possession or—although the programme is not quite clear on this point—be given ownership rights to the lands they farmed (Compare with the Land Programme Committee's proposal, and party executive's reporter in the debate, B. Eriksson).

Of ideological interest in this programme is the fact that by this the party definitely committed itself to a land policy which was not the same as the policy with regard to industry. As far as industry was concerned, Marx's slogan still obtained: first concentration in private hands, then socialisation. Regarding farming, on the other hand, it was established that concentration should be opposed and that small-scale enterprise and the right of ownership on a small scale should be supported. The entire Marxist scheme was rejected as far as farming was concerned. No inevitable developmental tendencies were noted. Political intervention was seen as something quite different and more than just a sanction of the progress of the production process. Here Lindhagen's "humanism" had clearly been victorious, even if the defeated were not conscious of that fact. In principle the reversal was just as remarkable as if the party had decided to oppose the tendencies to concentration within industry and declared its support for small enterprise and craft.

The debate at the party congress on land questions was characterised by an emphasis on tactics. A long line of speakers emphasised that it was necessary to win small holders and unpropertied farmers to the party. But the programme revision was also defended with arguments founded on fact. Above all it was asserted that to a certain extent small-scale production had shown itself to be useful, and that the independence of the small holders was valuable. Although no decisive opposition to the revision emerged, several speakers expressed reservations (Carleson, Adler, Lowegren, Rosling). They considered that even within farming large-scale production was superior, and that at the very least there should be experimental investigations into this point, before unconditionally accepting the value of small-scale production. Strengthening of the right of private ownership was in conflict with socialist principles.

The party executive had paid too much attention to Liberal and Conservative propaganda which maintained that socialism wanted to dispossess the farmers of their land. However, the alterations in the programme were decided upon without voting. From several directions there came the insistence that a special land value tax should be required in the programme (on the so-called unearned increment) but this demand was seen by others as likely to cause anxiety amongst the farmers and worsen the outlook of the party.

At the congress of 1911 yet another couple of points were altered in the area under discussion. On the suggestion of the party executive, who proceeded from a motion on the subject, the second paragraph of point VII was worded as follows: "The abolition of all indirect taxes—which weigh heaviest on the productive classes—above all by lively opposition to duties."

With this the principle of free trade, previously expressed only through a general repudiation of indirect taxes, was strongly emphasised. Fabian Månsson was foremost amongst the critics of the duty system. He expressed his views in a notable article, and in 1909 in the youth organisation brought through a declaration against duties. Månsson took as his starting point various points of view regarding the principle of free trade, which were hardly socialist. Quite simply, protectionism was a method by which a few owners and businessmen were able to tax the great mass of the people. "Duties are nothing less than sheer robbery. Parliament is used to force the poor to buy poor quality goods cheaply. There are only two types of people who support duties: thieves and idiots." Several contributions to the debate supported free trade. However, some speakers were of the opinion that for a short period and in certain cases protective duties were necessary and that workers in industries which depended on protective duties had difficulties in freeing themselves from short term egotistic motives. This was regarded as an indication of the advantages of duties. (Söderberg, Rosling, Johansson). The proposal of the party executive was accepted without vote. Furthermore, an addition was made to the point regarding protective legislation (IX), worded as follows: "Workers protective legislation to be brought about, without regard to sex."

An examination of the municipal policies of Social Democracy is outside the scope of this work. However, some main points of the municipal programme accepted at the congress in 1911 (a similar provisional programme had been decided on as early as 1908) should be mentioned here. In the introduction it was stated that the task of the municipalities had become of great importance for the realising of the socialist organisation of society. "Within municipal administration radical steps could be taken with the aim of transferring enterprises owned by private capital into the ownership or control of the state, and also to protect and support the poor classes in their struggle for improved conditions of livelihood." The primary demand was total democracy in the muncipalities.

In the following several concrete demands were made. In a section dealing with "municipal socialism" it was demanded that "business enterprises of a local character which are of general importance for the conditions of livelihood of the population and which exhibit monopolistic tendencies" should be transferred to municipal ownership and management. Municipal land policy should be aimed at increased municipal land ownership, particularly in those areas where townlike communities could be built. By means of suitable support and by themselves building municipalities should increase the number of dwellings, with particular reference to the needs of those of lesser means. The municipalities should be model employers, setting the pattern for other enterprises. According to the programme, municipal duties with regard to health services, social policy and education system should be extended, with particular reference to the poorer groups in society.

The municipal programme later remained unchanged, though an extensive revision of a formal nature was brought about at the Congress of 1928. The programme was not altered on the points mentioned at the congresses of 1914 and 1917.

From the beginning the parliamentary policy of Social Democracy was characterised by a formal correctness, by adaptation and by moderation. During the six years in which Branting alone represented the party, he introduced a practice, which remained unchanged, that the party grew from being a handful of representatives to being the strongest group in the lower house. Branting maintained a dominant position within the parliamentary faction, which consisted mainly of the older and more careful members, although at the party congresses he had to fight a growing opposition. Obstruction and demonstration were not part of the party's tactics. The Social Democrats took part in committee and plenary business in a reasonable and objective manner. Contributions of a principle or "high flown" nature were very rare.

The conventions of parliament were carefully respected. Moderation in proposals and motions was as conspicuous as this superficial adaption. In parliament the party did not press its more far-reaching demands. In general it satisfied itself with going one step further than the liberals with regard to those questions which were the order of the day. Until 1914 the liberals were the strongest left-wing party, and for a long period afterwards they maintained a decisive mid-position. Very early in parliament Social Democracy had the character of a radical reformist party, not of a party dedicated to the total transformation of society.

All of this was connected with several factors. The tradition of the Swedish parliament was that of calm and benevolent cooperation, and as such did not allow harsh treatment of the new party. At the same time it acted as a deterrent to wild behaviour and violent declarations. Men like Branting, Lindquist, Thorsson and Viktor Larsson fitted into this background very well, and soon gained personal popularity. The working methods adopted in the Swedish parliament made general debates very difficult, and favoured an informed detailed way of working. Partly because of this large ideological confrontations between the parties are very rare in Swedish politics. No general debate on socialism has ever taken place in parliament.

Cooperation with the liberals must seem natural to a Social Democratic party who wished to meet short-term demands advantageous to the working classes, and who rejected the idea of revolutionary propaganda which did not have immediate practical results. In the first place both the left-wing parties desired to achieve total democracy, and in other questions too they were largely in agreement, for instance questions of social policy, defence and temperance. There was a more or less open and systematic collaboration between the two parties during the period prior to 1920, with the exception of some short periods. This did not mean that there was no friction between them. In particular with regard to laws against propaganda hostile to defence, and against certain other types of agitation which were put through by the first Staaff ministry (1906) and also with regard to the position adopted by the liberals during the great strike. But collaboration was the rule. The Lindman ministry (1906–1911) was opposed by both parties. When the second liberal government (Staaff 1911–14) first made its appearance it was assured of the benevolent attitude of the Social Democrats, particularly because it advocated de-escalation of defence expenses.

Later conflicts occurred, mainly in the question of defence, but conditions at the time of the government's retirement strengthened the solidarity of the Left. As opposed to the Hammarskjöld government 1914–17) the Left largely pursued a unified policy.

Cooperation with the liberals was a result of Social Democracy's moderation, but it was also intended to strengthen and develop that moderation. Time after time a fear emerges in debates that due to demands which were too long-term cooperation might be endangered, and a sharp line of difference be created between the Liberals and the Social Democrats. This was thought to make the liberals less inclined to reforms and in that way reduce the chances of reaching political results which favoured the working classes. But not only political tactics but also the very political position itself must have been affected by the continuous respect for that which could be accomplished by parliamentary means, and for the strong involvement in practical detailed work.

Quite unconsciously the ideas of the Social Democratic leaders became oriented towards short-term matters, and problems of socialism in the real sense were pushed into the background.

All parties who advocate an extreme political opinion, and one which is totally rejected by the opposition, present a different view of themselves in parliament to the one they give to the people, that is if their behaviour in parliament is not only of a demonstrative character. The political appeals with which it was believed that a final victory amongst party supporters could be prepared would put a total stop to any gains the party might make were they used within the framework of parliamentary representation.

In order to secure concessions from the opposition, it is necessary partly to compromise, and partly—perhaps most important—to try to find common ground in arguments, and look for a common value basis. The resulting dilemma was clearly the foremost characteristic of the tactics of the Swedish Social Democracy. There was a definite gap between the mild appeals made by the party leaders in parliament on account of the positions adopted by the other parties, and the violent accusations and sweeping promises made to the working classes. This double policy does not seem to have meant difficulties for the leading Social Democrats themselves. On this point too the specific Marxist position to some extent constitutes an explanation. The large-scale propaganda stemmed from the general Marxist perspective, according to which the victory of socialism is a necessary consequence of development. In parliament many details were dealt with that were only peripheral to "development" as a whole. From the point of view of Marxism it was totally impossible to propose socialisation in parliament, because society was not yet ready for socialism. From the parliamentary point of view the Marxist belief was more a sort of source of inner strength that justified tactics and compromises. But in the long run it is difficult to maintain this attitude. The tactical line has a tendency to become involved with principles—the principle of meaninglessness!

The initiative taken by the Social Democrats during this period, and several other contributions they made can be seen as an attempt to achieve goals which were considered to be to the most immediate advantage of the poorer people, and in particular the industrial working class. That is to say, social policy stood at the helm. Without exception the party cooperated in the important social reforms which were accomplished in this period, though generally whilst maintaining a more radical attitude than the one which was accepted. For example with regard to the Work Protection Law of 1912—which included amongst other things regulations regarding the working conditions of women and children—and the law regarding general pension insurance in 1913. When the latter mentioned issue was taken up some Social Democrats moved that an attempt should be made to throw out the government's proposal, in order later to bring about better legislation. However, the majority of the party voted in favour of the proposal, whilst criticising it in part.

Several statements made by Branting at the conclusion of his contribution to the debate in the lower house were characteristic of the ideas regarding social policy which dominated in the party. He did not wish to criticise those who on principle had reservations about the proposal. "But if I think of us others, of we who usually discuss, weighing pros and cons, I think that it can be said that there exists here a dividing line between reformist and negative socialism. . . . There is also a little piece of common sense which says that even if one votes against this issue, it will be carried through all the same! Later one may attack the decision, and beating ones breast point out that one said no because of a desire to make things better for the working classes! For my part, however, I believe such a tactic to be unworthy of a mass party. We must make our decisions in a critical and solemn moment. We must decide now for the future how we should lay the foundations of the building of social insurance. The best thing is to come out into the open, to act as men and not hide behind one excuse or another." Above all it should be observed that in debates on social reforms these were never presented as something relatively unimportant, though this was common during the first phase of the movement. Neither was socialisation spoken of as the only cure.

The Social Democrats took the initiative to several economic and social reforms. Some of their proposals yielded no results, whilst others led to investigations and had some affect on legislation. To mention one of the most important examples, in 1905 the parliamentary group presented a motion regarding pensions for invalids and the aged. In 1908 they presented a motion regarding the 8-hour working day and the abolition of corn duties, in 1910 a motion concerning unemployment insurance and in 1913 a motion regarding a legal minimum wage. With the support of the parliamentary group, Lindhagen proposed several motions in connection with the party programme regarding the land question. In the debates on these motions, general social-reformist points of view were put forward which were not particularly characterised by the idea of socialisation. Such points of view were also the justification for this type of motion. In several instances the party received support from the liberals and their proposals collapsed due to opposition from the conservative upper house. The proposal regarding a legal minimum wage rested upon the idea that every citizen should have a livelihood fit for a human being. All parties should agree that "society is to be organised as a 'good home.'" Similar reasons were put forward in the all-embracing and comprehensive motion prepared by Rydén regarding the 8-hour working day. The physical and cultural development of the workers was in the interests of society, and increased leisure time was demanded if this was to be given the attention which was its due. This would also be to the advantage of production. Rydén ended his speech in the lower house, in which he defended the motion with the words: "The issue which I have allowed myself to present to the lower house for their consideration, is to me a great national question. I have asked myself the question: What is to be gained if we, in our country, have created the most advanced industry anywhere to be found if at the same time we have expended the capital in the form of the health and mental soundness of the Swedish people? What is to be gained if we create such an industry if the race, the physical strength and hygiene of the people is gradually worn down, or is damaged at the roots? I have demonstrated the signs of degeneration which already exist. I have pointed out the fact that the industrial worker himself, and his family life, are being ruined and for my part I believe that, whatever changes are going to take place in the patterns of home-life in future development such home-life will always be a stable part of the individual's existence." These points of view are the same as those expressed in 1846 by Macaulay the Whig politician, when he appealed for a legal limit to working hours. It has already been suggested that the Social Democrats did not take the initiative to more far-sighted steps in the direction of socialisation. And in the few cases in which the question of extending the rights of the state, or of new forms for state production came forward, general ideas of socialisation were not maintained. In the debates about the state's agreement with Grangesbergabolag regarding the orefields of the north in 1906 and 1907, Branting demanded that the state should have greater rights than in the proposals contained in the said provisions. He strongly criticised the government for submitting to plutocratic interests. However, his ideas were shared by representatives of both conservatives and liberals, and his arguments are by no means unique. As opposed to when the question of mines was taken up in 1897, this time Branting did not speak of a more general socialisation. Later, on several occasions, the party proposed motions regarding the abolition of the right to mining claims, and the replacing of this with a system of concessions. However, not even in these proposals was the demand for socialisation stressed. The tobacco monopoly decided upon in 1914 came about with the cooperation of the large part of the party. Existing differences of opinion, however, were not concerned with principles.

However, the press on the one hand asserted that the tobacco monopoly was the sign of the advance of socialism, on the other hand that it went against the ideas of socialism because it was not to the advantage of the consumers. It should also be mentioned that on a couple of occasions the Social Democratic group proposed motions regarding the extension of the right to expropriate for social ends, and that individual Social Democrats put forward a motion regarding the investigation of trusts and cartels. (Palmstierna 1910 and 1911), and also investigations concerned with control of the use of special natural resources at present privately owned (Lindhagen and others 1911). Both the latter mentioned motions, proposed by former liberals, contain quite an amount of socialist ideas. Palmstierna emphasised the concentration of capital and explained that gradually this must lead to intervention on the part of the state. Lindhagen tried to show that "industrial anarchism makes a rational use of natural resources impossible." The debates concerning these proposals were short and no contribution was made which was more connected to the program of the Social Democrats. Palmstierna in particular took up the question of the socialising of water-power (hydraulic power) both inside and outside parliament.

The period from 1914–1920 was a period of transition in Swedish Social Democracy. Internal conflicts became more severe, and led to the splitting of the party in 1917. Those who were sympathetic to the ideas of the Social Democratic Youth Organisation formed a new, left-wing socialist party which was strongly influenced by the victory of Russian communism. However, as early as in 1914 the majority of the party desired cooperation with the liberals, and after the election in 1917, in which the party largely maintained its position (86 Social Democrats and 11 left-wing socialists were elected) such collaboration became a fact. Under the liberal-socialist Edén minister (1917–1920), the constitution was made more democratic and certain social reforms were brought about which had been propagated for a long time. Conspicuous amongst these was provisionary legislation regarding the 8-hour working day. Collaboration with the liberals meant the sanctioning of the reformist tactics. But at the end of this period of collaboration, the question of socialisation was taken up for debate within the party. At the congress of 1920 the programme was revised and given a more radical orientation and the purely Social Democratic government which replaced Edén made the question of social transformation current once again by means of decisions made on the basis of several investigations.

Before entering into a discussion of the question of socialisation about 1920, let us stop for a few moments and look at the development of the party before that. The party's policy during the war years very largely was concerned with questions which were directly connected with the present situation. In particular an attempt was made to influence commercial and industrial policy so that it would benefit the poorer people. However, there is no reason to investigate these questions as they are not important as far as the general development of the party's ideology is concerned. Those aspects which should be noted from the point of view of the debate about economic and social ideas are the split in the party, the proposals regarding socialisation put forward in parliament during the war years, and the position adopted by the party regarding state control of the economy during the war—the so-called war-socialism.

Apart from questions of personalities and power, the differences between the party leadership and the youth organisation which led to the break-away by the left-socialists in 1917 were mainly concerned questions which were outside the social-economic area, in particular the question of defence. Therefore the split within the party can better be illustrated in other contexts. However, to a certain extent there was also a difference of opinion regarding the economic and social policy of the party. Z. Höglund and other representatives of the Left criticised the parliamentary group for not having worked to bring about the demands of the party with sufficient energy. It was not demanded that the question of socialisation should be taken up, because the time was not yet considered to be ripe for socialism, but it was considered that in the main the policy of the party leadership was characterised by a tendency towards the bourgeois, an increasing tendency to make compromises, and that mainly this was caused by collaboration with the liberals.

It should however be emphasised that questions connected with this did not play an important part in the party split. Neither was this split connected with any particularly Marxist point of view within the party opposition. Many leading men—Höglund, Ström and Carleson—concerned themselves with Marxist formulations, but others—for example Lindhagen and Fabian Månsson—were influenced by Marx only to a very small extent. During the summer and autumn of 1916, articles appeared in the new organ of the party Left ("Politik") which accused the party leadership of a developmental fatalism inspired by Marx. It was only after the split that a special left-socialist doctrine was developed, influenced by the communist interpretation of Marx. The situation regarding the conflicts before the split was characterised by the fact that certain member of the majority criticised both the party leadership and the opposition on the grounds of theoretical vagueness. In an article pertaining to the conflict, Engberg accused the party left, in particular Lindhagen, of having rejected social-economic determinism which was unconditionally connected with Marxism. At the same time he explained that the majority of the party should take much of the blame for what had occurred. Current politics had attracted all the interest, and theoretical questions had been put on one side. Neuman, another of the party's leading journalists asserted that the youth organisation, in that it had relatively small interest in economic questions, had in this respect connections with the traditional policy of the party. In the same way as did the party leadership, the young opponents used radical phraseology without making any attempt to involve themselves in the problems of which they spoke, nor to try to suggest solutions to them. The youth organisation "is merely a natural development of bourgeois radicalism in the guise of socialism which our party has always been, though perhaps not previously so clearly as at present. . . . Probably this does not seem to be a fitting comment to make, but the question is certainly called for: When do Herr Branting, and all the other leading Swedish Social Democrats who are one with him, intend to stop edifying us with the gesture, pleasant in itself, which is often the most convincing in authoritarian Swedish Social Democracy, and sit down at the table to try to get a socialist grip on at least some of the important economic problems of Swedish politics."

During the war years the Social Democrats and left-socialists suggested various proposals regarding state production and state monopoly. Some of these were the direct result of the situation during the war. Others were aimed at rectifying more specific errors. In these instances the underlying motivation was not characterised by socialist principles. Examples of this are the motions regarding a state galoshes factory, a state industrial programme for the refining of products of the state's forests, a state paper-industry, a state brickyard and a state monopoly of mineral oils. None of these motions led to a debate of any particular interest.

Certain others were of a greater importance with regard to principles.

At the 1917 parliament there was a proposal from the left-socialists regarding the establishing of a state merchant navy. In general the Social Democrats did not support the proposal, but in the lower house Rydén maintained that the socialisation of ship-owning would be recommended when this had more closely approached trust-formation. He said that he was convinced that "the iron grip which capitalism has on the large proportion of Swedish people forces state measures and state intervention of a degree quite different from that first considered possible." At the same parliament Palmstierna put forward a motion regarding the investigation of the state monopoly of corn import. It was stressed that due to the crisis a sort of state monopoly on corn import had occurred. The Standing Committee of Ways and Means rejected this, with reservations from the Social Democrats. During the debate, which ended with the rejection of the motion, Palmstierna expressed the opinion that the motion was an expression of a socialist way of thinking, but he also referred to several forms of state socialism which had already been realised, and said that it was only necessary to progress even further along the chosen path. At the parliaments of both 1917 and 1918 the Social Democrats introduced motions regarding socialisation with reference to two important industries—the sugar industry and the coal industry. It is sufficient here to rest at the treatment of these questions in 1918. The proposal regarding investigations into state monopoly and production and import of sugar were rejected by the committee concerned but the Social Democratic members demanded approval of the same, justifying their demand on the grounds of principles. "With those ideas that we harbour concerning the obligations which should be incumbent upon a society based on the norms of general justice, it must seem to us to be a goal worth striving for that industries for the production of commodities which exist within the country and which have reached such a monopoly position as that held by the sugar industry are in the hands of the state, in that state powers are such that they can regulate production to the advantage of *all* members of society, and without regard to private interests connected with various industries. The dearly purchased experience of the war years has allowed this to emerge in its correct light, and shown how not once has private interest in the face of the peoples' need chosen to depart from the viewpoint of private capitalism. . . ." In the debate in the lower house the Social Democrats alleged that this was a question of nationalising an already existing monopoly, and that therefore even those who on principle were opposed to socialisation could accept the proposal (Möller, Sterne, Engberg). The house made its decision in accordance with the reservations of the Social Democrats, but the question was rejected in the upper house. On the other hand, the question of an inquiry into the take-over of the coal industry in Skåne was accepted by the committee concerned, when the Social Democrats received the support of some of the liberals. Strangely enough, however, the arguments put by the committee were characterised by socialist ideas: It is a more and more common view that the real natural resources form a basic fixed capital or, if you wish, a capital that by its very nature is invested in a given nation.

Such capital should not be used with reference to the amount of profit which can be gained by private exploiters, but above all with full responsibility for both living and unborn human beings. . . . Therefore society must have control over natural resources. If they are exploited to the advantage of private profit there may be incalculable economic dangers for society in the future." In the debate in the lower house the Social Democrats were of the same opinion but they asserted that even from a social-reformist-liberal starting point the motion could be supported (Branting, Möller, Engberg, P. A. Hansson).

Several liberals, however, could not accept the motion, and it was rejected. When the proposal regarding a new water law was taken up at the parliament of 1918, the Social Democrats tried to maintain a greater right for the state with regard to the use of hydraulic power than did the Conservative and Liberal parties, in this connection presenting points of view similar to those they had put forward regarding the issues which have just been dealt with. At the parliament of 1920 the Social Democrats supported a proposal put forward by the left-socialists regarding an investigation into the nationalising of insurance. On the other hand the Social Democrats adopted a rejecting attitude regarding a more general suggestion of socialisation, which had been presented at the 1917 parliament by the left socialist group who had recently left the party. The proposal was based on the idea of an investigation into the extent and degree to which the state could extend state production and also raise state incomes "by the taking over of certain natural resources, industries, means of communication and private banks" and "partly safeguard the economic and social interests of other societies, and partly, and finally, create increased social and economic security for the people of the land." The motions of this nature which were put forward in both houses were criticised sharply by the Social Democrats. The party's members of the committee that prepared the motion in the lower house in particular were against the idea that a government that was not socialist should have the task of investigating problems of socialisation. Those presenting the motions were said to have overestimated the chances of a rapid transition to a socialist order: "the internal social development must have reached a certain degree of maturity before it is possible to think that it is possible to realise the Social Democratic view of society." Specific socialisation measures were however authorised, and the Social Democratic suggestion regarding this was referred to. Further, it was stated that "the social democratic parliamentary group has with regard to most aspects of the motions and in the order and in the way that it has been in accordance with the goals, cooperated in the rapid change of society in the direction of socialism, and it is to be expected that this group in the future too will give all its energy to winning this goal, the realising of which is their greatest task."

Therefore the motion must be rejected as "neither with regard to its general wording nor to the rest of its formulation" is it suitable as a starting point for the work of socialisation. In the short debate which took place in the lower house the Social Democrats took the same line. (Sterns, Palmstierna,

Nilsson), i.e. they were in favour of successive socialisation but were of the opinion that a general inquiry, in particular one entrusted to a "capitalist government," was unsuitable and they criticised details of the motives underlying this motion. No social democrat expressed his opinion in the upper house.

Undeniably it is quite remarkable the Social Democrats helped to reject first suggestion for a more general socialisation ever put forward in the Swedish parliament. Very likely more important motives than those stated in the debates and in the committee report lay behind the party's stand. There are certain statements which hint that the motion was considered to be tactically good. Social Democracy would be forced either to take exception to socialisation or to upset the liberals. One might assume that fear that the question of socialisation would dominate the 1917 election helped to decide the position adopted by Social Democracy. Partly this was concerned with achieving democracy in collaboration with the liberals, partly with the fact that at that time the principle of socialisation was a dangerous platform for propaganda, due to the tremendous lack of popularity of the system of commissions.

A debate on war policy, necessitated by the war itself, clearly exposed the fact that there were great and unclear differences of opinion regarding the meaning of the concepts of socialism and socialisation. This meant that the state regulated commercial and industrial life in a manner which for a long time had no equal in those lands which were at war (generally in a limited sense) and in those lands which were neutral, but affected by the war. Above all this concerned the regulation of distribution and consumption (rationing) but also often was concerned with large areas of production. Sometimes the state provisionally took over the running of certain branches of industry. However, what was typical for "war socialism" was that no expropriation or interference with the right of private ownership of a permanent principle nature took place. As far as Sweden was concerned it was mainly a question of regulating, often in detail, of distribution and consumption, but in our case too there was no lack of state activity in the area of production that had previously been the preserve of private enterprise (Fuel Commission). The system of commissions, which came to symbolise the wartime regulations, was generally considered to be necessary, but was also generally unpopular, partly because quite simply it was the external sign of the lack of commodities, and partly because commissions were considered to function expensively and inefficiently.

The position of Swedish Social Democracy with regard to war socialism can schematically be recognised in that at the beginning there was the tendency to see in it a step in the direction of socialism, though later this was generally seen as being of a non-socialist character. In several instances conflicting interpretations were presented in one newspaper after another. It is not possible to judge the extent to which the development of opinion depended on theoretical considerations, or was caused by the general discontent with the crisis commissions. Clearly the Swedish debate as the German debate was not a little affected by this. It should be remembered that in the bourgeois camp a development in the opposite direction can be discerned. At first it was denied that the crisis policy was socialist and later its unpopularity was used in the fight against the Social Democrats.

At the beginning of 1915 P. A. Hansson took up the subject of "War socialism" in a series of articles in "Social Demokraten." This did not involve socialism in its real meaning. "But it is a great overstatement to say that these general instances of interference have nothing at all to do with socialism. Call it nationalising, or making municipal, or state capitalism or whatever you like, but this does not alter the fact that certain concessions to socialist principles have been made . . . regarding the production and distribution of the products of labour . . . One cannot get away from the fact that an area which previously was in the hands of private ownership has been annexed, socialised by the state. . . . What remains is to extend the socialist nature of these measures, to fill the mould with a socialist content. By development in the direction of full democracy, by the assuming of power by the working class in the state and the municipalities we gain the means to make truly socialist what has so long been only half or quarter socialism." Two years later, also in "Social Demokraten" Nils Karleby presented the same opinion with even greater energy. Undoubtedly war socialism was an attempt to save capitalism, but to the extent that it involved the transferring of production and distribution from private capital to the state it was "an important precondition for the socialist organisation of society." When society made the plans, and all capitalists had to do was to pick up the profits, the road was being laid for socialism. "However, what is demanded is that the anti-capitalist masses possess the political power which allows them to fill the mould with their own spirit. From the point of view of socialist production the importance of the world war is that it has demonstrated the superiority of socially organised production and distribution over that of private capital." The same opinion was put forward in several other newspapers. At the beginning of the war "Ny Tid" wrote that war socialism was "an attempt to mobilise for socialism." When society became "the regulator of economic power what is it but the other side of socialism, although in a temporary and incomplete form." The crisis policy was seen as "socialism in times of necessity," as the "forerunner of real socialism." Certainly in the states taking part in the war, measures had been taken with the intention of strengthening the nation during the war, but they could also be used to increase the well-being of the people. "It is the great mass of the people who will give to various measures not only their democratic character, but also the aim of serving the general welfare of the people." According to the Örebro Kuriren, the government's decision in the question of provisions was "an important victory for the ideas of state socialism that social democracy attaches to this question." In the main war socialism involves "the acceptance of our point of view . . . small steps in the direction of socialism." In an article concerning "The war and socialism" the newspaper was ironic about the intervention by state authorities, which in point of fact was "pure socialism" though not admitted as such. "Up to now socialism has been that which it is forbidden to preach in the streets but which is discussed in the king's council. Socialism is growing on us, whilst the name frightens those who are not used to thinking, or who for other reasons cannot adopt a stand." It should also be mentioned that in the motion proposed by the left-socialists in 1917 regarding the taking over by the state of certain natural resources, the crisis policy was referred to as evidence of the practical possibilities of socialism.

All the reported speeches contain the same central theme. Regulation during the war was described as being socialist in form. In order for such regulation to mean real socialism it was further required partly that it had its basis in democracy, and partly that private profit interest should cease to exist. It was also said that a socialist government in the real meaning of the word should aim at general welfare, but basically this demand could only mean that regulation would be practised under normal conditions and not only in times of exceptional need. It was of primary importance in this reasoning that state production was seen as a natural form for socialism. At the end of the war and in the years following, such an idea was almost unanimously rejected. Everything that could be seen to differentiate the crisis policy from a socialist order was stressed. Private ownership had not been abolished. In the main it was only consumption, not production, that was regulated, whilst Social Democracy wanted to organise production in a planned fashion. The aim of the crisis laws was to save capitalism. How could it therefore be a question of socialism? As socialism meant well-being, even affluence, the "rationing of scarcities" that took place during the war could not be socialism. This became a common formula through which the key question in the debate was bypassed. These points of view varied in all the main party newspapers, and were also glimpsed in several parliamentary debates. In an unsigned leader in the summer of 1918 "Social Demokraten" wrote that "the conditions that developed during the period of crisis have nothing to do with the socialism that we Social Democrats wish to see realised in a future society. Socialism in the time of crisis . . . is only a forced emergency measure because non-planned production, together with other connected conditions which are all the results of the private capitalist system, have made the situation completely untenable. Real socialism does not dream of anything like forced submission to an oppressive rationing. Rather, it wants to estimate needs, which is quite another thing." In an article in "Ny Tid" in 1917, Sandler stated that regulation in the crisis period was proof that the socialists were right in their criticism of the private capitalist system, but that it did not mean an application of socialism's positive ideas. Possibly rationing of consumption was communism, but it was not socialism, because socialism wanted to plan production and liberate consumption. In a later article, the crisis policy was described as "quite simply an expression of the urge to survive of the bourgeois society."

"The socialist system of society is not a filing-system," wrote Engberg in "Arbetet," "It is the organisation of production for the needs of everyone, with complete abolition of all production having profit as its aim. Therefore it is not the state organisation of scarcity and hunger. . . . It offers freedom and independence to the unhappy." Under the heading "Is Herr Hammarskjöld a Socialist?", it was noted in Smålands Folkblad that the system of Commissions was introduced on the initiative of this government, and therefore could not be suspected of having socialist tendencies. What was intended by these interferences? It was intended that in a private capitalist society there was no other choice. . . . Had a socialist society existed all these instances of state intervention would not have been needed, because in such a case everything would have flowed normally anyway." Möller put forward the same ideas in an article in "Tiden." Socialism was aimed at an enormous increase of production, and would make all rationing and Commissions "of the present type" unnecessary. It was above all Engberg who, during a parliamentary debate on the Commissions, tried to show that they had nothing to do with real socialism.

In his rejection of the crisis policy as a form of socialism, Engberg asserted quite a different point of view from the one most commonly cited above, in the debate. He described the crisis policy as non-socialist quite simply because it was supported by the state. In parliament he said that "There must also be reasons to stress that we certainly did not think of favouring such a development as would mean that the various branches of production of society would be monopolised and, so to say, have their administrative top layers incorporated into the giant state bureaucracy. God save us from such a state socialist system! We want to get away from the pressure of the state—we do not see state production as any sort of ideal. State capitalism is a necessary transition period, a transition period that, thanks to the growing class struggle, we hope gradually to be able to defeat." In his newspaper, as in his speech regarding the crisis commissions, Engberg maintained that socialism wanted to do away with the state, not strengthen it, and that it had nothing in common with crisis policy. This way of thinking, natural from a Marxist view point, in this context involved a skirting of the issue. Quite clearly the question under discussion was how an action leading to socialisation could be brought about, not how the socialist society of the future should look. For the same reasons it could have been put forward in a debate regarding the right to vote that socialism was not concerned with the right to vote, because it desired to abolish the state.

In the main it is clear that in the debate in question, as in earlier debates on "state socialism," the key question was often ignored. Should socialism, either provisional or permanent, involve state (and municipal) production and regulation, or should it not? If, as would be natural with reference to the earlier actions of the party, this question was answered positively, the relationship between socialism and the crisis policy *from a certain point of view* could not be denied. If the question was answered in the negative, then new guide lines must be drawn up. Without doubt, the desire to take no part in the discomfort surrounding the crisis policy was one of conditions which caused the socialist leaders after the world war eagerly to discuss various possibilities for socialisation, which did not involve "state socialism."

At the county council and Elector elections of 1919 a special part of the party's manifesto was devoted to disassociating itself from the idea that commissions were a form of socialism. It is here stated that the commissions were depicted by the conservatives as a picture in miniature of the socialist society. "The impertinence in this exploiting of bourgeois ignorance about the real content of socialism is very clear, from the fact that social democracy has never aimed at state regulation of consumption. What social democracy wants is to create a new form of production . . . If the bourgeois statement regarding this is any more than a horrible bluff, it would mean that it was the right-wingers who brought about socialism in our country, and the Social Democrats who desire to abolish it! The truth is that as soon as circumstances permit we wish to get rid of the emergency institutions of the capitalist society, and the commissions themselves are one such institution."

During a period of about two years, from the end of 1918 to after the lower house election of 1920, the question of socialisation came to the fore in quite a different way than was the case either previously or later. The preamble to this was a heated debate in the Social Democratic press. A programme revision of 1920 brings up to date and makes more concrete the specific socialist demands. After this follows the preparatory decision on the part of the first Social Democratic government, and an election campaign regarding the question of a socialisation. The general conditions for this new orientation are clear. The realising in principle of political democracy in autumn 1918 meant that the questions which had been at the core of social democratic activity for twenty-five years had been solved. With political democracy came increased power for the party. In accordance with the new regulations, at the election to the upper house a third of the mandate was won (49 seats as compared to 19 seats earlier), and it could be counted on that the extension of the number of voters in the lower house would strengthen the position of the party in the lower house. Under such conditions it was inevitable that the question of the economic reorganisation of society was taken up because ideologically it was of central importance to the party, and it was said to have been put on one side due to the necessity of first winning political democracy. But the issue of socialisation was forced into the open for reasons other than this. The attempt to socialise in Russia stimulated an examination of the problem, even if the revolutionary methods of the communists were rejected by the Social Democrats. The left socialists who had broken away from the Social Democrats closely approached communism, and after this pattern they formulated a doctrine for socialisation that exposed them to criticism and competition. After World War I came to an end uncertain hopes regarding a new society everywhere became politically important. The Social Democratic parties revised their programmes and increased their propaganda, certain that what was called the failure of the capitalist system would offer new opportunities to socialism. In many parts of the world it was thought for some years that a period of extended, maybe eternal peace, would follow the war—a universal victory for government by the people and the building up of happy societies under the leadership of the democratic parties. It was in this atmosphere—a slightly rarefied atmosphere from the point of view of neutral Sweden—of great hopes that the Social Democrats operated.

The discussions proceeded from the fact that social reorganisation must follow political revolution. As was continuously stated, political democracy should be complemented with social democracy. The task of the Social Democratic party was extended and deepened. The issue was no longer to win preparatory successes and, by means of lesser reforms, improve the position of the working class. Now the issue was the creation of a socialist society. There were strong reservations to this positive line. Side by side with the front against the Conservatives and Liberals there existed a front against communism. This combination of radical aspirations and a rejection of the revolutionary and extreme position determined the ideological attitude.

One of the first and the most important contributions to the debate was an article by Gustav Möller on "The social revolution" in "Tiden," in autumn 1918. In this article, Möller criticised the idea of a social revolution, which he defined as "the abolition of capitalism and the accomplishing of socialism by revolutionary means." We will return to this aspect of his statement in a later chapter. The socialist society—"a society dominated by total democracy, in which economic exploitation in its real meaning does not exist"—could only occur as the result of action which had stretched over a long period. Since a majority had been won for socialism, legislation should be decided regarding the right to socialise "the industries, the nationalising of which the new owners of power consider to be important for general well-being, and that they should not be able to remain in private ownership and production." At the time of nationalising, which should take place successively, compensation should be given to the owners of the enterprises. When all important large-scale production has been nationalised, the development towards a society definitely free from exploitation should begin and in this way people be prevented from living on their interest.

This plan for the realising of socialism is closely connected to other of Möller's ideas. He stressed that poverty could not be abolished by means of an equal distribution of incomes in the capitalist society, because such a distribution would in itself only lead to an insignificant rise in the living standards of the masses. At the stage reached by the discussion at that point, this observation was important, because as hinted earlier, it was common, by means of drastic descriptions of economic differences, to create the impression that the problem of distribution was the basic issue. In that connection it was clear that the revolutionary path could not be accepted, because of necessity it must lead to decreased production for a long period, amongst other things because there was a lack of experienced technicians and administrators. In the main successive nationalisation would lead to a rationalising of production, in that squandering and unnecessary competition would disappear. First and foremost, socialism would mean a planned economy.

In important respects, the view of the socialisation issue which dominates Möller's article can, be said to be representative of the debate during that period. Of primary importance is the fact that the fatalistic concept of development as something independent of man was pushed out of the way to make room for a discussion of concrete issues, the precondition for which was belief in a meaningful freedom of choice. This was not expressly stated. One still spoke, following the Marxist tradition, about the party having to adapt itself to circumstances. "If it is written in the stars that the social system shall be socialist, than so be it. It is not in man's power to steer this development." This was a typical statement. But reasoning took place as if a choice between various lines of action did exist, and was not content simply to refer to "development," as had been common earlier in questions regarding the principle of socialisation. It is very likely that this change was caused by the communist revolution in Russia, after which it was difficult to explain that socialisation could only occur as the culmination of capitalism.

The idea that socialisation should take place gradually, and not as a total "expropriation of expropriators" became generally accepted. In this connection the Marxist perspective had been rejected on a very decisive point. One newspaper wrote that "Only a party of fools would dare to bring about general socialisation." Another explained that "those who speak and write widely of a socialist economic revolution taking place in Sweden in the near future are either fools or the provocators of the capitalist society." It became common to stress the fact that the realisation of socialism would require a whole epoch, that experiments must take place, that no dogmatism was allowed to hinder a reasonable adjustment. It was also maintained that under present conditions an equal distribution of income, would not be any great advantage, that the increase of production was of the greatest importance and that the working class should get rid of any illusions it might harbour about a rapid increase in well-being. The process was still sometimes described as a social revolution, but it was explained that this did not mean a violent, or even a rapid revolution. One author wrote that it was necessary to understand that the word revolution in this connection had the same meaning as when, for instance, a revolution within communications was spoken of. With regard to the question of the time for socialisation it was generally recommended that it should begin with trust-formed industries and certain natural resources (mines, forests), possibly even with banks and insurance companies.

In the reported article, Möller spoke in detail about socialisation as meaning "nationalisation." In the debate that followed, however, another line emerged strongly. With certain exceptions such as railways, post and telegraph, socialisation should not mean state control, but rather some other form of cooperative or social organisation of production. As the Liberals and Conservatives stated that socialism was similiar to the system of commissions and bureaucracy, it was answered that a nationalisation in the common sense of the term was by no means the intention. The explanation of this change is quite simply that theories about a type of socialisation without nationalisation—in the first place the English guild-socialism—became known to the Swedish Social Democrats. Several articles about guild-socialism were published in 1919, and the debate was much affected by the theory, even if only a few people accepted in its entirety. Wigforss was one of the most active guild-socialists.

There was no general conception of how socialisation without state control would appear. However, there was agreement that a bureaucratic rigidity should be avoided, that as far as possible private initiative should be protected, that the workers should have direct influence over the running of the enterprise and that in this way their interests should be joined to production. Cooperation was seen as a form of socialism and allocated an important place in the new society, both in the questions of distribution of goods and production. The guild-socialist way of thinking showed itself in plans to the effect that the various enterprises and branches of industry should form autonomous organisations, administered by boards comprising representatives of the state, workers and consumers. Wigforss spoke of a system of workers trusts under state leadership. "The state should fulfil an important task as a unifying and arbitrating representative of the working people in their capacity of consumers. Probably the various workers industrial organisations will cherish egoistic interest in opposition to those of the consumers, that is, the workers within other industries. Naturally the consumers should decide what shall be produced, and take part in decisions regarding what shall be paid for the goods. On the other hand, how production within each branch is to be organised will be decided by the workers within that branch. Through this form of socialism the workers interest in higher pay is maintained . . . every branch of industry becomes a gigantic 'mutual agreement' undertaken by the industrial organisation." According to Engberg, socialism would create "a society in which the cooperatively organised and administered apparatus of production is within the framework of a consumer-cooperation which embraces the entire society. Society's interests are guarded by the state. The administration of production is exercised by the producers. State bureaucracy becomes superfluous . . ." More detailed instructions were not given. Whether or not one reads the Swedish works or the basic works of English guild-socialism, it is extremely difficult to get an idea of what sort of organisation was really intended.

Economic or industrial democracy was demanded as well as socialisation. However, this expression was used in very varied meanings. Occasionally it seems (see Wigforss, for instance) that industrial democracy meant that the enterprise or branch of industry should be lead by representatives of different groups, in particular workers and consumers, and guild-socialism, for instance, could then be seen as a form of industrial democracy. Occasionally it meant some form of collaboration between workers and employers regarding the running of the enterprise, and in that case industrial democracy became something quite different from socialisation. By means of elected representatives the workers would achieve insight into the activities of the enterprise and possibly also some form of decision-making rights. Finally, certain writers saw the expression as meaning only that the workers would receive certain legislated rights regarding working conditions. In particular, the employers right to dismiss employees would be limited. Due to this, the debate is confused. However, the concept of economic or industrial democracy quickly became generally accepted and asserted.

Möller's pamphlet "The problem of socialisation" was representative of the points of view which dominated the latter phase of the debate in question. This pamphlet was the only work on the question of socialisation which was published by the party in connection with the lower house election of 1920. On several points this pamphlet was connected to Möller's essay on "The social revolution" mentioned earlier, but with revisions and additions. Möller stressed the great value of private initiative, and the danger that this would be decreased due to socialisation. In part, he said that the great ideas and the initiative behind them were not dependent on the economic desire for profit, in part socialisation should be so formed that independence was stimulated. The idea was not to organise production as a part of the state's activities. On the contrary, production should "be developed in self-governing forms, more or less as independent of the state's powers and those of the government and parliament, as is private production at present."

Within every branch of industry (within every enterprise, in a manner of speaking) the owner (society as a whole), the workers and the consumers should appoint a representation to make certain important decisions, and in addition elect the board or the administrative council. In this way "as good as complete self government" would be achieved. It can be seen that this way of thinking in its most important aspects is connected to guild-socialism, although this term is not used to describe it. The idea that the enterprise, or at least the branches of industry, should be more or less just as independent as in the present society is a strange one. How then can the planning of the economy take place? Just as earlier Möller insisted that the expropriation that led to socialisation should not take place without compensation to the owners. Clearly, this meant that exploitation would not be abolished immediately. "But I dare to appeal to the common sense in us all, if, when the process of socialisation has been once achieved, or at least has become very extensive, it is not tremendously easy to *do away with private exploiting capital by means of our tax legislation*. By means of a tax on inheritance or fortunes we could successively suppress them." According to Möller, socialisation should mainly embrace the trusts, the most important raw materials such as wood and iron, and also waterfalls and all power stations. A state bank should be established, but this should operate side by side with the private banks. Rapid socialisation of banks was dangerous because in that case the socialised banks would be made responsible for the industrial failure which took place due to lack of credit. In Möller's view the preparation for socialisation should take place through industrial democracy, amongst other things. An industrial council, should be set up for every branch of industry. These should include representatives of the capitalists (present owners of industry), the industrial workers, the state and the consumers. These industrial councils should have considerable power over production and should "form the starting point for a forced trust-forming of the capitalist industry. At the same time being active with regard to industrial democracy would mature the working class, making them able to be economic leaders, and mature production itself, ready for the take over by the state."

The entire Social Democratic debate bears witness to the clear fact that the party was not theoretically prepared for socialist action. A tacit or open criticism of the party's leaders also often emerges. These leaders have spoken of socialisations since the 19th century without analysing the problem and without making any attempt to make their views more precise. The youngest (and in that period rapidly advancing) of the party's theoreticians, Engberg and Karleby, expressed such criticism most strongly. In 1911 Engberg became the editor of "Arbetet," and in 1917 Karleby the editor of "Skånska Socialdemokraten." At the end of 1918 Engberg wrote that up to now the Social Democrats had had a liberal policy. "The socialist education is beneath criticism. There are no guidelines and programmes for a socialisation able to be realised practically. The socialist view of society has not penetrated the forces we have had up to now. It must be admitted openly and honestly that terrible sins have also been committed. Unprepared, we were thrown to our appointed tasks, and now we are groping in the dark without a steady light . . . Rather a reduced flock of clear-sighted socialists, conscious of their goals, than masses of parliamentarians with a strong feeling for the compromise of the day, and with the trump card of the demagogue in their hand . . . A party that is fourth-fifths hostile to the socialist view of life—such a party must travel a long road filled with suffering and purges before it comes to understand that the walls of the bourgeois castle are not stormed and destoyed by half-liberal eunuchs, but only by troups who are burning with the fire of socialist thought." In a further article, the same author wrote that socialism had "up to now been allowed to play the part of an ideal backdrop," without anyone bothering to try to make it more concrete. It might even be feared that the whole of the industrial working class would come to have a bourgeois view of life. "When a basic socialist attitude is missing, social ascent brings with it a decrease in the emotional atmosphere regarding the dominant social order . . . In the near future it will be shown that capitalism will come to understand splendidly the art of getting on with democracy." Karleby makes a similar criticism of the activities of his own party.

"It cannot be denied that there has been something vague, undecided, unsure and groping in the demands for socialisation put forward by social democracy up to the present time . . . Because we must honestly admit that we are badly prepared." In a characteristic article, the Örebro-Kuriren maintained that a general action for socialisation was out of the question "for the simple reason that our party has never seriously adopted a position with regard to this problem. Of course we have a programme for the future, but when that programme was laid down no-one dreamt that it would need to be realised in our time. It was not considered necessary to have contact with the demands of reality, or to have any deeper understanding of the problem."

The authors just mentioned considered themselves to be criticising Swedish Social Democracy from the Marxist standpoint. However, their own statements reveal the difficulties involved in the Marxist theories. Engberg preached Marx's determinism, but at the same time explained that the whole of the Swedish class of industrial workers could become bourgeois if they were not inspired by a true Marxist spirit. But how is this to be seen in relation to the class struggle and to the inevitability of socialism? If Marx was correct, is it possible that lacks in the training of the Swedish leaders, or weaknesses in their pathos can really be of any great importance? An increased criticism can be found in certain statements. Here, it is hinted that Marx's scheme helped to bring Swedish Social Democracy to an insecure and unclear position. Engberg wrote that Marx's theory "first the class struggle, then socialisation" involved a schematising which prevented the successive realising of socialism. Marx had been influenced by the "bourgeois mystique of revolution." A "constructive development of the Marxist view of society" was necessary. "Life is and must be the final teacher." A similar way of thinking can be glimpsed in Karleby. This also stressed that above all Marx's theory meant a demand for an analysis of reality, and a realistic policy based on that. In this connection a way of thinking was founded that describes the definite disintegration of Marxism, and which was to be very much evident in a later period. Marx was described as the thinker without dogma, whose real doctrine is observation of "development" and "life."

In many respects the Social Democratic debate in Sweden contains the same ways of thinking as the foreign debates and international discussions which took place at the same time. At the Second Congress of the International in Geneva in 1920, a resolution was taken on the issue of socialisation. To a great extent this expresses the same ideas as those dominant in Sweden at the time. "Socialisation must take place step by step . . . No matter how much socialists condemn the system of private profit they should not do away with it in any industry until they are able to replace it with a better form of organisation. Such a gradually occurring socialisation is generally incompatible with expropriation of private goods without compensation. The means required for this compensation should be gained by taxation of the existing classes. . . . In an economically advanced society with population concentrated in the towns, socialisation takes three main forms. The national, the municipal and the cooperative . . . A very important principle regarding socialisation is that it is controlled by the administration. This control is exercised by representatives chosen by the people. In all industries and branches of economy the administrative organs must be definitely separated from the political government." In general the administration of a branch of industry should be handled by a national representation, consisting of representatives of personnel within industry, the state and the consumers. Every enterprise should have a workers council.

The programme commission appointed by the party executive to deal in a preparatory way with the motions inspired by the 1920 party congress, decided in connection with a proposal (suggested at the 1917 congress, though not taken up at that time), to set in operation a general revision of the programme. As a result it was proposed that the programme should be extensively revised. The following people took part in the work of the commission: Sandler, Möller, Neuman, Engberg and P. A. Hansson (the latter as a substitute for Branting, who was unable to take part). Only Hansson, Möller and Sandler took part. In the final adjustment of the report Sandler probably formulated the justification for this. Some specially appointed experts also cooperated in the revision of the land programme. The comprehensive work of the committee was carried out in a month—7th July to 7th August, 1919. In the main the proposals of the commission were accepted at the party congress of 1920, in many instances without a more thorough debate. To a great extent the party received a new programme without so much as a difference of opinion or a public discussion.

The Commission suggested extensive alterations and additions to the general basic principles. In their proposal the congress made certain adjustments at the suggestion of the party executive which are of no interest as far as principles are concerned. The debate was extremely short and was concerned only with details. Apart from the final paragraph concerned with internationalism, the general basic principles were worded as follows (changes and important additions are in italics).

Social Democracy is distinguished from their political parties in that it desires entirely to reconstruct the economic organisation of the bourgeois society and bring about the social liberation of the exploited classes, ensuring and developing the spiritual and material culture.

The main cause of the evils of the civilisation of today is the private capitalist form of production, *placing the ownership of the means of production in the hands of a few, condemning the majority to a propertyless condition and a state of dependence,* and making the conflict existing between workers and capitalists into the *determining* feature of the present society.

In the *old days* the private right of ownership of the means of production was a *means of securing* for the producer that which he had produced. *Instead the capitalist private ownership has been a means for the possessors to deprive the workers of the fruits of their labour.*

Though in different forms this capitalist exploitation dominates the modern society and leaves no area untouched.

Mainly it leaves its mark on the development of all industrial countries. To the extent *that the petit-bourgeois social conditions are dissolved,* large-scale production replaces craft, the machine replaces the tool, world trade and mass production break down all market borders—to that extent the real producers become a class of wage earners, absorbing numerous elements from the middle classes oppresses by the development of capitalism, and is characterised socially by its lack of property and its insecurity with the consequent dependence and oppression.

The extraordinary advances of the labour process, the tremendously increased productivity of human labour, the constant opening of new areas of production, the entire capitalist development by which national fortunes have been multiplied,—all this brings with it on the one hand an unnatural amassing of riches, and on the other hand an enormous growth of the *propertyless working class.*

In addition capitalism shows itself unable fully to make use of the constantly growing productive forces. Lack of planning in the capitalist production is not abolished even with its most advanced forms of organisation. The increased economic order won by the forming of trusts does not allow the appropriate and complete utilisation of the productive forces. Exploitation continues to the advantage of an ever more concentrated and ever stronger power of capital.

But at the same time these circumstances and the fatal tendency in the development of society force the workers to form a counter-movement. They organise themselves *against exploitation, as producers* in Trade Unions and as consumers in cooperative associations, in a continuously *increasing* struggle between workers and *capitalists.*

The class struggle between the exploiters and the exploited is given a modern stamp. The working class becomes conscious of its historical mission as the bearers of a new order of production, liberated from profit interests, and appears as the leader of the exploited classes of the people, reduced by capitalism to dependence and insecurity.

Because it is not only the industrial means of production and the natural resources that have fallen into the hands of the capitalists. It also rules in other areas, in which the industrial large-scale form of production has not conquered. In areas where the old middle classes have been allowed to remain, they undermine their economic independence. It is not only artisans, small-merchants and those practising free professions who have become liable to taxation by the capitalists. In the form of bank and corporation capital the farming lands too are subject to its power. The real users of the land are put aside when not already in the capacity of wage earners on large farms they have the same social position as the industrial workers with regard to lack of economic freedom, and the duty of paying tribute to a constantly developing capitalism.

The conflict between the workers and the capitalists brought about by the industrial development are thus widened so that they become a conflict between the exploited and their capitalist exploiters that penetrates the entire society. However, with this comes a uniting of all the exploited classes that stand side by side in the class struggle. This class struggle will not cease until society has been reconstructed, so that the capitalist exploitation is entirely abolished, the class society collapsed and mass society abolished. On the other hand, this can only occur by doing away with the private capitalist right of ownership to the means of production and placing them under the control of society and in the possession of society, and *also by* replacing the present unplanned production of commodities with a *socialist* production planned after the real needs of the society and with *the intention of raising the level of affluence.*

This goal *can not be achieved without* a political struggle. *Therefore* Social Democracy wishes to *gather together and politically organise the exploited classes,* clarify *their role in social development,* the goals and paths of their class struggle, conquer political power and in the way and the order decided by the development itself, bring about the socialist organisation of society.

As was stressed by the commission, in working out the new statement of principles an attempt was made to be consequent in the means of expression chosen, and to be complete with regard to the main viewpoints. As earlier, three sections can be distinguished in the basic principles: the goals and development of capitalism, the final aim of socialism, the means of achieving this. In what follows, the most important changes and additions in connection with the report of this committee will be pointed out.

In the first paragraph the word "oppressed" was changed to "exploited." In this context, in several places in the programme the same or similar expression was introduced ("the exploited classes" "the capitalist exploitation" "capitalist exploiters"). The commission justified this by saying that "exploited" was a clearer and more precise expression than "oppressed." The intention was not to establish a connection to Marx theory of surplus-value. It was considered possible to speak of exploitation without accepting this theory. Hinted at in the new word, however, was a situation between the classes that was principally of the same character as that which Marx tried to establish in his surplus-value theory. Therefore the alteration meant a certain intensifying in the direction of radical Marxism.

In the second paragraph is a paraphrasing caused by the desire to attain greater precision of expression. In particular it should be noticed that the older formulation could lead to the interpretation that "the destruction of the petit-bourgeois society should be seen as the harmful fruit of the emergence of capitalism," which idea is directly opposed to socialist ideas. Therefore, the pharse referring to destruction of petit-bourgeois society was transferred to the fifth paragraph.

In paragraphs 3 to 6 capitalist development is traced, with special reference to industry. The fourth paragraph (introduced in 1911) was left out, as it broke the general line of the analysis. Instead, the situation of the farmers was dealt with in the tenth paragraph.

The seventh paragraph is new. The commission held that in the earlier programme an important link had been missing from the socialist chain of thought, i.e. the desire to create increased production. "In order that the basic principles should, in a balanced manner, present the important aspects of the socialist point of view, it was necessary to complement this point, in which it was established that the capitalist mode of production, whilst undoubtedly representative of a great economic achievement, has now become a fetter for productive forces. In this connection an unexpected opportunity was offered to deal with the new phase of capitalism's development (the building of monopolies), which could not reasonably find a place in a programme dating from the 1890s, but which should not be absent from a programme developed more than 20 years later."

The eighth paragraph corresponds to paragraph 6 in the old programme. Those changes which were made were essentially of a formal nature. Through this new paragraph the socialist ideas regarding the class struggle as a continuously developing process were further developed. In addition it was here established that in the present class struggle, the working class was the leading class amongst the exploited classes.

The tenth paragraph replaces the fourth paragraph of the old programme. The programme commission writes: "Here it was necessary to clarify that variant of capitalism exhibited by farming. Other middle-classes have also been mentioned in passing in practically the same terms as in the present formulation, but with the addition of the free professions, whose dependent position is equally clear. What needs to be put forward in this paragraph is, above all, the fact that the real practice of farming continues to be economically fettered, even if technically speaking they become united with their means of production—the soil. This falls through their fingers as property, exappropriated by the capital that dominates the credit organisations.

To the extent that the area of self-production shrinks, the farming producer becomes less certain that the product of his labour will be his, compelled as he too now becomes to place this upon a market dominated by private capital." With this paragraph, the presentation of the development of capitalism is completed. In the eleventh paragraph it is pointed out that the conflict between workers and capitalists stressed in the second paragraph has developed into a conflict between exploited and exploiters which embraces the entire society. The twelfth paragraph establishes the fact that thereafter follows a uniting of the exploited classes in the struggle against the exploiters. At the end of this paragraph a new formulation of the goal of socialism is made: the ending of capitalist exploitation, the fall of the class society and the abolition of mass poverty. This replaces the words "The fruits of labour to those who labour." The thirteenth paragraph corresponds to the seventh paragraph in the earlier wording. The first part of that paragraph was left out so that the formulation used here could give "direct expression to the fact that all is well in those areas in which means of production and labour are still technically joined, and that these areas are not really affected by the process of socialisation that is explained as being a necessary replacement of other areas of society." However, the commission further stated that it was clear that a high degree of exploitation by capital could take place in the so-called independent small farming or small craft. It was also quite clear that the social reorganisation, the necessity of which was proclaimed, could not come to an end with, for instance, the question of the exploitation of farming land, if it is believed that as long as the farmers managed to retain the fruits of their labour the land could be treated just anyhow—as a "private domain, sacrificed to self-content and lack of initiative." If planned production in accordance with the real needs of society was to be accomplished, then an important part of food-stuff production could not be placed "outside state possession, and state control."

In that paragraph it was said that the right of private capital to own the means of production would cease, and that these should be placed "under the control and in the possession of the state." The programme commission explained that the intention was to emphasise this in view of the common features of the state's organisation of small farming, small craft and large-scale production: "Capitalist ownership (which means exploitation) will cease in that the means of production will become the property of the workers. This can occur either in the form of small-scale production, in which the worker owns his means of production and uses it under the control of the state, or in the form of large-scale production, in which the workers jointly own the means of production, either by the joining together of groups or through the state itself." The words regarding the replacing of unplanned production with planned production should not, as in the formulation of 1911, refer to large production alone, but also to production in its entirety. Furthermore, the wording of the paragraph was changed so that the orientation of production towards the raising of the general level of affluence was stressed.

The earlier formulation was altered in certain details in the fourteenth paragraph. Amongst other things, a phrase was added to the effect that the role of the exploited classes in social development should be clarified. The programme commission wrote that this was "intended to hint that it is first when the masses are conscious of their role, and therefore understand the economic conditions under which they can reach one or another result, that the struggle yields the greatest gains to those who are struggling." The new basic principles are characterised in their entirety by greater formal rigidity than the old principles. From the point of view of their content, this means primarily an intensifying of the general Marxist perspective, a new interpretation of the development that is assumed to lead to socialism and a stronger and less simple presentation of the demand for socialisation.

Economic determinism still emerges clearly. The Social Democratic party is seen as a means by which to organise the political struggle made necessary by the economic change. It will unite the exploited classes into a community able to act decisively and effectively, it will clarify their part in social development and their activity in the class struggle, and after power has been assumed it will bring about socialism "in that way and in that form that the development itself indicates." It is noticeable that, just as earlier, socialisation is seen as an action which can only take place after power has been won. From this wide perspective it is not a matter of successively carrying through the socialist measures in collaboration with the Liberal and Conservative parties. Political power is seen as a weapon in the hands either of the exploiters or the exploited.

In the question of the social development leading to socialism, the new programme completes and perfects the tendency to a new way of looking at things that could be detected as early as in the changes of 1911. The idea of the conflict between the bourgeoisie and the proletariat had dominated the programme of 1897. The continued existence of the middle classes (in a way that did not completely agree with the Marxist scheme of things) had been admitted, but no great importance had been attached to it in the process of development. On this point the programme of 1897 was a half measure: Marx's theory of the disappearance of the middle classes was not accepted, but on the other hand, these classes were treated in the prognosis as if they were non-existent. The thoughts hinted at the formulation of 1911 are fully developed in the basic principles of 1920. The middle classes, too, are described as exploited and in conflict with the capitalist class. Unlike the formulation of the 1897 programme, the working class are not the only opponents of capitalism, but only the leaders amongst the exploited classes. A uniting of all groups against the small class of capitalists is predicted. Collaboration between the workers and others is seen not only as a means of bringing about democracy, but also as a uniting for the purpose of realising the socialist society, such a joining together being necessary due to the economic development.

There is a clear difference between this perspective and Marx's scheme. Certainly the theories of concentration and accumulation are retained—an "even more concentrated and mightier power of capital" is spoken of. These theories are connected to Marx with reference to the dissolution of the middle classes and the growing misery of the proletariat. In the 1920 basic principles, these theories were put forward in the section dealing with industrial development but were considered applicable even if the working class maintains or increases a given standard and the middle classes remain in existence. The theory of the exploitation of all other classes by the capitalist class appears, instead of the theory of impoverishment and the theory of the dissolution of the middle class. In this way a vaguer picture of the development of society is given, a picture that is also harder to criticise. It was not affected by evidence to the effect that the position of workers became better, or that the middle classes increased in numbers and importance. If it was admitted that the capitalists exploited all other classes there was evidence of a continuous and sharp conflict within the society simply by referring to the fact that the number of great fortunes and strong capitalist corporations had increased.

But what is meant by exploitation? It has already been stressed that in this connection exploitation as used by Marx was not intended (although this was often not the case in earlier socialist discussion), because Marx's theory of surplus-value was not accepted. That the word had another meaning is clear from the fact that the non-wage-earning middle classes were described as exploited. Marx's concept of exploitation was built upon the idea that labour alone created exchange value, and that therefore a leader of an enterprise employing workers appropriated the difference between wages and the value of the goods produced. Although exploitation was mentioned in the Erfurt programme for instance, only the exploitation of wage earners by the capitalists was intended. It is true that the word exploitation has been given meanings other than that used by Marx in national economic writings. As soon as the thesis of classical economy that labour is the creator of value is accepted, it is reasonable in certain contexts to use this concept. But there is no reason to assume that the programme commission accepted the classic theory of value which was generally rejected by socialist theoreticians too. Indeed, with this as the starting point (just as with Marx's theory of surplus-value) it was not possible to draw the conclusion that all social classes except the capitalists were exploited.

However, no attempt to define the concept of exploitation was made by the programme commission, either in the programme itself or in the motivations presented to justify the programme. If one wishes to understand what the commission meant then it only remains to examine more closely those particular cases which are cited as examples of exploitation.

In the third paragraph it was stated that capitalist private ownership has become a means for those in power to deny the workers the fruits of their labour. This thesis is a pure revision of Marx's theory of surplus-value. As it is not intended to be this, the question remains unanswered as to what is meant by this expression. This is also the case regarding the paragraphs 5–8 in which the industrial workers are described as the objects of exploitation. All that needs to be stressed here is that in the eighth paragraph the workers are described as being exploited both as producers and as consumers. In this connection it is hinted that—with reference to a norm that is not stated—partly they receive wages which are too low, and partly that they are forced to pay prices which are much too high.

In the ninth and tenth paragraphs it is stated that exploitation does not only involve the class of industrial workers. Here it is first established that exploitation does not necessarily involve ownership of the means of production, the use of which occupies the exploited. Exploitation not only occurs in the question of industrial means of production and the natural riches which "have got into the hands of the capitalists," i.e. are owned by the capitalists. Capitalism also becomes (and observe the new expression!) "the ruler in areas in which industrial mass production has not conquered."

And this "ruling power" (with regard to the content of which no more is said) offers an instrument for exploitation, just as the ownership of the means of production is such an instrument. By means of its domination, capitalism undermines the "economic independence" of the middle classes, at which, according to the following passages, exploitation takes place.

In this connection two categories of social groups are named. As far as craftsmen, small tradesmen and those who practise free professions are concerned it is briefly mentioned in a transitional passage that they "become liable to pay taxes to capital." It is not suggested what is meant by this. The phrase "liable to pay taxes" is taken from the programme of 1911 but in that programme it is only the small farmers who are mentioned as being "liable to pay taxes to capital." Regarding craftsmen and small tradesmen, does it mean that through competition the capitalists force them to reduce their prices? This seems to be unthinkable because the principle of large scale production is considered to be valuable. Does it quite simply mean that the chances of these social groups are reduced by capitalism? If so, Marx's prognosis of the disappearance of these groups is expressed in a very strange way. Or does it mean that craftsmen and tradesmen, just as other consumers, are exploited when they purchase from factories and wholesalers? Or does it mean that these groups must pay high interest on bank loans? Similar questions can be put with regard to the practice of the free professions. In accordance with what point of view are doctors, lawyers, artists and authors generally said to be exploited or to "be liable to pay taxes to capital"?

Farmers are the other category which were presented as the object of exploitation. Capitalism in the form of bank and company capital has placed "the farming land in its power. The real users of the land continue in economic bondage, paying tribute to capitalism that is steadily growing," even though they are not wage-earners on large farms. Here it was clearly desired to assert that industry and finance capitalism also exploits the farming class. No distinction was made between owners active in farming, independent farmers and lease-holders and small scale farmers who do not own the land—all of them are considered to be exploited. Probably it was partly the acquisition of farming by the corporations, and partly the mortgages on farming property held by the banks, that were referred to here, but no information regarding the nature of the process of exploitation was tended. In particular it should be underlined that the question of the right of ownership was not dealt with in this context. As far as farming is concerned, the owners of the means of production also belong to the exploited class, to the extent that they are neither bankers nor corporations.

Not even the large-scale land owners are mentioned as a group within the capitalist class. However, it must reasonably be predicted that owners who employ workers, or who lease out their land, were considered at one and the same time to be exploited and exploiters: exploited by the banks and company capital, exploiters of the agricultural labourers, lease-holders and farm-hands. But the system according to which the form of capitalism created under industrialism exploits all other groups, would have broken down had not the owners been given a place in the scheme of things.

From what has been said it emerges partly that the programme contains passages on which in the main it is difficult to get a grip and partly (and above all) that from the programme it is not possible to form an idea of what is really meant by exploitation. The concept around which the whole programme is built has apparently in no way been given any definite meaning by the authors of the programme. Wage-earners, the well-to-do small tradesman, the lawyer with a high income, the wealthy farmer—all of these seem to have counted as being amongst the exploited.

Which then are the exploiters? In the first place, private owners of large industrial concerns, business and bankers should be counted as part of this group. But it should be noted that it is mainly bank and company capital that are mentioned as the exploiters. The large proportion of those who are connected with this capital are in another context counted as being among the exploited. Therefore, the programme presupposes that a person can be (and in fact, is normally) both an exploiter, and one of the exploited. From this point of view a large part of the programme is meaningless. It should also be pointed out that whilst the exploited are not called proletarians (it would have been altogether unreasonable to have used such a term to describe, for instance, members of the free professions, or the wealthy farmers) the exploiters are labelled capitalists. With regard to one of the protagonists in the class struggle it was still possible to make use of the traditional Marxist term. This is clearly connected with the fact that the expressions 'exploiter' and 'capitalist' had lost all concrete meaning. They could only be given a circular definition—as a description of those who play an active part in the process of exploitation.

Psychologically this unthinking use of the concept of exploitation can be explained easily. In accordance with Marxist terminology, the concept had for a long time been used to illustrate the situation existing between capitalists and proletariat. As the social struggle was described as a fight between two categories (whilst at the same time departing from Marx's scheme by admitting the continued existence of the middle classes) it was quite natural to describe all groups apart from the capitalist class, i.e. all groups who desired to unite for the struggle, as exploited. In extending the dimension of meaning of the concept of exploitation, the same tendency emerges as that which was asserted by Danielsson thirty years earlier. That all except a few capitalists were part of the proletariat. Through a new means of expression the old conclusion was reached—that social democracy represented the interests of the majority against an inconsequent minority, and that the time was ripe for socialisation.

In Sandler's speech at the party congress (in this question he was the spokesman for the programme commission) he justified the proposal by saying that the party stood at the beginning of a new era. "We stand in the face of a new breakthrough—from this time onwards the problem of socialisation will dominate." The whole of the revision of the general basic principles can be seen from this perspective—that the problem of socialisation has been brought to the fore. The development towards socialism described in the basic principles is clearly considered to be nearing its end. It is on this point that the dominant position of the concept of exploitation has its main practical importance. That not only the wage earners, but also all the middle classes are said to be exploited was, in fact, asserted in the form of a historical perspective on the fact of socialism. The result is essentially the same as if (whilst maintaining Marx's scheme and with a more open violation of reality) one had stated that the middle classes had disappeared and that a few millionaires stood against the hungry masses.

However, the justification for socialisation is to some extent coloured by the (relative to Marx) new form attributed to the process of development. From his wide perspective Marx thought that the expropriators would be expropriated in a situation in which the system of production showed unsolvable inner conflicts. Despite the size of the productive forces the masses must live in poverty, and marketing difficulties lead to a crisis involving tremendous unemployment. Therefore, the socialisation of production would immediately lead to welfare for all, even if it was thought that this welfare would rise even higher during the socialist epoch that followed. Such a way of thinking could not be applied in an unaltered form, taking the starting points which had been accepted by the programme commission. Instead, in connection with the basic ideas contained in the programme, it was maintained that socialism would bring with it the abolition of exploitation, and mean changes directly connected with this. Further, it was asserted that exploitation could be abolished by means of "replacing the present planless production of commodities with a socialist production, planned according to the real needs of society and with the aim of increasing welfare." This assertion was only marginal to the programme's general way of thinking, but in connection with stress on the unplanned nature of capitalist production referred to in the seventh paragraph. The idea of an effective planned economy was brought to the fore, whilst the idea of a real distribution was not especially noticeable. Presumably such distribution would have been considered to be assured if exploitation was abolished.

With regard to the meaning of the socialisation concept, too, the programme commission presented a formulation that deviated from the general Marxist point of view. According to the programme, socialisation meant "abolishing the rights of ownership of the means of production by private capital and placing them under the control and in the ownership of the state." According to pure Marxism, the means of production thought to belong to capitalism would in their entirety be transferred into state control.

This point of view was also taken up in the programme of 1897. The 1911 formulation of the point in question reintroduces a difference between those cases in which "the means of production and labour are still joined in one and the same hand (independent small farming or small craft)" and those cases "in which modern production—large scale production—dominates."

In the first instance no socialisation is demanded. In the second instance, on the other hand, "private capitalist monopoly is to be placed under the control and in the possession of the state." The 1920 programme presents anew a common formula for all means of production. This was justified on the grounds that capitalist ownership (which involves exploitation) will be abolished by the transfering of the means of production into the hands of the workers. But, according to the statement of the commission, in reality a division is intended in connection with the predictions of the programme of 1911. The desired aim could either be achieved in the form of small scale production or large scale production. In the socialist society the worker will possess his own means of production. The word "possess" here must have meant the same as "own" (although ownership was probably intended to be subject to certain limitations), because in the strict legal meaning of the word possession would mean that these means of production were also owned by the state, and that the difference between small and large scale production as presented here would disappear.

What is new about socialism is that these means of production are used "under the control of the state." Thereby it was intended that small scale production, too, should be part of the socially planned production. Under large scale production "the workers will possess the means of production communally through group unions" (the influence of guild-socialism can be traced here) "or through the state itself." This division is naturally connected to the theory of exploitation that lies at the base of the programme. Only "The capitalist private ownership" (as the wording goes in the third paragraph), i.e. that ownership that is considered to be the basis of exploitation, must be completely taken over by the state, whilst ownership in general, which in the present society is considered to be the object of exploitation, need only be submitted to that control which is necessary for the most effective use of the means of production.

In the following the party programme of 1920 is discussed point by point, in so far as it is concerned with economic and social questions. In addition, an account is given of the most important points of view that emerged in the justification for their proposal given by the programme commission, of the report of the party executive regarding the proposals of the commission, and of the congressional debates. In those points on which no mention is made of any differences of opinion, the proposal of the commission was accepted without opposition (in certain cases after unimportant formal modifications). When it is considered necessary to make a comparison with the previous wording of the programme, the corresponding point in its original formulation is also presented.

Point VII

Previous wording	*Revised wording*
Progressive taxation of income, fortune and inheritance. Abolition of all indirect taxes—that mainly oppress the productive classes—primarily through energetically fighting custom duties. Considerable raising of the tax-free minimum existence. Development of the activities of the state and communes as producers and leaders of communication and distribution for the satisfying of general budgetary needs.	Direct taxation. Progressive income tax. Tax-free minimum existence. Higher taxation of unearned income. Private fortunes to be taxed progressively, particularly by means of inheritance tax. State capital formation to be secured at taxation. The surplus from state enterprises to contribute to satisfying budgetary needs.

Point VII of the 1911 programme was divided into two points of which that cited above deals with tax policy, whilst the following is concerned with trade policy.

In the question of taxation, amongst others, the programme commission stated that a definite distinction should be made between income which resulted from labour and income which did not. Socialism did not consider incomes resulting from land ownership, capital and market-profits to be legitimate, therefore believing that they should be highly taxed even in the present society. In the same way increases in fortunes which take place without any effort on the part of the owner (for instance through inheritance) should also be subject to particularly high taxation. In the fourth paragraph it was asserted that taxation should not lead to the reduction of capital resources which would occur if all taxes were used for current payments. A certain part of the taxes—"in particular all monies gained through inheritance tax"—should be reserved for capital building.

In its old form, the final paragraph meant that in the present epoch state enterprises should be severely limited, and that the growth and activity of state enterprises should be decided from a fiscal perspective. In accordance with the demand for socialisation that is made later in the programme, this formulation has here been altered. Point VII has remained unchanged except for one detail. In 1928 the words "and land value tax" were inserted into the third paragraph.

Point VIII

Free trade.

Foreign trade to be organised under the control of the state.

The programme commission was very decided in its opinion that the system of protective duties should be completely abolished. "Free trade is the breath of life for those enterprises which grow out of natural conditions and are run economically and rationally. It murders the useless! But the useless must be got rid of if society is to achieve the highest possible level of production. In a society showing the beginnings of socialisation the purging function of free trade is necessary. Social production is not able to exhibit its superiority if it grows up in a protectionist hothouse." Clearly the commission did not think that the second paragraph in this point involved any limitation of the first. The motives behind this are clearly and concisely stated: "free economic connections with foreign countries should be organized under the control of the state. The needs of the state, not those of private interests, are to dominate foreign trade." The point has not been altered.

Point IX

Accident insurance. Health insurance. Maternity insurance. Unemployment insurance.

The pensioning of the aged and invalids as well as children and widows' pensions.

This point corresponded to point X of the old programme. It has been retained unchanged. In 1928 it became number X.

Point X

Legislated 8-hours normal working day.

Prohibition of night work unless the work has to take place either for technical reasons or for the general welfare.

At least 36 hours consecutive leisure during one week.

Prohibition against the use of children under the age of 15 in industry. Also against all gainful employment that hinders obligatory schooling.

Protection against dangers at work. Labour inspection.

Public labour exchange, free of charge.

A satisfactory minimum wage level to be maintained by the regulating intervention of the state.

Legislation concerning workers' protection to be extended to home industry.

Freedom of emigration and immigration.

Labour protection and the advantage of social insurance to be assured also to foreign workers.

The rights of the working class to be assured by international agreements.

This point corresponds very nearly to Point IX of the old programme. What was new were the demands for the prohibition of all gainful employment that prevented obligatory schooling, and for a public and free labour exchange. Also the demands for the maintenance through the state of a certain standard of wages, for the extension of legislation regarding protection at work to cover home industries and for the regulating of the internal relations of the working class (the three final paragraphs). Regarding the question of the length of the working day, the previous formula of the "8 hour working day" was changed to the "8-hour normal working day." The programme commission explained that in this connection it was desired to establish that both shorter and longer working hours in certain fields and under certain conditions could be considered.

The proposal of the commission was accepted without alteration, although it was criticised on several points. A minority within the congress wanted the eight-hour working day to be the maximum working day, and also wanted the demand for free immigration and emigration to be removed. Some members had reservations against the demand for legislation regarding a minimum wage, maintaining that an official regulation of the standard of wages could only be brought about in a socialist society.

This point has only been altered to the extent that at the congress of 1924 a new section was added. In 1928 the point became point number XI. In points XII–XVI (after the congress of 1928 points XIII–XVII) as the commission stresses the party programme reverts to the specific socialist demands. Here "the basic guidelines were laid down for the socialist transformation of society." The commission explained that now the time seems "to be ripe for their formulation in the programme."

Point XII was worded: "The right to expropriate for society's needs." The programme commission writes that here "the instrument of justice that is demanded for the carrying through of the process of socialisation" is dealt with. The demand concerns "the right to expropriate within all areas of production, the right to expropriate both in questions of enterprises and of fortunes, the right to expropriate to the advantage of the state, the municipality and other administrative bodies, or for the union of groups (for instance cooperative organisations) under the control of the state."

The commission also took up the question of the compensation that should be allowed at the time of expropriation. At the time of a general expropriation of the fortunes of the ruling classes, it might be that no compensation would be given. However, it might also be suitable for a period of time to make the ruling classes into society's "rentiers." When private enterprises or branches of production were taken over by the state, in principle the value of the business should be paid to the owners, even if there were cases where the private ownership rested on such loose legal grounds that compensation was not justifiable. "When compensation is given, the peaceful advance of socialisation is best served if as a class the rulers bear the burdens of the redemption system. Naturally there can be no thought of the state being interest-receiver for an unlimited period, as the capitalists as a class will be abolished. The chances of this class painlessly adapting themselves to the productive society can be prepared by successively reducing interest, or by the claiming of the fortune first on the death of the owner."

The point has not been altered.

Point XIII

The following to be transfered into state ownership:

For the realising of a planned economy: all necessary natural resources, industrial enterprises, credit institutions, transport and communication routes.

Expert leadership of state enterprises with guarantees against bureaucratic management.

The participation of workers and consumers in the state's administration.

State control of those enterprises remaining in private hands.

This point is the most remarkable innovation in the political programme. The new paragraph was both directly and generally concerned with socialisation. In that way the central socialist demands were written into the political programme, and thus were described as being ripe for realisation. The programme commission wrote that here "the demand for socialisation within the greatest part of the economy, which bears the typical mark of capitalism" emerges clearly.

The commission took as their starting point the fact that socialisation was to take place gradually. "The political measures for socialisation would mean a fully conscious contribution to the continuing process of development towards socialism. Quite naturally, these measures must take as their primary point of departure the tendencies towards concentration reached by private capitalism. Where the development of production has already reached, or almost reached, the form of monopoly enterprise, conditions are ripe for socialisation." Large parts of the economy were still unripe for socialist management. Here, capitalism was still the most important factor in economic change. In these areas the state should intervene by controlling and promoting the movement towards concentration that signifies progress. It was a question first of ripening, later of socialising.

From the point of view of socialisation, the commission made several statements regarding principles, concerning the status of various means of production, and branches of industry. It emphasised that the possession of natural riches was of the utmost importance. Even if for organisational, practical reasons one or another strongly concentrated industry early became socialised, socialisation would nevertheless win its decisive victory only when the state came to possess the natural riches exploited by industrial production—the forests, mines and water-falls. "The economic preconditions are also such that the question of the socialisation of certain natural resources emerges as an immediate practical-political problem." In this context the land issue was not taken up, as it was dealt with in a special point of the programme. However, continued the commission, capitalism should not only be attacked at its economic base—raw-materials—but also in its most developed form—finance capital. In the area of credit, concentration had proceeded rapidly. "Already a couple of large banks dominate the greater part. The time for socialisation is clearly at hand." To a large extent means of transport and communication were already owned by the state, and to the extent that they were of importance for communications in general—all large railways, canals, floating ways—they should be put under the control of a planned administration, which embraced the entire country. This was also the case concerning the large steamship lines. Within industry there were many degrees of economic maturity.

Socialisation should be oriented towards the branches of industries and enterprises that are of most importance for the economy. With reference to commerce, which, with the exception of foreign trade, was not dealt with in the programme, it was stated that much of it could be socialised by the development of cooperations, and that important parts of it, in particular big business, would be integrated parts of the socialised production owned by the state.

The commission even dealt with the form the economy would take in the socialised society. The extension of social production could occur partly in the form of monopoly, partly in the continuing conditions of free competition. The state should have a legal monopoly position with regard to the extensive natural resources. Private capitalist finance institutions should not be tolerated. On the other hand, cooperative credit organisations could be of value. The circumstances were different with regard to industry. "There, state monopoly might be a temptation to uneconomic management. Therefore, the starting of new enterprises within a branch of industry that has been socialised should not be allowed. Socialisation can and should continue without the abolition of commercial and industrial freedom. There should be no legal hindrance to the consumers satisfying their needs in ways other than through socialised enterprises." In case the state enterprises were badly run, a large cooperative organisation could emerge as a competitor, even within production. In the same way, free-trade should be a splendid check on the uneconomic running of state enterprises. In this connection the commission touched upon the Marxist idea of the disappearance of the state in connection with the realising of socialisation. "To the extent that socialisation advances, the political power-state is done away with and becomes an economic state administration. . . . According to the foremost socialist theoreticians (and which was also emphatically stated by Engels) the socialisation that we strive after and which involves the end of exploitation must, by its very nature, result in the death of the power-state, with its unnecessarily elaborate bureaucracy." This statement is much too general to give any clear meaning. There is no reason to assume that the commission really thought that all centralised power would disappear in the socialist society. The statement that the power-state will be replaced by an economic state administration need only mean the self-evident fact that socialism would partly give to the state new functions and a new organisation. Finally, the commission dealt with the problem of administration in the socialist society. It was pointed out that experience from state-run enterprises had created justified fears that the running of socialised enterprises would be slip-shod, bureaucratic and uneconomic. In this connection guarantees could be assured "by avoiding the monopolistic forms, by avoiding rigid centralisation, by allowing plenty of room for cooperation, by giving the consumers a place in the organs of administration and by allowing enough freedom of movement to the leadership." Neither civil servants nor politicians, but those with the highest technical and commercial training should be placed at the helm of state enterprises.

Representatives of the whole society, of the workers, the employees and the consumers, should take part in the administration. "State management in its popular bourgeois meaning disappears, to be replaced by the self-administration of the socialised branches of production, representing various interests." Those enterprises that remained in private hands should be submitted to control in various respects. Supervision of dismissals, of the exploitation of the workers and the profits of capitalism. Regulations regarding waste and exploitation. The commission was of the opinion that the various forms by which the workers would be assured of influence over the administration of private enterprises would be examined more closely, and it was therefore suggested that the party congress should take up these questions for discussion.

The debate at the party congress regarding this central point of the programme was short and uninformative. However in his introductory speech Möller, the spokesman of the programme commission, put forward several interesting points of view. He stressed that at the abolition of exploitation, guarantees must be created that poverty would not increase. This statement illustrates very clearly indeed the difference between the old Marxist way of thinking and the ideas of the programme commission. Furthermore, Möller said that investigations had shown that the workers in the best positions now had just as large a part of the results of common production as would be given by a similar distribution of the results of production. It emerged that something more than the abolition of capitalism was required to create general affluence. The most important thing was to abolish the squandering of productive powers that is characteristic of the capitalist society. The boom that the war had brought to Sweden had led to no improvement in the situation of the working class. "Everything now points to the necessity of beginning to work for the socialisation of production and the abolition of capitalism." Socialisation should take place step by step, and compensation should be given to the owners and the expropriated. "It is a fact that practically all those who have had an economic or technical education hold capitalist ideas. But if we are to socialise we need these people and therefore we should see that we do not make them into the enemies of socialism from the beginning, because as such they would sabotage socialisation. . . . At the completion of the process of socialisation we must then make use of the taxation apparatus in order that the state can gain the capital that is given as compensation for the socialised means of production." The oft-expressed idea that socialisation should begin with the banks was not correct. If the state owned the banks, and if these refused to give credit to a certain industry, hostility would be aroused against the socialist organisation. However, a state business bank should be established that competed with the private banks, and in general one should begin with the socialising of the important natural resources. Almost all of those who took part in the debate agreed with these general ideas. Some of the difficulties connected with the socialising or control of industry were dealt with by some of the speakers (Engberg N. Eriksson). If the state decided that an enterprise was forced to cease production, there remained the question of the transfering of the workers to another enterprise. Duty-protected industries must, in the main, be discarded, and one would become forced to concentrate upon those industries that were able to withstand foreign competition. One of the speakers (G. Dahlberg) stated that a suitable starting point for socialisation would be large farms and company land; others were of the opinion that the land would not be the object of socialisation until much later.

In agreement with the proposal of the programme commission, a special debate on industrial democracy was arranged. This was opened by Wigforss, who reported upon the debate in other countries, in particular on the theory of guild-socialism. Wigforss agreed with guild-socialism and seems to have seen the introduction of industrial democracy as a step in the process of socialisation. Although the workers received more bread through state socialism, they still felt themselves to be isolated from the process of production. Step by step the workers could become the leaders of the enterprises. First they would be allowed to replace certain technical leaders, later they would also lead in questions of the distribution of products. The right of ownership of means of production would be in the hands of the state, but it should not emerge as leader of production. In the following debate various ways of giving influence to the workers and other groups with regard to the running of the enterprise were taken up, without any common line being formed. Some speakers reasoned that industrial democracy was a step towards socialism, whilst others wanted reforms (which would be of a much more unpretentious nature) carried out within the framework of the present system. From several directions it was pointed out that the concept of industrial democracy was unclear, and in the nature of a slogan, and the workers' own interest in this issue was questioned. A resolution was taken to the effect that the question should be examined.

The point in the programme just dealt with has remained unaltered.

Point XIV

Point XIV reads: "Society promotes cooperation." The programme Commission explained that cooperation did not imply only a temporary protection against capitalist exploitation but a form of organisation for the society of the future with great potential for development. It was stressed that Swedish cooperation had begun to organise even productive enterprises. In that way cooperation played an important part in the process of socialisation.

However, it could not render superfluous direct socialising intervention on the part of society. "But within the framework of the general socialisation plan it is wise to give increasing space to socialisation in its more compulsory forms that cooperation in its more advanced stages of development could bring about."

Point XV

Previous wording	*Revised wording*
(The preamble, which in the new programme corresponds to a few lines in the statement of general principles, is omitted.)	A Forced purchase of large land properties in private hands.
Private monopoly of special natural resources such as large forests,	Neglected properties to be confiscated by the state. The institution of entailed estate to

Point XV continued

Previous wording

mines, water falls and large peat fields to be transferred to the state. The system of concessions as a transition to socialisation. State land donations in reasonable cases to be recovered by the state. Important waterways for timber floating to be taken over by the state.

The state and the municipalities to extend their land possessions. Farming domains to be let either for large-scale production (by leasing to cooperative production or, until this can come about, to private individuals, with guarantees for the workers), or to small farmers, under terms securing their maintenance and legal rights. Building sites to be let with site lease-hold rights, option or repurchase rights.

The right of farm and forestry workers to associate to be maintained. Labour inspection to be extended to the large scale farming and forestry and to include inspection of dwellings. Under protected possession suitable lands to be given to agricultural labourers and others who wish to become small-farmers or to start cooperative farming. As a last resort this land can be acquired by expropriation of large farms (corporation domains, mansions).

Crofters, corporation leasees and farm holders on the land of others

Revised wording

be abolished; the state to acquire entailed estate.

The state's land donations to return to the state.

Dividing up of state land only if natural conditions render large-scale production unsuitable.

Letting out of the state's extensive land properties to private individuals to occur only with guarantees for the interests of society and the farm workers.

State lands intended for small-scale farming to be let out to the farmers with secure right of possession.

B

A system of concessions for land in private ownership placing control of land purchase in the hands of the state.

Crofters and leasers of private land to be protected by lease legislation. The land owner to compensate for new cultivation and land improvements.

At the demise of the land owner should the inheriters so wish, the state to buy the property in order to safeguard the chances of farming the land of their fathers.

Legislation regarding neglect to cover the whole country.

The 'own-your-own-home movement' to be placed entirely in the hands of the state.

Point XV continued

Previous wording	*Revised wording*
to be released as a last resort by expropriation. Users of the land of others to be protected by effective lease legislation. Independent small farmers to be supported against all types of power wielded by corporations and large scale owners. Cooperation between farmers and all other means by which the small farming can gain the advantages of large-scale production to be strongly promoted. Farming education to be promoted. Rational forestry. Credit for farming and dwelling purposes, particularly to the poor to be regulated directly by society (state and municipalities). Cooperative loan associations to be encouraged.	Against repayment the state to place means at the disposal of the own-home owner for the erection of buildings.

The programme commission wrote that central to land policy must be the facilitating of access to the land for those who, due to the fact that they work on the land, wish to build a home and livelihood. Also, to prevent the possession of land from being used as a means of gaining the fruits of the labour of others, and to protect the real uses of the land against capitalist exploitation and to safeguard the planned nature of production and also to increase production. In a capitalist society, large scale production was the means of gaining the fruits of others' labour. A land policy that desired to serve the working people must form large scale production so that exploitation was not allowed, and so that large scale production was placed under the control of the state. Cooperation and share systems should have been used. For the small holders (those who did not employ labour), on the other hand, farming was not an instrument for exploitation, and therefore the state did not require that they reject their right of ownership of the land. On the contrary, in many cases the lands in their use should be increased, so that by means of a rational production the necessary level of livelihood would be assured. Regarding this category of farmers it was particularly necessary to insure that their land did not fall into the hands of capitalist monopoly and speculation, and attempt to raise the level of production of the land. The commission emphasised that in our country small farming and large scale production must grow and develop side by side with each other, depending upon climatic and other circumstances.

The principles formulated by the programme commission are not altogether consequently made use of in the concrete demands laid down by the programme. There is a discrepancy between the basic principle of rational production, and the respect paid to the rights of private ownership. In this manner, only the forced purchase of the larger privately owned land properties is required. That the state should if necessary expropriate small farming, in order to make possible large scale production, was never brought up. Neither (as is shown by the paragraphs under "B") was it taken for granted that all large properties should be taken over by the state. According to the first of these paragraphs a system of concessions should be introduced for land purchase, and the justification given for this shows that it was taken for granted that even larger properties could be passed from one private person to another. In the second paragraph protection for crofters and those leasing the land from private owners was demanded.

According to the third paragraph, in certain cases the state could straight away intervene in order to make it possible for one who inherited land to retain this. On the other hand, regarding the entailed estate lands, it was required, without reservation, that this should become the property of the state, and no more detailed justification for this was given. Furthermore, it was not thought that all the large land properties owned by the state, and not to be divided up, should be run by cooperatives. On the contrary, the seventh paragraph under "A" presupposes that such properties should be able to be granted to private individuals, who in turn should be able to employ agricultural workers and who, according to the general argument, must become exploiters, even if guarantes in the interests of the farm workers were forthcoming. It was stated in the justification for this paragraph that the cooperative form should be tested on one or more of the state's properties. Before experience with regard to the suitability of this form had been gained, the properties should be leased out. The justification contains the following strange passage: "For the present, state-run farms should not be considered. This does not exclude of course that the society itself runs the farms, where there is reason to believe that these will be run to economic advantage." Here the idea of state farming is rejected, although the idea of the working of the land by society is looked on with approval. Possibly, it is meant that the desired form of farming belongs to a later stage, when socialisation is more completely established. Probably these inconsistencies in the proposals can be explained largely by the fact that the programme commission combined long-term and short-term requirements, without making this fact clear.

One of the guide-lines of the programme (though not consistently carried through) was the formation of new independent small farms, to the extent that this was suitable with reference to farming techniques. Forced purchase of large properties should, it is said in the justification for the proposal, be a means of liberating crofters, small-holders and lease-holders, and of supplying the agricultural labourers with land. In connection with this the demand was made that the properties in the ownership of the state, which from the point of view of farming technique should be divided up, should be given out to small-scale farmers with secure rights of possession.

This right of possession should be something very like the right of ownership. It should be valid for the entire life of the person in question, and should be able to be passed on to his survivors through inheritance. Further, according to the last paragraph of this point, the state should place at his disposal the means for the erection of buildings (own home).

The programme commission made several criticisms regarding the differences between the land programme of 1911 and 1920. Certain parts of the paragraph on farming in the earlier programme had, at the revision of the programme, been transferred to the second point in the programme (as had questions of socialisation, right to unite in organisations, inspection, cooperation, farmers' training and forestry planning), or had been referred to the question of dwellings and thereby to the municipal programme (land rights etc.). In the question of the freeing of crofters, lease-holders and small-holders, the new programme does not presuppose that this will take place by transforming the groups in question into land owners. Instead, a secure right of possession is suggested. Support of the peasants and farmers is included in the point regarding the system of concessions in relation to land purchase in the programme of 1920.

Point XV was accepted by the party congress with no debate. In 1928 it underwent an important revision.

Point XVI was worded as follows: "The distribution of incomes and fortunes to be regulated." In accordance with the suggestion of the programme commission this should be followed by a further more concrete clause: "The taking over by the state of private fortunes which yield a labour-free income to their owner." In their arguments justifying this, the commission maintained that socialism desired increased production, but also wanted a fairer distribution. When a socialist programme for production was being presented, therefore, the first outline of a programme of distribution should be formulated. "The state must strive to regulate distribution to achieve greater equality and justice. However, respect must be paid to the effect of this regulation on the increasing of productivity which is an essential demand if mass poverty is to be abolished." The commission considered that as socialisation of enterprises advanced, the income gap would become less without any particular measures being taken. However, direct state-intervention was also required. Above all the state should "maintain the right to more or less completely confiscate private fortunes gained from labour-free income." Closely connected to this was a strong limitation on inheritance rights. Finally, the commission pointed out that the taking over of private fortunes by the state opened new horizons for the realising of socialisation. "This can not occur only through socialisation of enterprises, but also through socialisation of fortunes. By this the state takes the place of the private owners or part-owners of the means of production that is represented by fortunes."

This proposal hardly seems to have been compatible with the principle of compensation for socialisation. Should the state first exapropriate an enterprise with compensation, and then take the compensation? A strange idea of the difference between enterprise and fortune lies behind this proposal. It is also worth noticing that it seems to have been thought that fortunes that were sufficiently large to give their owners a labour-free existence should be taken over by the state, but that lesser fortunes, giving a complementary labour-free income, should not. In the main this clause is one of the least thought-out of the entire proposal. The party executive, without motivation, suggested that it should be rejected. In the debate (Branting, Thorsson) it was said that the clause could be interpreted as a desire to confiscate all private property, and that therefore it was unsuitable. According to certain reservations put forward within the party executive the clause should be given another formulation: "The taking over by the state of large private fortunes," and "the taking over by the state of private fortunes to the extent that this limits the labour-free income of the owner to an existence minimum" respectively. The suggestion of the party executive was accepted. Thus, the non-informative point has been maintained unaltered.

Perhaps it has already been sufficiently pointed out that the programme of 1920 involved a very important revision of the Marxist scheme.

According to Marx's theory of society, the pairs of opposites proletariat-bourgeois and exploited-exploiters were identical. The new "general basic principles" was concerned only with the latter named pair, and used the concepts of exploiter and exploited in a very vague way, and one which was certainly quite different from that used by Marx. Instead of the idea of total socialisation at a given period of social development, the suggestion appeared of socialisation in certain areas, together with a more general planned economy. Measures in accordance with this plan did not agree with Marx's large perspective, and in fact were aimed at opposing the prophecied development. If part of production was socialised, and if planned economy was introduced with reference to those parts of production not transfered into state ownership, then the free play of the economic forces upon which Marx's predictions rested would be prevented.

When the 1920 party congress met, the liberal-socialist coalition government was already in the process of disintegration. The differences of opinion had become concentrated around the question of municipal taxes, and there was a general feeling that some solution must soon be reached. Thorsson, the Minister of Finance, supported by his party comrades, demanded that the question should definitely be solved according to certain guidelines which the Social Democrats considered to involve just appeasement for the poor groups of the population, in particular the industrial workers. The liberals wished for a provisional solution, in part along lines other than those recommended by Thorsson. The question was taken up for debate at the congress and a resolution decided upon that partly included the recommendation of Thorsson's proposal and partly expressed the willingness of the party to "take all the consequences that might be necessary for the carrying through of this reform," i.e., give the party leadership power, should the coalition break down, to build a purely Social Democratic government. It is clear from the debate in the social democratic press that the desire to propagate the idea of socialisation more freely, and to set in motion an investigation in this question affected the decision.

Some weeks later, at the beginning of March, 1920, Edén retired because of the question of municipal tax. After Edén refused to try to form a new government, the task was given to Branting who, in connection with the decision of the party congress, put himself in the foreground as a purely social democratic prime minister. In the government declaration it was stressed that in the first place the questions of municipal tax and dwellings would be dealt with. In several contexts it was underlined that the government would not try to realise demands more concerned with socialist principles. The government consisted only of Social Democrats, but the party's view of things was not so widespread that such a government was seen as parliamentarily obvious; "the fact will certainly force a strong limitation of the government's programme."

The proposal put forward regarding the question of municipal tax had "no particularly socialistic tinge." The limiting of the working programme became even more marked due to the time at which the government was formed.

However, the government considered that there were reasons to begin preparatory investigations "pertaining to the questions of penetrating social and economic changes that the time itself has made current." In particular the questions of industrial democracy and socialisation.

"I am convinced," said Branting, "that an objective investigation, without attention being paid to prejudiced opinions, of these lines of social development enforced by the productive strength of our people will indicate accessible ways of doing away with the present sharp conflicts in the society, and thereby lay the foundations for a better future for the whole of our nation."

In the main the parliament accepted the proposal of the government in the question of dwellings, but with reference to municipal tax it took the liberal line. However, the government decided to remain in power. On July 22nd an investigation committee was appointed for the questions of socialisation, industrial democracy and trust control. In the Cabinet the prime minister gave detailed statements with regard to the first two of these investigations.

With regard to the question of socialisation, the prime minister stated first that in the view of Social Democracy there was a fundamental lack in the private capitalist society—that to a very large extent production was outside public-control. "In the basic premises of the present social order there are no satisfactory guarantees either that production as an entity is given the most rational orientation possible, or that profit in the various branches is used in the way that is best from the national economic and social point of view. Free competition . . . has partly led to an uncontrolled and senseless competition that causes several superfluous jobs and therefore, in the long run, contributes to the fact that commodities become dearer, instead of cheaper, and in other instances partly prepared the ground for monopolies of several types, whose results have time after time shown themselves to be contrary to the clear interests of society." Furthermore, Branting reminded that since the world war the demand for an economic reconstruction of society has grown in strength. Sweden already possesses various different forms of public participation within production. State and municipal production, limited companies with the state as participant and controller (the manufacturing of tobacco and spirits), possession by both the state and private owners together (Grangesbergsbolaget). Various mixed forms should be noted by the investigation. It was necessary to "try to unite the advantages for the public, that could be reached by allowing free initiative the breathing space it needs, and the security in knowing that the good of the whole was being looked after, that it seems never could be achieved on the basis of the interests of private possessions. . . . A schematic socialisation of the total production is far from the way of thinking that has developed . . ." The investigation should be free to the extent that it could take up questions in those areas in which socialisation was called for, and questions as to the ways in which it was to be realised. The appointed committee, who received the title "Board of Socialisation," had extensive powers in the question of the forms the investigation was to take. The social democratic members, composing the majority, were originally Sandler, Möller, Steffen and Karleby.

Industrial democracy was characterised by the Prime Minister as "a new form of the situation existing in industry and similar enterprises between the owners of the means of production, the technical leaders of production and those who participated in the various aspects of production, in that the influence of the latter named groups with regard to the administration and general development of the enterprise should be secured, and thereby the (at present often absent) solidarity of the industrial workers with the production that is the fruit of their labour be promoted." A parallel to political democracy was to be found in the area of economics. Industrial democracy should be able to be introduced both in state-owned enterprises and those in private ownership, but for practical reasons the investigation should be limited to that production which was led by private persons or corporations.

Branting stressed that there were many very difficult problems involved in the forming of the new institute. Many different proposals had been put forward in the question of the composition and competence of the proposed representatives of industry. No definite line was established. In fact it seems from Branting's statement that the government lacked any definite concept of what industrial democracy should mean. In one context questions of the conditions of labour, not regulated by agreement, the revision of the current labour agreement, etc., were mentioned as possible tasks for the industrial representations. But in another context it was held that the most central question was that of workers, and officials, influence over the technical and economic administration of the enterprise. The former statement seems to hint that the aim was a very limited right to take part in decisions. The latter statement, on the other hand, (that is in fact in great agreement with the definition of industrial democracy as stated) suggests that industrial democracy would mean a sort of guild-socialism.

In the electioneering of the following months, prior to the lower house election, the central issue was the question of socialisation. In Conservative and Liberal circles the ideas of free initiative and the principle of private ownership were advocated, against the plans for socialisation that the decisions of the investigation committee were considered to make clear. Within

Social Democracy, on the one hand there was talk of the advantages of socialisation and evidence of strong radicalism, on the other hand the Conservatives and Liberals were accused of speculation, in that they were using fear of socialisation in their propaganda, despite the fact that no immediate plans for socialisation were contemplated. Therefore it should be pointed out that already prior to the decisions of the investigation committee, the leaders of the Social Democrats were conscious that these decisions would cause a strong reaction amongst the Conservatives and Liberals, and in that way create a basis for the election struggle. At a meeting of the party executive after the parliamentary session, Branting gave reasons why the government should remain in power, despite the defeat in the question of municipal tax. In this connection he stated that in particular the government should continue dealing with the Ålands-question. But he added: "The great questions of industrial democracy, socialisation and trust control should also be observed, which, due to the pressure of work, have not yet been brought forward. Initiative in these questions will quickly be taken, followed by statements that will be much opposed by the Conservatives and Liberals. After the publication of these statements a great bourgeois campaign against us will be instigated. Here we have the pattern for the election campaign. The election cry will be For or against social democratic ideas!" After the decisions of the investigation committee, the social democratic press stressed that because of these decisions the question of socialisation was brought into the current debate.

However, during the election campaign the socialisation propaganda of the party was characterised by a certain restraint and doubt. Even though the question of socialisation was in the foreground, it cannot be said that the electioneering was concentrated on this issue. The great energy and enthusiasm that developed some years previously in the struggle for democracy was not evident in this election campaign. It was often stated that there could be no immediate socialisation. Vague and reserved means of expression were common, with regard to the meaning of socialisation. The whole atmosphere in the party was characterised by a certain ambiguity. It may be asked whether the leaders of the party did not in fact consider the possibility of immediate action for socialisation, or whether, for tactical reasons only, they did not wish to bring this idea forward. Perhaps it was counted on that the election that would be of great importance from the point of view of socialisation would come only later, after the extended franchise decided by the government in relation to the lower house election had definitely been accomplished. In any case, it is certain that the idea of socialisation had such an important place in the propaganda that an election victory could be seen as evidence of the peoples' wish for socialisation. This was heavily underlined by the Conservative and Liberal parties.

It is noticeable that the election manifesto of the party, with its comparatively thorough treatment of questions in this connection, is characterised by a certain defensive tendency. Much space is given to a defence of the inquiries that had been instigated. Mainly there was criticism of both parties that could be said to be anti-democratic—the right-wingers and the left-socialists, the latter due to their proximity to Bolshevik Communism. These parties were said to wish to boycottt the investigations. Doubtless this was correct, to the extent that both these parties criticised the decisions made by the investigation committee, the right-wing because of its anti-socialism, the left-socialists because they demanded an immediate action for socialisation, and they saw in the investigations a means of avoiding this. But the rest of the bourgeois parties—the liberals and the new farmers party—gave the cold shoulder to the investigations.

Despite this, the manifesto tried to combine the results of the investigations with democracy by presenting criticism of these decisions as a part of anti-democratic propaganda. The election manifesto summarised the wishes of the Social Democrats with regard to the question of socialisation as follows: "Production shall, carefully and in a planned and conscious manner, be reorganized with the aim of furthering general affluence and economic justice in the society. The guiding principle of this organisation must be that all opportunities to increase production are utilised, because only in this way can general affluence be achieved, and the opportunities for capitalist profiteering decreased, finally to be abolished. . . . In the first instance it is necessary for the state to surrender its right of disposal over private monopoly and more important of the country's natural resources." It is noticeable that here the phrase "right of disposal," not "right of ownership" was used.

It was further maintained in the manifesto that the defeat of capitalism by socialism was in the interests not only of industrial and agricultural workers but also of many civil servants and smaller farmers. With regard to the land question it was stressed that Social Democracy protected the interests of the agricultural workers and small farmers against capitalism and the owners, after which the new land programme was quoted.

The points of view that have just been taken up varied somewhat in the press and in the election speeches of the Social Democrats. It was constantly maintained that immediate socialisation was out of the question, that Social Democracy was not tied to certain dogmas, but would judge each individual situation as it occurred.

At the same time, the value of partial socialisation measures was undeniable. In a speech on the 22nd August, Branting explained that the inquiry into socialisation was impartial, because even opponents were on the Board. However, quite naturally the directives must bear the traces of the social democratic government that prepared them. Regarding the advance of socialisation, Branting stated that it would be impossible to stop half way, and that this was also true for democracy. However, he added that Social Democrats did not hold by any dogmas, but on the contrary "as the real bearers of socialist thought (they) look upon the advancing economic development, whilst our forms only claim to be the expression of this development." This last thought, by which Social Democracy represented insight into the course of life, is, as usual, a recurrent theme—the only Marxist theme that can be traced. It was constantly asserted that the plans for socialisation did not include the smaller farmers. These points in the programme that were considered to appeal to small farmers and other small-holders were often underlined. At the completion of the election campaign, statements regarding socialisation seemed to have become more and more reserved. In one of his last election speeches on the 4th September, Branting said that the election campaign had been characterised by "a theoretical discussion of problems that are not at present current." It would be strange if decisions were made about the activities of the Socialisation Board before the results of the investigations had been published. However, Branting continued, "We are convinced the time is ripening for the socialisation of certain large concerns and natural resources, which according to general opinion should be transferred into state ownership. In this matter we have not severed all criticism with regard to the scope and the practical treatment of this question. . . ." Concerning the method of socialisation, on this occasion Branting said that possibly a start could be made by socialising 20 to 30 percent of certain more important industries, so that the state had control over the total production.

The impression given by the social democratic statements regarding the question of socialisation in the spring and summer of 1920, is the same as that given by earlier debates. From the beginning the party had held up socialisation as the important aim, without trying to clarify just what this socialisation would mean, or how it would be accomplished. This attitude was supported by the Marxist doctrine that saw in socialism the inevitable result of the free play of economic forces, and therefore was able to label every attempt to plan this as utopian. In fact, this doctrine led to an extreme form of utopianism. Socialism became a stimulating dream of the future, not a social construction built on the results of investigations and on theoretical reflection. Social Democracy, due to its rapidly gained position of political power and outside influence, was now in the position of being morally forced (even if not in a detailed way) to clarify its position with regard to that issue that was the starting point of the party's activity. It was unthinkable to continue to support the Marxist theory of developmental fatalism. A Social Democratic government could not explain that it had confidence in leaving development to capitalist tendencies. Neither could it completely apply itself to socio-political work that was characterised by bourgeois reformism. The ideological idyll under the protection of Marx's great perspective was at an end, and could never be revived.

A general insecurity must characterise all attempts to clarify, or more correctly to formulate, the ideas of the party, caused by this situation. Total socialism, that previously had been propagated without being made precise, must be replaced by concrete, partial and successive socialisation. Plans for action on foreign lines were quickly assembled. But time was short, as was the opportunity to investigate actual conditions, and the analysis of problems that could give these plans firmness and stringency. The entire debate had the character of an improvisation. In connection with this there was a continuous conflict between the new demands for realism and for the concrete, and the old utopianism. Therefore at the same time that it was attempted to form practical suggestions, there was also talk of allowing "development" to rule, and of adapting to "circumstances" as they actually were. It was only with great doubt that the leaders of Social Democracy abandoned the ivory tower of Marxism.

At the time of the election all the left-wing parties experienced a decline, whilst the right-wing and farmers parties grew. Social democratic representation in the lower house was reduced from 86 to 75 places. This defeat—the first suffered by the party—meant that the difficulties that have been mentioned were temporarily put on one side. But this seems also to have raised doubts regarding the idea of socialisation, and therefore was of importance for the future policies of the party. It was generally considered that propaganda in the question of socialisation had weakened the party's position, particularly in the countryside. Certain facts make it probable that this idea was correct, and that the criticism of the Conservative and Liberal parties that compared socialisation with a return to the methods of war economy was very effective. Since that time the question of socialisation has never been in the foreground in the way that it was in 1920.

After a period of delay, depending on foreign affairs (the Åland question) the Social Democratic government retired at the end of October. The most important reason was of course the election defeat. But it is characteristic of the party's position that the emerging economic crisis was also given as a motive for the change of government. After the war wages had risen, but now a period of wage depression and unemployment was beginning. During the negotiations of the party executive in the question of government, Thorsson, the Minister of Finance, stated that the situation made an early resignation necessary. His statement is so illuminating that it should be stated fully. "The economic difficulties are coming to a head. . . . It will be difficult for any government to rule during the coming period, but most difficult of all for a Social Democratic government. Should we continue to govern we would be forced to violate all too many of the points of our programme. This would only lead to an uproar in the country the like of which has never been heard. A government should be formed having the special task of dealing with economic problems. It must be stressed that the demand for increased wages must cease. But the question is, have we the courage for this? Quite simply, an economic policy other than the one we are able to put forward is necessary. Therefore we will serve the country best if we resign. . . . The economic situation being as it is today forces into the foreground the necessity to limit import. The alternatives of increased custom duties or prohibiting import must be considered. A Social Democratic government can not sit in power in such a situation. Quite simply the internal political situation in the country makes it necessary for the government to resign." A government whose Minister of Finance could utter such a statement could hardly be expected to lead an action for socialisation. Seen in relation to Thorsson's words, the entire debate regarding socialisation assumes the character of fiction.

The Disintegration of the Theory of Socialisation and the Victory of the Welfare Ideology

EVER SINCE 1920 Social Democracy as a whole has steadily advanced, although not so rapidly nor so continuously as at the beginning of the 20th century. The number of seats held in the lower house rose from 75 in 1920 to 112 in 1936. The only exception to this being the election of 1928. Since the abolition of graded franchise in municipal elections in 1918 in the years that followed the party claimed about 50 mandates in the upper house. At the beginning of the 1930s the number of representatives in the upper house rose to over 60. The advances were related to the growth of the industrial working class, and to the fact that support had been won from other social groups, in particular the agricultural workers. Not the least important is the fact that those social groups to which Social Democracy appealed most strongly had become increasingly active politically, and as far as participation in elections was concerned had nearly reached the level of other social groups. Party membership rose from 143,000 in 1920 to 368,000 in 1936.

The party leadership had been unusually stable. However, it is perhaps possible to speak of a change of generations in the middle of the 1920s when a number of leading party men (in particular Branting and Thorsson) died, and others retired from their positions. But even before that time a great many members of the generation that began its activity within the party in the first decade of the 20th century had attained important positions in the party council and the government. Later, that generation had formed the entire leadership. For more than thirty years the same names recur in congressional debates, brochures and newspapers. The second generation within the party were more numerous than the first, and to a greater extent has kept the leading posts within its own circle.

In the first Branting government party veterans in their 60s and representatives of the other generation aged from 35–40 sat side by side. In later years almost all Social Democratic ministers have been aged 50–60 years. In this respect the party has developed in the way that is common to all movements that at first advance rapidly and later are stable for a long period. It is probable that to a certain extent the political attitude of the party has been influenced by this fact.

When Branting died it was said in many circles that the internal conflicts that earlier were overshadowed by the authority of the ageing party chief would come into the foreground and threaten the unity of the party. This has not been the case. Conflicts have occurred within the party, mainly on the question of defence, but they have not lead to a lasting division such as that which occurred prior to 1917, and neither has the outward solidarity of the party been worsened. During this period quarrels within the party were so few and so insignificant that no attention needs to be paid to them here.

More and more markedly the desire for agreement and common understanding has dominated the internal debate of the party just as it has dominated the behaviour towards other parties. The resolutions of the party congresses on question on which there have been definite differences of opinion have been framed as compromises, and often have been able to be accepted by all. It is important in this connection that the new youth organisation that appeared after the party split in 1917 (The Swedish League of Young Social Democrats) unlike the earlier youth organisations, did not form the platform for a radical opposition, but on all important issues held the same opinions as the party as a whole.

Unlike the Social Democrats, the small extremist workers parties have split time after time, in connection with which group after group have joined the large party. In this way many of the leaders of the left-Socialist party, founded in 1917, have returned to Social Democracy. In 1923, after the founding of the Communist Party, the Leftist-Socialists returned, amongst them being Vennerström, E. Lindberg, and Månsson. In 1925 the so-called Höglund-Communists returned, amongst them Höglund and Ström. Persons who for several years denounced Social Democratic policy as the policy of traitors, and who strongly criticised the present political system, adapted themselves without friction to the moderate policy of the party. It was only in the question of defence that the former Leftist-Socialists and Communists represented an extreme position.

At the beginning of the 1920s Swedish crisis policy had, to use an expression often used in the crisis debates of the 1930s, a largely "negative" stamp. By means of suppressions an attempt was made to curtail government expenses and to create deflation by a restrictive economic policy. In their propaganda for deflation the Social Democrats first and foremost pointed to the high prices, whilst in conservative circles there was criticism of the high wages. The immediate damage caused by the crisis was mitigated by unemployment, and relief by so-called reserve labour, with its low wages, and also to some extent by government credit to banks and industrial enterprises. There was no systematic attempt to raise purchasing power or stimulate commerce and industry by promoting productive labour, or by government assistance to industry. Proposals from conservative circles regarding considerable increases in protective tariffs were rejected. On the other hand, increased tariffs on agrarian products were approved. However, due to circumstances not discussed here a rapid recovery took place. The number of unemployed that had reached a maximum of 163,000 in 1922 dropped to 55,000 at the beginning of 1923 and to 15,000–30,000 in the following years. Deflation proceeded with heavy decreases in the actual amount of money earned by the workers, though a certain rise in real-wages remained seen in relation to the pre-war period. The Price Index—with a base of 100 in 1913—was 376 in the summer of 1920, but 163 at the end of 1922. The Swedish crown regained parity with gold at the turn of the year 1922–23. A period of rapidly rising affluence followed the crisis.

The Social Democrats pursued no particular line during this period. The idea of a positive and expansive crisis policy of the type that was put forward under similar circumstances something more than a decade earlier seems not to have gained headway in the party. The only point on which a more definite opposition to the bourgeois was to be found was the question of unemployment benefit. The Social Democrats demanded much milder conditions for the obtaining of unemployment benefit.

During the years directly following the elections of 1920, the party's activity was of a purely defensive character. Of course it was explained that the crisis was a result of the capitalist system, but at the same time it was stressed that it was an international crisis and that an isolated socialisation in Sweden was not a way out. At the parliament of 1921 the party's parliamentary group maintained that the Social Democrats were "to a large extent dedicated to the defence of results that have already been won; any thought of advance was out of the question." The conservative stop-gap cabinet (led first by DeGear, later by von Syndow) that in October was appointed with the party's sanction met with loyalty, and even though it put forward proposals of which the party did not approve, was not criticised to such an extent as to endanger its existence. The government bills regarding raised tariffs met with opposition from the party but were carried through as far as farming was concerned, largely due to inter-party cooperation. The conservative plea for changes in the statute on working-hours was rejected. The Social Democrats motioned in vain for a grant for unemployment assistance that exceeded that asked for by the government.

The question of socialisation was broached in parliament partly in the

Budget Debate and partly in a debate occasioned by a comment of the Constitutional Committee regarding the authority of the Board of Socialisation. The cautious statements of the Social Democrats indicate that the question was in no way considered to be a pressing one.

Branting stated that at the present time a reaction was in the air, but that "a furthering of the demands of the unpropertied masses in society for another form of property distribution" could shortly be expected. When these questions became current once again it was important to have access to an investigation into "a rational transition to other social conditions." Therefore, the work of the Socialisation Board was oriented towards "a peaceful social development." Naturally, said Sandler, private capitalist society was in many respects defective, but nevertheless it was necessary to be on guard against throwing it away without being able to replace it with something else.

The decisions regarding the extension of the franchise to elections to the lower house (as per the agreement made at the autumn session of parliament) were definitely promulgated in 1921, and new elections were arranged for as early as in the autumn of that year so that the new provisions would be enforced. The election campaign was not concentrated on any definite issue. The main theme in the Social Democratic propaganda was a defensive one. In the election manifesto it was emphasized that it was necessary to prevent a reaction against the "popular policies energetically and successfully pursued by the Liberal-Socialist and Social Democratic leadership for three years." It was stated that amongst other things the reactionary aims included the raising of custom duties, the abolition of the statute on the 8-hour working day and the prohibition against strikes applied to certain groups of workers.

Outstanding amongst the reforms that were demanded were the procuring of independent farms for agricultural workers, crofters and small-scale tenant farmers, unemployment insurance and industrial democracy. Regarding the latter issue it was said: "If the voting masses give to Social Democracy the support that it needs in the election struggle, it is clear that political democracy must be supplemented by industrial democracy, which destroys the absolute power held by capital within production and elevates the worker from his position of cog in a machine to a position of participation and influence in industrial activity. In the approaching parliamentary session the Committee appointed by the first Social Democratic government of our country will submit proposals that should point the way to the further penetration of society by the spirit of democracy and democratic order."

With regard to the question of socialisation reference was made to the investigation that was in progress. The time would come "when the preparation for the disintegration of the capitalist society will become an absolute necessity." It was quite clear from the formulation used on this point that there was no intention of making current the socialisation issue during the next election period.

Election speeches and pamphlets, as well as election propaganda were characterised by short-term demands and points of view. Even if it was occasionally said that the capitalist system was the cause of the economic crisis, this notion was not presented as the justification for a rapid socialist reconstruction. In one of his speeches Branting said that the depression was caused by the fact that the desire for profit that was part of the present order determined the form of production. "We desire to abolish this basic fault. We understand that a deeply rooted system such as this cannot be replaced by another overnight. It is not the work of a day but the work of a decade that we are now preparing (through the Board of Socialisation). The socialist society that we wish to create will not be fashioned after any theoretical stereotyped model but will be built on experience—on life's own teachings." Moller formulated the party's aims as follows: "through industrial democracy the taking-over of the means of production." It was constantly emphasised that the socialist society must be built up through a policy of gradual reforms. On the whole the impression is that the socialisation issue was put forward rather less and in a somewhat more hesitant manner than during the election campaign of the previous year. The immediate pressing problems now came more to the fore. The parliamentary motions of the right-wing were a target for polemic that was absent in 1920.

At the election the Social Democrats won 18 new seats whilst all the other parties suffered defeats, and on the 13th October Branting formed the second exclusively Social Democratic government. Its programme was characterised by the same moderacy that characterised the first Branting ministry, but was phrased in even more general terms. The government said that it was "fully aware that it must perform the task of a national Swedish government of the people under particularly trying conditions." After this the economic crisis was dealt with.

As the inevitable result of the capitalist form of production a wave of violent economic depression has swept over us, bringing in its wake unemployment and distress for great masses of the people otherwise active in production. It should be observed that it was not directly stated that capitalism was the cause of the crisis, but of unemployment and distress. It was said that a new burgeoning of commerce and industry would occur "when it comes to the pinch . . . to realize the era of peace and common understanding." That is, the crisis could be overcome without socialism. The government requested increased assistance for the unemployed, and opposed raised custom duties and inflation. The big investigations should be completed. Social legislation should be maintained and those improvements of these suggested "which after careful examination of the nation's financial resources were deemed both desirable and feasible."

From the point of view of the party's ideological development the second Branting ministry is of less interest than any other Social Democratic government. It can possibly be said that its moderation and its relative inactivity marked a step in the turning of Social Democracy into a reformist party, with no distinct programme for the moulding of society. No remarkable or radical initiatives were taken by the government. No proposals at all of a particularly Social Democratic character were presented. An indication of this is the fact that after the parliament of 1922 the party's own newspaper said that the government could only nominally be called Social Democratic, and there was much irony in Liberal and Conservative circles as to the government's lack of radicalism. During the Budget Debate at the 1922 parliament the liberal leader said that the government was "bourgois to an unexpectedly high degree." In his reply, Branting maintained that in accordance with the programme proclamation, the government wanted a "Swedish national government of the people," and that it hoped to gather around it social groups other than just Social Democrats. The labouring masses had not viewed the accession of the government with any exaggerated expectations. "They fully realised that no big steps could be taken at present against the situation in the world that oppresses us as well as other countries. Under such circumstances we can not ask much of a government that in any case due to the pressure of conditions must constantly be aware of the necessity of a parliamentary sub-stratum for accomplishing the real and substantial things at hand, so that by putting itself in a definite minority position it does not jeopardise its own existence. I believe that amongst the Swedish labouring masses who have given their votes to our party there exists a high political training and an insight into the exigencies of the situation. I think that in relying upon this we have dared to put into practice a policy that is (to quote Herr Eden) as "bourgeois" as it could possibly be, in accordance with his description."

The conflicts at the parliament of 1922 were mainly concerned with questions that are of no importance from the point of view of ideological development. The government met with a noticeable defeat when its proposed trade agreement with Russia was rejected. The bill regarding the amount of unemployment assistance was approved as far as the size of the amount was concerned, but on the question of the terms of this disbursement the parliament supported a decision that was more restrictive than that desired by the government.

The controversy was concerned with the extent to which refusal to take the job offered in place of a worker engaged in a labour conflict should mean loss of compensation for the worker involved. One of the most interest government proposals was a bill (accepted by parliament) that extended government credit to private banks who found themselves in difficult circumstances. This bill was justified by the Social Democratic Minister of Finance on the grounds that the rights of savers must be protected. The bill was criticised by both Communists and Leftist-Socialists. In this and other cases the opponents on the Left could rightly claim that the current Social Democratic policy was to maintain and stabilise the existing order, not to disturb it. Gradually, Thorsson came to personify the governmental policy of thrift. Of particular importance in this connection is a government decision regarding a reduction of Committee routine in autumn 1922. This measure caused a much greater sensation than can be justified by its financial import.

The government's behaviour at the parliament of 1923 was proof of its desire to follow the moderate policy of reconstruction. However, as early as in April the government took upon itself to resign, since the Upper House rejected the proposal regarding directives on the question of unemployment that had already been accepted by the Lower House. The proposal had originated in compromise between the Social Democrats and a liberal group, but had also won certain support from other parties.

By resigning on this issue the government showed its desire to represent the interests of the working class. The acceding Conservative government, headed by Trygger, was met with bitter criticism from Social Democratic circles, but quickly showed itself willing to follow the policy of concord pursued by the retiring government. The statute on working hours was renewed with certain modifications. Due to the continued mitigation of the crisis, tension on the labour market was reduced. In the years that followed the political debate was concentrated around the question of defence.

Occasionally in the Social Democratic press a criticism of the second Branting ministry's "bourgeois" nature can be traced; but in the main it was stressed that the cautious politics of the government were approved of. The government was praised for its thrift, moderation and sense of reality. It was hinted that a more radical line would have meant a policy of adventuring that would have placed the social order in jeopardy. It was argued that without putting through a particularly socialist policy, the government nevertheless worked for the good of the working class, and hence for the good of the society as a whole. Occasionally it was hinted that the very existence of a Social Democratic government in a time of crisis was conducive to appeasing the workers, and therefore to social tranquility. In August 1922 the "Social Democraten" wrote: "For a year we have had a Social Democratic government. Has it not shown wisdom and moderation in the carrying out of its task? Is it not largely due to the government that our country has been able to come through the most pressing economic crisis we have ever experienced without any appreciable jolts worth speaking of? There is certainly no great risk that such a government will throw the country into a hazardous situation with unknown consequences. But on the other hand, it is of enormous importance not only for the suffering working class but also for society itself that in this way the road is opened for the working class seriously to assert their viewpoints, desires and interests." In an article entitled "Principen och livet" (Principle and Life) Engberg explained that the Social Democratic party "is forced to limit it's current demands so much that in practice there is room for them within the framework of liberal reformist policy. In principle demands always extend far beyond this framework, but the existing conditions makes it necessary to safeguard the form, when it is a choice between something or nothing." In some quarters it was contended that preferably the party should remain in a minority position for the time being. If the majority was won, either the party's reformist zeal would be blunted or the Conservative and Liberal groups would refuse to acquiesce to the reforms decided on by the Social Democrats. This strange reasoning seems to have been founded on the idea that if the party had the majority it would be morally obliged to try to carry through its general programme. On the other hand as long as the party only embraced a minority it was free to cooperate and make compromises with the others. It had not come to be seen as natural that a Social Democratic majority could consider other opinions yet still follow the moderate policy that was initiated when they were in a minority position. The majority was still regarded as the equivalent of a total seizure of power.

At the parliament of 1924, which was dominated by the defence issue the Social Democrats put forward some more extensive economic and social proposals. It should be stressed that in all certainty at least some of this initiative would have been taken even if the party had remained in a governing position. To a great extent the proposals resulted from the investigations that had first been completed in 1923. Thus many motions were based on the report of 1923 of the Land Commission appointed in 1918. On the whole these motions were concerned with the carrying through of large parts of the Social Democratic land programme. The opportunities for the corporations to acquire land were to be further curtailed. The usufructuaries should, under certain circumstances, have the right to redeem the area they cultivated and in general be assured of safe possession. The formation of new farms should be promoted, for instance through extended right of expropriation, and the institution of entailed estate was to be abolished. Several of the motions led to requests of parliament for inquiries and government bills.

The great importance ascribed to the question of industrial democracy within the party had expressed on several occasions during the preceding years. In the election manifesto of the 1922 county elections there was mention of "the great problem of industrial democracy, important for the entire immediate future of the working class," the solution of which "must lead to a necessary deepening of the entire process of democratisation in the society." The Investigation Committee appointed in 1920 and headed by Wigforss since October 1921 submitted its report in March 1923. This included a proposal regarding operating boards made by the majority of the Committee, with one exception composed of Social Democrats. Such Boards should be established in every enterprise of a given size, and be composed of elected representatives of the workers. The task of the Boards should be to "give the workers increased insight into production and an increased capacity for active partipation in promoting the production," and also to bring about "improved cooperation between the workers and the management of the enterprise."

The Boards should only act in an advisory capacity. In general, they should be given the opportunity to express themselves on questions of technique and business, and also on questions relating to the workers position in the enterprise. However, questions of wages and bargaining agreements should be dealt with as previously. A more precise description of the range of activity of these Boards was not stated in the legislative draft. It was stated that the entire proposal rested "on mutual good-will and cooperation." Should this be lacking then the proposed methods have clearly shown themselves to be impracticable and the problem must be attacked in other ways." Several of the Liberal and Conservative members definitely rejected the proposal. To them it was absurd to give "the workers insight or powers in areas that . . . must be reserved for capital and which, if surrendered, would deprive Swedish industry of its power to compete with other countries." An arrangement by which the employers would in some cases negotiate with the operating Boards, and in other cases with the trade unions, which perhaps might have ideas contrary to those of the Boards, would lead to misunderstanding and friction. "A continued development along the road embarked upon i.e. a gradual development of the general provisions in the collective bargaining agreements seems to us to be the fastest and most correct solution to reaching the desired goal of a trusting cooperation between workers and employers in the same enterprise." Johan-Olov Johansson, a Social Democrat, voted with the majority in the Committee but in a reservation explained that legislation in accordance with the proposal of the Committee could be expected to be ineffective because of the conflict existing between workers and employers. It could not be expected that the workers "would consider themselves called upon to give such advice and direction that on certain occasions of negotiations and instances of conflict would amount to a partial disarmament." A primary requisite for balancing the conflict between capital and labour was "that the workers maintain the right to participate in decisions on questions of the employment and dismissal of workers, on the supervision and allocation of the work and also with a right to participate in the management of the various enterprises."

As early as the spring of 1920 the party executive and the secretariat of the Swedish Federation of Labour (L.O.) had appointed a Committee of twelve members to inquire into the question of industrial democracy. After the Committee appointed by the government had submitted its report this "workers committee" convened to make a statement with regard to this. It was clear that several trade unionists were critical of the proposal of the committee, largely for the same reasons stated by Johan-Olov Johansson in his reservation. At the final meeting of the "workers committee," however, only eight members took part, and of these seven recommended in principle the adoption of the proposal of the governmental committee. However, the remarks made regarding this do not indicate any enthusiasm. Opinions indicated that only an advisory power for the operating Boards was conceivable and useful. "To the extent that one is clear that the right of decision in the hands of the Boards either would be meaningless, or would mean that the Boards became the organ for creating open conflicts for purposes which hitherto have not led to such conflicts, or finally a form of confiscation of property, to the same extent one should admit that the sensible course for development in this matter is mutual voluntary agreements." In practice the value of the operative Boards would primarily depend on the competence of the working class itself. Some minor alterations in the proposal were required. A reservation was made by K. D. Berg, who supported Johan-Olov Johansson. Amongst other things he said: "The only advantage to the workers in elevating this proposal to the dignity of a law is the increased insight into management that the members of the operating Boards would gain in that the employers would be liable to give them information regarding the position of the enterprise. But in many cases even this advantage may be illusory, because due to the present vague state of the law it allows the employers too many tempting opportunities for sabotage."

It is evident from the contribution to the debate just quoted, and from the debate in general, that there was strong doubt in the trade union movement regarding the proposal of the Committee. In fact, this proposal was extraordinarily restrained compared to the opinions as to the import of industrial democracy that were current a couple of years earlier. In the propaganda for this about 1920 it had been made to appear as a great step towards socialisation, or at least as a means of giving the workers considerable influence over the running of the enterprise. Now it had been practically reduced to a method of giving the workers information regarding the activities of the enterprise in question and in that way bringing them into contact with the employers. It is probable that many of those who supposed the idea of industrial democracy thought that it would prepare the way for socialisation by technically and economically educating the workers, but this long-term perspective had little relation to the current situation. Of the unclear measures proposed in the debate of 1920, that awoke great expectations, the proposal regarding industrial democracy was the first to fall to pieces, when an attempt was made to get away from generalisations and achieve stringency and precision.

However, at the parliament of 1924 the Social Democratic parliamentary group also submitted a proposal on the same subject. This simply amounted to a suggestion that the parliament should request of the Crown that legislation regarding the operating Boards should be prepared "essentially in agreement with the main lines put forward in the proposal of the government Committee." The second standing Committee on Laws rejected the motion under the reservations of the Social Democrats. Amongst other things the Committee maintained that no strong opinion in favour of the proposal was noticeable. The debates in the Chambers that took place at the end of the session were very brief and uninformative. In the lower house there were only three statements, of which one was from the Social Democrats. The motions were rejected without a vote.

During these years the Board of Socialisation was mainly occupied with investigations in connection with the debates abroad. However, in spring 1924 the Board presented a report entitled "State railways as a Public Business Institution," in which concrete suggestions were made regarding the management of the State Railways. The suggestion deal with the technical aspects of the problem of socialisation in a certain sphere. As the chairman of the Board, Sandler, put it, "the upshot is that the State railways should be a public enterprise owned by the State and under the control of the State, but independent of the State's political organisation with regard to leadership and management." The Board maintained that the business of the State could not be run rationally unless "administrative forms come into being that deviated from the state administration proper and that were caused by the very nature of business." The present situation was characterised by the fact that the State Railways had come into being as an extension of the state's general administration, at the same time as being the largest economic enterprise in the country. This situation was characterised by "a duplicity in the mode of operation that at bottom involves the constant interweaving of general state policy and the finance of State railways. This interweaving has made the State Railways into a hybrid of business enterprise and political administrative organ." The Board recommended a constitutional provision according to which the state's business enterprises should be administered separately and the fundamental provisions concerning this administration should be set out in special laws. Further a state railway law was proposed. According to this the supreme right of decision over the administration of the railways would be vested in an assembly of twenty-nine persons appointed by the Crown, the parliament, personnel employed in the railways and organisations concerned with traffic interests. This assembly should elect a council which in its turn elected a head. An aim would be an attempt to cover the costs of the operation.

The wages of the personnel should be decided by agreement.

There was a certain surprise that the first proposal of Board of Socialisation amounted to a limitation of governmental control over the state railways. Apparently when the proposal had been formulated liberal economic ideas as well as Guild-socialistic ideas had been considered. When the chairman of the Board presented the proposal at the party congress of 1924, he stressed that it "undeniably implies a reaction against the notion that everything in society can be legislated on. Behind the proposal of the Board hovers the idea that one must also rely on the efficiency of the freely operating forces, and on the fact that people in our modern organised society are to a considerable extent in the position of being able to look after themselves." There was no debate on the proposal in Congress. From the scant discussion on this question in the press it is difficult to ascertain with certainty the mood within the party. Within a short time the proposal of the Board seems to have been forgotten. No measures to revive it have been taken.

At the party congress of 1924 convening immediately after the close of parliament, only one question of socio-economic importance emerged regarding the programme. The programme commission suggested that the issue of industrial democracy should be included in the programme. In accordance with this proposal it was decided that Point X should be divided into two parts, A and B. In the latter was placed the passage previously included on this point with regard to international agreements for securing the rights of the working class, and also the following: "The workers to be assured of a share of influence in privately owned enterprises."

In its proposal the Programme Commission stressed that the demand for the solution to this question had come into the foreground during the last few years. "Regarding the meaning of the concept itself it was maintained that workers' influence might involve many degrees, from a real voice in the making of decisions regarding management and operation to rights to negotiate with employers about matters concerning the enterprise." In the guild socialistic enterprises the workers were their own employers, and the principles of industrial democracy employed in these enterprises clearly could not be followed in normal capitalist enterprises, in which it was impossible simply to transfer the right of decision making in matters concerning the enterprise, as this would imply that the workers themselves took over the concern. Therefore the settling of the issue involved difficult problems of organisation. In view of this, the programme should be so formulated that "neither in an upward nor downward direction does it limit that share of influence in the enterprise that is the workers' due. Here the course of development itself will set the limits, allowing greater or lesser influence depending on the conditions of production." Luterkort, one of the members of the Committee, drew attention to the fact that very different opinions had emerged regarding the meaning of industrial democracy. The heart of the concept, however, must lie in the legal right of workers in industrial enterprises "to a certain fixed extent to take part in the deliberations of the enterprise and exercise the right of decision making in questions in which they have an important interest of their own." Therefore, the programme should be formulated as follows: "The workers to be assured by legislation of the right to take part in the making of decisions regarding the administration matters of private capitalist enterprises." The party executive took the line of the programme commission.

The debate that followed showed that there were still great differences of opinion as to what was meant by industrial democracy. Some of the speakers criticised the arguments of the programme commission as they did not speak of any real right of participation in decision making for the workers. (Luterkort, A. Ström, Wennerström), whilst other speakers were in complete accord with the statement of the Commission (Engberg, Wigforss, Möller). A move to refer the motivation to the Editing Committee was rejected by 88 votes against 83, after which the proposal of the Programme Commission was approved. Thereby it was authoritatively established that industrial democracy would not mean the vastly extended powers for the workers that during the 1920 debate on the subject had been predicted in many circles.

The lower house elections of 1924 were dominated by the defence issue. The Social Democratic election manifesto that was thoroughly discussed at the party congress mainly dealt with this question. In addition there was a reminder of the party's proposal at the parliament of that year regarding the land question and regarding the risk that the law on the eight hour day would not be renewed when it expired in 1926, and also the proposals regarding the demands for unemployment insurance and industrial democracy. Nevertheless, the latter mentioned issue was only mentioned in passing and was not broached with anything like the same fervour as in 1921. On that occasion the party clearly had hopes of winning the majority. The electorate was appealed to, to "give the lower house such a composition that the existence of a Social Democratic government will not be dependent on the half-heartedness, hesitations and whims of a small faction of bourgeois left-wingers." In the election speeches and pamphlet material, questions of principle received scant attention. The question of socialisation was more definitely put aside that it had been at both the two preceding elections. The Conservatives and Liberals accused the Social Democrats of failing to clarify their intentions on this point.

The Social Democrats won only five seats, but the party's group in the lower house came to embrace no less than 104 representatives. The Trygger ministry was prevailed upon to resign on statements from both the large parties of the Left, and the third Branting ministry was formed on 18th October, 1924. In the government declaration the question of defence was discussed almost exclusively, as were attendant international questions. For the rest, the declaration contained only the following statement: "In the question of the social reforms demanded by the times, the indications of the election are not as definitely clear as in the question of defence. But the untroubled existence of a left-majority of a democratic character seems, however, to be a fact to which one is entitled to attach certain expectations. Therefore the situation offers essential analogies to the occasion when the previous Social Democratic government came to power. That government worked to promote meaningful social reforms that were later brought forward, and it is the intention of the present government vigorously to follow this policy." Thereby establishing that the government desired to conduct a moderate policy of reforms of the same type as that followed by the previous social democratic ministry.

In January 1925 Sandler became the prime minister in place of Branting, who died a month later. Thorsson who had been intended as Branting's successor as party chairman had died in May. P. A. Hansson was appointed party leader.

In the Budget Debate of 1925 the moderation of the government became the object of ironic commentary both from the Conservatives and from the Communists. The Conservative leaders in the lower house claimed that tactical reasons prevented the presentation of the issue of socialisation. On the other hand, the liberal leader explained, that in reality the Social Democrats no longer insisted on socialisation as the way to the increased general affluence for which they strived. The Social Democrats replied in evasive and divergent terms. According to Thorsson a party must submit its entire programme to the electorate. "When they have spoken they indicate the extent to which their demands could lead to practical results." In parliament the party could reasonably attempt only to achieve what was possible on the basis of the conditions of parliamentary strength. Engberg described the work of the party as "a policy of adaptation . . . It is adaptation to the actual current political situation, but also an adaptation to what the Swedish society, at its present level of social development, is approximately in a position to carry out with respect to the present situation regarding the balance of power between the classes." In reply to the comments of the liberal leader, Sandler stated that the liberals should be satisfied if Social Democracy assimilated liberal ideas. In fact it is true that "when the gunpowder smoke surrounding the political struggles has dispersed it may easily happen, as in the case of sensible people sitting down at the table and arguing economics, that they are thinking alike in many important respects." Moreover, Social Democracy did not see socialisation essentially as a series of legislative measures. "In the way of thinking that I am representing here, socialisation is quite simply a continuing process of development that is only partly adaptable to state intervention. To a very important extent this process takes place without we in the parliament lifting a finger to help it."

The question of defence was in the foreground at the parliament of 1925. However at this, just as at the following, parliament the government succeeded in bringing through a series of legislative drafts regarding agriculture, whereby certain parts of the Social Democratic farming programme were realised. General and definite prohibition of the acquisition of real estate by business concerns was announced. The right of tenants to purchase free of encumbrance their homes that were built on the lots was extended. A new form of granting the use of Crown land (secure copyhold right) was introduced in order to promote the formation of new farms. However, certain motions put forward by the Social Democrats and which went further than these, were rejected, amongst them being a proposal regarding the right to expropriate from corporations and big land owners in order to create new farms. At the parliament of 1926 the government took the initiative in several social-political reforms. Legislation regarding working hours was tightened. The old statute regarding the hiring of labour was abolished. Proposals concerning accident insurance and a sick relief fund collapsed due to dissenting opinions on technicalities.

The third Social Democratic government also collapsed on the question of the unemployment directive. The unemployment Commission had assigned the unemployed to work at a mine in Stripa, at which a strike was in progress. This caused great bitterness amongst the workers. There were differences of opinion as to whether the Commission's decision was in agreement with the government directive. The government revoked the decision but this was not accepted by the Conservative and Liberal majority in parliament. On 2nd June 1926 the government handed in its resignation and a ministry was formed by C. G. Ekman, and was supported by Liberals and 'free-thinkers.'

During a period of rather more than six years between the formation of the first Social Democratic ministry and the fall of the party's third ministry, Social Democracy had held governmental power for about four years. Since the party had shown itself ready to form a government with the support only of a minority, it was repeatedly confronted with the necessity of accepting the mandate of government. Due to its position as the largest party in parliament, and due to the impossibility of forming coalitions, the party tended to become the regular organiser of government. The practice of the first government was followed. Social Democracy in a governing position did not try to press the radical demands of its programme but contented itself with making proposals that could serve as the foundation for occasional collaboration with one or more of the Conservative and Liberal parties, and therefore lead to a positive parliamentary decision. Closely connected with this is the fact that the resignation of the ministries was not imputed to rejection of legislative bills, but to other reasons. The first government resigned due to defeat at the election, the second and third due to defeat in the question of unemployment, i.e. an issue in which the immediate and direct interests of the working class were at stake.

The first Social Democratic ministries have often been described as "experiments." This characteristic is correct to the extent that it might be said that the party accept a governing mandate "on trial," with a feeling that the Social Democratic policy in its real meaning could not be pursued, but that as no other government could very well be created, it might be an appropriate time to test what could be won through settlements with other parties. Such an attitude was natural during the period of minority parliamentarism, and it may also be traced in other parties. Even if in the Social Democratic press every governmental attempt was characterised as successful, the gap between programme and action caused unease. It was clear to all that the three governments had not succeeded in accomplishing anything of that which in debates and in the propaganda was held to be essential. A reaction set in against minority parlimentarism as such, and chiefly against Social Democratic minority governments, that were able to maintain their brief rule only through concessions and compromises. This reaction was clearly expressed in the debate on parliamentarism at the party congress of 1928.

However, this aspect of the problem is hardly the most important. It is likely that the attempt at government in the period 1920–26 on the whole confirmed and strengthened the moderate tendencies within the party. In a governmental position it was incumbent upon the party leaders to emphasise the difficulties and doubts inherent in a rapid reform policy, in contrast to value of unavoidable settlements and modest advances. The great hopes and the radical plans of 1920 disappeared. The generation of young politicians that ten years earlier represented doctrinaire socialism become involved with practical tasks and administrative routine. Yet again tactics determined ideology. The actions that originally were regarded as superficial and temporary became character and habit.

A survey of the general Social Democratic debate of these years gives the impression that the great principles which briefly dominated around the year 1920 swiftly receded into the background. The disintegration of ideology continued after the interlude caused by World War I, by the European revolutions and by the establishing of political democracy in Sweden. Marx was quoted less and less frequently and with greater reservations. In an article in "Social-Demokraten" in 1923, Erik Hedén asserted that Social Democrats could hardly call themselves Marxist any longer as several of the main points of Marx's theory have shown themselves untenable and have largely been discarded. It even happened that certain of Marx's basic tenets, central to his way of thinking, were labelled vulgar-Marxism. In a speech in the Budget Debate of 1925, Sandler emphasised that the Socialisation Board was influenced neither by Marx's system nor by the system of any other theoretician. De Man's book, "The Psychology of Socialism," was admired despite the fact that it implied a break with Marxism. Engberg, who was the foremost defender of Marx against de Man, mainly concerned himself in his criticism with semi-philosophical questions of slight interest to the political ideology.

Even Engberg admitted that Marx, who devoted himself to an analysis of capitalism, had not been of any enormous direct value for a Social Democracy which was concerned with constructive tasks. In the question of socialisation it was often maintained that the development itself must be the decisive factor, and that governmental measures were only of limited importance. Capitalism had not come to pass due to any decisions that had been made, said Sandler in one of his speeches, and neither could socialism be brought about in this manner. However, it is clear that "political disposals might be important with relation to certain aspects in such a continuing process of economic development" and "that socialists wish to take over the available means of political power." Engberg wrote that the path of socialisation should "be cleared and walked along bit by bit as demanded by the pressure of circumstances." These statements were obviously compatible with Marx's ideas on the inevitable victory of socialism, but did not involve an acceptance of Marx's social prognoses. It is clear that they were not in accordance with the declarations of 1920 regarding a rapid action in the matter of socialisation. A tendency also emerged to label all changes that were considered to be beneficial as socialism. Lindstrom wrote in 1927 that "It is necessary to create a wider concept of socialism. It could perhaps be summarised thus: the continuous adaptation of society to those things which are most expedient from the point of view of the ideas and interests of the citizens. Every advance that realises a higher degree of cooperation can be said to be an advance in a socialist direction." In addition it was constantly asserted that the question of socialisation would soon come into the limelight through the investigations of the Socialisation Board. Reference to these investigations served as the main argument in the debate on socialisation for more than fifteen years.

One of the strangest aspects of the ideological development of Swedish Social Democracy is that after 1924 the debate on industrial democracy, which had been presented with such incredible energy, gradually disappeared from the discussion. The immediate reasons for this might have been that the trade unions showed scant interest in the proposals that were presented in 1923 and 1924. The carrying through of these proposals was not regarded as having any particular material advantages. From the beginning the exchange of opinions in this question had been characterised by the utmost obscurity. As industrial democracy had been exalted as a method that would completely alter the status of the workers, it would usually have aimed at gaining influence in the running of the enterprise, which could not reasonably take place other than in connection with socialisation. However, the proposals that were submitted had by no means amounted to giving the workers a share in the management of the enterprise. They irritated the employers without waking any enthusiasm amongst the workers. The issue that in the election manifesto of 1922 was said to be "of decisive importance for the entire near future of the working class" had lost all current interest a few years later.

After the change of ministry in 1926 the Social Democratic party was outside governmental power for more than six years. The decision taken with regard to the Stripa mine called forth strong opposition against the 'free thinkers,' (i.e., liberals) who were deemed largely responsible for this, and it became common to speak of an incipient coalition of the Conservative and Liberal parties against Social Democracy. A tendency to radicalise the party's politics can be seen. However, the election defeat of 1928 counteracted this tendency. At the outbreak of the economic crisis the party had new problems to face. The struggle against the crisis provoked activities along lines other than those previously followed.

At the parliaments of 1927 and 1928 the Ekman ministry managed to win various successes with the support of alternative majorities. However, despite the fact that, as early as in the Budget Debate of 1927, the Social Democrats strongly censured the government's policy in the question of unemployment, they nevertheless supported the government's proposals on several issues. In the question of schools—the most extensive issue at the 1927 parliament—the "free thinkers" and the Social Democrats acted in alliance with each other. A Social Democratic initiative regarding amendments of the unemployment directive, by which the unemployed would not be able to be referred to work places at which there were existing labour conflicts, was rejected at the parliaments of 1927 and 1928.

At both these parliamentary sessions the conservatives unsuccessfully proposed that the Socialisation Board should be disbanded. The idea that within the Social Democratic party the socialisation issue was not considered to be a current question was repudiated by the party leaders. In 1927 Hansson said that unemployment was a reason to "examine the present mode of production and its only alternative, socialisation." Another reason was the conflict between political democracy and economic domination by the few. "In the long run a people who are competent with regard to political matter will not accept that the most important means for their existence be in the hands of a few rich men." During the 1928 debate on the subject the party leader maintained that if Social Democracy won the majority it would then "be confronted with the task of having to realise its programme . . . to the same extent that the Social Democratic policy becomes the leading policy, it will become the politics of the country." But at the same time the usual ideas were underlined that development towards socialism was taking place independent of all state interference, and that a rapid realising of socialisation by means of a series of legislative steps was inconceivable.

At the parliament of 1928 the conflict between the Social Democrats and the Conservative and Liberal parties was increased in a way that had important effects on the election campaign of that year. In a speech in the Budget Debate, P. A. Hansson laid down principles that boded an intensified radicalism in the party's politics. He compared the state to a home. "The basis of the home is community and solidarity. In the good home there are no privileged or deprived members, no pets and no step children . . . In the good home there is equality, solicitude, cooperation and helpfulness. Applied to the great home of the people and citizens, this would mean the breaking down of all social and economic barriers that now divide citizens into privileged and denied, into ruling and dependent, into rich and poor, into possessors and exploited, plunderers and plundered. The Swedish society is not yet the good home of the citizens. Certainly there is a formal equality, regarding political rights, but from the social point of view the class society still persists, as does the economic dictatorship of the few. At times the inequalities are glaring: while some live in palaces many deem it a privilege to be able to remain in their allotment-garden shacks even during the cold winter. Whilst a few live in affluence, many beg for their bread from door to door. If the Swedish society is to become the good home of its citizens class differences must be abolished, social care must be developed, an economic equalisation must come to pass in which the workers are given a share in the economic administration, and where democracy is realised and applied even socially and economically." The party leader briefly justified several demands that the party later embodied into motions. The question of socialisation was not of immediate urgency. "A more thorough socialisation, however, is part of the future of economic politics, perhaps even part of the very near future."

Due to deliberations regarding which there is a lack of more detailed information, the Social Democratic parliamentary group submitted several motions of a radical nature. Of greatest interest was a proposal asking for investigation "into the ways in which inheritance tax should be extended and reformed in order to bring about a limitation of the great fortunes and a more even distribution of property." In the extensive argumentation for this the inequality in the distribution of property was demonstrated and criticised. A more even distribution would create a higher living standard and a higher culture for those groups of people who lived in the shadow of the present conditions, and therefore such a distribution would reduce the social and political tensions. As one sentence in the motion puts it "Poverty can be endured with equanimity when it is shared by all." During the period that followed, this was continually quoted by the opponents of Social Democracy. "It becomes unendurable when daily it can be compared with the affluence of others, and as it is shown to be unnecessary, to be a temporary result of such social arrangements as are due to be altered." One means of achieving a more even distribution would be a tightening up of the inheritance tax. In particular, the motions referred to a suggestion of the Italian economist Rignano. According to this suggestion the first time a fortune is inherited it should be taxed lightly, but the second time it is inherited at least half of the fortune should go to the state, and at the third inheritance the remainder should be confiscated. However, this plan was only thought to be practical in a modified version. The objection that an increased inheritance tax would lead to reduced savings was met by the proposal that the funds acquired by the state through the inheritance tax should be set apart and capitalised. However, in the beginning they could suitably be used to pay off state debts. Those presenting the motion stressed that their proposal did not aim at any socialisation. All they desired was to increase the wealth of the state. In close connection with the proposal regarding inheritance tax, the Social Democrats also urged an investigation into the revision of taxes on income and capital.

Both proposals were rejected by an almost unanimous Conservative and Liberal majority. The discussion was concentrated on the question of inheritance tax. In Conservative and Liberal circles it was maintained that the proposal of the Social Democrats implied an approach to the Communists and an attempt to bring about socialisation in a devious manner. Wohlin held that the idea of a direct nationalising of the means of production had been abandoned due to the experience acquired in other countries, and to the inability of the Socialisation Board to formulate concrete suggestions. "In the intellectual confusion in which Swedish Social Democracy at present finds itself it has tried to advance along another easier and more comfortably accessible road i.e. that by relinquishing the idea of socialisation of the fixed means of production . . . try to achieve socialisation by another softer and subtler way, that nevertheless is just as dangerous, that is, by confiscating the results of the industriousness, efficiency and thrift of individuals. This confiscation has been disguised in the treacherous form of progressive taxation and increased inheritance tax." Lindman said that if one demanded socialisation more directly, one need not demand confiscation of inheritance, for should such confiscation take place, then in fact socialisation would be realised.

In certain contexts the Social Democratic leaders alluded to a tightened inheritance tax as a form of socialisation, but also stressed that they counted on support for their proposal from Conservative and Liberal quarters, because it did not go as far as did the principle of socialisation in its strict sense. A series of statements of Liberal politicians and scientists (mainly English, but some Swedish) were quoted as evidence of the injury caused by the unequal distribution of property, and the necessity of a reform. Wigforss, the author of the motion, said that the motion, is "to tell the truth quite simply a final attempt to stretch out a hand to the old bourgeois-Left. It is no more than an attempt to say: is there no chance that you, with your old Liberal ways of thinking, could openly admit that the conditions in society are not desirable, that it is not desirable that income is distributed as unevenly as is at present the case, and that you, as well as the Liberals in other quarters, have nothing against doing something to create a more even distribution." Hansson explained that the party, even though it held power, could not socialise more than certain branches of production which the course of development itself had rendered so ripe that state ownership and management would be advantageous. The current proposal was now so limited it should be possible to count on support even from Conservative and Liberal circles. However, certain Social Democrats justified the proposal in a way that could mean a confirmation of the Conservative and Liberal suspicions. "We need money for the social revolution," said Månsson. By "the social revolution" he seems rather to have meant a rationalising of industry, but the expression itself was likely to cause alarm. It cannot be denied that on the whole a certain ambiguity characterised the arguments of the Social Democrats. On the one hand the proposed reforms were presented as the introduction to a reformation of society. On the other hand, as a limited increase of a tax that in Sweden was lower than in any other country mentioned in the debate.

The party motions also included proposals for an inquiry into the establishing of a state commercial bank. It was argued that the power of the big banks over commercial and industrial life, called for a state bank that could borrow and lend in a fully businesslike way, and therefore serve as a guarantee against abusive practices on the part of the big banks. That this proposal was presented is surprising as several Social Democrats, prominent amongst them being Möller, both earlier and later asserted that a state commercial bank would mean great difficulties. Should such a bank refuse credit to industrial enterprises in difficulties, the state would be accused of causing the ensuing unemployment in the industries in question. The opposition parties joined to defeat this proposal. To a large extent the debate concerned the policies of the big Swedish banks towards industry. The Conservatives and Liberals defended the banks, the Social Democrats attacked them. The opposition parties saw the establishment of a state commercial bank as a socialist measure. The Social Democrats reacted strongly against this. "When speaking of socialism in this context it should perhaps be underlined" said Sandler, "that here it is not a question of whether or not a certain area of our economy should be socialised, but whether or not a branch that is threatened by monopolistic tendencies should introduce effective competition by a state enterprise in that branch."

The tendency to a rallying of the Conservatives and Liberals at that parliament was mainly manifested in the new legislation regarding labour agreement, by which disputes between the employers and the workers were referred to obligatory arbitration. With amazing energy the Social Democrats fought the agreement proposal, that was branded as an attack against the working class. A demonstrative strike was arranged prior to the taking of the government decision. This is one of the most remarkable examples of practical misjudgement within Swedish Social Democracy, for since the practical enforcement of the new laws they have been generally considered satisfactory. There were sharp conflicts between the Social Democrats and their opponents on the Right on other issues too, for example the question of local municipal taxation.

At the party congress of 1928, held shortly after the close of the parliamentary session, the acute situation was noticeable, above all in the debates on the election manifesto and in the terms for the building of a new Social Democratic government. These questions will be dealt with in another context. In the following the main questions of the programme that arose at the congress are taken up.

There were several motions regarding amendment or revision of the general basic principles, some of which were very far-reaching. Referring to his proposal at the congress of 1911, Lindhagen urged a general revision of the basic principles. Amongst other things should be introduced anew "a reminder of the indispensability of spiritual freedom and individual responsibility in the creation of a new world." The author of the motion drew attention to certain expressions regarding the "humanistic" ideas which had been introduced into the basic principles in 1911, but later were excluded at the great revision of 1920. In addition it was stressed that a more general fresh orientation of the programme was called for. What socialism really strived after was "economic, political and spiritual freedom." "On these premises, a grip on the necessary revaluations is secured. Many disguises of reality must be discarded and various conceptual confusions should make room for the truth . . . Let us bear in mind that at their conception Liberalism, Socialism, Communism and Christianity meant more or less the same thing, namely the victory of freedom in all the three senses mentioned above . . . In our time there is no organisation other than the socialist that is called and able to be at the forefront for the purpose of reorganising the world . . . The revaluations required for this purpose must begin with a revaluation of the programme. In several respects it is fossilised, loose, obscure and incomplete. A general revision of the programme is called for."

In his motion Lindström proceeded from more restrained and precise points of view suggesting that a proposal on new general basic principles should be prepared for the congress that was to follow. The justification he gave in regard to his motion may be supplemented with the ideas that he published simultaneously in other quarters. According to Lindström the main objections to the general basic principles were that "they overschematise the economic and social realities. It must be admitted that they connote a Marxist orthodoxy that can hardly be described as conforming to reality. The conflicting conditions in modern society are depicted in a remarkably rigid manner. This depiction should sooner logically lead to the acceptance of the theory of catastrophe, instead of serving as the fundamental substratum of a reformist tactic typical of Swedish Social Democracy . . . Here is an impending conflict between principles and practical action, that in the long run may affect the theoretical solution, as well as provoking displeasure with the content of the programme."

In his motion Lindström mentioned two examples in support of his criticism. When in the third paragraph of the basic principles it was said that "capitalist private ownership . . . had become the means by which the propertied denied the workers the fruits of their labour," it implied the concealment of the inescapable fact that "the process that the authors of the programme in the passages mentioned chose to depict has also included the formation of capital inevitable for every advance, the fruits of which have been to the advantage not least of the working class." Furthermore Lindström turned against the concept of exploitation that was characteristic of the principles in the programme. Nowhere was this given an economic definition and, in fact, neither could it be given such a definition. The word exploit now appears as a moral condemnation, without it being clear against whom it was directed. In another context Lindström further criticised several points in the principles of the programme. In the second paragraph it was said that the main defects of civilisation were caused by the capitalist mode of production, that placed the ownership of the means of production in the hands of a few. It would be absurd to make the form of ownership the most important factor for the economy of a society. "Here one meets a socialistic-dogmatic stupidity that is a worthy counterpart to the bourgeois-dogmatic stupidity, that believes that the private form of ownership is a prime necessity for a progressive society." Lindström pointed out that in its description of the present social conditions the party programme maintained that the propertied few became all the richer, while the working class became proletarianised." "But what is this other than the vulgar-Marxist theory of society that daily and hourly is denied in the practice of Swedish Social Democracy? The general basic principles give the impression that this conflict is of necessity intensified, and that no mitigating and mediating circumstances come into play. If such is the case, should not the whole matter quite logically lead to a theory of catastrophe? The Swedish Social Democratic programme of principles adds fuel to this theory of catastrophe. That the authors of the programme did not put forward such a theory can depend on nothing but the fact that they suddenly reminded themselves that there exists something called real life, whereupon in the nick of time they broke their train of thought." At the same time that Lindström put forward these criticisms of the programme, he insisted in his motion that certain questions that were not dealt with in the basic principles should be taken into consideration. In this way, following the pattern of certain modern programmes abroad, an analysis of principles should be made of the role of finance capital, of imperialism, and of the position of Social Democracy in relation to the state. In other of his statements Lindström made his ideas clearer. Amongst other things it should be emphasised in the general basic principles that socialisation "that is, production based on common social interests" would be apt to overcome the struggle between various group interests, and lead to an increase in production, and also that the Social Democratic party unconditionally stood on democratic foundations. The Programme Commission rejected these motions. Regarding Lindhagen's proposal it was said that a general revision of the programme could not take place without a directive, and that such a directive was not given in the motion, also that Social Democracy's desire for human freedom had already been dealt with in the first paragraph of the basic principles, reading "safeguarding and developing of the spiritual and material culture." Similar points of view were expressed with regard to Lindström's motion, to the extent that it aimed at supplementing the programme. Regarding the objections against the basic principles, the Programme Commission countered that no suggestion was made to replace the expression "exploit" with another expression. "The factual situation itself can not be removed from the basic principles without also taking away an essential part of socialist ideas. Before an alternative to the term "exploitation" is found it is of little value to discuss which term is best suited to be defined."

The Programme Commission took the line that here the question was simply the most appropriate way of expressing a certain "factual situation." But like the commission that had formulated the general basic principles, this

Commission did not attempt to establish what exactly the "factual situation" consisted of. It should be noted that in the main the Programme Commission was of almost the same composition as the Commission of 1919. Amongst its members were Sandler, Engberg, Hansson and Möller, and the report on this question had evidently been drawn up by Sandler, who was the author of the report of 1919.

The debate on this question, mainly carried on by Sandler and Lindström, offers practically nothing new over and above the statement of those who put the motion. There was no attempt to analyse more closely the concept of exploitation and other basic ideas of the programme. The rejection of the Programme Commission, affirmed by the party executive, was approved by Congress without vote.

Two amendments in the political programme were decided upon, and these should be mentioned briefly. There had been several motions regarding the question of land, amongst them one by Lindhagen, that in general terms demanded a more aggressive and radical land policy. The Programme Commission took the motion as the reason to propose an important formal revision of the land programme, and this suggestion was approved by Congress. In accordance with the proposal, Point XV of the programme was worded as follows:

Society to provide land for the formation of independent small-sized farms.
Sizeable landed properties to be conveyed into the ownership of society.
Speculation in land to be prohibited.
Social legislation on leaseholds.
Legislation on waste lands.
Promotion of intensified agriculture.
Promotion of reclamation of land and forests to be cultivated.

Skold justified the approved proposal and alleged that in the main this implied a more concentrated formulation of the requirements that were included in the present land programme. In this "important and unimportant points . . . were mixed together in such a way that it was difficult to decide what the party considered to be more or less important." In addition it was desired to win two material advantages through the proposed new text.

In the programme of 1920 it had been stated that allotment of the landed properties would only take place if natural circumstances made large scale production impracticable. In certain quarters this had been interpreted as meaning that the party was opposed to allotment of Crown lands for the building of own-homes, which was not at all the intention. The proposed new formulation got rid of this lack of clarity. Furthermore the revised wording had made clear that the party took the general economic ends into consideration, i.e., that it wished to "further measures that aim to extend the cultivated areas through new cultivation, and to create a higher increment and a larger lumber-capital in our forest lands."

In connection with the new local municipal programme decided by congress, a new point IX was introduced into the programme having the following formulation:

Local municipal self-government to be maintained.

Properties and other more permanent objects for taxation to contribute to municipal funds by means of a special municipal tax and special levies (compulsory contributions).

Controlled government appropriation to municipalities.

At the congress the issue of socialisation was only dealt with in passing. Prompted by a demand of one of the members of the congress the Clearance Committee proposed a statement that was unanimously accepted by congress practically without debate. It called attention to the fact that up to now the Board of Socialisation had mainly been occupied with general investigation and inquiries and that "the initiatives of another type that might have been expected from this Board have been limited to one enterprise which has already been socialised." Apparently these latter words refer to the report on the State railways. However, the resolution continued, the increased prestige of the party had forced the great question of organisation into the foreground, and the need of a practical economic programme of action had in the meantime grown unchecked. The main point of the statement was: "The party congress underlines the need of a programme of economic action that is more clearly formulated, and urges that in the light of the experience of recent years and the latest investigations of the Board of Socialisation (prior to the election of 1932) the party executive tries to draft certain guidelines for socialisation in our time, and also for the party's most pressing tasks in the area of economics." Evidently the statement is an indirect criticism of the delay in putting forward a programme of action on the part of the Board of Socialisation. It was now required that such a programme should be formulated within the next four-year period. However, the adopted statement seems not to have aroused any appreciable interest or attention. At the 1932 party congress one speaker claimed that probably several of the congress members present in 1928 had not attended to the question.

The election contest of the 1928 election to the lower house was the most heated since the election of 1914. The main contestants were the Conservatives and Liberals versus the Social Democrats. In several districts and wards the opponents on the Right assembled in a common electoral cartel, whilst the Social Democrats and Communists cooperated with each other. Several circumstances accounted for the fact that the election struggle was especially violent. The Conservative and Liberal attack on the Social Democrats was mainly concerned with plans for the distribution of income and property that it was thought could be read from the motion regarding inheritance tax and also from the manifesto, and from the cooperation of the Social Democrats with the Communists. Despite the fact that in this election the Social Democrats sharply criticised Communism, and stressed that the election collaboration was of a strictly technical nature, the right-wing propaganda often treated the two parties as if they were one. In addition the Conservatives accused Social Democracy of being responsible for the disarmament of 1925. It seems that the bitterness within Social Democracy was mainly caused by the decisions on the unemployment directive of 1926 that were forced through by the right-wing opposition, and by compulsory arbitration in labour disputes as from 1928.

The election manifesto of the Social Democrats was unusually comprehensive. It required nine pages in the report of the party executive as against two to four pages at other elections. The Manifesto had been discussed at the party congress that spring, though its final shape was given to it by the party executive. In introduction it was stressed that the Left had split and that a more decisive bourgeois rallying against Social Democracy was evident. In particular the decisions of 1926 and 1928 just mentioned were pointed out, and also the fact that several social-political questions had slipped by unresolved. Amongst other things the party demanded an extension of social insurance, and a land reform in accordance with the programme and with the proposal put forward in parliament. The latter issue was expressed in terms sharper than in any preceding election programme. By dividing large properties in public or private ownership into allotments new farms could be established, and small farms, crofts and dwellings extended into complete farms. For the majority of farmers the custom duties were without value. Further, amongst other issues, the manifesto dealt with the questions of defence and education. However, it was mainly two paragraphs at the conclusion of the election programme that signified a more radical party policy. After speaking of the necessity of infusing the meaning of political and Social Democracy into society, the manifesto continued: "Amongst the natural measures for realising this goal Social Democracy above all includes the transference into the ownership or control of society the great natural resources such as forests, mines and waterfalls. In addition, a modernised inheritance tax with the aim of distributing property more evenly and the attempt to assure the workers of co-influence in the enterprise in which they are employed. Social Democracy believes that an effective organisation of the state commercial bank is an effective means of suppressing the super-power of finance over commercial and industrial life."

These points made the issues of socialisation and industrial democracy into current questions, at the same time as they involve a fulfillment of the actions in the questions of inheritance tax and a state commercial bank.

Strangely enough these questions were dealt with only very briefly at the party congress. Möller, the Party executive's reporter, only reminded in passing that the draft of the election manifesto took up the question of the socialisation of certain natural resources. He justified the demand for a state commercial bank by saying that such a bank would "destroy the power of big capital over the economy" and therefore that it would be "a small step in the direction of the equalising of the conditions of power in society." Regarding the proposal in connection with inheritance tax he remarked that "it is many years since the bourgeois parties were as terrified as they are today, when the question of inheritance tax was taken up. . . . In the main one received a very strong impression . . . that one of the vital points had been touched upon, the touching of which makes them cry out loudly." This seems to have served as evidence of the aptness of the inheritance tax action, not as a sign of its danger. These questions were hardly mentioned in the debate. Only one speaker, Leo, touched on the question of socialisation. He considered that the point in connection with this should be formulated more precisely: "I am of the definite opinion that the manifesto should at least contain a warning to the people of the land that Social Democrats are now seriously determined to take action to create socialisation."

It was mainly Wigforss who took the radical line in the election. In three pamphlets ("The equalising of property and inheritance tax," "Poor and Rich," and "Ownership and socialism") he justified the proposal regarding inheritance tax and the demand for socialisation. In the former question he formulated several clauses that, even though they were surrounded by certain reservations, could justifiably be interpreted as evidence of the desire of Social Democracy to nationalise or divide up property. He spoke of the possibility of "a real accruing of fortunes by the state." "If there is something to divide up, and if there is the desire to do this to the greatest possible advantage, to create the greatest possible satisfaction, then there is only one rational rule to follow: divide it according to need. That is to say in practice—to divide it evenly . . . Wealth side by side with poverty means extravagance, because the rich can use the money for superfluous things whilst the poor have the bare necessities . . . There is no space for first class passengers in a sailing boat . . . The universal suffrage is incompatible with a society divided into a small class of owners and a large class of unpropertied. Either the rich and the propertied will take away universal suffrage, or the poor, with the help of their right to vote, will procure for themselves a part of the accumulated riches." These sentences seem to indicate a return to a principle of distribution that was seldom advanced in the Social Democratic debate during the period immediately preceding this one. At the same time that Wigforss justified an even distribution of property he also argued for a reduction in the property of the rich only, whilst these moderately well-to-do would lose nothing. This proved that in fact he was not prepared consistently to apply the principles that he admonished. Regarding socialisation Wigforss, like Marx, wrote that the entire industrial labour process was already "socialised" and that therefore nothing was more natural than that the means of production and the actual finished products should also be socialised, by placing them in "common" hands. "These 'common hands' may be the state or the municipality, or the free combination of the workers in an enterprise, it may be the workers within an industry organised in large organisations. All such forms express the desire to own and administer in common."

Several of the leading men of the party took another line. They concerned themselves mainly with the limited demands that were current within social policy and land policy. Without disclaiming the principles that were mentioned in the election manifesto, and in Wigforss' radical propaganda, they hinted that these were neither urgent nor timely and that at the election the electorate should not pay them any regard. Hansson attacked the unequal distribution of property as "a danger to society" and stated that in the motion regarding inheritance tax the party had indicated "a means of getting rid of the danger." But he also stressed that these questions should not be decided upon during the coming parliamentary period but rather that in this period questions should be taken up that did not concern the basic economic and social organisation of society. Sandler similarly expressed himself with caution. The inheritance tax proposal was not definitely formulated.

"Equal distribution and saving are both good things. You have to shift and shuffle towards a decent adjustment." The examination of the question of socialisation should proceed from the premise of economic expediency, and the need for flexible business-like forms of administration should be taken into consideration. Engberg explained that the right of ownership continuously adapted itself to the conditions of production and thus constantly altered. From the social point of view private property could be divided into two main types: "exploitation property" and "labour property." Only with regard to the former, the property of private capital, did the Social Democrats desire greater rights for the general public. Economic construction was not current policy. When reading through the report of the election speeches one receives the impression that the Social Democrats were under pressure from the effective bourgeois propaganda and thus were inclined successively to moderate their standpoint in the questions at issue.

The election was a serious defeat. The party lost fourteen places, of which most went to the conservatives. The losses were not caused by the fact that a considerable number of those who normally voted for the party now voted for another party, but rather by the fact that the party increased its election figures only to a very small extent. After the election the chairman of the party asserted that the action in the question of inheritance tax was probably the most important reason for the defeat. An investigation since carried out by the party executive suggests that he was correct.

The conservative government, led by Lindman, that assumed power after the election followed a moderate policy of cooperation and did not become the object of any systematic opposition from the Social Democrats. The Liberal leader and the essential parliamentarianism that he practiced were criticised much more sharply. In the main an inclination to retire from the radical policy that had been advocated prior to the election, and that many considered to have contributed to the defeat, can be traced in the party during the year following the 1928 election. In the Budget Debate in 1929 the Social Democrats behaved with great moderation. The party leader stated that there should be preconditions "for a certain cooperation between a conservatism animated by a real care for society and a Social Democratic eagerness to provide security and affluence for all." However, he considered that in the existing situation this idea could not bear fruit, as the Swedish conservatives were "more the guardian of privileges than the guardian of society." One of the labour-peace conferences organised by the government in autumn 1928, in which representatives of the employers and the workers participated, became the object of acknowledgment. However, the most important Social Democratic initiatives—amongst other things concerning the abolition of the 1928 law regarding labour conflicts, the new unemployment directive and the request for a proposition concerning unemployment insurance at the following parliament—were rejected. At the end of the parliament the parties not in government, for reasons that are of no interest in the present context, forced the resignation of Wohlin, the Minister of Finance. In connection with this, negotiations regarding collaboration between the Social Democrats and the liberals were initiated. These negotiations, that were partly caused by the desire to create a more stable foundation for the formation of a government, continued during the following period, and at the parliament of 1930 resulted in cooperation on several questions, mainly the issue of defence. However, no foundation for a new left-wing government appeared.

At the latter mentioned parliament the Social Democrats put forward a proposal in the question of unemployment. New guidelines were here drawn up for the treatment of this question, which presented the party's future crisis policy. The system of low wages and unemployment relief work was to be replaced by a system with more productive state-employment that, with regard to salaries and terms of employment, should be carried on in the same way as labour on the free market. The proposal was not accepted, but the parliament decided on a report that to a certain extent accepted the aims of those presenting this motion.

However, the parliament of 1930 was characterised by the crisis in farming that broke out in 1929 due to the international drop in the price of corn. The right-wing government presented proposals for a series of measures to support farming, primarily raised duties and obligatory mixing-in in milling, that is, the obligatory use of a certain percent of Swedish cereal. The Social Democrats criticised these proposals, partly from the general point of view of free trade, and partly because they saw them as intended to help only the more affluent farmers who produced corn for sale. The raising of duties was rejected due to cooperation between the liberals and the Social Democrats, whilst the forced mixing-in of Swedish cereal was carried through by a conservative majority. In such a position the Lindman government resigned and the liberals, who had adopted a definite mid-position, formed a ministry under the leadership of Ekman.

The election manifesto of the Social Democrats in the county-council elections of 1930 showed a clear retreat from the radical positions they had held in 1928. The party said that it opposed the attempt "to help only a small portion of the farmers by means of raised duties on provisions, and allow this help to be paid for by the consuming public as a whole, amongst which were hundreds of thousands of smaller farmers and the poorest people." However, the forced mixing-in of Swedish cereals was not criticised, which indicated that the party was willing to accept it. The party said that it had chosen to unite the left-wing parties around a limited programme for advance, but due to the position of the liberals, this desire had not been able to be realised. A solution to the social land question was placed at the forefront of the party's demands. One such solution would have the intention "of protecting the many small farmers and leasees against arbitrariness, and to assist them to profit from land clearance and soil improvement with the aim of creating opportunities for the extending of incomplete farming, so that these could assure the occupant of a livelihood, and also with the aim of opening accessible ways for building their own farms to agricultural labourers and others." However, no programme for settling the current crisis in farming was suggested. Further, the party demanded an unemployment policy in accordance with the motions put in parliament—unemployment insurance and increased old-age pensions. With this programme, which contained no point that went beyond the limits of social policy, the Social Democrats won a considerable victory. However, this did not lead to any change in the question of government.

The parliament of 1931 was characterised by general tension. The Ekman ministry, with the majority of those of uncertain colour, succeeded in putting through several important proposals, and a solution to two questions that had long been discussed (health insurance and the question of maternity benefits) was found. Despite the votes of the Social Democrats, an import monopoly on cereal was introduced. The Social Democrats motioned in vain in questions of unemployment benefit and unemployment insurance.

During the years before the great economic crisis the debate within the Social Democratic party indicates an extraordinary lack of clarity in the question of ideological guidelines. Since democratising was brought about, the party had been the strongest in parliament, it had taken the initiative (in collaboration with others) in successfully carrying through a number of meaningful reforms. But still, with the possible exception of 1928, the party had not gone beyond the bounds of social policy (or beyond the framework of bourgeois politics, one might say) in its proposals. The discussion on industrial democracy had faded away. Regarding the question of socialisation reference was made to the investigations that were taking place. It was generally presupposed that social democracy had other much more important goals than the proposals that were placed before parliament, but these goals and the means of achieving them were usually spoken of only in general phrases sanctioned by the ideological tradition. Did the party leadership follow some definite but unstated tactics, or did it in secret draw up precise goals, or did these means of expression disguise a void? The foremost representative of the party's youth movement, Richard Lindström, wrote in connection with the Fortieth Jubilee of the party that, "only those who for reasons of comfort, cowardice or ignorance ignore reality can deny that Social Democracy today is in the middle of a crisis." He spoke of "the growing lack of spiritual leadership and spiritual strength within the labour government." A new "spirit of investigation and regeneration" is called for if the party is to be able to "carry through its struggle for the ideas of socialism."

Two debates are especially useful in illustrating the situation. One of them took place in the social democratic press in 1929 and dealt with the principle of class struggle and questions in this connection. The other took place in the party executive in 1931 and dealt with the activities of the Board of Socialisation.

In the first issue of "Tiden" for 1929 Lindström wrote an article in which he discussed class and the concept of class struggle. Here he pointed out the wide generalisation that lay behind every class division and that was especially expressed in such concepts as bourgeoisie and proletariat. Joined to this was a criticism more tacit than real of the idea of the struggle that appeared so strongly in the propaganda of Social Democracy. To a much greater extent than previously the party should stress the importance of opinions, not only of interests. It should in name as well as in use become a 'peoples' party, i.e. a party that chiefly unites people around the ideas of socialism, without the old emphasis on the fact that every socialist ideal must be a proletarian ideal. An auspicious fate has allowed the party, for the benefit of itself and the country, to tramp underfoot the "theoretical basis." As far as sorting out the surviving theories is concerned, this people's-party mentality is a natural and strong point of connection." The aim of social democracy was to abolish class conflicts and the road for this was not prepared by continuously preaching a theory of class struggle. Earlier the leader of the party had put forward similar ideas, and in a series of articles had supported the most important aspects of Lindström's ideas. In close connection to the party programme, he stressed that exploitation was not only limited to the working class. Social Democracy was the representative of the great majority of the people who were in natural conflict with the small group of capitalists. The party should call itself a peoples' party and have as its aim the freeing of the people and the building of a national home for the people. Both the farmers and the middle-classes should be won over to the party. "Where the concept of class seems limited or isolated, there the concept of people opens the way to cooperation. Where the concept of class can easily lead to a weakening of responsibility in the face of that which exists, the concept of people orients efforts towards the utilising of those power resources that in cooperation can be made available for an immediate lightening of the pressure." Hansson warned "against a relapse into ways of speaking and methods of agitation that were as natural a couple of decades ago as they are now stale and designed to harm the progress of the party." There was no relinquishing of socialist principles. Several newspapers agreed with the party leader, often calling attention to the incorrectness of the Marxist social prognosis.

Engberg, who had been editor of "Social-Demokraten" since 1924 emerged as the chief opponent of these statements. In the main he took Marx's scheme as his starting point. The important class division occurred between those who owned the means of production and the propertyless. "The naked truth is that society is faced with a question of destiny: are the aspirations of the working class to triumph, or those of the capitalist class? Is that group, the leading class of which are the workers, to be the social order, or that group whose leading class is the big capitalists and big financial bourgeois to be allowed to continue to occupy their position of dominance?" The speech about a home for the people was taken from a young right-winger, Kjellén. It was desired in this way to indicate "a home for a people whose classes have fought out their struggle to the end and in that way done away with the class society." The slogan was "the formation of a concept apart from class reality. This does not extract the important aspects of the picture, does not join together the present and the future, does not bring into the perceptual range the class arrangements around which everything in society revolves. . . ."

To some extent this debate is reminiscent of the exchange of opinions regarding "class" and "people" that took place between Branting and Danielsson forty years earlier. However, its interest does not lie in the concepts themselves but in the fact that they reflect certain general ideas regarding the activity of the party. Even though Lindström and Hansson stressed that they did not intend any weakening of the "socialism" of the party, it is clear that their statements recommend a policy of cooperation that could hardly be thought to involve an action for socialisation. This is clear from Hansson's speech regarding the meaning of the concepts of class and people just quoted. It is also worth noting that those who supported the concept of people spoke of socialism but not of socialisation. The terminology that was recommended by Hansson portended the ideological justification given by Social Democracy for the crisis policy from the year 1933 onwards. After some years the party leaders spoke of the "peoples home" (which according to Hansson could be achieved by means of a "socialist" policy) as a reality, realised through the welfare policy of Social Democracy.

The work of the Board of Socialisation continued during these years without any proposal being made regarding the issue of fact. Several investigations were published, partly concerned with the question of socialisation in other countries, partly concerned with the Swedish establishment and conditions, with reference to which investigations such as those concerning the post office and forestry administration were considered necessary for the continued work of the Board. In a report given out in 1927 the Board recommended a certain increase of the state's right in the question of ore-findings, but the question of a more general socialisation of natural resources was not discussed. In November 1926 at the request of the government the Board gave an account of their plans. The Board had found an abstract analysis of different economic systems to be unsuitable. Instead they had oriented themselves towards concrete investigations within various areas. An investigation concerned with Swedish companies was one of the tasks at hand. In connection with this the Board would subject special groups of private enterprise to a more thorough scrutiny. Furthermore, an inquiry would be undertaken with reference to national fortune and national income. In an address of 1927 parliament asked if the Board would not in future do better to concern itself mainly with questions concerning the Swedish situation. In a communication of autumn 1928, at the request of the government, the Board stated that a "final summarising report" could probably be presented before the 30th June, 1931. In connection with this the government decided that the work of the Board should come to an end at that time. In 1929 the Board published an account of the balance sheets of Swedish limited companies. In its report of that year the Board informed of the fact that it had allowed investigations to be initiated concerning the Swedish electricity industry, paper industry and shoe industry.

The following year the Board said that these investigations continued and that work on the final report of the Board had begun. In June 1931 the government accepted that the Board be allowed to continue its work up to the end of March, 1932. In the Board's report of 1931 it is only stated that investigations concerning the previously mentioned Swedish industries were taking place and that work on the final report continued. The Board were not ready at the time mentioned, and in March 1932 the government allowed them to continue working, without remuneration for the members. The report of the Board in autumn 1932 merely continued the information that the work was continuing.

Before the decision allowing the Board to continue with their work until March 1932, the Social Democratic members of the Board had asked for advice concerning the pursuing of future work.

In February 1930 Möller presented an account of the work of the Board to the executive committee of the party executive. In the near future the Board was to adopt a stand with regard to the question of socialisation of the shoe industry. The Social Democratic members had intended to recommend the founding of a state enterprise sufficiently large to be able to meet the requirements of 25% of the market's need for boots and shoes, with the exception of so-called luxury shoes. Möller's report was followed by a debate on which further information is not available. No decision was taken.

Over a year later, in April 1931, the work of the Board of Socialisation was taken up for debate by the party executive. In his introductory speech, Möller said that such a debate was desired by the social democratic members of the

Board. The reason for this was that the work of the Board was coming to an end, and it was reckoned that the reports would be printed during the following year. First and foremost it was a question of an action for socialisation within the shoe and paper industries. "The Social Democrats on the Board have not adopted a definite stand with regard to the recommendations of the reports in these cases, and therefore there is still time for the party executive to give them information and directions . . . It can be expected that there will be great conflicts surrounding the work of the Board when these documents are presented. They could become the main point of the 1932 election movement."

It is not possible to write these reports from a political point of view, but we must consider that they will not make our political work more difficult. The political situation is at present favourable to us, and we should take no steps to make this worse. It is important that the Social Democratic members of the Board receive advice from the party executive before they are placed in the position of having to take a stand." After Möller's statement, Leo, the secretary of the Board, gave a report of the Board's activities in which in particular the proposal to found a state shoe industry was dealt with. Following this there was a thorough discussion.

The idea of action for socialisation was criticised by several speakers, not least by those who belonged to the radical wing of the party. Åkerberg was against the suggestion of a state shoe industry, because a result of this would be great unemployment. Engberg considered socialisation under tariff protection was unsuitable and in general rejected the idea. Höglund wished the party executive to advise the Board to make a more positive proposal. "The most sensible thing is for the Board of Socialisation to subject the idea to renewed testing, and that it writes its proposal in such a way that the party will not suffer from it politically." G. Branting took the same line. He dreaded an untimely debate on the programme of the Board, and in general seems to have considered socialisation only possible in a critical situation. E. Lindberg stated that the Board clearly felt itself forced to come forward with positive proposals. In Lindberg's view banks and natural resources should be of first importance in socialisation.

These arguments against socialisation were scrutinised in the speeches of Möller, Sandler, Leo and Wigforss, of which the first three were members of the Board. Möller stressed that everyone rejected the idea of socialisation just in that area to which he himself was connected. In particular this rejoinder should have concerned Åkerberg, who was the party's leading man in Örebro, the centre of the shoe industry. Möller continued that the question of socialisation of tariff protected industries meant great difficulties. It had always been the idea that compensation would be given at the time of socialisation. "But with redemption of tariff protected industries must also follow redemption of tariff profits which, so to speak, lie at the basis of the enterprise. This would mean weighing down the state enterprise with unreasonable capital expenses. From this point of view, the idea that tariff protected industries shall be redeemed is quite untenable. If we could not undertake a general redemption, but found that it is advantageous to have a footing within tariff protected industries we could do nothing other than build new enterprises." One solution might be to redeem only the best factories, but in that case the less good factories would demand redemption and the result would be that the state had a number of factories that must be closed down. A partial redemption was therefore unthinkable in reality. Möller added that the shoe-factories were out of date and that a rationalisation (involving specialising of production within large complexes) was therefore called for. Sandler described the situation as follows: "With great calm the party executive has accepted the information that we had not intended to socialise industry and farming in this country, but their feelings come to the boil when it is illustrated that there are particular branches of industry that are suitable for socialisation." If socialisation was desired then the only chance of bringing this about was within certain definite areas. A socialist society existed when socialist economics controlled the development. It was superstitious to imagine a society in which there was not more than one type of economy. The final reports of the Socialisation Board must be limited to Swedish conditions and the current situation. "We must not get caught up with what might happen in fifty years. By doing so the Board dare not have any ideas." In close association with Möller and Sandler, Leo reminded that if partial socialisation was not accepted, then the only alternative was total socialisation and clearly the time was not yet ripe for that.

Wigforss showed the greatest sympathy for making current the question of socialisation. Provided the Board made clear what the party would do if it came to power, the question of tariffs lost its importance. (Wigforss should have continued that Social Democracy wanted to bring about free trade). It should not be assumed that the party members were not mature enough to discuss practical socialisation. "If this idea comes into being, then a greater danger is that we retire from our socialist ideas. It is better then to say that socialisation is impossible . . . Should we not rather say that in a situation that is created by ruinous competition socialism is the only solution? . . . In general we should not be afraid to make the problem a current one. If by next year the crisis has not become a boom, then nothing would be more favourable." Höglund rejoined: "Wigforss says that if we retire at this moment we will become a liberal reformist party. But we don't have to give up the *idea* of socialism just because we do not accept these projects. It would be politically unpremeditated if we put these questions into the foreground in 1932."

The debate in the party executive was not followed by any decision that clarified the position of the executive. But it is likely that the atmosphere that was expressed during the debates was decisive for the actions of the social democratic Board members. No concrete proposal regarding socialisation was put forward in 1932, as had been intended, and since then no such proposal has appeared.

Certain aspects of the exchange of opinions should be underlined. The Social Democratic Board members proceeded from the idea that the first action towards socialisation would not have as its intention the taking over of existing enterprises, but only the founding of competitive state enterprises.

Earlier socialisation had chiefly meant the transferring of private enterprises into the hands of the state, but this was no longer the issue. The line now was that the state would compete with other enterprises and drive them out. Free competition, the risks of which were usually put forward in propaganda for socialisation, would be preserved. The state would participate in this more or less in the same way as a private enterprise run on rational lines and with unusual capital strength. If the state enterprises succeeded the result must be ruin and unemployment within a greater or lesser number of private enterprises. The reasons given for this line were mainly suitable in tariff protected branches of the economy. But to a certain extent they were also suitable in other cases. As Möller hinted, was it not so that socialisation in the form of redemption must lead to the state being forced to take over all enterprises, both good and bad, within the area involved? And would not such a general socialisation of a branch of the economy mean extreme economic difficulties?

To some extent this practical dilemma was touched on in the criticism of the socialisation proposal. However, the motive that was mainly put forward by the opponents of this proposal was another. The making current of the question of socialisation was seen to be dangerous from a political, that is party-political, point of view. It would not be suitable to appear in the election campaign of 1932 with a formulated programme for socialisation.

Wigforss protested that it would also be dangerous to relinquish the idea of socialisation. Would it not be suitable in a crisis that "is created by ruinous competition" to label socialism as the "only solution"? It seems that Wigforss was thinking of the principle in itself, not about the proposal, because the intention of the proposal was to widen competition. Höglund went further along the lines laid down by Wigforss. Was it not possible to reject the socialisation proposal, but at the same time maintain "the idea of socialisation?"

This could hardly mean more than that there continued to be general talk of socialisation without making clear what was meant by this, without causing anxiety by making the plans concrete. Socialisation should be used as a symbol but be dismissed from practical policy.

This statement illustrated the party's policy during the following years. The work of the Board was postponed after the government allowed them a new term. As earlier, there was talk of socialisation and of the instructions which were soon to be expected from the Socialisation Board. At the congress of 1932 the prospect of a clarifying investigation was once again held out. However, this investigation never appeared.

The reported debate clearly illustrated the whole problem that had characterised Swedish Social Democratic activity for a decade. The conflict between ideology and the desire for action appeared clearer than ever before. Was it to be impossible to bring about that socialisation that since the very beginning had been the goal of the party? Or due to the pressures of the past was a socialisation action to be suggested whose real value was doubted by the leaders, and that was generally considered to be dangerous from the point of view of the party's power position? Or was socialisation to continue to be put forward as the salvation of the future, whilst hinting that the meaning of this and the ways in which it was to be carried out would shortly become clear? The latter was chosen and the mystique of socialisation was maintained. But this tactic was reaching its limit. The Board of Socialisation could not be made into a permanent institution for the protection of the secrets of socialisation. The problem was solved due to outside events. The crisis increased the prestige of Social Democracy in the eyes of the people, and made possible a penetrating and meaningful action within the framework of the existing system—a policy in the grand style without socialisation. In the party executive debates it was said that socialism should be characterised as the saviour of the crisis. In fact, the crisis saved Social Democracy from its ideological dilemma!

During 1931 the economic difficulties became a general crisis. The number of unemployed that had been 32,000 in December 1930 rose to 89,000 in December 1931 and to 161,000 in December 1932. Unemployment reached its maximum in March 1933 when over 186,000 were registered as unemployed. Within farming, animal products (not much affected by the assistance measures decided upon earlier) were drawn into the crisis and prices of meat, milk and butter sank. The gold standard was departed from in September 1931.

Schematically speaking, two main lines appeared in the Social Democratic debate concerning the crisis. One of these saw the crisis as the "death throes" of capitalism, and used the Marxist scheme to explain its origin and predict its consequences. Only state action of the type that could be described as general socialisation or planned economy could reorganise and increase production. The crisis became a reason for socialisation in its real sense, for social production and planning. The other line placed the crisis in the context of capitalism but did not believe in the destruction of the "system" in the near future, and considered that more limited but directly relevant measures should be taken. The unemployment policy should be combined with a positive crisis policy directed at raising buying power, stimulating production and in various areas creating necessary technical and economic improvements. As a rule this crisis policy was not characterised as a form of socialism or planned economy. However, from the beginning it was in clear contrast to the idea that was common if not dominant, in Conservative and Liberal circles that the crisis should be met in the same way as earlier crises had been met, i.e. with general thrift that would make possible a new economic expansion, and an unemployment policy at the smallest possible cost.

To some extent the position was different with regards to the special farming crisis. At that time the Social Democrats hardly wanted to take any measures other than those that were immediately demanded to relieve suffering amongst the small farmers, whilst the bourgeois, in particular the conservatives and the farmers organisation, were inclined to want measures that would give a monopoly of the home market to Swedish farming.

In autumn 1931 the party executive appointed a Committee consisting of Wigforss, Sköld and Wennerström and having the task of formulating the guide-lines for the Social Democratic crisis policy. At the parliament of 1932 several motions were presented suggesting steps for alleviating the effects of the crisis, that were supported by these investigations. In total about 100 million crowns were requested for this goal, that is about twice as much as the government had suggested. The money was to be gained by means of loans, raising of direct taxes and reduction of the defence budget. However, the most remarkable aspect of the proposal was the demand for a revision of unemployment policy. Earlier the unemployed had been helped partly by direct finance, and partly by reserve-labour, i.e. labour that was paid with lower wages than the open market, that was not of any immediate necessity and that could not compete with other enterprises (mainly road work). In connection with earlier more limited proposals the Social Democrats now demanded that a large amount of the requested grant (about thirty millions) should be used for emergency labour, i.e. labour that was paid according to market wages and was concerned with enterprises that were of more direct use to society. Emergency labour had appeared before, but to a very limited extent. In accordance with the proposal amongst other things roads and bridges would be affected, also measures to improve forest areas, fishing harbours and also investigation of ore findings. By means of emergency labour skilled workers could be offered suitable employment which otherwise was not possible. This labour, plus other suggested changes in unemployment assistance, were, in the first place, justified by the need to relieve suffering and create necessary improvements in various areas. It was more economical to allow people to work than to keep them in idleness. In addition it was stated that the state grant to unemployment and to material for emergency labour would raise consumption and purchasing power and in that way generally effect the economy in a favourable direction. These points of view were put forward particularly strongly by Wigforss, who held a leading position with regard to the party's crisis policy. It was also hinted that the suggested measures would mean reflation, a limited rise in prices, which would be to the advantage of the farmers. This idea was not emphasised strongly, probably because a rise in prices could not be expected to meet with popularity amongst the industrial workers.

Regarding farming, it was maintained in the chief proposal of the Social Democrats that in the long run adaptation could be gained through a better organisation of the turn over of production and a decrease of the costs of production by means of rationalising. In this connection the state should participate through investigations and directives. However, immediate help to the farmers in the worst positions should be given in the form of cash, in principle to be repaid. Twenty-four millions were to be granted for this end. Tariff increases and similar measures were considered to be an unsuitable form of help for farming. Those placing the motions were of the opinion that this type of assistance would only increase the injustice. "Even the very wealthy owner shares in the assistance and often this is the greater the better the situation of the person receiving the assistance. On the other hand, this type of assistance leads to the fact that the citizens have to contribute to it without regard to their own economic position. As the contribution of the private individual to the assistance takes place in relation to his consumption, it may very well happen that the person who is well-situated contributes less and the worst-situated people contribute more. The method of assistance in question therefore goes against the principle of social solidarity."

The Social Democrats accompanied their crisis programme with a criticism on principle of the capitalist system, but also with an explanation of their willingness to cooperate in the crisis. In the Budgetary Debate of that year the party leader said that despite everything the situation in Sweden was better than in many other countries, and that the class conflicts had not reached the same intensity as in other places. Development towards an understanding between the parties should be forced further: "it is my personal and definite feeling that in the main it is never possible to create a happier state of affairs if at least the majority of the people are not joined in common labour for the general good." It is necessary that the possessing classes exhibit a real feeling of solidarity. Further Hansson stated that possibly the crisis was "a sign that a bad system had to collapse and leave room for a new and better system . . . in which the peoples' control over their resources is of such a nature that the intense disturbances which time after time expose us to terrible suffering could be avoided." Finally the Social Democratic speakers stressed that the party's proposal was not caused by ideas of class. It was intended to assist all who were in need, independent of their place in the production process. The party's first speaker in the debate in the upper house said: "The proposals that are to be found in the motion and in the reservation are not at all socialist in character. They are not formed in the spirit of class egoism."

In the main the Social Democratic proposals regarding unemployment were rejected, although they did lead to results in certain unimportant aspects. The criticism of these proceeded from the general idea previously dealt with. It was also asserted that the bringing through of the proposal would come up against great state-financial difficulties, and that emergency labour at market wages was intended to oppose an inevitable lowering of wages.

In the question of farming decisions were taken to give assistance that to some extent was connected with the Social Democratic proposal, but that was more limited. In the main the Conservative and Liberal parties followed another line. The grain regulations decided upon in 1930 and formed in 1931 were retained. A milk regulation was carried through with the intention of raising the profit of products. Several new or raised tariffs were decided upon, amongst others on eggs, potatoes and coffee. The decisions here mentioned, plus other similar decisions, were met by opposition on principle from Social Democratic circles. Several of the proposals put forward by the conservatives and the farmers party regarding customs and excise (amongst others in the question of cereals and margarine) were rejected due to collaboration of the Social Democrats and the liberals. On the other hand the government retained an extended power to raise tariffs if necessary despite the votes of the Social Democrats.

The government proposed and parliament decided, that a sum of 245 millions should be available for credit to banks (mainly Skandinaviska-Banken) that were threatened by failure on account of the crisis. In principle the Social Democrats accepted these proposals, though they wished for harder terms than those required by the bourgeoisie, in the first place a strong state control. That they took this position was justified by the fact that the banks must be saved, out of consideration for the deposit and so that unemployment would not increase further. However, the Social Democrats stressed that what had occurred was evidence of the weakness of the capitalist system, and of the need for state control of the economy.

At the party congress of March, 1932, those lines that had appeared in the crisis discussion in the party were dealt with. The proposal put by the party in parliament with reference to the crisis had not yet fully been dealt with, but it was already clear that it would not be accepted as the basis of a crisis policy. Under these circumstances it was clear that the congress must adopt a position in regard to the activities of the parlimentary group, and in connection with this indicate guide-lines for the coming election campaign. In addition the question of the making current of the principle of socialisation in connection with the crisis became the subject of debate and resolution.

The question of "the political situation on the eve of the election" was taken upon a speech of the party chairman. To begin with, he reminded that this time the congress met earlier in the year than was usual, and that therefore it was not possible for the party executive to present a suggestion for the election manifesto. During parliament there may occur events that would affect the content of the manifesto. On the other hand, the congress could make a general political statement particularly in connection with the motions put by the parliamentary group. After this, Hansson gave an account of the party's policies since the previous congress. Of importance in this connection is the fact that he placed the defeat of the 1928 lower house election and the victory of the 1930 municipal election in relation to the election programme on these occasions. From the events of 1928 it could be learned that "as far as launching penetrating projects is concerned, the party would be wise first to have really discussed these, so that it is not a question of going to the electorate only with an idea or a line, but also with a well-formulated practical proposal for the realisation of this idea." Comparing the election programme and the election victory of 1930, it could be seen that "what lies at the basis of confidence and secures our victory is no longer any radical way of speaking or loud appeals, but rather it is our attempt to put to the people practical proposals for the solution of issues that are of interest to them in their daily lives—a policy that is by no means new, a policy that does not exclude the idea that the duty to the future and to the greater aims that may never be neglected by a social democratic party, is fulfilled."

The crisis motion put at the parliament was the expression of this idea. "In this motion we see a splendid summary of our policy, that is a policy without reference to class or group, a policy for the whole people starting out from the correct idea that those in greatest need shall receive help first, and that as much help shall be given as lies in one's power." The party chairman warned against radical speeches before the coming election, which is of special interest with reference to the fact that he did not participate in the debate on the question of socialisation that took place later. After Hansson's speech the congress unanimously and without discussion decided that the editorial committee should have the task of formulating a proposal regarding the current situation.

This proposal was put forward shortly before the end of the congress, immediately after a decision regarding a statement in the question of socialisation, to which we will return later. The proposal was made by the party chairman and accepted without debate. In the main the statement thus decided "on the current political situation" involves an energetic recommendation of the crisis policy of the parliamentary group. "In the present situation Social Democracy sees as its foremost task to energetically work for a rapid and effective assistance to the groups of citizens who, through no fault of their own, have suffered from the results of the economic crisis." The statement begins with these words. In what follows the measures suggested by the party are further justified. The resolution maintained that Social Democracy did not only wish to put forward demands with reference to today, but also to give directions for the future. "In the latter respect Social Democracy goes in for such an economic policy, both regarding farming and industry, as is able to give security to commerce and industry and to the working people. However, in the conviction that the recovery of the economy presupposes the end of the violent restraint that has characterised economic exchange between people, Social Democracy is strongly opposed to enclosing and isolating measures by means of which the crisis is heightened and prolonged instead of being made milder and shorter." The policy of the party should not be bound by any class limits. "It does not wish to support and assist one working class at the expense of the other. In its work for advancement it does not distinguish between the industrial working class and the farming class, or between the work of the hand and that of the brain." This policy still met resistance from the majority in parliament. "When the Social Democratic proposal was dealt with, the Conservative and Liberal majority's unwillingness for a rational assistance and security policy on democratic lines emerged clearly. . . . An attempt is made to avoid an unprejudiced examination of the need to assist by constantly speaking of the need to save. . . . Against the opposition of the bourgeois parties to such a democratic policy we appeal to the Swedish people. We appeal for support for a policy that will give effective help to those who are oppressed and in need. We appeal to you to unite around a policy that in all areas wishes to maintain and develop democracy without reference to group or class interests, and in the interests of general security."

In fact, the statement recommended nothing more than a crisis policy on the foundations contained in the proposal of the Social Democratic parliamentary group. It is so formulated that the impression is received that from the point of view of principles an exhaustive picture of the party's programme of action in the face of the crisis has been given. A call to unite around certain reasonable demands is made, not a cry for economic and social reorganisation. There is no question of socialism or socialisation.

The points of view that were expressed in the great parliamentary motions of the party, in the speech at the congress of the party chairman, and in the statement regarding the political position that had been decided on, were not compatible with an attempt to bring through socialisation as the saviour from the present crisis. Those groups within the party who wished to make such an attempt had, in fact, already weakened their own position by not opposing the parliamentary proposal. Nevertheless, at the congress they attempted to make current the question of socialisation. The result was a statement deferring this question to the future.

The demand for socialisation was taken up in several motions. In the most detailed of these motions, and with which the Stockholm branch of the party said that it agreed, the crisis was interpreted as a sign of the breakdown of capitalism. Amongst other things it was demanded that congress should decide "that our party shall place the question of socialisation at the centre of its propaganda, its information activity and its measures," and also that the congress would make arrangements for the preparation of "a current programme of action in the question of socialisation." In another motion the formation of an economic ten-year plan for the party's activities was demanded, that would include, amongst other things, a detailed plan for socialisation. The report of the party executive regarding the proposal contained two different aspects. On the one hand, the congress should decide upon a general statement of principles regarding the question of socialisation with special reference to the crisis. In the view of the executive it was clear that the crisis exposed the fundamental lacks of the capitalist social order. "The acute need of people in a society filled to overflowing with unused productive resources gives the strongest possible reason to make clear in the daily propaganda of Social Democracy the tottering basis on which the welfare of the people rests as long as private interests dominate production."

On the other hand, socialisation should not be taken up as a current political question. "With reference to the impending practical work in regard to socialisation (to the extent that we are not already involved in this) the party should not adopt a position until the final report of the Socialisation Board is presented and has been scrutinised within the party." Therefore, the congress should refer the formation of a programme of action in the question of socialisation to the party executive and in doing so would test the ideas of the Socialisation Board.

Here it was hinted both that the policy already followed could be characterised as a sort of work for socialisation, and that socialisation in its real meaning was out of the question except in relation to a proposal of the Board of Socialisation. In its entirety the report of the party executive was based on the fact that the crisis should be used for socialisation propaganda, but not for socialisation action. The adopting of this position by a party that had put forward the idea of socialisation for several decades, was justified by saying that the Board of Socialisation had not completed its work. In 1932 as in 1920 the Board of Socialisation was a sort of ideological substitute for socialisation. A prerequisite for this idea must be that the Board would put forward a programme for socialisation that would guide the actions of the party.

In the fairly extensive debate—by far the longest that any Swedish Social Democratic congress has ever devoted to the question of socialisation—the most prominent members of the party took the party executive's line, whilst some less influential representatives expressed their sympathy for the motions. The party executive won. Nevertheless, the statement on principles regarding socialisation propaganda bore the traces of a desire to satisfy the wishes of the radical group.

The most prominent speakers following the line of the party executive were Sandler, Sköld, Engberg, Möller and Wigforss. In fact, the Chairman of the party had already clearly stated his agreement with this line when he warned against too much radicalism in connection with the coming election. Important differences emerged between the justifications given by the speakers in question. Sandler, who began the debate, strongly emphasised the importance of the work of the Board of Socialisation.

According to him there were several types of socialisation and various preconditions for realising them in various countries. Therefore, a thorough investigation was necessary as the starting point for this action. One method was to expect in the remaining report of the Board of Socialisation an industrial report and a final report. In the former the Board would adopt a position regarding such questions as the limitations of national socialisation, and questions regarding the suitability of total socialisation of an extensive area, or of partial socialisation that concerned only certain parts of a branch of the economy. In the final report were to be taken up "a long series of different questions of a principle nature that we will meet if we seriously begin the work of socialisation. One of these general questions is just how broad the socialisation action should be, and which of our various social lines of action should be united in harmony in order that together they might cause the changing of a society in the direction of socialisation. In this connection I think that it is not enough to discuss how the economy is to be organised and monopolised, but that it is also necessary to unite these measures with our policy in other areas—for example tax legislation, social legislation, school legislation etc.—in order to get something out of these various lines of action that are not always coordinated and that drives development in a certain direction." The various parties must take a stand with regard to the work of the Board of Socialisation when this Board had completed its work. Sandler hinted that under such circumstances too much impatience should not be shown. The main thing was a thorough examination. Moreover, as a secondary line in his speech Sandler stressed that Social Democracy was not to satisfy itself by analysing the course of events and waiting for the results of the interplay of economic forces. "We should get rid of the idea that we or our children will have the benefits of some sort of gratis-socialism, that the so-called development has placed in their hands." He ended by speaking of the action for socialisation that must eventually take place as "the main task of Social Democracy for the future."

Sköld represented a point of view that was coloured by scepticism and experimentalism. The crisis of confidence in the world did not depend upon capitalism but on nationalist and imperialist governments and people. It was quite possible that capitalism would survive the crisis even if it took another form. In every concrete situation Social Democracy should try to gain as much as possible for its aims, but one should not thoughtlessly demand immediate action. "It is better to sit and do nothing than do something silly!" It was dangerous to socialise bankrupt enterprises although in times of crisis these were easy to get. State control over banks would have been of small use during the crisis, because by means of such a control it was not possible to control bank deposits, and in the last analysis it was these deposits that decided financial movements. It should be made clear "that the question of socialisation is not solved to any great extent by parliamentary decisions. It is the economic forces that follow their grooves and break their paths that put us face to face with an accomplished fact. . . . In other words, I will say that we should be careful that we do not push socialisation too much into the forefront without making it clear for ourselves that to a very great extent we must seek public influence over economic life outside of parliament." Here Sköld seems mainly to have been referring to plans for new cooperative organisations within framing.

Engberg explained that larger economic units were necessary for a successful policy of socialisation. Small states could not accomplish much on their own. In order to maintain her economy Sweden was forced to place 30% of her production on foreign markets. "And it is because of this that in the present time I look upon the chances of socialisation as pessimistically as I do. Because we should not be blind to the fact that national socialism militarism and their common progeny protectionism, have drawn the small nations away from each other to the extent that the path towards larger units seems temporarily to be closed."

Möller pointed out the lack of clarity in the demands for socialisation that had been put forward. It did not help to speak generally of socialisation. It was necessary to make positive suggestions. As had been questioned, it was risky to socialise the banks because industrial enterprises that did not receive credit could in that way blame their bankruptcy onto the state. It was a great exaggeration to speak of a catastrophe of the capitalist system. In any event Social Democracy had no interest in causing such a catastrophe-situation. The party should try to win the majority and then gradually go over to measures of socialisation. "That condition that we do not explain today, that now we should start with one or another enterprise does not necessarily mean a complete helplessness regarding the chance of bringing about actual socialisation measures in a majority position. In that case it would be according to normal reformist principles." Socialism should not now be made into a central issue. "As long as the crisis lasts the very assistance measures themselves, as are presented in our motion for crisis assistance, by their very nature must occupy the central place in our programme." With particular reference to the importance of the municipalities in the process of socialisation, Möller criticised Engberg's ideas regarding the impossibility of socialism in a small country.

The most informative contributions to the debate were the extremely open speeches made by Wigforss. He began by reminding that at the congress of 1928 the party executive was given the task of formulating an economic programme for action,—a decision that of which perhaps a great number of the congress members had no knowledge. Now, when it was a question of formulating a statement in the question of socialisation, this must be so formed that socialisation appeared as a matter of actual urgency. Due to various difficulties and with reference to the work of the Socialisation Board, this had never been put into effect. Socialisation was to appear as "something that will help people even during the period in which we are now living . . . the question of socialisation must be paced in the foreground." But it was also undeniable that congress was not in a position to formulate concrete guidelines for a policy of socialisation. Wigforss stated that "within the party we are not yet clear as to which points we would attack if we really had the decisive power. . . . Let me speak freely for a moment. It cannot be helped that the whole of the history of our party has led us to a situation in which we have difficulty in forming positive guidelines.

Möller began by explaining that naturally we are entirely prepared for action in a revolutionary situation. I am entirely in agreement with him . . . If the party is forced to act, it will, without doubt, do so. But it is true to say that it is a long way between being forced to act due to a catastrophic situation, and otherwise to be satisfied with allowing the circumstances to develop and not acting because we are not completely in agreement . . . That in this situation we are forced to say that as long as there is no catastrophe we have no programme for action is naturally the party's weakness."

What were the causes of this situation? Wigforss' answer was that the party had two roots, Marxism and economic liberalism. Interpreted in the reformist way the Marxist conception led one to be relatively passive in the face of development. "We should follow, and when the time is ripe intervene and do something." On the other hand, economic liberalism had been the actual policy followed "and on every occasion it has been an obstacle as far as trying to give to the party a positive orientation in its economic policy is concerned. . . . Within the Social Democratic party one hears statements and reads speeches that show a certain concern for what is called a free economy. It is now almost impossible to find in the world similar ideas other than those held by the most stick-in-the-mud economic liberals."

Further, Wigforss stressed that two lines had been adopted in the socialist ideology, and that in fact these two lines did not agree. Socialisation (that is, the taking over of the means of production by the state) and planned economy. Socialisation could take place step by step and could be driven a long way without departing from the liberal system with free price-setting on the market as the decisive factor, without achieving a planned economy. Both these lines must be followed parallel to each other. But it must be remembered that planned economy could be brought about in ways that were objectionable to Social Democracy. Even a purely slave economy could be a planned economy. The question was to have a socialist planned economy instead of a bourgeois planned economy. Even the doctrine of free trade must be done away with, if it prevented plans for an organisation of the market and of the economy. Without going any further into the problem of socialisation, Wigforss ended by recommending a statement that would show the desire to make socialist ideals into reality. "What is missing in our Swedish Social Democratic party, just as in large parts of the international Social Democracy, is belief in our own strength, and to a certain extent this depends on a feeling of not knowing which paths we should take. If we could create certainty regarding the paths, we could also create the self confidence that is needed for our victory."

Contributions from those representatives who more decidedly sympathised with the motions that were put forward (such as G. Branting, Fabian Mänsson and Ström) did not require more thorough reporting. Whilst those speakers who could be seen as representing the party executive warned against underestimating the strength of the capitalist system, the "radicals" asserted that capitalism was in the process of disintegration. As Branting expressed it, "The economic catastrophe is not going to wait for the report of the Board of Socialisation." Therefore, it was necessary immediately to make plans for socialisation. No real analysis of how these plans were to be made was given. It was mainly banks that were mentioned as suitable objects for socialisation. There was undoubtedly something typical in the complement to the motion regarding an economic ten-year plan that was read by Uhlén, a member of the congress. That contained the following point: "Socialisation. The goal of the future: General socialisation. Immediate measures: A system for successive socialisation beginning immediately."

Fabian Mänsson accused the party congress of general conservatism. "I am of the opinion that this gathering is not mature enough to judge these things. To a great extent this gathering has solved its question of socialisation; it does not want to know about socialisation. What is true of the general public is also true of the labour movement. It is too conservative, too bound to tradition, yes, almost too indifferent to enter into such problems as demand young and new and fresh brains without preconceived ideas and without fear." Another speaker, E. Lindquist from Halmstad, said: "I think I can say that we who came here as representatives and who waited with the greatest interest to hear Sandler speaking on socialisation had expected a bit more than we got . . . What has Sandler to offer now? As far as I can see quite simply nothing . . . Our newspaper editors from Arthur Engberg right down to the smallest party newspaper for years have declared that the capitalist society is finished . . . But when one asks the party executive and the editors what they want to put in its place, they have nothing to suggest . . . In this context I would like to ask the newspaper editors to stop using big words and writing so much if they only do this to fool the workers and make them believe that it is possible to do more than is in fact possible."

The congress decided first in connection with the demand of the party executive that the editorial committee should have the task of formulating "a general statement of principles in the question of socialisation with particular reference to the economic crisis." After this a demand put by Branting, according to which the proposal put forward in the motion that the party "should place the demand for socialisation at the centre of its propaganda, its information activities and its measures," should be passed to the editorial committee for consideration, was rejected with 157 votes against 149. It should be pointed out that Branting's proposal, according to his own explanation, did not mean that the question of socialisation "in any way or in any form" should be made current in the election movement. Finally the proposal of the party executive concerning socialisation motions in general was accepted.

The statement suggested by the Editorial Committee that was read out by the party chairman was accepted without debate or voting. The statement was in the nature of a compromise between the majority and the strong minority who voted for Branting's demands. In time-honoured, Marxist coloured phrases capitalism was blamed for the existing situation. "The present crisis of world economy is the great crisis of capitalism. Never before has the capitalist system so clearly showed its inability to master the mighty forces of production that it brought to life. Workers, many millions of whom are unemployed, enormous amounts of inactive capital, stores and warehouses filled to overflowing, production apparatus extended and rationalised, but the elementary needs of the masses pushed to the brink and beyond of distress—that is the capitalist civilisation of today." After this picture of capitalism was more precisely drawn, the resolution stated that there was increasing doubt as to the system's ability to heal itself, and that the workers and other groups of the population as never before placed all their hopes on a thorough-going social change. "Swedish Social Democracy, conscious of this, sees as its unavoidable duty the organising of society's process of socialist change within the framework of our national economy and the social structure of the Swedish society. For this purpose a socialisation action is demanded, the accomplishing of which in changing circumstances now becomes the biggest, yes, the most important, task of the party." Socialisation must rest upon, and be brought through by means of, political, social and economic democracy.

However, the congress stressed that a socialist programme of action demanded very thorough preparation. "The promotion of socialist forms in the economy, and the transferring in that form of certain private capitalist enterprises, important for the welfare of the people, the taking of measures by means of tax, school and social policy to bring about a more even distribution and effective utilising of society's resources, the breaking down of privileges practised in the mis-used name of private ownership, increased security against exploitation to every honest contribution to production, increased democracy within all areas of society—*all* these lines of action joining with *one* aim: changing society in accordance with the idea of solidarity, *that* is involved in a socialist programme of action." The resolution ended with the words: "The situation is encouraging. Suffering weighs heavily on the shoulders of everyone. Only common labour can lift the burden and lay the foundations for affluence. The development and deeds that replace class advantages with the good and health of the entire people will be socialist."

When attempting to analyse the main points in the debate and the decision in the question of socialisation, it should first be underlined that half of the congress showed sympathy for the idea that the party should "place the demand for socialisation at the centre of its propaganda, its information activities and its measures." With a majority of only 8 votes of about 300 who voted, a proposal was rejected that was opposed by a unanimous party executive. However, it seems to be impossible to make more precise just where the conflict between the majority and the minority was really to be found. The minority, in the same way as the majority, did not wish to make socialisation a central point in the election campaign. Branting even said that the question of socialisation should in no way and in no form be made current at the election. The debate only shows that the minority were more eager than the party leadership and the majority, that the question be made generally current. The contributions of the leading party men suggest that within the party leadership the desire to press forward the question of socialisation was much less strong than the unanimous decision suggests.

Paradoxically this resolution can be said to be based on the idea that socialisation propaganda should be made current, but not immediately. It was understood that the election was not based on socialisation. But in the future the question of socialisation should be propagated with greater energy than before. And in time this propaganda should be followed by a making current of the question in another sense—the putting forward of the proposal to socialise. It must be assumed that the congress started from the idea that the report of the Board of Socialisation should lie at the base of this planning of socialisation activity, although strangely enough the resolution does not mention the Board.

If in one context one reads the statement "concerning socialisation and the economic crisis" and the statement "in the current political situation" it is difficult to believe that they have been formulated by the same editorial committee, and that immediately after each other they were decided by the same congress. One statement sounds like a revolutionary slogan, the other like a report from a Swedish parliamentary committee. One speaks in flaming words of the defeat of capitalism and the necessity of socialism, the other does not contain the words socialism and socialisation. In one, the socialisation action is said to be "the greatest, yes, the most important task of the party." In the other "Social Democracy sees as its main task to work with all energy by means of its policy for a rapid and effective help to those groups of the population who through no fault of their own have suffered from the effects of the economic crisis." One represents socialism as capitalism's victor and successor, whilst in the other Social Democracy appears as the helper in the economic crisis, that is, as the saviour of capitalism. One statement is supported by surviving Marxism, the other gives an account of the practical policy of Social Democracy. Ideology and reality had never before come up against each other so sharply. At one and the same time is proclaimed catastrophe and reformism. The small reservation that made possible the uniting of these ways of thinking was that the crisis policy should immediately (that is, at the election) be made current, whilst the socialisation policy should be taken up rather later even if in immediate connection with the crisis. Nevertheless, the difficulties in thus joining the two were clear. If the Social Democratic crisis policy succeeded this did not mean the defeat of capitalism, that was the basis of the demand in the statement regarding socialisation. The mass misery that in one resolution was said to lead to the extension and victory of socialism was in the other resolution said possibly to be able to be averted by a rational reformist policy.

From this point of view it could be said that both decisions very clearly and simply reflect the dilemma that characterises the whole of Marxist doctrine. From Marx's large perspective it is said that wealth and misery exist side by side until a catastrophe occurs. From his short-term perspective Social Democracy works for an improvement of the workers position within the framework of capitalism. How then can a catastrophe occur if Social Democracy is successful? In 1932 it was thought that the time of trial of capitalism had arrived. Marx's predictions seem really to have been fulfilled. The crisis that was occurring was considered as it was said in the Swedish resolution, to be "the great crisis of capitalism." But at the same time as in principle the demand for socialisation was intensified, measures against the crisis were recommended which had no particularly socialist character. To the extent that the policy was effective in the short run, the tendencies on which belief in an approaching catastrophe were grounded were opposed.

The question might be asked how members of the congress saw the incompatible statements that they unanimously accepted. Certain assumptions can be made from the debates themselves in congress and elsewhere. Probably it was quite natural for many vaguely to think that on the one hand one should try to divert the crisis by limiting measures, and on the other hand make use of it in an action for socialisation. The difficulty that this brought with it could not and would not be observed. It is also probably the case that the desire to make use of the crisis from a tactical point of view played a certain part in things. There was something tempting in at one and the same time offering temporary respite to the electorate—through the crisis policy—and future security and affluence—through the socialisation policy. One of these lines could be brought to the fore in competition with the Conservative and Liberal parties, the other in competition with the Communist party. But at the congress there were certainly many representatives who were in fact mainly interested in one of the two resolutions. As far as can be judged, Branting and Ström adopted a clear Marxist stand. Quite simply they saw in the crisis the catastrophe that had been predicted by Marx. To them the socialisation resolution must have seemed the most important. On the other hand at least certain members of the party leadership seemed to have been critical of this resolution, and seen the real expression of their ideas in the statement regarding the actual political situation. Possibly they relied on the fact that if the crisis policy succeeded the decision regarding socialisation would never be current. At any rate, it is unthinkable that the strong scepticism of for instance P. A. Hansson and Sköld could be united with a wholehearted reception of the socialisation resolution. It is also improbable that Sandler, Engberg, Möller and Wigforss, who warned against underestimating the strength of the capitalist system, would have agreed with the words in the resolution regarding the weakness of capitalism. However, together these two resolutions satisfied everyone; the combination of incompatible ways of thinking replaced compromise.

It is clear from this debate that great differences of opinion are to be found within the party, even apart from the two main points of view concerning the making current of the question of socialisation. What is above all noticeable is that those men who represented the party leadership exhibited great differences. Engberg's idea of the impossibility of isolated socialisation in a small country was criticised directly or indirectly by Sandler, Möller and Wigforss. Sköld expressed a general scepticism against state intervention that contrasted with the second speaker's belief in a future socialisation programme. Even between the ideas of Sandler, Möllers and Wigforss' existed deep-rooted differences. It was mainly on one point that there was relative agreement: the party was considered to be unprepared for a socialisation action and above all was said to lack clear lines in its economic policy. This was admitted more openly than in any previous debate. Neither did the speakers make any real attempts to dispel the lack of clarity that was so obvious. In the socialisation debate of 1920 a certain unity was achieved, at least in the question of which areas should first be placed under the administration of the state, and plans were made along the lines of guild socialism for the organisation of the socialised branches of the economy. Nothing was said of this in 1932. Lack of clarity was great in 1920, but it seems to have been even greater twelve years later.

In this context a line of thought put forward by Sandler, Möller and Wigforss, and made more precise by the latter, should be observed. Wigforss emphasized that the party had no economic programme of action but that it would certainly know how it should act if a catastrophe occurred. The party's weakness "is . . . that as long as there is no catastrophe, there is no programme of action." Sandler said that if "anything happens in the face of which it was necessary to act" one naturally could not wait for the Socialisation Board, but had to rely on one's own "socialist ideas and insight." By this he must have meant that the party had a current programme for its activities during the crisis, as is indicated by the parliamentary motions, but that it lacked a more general economic programme. However, a programme of action would appear if a catastrophe occurred. This way of thinking may appear strange. What would be the nature of the "catastrophe" at the appearance of which the party's programme of action would appear? And at the time of such a catastrophe, where would a programme of action come from, when in a decade of debates no such programme had been formulated? The explanation for these ideas held by two of the party's leading theoreticians can hardly be other than that they were still more or less thinking under the influence of the Marxist scheme of things. Catastrophe! For Marxism, this word symbolised the bankruptcy of capitalism and the victory of socialism. When the catastrophe took place the proletariat who lived oppressed and exploited would at last know how to act. The same picture was created by this magic word when also used by Möller and Wigforss. What should be done was not certain *now,* but *later* things would become clear. It should be added that even in everyday language the word catastrophe is often related to ideas regarding a simplifying of the problem situation that of necessity leads to a certain definite action.

A detailed investigation of Wigforss' illustrative and representative speech is out of the question here. One or two further points must however be commented upon. Wigforss considered that the lack of clarity and negativism of the party in the economic questions was due to what they had inherited on the one hand from Marxism, and on the other hand from economic liberalism. It may be added here that what Wigforss called economic liberalism can just as well signify an element of Marxism. Marx's scheme of development presupposed that economic liberalism would rule until it led to the collapse of capitalism. The developmental-fatalism taken from Marx meant, to express things in another way, that economic liberalism was accepted for the time being. Wigforss further noted that a definite distinction must be made between socialisation and planned economy. Important areas could be socialised without planned economy being possible as a result. Here the difficulty that meets reformist socialism as opposed to Marxism was touched upon. From Marx's large perspective socialisation should be complete, and therefore naturally mean planned economy. Having put forward the weaknesses and difficulties of the party, Wigforss goes directly to the demand that the idea of socialisation should be made current. At the same time he stressed that if the party achieved clarity regarding its aims, it would win self-confidence and therefore the certainty of victory. The strangeness of these statements lies in the fact that Wigforss, like many others, obviously lacked a clear idea of how socialisation would take place, and what it should mean, but that nevertheless he considered that clear lines would be achieved if only the demand for socialisation was decided upon. On this point he seems to have been representative of a great proportion of the party.

At the congress the land issue came up mainly through a motion put by Lindhagen in which he demanded that the congress should stress the importance of the state's right of expropriation for the establishing of small farming. On behalf of the party executive Sköld said that the demands of the programme on this point naturally should be realised, but that the present situation made action for the creation of farming unsuitable. "In a situation in which the great number of the country's farmers find themselves in economic misery, the like of which history has never before seen, and in which above all it is impossible to make a livelihood by farming. . . . it is certainly no rewarding task to make proposals for measures by which new groups of the population should become farmers."

It had been shown that the lessees were not desirous of making use of their opportunities to redeem the land they leased. In the question of land acquisition under these conditions the party must orient itself partly towards getting land for the forestry workers that could help to maintain them, and partly to making self-supporting those small farms whose owners were dependent on carting-jobs in the wood industry and also on other ways of making a living that were threatened by the crisis. On the other hand it was at present meaningless to work to create entirely new farms. Sköld's ideas won almost total support. Two statements in the land question were accepted. In one it was generally maintained that the party and its parliamentary group should make use of all suitable opportunities "to create better changes for those without private means, or with very little, if they so wished to be possessed of land to use in order to create more secure forms for the land possession of the working farming population, and also to obtain state control over the use of farming land in the general interests." To this end expropriation for land acquisition should be used if appropriate. The situation of the forestry workers was dealt with in the second statement: "No one is hit harder than the forestry workers by the present crisis. This group of workers has lower wages than any other despite the fact that the work is clearly of a seasonal character, and in addition have suffered great unemployment. Undoubtedly, it would be a great relief to many a forestry worker if he could come into possession of his own dwelling and sufficient cultivated land so that he could largely maintain himself with regard to farming products. Therefore, the congress states as its opinion that as the party works to bring through its programme regarding the question of land, special strength should be alloted to gaining a rapid solution of the question of land for forestry workers. By doing this the disinclination of the land owners to relinquish necessary and suitable land should, to the extent that is necessary, be broken, by placing the right to expropriate land for the required end in the hands of the state."

Further, in connection to several motions and at the suggestion of the party executive, a statement in the question of agricultural labourers was decided upon. In this statement the party's position with respect to this group of workers was developed more fully and with more concern for principles than on any earlier occasion. The statement started with the explanation that as the goal of its activities the party set forth "the political and economic freeing of the working classes," and that its social policy of welfare did not concern any given group "but rather all groups who suffer from the capitalist system." The demand for special legislation for certain groups that occasionally had been put forward, had been caused by special circumstances that had created special needs for protective legislation for these groups. As a reminder of this the congress wanted to state, "that it now seems to be necessary to direct particular attention to the agricultural labourers and their conditions." The working programme that was set out in the following dealt with continued action for the regulating of the working hours of agricultural labourers, the placing of this group on parity with other working groups regarding unemployment assistance and insurance, measures for improvement of the living conditions of the agricultural workers, and protection against eviction in connection with labour conflicts. Finally the party organisation was exhorted to take special measures in order to spread the knowledge of the party's policy and intentions amongst the agricultural workers. The statement of the congress was accepted without debate after a speech by Möller who presented the party's case. According to Möller, the question of agricultural labourers was the most important issue with regard to the future possibilities of the party. If the agricultural workers voted Social Democrat to the same extent as the industrial workers, the party could definitely count on a majority. During the most recent years increased political interest can be noticed amongst the agricultural workers. "This is perhaps the most encouraging sign of a political innovation that at present is generally to be found in our country."

Finally it should be mentioned that a motion was placed that at this point in time appeared to be an absurdity, regarding the regulation of the manufacture of margarine to the advantage of butter production. The party executive rejected the motion on the grounds that such a regulation would lead to the fact that an important commodity would be made dearer without the situation of the farmers being improved. If the price of butter rose, then there would be a reduction of consumption. As Sweden produced more butter than was consumed within the country it was unlikely that by reducing the manufacture of margarine such an increase in butter consumption would take place that the price of butter within the country would be freed of the influence of the price of world trade. Sköld, who presented the case for the party executive, stated that the motion clearly sprung from the National Confederation (Riksforbund) of the rural population, and in some way had been smuggled into the party branch who proposed it. The motion was rejected without debate.

As did the resolutions of the party congress, the Social Democratic election campaign at the lower house election of 1932 took two main lines.

Capitalism was represented as being the cause of the crisis and it was hinted that it must be succeeded by socialism, but crisis assistance of the type that was demanded in the Social Democratic motions at the parliament of that year were presented as the goals of the current policy of the party. The party's election manifesto began with a general description of the situation. "The weaknesses and dangers of the system of private capital are exposed as never before. Wealth in the form of natural resources capital and labour is greater than ever. This, together with the fantastically highly developed technology, should lead to a richer and easier existence for man . . . Instead we watch a crisis develop, seeking its victims in all parts of society. In a capitalist system the powerful productive forces could not be ruled. Right in the middle of the superfluity of all that man needs to produce there is misery and unemployment almost without parallel." However, from this the conclusion was not drawn that a socialist system must be established. The words socialism and socialisation do not appear in the manifesto. Partly the tariff system was criticised as was the demand for increased armament, and partly help for the victim of the crisis was demanded by means of emergency measures and financial support to a greater extent than previously. The demand for thrift was now allowed to lead to the fact that productive expenses were limited. Amongst those social reforms that were taken up in the manifesto, in addition to crisis measures, were unemployment insurance, raising of old-age pensions and regulating of the working hours of agricultural workers.

In general the election propaganda followed the same lines. However, the question of socialisation was taken up and dealt with in a series of proposals, partly in reply to the statement of the Conservative and Liberal parties to the effect that the Social Democrats dare not make this question current. A tendency to see the party's crisis programme as the expression of socialist principles can be traced, but at the same time to shelve the question of socialisation in its real meaning. In an election speech the leader of the party stated that the Conservatives and Liberals asked why the Social Democrats did not place the electorate face to face with the problem of the realising of the socialist order of society. In fact, he continued, the Social Democrats had taken up precisely this problem. In the eyes of the party the Kreuger crash and other events showed "the danger of allowing power over the economy to lie uncontrolled in private hands. Should we not soon be ready to say that there must be an end to such an order, and instead create an order than can rationally make use of the resources of society in order to secure bread and work for the masses. If the questions are put in this way, then the election movement is to be seen as a trial of strength between capitalism and socialism." However, Hansson did not put forward any sort of demand for socialisation, but only recommended the Social Democratic crisis programme. In other contexts he stressed that a socialisation action was out of the question and that no plans for such an action had been able to be formulated. In a pamphlet Wigforss justified the proposal of public labour as a means of relieving the effects of the crisis and of creating increasing purchasing power, therefore mastering the crisis. But moreover this demand was "an expression of the endeavour that supports the socialist movement to liberate the productive forces from the fetters in which the private capitalist system has placed them, to free man from being a servant of the economic organisation and instead put him in a position to rule it." Möller and Sandler expressed the most common criticisms of capitalism and spoke of the need for a social reorganisation, but tried not to present the demand for socialisation as a current demand. As Hansson and others, Möller stated that socialism was a consequence of democracy: "A joining of democracy and private capitalism is an insoluble paradox . . .

from which it follows . . . that private capitalism must give way . . . that political democracy must be complemented by economic democracy."

In connection to his statement at the party congress Engberg explained that an isolated socialisation in Sweden was unthinkable. "Because, let us speak honestly, the realising of socialism is at one and the same time the planned organisation of the world economy and the planned integration of the national economy in the world economy." Again Vougt characterised the crisis policy as socialism. "The intervention of the state in the situation of private individuals for the common good of the peoples economy is for us practical socialism. To create work for man, to give him the chance of earning his bread, that is practical socialism." Only a few individual representatives of the radical wing of the party tried to make the demand for socialisation more concrete. It was G. Branting's opinion that as early as at the following parliament the question of the creation of a state central bank could be taken up, and also the question of nationalising brewing, the trade in drugs and insurance.

However, the main problem in the election debate was the question of immediate and useable measures against the crisis. As justification for the Social Democratic line there was criticism of the policy and crisis programme of the Conservative and Liberal parties. A certain doubt could be discerned in statements in the propaganda in connection with thrift. On the one hand this demand was generally agreed with, on the other hand the enormous state grant that was required to meet the crisis was said to be necessary, and in the long run productive. Certainly Wigforss represented a widespread, but not altogether openly-expressed idea when in the radio debate prior to the election he said: "We believe that the general thrift panic makes the crisis worse instead of making it milder." Above all the tariffs and the proposal to raise them were criticised. For many Social Democrats it seems that the policy of economic isolation was the main reason for the crisis, even if this was said to be the fruit of the "system." Hansson stated that the tariffs formed an extra tax of the poor and had the effect of paralysing large parts of the economy. According to Engberg "the most important thing at present in Swedish politics . . . is the resuming of the free trade front in parliament." A series of notable and theoretically formulated attacks against protectionism were made by Örne. The bourgeois farming policy was said only to favour the better situated farmers who sold corn, and was to the disadvantage of several small holders who produced less corn than they needed. Sköld wrote that the demand for the limiting of margarine production is "an attempt to ruin the livelihood of the poorer classes with edible fat, and amongst the poorer classes could be counted many smaller farmers . . . And it is directly damaging for farming because it removes from our dairying a spur to technical development." Sköld summarised his opinion in the following passage: "The bourgeois policy for improvement of animal production has not shown itself to lead to the goal, the bourgeois policy supports vegetable production that is to the advantage of the larger farmers, but to the disadvantage of smaller farmers." In its entirety the polemical line in the Social Democratic propaganda means that the capitalist order was accused of being the cause of the crisis, and that the Conservative and Liberal policy was said to be aimed at worsening the crisis, rather than overcoming it.

The Social Democrats won fourteen new seats and thereby had 104 representatives in the lower house, whilst the Conservative and Liberal parties received in total 118 mandates. Since the attempt to create a bourgeois coalition government had failed, the fourth entirely Social Democratic government was formed on the 24th September.

At its initiation the government explained that it counted on cooperation with the other parties. However, "as the foundation of its work (it would) place the programme that the Social Democratic party had presented to the electorate, as the expression of what they consider to be necessary and correct in the present situation." The economic crisis had been intensified due to the policy of enclosure, and an active policy should be followed in order to break down the barriers that divided the people.

Unemployment should be opposed, amongst other things by means of productive labour that would partly create new opportunities for work, partly "encourage the free enterprise to increased activity." The difficulties in farming must be met by measures for making production cheaper and assisting in the selling of products. Within social policy questions of unemployment insurance and improved old age pensions were placed in the foreground. "A strict policy of thrift is necessary but should not ignore the general payments that in the long run are the most productive; those that help to maintain the physical and spiritual health of the people." The question of socialisation was not dealt with directly, but its existence was hinted at in the following passage: "In our country circumstances that are both morally and economically trying have made current the question of state control over the administration of the state economy. The government finds it natural to pay particular attention to this question."

At the parliament of 1933 the government presented a crisis programme of such a penetrating nature that, whilst directly connected to the proposals of 1932, it meant a new orientation in Swedish politics. About 160 millions should be granted to emergency labour, and 40 millions to unemployment help of a different nature. The government would have great freedom with regard to emergency labour. Amongst other things the grant might go to the building of dwellings, to municipal labour and to loans or subventions to private enterprises. It was reckoned that about 90,000 workers would in this way receive employment, and it was assumed that orders in connection with the work would be made to industry for nearly 70 millions which is why a great number of workers apart from those directly employed in emergency labour would be helped. Reserve labour, that for the time being was to be retained to a certain extent, would be paid according to the current wage paid to unskilled labourers, not with a lower wage as had been the practice earlier. Means for the crisis assistance were to be raised by loans. Therefore raising of both direct and indirect taxes was suggested. The taxation scale for inheritance tax should be raised so that an amount more than double the amount previously obtained in this way would be received. Several economies were made with regard to current expenses.

The main justification for the government's proposal is to be found in the speech of the prime minister when the proposition was presented. "If emergency labour is to be of real importance as a means of effectively supplying work and stimulating the enterprises and economy in general, in a time of widespread unemployment, then it must be on a much wider scale than has been the case up to now. . . . A serious attempt to get out of the current stagnation should be made. This can now be expected as the result of individual initiative alone. The general paralysis restrains everyone. . . . The fearful and blind abstemiousness in all quarters has not counteracted stagnation and impoverishment but rather, as far as can be ascertained, has had a diametrically opposed effect. The setting in motion of general labour in a sufficiently wide scale, both state and municipal, should both directly and indirectly give labour and incomes. Various enterprises would be occupied in producing the materials for use in these jobs and therefore private enterprise be stimulated. However, . . . by direct loans or support the state should also encourage productive labour that has been set in motion by private individuals. It is my hope that by means of such steps it will be possible, not only to give employment to considerable numbers of unemployed, but also to break down stagnation and open the road to recovery and economic reconstruction." A thorough theoretical explanation for this positive crisis policy was given in an appendix to the Government budget proposal made by Gunnar Myrdal, professor in national economy.

The government's unemployment policy was said to be of immediate value even from the point of view of farming, as it was oriented to increasing the demand for farm products. In the question of farming the government started out with the idea that the corn regulations decided upon earlier should be maintained. This was mainly because the regulation had existed for so long that deviating from it would mean too great a disturbance of the situation. The fall in prices in certain areas would be so great that a crash might result. However, the state measures should be seen as a temporary intervention that would be discarded as soon as conditions allowed. In connection with the milk regulations that were introduced in 1932 an import monopoly on milk and dairy products was suggested. In addition the government recommended amongst other things a grant of 10 millions for loans to farmers.

As in previous years the Social Democrats characterised their policy as a policy of cooperation. It was a question of helping all social groups by doing away with stagnation. In the Budgetary Debate the prime minister said that it was not a question of bringing about a socialist order. "I do not think that a socialist government has any reason just now to sit down and think about how it is possible to build up a socialist society. Whatever government is in power has its hands full with serious tasks concerned with the near future. And a government that is aware of its duty will apply itself to these tasks."

It is not possible here to go any deeper into the debate and actions centering about the government proposal. Within the bourgeois parties—mainly the conservatives and the bourgeois left—a general criticism of the Social Democratic point of view was put forward, even if there was an inclination to meet this to a much greater extent than in the previous years. The high taxes were seen as being aimed at getting rid of the advantageous effect that the emergency labour and other supporting measures could have on the state of the market, market wages for relief labour were seen as preventing a necessary decrease in wages. The financial programme was even called an attempt at confiscation of private property more diligently thought out than had been the case in 1928. The government was said to have neglected farming. A further series of regulation measures to the benefit of farming were demanded by the right-wingers and the farmers party. Criticisms of various aspects of the government proposal came from those holding varied points of view.

The crisis proposal was referred to a special committee who later came to be called the Welfare Committee. However, the decisive negotiations as to an agreement took place between the government and the party leaders. This resulted in an agreement on 27th May between Social Democracy and the Farmers Party ("horse trading"). This meant that in the main the Farmers Party agreed to the government's unemployment programme, whilst the Social Democrats accepted several suggestions from the Farmers Party regarding further supporting measures for farming. The agreement became the foundation for the government decision, which was even accepted by some liberals. 180 millions were granted to the fight against unemployment, of which 100 million went to emergency labour. The directive regarding unemployment assistance was made milder. A rise in taxes was decided, although not as great a rise as the government had suggested. In the main, loans were used. Amongst other things it was decided in the question of farming that the price of butter would be maintained at a certain minimum and that in this context margarine excise would be introduced, also, that with regard to several other farming products the prices would be stabilised or raised by various types of regulations. Yet another step was taken in the direction of a general state price-setting in this area, and a monopolising of the home market for the domestic products.

During the negotiations the parties had come close to each other on various points, and the parties that were outside the final agreement could hardly be said to have a different base from their opponents in the question of principles. The government decision was preceded by an intense debate and followed by a widespread press polemic, but did not lead to any general intensifying of political conflicts.

From the Social Democratic point of view the crisis agreement definitely meant that the party had on the one hand succeeded in realising its plans for unemployment policy much better than they had expected, and on the other hand that important points both in the general programme and in the election programme of 1932 had collapsed. The principle of free trade that had been of such importance in the electioneering was given up, and the farming regulations that previously were criticised were extended. The most typical example of the change is perhaps the idea of a margarine excise which whilst having been rejected as an absurdity at the congress of 1932, was realised with the cooperation of Social Democracy a year later. If a comparison is made between the Social Democratic election pamphlets from the lower house election of 1932, and the 1934 county-council elections it is seen that on several points arguments that were not accepted in 1932 were energetically promulgated in 1934, and that ideas that at the former election were seen as decisive, at the latter election were either ignored or criticised.

A more or less unanimous justification for the position adopted by the party was given in parliament and in the public debates. The fact that two great parties who earlier had mainly opposed each other were now united with regard to certain vital questions was given great importance. It was often asserted that Social Democracy and the Farmers Party represented both the largest producing groups in the country, and that therefore their collaboration had a wider significance. P. A. Hansson wrote in 1934 that both classes had achieved greater understanding of each other.

"If the psychological results of the agreement are taken care of, then the future effects may be of importance. In general nothing is more natural than cooperation between both the large groups of citizens in questions regarding which democratic disposition and a love of freedom are common." Often the idea of cooperation between "the working groups of the population" was held up as a main motive in social democratic policy that now really had been realised and the great agreement was said to lie at the basis of a continuing connection. The idea of cooperation, and the active policy that was made possible through this, was of value with reference to the consolidation of Social Democracy in a time of international crises and victories in antidemocratic directions.

More particularly the agreement was first and foremost justified by the fact that it meant that the Social Democratic unemployment programme was accepted on all important points. The farming regulations were defended, to some extent along different lines. It was the price of aid to the workers. In the present situation it was the only way of lessening the difficulties of the farmers. Even if in principle protectionism was incorrect it might occasionally be a necessary measure in times of crisis. At the same time as it was asserted that the agreement was to the advantage of the farmers, it was stressed that they were not helped to any unreasonable extent. Sköld wrote in 1934 that the policy that was adopted meant that the farmers had to be satisfied with a reduction in income of a fourth, despite the support. "There is certainly no more important group in our country that has had greater decrease of living standards due to the crisis, and none who has made greater sacrifices." But the farming policy was also justified on the grounds of more general principles. It was said to be a natural complement to the unemployment policy. Wigforss wrote that the crisis agreement may be characterised so that the expansionist and reflationist line was victorious, not only with regard to the unemployment question but also in the question of land. When the purchasing powers of the workers rose, farming products, to a relatively great extent, could gain a market within the country, which justified the protection policy. On the other hand the improved conditions of farmers would mean that sales of industrial products rose.

As early as in the summer of 1933 a certain improvement in the state of the market took place. The situation rapidly improved in 1934 and the years that followed were characterised by a favourable industrial market. In 1933 the number of unemployed was on average 164,000, in 1934 115,000 in 1935 62,000 in 1936 36,000 and in 1937 18,000. The extent to which the state crisis policy was of importance in the improved condition of the market is disputed. In general it is believed that it hastened and strengthened a tendency to the better that had other causes. It is undeniable that the fears expressed by the critics of the crisis agreement showed themselves to be groundless. It is also without doubt that the crisis policy immediately relieved the situation of the groups that were most badly hit, and that by means of emergency labour and other measures considerable improvements regarding, amongst other things, dwellings and communications took place. It is probable that the active and energetic state activity raised the government's power and the authority of the entire democratic regime.

During the following years the government completed the policy that had been started, mainly with the collaboration of the Farmers Party though without any particular opposition from the other parties. With the improved state of the market the question of unemployment was pushed into the background. Time after time farming policy was extended by new decisions that regulated prices of farming products and gave to Swedish farming a more complete monopoly of the home market. The most important socio-political reforms were the introduction of unemployment insurance in 1934, and the raising of the old age pension in 1935. With reference to the latter mentioned decision the government was not able to carry through its proposal in its entirety. Therefore a new proposal regarding old-age pensions was put forward at the 1936 parliament. The opposition of the bourgeois majority was the main reason for the collapse of the government.

In the speeches of the members of parliament, especially the prime minister, in these years, it was constantly asserted that the crisis policy that had been brought about was a policy of cooperation, a peoples' policy, whose goal was to satisfy the interests of various groups in society, and to work for general welfare. The class struggle was not mentioned. Instead it was stressed that the feeling of community was strengthened and ideological conflicts reduced. When the question of socialization was dealt with the fact that it was not a current question was stressed. In one of his speeches in 1934 the prime minister stated that in a general sense the groups in society were nearer to each other than before. Deep conflicts were still to be found, but a considerable evening-out had taken place and the common platform had broadened. An increased state control of the apparatus of production was demanded, and it was here that socialist points of view entered into things. But it was necessary to proceed carefully. "We don't recommend any adventurous experiments, knowing full well that those who would suffer most intensely from a failure are just those masses whose position we desire to improve. We don't want any violent change, but only a purposeful and careful preparation of a development towards greater perfection of democracy in all areas." In a speech in the Budgetary Debate in 1935 Hansson explained that in the opinion of Social Democracy, society was to be looked upon as "an organism in the act of continuous development." It was necessary "to adapt the policy to the stage of development of the society at a given time, at the same time as one attempts to act in order to prepare and assist the coming smooth development. Therefore in our times a social democratic policy can very well be a policy that quite particularly attempts to make use of the immensely valuable strength that lies in private initiative and private enterprise, together with the state and social contributions. . . . I am convinced that if we now have not only a great theoretical discussion but a great practical discussion on, for instance, socialisation of certain areas, it is possible that in the long run we are right, but for a time, a rather long time, we would destroy the forces in a rather fruitless discussion to the detriment of the cooperation with other forces by means of which could now come important results." In the Budgetary Debate of the following year the prime minister expressed himself even more clearly in the question of socialization. "By no means do I believe that we have reached that degree of social development at which an extensive socialization could with advantage be begun." As in England the bourgeois parties in Sweden should be clear that the old liberal ideology was not tenable, and without prejudice test how greater security can be gained by means of state intervention. "We would willingly, we Swedish Social Democrats, to the same end agree to give all possible encouragement to private enterprise that will still have its tasks and that will definitely remain in existence for a long time, even in the form of private enterprise." "A successive abolition of the economic conflicts and in that way a gradual settlement of the class struggle" could be imagined. An improvement of society could only take place "through cooperation between various groups, between various classes."

In 1933 two of the committees appointed by the government (of which one completely and one in the main was composed of Conservative and Liberal members) asked whether or not import and business concerned with coffee and petrol should be monopolised by the state. The proposal was justified using financial, organisational and trade policy conditions. In the report the question of socialisation was not dealt with. However, the proposal was criticised in large areas of the bourgeois press as evidence of a tendency to socialisation. At the County Council Election in Stockholm 1935, the question of monopoly was important, and the election defeat of the Social Democrats was generally considered to be connected with this. What is important in this context is that the government's representatives time after time rejected the idea that investigations into coffee and petrol monopoly meant a boost for socialism. The question of monopoly was not presented to parliament.

In the main the Social Democratic discussion even outside parliament followed the guidelines of the government. But other tendencies can also be traced. At the same time as it was stressed that in its real meaning the question of socialisation was not a current one, one was inclined to label the policy that had been carried through as a sort of socialisation. Under the heading "We are socialists!", Ny Tid wrote that in contrast to other parties the Social Democrats tried to make the crisis policy planned and effective. "This is our socialisation. In this way we are socialists. Our socialism and our socialisation is the realising of the idea: The support of all fit members of society by creative wholesome work." An article in Örebro-Kuriren is even more characteristic of the existing uncertainty in the use of the concept. When a bourgeois newspaper took up the question of the position with regard to socialisation adopted by social democracy, the Örebro-Kuriren answered that the expression socialisation was in fact a slogan "a scarecrow for ignorant children." In fact, socialisation could only mean "manipulations" by which society was made socialist, and such "manipulations" were unreasonable. Moreover, socialisation was not the main point in the Social Democratic programme. "It is necessary to look right up to Point XII in the political programme before reaching something that smells of 'socialisation.' Furthermore, socialisation was only demanded to the extent that was necessary for the creating of a planned peoples' economy. Planned economy, however, was a tricky point. All the peoples of the world are tackling this problem. Behind Nazism in Germany, fascism in Italy and Roosevelt's experiments in America there are clear attempts to create a planned economy." Finally it was maintained that a rather extensive planning of the economy had taken place in Sweden with the collaboration of all parties. "We are sliding inexorably into a society in which cooperation between the nation and the people is a categorical imperative. One may call this socialism or prefer to call it private capitalism—in reality it amounts to the same thing. We all help to promote it." A third newspaper said that Marxism "had been a danger for the working class, which sought to participate in the good of society and attempted to gain influence in national decision making. . . . Social Democracy can take all the accusations that it is 'becoming bourgeois' very calmly. . . . When one has got so far that one admits that there is a problem of economy for all of us, then no movement should need to place its own labels on questions and decisions, then one has achieved a community of the people without the decree of power." It was often stressed that not only a majority, but the vast number of people, must accept the idea of socialisation before it was put into practice.

The voices raised for a more radical policy were not heeded. The previous Communists, of which several were now in prominent positions within the party, were in complete agreement with the policy of cooperation. At the congress of the Youth Organisation in 1934 there were motions that the organisation should formulate "a youth socialisation programme" and that its propaganda should be concentrated around this question. The Council of the Youth Organisation rejected these proposals. In its speech it emphasised that in certain areas the principle of socialisation had already pushed its way comparatively far into Swedish social life. The demand for socialisation had not been given more space within the practical work of the party due to "a general political situation that has pushed other, and up to now more pressing, problems into the foreground." The youth should study the question of socialisation, but not take separate initiative. The chairman of the organisation, and other speakers, labelled the government's policy as a step in the work of socialisation. The decision was based on the idea that one should follow the development of the problem of socialisation and spread knowledge of this, and also "on all occasions desired by the party place the strength of the youth movement at the disposal of the realising of the demand for socialisation within the Swedish economy." It was clear that an overwhelming majority within the Youth organisation backed up the government's policy.

Three members of the Board of Socialisation, Möller, Leo and Sandler, joined the Social Democratic ministry of 1932. Nevertheless no changes were made in the composition of the Board. How the work of the Board was successively wound up is seen clearly from the parliamentary records of the years that followed. In 1933 the Board informed "that work on the final report of the Board, and work on the investigations of the Board concerning Swedish industries had to a certain extent continued during the year." In 1934 the Board said that work on the final report was in part proceeding. On 9th January, 1935, the government decided that the activities of the Board should cease on 31st January of that year, and gave to Sandler, the foreign minister, the job of "as soon as circumstances allow, partly to give out a draft of the report of principles of the problem of socialisation, and ideas connected with this, (to the extent that preparatory work on this had been carried out), and partly to present a summarised account of the activities of the Board of Socialisation."

Since then Sandler has presented two investigations (apart from certain writings on the question of socialisation in other countries) that are said to form "the draft of the report of principles." The first of these came out in 1936 under the title "The problem of Socialisation: general views," and the other in 1937 entitled "The problem of Socialisation: economic problems and factors." In both these writings a foreword informs that they were intended to lay the foundation for the report of principles of the Board of Socialisation, and that therefore they were drafted in the name of the Board of Socialisation. Sandler informs, however, that the Board has not carried out any final checking of the writings, which is why the author is solely responsible for their content and form. In fact the Board as such had not given out any report of principles. As a matter of fact, to judge by the foreword what is now presented is only a part of the account with which Sandler proposes to terminate the activities of the Board.

Nevertheless what is more important is that the writings in question do not form a report on socialisation of the sort that earlier was generally thought of as being the main result of the work of the Board. No plan either for partial or general socialisation was presented. The author neither recommends nor rejects an action for socialisation. In the main the question of socialisation in Sweden was not discussed. The writings may be seen as a series of general essays on the subject of the problem of socialisation and related questions.

A reminder of some main points in the first paper, that was more concerned with principles, is called for. It begins with a discussion of the concept of socialisation. The main thing here is a definition found in a German political handbook that clearly contained evaluations. Sandler points this out, and in connection with this makes the statement that it is not possible "to deal with social problems without, from the very beginning, bringing in certain evaluations"—a statement that is clearly correct if by "deal with" one means "make proposals" or "act" or similar, but just as clearly incorrect if in this connection "define" or "analyse" is meant. After this, and clearly influenced by Myrdal's work "Science and politics in National Economy," though this is not quoted, the author presents the values from which he proceeds. It seems that he believes himself able to give an objective account of these values. The values in question are 1) economic liberation—that is, liberation from "the fetters of scarcity." 2) livelihood for all the members of society, 3) utilising of the capacity of all, 4) a feeling of comfort through a certain measure of freedom, 5) the chance to advance, 6) security, 7) that a minimum of revolutionary means be used for advance.

The author assumes that these norms, in themselves emphasing values and thus accepted by all (which is why they can also result in very different structures of society), are clearly intended to offer some guidance for political activity. At the same time it is maintained that the norms are in conflict:

"affluence and freedom, advance and security could come into conflict." This is said to depend on "the deep irrationality of man." Clearly a misunderstanding is to be found here. It is not irrational to demand good food, a lot of food and non-fat-forming food but in an individual case there can clearly be conflict between these requirements. After this, and without being hampered by the scepticism he expressed earlier, the author writes about various types of socialisation. With regard to the subject of socialisation one can distinguish between state enterprises, autonomous social enterprises, guild-organisations and consumer-cooperative enterprises. With regard to the object, between the socialising of ownership, of production, of produce, and of the control of society. Finally some general statements were made regarding socialisation and the population problem, but without the author explaining what he means by socialisation in this context.

It should be clear that at least as the starting point for socialisation, this work is of small value. What is interesting in this, just as in the second part of the draft, is that almost no regard was paid to the programme of Swedish Social Democracy, and that statements are continuously made that show that the author considers the statements regarding the development and structure of society to be found in the programme to be incorrect or misleading. The very method in which Sandler treats his subject is incompatible with the social prognosis that is given in the basic principles of the programme. The report on principles is not an unimportant stage in the development of the ideology of Swedish Social Democracy, when one considers that it was Sandler himself who was the author of that programme and of the justification that was given for the programme.

In "Tiden," 1937, Karl Fredriksson, an author active within the Social Democratic party organisation, gave an analysis of the party's position regarding the problem of socialisation. This can be seen as a summarised expression of the situation that occurred after the victory of the welfare ideology and the winding up of the Board of Socialisation. Fredriksson reminded that in 1932 the party congress said that "an action for socialisation was the biggest, yes the most important task of the party," and added: "If one is very eager that there be agreement between our theory and our practice, one might say that through our practical economic policy we have acted in agreement with this declaration. But it was not milk regulations, cost-of-living index locality regulated pensions, maternity benefit and childrens' allowance that was the main aim of the congress declaration of 1932. The real intention was that we should set about transferring important means of production into state ownership. And that something would happen just as soon as the Board of Socialisation was ready with its work. Five years have passed since then. There has been no particular hurry—with the approval of the party we have allowed the members of the Board to edit the final report in their spare time. . . ." In practice the question of socialisation had always taken a second place in the party's politics. "No doctrine of socialisation but the manifest and immediate needs of the poorest groups of the population have indicated those tasks to the solving of which first and foremost we direct our strength." It could possibly be said, continued the author, that in the long run a penetrating action for socialisation would be of greater value than successive reforms. But in this respect it was not possible to feel convinced.

Partial socialisation could not be expected to yield great immediate advantages. If it was possible to assess this, these would first come when a coordination of the entire apparatus of production took place. But directing ones' energies to this would not be "particularly attractive as political activity." If it had taken seventeen years to investigate the question of socialisation people might suspect "that it might take a hundred years to really socialise as much as is necessary in order that the effects can be felt. People don't want to wait so long. At least not as long as there are immediate practical tasks in which the application of political power can be expected to give manifest results in the considerably nearer future." The fact that one chose the short-term points of view, and therefore in principle aimed at a social policy or welfare policy, did not need to mean that the question of socialisation was discarded. "It only means that socialisation becomes what it should be—not an unavoidable principle, but the alternative of choosing or not doing so, all because a socialised production in the special case brings us nearer to, or removes us from, the material and spiritual freedom that is our real goal." With these rather obscure words one of the clearest and most honest analyses of the state of the problem of socialisation that has ever occurred within Swedish Social Democracy is completed.

In the autumn of 1934 the question of population, earlier to be noticed mainly in specialised circles, became a current political question. Through their work "Crisis in the question of population," Alva and Gunnar Myrdal started a general and lively debate. The authors stressed that nativity had dropped so low that within a few decades there would be a reduction of population if the number of births did not rise considerably. Large-scale immigration from other countries would threaten the social and cultural level of the country, and for the working classes in particular bring with it a decrease in standards of living. The solution to this was not in legislation against contraceptives and other measures making free birth control difficult. On the contrary, all such regulations should be abolished. In the long run an improvement of the situation was only possible by means of a rise in general welfare, and a policy that favored child-bearing.

An increase in the building of dwellings through state and municipal initiative, plus measures to improve the position of mothers, and reduced family costs for the maintenance and upbringing of children, were some of the reforms that were immediately necessary.

But in addition a meaningful levelling of incomes was demanded, and a planned economy that increased production. "If one wishes to stop the fall in number of births, there is no other means than a very radical distribution and social policy, and in its turn this can not be brought about in any other way than on the basis of a radical production policy that increases the effectivity of production to the level of the technical opportunities." The population question was "the strongest argument for a penetrating and radical socialist reforming of society. The question of population will raise tremendously the political demand that social circumstances in our country should be changed to such an extent that once again citizens will want to bring sufficient numbers of children into the world in order that our people will not die out."

The principle demand for measures in the question of population was intended to gather a wide following. From the national point of view nothing could be more important than preserving the nation. The groups that particularly represented this point of view also proved their desire for action, even if it was often maintained (with reference to the fact that nativity had decreased at the same time as welfare had increased) that the means of creating a change was not a raised standard of living, at least, not mainly so. As the Myrdals reminded, from the social-radical point of view the question of population in any case appeared as a support for the demands for reform that had been put independently of this. Within Social Democracy, the question of population had hardly been discussed earlier. In general one should have adopted more or less the same general standpoint as Professor and Mrs. Myrdal. One had worked for the right of free birth control but also maintained than an effective use of the country's resources would very much reduce the need of such a control. Now the party mainly associated itself with the demand that was put forward. The national as well as the social radical points of view were underlined in the debates, even if in some circles advocates of increased nativity were suspected of desiring national isolation, and in the main of advocating nationalism.

At the parliament of 1935 several motions were put forward regarding investigation into the population question, and a positive decision made with which almost all agreed. In the short debate it was underlined by the Social Democrats that for a solution of the question penetrating social reforms were required. After this the government appointed a population commission, the directive of which made possible the comprehensive treatment of the problem. During the years that followed the population question, as the earlier crisis, came to widen the framework of socio-political activity. Important intervention could be justified on the grounds that it was necessary, if a return to "normal" conditions was to be made, i.e. to a population of stationary or slowly growing size.

In its entirety the Party Congress of 1936 expressed the situation that had arisen through the successes of the Social Democratic government, the lessening of the economic crisis and the worsening of the international situation. The only questions that awakened greater interest were those questions connected with each other regarding the resignation or continuation of the government, and the position adopted by the party with regard to defence. All proposals regarding programme changes were rejected, usually after little or no debate. The economic and social questions now raised little interest, though they had taken a prominent place at the previous congress.

The treatment accorded to a motion regarding revision of the general basic principles is very illustrative of the party's ideological development. In this connection the actual content of the motion is of no interest. The motion was presented by a private member of the Stockholms branch of the party and contained only a detailed criticism of the basic principles. In general terms this was rejected by the Programme Commission and the Party executive. However, one member of the party executive, K. J. Olsson, had reservations, and demanded that the newly elected programme Commission and Party executive should have the task of carrying out a general revision of the programme. Amongst other things he maintained that the formulation of the general basic principles did not give a completely correct description of the existing condition, and in several places gave reason for misunderstanding and ministerpretation. Wigforss and Möller appeared as representatives of the Party executive against the proposal for a revision. They did not defend the general basic principles in their present form, but considered a revision unnecessary. Even if certain points needed to be revised, said Wigforss, it was not clear how the revision should take place. "I believe that things develop rapidly, that perhaps rather soon a new situation would demand a new revision and from that point of view it is perhaps just as well to allow the programme of principles to remain as a historical document and concentrate our efforts more on the formulation of the immediate measures that must still be the most important task of the party." Möller stressed that only individual voices had been raised for a revision, and that the programme commission on its own initiative could suggest changes, if at the next congress this should show itself to be necessary. Olsson and Lindström spoke in favour of a revision. The former said that the main argument against revision was that at present this did not seem to be called for. But if the present time was not considered suitable, the question must be asked under what circumstances a pressing need for revision could be thought to exist. "To that I must then answer that either it would be when such a lack of agreement between the party's practical policy and its programme had occurred, so that the situation was quite untenable, or when such a strong demand from the members had been made that quite simply we could no longer avoid reformulating the programme." However, it would be unfortunate if the party found itself in such a situation. It would be best if the programme revision could take place in peace and calm and without external pressures. In the main Lindström put forward the same points of view. After the debate, that was particularly brief, the motion for the rejection of the proposal was accepted with 151 votes against 147. Two circumstances are of special interest in this context. Within the party leadership rejection was justified by saying in the main that the whole thing was of relatively small importance. The speech made by the party executive's spokesman, Wigforss, was based clearly on the fact that the programme of principles was not to be made into anything of great importance. It should remain as an "historic document." If it was to be adapted to the changing circumstances then perhaps before long new changes would be required. As the programme of principles was intended to present the party's basic view of the development from capitalism to socialism, this justification must be interpreted as an explanation that the basic view was other than it had been in 1920, and in fact was constantly changing. Furthermore, it is remarkable that despite the position adopted by the party leadership, and the brevity of the debate, nearly half of the votes were in favour of a revision. This seems to show that outside the party leadership the general basic principles were still seen as a meaningful reality, and because of that it was desired that their formulation should be in agreement with the current ideas of the party.

Several motions aimed at making the demand for socialisation current. In one motion it was demanded that the programme of action concerning control over the private building of monopolies should be drawn up. The party executive said in their statement (by which the motion was to be considered answered) that clearly at every point in time there was a need to allow the guiding lines of the party programme to be formulated in concrete suggestions. However, continued the Party executive, "experience should have shown that such a formulation practically speaking must occur in connection with the continuing political activity of the party, and must be strongly influenced by the economic conditions prevalent at a given time, and the problems that due to this require solutions." There was no reason to compile a special programme of action on this point. In another motion a statement regarding the socialisation of credit institutions was demanded. The party executive suggested a statement regarding the desirability that the state's influence and control over credit institutions be extended. According to the justification given for this both "methods and procedures should be decided according to the existing conditions at every given point in time." Regarding this, and other motions on the question of socialisation, the report of the party executive was accepted (that throughout contained general statements not binding to anything in particular) unanimously and without debate. Wigforss, the spokesman of the party executive gave a brief account of the motions and the ideas of the party executive. There was no criticism concerning the fact that the Board of Socialisation had not presented their final report.

The question of population, too, came up before the congress. A local branch of the party insisted on a congress statement "against the fact that the party supports a policy that directly aims at increased nativity." According to the motion there was no reason to fear a population reduction, and there was an attack on the "alarming, frightening calculations" that had been made. The party executive (whose statement was to be considered as an answer to the motion) referred to the investigation at present under way and added that "within the party there is total agreement that the basis for the preservation and strengthening of the people must be sought in conditions of living that allow security, confidence and courage."

In the debate that ended with the unanimous acceptance of the proposal of the party executive, only Möller and G. Myrdal spoke. Möller expressed more exactly a line that often appeared in the earlier Social Democratic discussion: "I must say that I do not for a moment hesitate to frighten as many conservatives and members of the Folk-party and of the Farmers party as you like with the threat that our people will die out, if by that threat I can make them vote for social proposals that I present. That is my simple view of the population question, and it is sufficient for me." Myrdal put forward the same points of view he had put forward in his book, but particularly strongly he asserted the importance of the population question as a means of propaganda for social reforms. The reforms in the population question that were demanded would lead to such social conditions" that people in general and with a feeling of responsibility could do what most of them want to do, that is have a normally large family something between 2 and 3 children. . . . The most important thing in the population policy is naturally that it gives a new argument should that be needed (we do not need it) for creating greater economic security for the families."

In agreement with the ideas of the party congress the government made its continued existence dependent on the fact that the question of old-age pensions was solved in accordance with the guide-lines it had laid down. When the Conservative and Liberal parties rejected the proposition, on the 15th June the government asked for its resignation to be accepted. However, as in principle the government had accepted the solution of the defence question that was decided by parliament (although it refused to cooperate in this due to the fact that parliament rejected the proposal in the question of old-age pensions) the government crisis did not mean any intensification of the conflicts between the Conservative and Liberals and the Social Democrats. The new government was formed by the Farmers party alone, which was a guarantee that no break with the welfare policy would occur. The government, that during its short term in office did not take any remarkable measures or any great initiative, was not criticised within the Social Democratic press, but rather was treated with a certain sympathy.

This circumstance led to the fact that the entire election movement of 1936 was relatively calm. Although there was great electioneering activity, the conflicts between the parties appeared less than at the previous election. A decrease in tension can be noted that under the continuous intensifying of the international situation that took place in the years that followed gradually was changed into a national policy of cooperation.

The main point in the election propaganda of the Social Democrats was reference to what the party had accomplished in previous years, and a promise of continued "welfare policy." It was maintained in the election manifesto of the party that the crisis policy that was adopted by the Social Democratic government partly contributed to the improvement of the economic conditions, and partly had enduring results in the form of cultivation measures within farming and forestry, improved dwellings and the building of new dwellings, and extended communications. The citizens were exhorted "to unite around an energetically continuing welfare policy."

Experience had shown that the state could and would positively cooperate in the making secure of the peoples' livelihood. Therefore crisis preparations must be arranged without delay. Even more important was to prevent a new, penetrating crisis. "This can only occur through cooperation between the privately owned parts of the economy and the representatives of the state, with the aim of gaining a better hold on the economy by means of general inspection and control." The prospect of a series of reforms of limited extent was held out. For the maintainance of agriculture the party wanted to cooperate "in continued security and regulating measures with flexible adaption to changed circumstances and with just consideration between the various farming groups together, and also between the farmers and other groups of the people." Craft and small industry would be supported as a natural link in the attempts to increase the opportunities to work. The questions of working hours and labour protection would be taken up and a legislated holiday introduced. The proposal regarding increased old-age pensions that had been rejected by the government should be passed. Work should be completed "with regard to working hours and conditions of labour, to give agricultural workers, white-collar workers, home-helps and other deprived groups a share in the social welfare." Questions that were not of an economic or social nature were hardly touched upon in the election programme.

The same points of view dominated the election pamphlets, election speeches and newspaper articles. The sixteen pamphlets given out by the party almost exclusively dealt with welfare policy and its realisation. On the election posters a comparison was made between unemployment in Sweden and in other countries, and in words and pictures it was shown that new dwellings had been built, railways electrified, bridges and harbours created all due to the Social Democratic crisis policy. That this policy was the main cause of the improvement of the economic situation could hardly be asserted in responsible circles, but without doubt certain descriptions were intended to give this impression to the electorate. On no earlier occasion has a party in our country so systematically based its election propaganda on what has already taken place, and on the idea that the future policy should continue upon the same lines.

It is taken for granted that no demand for socialisation was mentioned in the election campaign, and that socialisation was not held out as the future goal of the party. Nevertheless, in many speeches the socialisation question was dealt with, and the formulation on principle of the party's economic policy on the whole. Often such speeches led to statements in Conservative and Liberal circles to the effect that in reality Social Democracy aimed at socialisation. This line was taken up in the bourgeois propaganda as a counter to the continuous mention of the welfare policy found in Social Democratic propaganda.

Nowhere in the election manifesto can the words socialism or socialisation be found. Nevertheless, in a few general formulations the principle guidelines for the economic policy are given. According to these Social Democracy wants to "promote all sound enterprise, private and general, that wants to make use of our rich possibilities for the good of the nation's economy. The general inspection and control is to be aimed at promoting the correct utilisation of national resources, but prevents speculation prompted by the desire for private profit that may result in putting into jeopardy the results of responsible conscientious work for the good of all. We do not hide our belief that the technical and economic development will make necessary production forms giving greater room for state influence. But we see as our task the support and stimulation of the economy in those forms that at every given time are most expedient to secure and raise the livelihood of the people. Our deeds deny the statement, intended to frighten, that we wish to inhibit enterprise. We desire no other intervention than that which is justified with regard to the general good and the welfare of the people." This passage is to be found between the account of the party's activities during the previous election period, and a presentation of the current political requirements. In its brevity it is the most interesting part of the election manifesto, from the ideological-policy point of view.

Here it is stated that the party will allow its policy immediately to be decided by regard to "the general good and the welfare of the people." No other more precise basis of the party's activities is given. The party has decided to promote private as well as general enterprise, as long as it is "sound." Certainly the party is of the belief that "the development" will make necessary forms of production with greater state influence." But the party desires—and here is the core of the whole thing—to support the economy "in those forms that at every given time are most expedient to secure and raise the livelihood of the people."

In a way this passage can be said to mark the end of the ideological transformation of Social Democracy. According to Marx and the older Swedish doctrine, socialism would succeed capitalism, when the latter was no longer rational, when the development of the productive forces demanded a new form for the exploitation of nature. With reference to this Social Democracy had propagated socialism but maintained that this could first be realised only when development rendered society ripe for such a change. However, in practice as soon as the party had achieved a more important position of power it had acted to limit the anomalies that were considered to arise from the capitalist system and in plain words to remedy lacks in that system.

Now this policy is put in a Marxist context in that the party is said to be guilty of supporting the economic forms that at a given time are the most expedient. The party should support the capitalist system as long as it is expedient. Does this mean that in that way the party is the defender and protector of the capitalist system? From one point of view, that for most people seems to be natural, the answer must be in the affirmative. If Social

Democracy and the bourgeois parties, i.e. just about the entire population, use their strength to "support and stimulate" the existing system, its defeat seems to be improbable. But to the convinced Marxist things need not be seen in this light. In his view "development" will inevitably lead to socialism, even if right up to the very moment when it seems impossible to maintain capitalism Social Democracy supports this form of production.

There is no reason to analyse the passage in question more closely. Its strangeness can really be said to lie in the fact that at one and the same time are to be found the idea of the free play of forces—"development"—and a state intervention of great importance.

Naturally this passage, just as other similar statements, cannot be seen as representative of any well-thought-out idea. Probably it has been thoughtlessly written down, without being subjected to any closer testing. It is remarkable not merely as an ideological curiosity, but because, as will presently be shown, it recurs in authoritative statements. Here developmental fatalism has direct links with short-term policy. In the resolutions of 1932 an ideological and a realistic line are to be found side by side. Here, a vague expression of the Marxist-ideological line has been used to support a current and realistic policy. Seen from this perspective, other points in the programme are also of special interest. In particular it should be remembered that the party promised to support craft and small industry in order to increase employment chances. Mark well that here it is not a question only of assisting groups of persons within various professions by support or assistance against exploitation. The party preferred to encourage craft and small industry in order to improve the general economic situation. Social democracy, whilst, in its general basic principles, in accordance with Marx, still speaking of the inevitable collapse of this form of production due to industrialism and capitalism, now commits itself to assisting it. One was now ready to promote small-scale production, within industry as well as within farming—a thought that some years earlier was considered to have been perhaps the clearest evidence of a deep lack of economic knowledge, of a petit-bourgeois attitude, and thereby of an attitude that in a very special way was outmoded.

The question of socialisation became more directly and thoroughly discussed in newspaper articles and election speeches. Two points of view were continuously put forward, as was hinted in the reported points of the election manifesto. On the one hand it was said quite simply that Social Democracy desired the general good, that it was not bound to dogma and that it supported private or public production, depending only on which form was the most suitable in a given situation. On the other hand, it was maintained that the economic revolution of society takes place independent of state intervention, that it is a process occurring apart from politics in their real sense. As an example, several articles appearing before the election in Social-Demokraten could be mentioned.

In a leader on "Free enterprise" the party chairman wrote: "the question is not freedom or force, private enterprise or state regulation. The question is how the good of all can best be promoted. What we must strive after is a good national economy guaranteeing security for all and with the possibility of raising the general level of welfare . . . Certainly for a long time to come private enterprise will be of decisive importance for the national economy. We Social Democrats are not hindered from admitting this either in words or deeds." In an article entitled "Socialisation and election" Hansson wrote that on the grounds of bitter experience, the party was accused of wishing to keep the demand for socialisation out of the election campaign. This was not correct: the principle of socialisation had not led to election losses. The party's position with regard to the issue of socialisation was caused by quite different motives. "For our entire view of society the change of productive forms appears as the result of a development that creates the conditions for higher forms of production, and makes these into necessities. From that follows naturally that we do not see the process of socialisation as depending on any decision made, possibly by a small and perhaps temporary parliamentary majority. Rather, we see as our task the maintaining of the state of political preparedness at all times, as thus allowing ourselves to meet the demands of the economic and technical development . . ." With even greater energy Engberg, somewhat later, expressed the same ideas in an article on "Socialisation." The conservative and liberal opposition was accused of seeing some sort of concrete measures in socialisation. "They talk nonsense about the possibility of a Social Democratic parliamentary majority making some sort of decision to socialise, and putting this decision into practice . . . By socialisation it meant nothing other than the continuous adaptation of the economy by the state according to the demands of the national economy. In our country this adaptation has been going on for a long time . . . Socialisation is not something imminent but rather a continuous process. When the conservative and liberal press mutter against socialisation, then they attack the main tendency in the development of our society."

These ideas were made much use of in answer to the conservative and liberal statement that Social Democracy wished to socialise. It was explained with real indignation that the party did not act according to any theory that was considered true for all times and in all circumstances, but rather judged the merits of each situation as it occurred. Social Democracy did not wish to socialise for the sake of socialisation—it is conscious of the dangers of regulation and intervention. What was necessary was to adapt according to development, to act in the way that the development itself indicates.

Socialisation is not something that occurs through laws and parliamentary decisions. These statements seem strange, considering partly the fact that the party considered that its own crisis policy, brought about by parliamentary decision, had led to very important results, and partly that the Board of Socialisation was considered to be of such importance. What was the point of investigating the question of socialisation, if socialism did not depend upon any decisions, but upon development? However, such reasoning became possible in that various different perspectives were adopted. The policy of welfare was seen as a short-term policy, something apart from "the development." On the other hand Socialisation was again placed in a great deterministic perspective, and to a large extent became a matter of "development."

Another tendency could also be traced in the debate. The traditional value-laden words socialism and socialisation were used about the policy that had been followed, and also about the policy that was being recommended. This tendency is clearly not a new one. In the preceding, many examples have been mentioned illustrating the watering-down of the concepts in question. But in the debate concerned with the election of 1936 many more examples than earlier are to be found of a terminological revolution. It is typical that in the quoted article Engberg spoke of socialisation as a certain form of production, and as "the continuous adaptation of the economy by the state according to the demands of the national economy." If the expression is used in the latter sense, then it is quite simply the same as development itself. It had long been argued that socialism is a fruit of the development. Therefore, it is very easy to label development as socialism. It was particularly easy to see in the reform policy that the party followed, and looked as if it would continue to follow a form of socialism or socialisation.

Hansson, in at least one of his election speeches, maintained that lately socialisation had made great strides forward. He said that even attitudes had been socialised. In one newspaper it was said that by socialisation the conservative and liberal parties meant a transferring of all important means of production into the ownership of the state and municipalities. However, this was an incorrect idea. Socialisation "is in the first place an attempt on the part of the state and of society to create good conditions of living for the people . . . What is a planned reform policy, with the aim of socially draining society and creating increased protection for the people against social and economic accidents, other than a link in the process of socialisation?" According to another newspaper, it could very well be said that a realising of "these (recommended in the election manifesto) reforms and measures, that all aim at improving the national economy, is a realisation of socialism. This is what we mean by socialism." Wigforss criticised the party's opponents because they wanted to attack "socialism," despite the fact that this concept could be used in many ways, instead of speaking of welfare policy, which term had a clear meaning. But he added that the Social Democrats should be judged with regard to what they themselves called socialism—that is, welfare policy.

Myrdal, who was not weighed down by the Marxist traditions of the party, explained in one of his articles that a regulation of consumption with regard to needs and resources was socialism, and in an election speech defined the concept as follows: "We desire, without any doctrines that put blinkers on us, but also without any false prejudices, to do all we can, all that can reasonably be done, to make more effective, to make more stable, to strengthen the economy. This is what we mean by socialisation."

Naturally there are justifications for using the words socialism and socialisation in this way. What is strange is that the words are used in quite different meanings. Socialisation is sometimes spoken of in the old sense as state take-over of the means of production, sometimes in accordance with old liberalism, the word development is meant, in the sense of state intervention, sometimes it is social policy and social reforms on the whole that are intended. Socialisation therefore can sometimes mean something that one can do, but does not wish to do, and sometimes it can mean something that one wishes to do, but is unable to do, and sometimes it means something that it is in the process of being done. It should be added that certain uses of the concept are in diametrical opposition to the earlier use of the words within the party. In the earlier debate, social policy had been seen as something that differed in principle from socialism. Social policy was detailed reform within the framework of the existing system, socialism was a new "system." Regulation of consumption had been seen as something quite foreign to social democracy, which perhaps emerged most clearly in the debates about crisis economy during the world war. By socialisation one had meant the state organisation of production, although now this is out of the question.

The central points of the election programme and campaign of social democracy should be emphasised and made even more precise. Quite definitely, and with reference to the programme, the party rejected the idea that its policy meant a successive realisation of a definite social doctrine, and accepted the principle of judging each situation on its own merits, with regard to welfare of the general good. Naturally, the idea of working for the general good had appeared earlier. But at that time welfare had been seen as being only able to be realised through socialism, and thus socialism had been the aim. Now, welfare was the direct goal of the party, being at times said to be the same as socialism, because of its final result. As socialism aims at general welfare, what is done to attain welfare must be socialism. Mainly, this meant a fantastic ideological weakening. The concept of socialism had had a certain tendency to the concrete, the concept of welfare was, by its very nature, purely an evaluative expression—a word by which all parties and all people describe their desires. Quite simply, action with regard to the general good is a suitable or correct or valuable action. The expression says nothing about the objective content of the action. But in addition the new ways of characterising the goals of the party had a remarkable symbolic content. As welfare was introduced as a direct and decisive motive, it is clear that one orientation rests on established foundations, that it sees reforms and measures as a detailed complement of an order that in the main is satisfying. When the welfare point of view is taken society can be seen as a totality, one stands above conflicting interests and ideas and is able to judge between them. But this point of view is only possible when a state of harmony exists, and when it is a question, by means of small incidences of intervention, of securing this harmony or re-establishing it when it is disturbed. The idea of welfare becomes a symbol of the desire to maintain a state of a political regime of a social order. On the other hand, when an ideological programme intervenes before the idea of welfare, this means that the state is seen as unharmonic to such a great extent that a transformation must take place in order to create the relative harmony that is a precondition for the immediate application of the idea of welfare.

The ideological discrepancies just dealt with should probably be seen in relation to another condition. In the Social Democratic programme at that time, and especially in the election campaign of 1936, the party leader was placed in the foreground in a way quite different from earlier. To a great extent this depended quite simply on the fact that Hansson—as did Branting earlier—acquired increasing authority, in particular because of his long and successful term as head of the government. But this should also be seen from a point of view more connected with principles. The more developed the ideology of a party, and the greater the importance accorded to this, then the less reason there is to emphasize the personality of the leader. When a party quite simply says that it strives after general welfare, then the personal aspects must be important. It becomes necessary that the persons acting on behalf of the party have great ability to decide in individual cases what is demanded by welfare, because there is no longer any ideology that clarifies this. Complete power of attorney presupposes great confidence in the person holding such powers.

The election of 1936 was a great success for Social Democracy. The party won 46% of the votes, and 112 seats. As socialists and communists together won 11 seats, this meant that the Social Democrats alone were in the majority against the Conservative and Liberal parties. However, when the party leader formed the new government, negotiations were begun regarding collaboration with the Farmers party, and on the 28th September a coalition government came into being, formed by the two parties. In the parliamentary explanation this stressed the need for cooperation "between representatives of various ideas and interests, parties and classes." This presupposed "that citizens working within various branches of the economy have equal rights to have their voices heard and to be cared for by the state, at the same time as the underprivileged groups of the people must clearly have their needs met as a matter of great urgency."

Several measures were held out, that involved a completion of the welfare policy. In a statement of principles it was established that in its work the government was not bound to any particular social theory. "The great question of an improved national economy will be tested by the government without preconceptions as to which paths should be followed. This proceeds from the difficulties with which the economy and the people clearly have to struggle. The government does not desire any social measures that hinder private enterprise from making contributions that are to the good of society. But with regard to limited private interest it does not reject such measures on the part of the state as are clearly to the advantage of the great majority of the citizens."

Latterly, what has been the part played by Marxism within Swedish Social Democracy? In the main the preceding description gives the answer to this question. Much earlier Marx's economic theory in its real meaning had been rejected. His social theories have less and less been cited, and in a much milder form, although in the party's programme of principles they are still a main point. In 1931 a prominent Social Democrat could still write with full justification "that on no point has modern Social Democracy as a whole freed itself of Marx's ideas, as much as in the question of the theory of catastrophe and the related idea of exploitation."

These ideas are hardly mentioned any more except as the proof that Marx is outmoded. It was only during the economic crisis at the beginning of the 1930s that Marx's social theories experienced a renaissance in Sweden, as in other places, to the extent that some Social Democrats (usually young party men, outside leading circles) then believed that the catastrophic crisis predicted by Marx had come. This point of view to some extent affected statements on the question of socialisation at the congress of 1932.

However, during the period in question the most important change in the relationship to Marx is that the theory of class struggle was gradually rejected by the leading groups. During the recent years in particular the so-called "peoples home ideology" for which the party leader is the foremost champion became popular in debates. This means that the harmony that in Marx's view would occur after socialism had been realised was said to have been achieved, or able to be achieved through Social Democratic reform policy. In that way the theme around which Marx's entire construction of history is built was rejected.

This does not mean that Marxism's part in things is ended. It should first be stressed that Marxism surely appeared more in what one might call the simpler propaganda than in the authoritative and responsible explanations that were presented. Myrdal wrote that Marxism "has disappeared between soothsayers, who in accordance with the old recipe smiled at each other in private but in the public polemic, and even more in the peoples' agitation, its entire and emphatic social protest has been allowed to remain . . . This duplicity has certainly been a great psychological difficulty for those active in the movement. They have had to show one face when they dealt with other opinion and interest groups, and another when they spoke to those from whom they received their assignments—the workers. This has hardly been dishonesty in the usual sense of the term—rather a feeling for style and tradition." This was written in 1932 and by 1940 it seems to be rather out of date. Social Democracy had now gone much further in openly proclaiming short-term points of view, and also in indifference to the old ideology. But the basic way of thinking is important. Social Democrats, even if they have not proclaimed Marx's theories, have in their propaganda used a phraseology that in fact presupposes the acceptance of these theories.

The great slogans have been taken from Marx, they have symbolised Marxism and stimulated ideas in accordance with Marx's perspective. It is sufficient to mention words like "capitalism" and "socialism" "bourgeois" and "proletariat" "exploitation" "petit-bourgeois" "concentration of capital" "class struggle" "class society." Several of these words have meaning only through Marx's conceptual scheme, others are given a special tone through Social Democratic electioneering because they are part of this scheme. Even more formulated ways of thinking having a connection to Marx have been more common in popular propaganda than in the more binding declarations that are to be found in the election manifesto and the congress resolutions. As Myrdal pointed out, this has certainly not meant any dishonesty. Several of the present leaders were convinced Marxists in their youth. Probably they have not always been clear that they had ceased to be this. The traditional Marxist phraseology has appeared as a natural means of expression on occasions when the future path was traced and the great perspective unfurled. In addition the historical physical ideas from which Marx's more precise economic and social theories were formed have maintained their authority to a much greater extent than have the theories. As a rule the materialist conception of history seems still to be considered an important and correct theory, even if its essential content is seldom stated with conviction.

A general atmosphere of economic determinism has surrounded the Social Democratic debate. It is sufficient to remember the continuous talk of "development" as some sort of independent active force. It is impossible to investigate the extent to which this idea has influenced the positions adopted in individual cases. A positive attitude to a reform is expressed often by saying that the reform was ripe, or that it lies in the clear line of development. Proposals that are considered to be too far-reaching are rejected, this being justified by saying that one must not run ahead of the development. During recent years "development" has been mainly used as an argument for a moderate, principally conservative, policy. This was particularly the case during the election campaign of 1936. In this context the most important factor is that determinism itself had become a factor of importance in Social Democratic ideology, even if on many occasions it was criticised by the party's own theoreticians.

The discussion that directly concerned Marx and his importance for Social Democracy has been slight. The general tendency is to characterise Marx as the founder and inspirer, but to stress that his system is characteristic of its age, and therefore to a certain extent out of date. A certain uncertainty characterises this attitude. Sometimes Marx is presented as the great ideologist of modern Social Democracy, sometimes as a pioneer without current importance. In one case one thinks of those parts of Marx's theory that are accepted, in the other case of those parts that are rejected.

Some examples will illustrate the situation. To some extent in connection with de Man, in an article series in 1928 de Vougt put the question: should Social Democrats call themselves Marxists? The reply was negative. On certain important points Marx's theories have been rejected, and it would be risky to identify with a system that basically one did not accept.

Several years later the same author wrote an article in connection with the fiftieth anniversary of Marx's death. Here Marx's important contributions were stressed, but also that which was untenable in parts of his ideas. The result was a characteristic formulation: "Our party stands—and stands with honour—on a Marxist base, but it does not need discussions of Marx's theses." Somewhat later de Vougt dealt with the criticisms of Marxism made by two Social Democrats (Viktor Svanberg and Alf Ahlberg—both outside politics) in a lecture and a questionnaire reply, which were indignantly denied by several young Marxists. The latter was said to be unjust. "Therefore it is also clear that we consider the actual theory of class struggle, as well as Marxism in its wider sense, to have been discarded from the party's practice. The movement stands and stands securely on the basis of the community of people." On the latter mentioned occasion other newspapers also expressed themselves. In "Social Demokraten" G. Branting declared himself as in accordance with Marx, almost without reservation. In 'Ny Tid" Lindström agreed with the criticism of Marx, but added that Marx's theory contained many thoughts that were still useable. Marx should not be seen as an infallible master, but as a prominent researcher whose ideas have been tested without preconceptions. He should be seen in the same historical perspective as, for instance, Bentham and John Stuart Mill. The "Örebro Kuriren" took more or less the same line. In that newspaper it had earlier been said that Marx "gave us a working method, a way of thinking that is valid, though limited in time. At the present time we have overcome Marx, just as we have overcome Jesus of Nazareth and Immanuel Kant. But just as neither of the two latter could be removed from history without humanity feeling hopelessly impoverished by this, neither can Marx be removed as if he were just any author. . . ."

As has been shown earlier, the concept of socialism during recent years has often been weakened in such a way that it has become the same as social care, or general welfare or similar. A similar, though not so wide tendency to weakening, can be traced in the question of Marxism and the various Marxist theories. Marx was changed from being an original ideologist to a preacher of self-evidences. Karleby, in "Socialismen infor verkligheten" is the person who has most energetically interpreted Marx in this way. Here, the material conception of history is said to have been "a theoretical expression of that view that a person with normal common sense has of historical occurrences." According to Karleby, what a person with common sense thinks in this case could be summarised in the phrase that man himself creates his own history.

The fact that Swedish Social Democracy has become Marxist does not depend on the study of Marxism but on the fact "that from the beginning Marx has theoretically expressed that which comes naturally as a view of modern society to the working class" (compare the labour movements of England and America). Socialist or Marxist theory is "nothing more than all theory . . . correct observation of facts, logical consistency in their interpretation . . . A contribution to an investigation, a study of a practical economic or actual problem that is characterised by sufficient knowledge of the thing at hand, logical clearness and proper attention to all the facts concerned is a work that can be counted amongst socialist theory. . . ."

According to this way of thinking, all sensible thought is Marxism. The truth is always Marxist. The deductive process is of the type that was previously pointed out: Marx desires to think sensibly, therefore it is Marxist to think sensibly. The fact that other thinkers have also had this ambition is overlooked. Certainly this way of interpreting Marx has not become dominant, but time after time the idea is put forward that in the main Marx's theory is the demand for clear and realistic thought, and that above all it is against every form of dogmatism. In this way Marx becomes a symbol of truth, of the intelligent adaptation, reality and life, and without difficulty can be made into a guarantee for any point of view.

Finally, it should be established that a large and growing number of the party are quite outside of Marxism. The traditional connection to Marx has in recent times mainly appeared in party men who are now largely middle-aged and who have taken active part in the work of the party since the time in which Marxism was the self-evident starting point of all theoretical debate. Many of them have been amongst the leading men of the party without taking part in internal work—such as Undén and Nothin—have apparently been completely uninfluenced by Marxist ideas. This is also true for the one prominent social researcher who played an important role in the Social Democracy of the day: Myrdal. The fact that the intellectuals who did not accept Marxism did not criticise it, seems to depend on the fact that they saw it as unimportant for the political orientation of the party. For many of the more prominent representatives of the working class in the party Marx was apparently no more than a name. Within the younger generation some convinced Marxists have appeared, especially during the crisis debate at the beginning of the 1930s, but on the whole the Social Democratic youth has followed in the tracks of their elders and turned their interests towards problems that lay near at hand, without attempting an ideological justification in the grand style.

Summary

When Social Democracy appeared in Sweden, it turned first to the working class who were an insignificant part of the population of the country. From its inception, therefore, great and immediate advances were impossible. In addition, under the terms of the constitution the greater part of the working class were denied legal political influence.

However, in its most important aspects the ideology of Swedish Social Democracy was shaped without reference to Swedish conditions. Marx's ideas, connected as they were to the old English industrialism, dominated totally. Swedish theory was hardly more than a popularised and simplified version of Marx. The social prognoses according to which free enterprise—the capitalist system—inevitably led to a situation out of which socialism would develop, were entirely accepted. The question was to make the working class conscious of the "historical mission" that would be theirs when capitalism collapsed, and, through political reforms of the constitution, to prepare for the inevitable assumption of power.

Attached to this concept were certain ideas which, even though they had been rejected in their original schematic form, stalked the development of Swedish Social Democracy like a spectre. Capitalism and socialism were regarded as entirely different social systems. The transition from one to the other must occur in a very decided manner. Capitalism would be replaced, or succeeded, by socialism. However, in this connection there was no necessary link with the Marxist theory of crisis in its real sense, but the idea that once won, the victory of socialism would be total implies a domination of the social organisation. It was not predicted that the party would gain a strong position of power without the majority, and even less that once achieved a majority could again be lost. Victory meant total victory, that a new world opinion had become powerful, that the road was open for socialist action. Another socialisation did not necessarily follow this victory. Even earlier the idea of partial and successive socialisation measures had been expressed. But these would be realised by a dominating socialist movement, calculatingly utilising the state apparatus for its own ends.

How socialisation would come about, and how the socialist society would be created was rarely discussed. According to Marx such a discussion was utopian and unscientific. Certainly it was possible to predict that the new society would come into being, but not the forms that it would take. Instead of making concrete plans, therefore, one described in general terms the society of the future as uniting on the highest level welfare, freedom, happiness and culture, and thereby, in the eagerness to make plans that were of a non-utopian nature, yielded to an even more marked utopianism.

As a practical movement, Social Democracy was concerned with short term goals. The main tasks were limited social-political reforms and above all a general political democratising. Due to the expansion of defence, a new area for party activity developed at the beginning of the 20th century. The demand for a restriction on armaments, which idea led many people to a defence nihilism, became a major theme in the propaganda of the party directed at the discontented groups. An unusually rapid advance took place. Through the Trade Unions the class of industrial workers joined the party. The extension of the franchise in various phases made it possible to make political use of this success to win the people. Industrialisation increased the numbers of working class, and in that way strengthened the party. In a few decades capitalism, which at the inception of the party existed more in theory than in practice, became an important part of the Swedish economy, and its victories within the economy caused the victories of Social Democracy within politics.

The Marxist theories were quickly rejected in their more pronounced form. This even included the social prognoses originally considered to be fundamental. The beliefs regarding the disappearance of the middle class, and the exploitation of the proletariat could no longer be upheld. Through its policies and through the concessions and initiative that these occasioned in its opponents, Social Democracy itself opposed that intensifying of the class conflict that was the very cornerstone of Marx's social theory.

Industrialism, and the entire reconstruction of society connected with this, created a new middle class and increased the affluence of the working class rather than gradually driving the unpropertied masses to the edge of starvation, as had been predicted. Within farming the expected tendency towards concentration did not appear, and the number of independent farmers did not show any absolute decrease. Whilst retaining great parts of the Marxist conceptual apparatus Social Democracy reaped the consequences of this when, in 1911, it declared itself the defender of the farmer, and in 1920 the defender of all "exploited" classes.

Whilst the more precise Marxist doctrines grew weaker, the emotional and intellectual atmosphere enmeshing these doctrines remained. The concept of historical materialism, historical determinism and the associated developmental fatalism, the principle of class struggle and the belief in a total system change, in the victory of socialism and the realisation of the ideal society, all this lent colour and strength to Social Democratic declarations. Though the party leaders energetically and effectively worked for reforms in current (policies) they were inspired by, and infused their supporters with, the feeling that the great, the real, the true for which they fought was something more, something eternally more vital.

"Socialism" did not consist of social policy, nor of democratic reforms, nor of work towards peace and disarmament. Rather it consisted of a tremendous innovation that one day must come to pass. In a way that made comparisons with religious movements natural a concern with today was united with a belief in a future, in which were mingled all the ambitions, hopes and dreams of the poor classes.

Of what was this socialism composed, and how could it be achieved? An answer to this question was refused, on the same grounds as previously. The very fact that the question had been put was in itself proof of a lack of a socialist insight. During that decade no work was published in which an attempt was made to deal in a concrete and complete manner with the actual realisation of socialism and the organisation of the socialist society. The nearer one approached political power, the more problematical this attitude became. It could be defended just as long as the Marxist predictions were accepted, as long as a revolution was expected as the solution of the internal conflicts of the capitalist system. For Social Democracy, accepted both by the majority and the leaders on terms quite different from those stated by Marx, it was necessary when holding a position of power to have a programme of action. Socialism could not be maintained merely on the grounds that it was a mystique, a holy word, characterised by secrets known to no one.

A temporary solution to the difficulties was reached in 1920, at the first party congress to take place after total political democratisation. In the new programme and the appended commentary the idea of socialisation of the important means of production was presented as an issue of immediate importance. However, the debate preceding and following the programme revision indicated that there were varied opinions with regard to socialisation and the socialist organisation, and above all that these were unclear. The first

Social Democratic government appointed a committee to attempt to achieve clarity.

Whilst the work of this committee was underway, the party continued its short-term political activity. Three Social Democratic minority governments were formed, on the principle that one should try to bring about socio-political reforms in collaboration with other political opinions. The party stressed its desire to have a united policy and to protect the interests of all groups in society. By means of compromises and agreements, the idea of class struggle was put aside. When for several years in a row the party found itself without governmental power, this did not result in any alterations in the policy they had followed.

The radicalising that was noticeable prior to the election of 1928 was only a temporary deviation. After the election defeat there was a return to the idea of a united policy and limited demands for reform. The favourable state of the market following the brief post-war crisis made this ideology acceptable. During the whole of this period (1920–1932) tendencies to a weakening of the concepts of socialism and socialisation can be traced. It was explained that socialism could not be achieved by means of political decision, but only through a continuous development of society outside of any state intervention. Social development thus spoken of did not mean, as earlier, an intensified conflict eventually leading to a decisive victory for the proletariat. On the contrary, it meant increased free cooperation within the framework of the existing system—mainly through cooperation and trade agreements. However, the idea of socialisation in its real sense was maintained. With regard to this, reference was made to the Socialisation Board, whose final proposals, year after year, were said to be expected within the near future. The Board became the official expression of the declared socialist ideology that remained a symbol for the aspirations of the party remote from the current political work. In this way the hidden intentions of the Social Democrats would be made evident.

The Board worked slowly. It submitted a series of investigations of secondary interest, but took a long time about the final and positive statement that everybody was waiting for. In Conservative and Liberal circles this was said to be because Social Democracy either would not or dare not suggest socialisation. The Board's activities began to be looked upon as a means of gaining time, and if possible of disposing of the entire issue. In Social Democratic circles there was talk of enquiries of a comprehensive and complicated nature. However, at the beginning of the 1930s the Board, according to its members, was ready to begin working on certain concrete proposals. A decision had to be reached. It appeared that many of the party leaders feared that such proposals would have a detrimental effect on the party's chances in the coming election. There was no sign that any significant group within the party demanded an immediate action for socialisation with any enthusiasm. According to one opinion, probably the most common, it was desired to maintain "the idea of socialisation" without submitting completed plans, i.e., to continue to put forward a general socialisation propaganda without committing themselves to anything in particular. Once again the question of socialisation in its real sense was shelved for further consideration.

In such a situation, in which a clear conflict between ideology and practice seemed unavoidable in the very near future, the economic situation became worse in such a way that the question of the mastery of the crisis came into the foreground. This situation was to be of decisive importance in the future policy of the party. With the support of the general welfare-motive basic to social policy, it became possible to work towards a much greater intervention than was previously imagined. The framework for a policy of compromise and unity was extended in that all measures that could be seen as directly aimed at a settlement of the crisis were immediately adopted. It is true that an extreme group within the party saw in the crisis a sign of the approaching defeat of capitalism, and wanted to make "socialisation" the key word in the propaganda. But the party leadership worked for a more short term policy that would integrate unemployment assistance in a larger scheme for overcoming crisis. Both ways of thinking were satisfied at the congress of 1932, each having their own resolution, but the platform of the election work of the party was the demand for immediate active measures against the crisis.

With the Social Democratic election victory came a crisis policy, in collaboration with other parties, of a more embracing and comprehensive nature than that suggested earlier. As the crisis was followed by a new period of boom the prestige of the party was strengthened, and the carrying through of the policy received the sanction of the people. In many circles the changes that had been brought about were regarded as being a sort of planned economy or socialisation. In other circles it was asserted that through the crisis policy the party had shown itself able to follow the line of "development" itself and that in a deeper sense they had acted consistently, even though no particularly socialist activity had taken place. When a state of welfare returned the demand for socialisation in the real sense was deadened. Due to the victories that had been won, and the continuing reform work within the framework of welfare policy, the ideological problems were placed in the background. When the Board of Socialisation was dissolved, without the proposals announced some years earlier having either taken place or been promised for the future, there was no opposition and almost no astonishment.

From the beginning Swedish Social Democracy was socialist in the sense that the taking over of the means of production by the state was its basic idea. Other more accessible demands, however, were those that were considered more important from the point of view of political activity. The principle of socialisation was not introduced as a question of current interests, and there was a considerable gap between theory and practice. It is only in later years that a levelling has taken place, in that the demand for socialisation has been removed even from the large perspective, the ideological debate. To the extent that at present the possibilities of isolated socialisation measures can be seen, they are seen from the perspective of the general welfare ideology that replaced the socialism that was characterised by the theories of Marx.

The State and Democracy

From a Democracy of Tactics to a Democracy of Principles

According to some socialist ideologies, the state has been an instrument of class oppression and the victory of socialism will replace the coercive system of the state with the free interaction of individuals. This line of reasoning was defined by Marx and Engels. They regarded the state as an intermediate stage in the history of mankind, between primeval poverty and freedom and the affluence and freedom of the future. In terms of their Hegelian philosophy, the advent of socialism would enable society to free itself from the fetters of the state. This concept is particularly essential in the ideology of Engels and later in that of Lenin; it provided a source of important precepts for political action. Lassalle has been regarded as the antipode of Marx and Engels, for he envisioned socialism as the realization of the true concept of the state; in his brief span of activity as a socialist agitator he concentrated exclusively upon demands that could conceivably be satisfied with the aid of the state as it existed.

The thought of abolishing the state has not been expressed in any program of the Swedish Social Democratic party. This idea has only been intimated in certain party terminology, especially in the use of the word "society" (*samhälle*) in contexts where the word "state" would be the natural choice of common usage. This idea has, on the whole, played but an insignificant role in Swedish discussions. However, the early debate on this question reveals a certain difference of opinion. Following the pattern of Lassalle, Palm held that "the concept of the state . . . is first realized through socialism and is only realized through socialism," whereas Social Democrats who were influenced by Marxism avoided the word state as denoting the future society and at times suggested that this society would not have the character of a state in the true sense. The notion that the state would disappear was at times proposed by the semianarchistic movement that temporarily won acceptance in Social Democratic circles. In his commentary of 1901 on Engels' paper "The Development of Socialism from a Utopia to a Science," Branting contradicted Engels by asserting "modern socialism [has] little or nothing left of this theoretical aversion to the state as such." Social Democratic theorists have since referred to the abolition of the state as the conclusion of the development predicted by Marx only in clearly exceptional cases. This view has sometimes served as a suitable retort to the accusation that socialism wants to make the state dominant. Today it is commonly pointed out that this idea lacks—and always has lacked—significance for Swedish Social Democracy.

Closely connected with this question has been the problem as to whether socialism should use the means made available by the state to bring about a socialist order. Should one participate in or remain aloof from politics until the society—socialism—is realized? Here Marx, who regarded the capture of political power as a necessity and who believed that the state would be retained for a limited period under socialist leadership, was in disagreement with anarchism, which anticipated that revolution would be achieved through other means and that state or state-sanctioned action could be completely bypassed. Ever since Palm's first address, Swedish Social Democrats have been virtually unanimous in their reply to this question as well. The Marxian line has prevailed; its sole opponents were some semianarchistic Young Socialists who were excluded or otherwise disappeared from the party in the early 1900s. The capture of political power has become established as one of the party's general principles.

How, then, was socialism to achieve power? By legal or revolutionary methods? In accordance with democratic forms or not? As suggested in another context, this question can be broken down into several component problems. During the productive years of Marx and other early ideologists, no European state was a democracy. Some foresaw a peaceful, legal victory for democracy; others contended that revolution would be necessary. Both views won supporters among the Social Democrats. According to one revolutionary line, socialism would assist in the establishment of democracy through violence; within democracy the socialist goal would be attained by peaceful means. This was the political or democratic revolutionary idea approved as an instrument of socialism. According to a variation of this idea, by the time the democratic revolution took place socialism could be assumed to be so strong that by virtue of its majority sway it would take over the power of the state and begin to implement socialism. Marx used the phrase 'the dictatorship of the proletariat" in certain contexts to denote the situation that would then arise. Thus the political revolution would immediately become a social revolution. This reasoning could be turned to a singular use. One could assume that once the revolution had succeeded, socialism would take over power without first receiving formal democratic legitimacy. Socialism would simply seize power after the revolution. It was unnecessary to justify such a line with antidemocratic arguments. Since the presumption was that the will of the people could not be established by elections before the revolution, it was possible to describe the socialist rule emerging from the revolution as representative of the masses without closely questioning its popular support. Occasionally, however, it was explicitly asserted that socialism would seize power despite its minority standing and the expression "the dictatorship of the proletariat" was applied to this situation. (Communism has oscillated between the latter lines of thought.)

The revolutionary idea took still another, completely different form. Some contended that if democracy were achieved without a social upheaval—whether by peaceful means or not—a revolution to carry through socialism would be indispensable. They thus recommended an isolated social revolution, so to speak. Victory would be won in two stages: 1) democracy, possibly by a political revolution; 2) socialism, through a revolution. As a rule, those who contemplated this tactic probably assumed that once the social revolution had been carried out, a majority of the people would be won over to its aims. They presupposed that the economic pressure that would be exerted by the bourgeoisie and its influence on propaganda media would prevent socialism from acquiring power in a democratic state.

These ideas were not defined by socialist theorists if acknowledged authority. It was a simple matter to cite Marx to substantiate all the divergent lines mentioned above. The field lay open for the controversies on tactics that have pervaded socialist debate.

The relation of this question to the problem of the class struggle is obvious. According to Marx's major perspective, at a certain stage the expropriated, exploited class would turn against its masters and expropriate the expropriators. From this perspective it was logical to expect either a combined political and social revolution or, which was less conceivable, a social revolution within a democracy. Socialist collaboration with other groups was considered out of the question. According to Marx's minor perspective, there were a number of different classes which could, for various reasons, be grouped in different ways. If this perspective was applied, the natural course would be first, the achievement of democracy by either peaceful or violent means, second, the gradual, peaceful realization of socialism within the compass of democracy. Cooperation with other groups was conceivable both to win democracy and to function successfully within democracy.

Common to all true Social Democratic movements is the value they place on democracy—universal suffrage and civil rights—as the vehicle for action in the nonsocialist state and their supposition that, to the extent that it did support political institutions, a fully developed socialist society would have a democratic character. Differences between these movements have centered around whether or not revolutionary methods should be used to achieve democracy and whether such methods, and others that are not part of standard democratic machinery, should be used as a last resort to transform the democratic state into a socialist state. Since socialism was held to be the ultimate goal, it was natural to regard nonsocialist democracy as a tactical tool. In the main, this view of democracy has exerted the greatest influence before a democratic form of government has actually been established. Once democracy has been obtained, it has progressively come to be regarded as valuable in itself, and as something that has to be preserved under any conditions.

The early debate among Swedish Social Democrats is a good example of the lack of clarity just indicated. It is frequently difficult or impossible to determine the meaning of certain statements, or whether they were even intended as expressions of a specific thought. Does "revolution" mean a political or social revolution, or a revolutionary action that comprises both a political and a social upheaval—a "permanent" revolution, to use the expression that Trotsky made famous? It is frequently evident that the alternatives at hand were not examined and that a mode of expression was adopted without specifying what it really meant. At times "proletariat" was used in the true sense of the word, that is, as a term characterizing the industrial working class; at other times it referred to all people who earn their livelihood through their own work—or at least to all those who do not earn high wages. This made it possible to present the party as the great party of the people, of the masses, even though the proletariat in the usual sense of the term constituted but an insignificant part of Sweden's population. Discussions of cooperation with other parties or groups reveal a similar lack of clarity. It enabled its practitioners to characterize all nonsocialist groups as belonging to one reactionary blot without any suggestion of the probability that these groups constituted almost the entire population.

This obscurantism was most striking in references to revolution or universal suffrage as the means of securing victory. That revolution was completely unthinkable and that universal suffrage would, at the time, hardly give the party more than an occasional seat in the Riksdag were facts that apparently went unnoticed. The peculiarities in the reasoning would, however, be partly hidden by the rapid pace of Sweden's industrialization: by the time universal suffrage had been won, the working class was big enough to supply the foundation for the largest party in the Riksdag.

The above indicates that early Social Democratic debate in Sweden was peculiarly unreal. Proceeding from a scheme that was mainly Marxian in origin, participants in discussions of the problems paid little attention to

Swedish conditions. Marx's commanding attitude was reflected in the party. Just as Marx, surrounded by a handful of friends, established rules for all of Europe's working class—which didn't even know his name—so a group of young Swedes, whose supporters constituted about one thousandth of the nation's adult population, spoke as if they commanded—or would soon command—a majority poised for action.

In two addresses given during the autumn of 1886, Branting presented the view on the question of tactics that would later play a definitive role in his work. The foundation of his thinking was most clearly set forth in an address entitled "Why the Workers' Movement Must Be Socialistic" that was given October 24, 1886. After explaining the aims of socialism, he posed the question as to how these aims were to be achieved—"through revolution or reform?" The realization of socialism would obviously mean a revolution in the sense that a new social order would be brought into existence. But he declared that if revolution was thought of as being "something connected with street brawls, murder, and plunder, then socialism as such is so far from being revolutionary that it must instead be characterized as reactionary, in the true sense of the term." Socialism did not hold private individuals responsible for bad social conditions, and therefore the idea of "inciting to random assaults on the persons or property of individual opponents" was alien to socialist thinking. Yet socialists could not promise to pursue only legal courses of action whatever the circumstances. If the upper class refused to grant universal suffrage and, as in Russia and Germany, deprived the working class of its civil liberties, then it would be the duty of socialists to crush such tyranny. The bourgeoisie, which had gained power through a series of revolutions, should not be surprised at this view. "If, however, the upper class were to respect popular will *even when it demanded the abolition of its own privileges,* then socialists would not be the ones to resort to unnecessary violence. But the first requirement for a peaceful workers' movement is that it have some way of asserting itself. *Universal* suffrage is therefore the price that the bourgeoisie must pay for its dissolution by administrative [action] rather than through bankruptcy, brought before a revolutionary tribunal."

These statements suggest that Branting considered revolutionary methods a necessity if suffrage were not granted, but that he rejected the thought of revolution under other circumstances or for other aims; in other words, he accepted the bourgeois-democratic revolution but rejected the social revolution. Still, his statements are not entirely clear. He flatly opposed only one kind of "revolution," that involving murder, plunder, and random assaults—which no one seriously considered at the time. He further declared himself in favor of violent methods under only one condition—the imposition of legislation discriminatory to the workers—but this was a stand that even many nonsocialists would have considered justifiable. He never gave a direct answer to the question as to whether socialism would employ only peaceful methods once democracy had actually been implemented. He only said that in this event socialists would not "resort to unnecessary violence." As on several other occasions, Branting was apparently anxious to maintain relations with both the bourgeois democrats and the revolutionaries within the party.

This address did not explore the question of collaboration with nonsocialist groups in any detail. Branting only stressed that, although it shared many views with the bourgeois democrats, the working class could not act "as a tail at the end of the liberal or radical bourgeoisie," for the liberal program was inadequate and lacked the scientific, purposeful direction of the socialist program. However, in an address on "The Prognosis for the Near Future" given some weeks earlier, Branting had thoroughly discussed the question of such collaboration. In this address he assumed that there would be a period of reaction against the demands for freedom and popular government, and supported this assumption by citing the legal proceedings instituted against Palm, together with certain hints of countermeasures against socialists, as evidence of such reaction. Further, one could expect a change in the system of government, a kind of monarchal dictatorship in line with the Danish pattern. In Sweden as in Denmark, socialism therefore should "for the time being arrive at a cease-fire—no, more than that—at a defense alliance against attack, although, and note well, on the basis of equal rights and including those elements from the third estate which have not yet completely lost the revolutionary spirit but wish with sincerity and strength to oppose the aggression of the upper class." Branting added that socialism should be able to reject the "temptations of the Right, with its pseudosocialistic phrases and proposals which will most certainly not be adopted." (In all probability he was referring to the so-called state-socialist proposals, such as those common to Bismarck's sociopolitics. More general reasons for collaboration with nonsocialist liberalism were also given. Sweden was an underdeveloped nation in which the middle class was still an important factor. "The working class needs all the help it can get from this quarter, just as the middle class, in turn, needs the support of the workers in order to hold its ground against their common foes. Bourgeois radicalism and socialism shared a common goal in the fight for universal suffrage, and for the time being, this was the most vital goal for them both.

From time to time Branting made statements that did not agree with the views just cited. He would, for example, speak of "social revolution" in a manner that suggested that he was referring to a revolution in the usual sense of the term, not to a peaceful revolution. He maintained that it was futile to expect anything of the Riksdag and anticipated that the workers, "[rallying] around the red banners of the class struggle and Social Democracy, [would] create a force that could outweigh [the force] of the others, that could at a given moment step forward and say: give us our rights, or we will seize them anyway." During Branting's years as editor of the chief party organ, *Social-Demokraten* sometimes carried articles of a patently revolutionary tenor. On one occasion Branting maintained that it was impossible to establish universally valid rules for party activity.

In any event there is no denying that Branting regarded the attainment of universal suffrage as the primary objective and that he believed that both democracy and socialism could be won through peaceful means. When he threatened violence, it was in regard to the struggle for universal suffrage. As was true of many nonsocialist liberals, Branting apparently thought that violence for the purpose of achieving democracy could be morally sanctioned. The importance Branting attached to the franchise is clearly expressed in the so-called Lill-Jans resolution that he proposed and which was adopted at a meeting on July 10, 1887. This resolution asserted, among other things, that "universal suffrage is an indispensable condition if the people are to become masters in their own house through peaceful means and reform society according to their needs instead of essentially only serving the interests of the upper class, as is that case at present." The resolution concluded that "the speedy granting of universal suffrage is the only way to a peaceful solution of the great Social Question. . . ."

It cannot be said that Danielsson held a plainly revolutionary standpoint at this time. His position on the question of tactics was even less definite than Branting's; the comments he did advance on this question do not testify to a consistent or thoroughly considered conviction. It is, however, equally indisputable that he evinced stronger social revolutionary tendencies than other party leaders. At times he did assert that it was conceivable that the social revolution might be achieved without violence. "A social revolution is imminent," he declared in an address given in Stockholm in 1886. "This time the proletariat will accomplish it—by violent or peaceful means, depending on the position the ruling class adopts." At southern Sweden's workers' congress of 1888, Danielsson made an obscure speech on the tactical question. One speaker interpreted it as meaning that Danielsson "wanted a violent revolution." Danielsson protested that he had been misunderstood: should violence become necessary, it would be because of the upper class, not the workers. Danielsson later wrote in *Arbetet* that the workers should not use violence until peaceful means had proved impracticable. These statements are, however, contradicted by many others that suggest that Danielsson had little faith in parliamentary methods and really considered revolution necessary and desirable. At a meeting for the unemployed held in Stockholm early in 1887, he spoke of revolution as a "world-shaking storm" that would soon break out. The whole tone of the speech bespeaks a kind of militant exultation. In yet another speech he declared that the revolution "must come and we should recognize that we must fight for it even when [doing so] involves more than words and demonstrations." More indicative of this contradiction are Danielsson's many articles in *Arbetet* that proffered revolutionary opinions. One should strive to win the franchise; through it, one might obtain minor social reforms. Parliamentary activity was nevertheless of secondary importance. One article described democracy as "a huge historic lie"; without economic equality, political equality was an illusion. Yet another article characterized parliamentarianism as "the modern [form of] rule in the class state." The legislature passed only those laws which directly or indirectly benefited the ruling class. "Irrespective of the state of the franchise in a nation, legislatures everywhere have the character of upper-class commissions of public safety, nor can they ever have any other [character] in a class state." A Scandinavian trade union congress was scheduled to convene in Copenhagen in the summer of 1888; Danielsson—in opposition to Branting—advocated that Swedes refrain from participating in the congress. One of the reasons he gave for his stand was that Danish socialism, which collaborated with radicals and gave priority to parliamentary work, was no longer a revolutionary party. The Danes had lost "socialism's most essential character, that of the philosophy of a revolutionary societal class in the light of which daily political events become but of secondary importance and, in any case, can only serve to illuminate and inform. Take away this character of socialism, change it from a new theory of society and the world into a paltry political program for a purely parliamentary party, and at that instant the enthusiasm in the workers' core will be extinguished and the ideal of the social revolution degenerate into a pursuit of 'reforms' that will consume all the workers' interests." The splendid thing about socialism, continued Danielsson, was it "never for a moment demeans itself by playing the role of a parliamentary party but retains its social-revolutionary tendency under all circumstances. These and similar statements are far from clear, but they suggest that Danielsson envisioned not only a revolution to attain democracy but also a social revolution to make socialism into a reality. Yet one cannot completely rule out the possibility that even in this context Danielsson interpreted revolution to mean a peaceful reformation of the order of society.

Danielsson also made contradictory statements in regard to the question of collaboration with nonsocialist democrats and radicals. In the first issue of *Arbetet* he addressed himself not only to the workers but also to the middle class, which was said to be dependent on big capitalists and landholders just as the workers were. In the course of his polemics against Swedish participation in the Copenhagen congress, he criticized the Danish workers' party for "compromising with these political subentities who call themselves liberals, radicals, Europeans, or whatever." In an article that appeared early in 1889 he vehemently attacked the idea of collaboration with the liberals. The enmity between workers and liberals was irreconcilable, "for so far as we can judge, 'liberals,' meaning the whole motley crew of manufacturers, businessmen, professional politicians, newspaper editors and the members of the vegetating, middle class that is usually included under the designation 'free traders,' are as a rule, without opinions and readily reconcile themselves to the most reactionary government since their main aim is always economic security." Social Democrats should, however, collaborate with a truly radical party if one were formed. Although he did not express himself precisely, Danielsson obviously stood well to the left of Branting on this question as well.

In the discussion on participation in the Copenhagen congress, Palm sided with Branting and Sterky with Danielsson. This alignment was probably a manifestation of more general tendencies. Palm concentrated all his agitation on the cause of universal suffrage, and his speculations on recourse to revolutionary methods at this time were most likely limited to the thought of a revolution to attain the franchise. In a debate with Anton Nyström in the beginning of 1886 he declared that Social Democracy wanted to achieve its goal by lawful means but that it would have to resort to other methods if those in power were, for example, to suppress freedom of speech. This interpretation is in complete accord with Branting's view, as expressed somewhat later. In at least one article, however, Palm wrote about "the social revolution" as if he were referring to a violent rebellion. In 1886 Sterky wrote in *Social-Demokraten* that Social Democracy wished to achieve its ends by peaceful methods. State expropriation of the capitalist-owned means of production need "not necessarily be carried out through violence." Here Sterky was obviously entertaining the idea of a revolution, not to attain democracy, but to achieve socialism.

The newspapers *The Voice of the People* (*Folkets röst*) and *The Proletariat* (*Proletären*) frequently carried articles and editorials in a revolutionary vein. *Folkets röst* constantly expressed the thought that a violent kind of revolution might be necessary if the bourgeoisie did not yield. On occasion it was intimated that bourgeois concession was conceivable, but as a rule violence was regarded as the course that would probably have to be followed.

"The bourgeoisie is our mortal enemy," declared one article. "We must not rest until it is overthrown, we must fight our enemy, and in the end we shall be victorious. Compromise is of no avail, we should always remember that we have an irreconcilable foe that must be unconditionally destroyed, for as long as this enemy (the bourgeoisie) exists, so must also class hatred exist. . . ." Elsewhere we read:

> that all signs indicate that the despoilers, with the police and military in their pay, will not relinquish the rights they have extorted except through a social revolution. . . . The demand of the masses to enjoy both political rights and the total fruits of industrial development ushers in the last phase of the revolution. This is precisely what the struggle is all about, and it is sure to be a hard [fight], just as surely as the just cause of the people shall win, even if only after bloody battles. All good, noble, and great reforms have been advanced through bloodshed. . . .

Similar, though perhaps slightly less vehemently worded views can be found in *Proletären*.

The discussions of the period are, on the whole, characterized by threats of a revolution, whether democratic or social. Socialism would be realized, preferably through peaceful means, but if this proved impossible, then through violence. The differences in outlook that existed arose partly because some contemplated only a democratic revolution, others a social revolution, and partly because of different ways of appraising the possibility of reaching the goal by peaceful methods. Democratic reforms were regarded as a means to achieve socialism; at times the franchise was not thought of as a basis for concrete political activity but only or chiefly as an instrument of propaganda. Those in power were to be held responsible should a revolution take place, for by making concessions, they could avoid such subversion. The agitation that was carried on by word of mouth was very likely even more revolutionary in tone and more impassioned than that reported in this account, which is mainly based on newspaper articles, would indicate.

It should be strongly emphasized, however, that the revolutionary ideas that were advanced were neither fully developed nor sharply defined. Whether the discussion concerned a democratic or a social revolution, it was most likely commonly assumed that a revolution would have to have the support of a majority of the populace. Revolution by a "class-conscious minority" or the establishment of a dictatorship based on such a minority did not enter into the discussion. That democracy would prevail in the socialist state was regarded as self-evident. The import of the revolutionary terminology used at this time was thus entirely different from that employed in communist doctrine as developed later.

The constituent congress of the Social Democratic party deliberated on the tactical question and laid down the party line in explicit resolutions. Data on the genesis of the various resolution proposals and on the attendant debates are, however, most incomplete.

On Branting's initiative, the Social Democratic Union in Stockholm had called for a statement on the franchise question. The introduction to the resolution that was unanimously adopted pronounced a certain amount of scepticism regarding the significance of the franchise. The congress recognized "that class oppression can exist just as easily in nations with the franchise as in those without it"; it claimed that it entertained "no illusions about the immediate results of the introduction of universal suffrage" and described the franchise "as only a means, not an end." The congress then announced that it demanded the franchise "as the most important and most educational political right in the present society" and that it concurred with the Lill-Jans resolution of 1887 which, among other things, designated the prompt concession of the franchise as "the only way to a peaceful solution of the great Social Question." Another resolution recommended coincident demonstrations for "the natural civil rights of the working class."

It would be fruitless to attempt a closer analysis of the wording of a document that was probably drawn up in haste and whose authors left no record or comments regarding its real purport. It is, however, apparent that the resolution was a compromise that had not been thoroughly worked out. Some contradiction exists between the statements made by the congress itself and the statements with which the congress said it concurred. The statements issued by the congress itself express a view which, at that time, found its chief spokesman in Danielsson. The demand for the franchise per se was notable in this view because of the emphasis placed on its educational value; universal suffrage was not described as the principal means for the transformation of society. The Lill-Jans resolution clearly bore the stamp of the more positive evaluation of the franchise for which Branting was the chief spokesman.

The resolution on "the violence question," as it is called in the minutes, was proposed by Branting and was unanimously adopted without any real debate. It read as follows:

> The Congress declares that, in its efforts to organize the Swedish working class for the seizure of political power, Sweden's Social Democratic party wishes to employ only those means which are in agreement with the people's natural sense of justice. The modern program that we have proposed and which we are working for is the best evidence that we ourselves by no means aspire to a violent revolution. The Congress explicitly rejects the rash plans that our enemies sometimes ascribe to us and

> which would have us wish to hazard the entire workers' movement by attempting a violent coup [d'état] of one kind or another without sufficient support among the people. To the contrary, now as before the party wishes to use all its influence to prevent imprudent, violent outbreaks of popular discontent that could not be backed by sufficient might. Revolutions can never be "made"; but should the blindness and egoism of the rulers provoke a violent revolution as the self-help of despair, our position will be a foregone conclusion and we will be prepared to do all to capture and preserve for the people the most valuable fruits of the struggle [that we can secure] in order that their sacrifices shall not have been in vain.

Branting based his defense of this resolution on the need to dispel misunderstandings and false rumors regarding the party's goals and methods. The barb of the resolution was obviously aimed at the pro-violence agitation that was being conducted in some quarters. Accounts of the party's history have irresponsibly interpreted the resolution as clear acceptance of the line of peaceful agitation on principle. It supposedly confirmed the "strictly pacifist tendency" of the movement and signified "a rejection of all ideas of plans for a coup." Such analyses of the resolution have been influenced by the parliamentary, pacifist tactics that the party has since pursued and stressed with increasing firmness. In effect, the wording of the resolution of 1889 brands it as an equivocal compromise formula; it testifies to the fact that the idea of violence was far from alien to Social Democracy of that day. Almost every sentence in the resolution hints at the possibility of violence, even though peaceful tactics may be accorded a kind of vague precedence. The first sentence simply states that one wishes to employ methods that are "in agreement with the people's natural sense of justice." This does not state anything concrete. The resolution goes on to explain that one does not aspire to a violent revolution; in other words, the congress takes into account the possibility that peaceful methods may prove sufficient. The next few sentences are particularly obscure; in fact, they give one the impression that they are the product of a studied, deliberate attempt at obscurity. Not all violent coups are condemned; only those that are undertaken "without sufficient support among the people" and which would therefore "hazard the entire workers' movement." The party claims that it wishes to prevent violent outbreaks, but its claim extends only to outbreaks "that could not be backed by sufficient might." All that is really said is that one ought to avoid revolutionary attempts that have no prospects of success: the most inflamed revolutionary could endorse this proposition. To be sure, under the existing circumstances this sentence did imply a rejection of the idea of violence: no one could really expect that a party with 3000 members would be able to carry out violent action, but everything might be possible in the future. What is more, the last part of the resolution stresses that should a violent revolution spontaneously erupt, the party would be prepared to join forces with it. In sum: in the prevailing situation the party did not wish to pursue revolutionary tactics that had no prospects of success, but such tactics might conceivably be used once the party's instruments of power could provide the conditions necessary for success. Even before these conditions could be fulfilled the party was prepared to join a revolutionary movement should one emerge in spite of the party's scepticism toward its potential. It would be absurd to describe these as strictly pacifist statements; such a designation could only be explained by the common tendency to assign to the party's early positions ideas that would govern its activity at a much later date.

Sharper controversy arose over the tactical issue in its more limited sense of collaboration with other political persuasions than over the questions of the franchise and the use of violence. An equivocal compromise that lent itself to different interpretations by various factions was hardly possible in this case. Some decision had to be made as to whether collaboration with other parties would be permissible or not. The two main proposals were in direct conflict. Branting's proposal began with the following statement: "The Congress fully recognizes that in comparison with the revolutionary Social Democratic Workers' party, which is the political expression of society's propertyless working class, all other political parties tend more and more to become one single reactionary mass." But the proposal immediately continued by asserting that "in an economically underdeveloped country such as Sweden, the Congress nevertheless considers that it would be premature to pursue independence of other parties, which is always necessary, to the point of refusing all collaboration under any conditions. For the time being therefore, collaboration at elections and in agitation for the franchise . . . for specific, immediate objectives, shall be permitted with groups that show that they seriously wish to protect and extend the people's rights. . . ." The prerequisites for such collaboration were the concomitant recognition of the equal standing of Social Democracy as a political party and the acceptance of the conditions by the party's representatives, who were always to be consulted in such cases.

Sterky's proposal was brief and to the point: "Since Sweden's Social Democratic Workers' party is a propaganda party, i.e., [considers] its main objective to be the dissemination of information about Social Democracy, and since participation in elections is a good vehicle for agitation, the Congress recommends election participation, but only when some definite result may be achieved or when it at least affords a field for propaganda. But when all other parties are reactionary in relation to this party the Congress repudiates all collaboration with other parties." A proposal brought by Palm did not totally reject the idea of collaboration but referred to elections only as vehicles for agitation: Palm later voted for Sterky's proposal. Prior to the congress Danielsson had sent a proposal to Branting which emphasized that the party was "a revolutionary and not a parliamentary party" and that, in comparison, all nonsocialist parties were "reactionary masses." Yet Danielsson conceded that limited collaboration might be possible under the supervision of the party administration. Danielsson's proposal was not brought up for consideration at the congress, nor was it intended to be. The substance of Danielsson's proposal is just about the same as Branting's and it was most likely the basis for the latter's recommendation. The congress finally voted in Branting's and Sterky's proposals. The former won, 35 to 11. Thorsson joined Sterky and Palm in the minority at the vote.

This resolution has also been subject to interpretations that may be understandable in the light of the party's subsequent development but which are nonetheless incorrect. According to Höglund, the resolution laid down "the main political-tactical precepts the party would follow until the third Social Democratic government had been defeated, at which time the catchword, the single reactionary mass, which had been spurious in theory as well as a practical obstacle to productive Social Democratic political maneuvering, literally became a reality in the form of the bourgeois rally against the working class." Nordström spoke of "the cautiously adaptable main political-tactical line that the party would follow until the time when Social Democracy, in its capacity as the executive party, would have to master entirely new tactical problems." It was thus maintained that in this resolution the congressional majority and Branting in particular anticipated the party's subsequent development, which was oriented toward purely parliamentary tactics and collaboration with other parties.

We should first note that everything indicates that Branting's proposal was based on the same desire for mutual understanding and compromise that distinguished his proposals on the questions of the franchise and violence, both of which had been readily adopted. His demand seems like an overworked version of Danielsson's proposal; in effect, the proposal chiefly expressed the "semiparliamentary" line that Danielsson represented. There was no recommendation of collaboration with other parties from a long-range point of view. Limited, short-term collaboration was justified on the ground that, in economically underdeveloped Sweden, the nonsocialist parties did not yet constitute "the single reactionary mass" which the theoretical premise dictated they would become. Collaboration was conceivable "for the time being." Its main purpose would be the attainment of popular government; there was mention of collaboration at elections and in agitation for the franchise with groups that "wish to protect and extend the people's rights." According to the resolution, such collaboration would be impossible later on when Sweden's socioeconomic development was further advanced. The resolution did not anticipate future tactics; moreover, the actual course of development turned out to be the direct opposite of the resolution's prognosis. Branting contemplated limited, short-term collaboration for the purpose of democratization, which would be followed by sharp conflicts. Actual events, however, have demonstrated growing collaboration, even for the realization of demands other than constitutional reforms, and an increasingly tangible *détente* between Social Democrats and nonsocialists. It would be a complete distortion of the purport of the 1889 resolution to read into it a prophecy regarding party tactics from the time of collaboration with the left in the early 1900s, to the alliance with the Independents on certain issues in the 1920s, through to the coalition government formed with the Farmers' party in the 1930s.

Sterky's resolution proposal uncovered the prevailing differences of opinion which had been obscured in the franchise and violence questions by ambiguous formulations. This proposal was based on an outlook that had been expressed in the franchise resolution in its stress on the educational value of the franchise and on its use as a tool of limited effectiveness, and in the resolution on violence in the many hints of revolutionary action. The proposal held that the party should be a party for propaganda and that electioneering be regarded as a means of agitation; in other words, the proposal did not anticipate that the party's objectives could be reached through parliamentary-democratic methods. From this point of view, collaboration with other parties naturally had to be rejected. If one contemplated the possibility that victory might be won by *either* revolutionary or peaceful means, one would have to accept collaboration as a method of attaining universal suffrage. If, on the other hand, revolution was regarded as inevitable, collaboration with nonrevolutionary parties would be meaningless.

In summary, the import of the position of this congress on the so-called tactical questions thus appears to differ from the tenor of previous statements. It has been maintained that the congress represented a victory for the democratic-pacifist-reformist line, that is, for the line that regarded attainment of the franchise as the essential condition for the reformation of society, that repudiated violence, and acknowledged the value of collaboration with other parties. In reality, however, this line did not emerge victorious. The outcome of the congress was a compromise: it demanded the franchise but did not exalt it; it repudiated plans for violence but only to the extent that such plans were unfeasible; it accepted collaboration but only provisionally, and then only to attain certain objectives. This could provide a basis for agreement on the questions of the franchise and the use of violence, but not on the question of collaboration. A definite decision had to be reached here. It was not possible to recognize two alternatives simultaneously as had been the case in regard to violence. Branting's victory on this issue was not a victory for the reformist line but for the general line of compromise. A victory for Sterky, on the other hand, would have meant a triumph for the revolutionary line and the consequent rejection of compromise.

Among the other resolutions passed by the congress was an exhortation to arrange for demonstrations on a certain day "more effectively to rouse the classes in power to a speedier realization of the natural and civil rights of the working class," and to see to it "that citizens in uniform under no pretexts lend themselves to violence and against the freedom rights of other citizens." This resolution was considered one of the best proofs of the party's revolutionary intent.

After the congress had adjourned, Branting—who had introduced the winning resolution proposals on all the tactical questions—expressed his great satisfaction with the accomplishments of the congress. He noted that the different factions within the party had been considered during the formulation of the resolutions and that existing tensions, especially those between Stockholm and the province of Skåne, had thereby been relieved. Danielsson, who was in prison during the congress, also professed to be quite satisfied with what had been accomplished, but he criticized the resolutions on the ground that they were not representative of the party's left wing. He contended that the party had not made its revolutionary character sufficiently clear and that the rulings of the congress principally constituted a compromise, "an arithmetic mean" between the various groups in the party.

It is not surprising that the government viewed the party's first resolutions as a revolutionary threat to the *status quo*. A bill for legislation to deal with socialism was the cabinet's answer to the congressional resolutions. This bill, which was introduced in May 1889, would have made it a criminal offense to instigate "measures that imply a threat to the order of society or a danger to its existence." As already noted, this far-reaching demand was not approved by the Riksdag.

The questions of the value of universal suffrage, of the potential and necessity of revolutionary action, of the advisability of collaboration with other parties were the subject of considerable debate in the period between the party congresses of 1889 and 1891. Without delving into too much detail, let us try to determine the main lines of argumentation. We shall first review the discussion that took place within the party leadership, then turn our attention to the controversies that arose with the emergence of the anarchist faction shortly before the congress of 1891.

During this two-year period, Sterky, Danielsson, and Branting represented three relatively divergent lines of thought. Sterky advocated extreme "radicalism." His standpoint can be summarized as follows: electioneering and parliamentary activities are of value only because of the opportunities they offer for propaganda; there can be no collaboration with other political persuasions; power must be seized by revolution. Sterky presented these arguments with particular clarity in a *Social-Demokraten* article of February 1, 1890. His justification of revolutionary tactics is especially significant:

> The working class cannot gain power through the ballot. Even if one were to suppose that the franchise became universal and without restrictions, the working class would still not attain power thereby, for it would still be too economically dependent on the capitalist class to use its vote. Yes, suppose that even the fantastic should occur, that the working class could send a majority to the legislature; not even by doing this would it obtain power. One can be sure that the capitalist class would then take care not to continue along a parliamentary course but would instead resort to bayonets. And were the working class then not fully cognizant of its mission and stripped for battle, it would surely be the last time it would ever have any association with parliament.

These words convey an outlook that may have flickered faintly in various quarters in the 1800s, but which has gained particular importance in recent socialist debate. The fact that the working class comprises the mass of the people is not decisive; pressure exerted by the upper class and propaganda will prevent the workers from becoming socialist. It follows that a revolution to achieve what the working class *really* wants will be necessary, even if the workers have not thusly expressed themselves at the polls. This, in very abbreviated form, is the modern communust doctrine of the proletariat dictatorship. And the complement of this idea is the assumption that should the workers gain a majority in the legislature they would be violently suppressed by the ruling class. The fascist and national socialist revolutions have frequently been cited as confirmation of this theme, which recently has been energetically espoused by certain extreme groups within the English Labour party. In Sterky's opinion, only a revolutionary action when the time was ripe—whether before or after the franchise had been won—could provide a solution. Yet Sterky does not touch upon the difficulty this presents. Could the socialists, although they had not yet won over the working class, really bring about a revolution when it was even thought improbable that a socialist working class with a majority in the legislature could defend itself against illegal measures taken by the upper class? Sterky again presented his views at the Scandinavian Workers' Congress in Oslo in the summer of 1890. He then proposed a resolution that "participation in elections and in parliamentary work is solely of significance in regard to agitation and thus cannot be used to effect anything at all of direct, practical value for the working class" and that "such participation . . . in collaboration with bourgeois parties or groups demoralizes the participants, especially the workers' representatives." What is remarkable about these statements is that they specifically declare that nothing can be won for the workers through parliamentary action; in a bourgeois society, social reforms are accordingly considered unobtainable or of little value.

During this period Danielsson was shifting from a more or less revolutionary view to increasing recognition of the value of parliamentary action. His relativism on the question of tactics was stressed in a newspaper article. "We are sceptics, opportunists, in regard to tactics. To dogmatically determine certain tactics would be folly for all parties and under all circumstances, and during the period of transition that society is now passing through . . . it would be an even greater folly to establish a dogma regarding tactics that would bind the party to act according to the same routine under all conditions." At the Scandinavian congress of 1890 he appeared against Sterky and declared that the workers could greatly profit from political victories. He further recommended participation in elections with nonsocialist parties that featured universal suffrage in their platforms. His stand on the Swedish elections of 1890 conformed to these assertions, and he succeeded in obtaining the participation of the workers in the city of Malmö in the elections.

Yet it often appears that Danielsson was of the opinion that power would only be gained through revolutionary methods. An article that appeared in the autumn of 1889 is typical of his imprecisely formulated statements. "I do not believe in parliamentarianism, no . . . not even in a people's state. But I have not sworn to anything. . . . let us try [participation in elections], we *must to the utmost* do our duty in order to prevent unnecessary violence during the resolution of The Social Question." On one occasion he wrote "that the workers' party could not be parliamentary, but must be a revolutionary party" and that "a revolution must take place on the street and not in parliament"; on yet another occasion he maintained that any "real result could probably not be achieved" without revolutionary uprisings—in other words, without bloody sacrifices by the embattled working class. It is impossible to determine whether he envisioned that such revolution would occur before or after universal suffrage had been secured.

Branting's statements during these years reveal no trace of change from the position described. Like Danielsson, he stressed his relativism in regard to tactics. In the autumn of 1889 he wrote: "I do not consider certain party tactics as absolutely true or absolutely false, but as suitable or unsuitable, according to the situation." He completely supported the resolution passed at the international congress of 1889 which asserted that the parties in countries where workers were deprived of the franchise should use "all methods possible" to obtain their right to vote and hinted at the acceptability of even violent methods on such occasions. In an address given in 1890 in memory of the capture of the Bastille, Branting went so far as to openly threaten revolution. Even if the lower house should become more well-disposed toward the people, the rule of the upper class in the upper house would remain intact. Therefore, Branting claimed, events will take their usual course; "when the people mature they begin to act, even without the gracious permission of the police. . . . We must . . . ever more gravely come to accept the thought that we may even have to risk our lives, if necessary. . . ." To criticisms of this address that appeared in *Göteborgs Handels-och Sjöfartstidning* Branting replied, somewhat vaguely, that if the suffrage movement promised never to abandon a legitimate basis it would be a "castrated" movement. However, the only medium of exerting pressure for the franchise that he now suggested was "a swelling popular discontent that will not accept everything." At times Branting also seems to have considered a revolutionary conflict necessary—even if the franchise were achieved by peaceful methods. In answer to Sterky's statements of principle on the question of tactics he granted the probability "that the entire upper class will finally close ranks for a last battle for survival." Until then, however, the workers should strive to improve their position through parliamentary action, for "the higher it [their position] is, the more sure the transition to the socialist society." Yet, on the whole, Branting displays a more optimistic and modern outlook than Danielsson. He apparently expected that purely pacifist tactics would suffice to reach the objectives of the party. He constantly and vigorously emphasized the value of collaboration with other parties to achieve universal suffrage.

During and after the 1890 elections, and especially during the spring of 1891, the question of tactics was discussed from somewhat new viewpoints. The semianarchistic group that appeared within the party completely rejected parliamentary activity, which it considered not only ineffective but downright harmful. "Parliamentarianism diverts from the objective, cultivates election fever and candidate hunger, and entails financial expenditures that could be used to educate and prepare the people," Bergegren declared in a speech given February 1, 1891, according to a report that he himself approved. Party activity should aim, through propaganda and organization, at preparations for revolution. No definite guide was provided for the form of revolutionary activity, "the direct action." Bergegren evidently first clearly declared himself in favor of individual terrorist activity during the party congress of 1891. *Under röd flagg* (*Under the Red Flag*), like other Social Democratic newspapers, usually referred to violence and revolution only in the most general terms. Their credo was not unlike that advanced by Danielsson in *Arbetet* (*Work*) some years earlier. At times the ultimate goal was said to be the elimination of the very organization of the state.

The propaganda of the anarchists led to lively polemics. All the party leaders—Branting, Danielsson, Palm, and Sterky—took exception to it and stressed, albeit from somewhat different viewpoints, the value of election participation and parliamentary activity. Nevertheless, the agitation carried on by Bergegren and his cohorts soon made an impression on many party members; this is evident from the strength that the semianarchistic group was able to show at the congress of 1891.

The use of strikes as a political weapon presented a particularly complicated problem. In the autumn of 1889 Danielsson referred to general strikes as "the natural form of the struggle for the imminent revolution in societal conditions." At a party meeting held in the spring of 1890, the first congress of the northern and central districts, it was proposed that if universal suffrage were not granted within a certain period of time "a general work stoppage" be used as a form of coercion. No decision was reached on this, but one year later Bergegren brought up the idea of general strikes. In an address given in February 1891 he urged the workers "to prepare themselves for a general strike that will express in action the revolution that has been and is under way." Somewhat later *Under röd flagg* described the general strike as the "most powerful weapon" of the working class. "When the great masses, bound to slavery by wages, come to realize this, then the hour of freedom will have struck, then the old capitalist society will be smashed and a new chapter in world history will have begun." It would be absurd to employ this weapon for "a triviality" like universal suffrage. "Such a course of action would be about as astute as shooting with a cannon in order to be able to shoot with a rifle." Both *Arbetet* and *Social-Demokraten* supported the idea of a political strike on a large scale, but for more limited purposes. Danielsson now realized that an absolute general strike would be impossible. At best it could include workers engaged in manufacturing but not those employed in distribution. The ruling class, with its police and military forces, would carry off the victory. "It would become a hunger contest between two classes, one of which has control over food and servants while the other has nothing." A strike could shut down one vital branch of industry and the strikers be supported "by the rest of the workers within the country or in Europe." "This form of general strike is a wrench in the heart of society and, correctly used, although it may not completely break the power of the bourgeoisie, it can nevertheless force such workers' reforms as universal suffrage, the 8-hour day, and international protective legislation." Pehr Eriksson, in a *Social-Demokraten* article, expressed a similar view: a general strike could achieve certain political and economic results but not "a Social Democratic order of society."

In these circumstances, the 1891 party congress was mainly concerned with the position of Social Democracy on anarchism and with related questions of tactics. The debate on anarchism and the resolution giving the party's position on this issue was discussed in a previous chapter. Let us bear in mind that the vote repudiating anarchism passed by only a fairly narrow majority: 28 to 11, with 12 abstentions. Further, that the debate on the tactics of anarchism was extremely vague. One is left with the impression that not even the party leaders had read the main body of literature in the international debate. On this issue Branting stated only that, in contrast to Social Democracy, anarchism repudiated all political activity. While underlining his own scepticism regarding "parliamentarianism," Danielsson criticized the anarchists' aversion to all forms of parliamentary work.

Several special tactical issues were also treated. Debates were organized and special resolutions passed on such questions as "Parliamentary Tactics or Violent Methods?", "The Question of Violence," "The General Strike," and "Winning Universal Suffrage." This classification of issues, which was mainly determined by their connection with various proposals, produced some strange results, among them the repetition of arguments. Nonetheless, this account must consider each issue separately.

The views that emerged from the debate on "Parliamentary Tactics or Violent Methods?" were largely connected to other questions of tactics. Danielsson's resolution proposal won, 38 to 10, over that supported by Luthman, Bergegren, and other delegates friendly to anarchism. The first two paragraphs of the winning resolution read as follows:

> Since the Social Democratic Workers' party is a revolutionary party that strives for a fundamental transformation of the present bourgeois society it must consider the possibility that organized violence may become the ultimate liberator of the suffering proletariat. But as long as the peaceful means of universal suffrage has not yet been tested, the Congress expressly declares its disapproval of all kinds of dynamite agitation and brands as traitors to our principles those agitators who incite the masses to acts of violence against private individuals.

The resolution then underscored that, in view of the experiences of other nations, parliamentary activity "must be considered a good method for agitation and as effectively promoting the party's development even from other points of view. . . ." The party therefore ought to participate in elections as soon as the franchise became universal or "substantially" broadened, "but only as a completely independent party and without abandoning its basic opposition to the bourgeois parties because of the workers' momentary demands on society." As long as the existing regulations governing the right to vote for representatives to the lower chamber were in effect it would be up to the party locals to decide whether participation in those elections should take place. No particular mention was made of elections under the existing system. The resolution concluded with an exhortation to the party's agitators to the effect that "while awaiting universal suffrage [they should] energetically and systematically conduct purely socialist propaganda." This proposal was supported by Branting, Palm, Sterky, and Thorsson, among others. A short counterproposal was colored by a vague anarchist tendency. Its principal message reads as follows:

> Since a growing number of people must recognize that the sound development of society is possible only when all its members . . . are afforded the opportunity to develop fully and freely and to enjoy the fruits of their communal efforts, it obviously follows that—in view of the extremely miserable conditions of existence of Sweden's working class and the rapid, comprehensive proletarianization of the members of society just referred to that is continuously taking place—the snail-like course of parliamentarianism cannot correspond to the people's opinions and needs.

As mentioned, by and large the same delegates that supported the unsuccessful, generally anarchistically toned resolution also voted for this proposal. Yet it is interesting to note that the alignments shifted from one roll call to the next. Löfgren, who had first cast his vote with the minority, now voted with the majority; Janhekt, who had first been neutral, now joined the minority; Hedberg switched from the minority to a neutral position, that is, abstained from voting. Thus the controversy on the question under discussion did not become just a continuation of the contest between pure Social Democrats and "anarchosocialists."

The discussion brought out sharp conflicts. The minority speaker declared that the franchise was valueless: "nonsense such as universal suffrage is something that does not affect me in the slightest." There was general talk of revolution, strikes, and violence as methods of reaching an objective. Bergegren was the foremost spokesman of the tactic of physical assault: "as far as I am concerned, I think minor murders are altogether commendable, and such attacks strike terror among the rulers of society. We should infuse ourselves with the poison called hate so that we will be ready for any violence whatsoever." Branting did not completely reject violence but believed it could be considered only for the purpose of winning universal suffrage, not to force the breakthrough of socialism; he considered individual acts of violence utterly reprehensible.

> For my part, I shall state that my references to seizing our rights by evil or good [means] and the like, always and solely concern the ways of giving public opinion the *normal foundation* to rest on through *universal suffrage.* An absurdity such as considering recourse to violence in order to force a socialist societal order on the people at the present stage of development has never for a moment occurred to me.

Other majority speakers sharply criticized the references to minor murders and attacks on private citizens, but also voiced their doubts regarding the potential of the parliamentary course. Danielsson made it known that he had learned to appreciate the value of parliamentary work because of the training it offered party members in preparation for their exercise of power after the revolution. When, in the previous debate on anarchism, he had asserted that "the end of the class society will most likely be characterized by the revolutionary dictatorship of the proletariat," he was obviously not thinking of a victory for socialism through peaceful means. The same general line was held by Sterky, who claimed he was not afraid of revolution but still emphasized the educational value of electioneering as well as the impossibility of immediate recourse to revolutionary action.

The majority was divided on the questions of participation in elections under the existing order and of collaboration with other parties. Branting was in favor of participation in elections and cooperation with other parties at elections; Danielsson was in any event in favor of electioneering activities; Thorsson, on the other hand, considered participation under the existing conditions to be meaningless, and wished to limit party activity to propaganda.

Before commenting on the resolution that was passed, let us briefly reconsider the closely related decision that was reached on "the violence question." This question was treated separately because the Social Democratic Union in Stockholm had demanded that "if the consensus of opinion should prove to include so-called *action propaganda,* then the [local] organizations should hold discussions as to *which* violent methods are the most practical and fully feasible." Since the same general topic had already been thoroughly discussed, the debate on this point was not extensive. Branting, however, proposed that the answer to the motion simply be the resolution on violence passed by the congress of 1889. Bergegren once again suggested the following:

> Since the question as to whether the workers' party should change over from words to action is regularly posed by so-called moderates as well as by so-called radical speakers, the Congress urges party organizations to seriously reflect on which methods the working class ought to use to reach the goals the party has established as Social Democratic, and, if the majority should be of the opinion that the party will one day need to resort to violence, that the organizations hold discussions as to which methods of violence can be considered the most practical and, at the same time, the most feasible.

It must be noted that violence was not directly recommended, but that it was obviously assumed that violence could and most likely would need to be employed as a weapon. Branting's proposal won, but by an astonishingly narrow margin: 29 to 19, with 2 abstentions. Several participants (e.g., Löfgren, Dahlberg, Hagberg) who had voted with the majority on the party position on anarchism as well as on the issue "Parliamentary Tactics or Methods of Violence?" now moved over to Bergegren's side.

The resolutions considered here have not been subject to a real analysis, but they have often been characterized as a victory for the reformist-pacifist school of thought. The decision just discussed has often been bypassed or only briefly mentioned, despite its significance for the party's position at that time. A distorted interpretation of the tactical question at the time has become generally accepted.

The two resolutions discussed, which we shall subsequently refer to as numbers 1 and 2, together with the generally anarchist resolution, obviously represented a defeat for the so-called anarchist faction. However, as has been justly noted, the defeat may have been obvious, but it was not devastating. The anarchist line seems to have been comparatively stronger in Sweden than in other countries such as Denmark, Norway, Germany, and France. Still more noteworthy is the fact that a significant minority within the party totally repudiated legal, peaceful methods.

It is also important to realize that the victory over anarchism was not a victory for pacifism over violence nor for reformism over the revolutionary line. The approved resolutions implied an acceptance of violence under circumstances that were not clearly specified. This has already been noted in regard to resolution 2, which simply repeated a ruling of the 1889 congress. This compromise resolution, which was passed unanimously in 1889, received only 60 percent of the votes in 1891, at which time the minority voted for a proposal that directly recommended local discussions regarding suitable methods of violence. In respect to acceptance of the possibility of violent tactics, resolution 1 was still more specific. It stated that the party must "consider the possibility that organized violence may become the ultimate liberator of the suffering proletariat." The subsequent repudiation of "dynamite agitation" and "acts of violence against private individuals" by no means implied abandonment of the revolutionary line. Oddly enough, sheer anarchist violence—which was the kind of violence in question—was held to be objectionable only under existing conditions "as long as the peaceful means of universal suffrage has not yet been tested." As a rule, however, it seems that the majority generally wished to renounce anarchist violence (murder and attacks) and considered a violent course unsuitable if universal suffrage could be won through peaceful means and if it would lead to victory for the party.

The attendant debate illuminates the import of the resolution. Not one of the speakers absolutely condemned violent action on principle. The most "reformist" position was held by Branting, who contemplated the possibility of using violence to achieve universal suffrage, but apparently believed that only pacifist tactics would be in order once the franchise had been won. As a rule the spokesmen for the majority adopted a different approach. In their view a violent revolution would be necessary to win the ultimate victory and the realization of socialism—regardless of when and how universal suffrage would be achieved. Danielsson and Sterky had clearly expressed this opinion, and it was surely hailed by many other delegates who voted with the majority on both decisions. Because the congressional report is incomplete it is impossible to examine this point in detail. It is particularly hard to determine if those who spoke of violence referred to it in Branting's sense of the term—to win the franchise—or in Sterky's and Danielsson's sense—to revolutionize society. For example, Braun, one of the spokesmen for the majority, spoke in a general way about "the gains of general strikes and revolts."

Schematically the congressional delegates thus represented three different views. One thought elections and parliamentary activity to be valueless; this anarchist faction lost by a large majority through resolution 1, but in the vote for resolution 2 it gained the support of some delegates who thought it best to immediately deliberate on the question of violence, even though they did not wish to exclude a parliamentary course. This group can be designated as the left wing of the faction led by Sterky and Danielsson. According to their view, the possibilities implicit in the parliamentary course should be utilized, especially with a view to the opportunities they offered for education and political training. However, this course would never achieve the objective; in the last analysis seizure of power would have to be accomplished through revolution. The third view was principally represented by Branting: violence might be needed to win universal suffrage but should not be used thereafter. The two last views agreed on two vital points concerning the situation at hand: they rejected individualistic, anarchist violence, and they wished to utilize parliamentary opportunities. However, in all probability the anarchist line, together with the Danielsson-Sterky line, represented a majority at the congress. The suggestion that reformism should have won is therefore absurd: both the resolutions in question acknowledged justifications for violence and many probably expected that socialism would be realized through a violent revolution.

The statement on participation in elections in resolution 1 is clearer than the corresponding declaration of the 1889 congress. A distinction was now drawn between tactics to be used for the duration of the *status quo* and tactics to be used after a universal or considerably broader extension of the francise. For the duration of the *status quo* it would be up to local organizations to decide on participation. No specific pronouncement on this subject was made in 1889, but the resolutions of the congress regarding the franchise and collaboration with other parties indicate that participation in elections was thought desirable. The formulation of the resolution was in all likelihood influenced by the differences of opinion that came to the fore within the majority. The resolution did not mention collaboration under the prevailing conditions. In the future, when the franchise had been broadened, the party ought to participate in elections "as a completely independent party." Thus we have the rule that is implicit in the 1889 decision, according to our interpretation: collaboration with other parties at elections could be considered only as a tool to gain universal suffrage. This underscores the unjustifiable nature of allegations that Social Democracy at this time had already committed itself to the course of collaboration that it would pursue in later years.

Two additional resolutions that are of interest in this context were passed by the congress with almost no controversy. One concerned the general strike. Without specifying their wishes, certain local organizations had demanded a statement on this issue. The congress declared "that if not a general, then a highly organized large-scale strike aimed at one of the most vulnerable points in the social organism can be used under appropriate circumstances as one of the tools [with which] the workers' party can [carry on] propaganda and [gain] power in order to realize the political and economic demands that have ripened in the consciousness of the people." The resolution continued with the assertion that no definite time for the large-scale strike should be set; the time should be determined by the political and economic situation. Neither the resolution nor the attendant debate discloses details as to what this large-scale strike was thought to involve. Since the anarchosocialists had called for strikes as a revolutionary instrument and others regarded strikes as a way of bringing about universal suffrage, it was natural that the question be broached. The general character of the formulation of the resolution made it acceptable to both groups.

In view of other decisions and debates at the congress, the resolution on the franchise is formulated in a surprisingly positive manner. The first paragraph reads as follows:

> Referring to the statements of the prior party congress and of the International Social Democratic Congress in Paris regarding the benefit and necessity of the democratization of the working class and of society as a whole to the effect that the first point in the current program—universal suffrage—be fulfilled as soon as possible, the Congress determines that the Swedish Social Democratic party's agitation among the masses . . . for universal suffrage shall continue in full force.

The resolution then assigns party delegates the task of organization of elections to a "people's parliament"; following a Belgian model, elections based on universal suffrage would choose an assembly whose principal work would be the preparation and dissemination of propaganda for the franchise. Should this people's parliament, which was scheduled to convene concurrently with the regular parliament in 1893, not succeed in garnering universal suffrage, then, if possible, a campaign was to be launched for a large-scale strike in the summer of 1893. This strike should preferably "be aimed particularly at the social class that has been the principal source of opposition to the reform." In this event a new people's parliament was to be held in 1894; this parliament should have "such a broad popular basis and be so imposing that further opposition from the side of the 'law' would be unthinkable." The resolution concluded with the following odd pronouncements:

> The Congress also resolves that during this interval—a period of respite for society's rulers—party agitators should prepare and to the greatest possible extent organize Sweden's working class for the eventuality that the above-mentioned means of coercion will be used. Finally, in view of the zeal shown in some quarters that crusade for the noble aim, "the defense of the fatherland," the Congress urges the workers of Sweden to organize and train in voluntary rifle clubs wherever it is possible to do so.

This resolution was passed without a vote; only Bergegren was opposed to it. It did not meet any opposition from the anarchists because they considered that they could not adopt a position that ran directly counter to a declaration of principle for universal suffrage.

It is strange that the resolution refers to a certain date for the large-scale strike which was to be used as a method of coercion for the franchise despite the fact that the large-strike resolution first passed had pointed out the inadvisability of fixing such a date. This inconsistency may have been connected with the general vagueness regarding the purpose of the strike recommended in the large-strike resolution, which was not specifically concerned with a strike for the franchise.

The last part of the resolution, which recommended the formation of rifle clubs, is even more curious. Considering the sentiments prevalent in the party, this advice cannot be interpreted as a display of interest in defense. The only comments on the resolution appear in an article written by Palm more than six months later. It indicates that Palm, who had declared his opposition to the decision, assumed that the contemplated rifle clubs were intended for use in the event violence should break out, and there is no reason to challenge this interpretation. Palm, together with Branting and Danielsson, had been a member of the committee that prepared the proposal for the resolution; moreover, this line of thinking is in complete agreement with the general position adopted by the majority at the congress. It is surprising that Branting contributed to the preparation of a similar proposal, but this may have been part of a compromise reached between himself and Danielsson.

On the whole, the position of the 1891 congress was to the left of that of the 1889 congress—a change that was primarily due to the position that the anarchist line had gained within the party. There is no point in trying to construct explanations for the anarchist gain: in such a small party the impact of personal influence alone could lead to significant shifts in position. Despite sharp controversy on the question of tactics, the party's plan of action for the near future had been drawn up by virtue of the emphasis placed on the importance of agitation for the franchise. In practice, this resolution—not the statements colored by revolutionary ideologies—came to be of importance.

Although the majority at the congress definitely rejected anarchism no attempt was made to exclude the anarchist group from the party. In the course of the debate Branting declared "for my part, I most emphatically vindicate myself against being included in the same party as a Hinke Bergegren." However, according to an article by Danielsson published after the congress, "the party leadership in Stockholm" did not wish to exclude Bergegren—an attitude that Danielsson himself deplored. When, in the course of the following years, the bourgeois press held the party responsible for Bergegren's agitation, party leaders tried to absolve themselves of blame by citing the resolution of 1891. But the fact remained: Bergegren continued to be a party member and thus was regarded as an exponent of the party by the outside world.

The party congress of 1891 marks the end of the first phase in the development of the constitutional philosophy of Social Democracy—a phase characterized by great uncertainty regarding the methods to be employed in party activity. During the subsequent period and until the franchise reform of 1907–1909, party efforts were devoted more and more to increasing the political opportunities of the working class within the framework of the state as it existed. From the point of view of its practical operations, the party mainly became associated with its support of the franchise. Its membership increased from between 6000 and 7000 in the early 1890s to over 100,000 in 1906–1908. Efforts to solve the question of the franchise pushed the idea of revolution into the background. Concentration on one specific mission led automatically —and more surely than debates and resolutions—to the party's impregnation by the pacifist, reformist line. As far as the party majority was concerned, any discussions of extraparliamentary methods of coercion dealt only with methods of a nonviolent nature; the purpose for which they might conceivably be used was said to be the franchise, not a social revolution.

A plainly revolutionary faction that was hostile to parliamentary action nonetheless persisted within the party and was particularly assertive in the early 1900s. This faction seldom came to the fore in the press and at congresses, and Branting and other majority leaders repeatedly declared that it had no right to represent the party. Thus, it gradually assumed the character of a party within a party, and the propaganda it issued was cited by the bourgeoisie as evidence of the dangers of Social Democracy. Yet not until Bergegren and Schröder's expulsion from the party in 1908 would the effects of the real schism that had long existed make themselves felt.

Let us first consider the discussion of tactics among those within the majority who accepted—and to an increasingly greater extent accepted *only*—the pacifist line, and thereafter turn our attention to the revolutionary line.

The increasing dominance of reformism within the former group was partly due to Danielsson's change in position. Although he still issued isolated statements that were revolutionary in tone, Danielsson increasingly leaned toward moderation. In the summer of 1891 he declared "that a more or less peaceful settlement with the upper class would be in the best interests of all humanity" and that is was the duty of Social Democracy to do everything "to avoid a bloody catastrophe"; in order to be successful, a revolution "must 1) be international, 2) take place simultaneously in all parts of a nation, 3) have the support of a majority of the people." This, in fact, meant a distinct repudiation of revolutionary agitation. One year later he published a much noted article in which he clearly stated that in the course of the five years since his arrival in Malmö he had "changed his mind on some important questions." He had lost all faith in a "single revolutionary mass"; he was a firm supporter of "parliamentarianism"; and he hoped that in at least some countries The Social Question might be solved through parliamentary means. Collaboration with other groups with democratic goals was recommended as a means to achieve both political and economic reforms. "I regard the securing of the state and municipalities [*kommunerna*] to be the only rational tactic for a Social Democratic party." Branting responded to this article by noting that Danielsson's views corresponded with the standpoint to which a majority in the party already subscribed, but also expressed certain apprehensions that Danielsson would come to lean too far to the right—a misgiving that was evidently prompted by Danielsson's unrestricted demand for collaboration with other groups.

Sterky criticized both Danielsson and Branting, asserting that the Social Democrats were a revolutionary party, that their main task at present was to pave the way for socialism through propaganda, and that parliamentary activity must be regarded in this light and not as a means of reaching lesser goals. Yet even Sterky's article suggests a reformist line of development. Although he stressed that the party should be independent vis-à-vis other parties, he did not mention any necessity for revolutionary action.

The positions of the three party leaders were again defined at the Scandinavian Workers' Congress in Malmö in 1892. This congress adopted a resolution that explicitly recommended parliamentary activity. In the course of the debate on this resolution, Sterky expressed the opinion that the nonsocialist groups should be regarded as "a single reactionary mass" and that collaboration with such groups was impossible. Danielsson called this view a "class prejudice" that Marx himself would probably not have accepted in the situation at hand. Social Democracy ought to try to win over the "borderline class" that lay between the proletariat and the bourgeoisie. "Our party must be a negotiating Social Democracy." Branting adopted a conciliatory position. The first order of business was to win the working class, then the middle class. It was therefore inadvisable to speak of "a single reactionary mass"; the party should instead assert itself as a party that dealt with practical matters.

The people's parliament recommended by the 1891 congress took place in 1893 through collaboration between Social Democrats and the New Liberals who called for democratization. More than 150,000 persons—even women were granted the vote—participated in the election of this assembly. Twenty-eight of the 123 representatives elected were Social Democrats, among them, Branting and Danielsson. The party played a prominent part in the transactions of the congress. Of particular interest in this context is the Social Democrats' proposal for an investigation into the possibility of using various measures to exert pressure—strikes, rifle clubs, refusal to pay taxes or do military service—and that the people's parliament subsequently resolved to exhort those groups working for the cause of universal suffrage to discuss independently appropriate methods of exercising such pressure. The resolution did not, however, specify the particular measures that the Social Democrats had recommended and which had occasioned some wariness among many nonsocialist supporters of the franchise. A new people's parliament was to be held in 1896.

Such was the state of affairs when the party congress convened in 1894. The franchise was now the central issue; there was no debate on reformist versus revolutionary tactics. The resolution regarding the franchise was far more positive than the declarations that had been adopted in 1889 and 1891: universal suffrage was described as "one of the most important means toward the realization of the Social Democratic program in its entirety" and should therefore be featured in all agitation. For the first time an authoritative, uncontroverted statement was made to the effect that it was conceivable that socialism might be attained through the franchise. Another resolution adopted at this congress declared that party organizations should campaign for the rights of assembly and demonstration, which seemed to be in jeopardy because of certain official decrees, and that arrangements be made for mass demonstrations for the franchise to be held at the people's parliament of 1896.

In regard to pressure tactics to win universal suffrage, the congress passed a resolution (of which Danielsson was the principal author) "that, if even the pressures brought to bear by the people's Parliament of 1896 should prove fruitless, a repeated rejection by the Riksdag of the motion for universal suffrage be answered by a work stoppage within those branches of industry where a general strike could prove effective and beneficial, and that, if possible, such a strike commence immediately following the proclamation of the decision of the Riksdag." Branting proposed an addition to this resolution that would permit the party leadership to postpone the strike from 1896 to a later date, should this prove necessary. The congress declared that it did not believe "in the possibility of a general strike in the true sense of the term" and cautioned against a strike of agricultural workers because it would not be feasible and "from a general social point of view not . . . advisable." The congress further declared that it placed its main hopes in "the workers in the rest of Sweden's large natural industries, mining, manufacturing, the iron and wood industries, with the support, if possible, of the workers engaged in the communications industry. . . ." Finally, a recommendation to participate in the election of members of the Riksdag was passed without reservation: collaboration "with other free-thinking parties" could take place under the condition that "Social Democrats are recognized as a political party and one of the chief points in the party platform be accorded serious consideration." Joining forces at elections with groups that advocated universal suffrage was thereby generally accepted.

The 1894 congress marks the natural evolution that had taken place within the party following the organization of concrete measures for attainment of the franchise. A moderate course on all questions—the evaluation of the franchise, participation in elections, collaboration with other groups—was now accepted without controversy. At the same time, the revolutionary line, which had probably claimed a majority within the party at earlier congresses, was no longer of any consequence.

It could also be said that the party had grown to accept the idea of a general strike as a method of coercion without first determining whether it would actually be possible to organize a comprehensive strike and without thinking through the problems that such action would entail. Belgium's general strike of 1893, which had come to be cited as a model for strike action, had been based on conditions that were entirely different from those existing in Sweden. Industrialization in Belgium was incomparably more developed than in Sweden, and the Belgian workers' movement was far stronger. It must have been obvious that there was little likelihood that Sweden's Social Democrats who, in 1894 still numbered less than 8000, would be able to carry out a strike of significant proportions within the near future. Nor do we have reason to believe that the party leaders who had been commissioned to prepare such a strike to be held in 1896 actually did anything about it: neither published reports nor the unpublished records of the leadership contain any evidence of such measures. Immediately after the congress had adjourned, Branting published an article that indicates his scepticism regarding the possibility of realizing the resolution passed by the congress.

Nevertheless, before the elections to the people's parliament of 1896, the party leadership expressed the opinion that the demand for large-scale strike action be included in the party platform; this policy was subsequently followed in Stockholm and in most areas in central and northern Sweden. Now it was Danielsson who declared his opposition. He believed demands for a large-scale strike might divide the franchise movement and doubted that an effective strike could be organized. He pointed out that, in reality, a large-scale strike must mean revolutionary attempt, and that such an attempt would not only be unjustifiable in view of the opportunities for the working class to make its voice heard through other means, but would also be dangerous and without any prospects of success. Danielsson was by now also inclined to "reach the goal of universal suffrage in two runs," that is, to begin by concentrating on a limited reform of the franchise. Party organizations in southern Sweden by and large adopted Danielsson's negative position on the strike question. Danielsson was sharply criticized by Branting, who said the former was on the way to "the motley, jumbled realm of the middle class," and that he, Branting, was on principle sympathetic to the idea of a large-scale strike. Branting did not question the advisability of setting a specific date for the strike—that is, immediately after the people's parliament of 1896.

The second people's parliament aroused less interest than the first. The electorate numbered approximately 130,000. Thirty of the 146 members were Social Democrats, proportionately somewhat less than in 1893. Prior to the parliament and following the decision of the 1895 national convention on the franchise, non-Social Democratic franchise supporters had sent questionnaires to corporations and to private individuals regarding the advisability of using certain coercive methods—particularly a large-scale strike—to force through a reform of the franchise. It became evident that a large proportion of the nonsocialist proponents of the franchise were definitely opposed to the thought of such a strike: this may have been the reason why many of them refrained from working for or participating in the elections to the people's parliament. Branting's motion that the people's parliament issue a declaration of principle in favor of a large-scale strike was rejected in committee. Then Branting and other Social Democrats—including even Danielsson—demanded that the parliament relinquish to the workers' organizations the responsibility of preparations for the use of the strike weapon, should such action seem appropriate. In practice, this meant that the nonsocialist proponents of the franchise would bind themselves not to oppose agitation for a large-scale strike. This proposal was defeated, 67 to 63. After this defeat, Branting declared that he did not wish to join in setting a date for another people's parliament because this institution seemed to have steadily lost its significance. Within the party as a whole, a critical disposition had developed toward the nonsocialists in the franchise movement. It is interesting to observe, however, that this did not stop the Social Democrats from seeking nonsocialist support at the 1896 elections to the lower house in Stockholm and Malmö—the only places where the party had placed its candidates on the ballot. Branting won a seat at this election, largely by virtue of Liberal votes.

Ensuing developments indicate the party's reluctance to realize large-scale strike plans. Unlike the congress of 1894, the 1897 congress did not pass a resolution on such a strike. It resolved, without debate, simply that party members should "in all ways through agitation and organizational activities work toward the dissemination of the idea of a comprehensive work stoppage as being the most effective means of exerting pressure to secure universal suffrage." Shortly before, a similar resolution had been adopted at a Scandinavian workers' congress, at which Danish and Norwegian workers were instructed to help their Swedish brothers if a large-scale strike should take place.

The party administration was authorized to arrange for the party organizations to vote on whether the party should participate in the next people's parliament. A third parliament never did take place, partly because of the hesitation evinced by Social Democrats. On the other hand, in 1899, nonsocialist supporters of the franchise petitioned the king for reform of the vote. The Social Democrats, who did not want to avail themselves of this course of action, generally disassociated themselves from the petition, but Danielsson recommended that they support it. The party congress of 1900 issued a new proclamation on the question of the franchise, but it amounted to little more than a repetition of earlier resolutions.

By this time more practical considerations regarding a large-scale strike were being aired. In February 1899 the party administration decided to begin an investigation into the prerequisites for an effective strike to further the cause of the franchise. Private conferences were arranged with district representatives to analyze which occupations might best lend themselves to such a strike, which would be the most advantageous time for the strike, and how the resources for this action might be obtained. At a later conference, which was also open to persons not in the party administration, it was decided that the administration should pursue vigorous agitation for a strike. Special attention was to be given to railroad employees and other transportation workers. The strike issue was examined at several subsequent conferences. Following the 1901 session of the Riksdag, which had enacted a new organization of the army but had not, as demanded by the radicals, also solved the question of the franchise, agitation for a large-scale strike became all the stronger. At a special conference on the franchise that was held in Malmö in August of 1901, it was decided that the strike issue would be taken up by workers' organizations and that a special fund for a large-scale strike would be created. A somewhat later decision directed that a revote on the strike issue be taken by these organizations and that the results be reported to the party administration.

As directed by the congress of 1900, a party conference convened in Stockholm in April, 1902. Except for the smaller number of delegates, it had the characteristics of a party congress. The Riksdag then in session was to deliberate upon a bill for franchise reform comprising conservative guarantees that were unacceptable to the Left. The party conference, however, concerned itself only with the strike issue. It was established that about 90 percent of those who voted in the workers' organizations were in favor of a large-scale strike, but participation in this vote had been scant (about 20,000 of the party's nearly 50,000 members voted).

There was considerable difference of opinion at the conference. Branting declared himself definitely opposed to a large-scale strike: he did not believe it would be possible to accomplish, and wished to limit the methods of coercion to demonstrations. Several party leaders such as Thorsson, Blomberg, A. C. Lindblad, Nils Persson, and Aug. Nilsson sided in the main with Branting. Some criticized the leaders for not wishing to carry out the strike that they had long advocated and for not having drawn up plans for the strike. Among the supporters of the strike were Herman Lindqvist, Palm, and Kata Dalström. It should be noted that practically all proponents of the strike apparently supposed that it would be purely in the nature of a demonstration and would be lawfully conducted. However, one speaker urged that the party demand more than universal suffrage: that it also demand the abolition of the upper house and of the monarchy itself. Another speaker expressed the hope that the demonstrations would lead to revolts.

The decision of the conference was a kind of compromise. Large demonstrations were to be organized; during the period when the franchise question was on the floor at the Riksdag, these demonstrations would be enlarged to include work stoppage to the extent that this was practicable and seemed appropriate as a coercive tool. In regard to voting regulations, Branting—the only member of the Riksdag—was inclined to accept a compromise (the so-called *kommunalstrecket*), but it was decided that the party would continue to pursue the principle of universal suffrage without any restrictions.

The program of the conference was carried out more successfully than many had anticipated. Large demonstrations were arranged; because of minor skirmishes with the police and the arbitrary behavior of the law enforcers, the demonstrations won a great deal of publicity. During three days, from May 15 through May 17, approximately 100,000 workers conducted a peaceful, orderly strike. It is probable that the demonstrations and large-scale strike helped educe the Riksdag's decision to conduct an investigation into the question of universal suffrage.

In the course of the ensuing years, until the positive decree on the franchise in 1907, the use of a large-scale strike as a coercive tool was frequently the subject of debate. Considerable uncertainty about the use of the strike was manifest, particularly among the party leaders. In 1904 another vote was taken on the question. Less than half the party members voted. A bare majority did indicate that it favored such a strike on principle, but most did not wish to strike without compensation, nor—in response to a question asked of them—were they willing to allow the 1905 party congress to announce a large-scale strike of undetermined duration. In accordance with this consensus, the 1905 congress decided that, should the occasion arise, the party administration would later convoke an extra party congress to deal with the strike issue. Early in 1907 the party administration arranged for a second revote on the strike question; this time approximately 50 percent of the party membership voted, and of these, two thirds favored a new large-scale strike. An extra congress convoked by the party leaders took the issue under consideration in April, 1907. The outcome of its deliberations was fairly general agreement that a new large-scale strike was inadvisable or unfeasible, especially since the constitutional reform proposed by the Lindman cabinet could be considered a great step forward. The congress decided that no large-scale strike would be held under the existing circumstances. It nonetheless allowed that strikes might be used in the future as weapons to further the franchise and other causes related to the rights of the working class. However, with the passage of the first great constitutional reform in the spring of 1907, the strike issue lost all urgency.

Concurrently with the cause of universal suffrage ran the fight for civil rights, particularly freedom of expression, demonstration, and assembly. There is no reason to closely examine this struggle here. It was meaningful from the point of view of practical politics, but was of less moment for the party's ideological evolution. We may simply note that the Social Democrats followed the same line of thinking as the Liberals: freedom was not only a prerequisite for the party to function successfully but was a value above discussion—the distinguishing feature of a civilized nation.

After the congress of 1891, the strictly revolutionary faction in the party remained in obscurity for a number of years. As mentioned, the newspaper *Under röd flagg* ceased publication in June 1891. In the same year, Bergegren became editor of *Proletären* in Norrköping, where he continued his antiparliamentary activities. According to the propaganda he issued, the party leaders, who were in favor of participation at elections, deliberately deceived people so that they could "under partially changed conditions, sneak into the Riksdag comedy as fellow players." He regarded universal suffrage as being of little value since "the great mass of people is still led by religious fantasts or liberal swindlers." Bergegren left *Proletären* in January 1892, after which he did not appear in political discussions for several years. He was succeeded on *Proletären* by Rydgren, who wrote in a semirevolutionary vein and was subsequently sentenced to a prison term for libel against the Riksdag. After one additional turnover in editorship, *Proletären* adopted a more moderate policy until it ceased publication in the spring of 1893.

Beginning in 1891 and for some years thereafter, Palm was really the main spokesman for the antiparliamentary line. Primarily because of conflicts with coworkers, Palm left the editorial staff of *Social-Demokraten* in the autumn of 1891, after which he assumed the role of a kind of leader of the opposition. He put in appearances at various gatherings, and, in November 1891, again began publishing—this time, *The Will of the People* (*Folkviljan*), as the voice of a secret organization with vaguely revolutionary aspirations. He used this organ to accuse Branting and other party leaders of being power-hungry, to declare his sympathy for the anarchists, and to deride parliamentarianism. When, after a little more than a year, *Folkviljan* had to close down, Palm sporadically issued new, even more extreme publications. Besides the abuse they leveled against Social Democratic leadership—and Branting, in particular—these publications mainly carried scornful attacks on all parliamentary activity. All representative bodies were said to be corrupt: "by their bargaining and venality they poison the social organism and bring disgrace upon nations." Workers were urged to abandon resolutions and demonstrations in favor of action. In the future, governments would be administered by specialized departments and important decisions would be reached through popular referendums. Certain elements of anarchist and syndicalist theories can be detected here, albeit in a most primitive form. There are some traces of the influence of Palm's propaganda, but on the whole this seems to have been inconsequential. In 1892 Palm was expelled from the administration in the northern and central districts and was declared unworthy of a position of confidence within the party; this measure was subsequently confirmed by a vote among party members. However, the party could not disclaim all responsibility for Palm's activities, especially not after his reappointment as agitator by the party administration in 1895. Prior to this action Palm had promised he would not agitate publicly for secret organizations and would stress the merits of securing the franchise.

In 1892 a young worker, Arvid Björklund, attempted to give a more thorough and theoretical rationale for the revolutionary position in a pamphlet entitled *Why Are We Revolutionaries?* (*Varför äro vi revolutionära?*). The main points in this pamphlet deserve to be reviewed, not because of the impact of the pamphlet—which was probably negligible—but because it offers by far the clearest exposition of revolutionary thinking based on Marxian doctrine (although deviating from Marx on several vital questions) presented in Sweden prior to the appearance of Bolshevik agitation.

Björklund takes Marx's theories of accumulation and impoverishment as his point of departure. The capitalists become fewer in number and richer, the proletariat becomes greater in number and poorer. Attempts to counteract this trend through trade unions really only worsen the workers' lot because they lead to a stepping-up of technical efficiency which, in turn, makes possible the use of cheaper labor (women and children). The day is approaching "when a few, wallowing in the effulgence of riches, will rule an enslaved humanity." Even if the workers should succeed in winning universal suffrage their position will nevertheless remain unchanged. Those who possessed economic power could, in various ways, also secure political power, and workers in democratic states would therefore be as oppressed as those in despotic states. "Universal suffrage is . . . the safety valve that those in power will most certainly use should the ferment grow too strong. If public opinion then holds that we can reach our goal via the parliamentary route, then one can rejoice in victory and the rulers can continue as before in peace and tranquility." An upheaval is therefore necessary to a realization of the socialist society. The objection is raised—writes Björklund—that industry is not developed sufficiently to permit a socialist system of production. Yet if one is a socialist, such an objection must appear ridiculous. "Does one then consider socialism incapable of developing production? Is not a socialist society the best safeguard for sound progress? Would not discoveries and inventions, which make big industry possible, grow enormously in scope in a society where no one's aptitutdes were stifled but allowed to develop freely; where information would be available to all who thirsted for knowledge . . . ?" It is also said, continued Björklund, that "one stage must be succeeded by another . . . that capitalist production is a legitimate transitional stage." In fact, one believes in eternal progress. Yet "the teaching that progress is eternal is humanity's worst enemy. It leads us to sing the praises of progress while we march to our destruction." For capitalist development means an increase in misery for the great majority. And as their misery grows, the mass of people will become more apathetic and listless. At the same time, steady improvements in the techniques of warfare afford the ruling few even greater possibilities to maintain their power. If a revolution is to take place, it must occur soon. If this cannot be made clear to the workers, then this civilization, like those before it, will become petrified or go down in ruin. "Either we succeed in [carrying out] a well-planned revolution—yes, then humanity will be saved—or else we fail, and humanity is doomed. We will then have done all we could to avoid destruction; we will have done our duty."

Because of influences that are exceedingly difficult to specify, the youth movement that developed in the 1890s exhibited extremely radical leanings in regard to the question of tactics and many other issues. The first Social Democratic youth club, which was formed in Stockholm in 1892, displayed its radicalism by, among other actions, siding with Palm in the intramural struggle then being waged. After the youth clubs joined to form the Socialist Youth Union in 1897 and publication of the newspaper *Fire* (*Brand*) had begun in 1898, the movement evolved under Bergegren's leadership along an increasingly antiparliamentary and revolutionary, semianarchistic course. One of the messages of the first *Brand* issue was that the parliamentary tactic "leads to hypocrisy, inertia, and cowardice. . . . The forces of democracy are impotent in the face of capitalist power. . . . Capitalist power can be overthrown only by the social revolution." There were also hints that isolated acts of violence might be justifiable. "Why not defend an action based on honest and noble emotion, even if it is forceful and violent? Think of how strong the oppression is—can it not elicit acts of violence?"

Propaganda for violence, sometimes articulated but usually veiled, appeared throughout the paper. In its relations with the party majority, however, the youth movement used evasive tactics. In response to criticism of their antiparliamentary agitation, the "young socialists" stressed that their movement did not absolutely repudiate the value of parliamentarianism, but that it wanted to keep the way clear for the revolutionary line as well. They pointed out that this attitude had been espoused by leading "conservative Social Democrats," and that their union thus worked in accordance with party traditions.

In the early 1900s a quickening of radicalism was noticeable in the youth movement. It was mainly expressed in antimilitary and antireligious propaganda. But a comparatively new element in revolutionary agitation had been added. As was the case briefly in the early 1890s, the idea of a revolutionary general strike became a rallying point for antiparliamentary factions. These adopted the plans for a large-scale strike which were upheld by the party as a whole, but wished to turn the proposed strike into a social revolution rather than use it only as a means of coercion for the franchise. In a few years this line of thinking would become a central question in the debate on tactics.

A more developed theory of a revolutionary general strike appeared, as far as we know, for the first time in 1903 in a long, unsigned series of *Brand* articles entitled "The General Strike and the Social Revolution." The series drew upon Swedish experiences to some extent, but its main inspiration was obviously syndicalist doctrine, primarily as conceived in France. To begin with, parliamentary tactics were subjected to detailed criticism. Such tactics, it was said, had never produced results of any value but had, on the contrary, led to neglect of the workers' movement. Revolution alone leads to the goal. However, the traditional form of revolution, "barricade revolution," is not practicable: the revolution must be economic and social, not only political in scope. The modern weapon is the general strike, which "is nothing more than the social revolution itself." It can paralyze all production, communication, and consumption. It is a matter of "forcing the total disorganization and destruction of the capitalist order of society and thereby its complete collapse, after which the proletariat, through the organs of its trade unions, will take over the means of production—all economic power." The general strike will automatically be transformed into a revolution when hunger drives the masses to action. Its advantage over direct violent action lies in the fact that "it can begin entirely legally and without danger to the proletariat. It can thus count on the support of several thousands who lack the courage to go out and fight on the streets." The military will ally itself with the people, and serious battles need not occur. Partial strikes are only of value as preludes to the general strike.

In the course of the following years, the general strike—together with antimilitaristic and antireligious features—became an important ingredient in the propaganda published in *Brand* under the editorships of both A. Jensen and Hinke Bergegren. In 1904 there appeared a translation of the anarchist Roller's pamphlet, *The Social General Strike,* which had served as a source for many *Brand* articles. At a congress held in 1905, the Socialist Youth Union issued the following pronouncement:

> With regrets that parliamentarianism has been advanced in the Social Democratic workers' movement as the only sure way toward the liberation of the working class . . . the Congress declares that societal developments increasingly indicate that the most effective weapon at present available to the working class in its struggle against a class society of mounting ruthlessness is the general strike, and the Congress urges all members of the Union to develop a vigorous agitation to disseminate among all of Sweden's workers the idea of the necessity of the use of this weapon.

Proposals of a strike against military service were linked to the idea of a general strike; we shall return to this question in another context. In the course of the following years, especially 1906–1908, the general strike was the subject of much heated discussion. The tactical conflict became in the main a conflict between the revolutionary general strike versus parliamentarianism.

The general strike provided antiparliamentary groups with a natural substitute for naked violence. It might even be said that the general strike was used as an ideological cover-up for the thought of violence, as a camouflage. As in French syndicalist discussions, the strike was advanced as a legal means which would therefore not immediately be countered by suppressive measures. At the same time, however, it was assumed that the strike would lead to open strife and thereby to revolution. As pointed out in *Brand* articles, the basically peaceful character of the strike would lure even those workers who recoiled from direct action onto the road to violence. Other concepts characteristic of syndicalism—such as the theories of a moral elite and the myth of a social stimulant—gradually clustered around the idea of a general strike, but these did not attain any importance until later, when the young socialists formed an independent party and syndicalism emerged as a special movement.

The idea of a general strike gained no support outside the young socialist movement. It was described as a form of anarchism and thereby as basically antisocialist. As a rule, those who divorced themselves from this idea went even further than the resolution passed by the International in 1904. The first comprehensive criticism seems to have been offered by Branting in a series of articles (largely based on a Dutch work by Mrs. Roland-Holst) that appeared in *Social-Demokraten* in 1906 and was later published in the form of a brochure. Branting wrote that, according to the Social Democrats, the working class can "overthrow the existing society only when the process of production has reached a certain degree of development which makes it ripe for a socialist system of production." As a means toward this "the proletariat must *seize the power in the state* and reform the state to suit its purposes." The anarchist basis of the thinking of proponents of the general strike was demonstrated by the fact that they never referred to the functions of government once socialism had been realized. "One can say that devotees of the general strike are economic *blanquister* who believe in the power of a sudden revolutionary *coup* to transform society. They fall into the very same unhistoric view from which Karl Marx, to his everlasting credit, liberated socialist theory." A general strike would be most dangerous to trade unionism. Interest in achieving limited improvements in the conditions of the workers would disappear. Local strikes would be regarded as preludes to a general strike and would therefore be extended in a way that would jeopardize their success. The new theory would impede the entire workers' movement by relegating to the background the idea of educating and organizing the masses for the exercise of political power. Branting agreed with Mrs. Roland-Holst that "the idea of a social-revolutionary general strike affects the mental state of the working masses in about the same way as *sensational novels affect youth*. It makes them overly tense, it closes their minds to the realities of the development of society, it destroys all healthy interest in daily life, and keeps them from the promising contest of the moment." Branting concluded his presentation by describing the theory of general strike as "a children's disease, and nothing more. . . . But not all of us have to suffer through all children's diseases, and our Swedish workers' movement really ought to be adult and mature enough not to be susceptible to such epidemics."

Other prominent Social Democratic newspapers followed the same line. *Arbetet* compared the belief in a general strike with belief in miracles, and declared that it was natural "that this new faith in miracles . . . should claim its most numerous and ardent followers in those countries where [the level of] popular enlightenment is lowest and where consequently all kinds of miracle worship flourish." *Ny Tid* stated that a general strike was unnecessary if the military and the general public allied themselves with the workers, and that it would be folly to attempt it if they did not.

The general strike was the object of particularly thorough criticism by two of the leaders in the new youth union, Höglund and Möller. Höglund expressed the same opinion as *Ny Tid:* if the great majority of the people had been won over to socialism, then a general strike would be superfluous; if not, it could hardly be carried out. It would be unreasonable to believe in the possibility of enticing the workers with the distant objectives of the general strike without attempting to secure more immediate advantages for them through parliamentary-political channels. Socialization would be possible if the workers won a majority and the power of government; they could then successively realize their demands through the machinery of government without encountering concentrated opposition from the capitalist class. But socialization could not be established through a coup. Even if a general strike should prove successful, the trade unions would not be able to take over production. Dock workers would not be able to manage a shipping business; miners did not have a command of the organization of ironworks.

After the expulsion of the young socialists from the party there was no propagandizing for a revolutionary general strike *within* Social Democratic circles. The large-scale strike of 1909 obviously had no revolutionary aims, and this was explicitly underscored by party leaders. During the subsequent period, the idea of a revolutionary strike was adopted primarily by the syndicalist movement organized in 1910, and also by the Young Socialist party, which emerged from the Socialist Youth Union in 1908.

The revolutionary and anarchist development of the young socialists in the early 1900s and, in particular, the formation in 1903 of a new youth movement that was better able to cooperate with the party leadership brought to the foreground the question of accommodation with the extreme minority. Its activities were frequently alleged to be detrimental to the party, and Branting and other party leaders repeatedly disavowed responsibility for the propaganda circulated by the young socialists. However, as long as the young socialists remained within the ranks of party membership, such disclaimers were relatively ineffective. Still, the party leadership was long reluctant to take drastic action. A proposal was advanced at the 1905 congress that would give the party administration the possibility to expel members; the proposal was patently directed at the young socialists. Pursuant to this, the administration prepared a resolution proposal asking that the congress confirm certain statements agreed upon at the 1891 congress: the repudiation of anarchism and the clause in the resolution on the violence question which stated that the party wished to use only such methods "as correspond to the people's natural sense of justice," and that the party regarded its present platform as testimony to the fact that it did not aspire to "a violent revolution." In addition, the congress ought to declare "its keen disapprobation of [a situation in which] persons who wish to consider themselves party members have conducted flagrantly antiparliamentary propaganda."

The remarkable thing about this proposal is that the party administration attempted to represent the parliamentary line as the traditional one for the party, and extracted only those statements from the rulings of the 1891 congress which supported this view. The administration was sharply criticized in ensuing debates on the ground that its proposal tended to split the party. On the other hand it was asserted (by, for example, Kata Dalström and Rydén) that an accommodation was necessary. A decision was made without a vote to strike the entire matter from the agenda. In all probability the administration abandoned its proposal for fear of shattering the party.

The presence at the congress of numerous partisans of the young socialists was demonstrated on another occasion. In a debate on socialist agitation among the military forces, Branting declared that the party would give its cooperation only to the Social Democratic youth movement, not to the young socialists. No fewer than 56 of the 173 delegates to the congress entered objections to this statement. There was, however, no evidence of sharp opposition from the young socialists during the rest of the congress.

Intraparty tension rose rapidly during the next few years. Toward the end of 1905 the young socialists published *The Yellow Peril* (*Gula Faran*), which explicitly called for terrorism. "Nothing is criminal to truly revolutionary socialists. . . . Our motto is: the dagger in the flesh." This publication was defended by Bergegren and Schröder, who were the most prominent figures within young socialist ranks at the time. The following year the police uncovered certain plans for a bank robbery that seemed to be connected with young socialist propaganda. Young socialist leaders were even supposed to have taken direct part in planning violence to individuals. The embittered strife between Social Democrats and young socialists that resulted from the discovery of the plans culminated in the administration's decision to suspend Bergegren and Schröder from the party for the time being. A definitive decision on the question was reached at the congress of 1908. Prior to the congress, a vote taken within the party revealed that 20,000 were in favor of expelling the two, and 8,000 were against expulsion. The congress ruled in accordance with the administration proposal, 227 to 69 in the case of Bergegren, and 233 to 44 in the case of Schröder. The spokesmen for the majority stressed throughout the debate that those who rejected parliamentarianism should not be members of the party. However, this question did not dominate the debate. The subject of most discussion was the tone of the publications issued by the young socialists and their attacks on individuals in particular. A statement issued by the administration declared that Bergegren and Schröder's "propaganda is obviously contrary to the established general principles of Social Democracy, which, following the pronouncements of the international congresses, include political and parliamentary action as one of the chief instruments in the struggle for a better order of society. . . ." It must be emphasized that Branting did not consider that belief in a general strike of itself disqualified one as a socialist, but that persons who believed *only* in a general strike naturally did not belong to the party. After the congress had adjourned, the young socialists united to form a party of their own.

This exposition indicates that party policy in regard to the methods to be used to obtain power underwent a fundamental change during the period under consideration. The main objective of the majority became political equality; revolutionary ideas faded into the background. The expulsion of the leading young socialists was to some extent connected with this change, but we must bear in mind that this was not the only source of friction between the Social Democrats and the young socialists. In 1891 a majority at the congress had renounced the anarchistic line without thereby rejecting revolutionary tactics; in 1908 it was possible to vote against the young socialists without supporting reformism.

As a matter of fact, there is no resolution, no program modification, no debate that can symbolize and substantiate the transformation in the party. The change was slow, and was not accompanied by definitive or salient declarations; in many instances, even those immediately concerned were probably not aware of the successive shifts in standpoint. The magnitude of the change is best illustrated by comparing the debates around 1890 with those that took place in 1900. The revolutionary or semirevolutionary statements that were commonplace around the 1890s have no counterparts in the large Social Democratic newspapers of a decade later. The "big" question of tactics is now considered only in exceptional cases, and then only in conjunction with a reassertion on principle of the reformist-pacifist line.

Branting had been of a democratic propensity from the start, and this bent grew stronger with time. His most comprehensive contribution to the franchise question, the pamphlet *The Franchise and the Workers' Movement* published in 1896, does, indeed, state that the franchise is not primarily a goal but a means for social reform, but there is no mention of revolutionary measures, whether to achieve democracy or to bring about socialism. In the Riksdag debates on the issue, Branting sometimes expressed himself with surprising moderation. In the 1899 Riksdag he justified the demand for the franchise in a manner that was hardly distinguishable from the Liberal approach; he based his defense on the principle of individuality and on the value of "equal political rights for all members of society." Universal suffrage was not as dangerous as its opponents believed. The experience of other nations showed that the oppressed classes did not use the vote to overthrow those in power. Branting gave Germany as an example. Here, those with power continued to be in power despite the franchise, "but the difference is that there the workers have . . . a way out whereby they can, on legal grounds and without disrupting the society, increasingly look after their interests as *they* see them, and not as their guardians see them." The wish to present universal suffrage as a reform that was harmless from a nonsocialist point of view is even more obvious in Branting's statements during the 1902 debate:

> The education of the masses is slow work. And while this educational work is in progress the workers will coincidentally come in touch with the realities of the society which they are sometimes a part of and sometimes not. They thereby get an opportunity to distinguish abstract schemes which—in the beginning, when they [the workers] were completely on the outside—may have seemed easy to carry out, but which, when they are to be translated into reality, reveal that they comprise a whole series of reforms that are to be implemented, first one and then the other. . . . Among the workers there are many who are conservative, liberal, radical, and socialist, in other words, all possible shades and groupings.

In a subsequent address at the same Riksdag, Branting emphasized that the strike for the franchise had not implied any threat; it had not been conceived "under the false impression that one could, in one assault, storm the gates behind which the ruling few had entrenched their privileges." This and later remarks suggested that a solution to the franchise question would strengthen nationalist sentiments. At times Branting did refer to the class struggle in the democratic society, but he concomitantly underscored his hopes that it could take place in a humane way. His many comments on the question contain very little that is provocative and nothing that bears the stamp of revolutionary phraseology. The same applies to Thorsson and Lindqvist's contributions to the Riksdag debates.

In *Social-Demokraten,* Branting and others time and again declared their unqualified support of the parliamentary line. A Branting editorial that appeared in 1903 asserted that a certain superiority vis-à-vis parliamentarianism was one of the children's diseases of the workers' movement. Such an attitude was especially natural wherever workers did not have the vote. In Sweden, however, it had been "completely repressed by the very struggle to secure the franchise." Several articles programmatically defended the whole reformist idea that Social Democracy would successively impregnate society through democratic forms. In a series of articles published in 1907, Ågren wrote that following the revolutionary line one would have "condemned at least one generation to increasing social torment." "Universal suffrage and the parliament are the safety valve on the social boiler; if it is present and is allowed to function, well, then there will be no explosion, no matter how much is written about a revolution; if it is not present, there is danger of an explosion, and then the tactic will be different."

Other publications representative of the party majority largely conform to this picture. As may be gathered from preceding pages, Danielsson was a convinced reformist during the years immediately before his death in 1899. Sterky most likely underwent a similar conversion. Signs of a change in his attitude can be traced as far back as 1892. His last published document, *Socialism, the Liberator of the Working Class* (1899), contains no references to the necessity of violence or revolutionary action; instead, emphasis is placed on the value of the franchise, not only from the educational standpoint that Sterky had advocated earlier, but as a means of gradually implementing the workers' demands. The Social Democratic press of the time used the word "revolution" to signify a peaceful reformation that would take place gradually. One could thus call oneself a revolutionary and at the same time repudiate all aims commonly regarded as revolutionary.

The condition essential to the development in the direction of pacifism, reformism, and democracy was the actual work devoted to winning the vote. There is good reason to speak in this context of the interaction between theory and practice. Agitation for the franchise could be conducted successfully only if the vote was presented as important. It was impossible to arouse followers to fight for democracy at the same time as one asserted that the objectives of the party could not be realized within the framework of democracy. In order to direct the attention of the groups controlling political power to the demands for democracy it was necessary to promise observance of the required conventions. One could not demand democracy and also imply that this same democracy would provide a base for revolutionary propaganda. The performance of the party and of Branting, in particular, at the Riksdag illustrates this point. Here one had to prove that democracy provided a safeguard against unparliamentary and illegal tendencies and even that it would probably not lead to a socialist takeover within the foreseeable future.

The above does not mean to imply that the party leaders changed their message without a concomitant change in their own views, that they simply pretended to be democrats. On the contrary. The internal imperative that carried the franchise movement into democracy, was also at work in the minds of the leaders. The idea of revolution, which had occupied a prominent place in their outlook in the 1880s, had faded into reminiscence or appeared as a dim possibility sometime in the future. They became democrats by working for democracy. To claim, with Sterky and Danielsson, that the struggle for the franchise and political power was valuable solely from an educational standpoint was tenable only under the condition that this struggle failed. Once one had won the vote and power, or rather, as soon as there was a possibility of winning them, this standpoint disappeared as if it were a phantom. In a way, therefore, these developments proved that the unmitigated revolutionary and antiparliamentary minority was right: the majority had become the captive of the very democracy it had formerly regarded as only a tactical instrument. The majority had lost the freedom it had thought it would be able to retain; the "big" question of tactics—peaceful versus revolutionary measures—solved itself in the course of the work on behalf of democracy.

Other factors helped accelerate the change in the party's attitude. Collaboration with nonsocialist democrats seemed natural under the circumstances, and this interplay tended to instill in Social Democrats some elements of the democratic principles that distinguished liberalism. The evolution of international socialism in a reformist and democratic direction also influenced the Swedish leaders. For various reasons, Branting—who had always inclined in this direction—acquired an increasingly stronger position in the party. In addition, the growth and consolidation of trade unionism demonstrated the possibilities of peaceful measures.

The party's development should also be considered from another point of view. Early Social Democratic debate had an element of unreality, of play; it was more akin to speculation, which did not entail any commitments, than to the evaluation of alternative plans. A general's staff without an army debated with the air of irresponsibility that comes with the certainty that direct action is impossible within the immediate future. The course of the debate was determined by the fact that the participants were young men without real practical experience or theoretical instruction who regarded some of the writings of Marx and Lassalle as the basis of all rational action. As long as the movement was of no consequence and could not exercise any influence, such a position was tenable. As the party grew, the situation changed. Its main support was derived from trade unions, which were striving for improvements in the living conditions of the working class. The thousands of workers who flocked to the party in the 1890s and early 1900s had a short-range interest in politics and were concerned with political and social reforms that could be quickly implemented. The fantastic aspect of the revolutionary ideas was then manifest. Even the organization of a large-scale political strike presented enormous difficulties. Here, as on other points, the doctrines of the leaders were adjusted to the wishes of the masses. Once the movement had gained sufficient influence to actually accomplish something the reformist line became predominant. Revolutionary ideas played a part as long as they could not conceivably be realized.

Lastly, the fact that its efforts in behalf of democracy made socialism democratic and that democratization itself could proceed peacefully was connected with the character of the Swedish government. To be sure, the worker's movement did encounter some opposition to its agitation and its endeavors to organize the working class, and it interpreted this as attempts at suppression. It is true that Social Democratic speakers and journalists were prosecuted and sentenced, that demonstrations and meetings were often obstructed by the police, that attempts to organize were hampered by private individuals whom the state could not prosecute under existing laws, and that some new legislation was passed curtailing the right to agitate in certain areas and prohibiting the use of certain weapons of combat, particularly in trade union conflicts. Yet it cannot be denied that political freedom was comparatively far-reaching. One might discuss whether or not the laws governing freedom of the press were occasionally used against the Social Democrats. The fact remains: the firm guarantees for freedom of the press prescribed by law were by and large respected, and even violent attacks charged with revolutionary threats to the *status quo* could be published without official intervention. Anyone who has studied the Swedish press of the 1880s and 1890s would consider it absurd to charge the Swedish government with suppression of this freedom, and the same applies to other areas of activity. The constitutional Swedish state, with its bureaucratic legalism, was less severe in its treatment of socialist endeavors than many other governments, including the democracies of France and the United States. The freedom that prevailed in Sweden provided a barren soil for the growth of a strictly revolutionary movement forged from a feeling of oppression.

The representative reform enacted 1907–1909 through the efforts of the Conservative Lindman cabinet came at a time when reformism was predominant among the Social Democrats. The reform signified a victory for the policy then being followed and thus reinforced the reformist line. Complete democracy had not been realized, but the opportunities available to the working class to exercise influence on the legislature had increased immeasurably. The right to vote for representatives to the lower house had been extended to comprise the great majority of adult males. The upper house became somewhat more democratic, but Conservative rule was maintained through the system of apportioning votes at local elections according to income and wealth. A proportional electoral system was introduced. The primary objective of the party became the complete democratization of the legislature and government.

The Social Democrats had accepted a democratic policy and might therefore be considered a democratic party—with one important reservation. As indicated in one of Branting's statements quoted earlier in this chapter, democracy still remained more a means than an end to the Social Democrats. They still regarded democracy primarily from a tactical viewpoint as being the best road to socialism. This meant that democracy was not firmly rooted in the party. It seemed conceivable that the party might again change policy and give priority to socialism if democratic methods did not prove practicable. In reality, the opposite took place. Democracy ceased to be a question of tactics; the new policy was socialism, but only if it could be achieved within the framework of democracy.

After passage of the franchise reform, the party continued its efforts to bring about complete democratization of the legislature. It held that the upper house ought to be abolished or restructured on the basis of universal and equal suffrage at local elections; the right to vote for representatives to the lower house ought to be extended to women and to those excluded by tax rate criteria. Social Democrats thought it self-evident that even the executive branch have a democratic foundation. Gradually and with increasing decisiveness, the Social Democrats allied themselves with the liberal party's demand for parliamentary formation of cabinets. The second Liberal cabinet, 1911–1914, was supported by the Social Democrats. When, in February 1914, this cabinet was forced to resign because of its conflict with the king, both Liberals and Social Democrats bitterly attacked what they considered an attempt to revive the personal power of the monarch. World War I, however, temporarily helped reduce tensions in regard to constitutional as well as other conflicts.

Party activity consistently adhered to parliamentary-reformist policy. Of special note is the party's view of the comprehensive strike of 1909 as economic in nature. Social Democrats most firmly dismissed all charges that they wished to use the strike as an instrument to gain political power. The strike itself was characterized by the workers' quiet, disciplined performance.

This period did not produce any thorough-going debate on party tactics or on its position in regard to democracy. However, a discussion that took place in the lower house during the 1909 Riksdag is of interest. The discussion, provoked by an interpellation, brought up the question of the aims of the Social Democrats and in particular their position on the use of legal versus revolutionary tactics.

Prime Minister Lindman asserted that the Social Democrats could not be compared with other political parties because their aim was the abolition of the existing society. The Social Democrats still harbored a revolutionary line. However, the government considered that, by virtue of existing and proposed legislation it "has sufficient resources at its disposal to counter violence to itself if only the laws are applied without indulgence and the resources that the state has at its disposal are used. Therefore, should the Social Democrats seek to realize their teachings through the way of violence, they must be prepared for the consequences."

Several leading Social Democrats rejected the allegation that the party contained revolutionary tendencies. Lindblad maintained that the party did not believe in the possibility of reorganizing the economic system through a violent upheaval but added that a peaceful course of development was dependent on the willingness of the established classes to reform. Hamilton, the minister of the interior, interpreted this as an acknowledgment that the party was prepared to resort to violence if its objectives could not be realized through peaceful measures; Lindman's comments were in a similar vein. Referring to the platform established in 1897, Branting took exception to the idea that the party aimed at revolution and that society would need to resort to special measures to protect itself. Branting claimed that Lindblad had only wished "to emphasize that the roads a surging popular movement may take are ultimately decided by those in power. And this is not a matter for dispute with one sole Social Democrat, but with all of history, which testifies [to the truth] that if one societal class all too insolently and all too long opposes the people's demands, then it bears the responsibility if developments follow not peaceful but violent paths." Sv. Persson and N. Berg, speaking in Stockholm and the town of Munkfors respectively, upheld parliamentary tactics without reservation. Persson declared that the use of violence would surely mean the downfall of the party and that the parliamentary course was the only feasible one. "And the tactics that we who are called the leaders have embraced in this case [are the tactics] we have always embraced. We have never encouraged the workers to use any methods of violence in their social struggle."

The dissensions that gradually developed between the party leadership and the new Social Democratic Youth Federation formed in 1903 to some extent concerned the value of reformist tactics. There was no sharp, deep schism between the two, as there had been between the Social Democratic majority and the young socialist minority within the party. The youth movement upheld parliamentary methods and did not conduct any propaganda for violence. As previously noted, the leaders of the movement definitively rejected anarchist and syndicalist ideas. The dissensions that did arise concerned the nature of parliamentary activity, the "minor" tactics, and they sometimes assumed the character of disagreement on principle. Leaders of the youth movement such as Höglund and Ström demanded that party representatives in the Riksdag call for radical reforms; they were critical or dubious about collaboration with the Liberals; and they were particularly anxious that future plans overrule the expediencies of daily politics. We may state schematically that this group wished to gain power through parliamentary means—although not entirely without reservations—but that it concentrated on the takeover of power more rigorously than did the "right wing" of the party. Its point of view was reminiscent of the positions held by Sterky and others twenty years previously. Just as Sterky had wished to use political activity as an instrument for agitation and education, so the leaders of the youth movement regarded parliamentary work primarily as a means of attaining the power necessary to the realization of socialism.

In the early 1910s the dissension became more fundamental. It expressed itself in part in the debate on "cabinet socialism," and in part in the general attitude to parliamentary activity. The publication of the youth federation defended parliamentary pursuits but warned against overestimating their value and against concentrating on scoring successes in the Riksdag. For example, in an article entitled "The Value of Parliamentarianism," Höglund wrote that the young socialists' criticism of parliamentary work had contained "some requisites of truth" and that the danger of overestimating the potential of parliamentary efforts did exist. Höglund continued, somewhat unclearly, to state that The Social Question would be solved "through" the Riksdag, not "by" the Riksdag, "but only by the exploited classes themselves, who must be organized, socialistically educated, and determined in purpose in order to benefit from political power." One ought not to compromise in order to gain minor victories and convince others that the party is harmless. "For these gains are bought at the expense of something far more valuable: our clear, irreconcilable position of opposition to the whole bourgeois society. . . . The most important parliamentary task of the Social Democrats at present is . . . socialist agitation on a grand scale." Democracy was described as a means of implementing socialism, not as an "end in itself." This viewpoint had to be kept alive in the struggle for democracy. At times Höglund hinted that perhaps not even total democracy would suffice for the realization of socialism, but that it was nevertheless the first requisite for such a realization.

The same general trend of thought—distrustful of parliamentarianism although not directly antiparliamentary—was expressed, for example, in articles written by Lindhagen, who had now aligned himself with the party's left wing. Still more extreme articles appeared in *The Storm Warning* (*Stormklockan*). Shortly before the elections of 1911, Hannes Sköld wrote that winning seats in the Riksdag was of little import, that the Social Democrats in the Riksdag should use this tribunal simply as an arena for agitation, and that the first concern was to win over "not the national parliament but the parliament of the streets, the masses, the working class."

The 1912 congress rejected a proposal in which the youth federation would have declared itself against the statement formulated by the 1891 congress regarding "the possibility that organized violence could be the ultimate liberator of the suffering proletariat." In the course of the attendant debate, representative speakers contended that one should not completely reject the idea of using violent methods under certain circumstances. Some moderate party publications accused the youth federation of plainly revolutionary tendencies —without doubt an exaggerated supposition.

The intensification of the conflict between the party leadership and the youth federation that finally ruptured the party in 1917 was in part due to the dissension described. Of particular importance was the resolution of the congress convened by the youth federation in 1916 to prepare for the use of extraparliamentary, possibly even revolutionary methods in the event of war. The fact that the party leadership would have no part of this resolution signified that it repudiated revolutionary tendencies.

Elimination of the minority, which emerged as an independent, Left Socialist party, tended to secure the supremacy of parliamentary-democratic principles in Social Democracy. Nevertheless, different circumstances pushed the question of the use of extraparliamentary measures into the foreground during the period immediately following the party split. In the spring of 1917 and late in the autumn of 1918, the idea of revolution or, in any case, of extraparliamentary action on a large scale acquired a new urgency. Yet the objective on both occasions was complete democracy; there was no thought of "social" revolution.

The revolutionary tendencies current in the spring of 1917 were most likely mainly stimulated by the high cost of living and by difficulties in obtaining food. A bitter mood of discontent prevailed, and in many places it gave rise to spontaneous so-called hunger demonstrations, which sometimes ended in street fights and incidents with the police. Social Democrats and even Liberals regarded the policies of the Hammarskjöld cabinet as inept and probably anticipated that the formation of a leftist government that must follow a democratic breakthrough—that is, the democratization of the upper house and the monarch's recognition of parliamentarianism—would be able to alleviate conditions. But the Social Democrats must also have seen the necessity of exploiting popular discontent to the party's advantage by conducting a radical opposition—a view that gained particular importance because of the competition offered by the Left Socialist party. Resentment at the high cost of living could in this way be translated into the demand for prompt democratic reforms. Finally, as in other countries, the Russian Revolution also helped create a revolutionary climate of opinion.

Party spokesmen in the Riksdag made statements containing little-disguised threats of violence. The first such statement occurred in the course of the debate on the abolition of "the forty-vote scale," [A system of apportioning votes at elections to the upper house whereby one elector could receive as many as forty votes depending on the size of his income.] that is, on the democratization of the upper house. Hallén then spoke of "a revolutionary mood among the people that is erupting under the pressure of the growing poverty in thousands of homes." If the upper class does not sacrifice its political privileges, he continued (with the full endorsement of his fellow Social Democrats), "then the political struggle in our country, whether or not we ourselves so desire, will absolutely be fought with entirely different weapons which, as the experience of history and of modern times bears witness to, will sweep away the last remnants of reactionary rule in our nation." Branting offered the same line of reasoning, if more moderately expressed:

> It is certain and true that in this nation we ought and wish to shape our development to the greatest possible extent in accordance with the loyal, completely legal course that has of old been a good Swedish tradition—I am certain that I have behind me the full support of the party whose chairman I am honored to be when I express this absolute loyalty to peaceful paths. But situations exist in which the obstinacy and obdurate blindness of the opposition force even those who would pursue these paths to deliberate on how to break this opposition.

Some weeks later Social Democrats criticized the establishment of a kind of safety corps to supplement the regular police force in the event of public disturbances (particularly the May Day demonstrations). Social Democrats pledged their cooperation in maintaining order, but also intimated that the revolutionary mood of the people could become dangerous if provoked by the use of extraordinary measures.

At the same time, Branting directed an interpellation to Prime Minister Swartz in which he exhorted the government to abolish the forty-vote scale and introduce universal suffrage for men and women at elections to the lower house. In this context, he cited the Russian Revolution and the democratic movements in Germany, Austria, and Hungary. Branting asserted that Swedish workers would not accept deferment of the realization of democratic demands for an indeterminate period. Consideration of "peace in society and the possibility of harmony among our people" should induce the cabinet and the majority in the upper house to assist in bringing about constitutional revision.

Branting's interpellation was answered June 5. Swartz called attention to the impending elections to the lower house. A large demonstration outside the Riksdag, which led to large-scale intervention by the police, underscored the gravity of the situation. By this time, however, the vague plans for extraparliamentary action which the Social Democrats had previously contemplated had receded to the background, and Branting stressed that the elections to the lower house should prove decisive to the solution of the constitutional question.

The semirevolutionary climate found its main expression outside of the Riksdag. The resolution adopted at the May Day demonstrations had an ominous ring: "Let those in power know that in times such as these the working class will not hesitate for one moment to use the weapons that may prove necessary to break the opposition of a ruthless, class-egoistic few if [these few] by means of unjust money minimums continually attempt to block progress." *Arbetet* commented that the resolution was intended to remind those in power that the people "are staunchly determined to seize their rights by force if they are denied."

May 7 a so-called working committee was established by the executive committee of the party administration, the confidential council of the Riksdag group, and the Secretariat of the Confederation of Trade Unions (*Landssekretariatet*). The committee was composed of seven members, with Branting as chairman. Its task was to unite the popular movement "and direct it in the manner [that ensures] the most lasting benefits for the whole workers' movement." Of first concern was the transformation of the hunger demonstrations into demonstrations for democratization. The committee's circulars urged the workers to avoid "meaningless attacks" but also intimated a readiness to resort to methods other than parliamentary ones, "Threats are alien to us," declared circular 1. "But we are familiar enough with the mood of the people throughout the nation. Recently, on May 1, the working class demonstrated its capacity for self-discipline in a most admirable fashion. But when these masses now demand their due rights—who could believe that they would permit themselves to be dismissed with a no or with evasive words, or with a little finger, when it is the whole hand that must be given."

Following the prime minister's response to the interpellation on the constitutional question, the committee issued a statement declaring that elections to the lower house ought to decide the solution to the question. The committee reported that the question of arranging "a political general strike movement" had been discussed, but that such a movement had not been considered appropriate or feasible. It pointed out that industry was working under difficult conditions, and that a large-scale strike would therefore probably cause a shutdown of many business concerns, with the likelihood that they would not reopen within the near future. The *Landssekretariat* had firmly rejected the idea of a large-scale strike for this reason.

The existence of sharp divisions of opinion within the party leadership was revealed in the remarkable debates that took place at the meeting of the party administration May 20–23, 1917. Here the revolutionary issue was openly and thoroughly discussed. Palmstierna was the first speaker to call for an investigation of the situation from this point of view: "The question is not . . . large-scale strike. Instead, we are faced with the question of revolution. Have we examined the possibility of this? If it is shown that no possibilities exist, then we need only record this. The speaker was sceptical about the possibility, but an investigation should be made. . . ."

Rydén was more positive. Social Democrats would forfeit a historic moment if the battle did not continue "with all the means at our disposal." If the Conservative cabinet remained and refused to accede to the demands presented in Branting's interpellation, Social Democrats would have to resort to force. "The natural first step will be a general work stoppage ordered by the political leaders; trade union leaders can and should be kept out of it. The speaker was not blind [to the possibility] that such a work stoppage could culminate in something else. Then there is the question of the position of the military forces. The officers' corps is against us, and the dependable ones have been removed. But the bulk of enlisted men and junior officers is on our side, and in such a struggle we could with certainty count on the cooperation of a great many bourgeois elements." Recoiling at the thought of the sacrifices would accomplish nothing. One had to be ready to use methods "that decisive times might necessitate." Several of the younger leaders, such as P. A. Hansson, Möller, and Sandler, took roughly the same stand.

Leaders of the trade union movement, Lindqvist, Söderberg, and Thorberg, for example, definitely advised against large strikes and revolutionary attempts. Lindqvist contended that "the people will not get more bread or shorter working hours through large-scale strikes or revolutions." Thorberg attacked revolutionary proposals as unreasonable from a practical standpoint. "The mood that has been created in the nation may compel the preposterous to happen as a punishment to the people and as a warning to various agitators. But we should all clearly understand that we are not equipped for a battle using all methods." Thorsson could not concur with "Rydén's view that from the start activities should have 'a revolutionary orientation,' so to speak. One large-scale strike with support is unthinkable, another large-scale strike results in revolution." C. E. Svensson and Åkerberg, among others, held a moderate line. The latter offered the reminder that the popular movement had emerged from the people's need and that the random plundering that accompanied revolution would only aggravate that need. Branting made an appeal for unity. His comments on the heart of the matter were designed to mend the differences between the contending groups. "It is proper that the people's movement be rumbling outside. It is the backbone of our influence. If the others have some respect for this mood of the people, we should understand how to use this, and we ought to make it clear that the moment the Right takes a brusque attitude of rejection, we will renounce all further responsibility for developments."

The outcome of the debate was a resolution that was adopted without a vote and which represented a victory for the moderate line. The party administration expressed "its certainty and expectation that the mood among the working class which now assumes such strong expressions, will prevail until a thorough constitutional reform has been secured even in our nation and thereby the foundation for a true democratic order under which our people, unfettered by unjust privileges for the few, can carry out the vital social reforms that the times require." It was accordingly established that the popular movement which the party had previously attempted to strengthen and incite would not be used for revolutionary action. The main consequence of the people's movement and of the party's participation in the movement was undoubtedly, as intimated in the annual report of the party administration, an improvement in Social Democratic prospects at the elections to the lower house in 1917.

The constitutional question came to the fore at these elections. In a manifesto issued prior to the elections, the Social Democratic party demanded, with extraordinary severity, the abolition of the forty-vote scale and the establishment of universal suffrage for the election of representatives to the lower house. "Does not our nation smart with shame [at the fact] that, when all of Europe augurs the breakthrough of democracy and liberation as never before, our Swedish people should nonetheless patiently remain under the guardianship of the rule of business and estate holders, of big capitalism and bureaucracy, all welded together in the majority that now sits in the upper house." If the elections scored a victory for the Left, further resistance to a reform should be precluded. "To engage in attempts to again brush aside the demands of the people would, under such circumstances, constitute such brazen defiance that it would almost certainly rally all of Sweden's working people to a movement far more serious than that which this spring elicited the recognition that the elections should now be considered decisive."

After the election victory and the formation of the Liberal-Socialist government, all revolutionary tones disappeared from Social Democratic agitation for a while. This was most likely the result of several interacting circumstances. The change in government alleviated the anxiety of the masses; the Liberals rejected extraparliamentary methods; the Bolshevik revolution changed the Russian example from a model to a warning; the democratic movements in Germany and Austria did not, as anticipated, meet with immediate success. The Finnish Civil War also tended to modulate the prevailing mood toward caution. It is important to remember that in their discussion of the Finnish war, Social Democrats emphatically stated that a revolution was under no circumstances justifiable in a democratic nation. The only revolutionary elements in the debates on the constitutional issue at the regular session of the Riksdag of 1918 were those injected by the Left Socialists. In response to a Conservative charge that the Social Democrats were guilty of revolutionary tendencies, Engberg, a representative of the party, declared that "Swedish Democracy, in its nucleus here in the Riksdag, is not going to avail itself of extraparliamentary measures unless the Right pursues policies that make such measures simply unavoidable."

In answer to Left Socialist criticism that the party was unwilling to use forceful methods—their immediate argument concerned a check on taxation and appropriation by the lower house—Branting declared that such methods could not be employed without Liberal support. "For my part I do not doubt that, confronted by continued obstinacy from the Right on this question, a sufficient number even within the Liberal party will become convinced that one cannot stand and tread on the same spot." However, the government's proposals on the constitutional question were rejected without any special attempts to force concessions from the Conservatives. Special attention should also be paid to the fact that the manifesto issued prior to the county council elections in March 1918 did, to be sure, vigorously advocate democratization but it in no way suggested that extraparliamentary methods might be used.

The situation again changed in the autumn of 1918. The victories of the Western powers and the revolutions in Germany and Austria-Hungary influenced public opinion in the same direction that the Russian revolution had done one and a half years before. As the party administration noted in its annual report, the Left now believed that "the societal groups that opposed the struggle for democratization in our nation and that were concentrated in the upper house . . . lost their stronghold in the world concomitantly with the overthrow of the German reactionism, and they must realize themselves that any attempt to keep Sweden as a kind of reactionary oasis in Europe is doomed to failure." In mid-September the government gave notice that it would again attempt to effect a constitutional revision, and that the question of reform of the franchise at local elections would be presented at an extraordinary session of the Riksdag.

A resolution passed at a number of meetings arranged by the Social Democrats contained threats of revolutionary action which went much further than any previously published statements. It maintained that "the organized violence in the Europe of capitalism and autocracy . . . had fallen on its own sword." The rule of the few was being abolished everywhere, and the people were on the verge of a new era. "The moment has come for action to realize and secure a democratic and socialist order, to be reached by lawful paths. But if we indicate these [paths] as preferable from all points of view, then the Swedish working class must anticipate, now as always, that the attitude of the privileged classes may steer developments along entirely different paths which may force the workers and others among the common people to mobilize all the force they can muster to break the opposition. The responsibility for such an undesirable turn of events would then rest on those societal groups which stubbornly and without appreciating what the situation here and elsewhere in the world requires oppose the demands and needs of the new era." The resolution urged the party administration and Riksdag representatives "to organize immediately an action that will without delay break the opposition of the privileged classes and lead to full democracy in Sweden's societal life." The resolution further set up minimum demands: democratization of the legislature, a referendum to conclusively decide the question of the establishment of a republic, and a series of other reforms, such as the eight-hour work day and discontinuation of compulsory military exercises. Perhaps the most unusual feature of the resolution is its wording, indicating that the threat of extraparliamentary action was not limited to the implementation of democracy, but applied to other reforms as well. It even referred to "action toward the realization and securing of a democratic and *socialist* order." Yet it is certain that, in effect, the threat of revolution was considered justified only because democracy was not complete. The conclusion of the manifesto contains a definite declaration of principle for democracy that repudiates "Bolshevik-antidemocratic speculations of an Eastern pattern." Perhaps politics dictated the use of vague, ambiguous wording. Especially in view of the keen competition offered by the Left Socialists, it may have seemed politic to link the demand for democratization to other popular reforms.

A manifesto published November 15 following deliberations between the party administration and the representative body of the Swedish Confederation of Trade Unions (*Landsorganisationen*) generally repeated the demands in the resolution just discussed. Special reference was made to the German revolution. There was mention of the possibility of special "measures to look after the rightful demands of the working class," but there was also a warning against "every dictatorship of a minority, irrespective of the social class in whose name it rules." The conclusion of the manifesto emphasized that opposition to the demands laid down would only result in an increase of those demands.

On November 23 the cabinet bill on the question of the franchise in local elections was introduced in the Riksdag. During the special "referral" debate before the question was remitted to a committee, Branting declared that no essential part of the current demands could be surrendered. If attempts were made to pare down the program, the parliamentary course would no longer be practicable: "the Right itself would realize, if it looked around, that we of the Social Democratic party here in the Riksdag have no possibility whatever of holding back the storm which, in such a case, would spontaneously break over the nation." While the Riksdag was deliberating the constitutional question, the Social Democratic press was ominous in tone. It openly proclaimed that revolution was inevitable if the Conservatives did not accede to the demands. The government program was frequently characterized as a minimum program which in no way lent itself to bargaining; even the demand for a republic was described as urgent.

Even though the Riksdag deliberations resulted in a settlement that somewhat modified the demands of the left, the fundamental demand for democratization emerged completely victorious. Party leaders could thus actively support the settlement reached by the Riksdag committee and, at the same time, stress the necessity of additional constitutional reforms in the future. A manifesto signed by the party administration, the representative body of the Confederation of Trade Unions, and the Riksdag group expressed regrets that certain concessions to the Right had to be made. "But we have regarded it as our duty to act in such a way that the Swedish working class, except for absolutely compelling reasons, need not assume difficult and inestimably great sacrifices, as might have been the case if the differences had remained irreconcilable to the last."

Since the democratization of the legislature enacted in 1918 and implemented during the ensuing years through constitutional reforms and the attendant complete breakthrough of parliamentarianism, the Social Democratic party has not sustained any ideas of revolution or of any extraparliamentary action. Democracy has been accepted without reservation as a working form of government; the possibility of a social revolution in the sense of a seizure of power by extraparliamentary means to achieve socialism has been repudiated.

This position was crystallized in the debates that took place 1918–1920. The Russian Communist regime and the attempt to establish communism in Finland through violence gave the party's spokesmen cause to explicitly state their views. Efforts to bring about socialism by undemocratic methods were criticized on two grounds, as deviations from the course charted by Marx, and also as deviations from democratic principles. Marx, it was said, based his thinking on the supposition that socialism could be realized only when it came to be embraced by a majority of the people as a result of socioeconomic developments. The dictatorship of the proletariat that Marx had in mind was a socialist majority rule according to democratic forms, not a dictatorship of a minority. To try to socialize society without majority support was to try to move ahead of developments, to force through socialism before society was ripe for it. Such an attempt must necessarily be transitory; the illusory nature of the socialist victory would be revealed and a capitalist regime would be reinstated. "Socialism cannot be forced ahead as thought it was an artificial hothouse plant," wrote Karleby, who concisely expressed this line of thinking; "it must grow in freedom, strong and firmly rooted in the needs of society. An attempt at dictatorship before economic realities provide the genuine conditions for the political rule of the working class can endure for a while, though subjecting the revolution to enormous dangers." The manifesto issued by the party in reaction to the Finnish Civil War in 1918 vented the same view:

> An armed uprising against a national assembly chosen by the people on the basis of the broadest suffrage in a nation where the people's democratic right to self-determination seems so firmly rooted that it cannot be threatened in the future ex-

cept possibly by external violence—to us such a deed represents a denial of the fundamental concept of democracy, a proclamation of the violent might of a minority over a majority of the people, which could be turned against us by every privileged rule of the few or capitalist dictatorship. . . . This entire view is ultimately derived from the anarchist illusion of the creative power of "the purposeful minorities," although ever since the days of Marx, socialism has contradicted this by its teaching that the new society must not be the work of a few guardians but of the socialistically enlightened working class itself.

Branting's speech on "Democracy or Dictatorship" held at the meeting of the Stockholm workers' commune, October 28, 1919, is an authoritative declaration of the party's predemocratic spirit. Before World War I workers' movements in all nations strived with growing determination for the democratic cause and for practicable reforms within a democratic framework. The war had caused certain groups in the movement to revert to primitive, long-discussed currents of thought. Foremost among these was Bolshevism, which, said Branting, with its doctrine of the expropriation of property by violence, "regresses to the time before Marxist theories." "The whole developmental idea of socialism is discarded in Bolshevism." The Swedish party had always connected socialism with democracy. "But now one protests that democracy is just humbug, formal democracy, dictatorship of the middle class. Yes, but it is nevertheless a fact that we Social Democrats have always pointed out that political freedom and political democracy are not enough. Our goal is a new system of production that eliminates the class difference characterized by poverty on the one hand and wealth on the other. Now one wants us to throw away what democracy there is. Should one instead not try to make democracy penetrate deeper and bring about true equality?" It would be dangerous to attenuate the workers' democratic sentiments, for then the other classes might recapture their lost power. "There is no doubt that democracy will facilitate the implementation of socialism at the same time as it educates and trains the workers [to deal with] general and immediate problems. The [degree of] maturity of the working class can be ascertained from the decisions that enjoyment of universal suffrage will yield. These decisions will also indicate when the working class is [sufficiently] mature to proceed to a socialist order."

An article by Möller that propounded the precepts for the party's tactics delivered a sharp criticism of the very concept of "social revolution." Socialization meant a change in the system of production, which was possible at a certain stage of development. In order not to disturb the production process, this change must take place successively and over a long period of time. In a democracy the prerequisite for the onset of socialization would be majority support of socialism. It would be absurd to term such a change a revolution, for revolution meant just the opposite of evolution—a certain method of quickly effecting an upheaval, not a slow process of development. The revolutions that the Bolsheviks brought about or sought to bring about were really revolutions in the ordinary sense of the term—attempts to enforce the socialist society without delay. Such revolutions could only cause a disruption of production and the entrance of a reaction. "That is to say, social revolution conceived as a shortcut to the socialist society would prove to be a typical back road. 'The social revolution' is, in other words, nonsense." Möller's article was criticized by the Social Democrats on the basis of Marx's conceptual scheme, but even Möller's critics approved his fundamental ideas.

Engberg, another young theorist, based his unconditional support of democracy on other propositions more closely connected with Marx's thinking. For socialism, democracy was not an end in itself but rather "a more rational basis for the class struggle." Socialism's demand for incipient nationalization of the means of production was in harmony with the purpose inherent in the historical forces of development. "But it is just here that democracy becomes of decisive importance. The struggle for the state is political. Its outcome is therefore to a very great extent contingent upon the possibility open to society's members—whose proletarianism has been brought about by the capitalist process—to exercise their proper influence on political decision-making. If democracy is achieved, the growth of capitalism means a corresponding mobilization of voices *against* the capitalist system itself. Democracy therefore contains an automatically operative device that heightens the opposition to capitalism in proportion to the development of capitalism."

Engberg apparently envisioned a continued capitalist development that would be accompanied by proletariarization and growth of the socialist party. In a later article he declared: "We now dare to state, however, that if full political democracy prevails in a society, that is, if the interests that really exist can be faithfully translated into influence on the government, adjustment of political vestments according to conditions of production need never take the form of revolution. . . . In other words, after the victory of political democracy, the working class ought to dispel the idea of a violent upheaval."

An essay written by Wigforss in 1920 represents one of the most subtle, reflective insights into the problems at that time. The essay was intended as a point of departure for a thorough discussion, but such a discussion never materialized. Wigforss was somewhat sceptical of the generally accepted view that under a democratic system the position adopted by the majority in the Riksdag would be a sure indication as to whether the people were ready for socialism or not. "A people that is not ready for socialism because one half of them plus one vote *against* [it] will not be ready if one half of them plus one vote *for* it." It would be more logical to regard the majority principle as a rule of the game, brought into play to provide for the maintenance of peace in society. Yet if one accepted this, it would also be natural to demand that in the competition for votes, no party or line have a starting handicap. As a rule, however, the requirements of democracy did not go this far, for this "would, of course, mean *advance rejection* of *all* the real privileges which it is precisely our intention to eliminate with the help of the majority won [in the legislature]." Nonetheless, certain minimum conditions were required to prevent too great a disparity between the prospects of the various lines. A certain amount of instruction for all citizens was needed if they were to form opinions on different social issues. To attain this, greater economic equality was also needed. The same applied to the area of industrial production. "Society rests on economic foundations to such a great extent that for the power of government to be in the hands of those who own nothing while the economically dominant are politically powerless must be considered an anomaly and can be regarded only as a transitional stage." Wigforss therefore believed that, together with universal suffrage, increased economic and industrial democracy represented the minimum conditions for a peaceful development. To thus complement that which had already been gained a certain amount of extraparliamentary pressure might be needed, even under formal democracy; this, however, in no way implied revolution. Wigforss continued along more general lines: consideration of the minority, or rather, of the minorities, was necessarily linked to a democratic order; as was true of national or religious groups, a group united by economic interests demands a certain amount of respect for its interests, even if it is in the minority and cannot be expected to willingly comply with majority decisions under all conditions.

These expositions reveal two different, if not altogether clearly defined lines of thought. According to one, democracy represents an opportunity for socialism, once it has acquired sufficient strength, to take over the power of government and put socialization into operation. The triumph of socialism is regarded as the consequence of an economic development that brings the majority of the people in a capitalist society into the socialist fold. According to the second line, the role of Social Democracy is gradual, progressive reform within the framework of the existing regime. It presupposes a certain mutual respect between social classes of one another's "rights," and that, even when it has won a majority, socialism will strive for mutual understanding and agreement with other groups by granting them certain guarantees, a certain "autonomy," to use somewhat of an overstatement. There is no question of a "victory," "a power takeover," in the usual sense.

These lines of thinking are related to two competing currents in democratic ideology: the majority principle and the tolerance principle. As a rule, democracy is thought of as a combination of these principles: it is the majority that decides, but within certain limits. This was a natural combination to the liberal mind, but it posed a problem for socialists, with their demands for subversive measures. Wigforss' parallel between societal classes on the one hand and national and religious groups on the other is illuminating. In theory, application of the tolerance principle to national and religious groups does not present a problem as long as there exists a desire for continued association. But its application to societal classes, strictly speaking, means retaining the *status quo*. Since socialism's goal is to change the *status quo* by political action—notwithstanding the thoughtless but often cited idea that politics only mirrors economic conditions—it cannot accept the tolerance principle in its liberal form. The tension thereby produced can, from one point of view, be said to be the core of the socialist position on the problem of democracy.

It would be superfluous to demonstrate through citations that Social Democracy maintained and gave increasing emphasis to its democratic position during the following years. Every manifesto, every speech, every document that treated democratic questions testifies to this. As the party leader affirmed at the 1932 party congress, "To Social Democracy, democracy is the *principle, the vital air,* the only order under which its ideals can be realized in spirit and substance, the only way in which human beings who are free and enjoy equal rights can live together in society." Around 1920 one might have been tempted to think that the strong emphasis on the value of democracy was due partly to the recent and complete establishment of this governmental form and partly to the expectation that democracy would soon lead to measures of a more truly socialist nature. In reality, democracy has instead become more firmly rooted in Social Democracy since it has been shown that democracy will not result in socialism within the near future. This development should be viewed in light of the Social Democrats' attenuation of their specifically socialist demands or deferment of the same to an indefinite future. It would be only a slight exaggeration to claim that democracy has filled the ideological void left by socialism. In studying Social Democratic newspapers and pamphlets one is struck by the fact that some decades ago the value-charged word above all others was "socialism"; now, it is "democracy." This can largely be explained by an international trend that has placed Social Democracy on the defensive and by the threat that Social Democracy perceives in the new ideologies that have had demonstrable success in other countries. There is a great difference between the Social Democracy that regarded itself as history's chosen ruler of the future and the Social Democracy that has witnessed the destruction of a series of powerful sister organizations in other countries and that must consider the repulsion of modern dictatorial movements as one of its main objectives. As did the example of Bolshevism before, so have the later examples of Fascism and National Socialism heightened the Social Democrats' cognizance of democracy. It should be remembered, however, that the consolidation of the democratic line in Social Democracy is paralleled by the acceptance of democracy by the Swedish Conservatives. Interaction between the two parties has generally secured the position of democracy. The predominant trend in Swedish politics has been a convergence toward the middle, not the provocation of extremist tendencies.

The construction of a special Social Democratic ideology has followed the acceptance and use of democratic forms. Not that the Social Democrats to any important degree enlarged upon the justifications for democracy that had previously been advanced by adherents of differing currents of thought. Democracy per se became the subject of theoretical discussion and reflection. Early Social Democrats characteristically viewed democracy as a better and safer way to attain socialism than revolutionary subversion. In their support of democracy, their successors have displayed the kind of dedication that had once been reserved for only socialist doctrine. One gets the impression that only during recent decades have the Social Democrats discovered—and from time to time proclaimed with the joy of discovery—the special ideology of democracy.

Most important has been the realization that democracy presupposes cooperation, settlement of differences, reciprocal concessions. One indication of the Social Democrats' outlook is that one of the party's young theorists, referring to a work by Morley (one of English liberalism's classic figures), wrote a systematic defense of compromise as the working formula of democracy. Still more significant is the fact that the party leadership and Social Democratic governments have consistently justified important proposals by citing democracy's vital need of resolving differences through mutual understanding. (This, of course, does not mean to imply that the proposals mentioned can be regarded as concerted solutions from a factual point of view.) Examples of this approach are the proposals on national defense in 1925 and 1936 and the agreement reached on emergency policies in 1933. The second Social Democratic cabinet described itself as a "Swedish popular national government." The 1936 coalition cabinet, formed under Social Democratic leadership, introduced its policy statement with these words: "in a time of unrest and insurrections in the life of people and nations, when democratic and parliamentary governmental forms have been displaced or threatened by dictators, it appears more imperative than ever to safeguard popular self-government in our own nation by providing the broadest possible support for the work of the government." The interesting part of this pronouncement is not the desire for concord per se but its designation as an essential ingredient in a democratic system. In similar fashion—as the following discussion will reveal—the Social Democratic standpoint on the problem of principle regarding parliamentary cabinet formation has been contingent upon the desire that the system function; the problem was viewed not only from the party standpoint but also from the standpoint of democracy.

P. A. Hansson gave these viewpoints particularly forceful emphasis. Branting's successor as party leader followed the line laid down by Branting during the debates on the franchise. Branting had spoken of a relaxation of tensions and collaboration after the franchise had been won. Hansson began with the premise that Branting's perspective should be translated into practical politics. During the period of minority parliamentarianism he underscored the need for collaboration between the parties, which would make possible the establishment of a stable majority government. In the debate in 1931 he affirmed the necessity for "a deeper feeling for the obligations of democracy which, in the first place, include an honest willingness to cooperate for the general good." His speeches, published under the title *Democracy* (*Demokrati*), echo time and again the idea that the desire for concord is vital to democracy. The success of the Scandinavian democracies, he declared in a speech in Copenhagen in 1935, is attributable to the fact that "socialism and bourgeois democracy . . . have never come in conflict with one another; the bourgeois democrats have not permitted terror of socialism to cause them to abandon their democratic ideals, the Social Democrats have not deserted bourgeois democracy for fear of contagion. Instead, their forces have united to solve common democratic questions. . . ." In another speech he declared that unchecked majority rule is just as much of a dictatorship as minority rule. "Dictatorship is and always will be dictatorship, even if it is briefly or permanently supported by a majority." In a paper commemorating the party's fiftieth anniversary, Hansson described democracy as the antithesis of power politics and stressed that the majority must constantly consider the minority in a democratic state. The clearest and most concrete illustration of this thinking, which meant converting the tolerance principle into a policy of reciprocal accommodation, is the formation of the coalition cabinet in 1936. This was the first time the Social Democrats enjoyed a position of power in the lower house, and they immediately sought organized collaboration with another party. A few decades earlier even the most reform-minded Social Democrat would have considered this tactic preposterous.

The firm adherence to democracy, and thereby to legality as well, was pronounced even when dissension between the Social Democrats and nonsocialist parties was severe and the debate sharp. During the six-year-period (1926–1932) when the Social Democrats were not in the cabinet the party press did inveigh against the nonsocialist cabinet in power, but the censure did not extend to the system itself. The Social Democrats demanded, above all, a stronger, more stable government—whether it be backed only by the party, or by collaboration with independents, or by a nonsocialist block. In the course of the 1928 controversy over work stipulations, extraparliamentary pressure in the form of a strike demonstration was organized in a matter of hours. This was the sole occasion of such extraparliamentary pressure during this period, however, and it was made clear that the strike was only a demonstration of opinion. When the question was on the floor in the Riksdag, party spokesmen did, to be sure, point out the risk that the proposed legislation would aggravate social conflicts. Yet the party leader, with the endorsement of the whole party, declared that the Social Democrats would try to prevent "poisoning" the spirit within the trade union movement—even if the legislation were passed. During the impassioned debate on the Ådals affair, party representatives affirmed their opposition to all violence and, in particular, to the propaganda for violence circulating among the workers.

It should be noted that certain elements in the social democratic debate in other nations regarding the problems of democracy have been given only fleeting mention in Swedish discussions or none at all. In recent years in England and France in particular, it has been commonly assumed that at a certain level of social democratic reform—especially when measures to implement socialization would be attempted—the "Establishment" would organize violent countermeasures. In other words, in a democratic state social democrats could peacefully accomplish their purposes only to a limited extent. The more or less clearly formulated conclusion is that social democrats must be prepared to resort to extraparliamentary action or, at least, to methods that could not be considered democratic in the usual sense of the term. The reasoning is obviously connected to Marxian concepts of a clear-cut, irreconcilable conflict between capitalism and socialism, but it was also stimulated by European fascist movements as commonly construed by socialists. These ideas have received only occasional attention in Swedish debates. It can be assumed that the lack of interest in them was related to the absence of any real plans for socialization and to the distinct ineffectualness of the fascist tendencies that had appeared. In accordance with their pessimistic attitude toward democracy's potential, social democrats in other nations also believed that if they controlled a majority they would force through legislation that would provisionally put the ordinary parliamentary system out of operation. What they had in mind was the adoption of legislation granting the government the authority to rapidly effect fundamental socialization measures and to take effective action against any opposition that might arise. The idea of the dictatorship of the proletariat recurs here in diluted, veiled form. This idea has not, to the author's knowledge, been included in any Swedish exposition. Swedish Social Democrats as well as members of other parties in the country considered simplifying parliamentary operations, but this did not imply any intent to use a Social Democratic majority to restrict the opportunities of minority parties through a power concentration in the government. The absence of such ulterior motives is an indication of the party's unconditional acceptance of democracy.

Socialist debaters in other countries not infrequently give the word "democracy" a connotation that can be used to cover up antidemocratic motives. One can detect this connotation in the Wigforss quotation cited. It suggests that democracy is not complete if it does not extend to the economic and social as well as to the political sphere. At times the term "formal democracy" is used with a tinge of scorn to designate purely political democracy. Accordingly, one could call for sweeping economic and social reforms—even socialization—on the grounds that they were a necessary part of democracy. One of the interesting aspects of this tendency is that it shows the high value-content that the word "democracy" had acquired: socialism is now demanded as a natural consequence of democracy; previously, democracy had been regarded only as a means toward socialism. The import of this connotation lies in the possibility it affords groups that do not unconditionally respect democracy, in its usual sense of popular government, to act as advocates of "true" democracy—in the sense of equality or socialism, for example. If one pursues this line of thinking, one can even call dictatorships democracies—as the communists do. Such disguised antidemocratic tendencies have at times appeared in Social Democratic debate, but it has by no means been a characteristic feature of the debate. Swedish Social Democrats have discussed social and economic democracy as future objectives that should be reached—but only through the means provided by political democracy. This form of expression, which can scarcely be misinterpreted, is exemplified in a statement made by the party leader in an address delivered in 1931:

> An [observation] has been made . . . to the effect that only when democracy becomes socialist will it acquire great significance. Once again, an attempt to blot out feeling for democracy [as it exists] now. Obviously, democracy will become socialist. . . . We are working to extend it in the social and economic spheres, but the prerequisite for this consummation is that we preserve that which we have already won. One could also say that that the only way to win a popular majority for this extension work is to evince loyalty to the democracy that has already been won through struggle.

The development of Social Democracy into unqualified acceptance of democracy per se has not displaced any main points in the party program, which, on the whole, has received priority in the interchange of opinion.

At the 1920 party congress, in connection with a general revision of the party program, the party administration presented a proposal that clearly indicated that no action toward socialization would be contemplated without the support of a majority of the citizens. According to the suggestion of the program committee, the first sentence in the party's statement of principles was to have the following wording (which is not very different from the earlier formulation): "The Social Democratic party differs from other political parties in that it wishes to transform completely the economic organization of bourgeois society and bring about the social liberation of the impoverished classes, toward the securing and development of material and nonmaterial culture." The administration recommended that the words "supported by the will of a popular plurality" be inserted before "bring about the social liberation of the impoverished classes." The spokesmen for the administration (Branting, Engberg, Karleby) were of the opinion that since the sentence as formulated by the program committee clearly defined the difference between the Social Democratic party and nonsocialist parties it would also be necessary for the formulation to distinguish between social democracy and communism. Insofar as democracy was, in fact, a vital part of the party program, it should be stressed in the statement of principles. Representatives of the majority in the program committee (Sandler, Möller) adopted the same position in regard to the democratic principle, but they did not believe that a declaration espousing democracy would be appropriate in the context: the statement of principles should only define the party's fundamental position on economic development. Sandler charged that it would be inconsistent to refer here to the will of a popular plurality "for the will of the Social Democrats to implement socialism is just as steadfast, even if we are in the minority." The brevity of the account of this line of thought as reported in the congressional record renders it patently illogical. In reality, the wish to bring about socialism was assumed to be dependent on the provision that this wish be shared by a majority of the electorate. All the same, the congress resolved without a vote to ratify the proposal of the program committee as it stood and the recommended amendment was not adopted.

Nonetheless, the debate on this question demonstrated that total concurrence did exist in regard to the heart of the matter: socialization without a popular majority was deemed inconceivable, that is, there was complete agreement that the party wished to implement its program only through democratic forms. In addition, the congress adopted other amendments that affirmed the democratic viewpoint. The second article in the program included, among others, the term "popular self-government." No differences of opinion arose on this point.

Subsequent party congresses have given only passing consideration to questions of constitutional principle. A motion advocating measures to ward off a parliamentary crisis was made at the 1928 congress. In rejecting the motion, the party administration declared that "the political program of social democracy is thoroughly infused with the idea of democracy but it contains no article in which the party formulates the system that it considers best for the exercise of government power." The parliamentary system of government "in the traditional sense" was not "automatically" included among the party's objectives. Under existing conditions this system was the most suitable, but in the classless society that the party was striving to achieve, another system for the exercise of government power, based on a democratic foundation, might prove preferable. The exact implications of this proviso were not explained during the debate; Möller, the spokesman for the party administration, used phrasing as ambiguous as the above. A motion for revision of the party program made at the 1936 congress brought up the idea of complementing the general policy statement with the declaration of the party's democratic principles that had been proposed by the administration in 1920. According to this proposal, the words "without use of violent methods" were to be inserted in the first paragraph of the policy statement before the wording that defined the party aims. The proposal was rejected in its entirety. The administration referred to the resolution of 1920 and added "Our party chose the democratic course from the start, and has, with the passage of years, ever more firmly stressed its democratic position. There is no need to record this by altering the program."

Yet prominent members of the party and particularly of the youth movement have asserted that a more complete and more principle-oriented declaration of the party position vis-à-vis democracy should be included in the program. "It would be beneficial," wrote Lindström, "to establish that to Social

Democrats democracy is not only a method but also a principle." When, in the course of their program revision in 1937, Dutch Social Democrats adopted a statement regarding "democratic socialism" and its meaning, some Swedish Social Democrats maintained that their party ought to follow this example.

The Recognition of Parliamentarianism

THE SOCIAL DEMOCRATS' acceptance of the responsibility of government, whether alone or in collaboration with other parties, became a central point in the debate on party tactics. Since the democratic line of action had been recognized, since a substantial measure of democracy had been gained, and since the party had attained a certain amount of strengh within this constitutional framework, a singular dilemma presented itself. On the one hand, by virtue of the unwritten law of parliamentarianism, the party had the right and the duty to engage in cabinet functions; on the other hand, such functions offered the possibility of realizing certain demands, or at least tended to contribute to an increase of radicalism in government policy. But if cabinet socialism was accepted, even though the party could not proceed to a realization of socialism, then the teaching of class struggle in its more stringent form had to be definitively abandoned. According to this teaching, cabinet socialism can be nothing but an absolute anomaly: the class that is supposed to overthrow the ruling class participates in the administration of the government—which is the primary medium of coercion of the ruling class.

It is difficult to clearly distinguish between, on the one hand, the discussion of Social Democratic formation of a cabinet which revolves around this theoretical dilemma or is in any case connected with it, and, on the other, the more concrete debate focused on the situation at hand. However, as far as possible, this distinction will be made; in this context only those questions which concern matters of principle will be treated.

The idea of cabinet socialism hardly entered the debate in Sweden prior to the 1911 party congress. However, at the international congresses in Paris in 1900 and in Amsterdam in 1904 the Swedish delegations had voted for the less rigid of the resolutions proposed. At the final vote in Amsterdam, which decided in favor of general repudiation of cabinet socialism, the Swedes abstained. Even though Branting's congressional reports are intended to be nonpartisan, they nevertheless disclose his sympathy with the reformist line.

Further, his commentary of 1902 on Engels' *The Transformation of Socialism from a Utopia to a Science* contained definite affirmations of the practicability of cabinet socialism. After emphasizing that the transition to a socialist society need not take "the form of a catastrophe, a furious battle against 'the one reactionary mass,' " Branting contended that "it can, on the contrary, lead to cooperative government on a positive program of reform between the socialist workers' party and reasonably related political factions, as we have already seen . . . in many places in Europe."

The possibility of Social Democratic participation was evidently not entertained in any quarters when the Staaff cabinet was formed in 1905. However, after the Social Democratic victories at the polls in the 1908 election, the question of Liberal-Socialist collaboration in the event of a cabinet crisis had to be seriously examined. The matter was discussed in the press in the autumn of 1908, and in December of the same year the party administration dealt with the party's position toward the cabinet that would be formed when Prime Minister Lindman would be forced to resign. It was almost unanimously agreed that the party ought to support a Liberal cabinet; Branting merely noted in passing that collaboration in the actual composition of the cabinet was unthinkable: "in regard to the question of the inclusion of a Social Democrat in the cabinet . . . this must not take place. . . ." There was no exchange of opinion on this point; that the party would refrain from involvement in the cabinet was probably considered self-evident. When, around the same time, the newspaper *Dagens Nyheter* maintained that Social Democrats should not shirk cabinet responsibility, Branting answered that the paper "completely ignored the difference between seeking a position of power as the controlling and driving force in a people's legislature and the assumption of some kind of partial responsibility for a policy that essentially aims at a conservative development of the established order with its privileges for the established minority."

In anticipation of the impending elections of 1911, which, it was presumed, would result in victory for the Left, the question gained a new sense of urgency. The following resolution was passed without a vote at the party congress that convened some months prior to the elections:

> Pursuant to the resolution [adopted] at the international congresses in Paris and Amsterdam, this Congress declares that the entrance of Social Democracy into a bourgeois cabinet is not advisable but can only be an "exceptional emergency measure in forced circumstances" and under any conditions ought not to occur without the approval of such a step by the Social Democratic Riksdag group and the party administration. The partisan who, lacking such a mandate, nevertheless enters into a bourgeois cabinet, is thereby considered to have left the party.

It was further resolved that "a two-third majority shall exist both within the Riksdag group and within the party administration for approval of entrance into a bourgeois cabinet." The resolution was proposed in conjunction with consideration of the question of the activity of the Riksdag group, and was scarcely subject to any debate. Only one speaker, Fabian Månsson, declared that every statement regarding cabinet socialism was superfluous. Branting approved the proposal but stressed that an invitation to participate in the formation of a cabinet must be seriously weighed.

After the elections, which resulted in an increased majority for the Left with the Liberals as the largest party, the executive committee of the party administration took the question under deliberation. The immediate reason for this was the expectation that Staaff would call for the party's cooperation. The committee was unanimously agreed that such collaboration should not take place, but several committee members such as Branting, Lindqvist, and Palmstierna emphasized that their position was determined exclusively by practical considerations, not by reasons of principle. It was decided that the members of the party administration and the Riksdag group should be questioned by telegram. Sixty-three of the answers received indicated support of the committee's view; six replied to the effect that the party ought to place itself at Staaff's disposition. The latter group included, among others, Steffen, E. Kristensson, Linders, and Nilsson in Tånga. When Staaff extended an invitation to participate in cabinet formation, Branting declined. However, negotiations were made regarding the policy and composition of the new cabinet, and these led to some promises of support from the Social Democrats.

Lively discussion by the party press followed this decision. Vigorous opposition to the negative attitude toward Staaff's invitation did appear in some articles. In *Arbetet* Aug. Nilsson wrote that Branting's exaggerated loyalty "makes him now, when it really counts, a party politician and not the statesman that the head of our party ought to be." Observance of the congress' resolution on cabinet socialism meant that the party would be rendered impotent. "Social Democracy has thereby degraded itself to a second-class party restricted to verbal gymnastics in or outside of the Riksdag but without the power and without the responsibility to which it is entitled by virtue of its outward greatness and the political situation." Nilsson wrote that a strange idea prevailed within the party, namely that it would be relatively easy to seize all the power of government in one stroke, but that it would be exceedingly difficult to effect cabinet socialism. "For my part, I suspect that astronomical difficulties will present themselves on that fateful day when the Social Democratic party . . . without preliminary attempts, takes over the entire machinery of society, not simply to let it [continue] functioning as it had been, but committed to the obligation to make everything seven and seventy times better. I simply do not believe in that day. It is a romantic notion that we ought to have grown out of long ago." N. S. Norling and H. Åkerberg, writing in *Arbetarbladet,* definitely declared themselves in favor of cabinet socialism. The party needed experience before it took over the power of government. The belief in the corrupting influence of parliamentarianism contained weaknesses. "Shame . . . on the party that cannot get through even the hell of parliamentarianism with a bright and shining coat of arms. It would not be worthy of the noble task of guiding humanity into the promised land."

A conciliatory view, which had little to do with principle, was espoused by most of the prominent figures in the party and by the most influential newspapers. Writing in *Arbetet,* Rydén stated that in view of the existing circumstances—among others, the party's need for further parliamentary development—one should decline this time, but that this refusal would not have any real basis in principle. *Ny Tid* and many other newspapers represented approximately the same viewpoint. The actual rift on this question within the party was sometimes cited as the real reason for not participating in the cabinet. In all likelihood Branting was counted among those who considered the purely practical reason to be decisive. After the elections he wrote an article in *Tiden* in which he suggested that Social Democratic collaboration in the formation of the cabinet was a possibility at some future date when the party had grown in strength. The views of the party press were reflected in *Social-Demokraten,* but it did not offer a clear-cut editorial statement on the matter. In one of his speeches Branting expressly pointed out the difficulties that might arise if a Liberal-Socialist cabinet were confronted with a direct conflict between capital and labor. In such a case the Liberals would probably drift over to the capitalist camp. The experience of the large strike of 1909 very likely increased the anxiety among moderates such as Branting vis-à-vis coalition with the Liberals.

Some party factions repudiated the thought of collaboration with greater firmness and based their stand more clearly on principle. Foremost among them was the youth federation and its leaders, together with radicals such as Lindhagen and Carleson. The former spoke of the stupefying effect of power and described the seemingly powerless movements as being the ones that really were the most potent. Within the youth movement, where a half-derisive attitude toward parliamentarianism now prevailed, many charged that cabinet socialism implied or would result in a departure from the principle of class struggle. The party would definitely drift into revisionism, which was tantamount to abetting conservatism. At the congress of 1912 the federation adopted a resolution that underscored the party's decision of 1911 against cabinet socialism and decried "the obvious contempt for the resolutions of the party congresses that has manifested itself . . . in the party press in the course of the debate in question." Some claimed that a period of Liberal rule was necessary as a kind of rehearsal for the victory of socialism. The generally held precept was that the party should not become involved in the cabinet before it had gained a majority in the lower house. In an article that was typical of his attitude, Carleson wrote that Social Democrats must not forget "the line of demarcation has been drawn between us and the nonsocialist world. This is not only a question of adding or subtracting so and so many meters of radicalism to or from the dimensions of the program—by its very origins and its aims Social Democracy differs in kind and essence from the nonsocialist parties in regard to its fundamental concept of society, and we cannot becloud or obscure this difference with impunity. . . . The moment of power when responsibility for the government can be demanded of us will occur at the very earliest in conjunction with our majority in the lower house and preferably also with at least a fairly strong minority in the upper house."

The most moderate and thorough-going rationale for the line that was on principle opposed to involvement in the cabinet was that presented by Sandler in a *Tiden* article. He claimed that it was unreasonable to speak of a coalition as a natural consequence of the parliamentary tactic: it could just as well be said that coalition of all parties was a consequence of parliamentarianism. The cabinet differs from the Riksdag and from committees in that "it shall *govern,* and this must be done [in accordance] with a policy." A Liberal cabinet could only govern according to liberal philosophy; socialist collaboration in such a cabinet would thus mean that the Social Democrats accepted responsibility for liberal policies. Of course the two parties did have some program points in common, but the Liberals were bound by their promises to the electorate to implement these irrespective of whether or not the Social Democrats participated in the formation of the cabinet. Cabinet socialism would be called for if liberalism adopted so much of the socialist viewpoint that the difference between the two parties became one of degree, not one of kind, or if a new bourgeois party with similar socialist tendencies should arise. "There must first be a breakthrough of our fundamental concepts among the electorate. Then it will behoove the Social Democrats to assume the duty of forming a cabinet, whether alone or in collaboration with a party that accepts the *Social Democratic* government program. . . . In any case: coalition government is impossible as long as Liberalism is liberal and Social Democracy is socialist."

The untenable part of this argument (which some years' experience refuted) is obviously the view of socialism and liberalism as two separate philosophies that do not permit any reciprocal accommodation. As a matter of fact, many questions then current might have lent themselves to compromises between the two parties. Further, advocates of cabinet socialism contended that participation in the cabinet would enable the Social Democrats to influence the Liberals along a certain line far more effectively than they could without such participation. Sandler himself contradicted his own attempt to set up the problem as though it could be "solved" by certain logical deductions when he ventured the possibility of a coalition with a nonsocialist party sometime in the future. The contradiction is to some degree obscured by the qualification that such a cabinet would be based on "the Social Democratic government program"—an expression which, if carelessly read, could be interpreted as synonymous with "the Social Democratic program." This could not have been the interpretation intended, for then the party with which collaboration was thought conceivable would be Social Democratic.

The above, of course, does not mean to indicate the author's opinion as to the feasibleness of a coalition government in 1911. The author's intention has simply been to record the fact that—insofar as coalition with a nonsocialist party was thinkable—the problem was not of a kind that could be resolved by applying a few general principles: it was merely a question of expediency.

The autumn of 1914 ushered in a situation that made continued renouncement of participation in the cabinet appear impossible. The elections in September of that year had made the Social Democrats the most powerful party in the lower house: the party could now claim 87 mandates, against the Liberals' 57. The conservatively disposed Hammarskjöld cabinet could, at best, be expected to remain until the end of the war—which was generally presumed to lie in the not-too-distant future. Early in October 1914 the party administration met with the Riksdag group's confidential council and with the editors of the party press for deliberations on the situation. Branting opened the debate. The government in power ought to remain until peace had been declared; the problem was to decide how to deal with the situation that would then arise. The natural course seemed to be a leftist cabinet with representatives of both parties. Social Democrats could not disclaim responsibility; doing so would result in a continuation of Conservative rule, and at the next election the electorate would be of the impression that "voting for the Social Democrats did not produce any concrete results." A series of speakers such as Lindqvist, Rydén, Thorsson, and Bernhard Eriksson agreed with Branting. Fabian Månsson was dubious: the king's power play "will not become weaker or less treacherous with a mixed cabinet. When such [a cabinet] was one year old, we would have a new farmers' demonstration march, an armed one." Some Social Democrats—Ström, Vennerström, Sandler—were of the opinion that a purely Social Democratic cabinet was preferable; they intimated that such a cabinet should prepare a relatively radical program and, if need be, fall with it. It was decided to open negotiations with the Liberals. Further, in accordance with Branting's proposal, the party administration decided—13 to 5—to announce "that if agreement is won on a common program of action, our party is prepared to take part in the formation of a left-oriented cabinet, either by supporting a Liberal cabinet or by forming a coalition cabinet or a purely Social Democratic cabinet." The minority voted in favor of leaving the question of cooperation open until after the negotiations with the Liberals had been concluded. The press was informed of the main points in the decision of the party administration—but not of its statements on the cabinet question.

Soon after the opening of negotiations with the Liberals the question was broached at the party congress which, having adjourned in the beginning of August, had again convened at the end of November. The debate took place behind closed doors, but most of the minutes have since been published. Branting reported on the program that was considered a basis for negotiations with the Liberals and gave an account of the administration's rationale for its position in the beginning of October. He pointed out that a case such as the one at hand had not been brought up at any international congress, "for until now the only cases that have occurred have been those where a Social Democratic hostage was to be installed in a Liberal cabinet, cases such as the one that our Swedish party declined in 1911." Now it would be "the socialist majority within the left bloc that would have the last word in the cabinet." If the party did not agree to cooperate with the Liberals, the 1917 elections could result in a Social Democratic defeat. "For one can easily understand that large groups of electors would not wish to continue to support a party about which one could say, with some justification, that it bore the responsibility for continued rule by the Right."

Höglund was the main spokesman for the opposition. Not even if the party had a majority in the lower house would it be self-evident that it could take over the power of government. Coalition with the Liberals would undoubtedly conflict with the generally antirevisionary principles established by the Socialist International. Such a cabinet would be forced to approve the recently passed resolution on national defense. "We would have to refrain not only from the implementation of our socialist demands but also from the implementation of our democratic program. What stand would we take on the king's power? Can a Social Democrat take the oath of a cabinet officer? . . . If one cannot fully realize democracy and abolish the king's power, what will then happen to socialism?" The most natural course of events would be the formation of a Liberal cabinet, but if this could not take place the Conservative cabinet ought to remain. "It might be more advantageous to have a Conservative cabinet that was pressured by strong opposition from the Left than to have a left-oriented cabinet pressured by strong opposition from the Right." Under all circumstances, the Social Democrats must refuse: otherwise their party would become "a bourgeois reform party."

In the main, the debate revolved around the views presented here. The final battle concerned two resolution proposals. Both approved negotiating with the Liberals on collaboration. According to Rydén's proposal, which reflected the opinion of the party administration, the last sentence of the resolution should read as follows: "If agreement is reached on a common left-oriented platform and the party administration and Riksdag group find that the situation calls for Social Democratic participation in the formation of a cabinet on the basis of this platform, the Congress hereby grants its consent." The proposal advocated by G. Björklund concluded with these words: "To the contrary, no reasons have been presented that the Congress can accept [as justification] to assent to the party's participation in the formation of a Liberal-Social Democratic cabinet, no more than the Congress can recommend a Social Democratic cabinet in view of the dynamics of power in parliament and elsewhere that the working class can develop at present." Rydén's proposal won with 90 votes to 58 for Björklund's. The majority included most of the party's older leaders and some outstanding young members such as P. A. Hansson, Sandler, and Åkerberg. Opposition to the successful proposal was mainly composed of representatives of the party's extreme Left.

The debate conducted in the party press before, during, and after the congress contained little that could be added to the congressional discussion. It emphatically rejected the thought of forming a purely Social Democratic cabinet; this alternative should not be considered even if a coalition or a purely Liberal cabinet proved impossible. Supporters of cabinet socialism asserted that the main task at hand was to ward off reactionary plans and that socialist cabinets could be most useful from this point of view. Writing in *Social-Demokraten,* Örne declared that if the party refused to work along this line "in order to accommodate people whose entire strength lies in the present impracticability of their positive demands, even if we had a one-chamber system and a republic, this would be a terrible disappointment to all the voters who believe that it is more important to do some kind of direct good than to demonstrate." Those hostile to cabinet socialism frequently called attention to the risk that the party would have to carry out the new national defense plan that had been forced through by Conservatives.

Negotiations with Liberal leadership did not culminate in a cabinet change. The two parties had entered into negotiations with the expectation that the present cabinet under all circumstances would soon resign now that the war had ended. The resolution of the party congress regarding these negotiations nevertheless represents the conclusion of the first phase of the discussion on cabinet socialism. The basically negative view had been abandoned, even though the party had not yet declared that it had the same rights and obligations regarding cabinet formation as other parties. Following the meeting of the party administration in October, a newspaper proclaimed that "A new epoch in the history of Social Democracy began with [the passing of] this resolution. A Social Democratic party declares that independent of all compelling circumstances and all sheer emergency situations it is ready to send representatives to the nation's governing body and accept all the consequences of the party's action that might result." As indicated, it was the first time a Social Democratic party had delivered such a verdict.

The coalition government that had been anticipated in 1914 did not materialize until after the 1917 elections. The incisive exchange of opinion within the party administration attendant upon the formation of a cabinet did not project any opposition to Social Democratic participation; the question of principle regarding cabinet socialism was not even touched upon. Total unanimity could be attained now that the extreme left wing had left the party. Party organs justified Social Democratic membership in the cabinet by citing the necessity of establishing a firm parliamentary base for the cabinet's work; this would, in turn, safeguard the process of democratization that was the most immediate and important objective to Social Democrats and Liberals alike. As the party administration expressed it, the party followed "the road that concern over the future of democracy in our nation prescribed." A few isolated voices alleged that the position of the Social Democratic cabinet members was extraordinary from the point of view of the party's general principles. One newspaper contended that "They must be prepared to leave their seats in the cabinet and return to their places at the barricades of the class struggle the moment that the conflict between liberalism and socialism comes into the open." However, such reservations were few. The problem as to which party—the Liberal or Social Democratic—ought to take over the leadership and build a majority in the cabinet was disputed both within and outside the party. Occasionally a party newspaper would intimate that Branting ought to head the cabinet, but most newspapers unequivocally asserted that the Liberals, who were able to tip the scales in the Riksdag, should have the main responsibility. A totally Social Democratic policy was obviously not feasible, a fact that was quickly established by the party's foremost organ:

> In our opinion the situation thus requires a left-oriented cabinet—formed with the most immediate purpose of implementing the demand for constitutional revision insofar as this [demand] won at the election—a bloc cabinet [composed] of Liberals and Social Democrats under Liberal leadership, but [one] in which our party has sufficient representation and can assume its whole share of responsibility for [ensuring] that the breakthrough of democracy in our nation at last becomes a reality, and a secured reality. . . . Just as the advance made by an army must be decided by the pace of its slowest components, in a Liberal-Socialist coalition it will not be the party that is farthest to the left that can determine what both should jointly strive for at first.

Social Democratic recognition of cabinet socialism met with caustic criticism from the new extreme-left party, the New or Left Socialists. The criticism was, of course, contested. Engberg and Möller's arguments in defense of the Social Democratic position are of particular interest. Writing in *Social-Demokraten,* Engberg developed an original, sweeping perspective that undoubtedly was a retrospective rationalization of the Social Democrats' actions (his views had had no currency at the time of the actual cabinet formation). According to Engberg, if one was a Marxist, one was necessarily a cabinet socialist. Marx had not stated this correlation, but conditions had changed drastically since his time. The growing tendency had been toward a concentration of capital under state protection and control. Private capital had to a great extent been converted into government capital, managed by a handful of banks: private capitalism had become government capitalism. Socialism must therefore meet capitalism on a new front. "Confronted with government capitalism, the object of the policy of the proletariat is not to destroy the state but to try to master it in its capacity as the administrative agency of capital." Cabinet socialism was a sign that Social Democrats had instinctively understood this state of affairs.

Engberg's reasoning is strange. Social Democrats had always aimed at capture of government power. There was nothing new about that. But the necessity of a coalition government in a specific case does not at all follow from the first, very general viewpoint. Engberg apparently discarded this opinion after a while; in any event, he subsequently regarded cabinet socialism from a more modest perspective.

On the other hand, Möller's defense of the coalition, which was published in *Tiden,* was principally a concise synopsis of the reasons presented in previous discussions. A completely Liberal cabinet might have been the best solution from a Social Democratic standpoint, but such a cabinet could not be formed simply because the Liberals had refused to accept responsibility alone. Had the Social Democrats declined to participate in the cabinet, the king would have been given a free hand and a right-wing cabinet would probably have resulted; "we would have relegated the lower house to the trash heap and conceded that cabinet formation must be an act of royal favor. . . ." Social Democratic cooperation was therefore necessary, partly to sustain the parliamentary system itself and demonstrate the capacity of the Riksdag to build a foundation for a government, and partly to set in operation cabinet activities for the realization of democratization. A totally Social Democratic cabinet was unthinkable: the party did not have a majority in either house and its bills would therefore meet with defeat in the Riksdag. Möller thus postulated that the Social Democrats could not conceivably form a minority cabinet without incorporating a thorough-going socialist program.

Möller continued: "the ultimate reason for the inevitability of Social Democratic cabinet socialism" was "the nation's political backwardness." In other countries democracy had been put into effect by bourgeois liberalism. In Sweden "the bourgeois class has mostly been antidemocratic, and the result is that we have acquired a strong and large Social Democratic [party] that must assume the work accomplished by the burghers of other nations." The idea is interesting because, like other vindications of the party's tactic, it indicates that one considered Social Democratic participation in the cabinet to be a unique phenomenon, caused by the need for democratization. The Social Democratic party was still not thought to have the same parliamentary obligations as other parties.

In Möller's opinion, the Swedish Social Democratic party had not acted contrary to the Amsterdam resolution, which only prohibited socialist parties from "vying for a share of government power within the bourgeois society." The party had not vied for a share in the power of the government: "political conditions forced this share on the party." As the account of the Amsterdam congress indicates, this argument is not tenable. The French version of the resolution openly states that Social Democratic parties "should not accept" a share of government power, and the entire congressional debate demonstrates that the use of the words "aspire to" in the German text—on which the Swedish version was partly based—was not ascribed any special significance. According to Möller's interpretation, the resolution would be totally meaningless, for participation in a cabinet can always be said to be necessitated "by political conditions."

Following the passage of the democratization program, a debate on the dissolution of the coalition government began in the autumn of 1919. However, since a new program for the cabinet's work had been drawn up, it was decided that the coalition continue for the time being. It is important to note that objections were raised both in the party press and by members of the party administration against prosecuting the policies of the coalition cabinet on the grounds that a clearer distinction had to be made between Liberal and Social Democratic policies. Engberg championed this objection with particular ardor in his articles in *Arbetet*. One ought to dissolve a connection that made "the *Liberals'* program the official order of the day of the Social Democrats." Contrary to assertions made two years previously, government power was now declared to be of secondary importance. "The preponderance of socialism's work lies once again neither in parliament nor in the cabinet. It lies in the economic class struggle itself, it lies in the growing pressure that the unpropertied are exerting against the wall [that separates] the people and property." A recurring opinion held that the party ought to break with the Liberals, design a clear-cut socialist program (it was expected that a program revision would occur at the 1920 congress), and fight for this program in the role of the opposition at the coming elections in 1920; these steps would make a Social Democratic majority in the lower house probable, or at least possible. "Let the bourgeoisie take control, let the Social Democrats [then] step forward without restraint and show the nation the conditions that compel a socialist orientation—and [let] the bourgeoisie know that the time is not far off when the majority will be found on the side of socialism." So reads a typical editorial in *Skånska Socialdemokraten*. In some quarters one also contemplated the possibility that the coalition cabinet might be succeeded by a completely Social Democratic cabinet, and some urged that such a cabinet offer an unadulterated socialist program.

The party congress that convened in February 1920 thoroughly explored the question "Social Democracy and government power," but deliberations took place behind closed doors; no minutes were printed, and the unprinted minutes (which were certainly then extant) have since disappeared or, in any case, have not been discovered. At this time definite disagreement between Liberal and Social Democratic cabinet members manifested itself in their stand on local taxes. Liberal members would not approve the bill that Thorsson, the minister of finance, wished to introduce. The congress proclaimed its unanimous support of the bill and declared that the party was "prepared to accept all the consequences that might be necessary to advance this reform, and leaves it to the party administration and the Social Democratic Riksdag group to decide accordingly [and] in view of the situations that may present themselves." Some weeks later the first Social Democratic minority cabinet assumed office. As expressly affirmed in its policy statement at that time, it did not intend to present any specifically socialist demands and was in no way a militant or demonstration-minded cabinet. The policy statement avows that the cabinet is "composed exclusively of Social Democrats, but not because the general philosophy of our party has already won the following within the nation and among the people's representatives that would make such a cabinet a matter of parliamentary course. This fact necessarily dictates very great limitations in the cabinet's program." The cabinet remained even after its bill on local taxes failed, but it fell after the party's defeat in the autumn elections.

One's general impression of the discussion in the press on the formation of the first completely Social Democratic cabinet is that many in the party were hesitant or reluctant about the responsibility of government at the start, but that the secret debate at the 1920 congress produced fairly widespread adherence to the line then ratified.

Among the reasons presented in justification of this line, the following were apparently the most decisive. Much importance was attached to the question of local taxes, and it was presumed that it would be resolved more favorably from the party's viewpoint if the Social Democratic line provided the basis for the bill concerned. Acceptance of the responsibility of government would show that the party had the capacity to manage political leadership; this theory was fanned by the doubts concerning the party's capabilities expressed by some bourgeois newspapers. And, above all: the Liberals refused to form a cabinet. The Conservatives, who had just been vanquished and had fought against parliamentarianism and democracy, could not be considered for the cabinet. An interim cabinet, following immediately after the breakthrough of the principles of parliamentarianism, would symbolize a failure for democracy. Under the circumstances, the only possible solution from both a parliamentary and a political point of view seemed to be a Social Democratic minority cabinet.

Between 1911 and 1920 the party position on parliamentary cabinet formation thus underwent a significant transformation. In 1911 it unanimously supported the principle-based recommendation by the party congress against coalition with a nonsocialist party. The normal requisite for a Social Democratic cabinet was then apparently presumed to be a majority in the legislature or, in any case, in the more democratic of the two houses. However, in conjunction with the cabinet crisis in the autumn of the same year, some quarters called for Social Democratic participation in a cabinet of Liberal formation and leadership. Following the resignation of the Conservative cabinet in 1914, coalition between the two left-oriented parties was acknowledged as suitable. Three years later this thought was realized without encountering any opposition within the party. And in the spring of 1920, the party was prepared to form a completely Social Democratic minority cabinet that did not include any specifically socialist features in its program.

This transformation is manifestly a result of the acceptance of the parliamentary system. In 1911, when the Liberals were the foremost representatives of the Left, Social Democrats could still demand respect for the wishes of the Riksdag in regard to cabinet formation without becoming further involved in such formation. In 1914 and 1917 this was no longer possible. Since the Social Democrats had become the leading party of the Left, the Liberals refused to govern alone: the Social Democrats had to choose between a Conservative or, in any event, a nonparliamentary cabinet, and a cabinet formed by the Left bloc. By 1920 the situation was such that either the demand for a parliamentary cabinet had to be relinquished or the Social Democrats had to assume responsibility for the government alone. The inner logic of events in 1920 compelled the party to take action that would have been considered beyond the realm of possibility some years earlier.

In forming the 1920 cabinet, the party seemed to acknowledge that it had the same obligation to cooperate in the functioning of the parliamentary system as other parties. It is true that the cabinet resigned in 1920, even though the party was still strongest in the Riksdag, but this could be vindicated by reference to the vague rules of minority parliamentarianism, which indicated that a party that had suffered an election defeat ought to step down.

A few years later, however, signs of doubt again arose as to the parliamentary duties incumbent upon the party. Before delving into this, we shall briefly consider an unusual proposal presented by Engberg in 1921 in *Arbetet.* The proposal aimed at lightening the burden of parliamentary responsibility. Engberg thought it inadvisable to consistently involve party leaderships in parliamentary cabinets. If a left-bloc cabinet were formed, party members outside the leading clique should be accorded cabinet seats. This would give greater freedom of action to the parties that collaborated in the cabinet. "One [thus] ensured, *first,* that the cabinet would be truly parliamentary, *second,* that the desired general policy would be guaranteed, *third,* that the parties would not have to behave as though they were handling broken glass when acting upon several questions presented by the government, *fourth,* and lastly—and perhaps not least important—that the party leaders would be afforded the freedom to express the party stand in certain situations without thereby placing the cabinet in an awkward and false position."

This argument did not seem to attract much support, and it has not been applied to the formation of any cabinet. On the contrary: all parties have taken it for granted that their leaders ought to sit in the cabinet. The argument is of interest as an expression of the wish to obtain parliamentary cabinets without thereby assigning any parliamentary responsibility to the parties —a kind of pseudoparliamentarianism. During the parliamentary periods in Italy and Germany on the other hand, this method was applied on several occasions. The parties sent second-class representatives to the cabinets, and did not consider themselves completely involved in cabinet work. Not without cause has this practice been regarded a sign of the disintegration of parliamentarianism in these countries prior to the establishment of dictatorships.

No significant exchange of opinion on the principles involved in the relation between the party and the cabinet took place during the next few years. Cabinet socialism was definitely acknowledged. The policy line aimed at a takeover of executive power that had been prescribed by the 1920 resolution was further pursued. General unanimity in the party regarding cabinet socialism prevailed at the time of the formation of the next Social Democratic minority cabinets in 1921 and 1924. The consensus of opinion also held that the cabinet ought to adapt itself to its minority position and conduct the same moderate, compromise-oriented policy that the first Branting cabinet followed.

There was no question of a militant cabinet that would fight for specifically Social Democratic causes. The cabinets fell because of the party's defeat on the unemployment issue, that is, on an issue that led to sharp differences of opinion between social groups but that did not implicate essentially socialist views to any important degree. The party's parliamentary activity during this period gives one the impression that it adapted to circumstances without deep analysis or reflection in the same way that other, less characteristically ideological parties adapted themselves. The period following the 1920 elections did not seem to be an opportune time to press demands for socialization, and the 1924 election was dominated by the national defense issue. Widespread satisfaction with the objectives that had been won—primarily democratization and the standard work day—had placated reformist zeal. The softening of the party's demand for reform was probably also due to the relaxation of tension that the older party leaders now experienced after a decade of bitter struggle. Branting's interest in and contribution to foreign policy gave the party a prestige within its own ranks and to outside observers as well that many felt did not correspond to the party's achievements and strength in domestic policy.

During the Ekman cabinet, 1926–1928, debate on the cabinet problem again gradually gathered momentum. The causes were several. There was the growing consciousness of the inability and reluctance exhibited by the three Social Democratic cabinets (1920–1926) to conduct Social Democratic policies or even to present specifically Social Democratic demands. What, it was asked, had been won by these ventures? Together with other parties, the Social Democrats also realized that the Swedish system of government tended to develop into a systematic minority parliamentarianism—a possibility that was scarcely considered while the struggle for democracy was going on. The Ekman cabinet remained in office by taking advantage of vacillating majorities, and its supporters began to formulate a theory about "weighted parliamentarianism." His relative stability became a source of irritation to the Social Democrats who, despite incomparably stronger parliamentary backing, had been forced to relinquish executive power three times in the course of less than five years. Confronted with the Ekman cabinet, which they alternately criticized and supported, Social Democrats and Conservatives alike experienced a mixture of aversion and helplessness. After compulsory arbitration in litigation was legislated in 1928, the Social Democrats' attitude toward the cabinet was more negative than ever.

The foregoing suggests which issues were queried in the new debate. There was no further discussion as to whether Social Democrats could accept executive responsibility in a middle class society or whether, in the capacity of the executive party, they could collaborate with other parties. The first question was how to build a more stable executive that was based on majority support; second: were the Social Democratic minority cabinets worthwhile? Should the party take control of the government only if it had a majority, alone or together with another party? There was obviously no logical connection between these questions. One avoided the problem of what the Social Democrats should do if they decided that they should not form a minority cabinet and if a majority cabinet, with or without Social Democratic cooperation, proved impossible to achieve. This kind of indecisiveness clouded the entire debate.

We shall not pause to review the statements made on these questions in speeches and in the press, but we should bear in mind that many shades of opinion were expressed. Some criticized Ekman's "skipping parliamentarianism"; the party's main concern should be the establishment of a majority cabinet, possibly even by rallying nonsocialists. Others stressed that the Social Democrats could not again accept a cabinet commission without majority support in at least one house. One often cited the English example of 1924 when MacDonald's minority cabinet was considered a failure and a new experiment along the same lines unthinkable. Yet there were some who advocated that the Social Democrats form a new minority cabinet when the opportunity arose. The mainstreams in the debate were clarified at the party congress of 1928. The penetrating exchange of opinion on the cabinet question that then took place is one of the most interesting in the history of the Swedish Social Democratic party.

The workers' commune from the northern city of Sundsvall presented a motion at the congress that—without offering a proposal on the specific issue at hand—demanded that the cabinet question be submitted to debate and that directives for the party's position be drawn up. The motion stated that the Liberal-Independent cabinet in power carried on "a vegetative existence, without a parliamentary basis, through the system of 'skipping majorities,' which must undermine confidence in and respect for the executive power as well as for parliamentarianism." Following a report on the several opinions within the party, those proposing the motion declared that "the workers' party could best promote the interests of the working people by taking the position of an opposition party in order to advance and convert into political reality its own thoroughly studied and practically designed program on all important issues." The party's forces would thereby be assembled and the conditions for a stable majority would be provided. Although it was not made explicit, the underlying thought was that the party should not assume cabinet responsibility without a majority in the lower house.

The response of the party administration to the motion was not clear. It indicated that the cabinet problem ought to be examined "bearing in mind that increased stability in the course of action of Sweden's government [is a goal] to aspire to on general political grounds and that the standard requisite for government responsibility ought to be the possibility of realizing a positive if limited program." Only a concrete situation could show whether forming a cabinet could be a useful means of advancing the party's aims. Accordingly, the congress should only state "that the party tribunals must . . . examine the question in each case." Engberg and Vennerström proposed essentially the same notion, but offered different explanations for their stand. The significant part of their justification was the statement that the cabinet problem should be evaluated "with the view that cabinet formation ought to take place on the basis of majority support in the lower house." According to the debate, this implied that a cabinet might be formed even with the support of another party.

Wigforss, who introduced the comments of the party administration, accented the party's responsibility to forward the functioning of the parliamentary system as other parties did, and also the danger of taking over government power without the possibility of accomplishing something that the party considered of real value. He condemned Ekman's parliamentarianism on the ground that a cabinet ought to be based on majority support. Wigforss indicated four cases in which Social Democrats ought to take on the responsibility of government:

1. If the party obtained a majority in both houses.

2. If the party could enter into a coalition with another party and thereby form a majority cabinet. Because of differences with the Independents, however, this case would most likely not arise.

3. If a Social Democratic cabinet—although a minority cabinet—found it possible to "realize a positive if limited program." To clarify the wording used by the party administration, Wigforss stressed on the one hand "that the wording represented a check against a repetition of the attempt to form a Social Democratic cabinet on such unsteady foundations as those present at the 1926 Riksdag," and on the other, that the demand for a "positive" program could be kept to a minimum, for example, to the legislation of unemployment insurance.

4. A Social Democratic cabinet might be justifiable in exceptional cases even though it lacked the qualifications necessary "to win a positive and immediate end." Such would be the case if the other parties refused to assume command of the government and announced that it was the Social Democrats' responsibility. But in this case, the party that controlled the government should really declare its ambitions and let the people know what it wished to accomplish in a future majority position. In a sense, the cabinet was to be formed "for the purpose of demonstration"; it was to be "a cabinet for agitation, a cabinet for [dissemination of] information." However, the cabinet was not to declare all goals that could be included in a socialist policy, only "those which it objectively considers to lie within the realm of possibility—for example, those which correspond to the nation's economic condition." This line of thought was evidently influenced by events in Norway. In the spring of 1928 the Norwegian workers' party had formed a minority cabinet that laid down a radical program and was immediately thereafter overthrown by nonsocialist parties. Note that Wigforss considered this alternative to be applicable even when the Social Democrats had a majority only in the lower house. A policy of agitation of the kind indicated would then "be the natural preparation for the contest against the upper house or against the present majority in the upper house, which would naturally result from such a majority position in the lower house."

Wigforss' comments won general support, even from the minority in the party administration. However, one speaker (Elof Lindberg) claimed that he felt "that there was something suspicious buried somewhere in this question," but that "he couldn't possibly discover it." A retrospective study of the discussion readily reveals contradictions in Wigforss' presentation.

To expose these contradictions one might first postulate that the Social Democratic party ought to have the same cabinet responsibilities as other parties, as Wigforss apparently assumed would be the case. This idea cannot be sustained. In theory the party should form a cabinet if it could implement a positive program in spite of its minority position. These words could naturally be so interpreted that they would never prevent the Social Democrats from forming a cabinet. But Wigforss presupposed that these words would set a definite line of demarcation. It seems probable if not certain that, in his view, the previous Social Democratic cabinets would never have transpired if this demarcation had been acknowledged at the time. Even if the given requisite were not fulfilled, the Social Democrats could form a cabinet in exceptional cases, but this cabinet would be in the nature of a demonstration and could be expected to be forced to resign immediately. It could therefore happen that, although they were dominant in the Riksdag, the Social Democrats might refuse to form a cabinet for any purposes other than agitation and demonstration. The party would thereby place itself in a special category of its own making, with the assumption that other parties would feel obligated to assume the responsibility of government even though their chances for success in the Riksdag were as small or smaller than the Social Democrats' prospects. This reasoning is all the stranger in view of the fact that an interim cabinet of the Ekman variety was considered inadvisable from a parliamentary standpoint. Should the Conservatives take over executive power? Why shouldn't they also decline or limit themselves to a short-term demonstration cabinet? The reasoning can be explained to some extent by the implicit idea that a militant Social Democratic cabinet could force a rally of nonsocialist parties. But mark well, the alternative of a militant cabinet was thought possible even if the Social Democrats had a majority in the lower house and could therefore be replaced only by a nonsocialist minority cabinet. Were Wigforss' directives translated into actual practice, the Social Democrats—by disclaiming the responsibility that was considered incumbent upon other parties—might render a parliamentary system inoperable.

The ambiguity in Wigforss' reasoning can be illustrated in another way. A Social Democratic cabinet without majority support might be established if it had a possibility of realizing even a very limited program—and in exceptional cases, even if this condition were not present: in this event, the party was to present its entire immediate program in order to demonstrate its intentions to the voters. In one case, the party would settle for a minimum, in the other, it would demand a maximum. A cabinet that found it could not accomplish anything would suddenly demand everything. How were negotiations with other parties to be conducted under such circumstances? What would be the cast of the internal operations of the cabinet—or of the contemplated cabinet? Here the lack of well thought-out premises appears so flagrant that the absence of criticism during the congressional debate can only be ascribed to a desire to avoid conflict on this issue.

The speakers who agreed with Wigforss emphasized different points in his address and thus achieved an illusory consensus. The party leaders stressed "that a party with the standing that the Social Democratic party has acquired cannot claim a privileged position in regard to responsibility for the government of the nation." Hansson then offered a vindication of the party's formation of the cabinets of 1920, 1921, and 1924. The Social Democrats had never formed a cabinet "for the pleasure of ruling"; they had always expected that they would realize essential demands with the cooperation of other groups. It would not be advisable to fix "any restrictions on the ways to deal with different situations that might arise." Hansson had no objection to the establishment of certain "general principles" as long as this did not create a situation such "that the party does not have the possibility of utilizing every situation that presents itself in a way that is most advantageous to our people." Without specifically saying so, Hansson—although concurring with Wigforss' more general statements—avoided endorsing the special conditions given in Wigforss' introduction. In other words, Hansson followed the strictly parliamentary line, which placed the Social Democrats on a par with other parties in regard to the right and obligation to assume cabinet commissions. Sandler was of the same opinion, declaring that "one must never think that the need for judgment and dexterity in political matters can be replaced by congressional resolutions that restrict one's [scope of action] in situations that [such] congresses cannot anticipate." Other speakers (O. W. Lövgren, Olaf Olsson) also aligned themselves with these two representatives of previous Social Democratic cabinets.

Engberg and Vennerström, among others, concurred with Wigforss' introductory remarks from entirely different points of view. Vennerström claimed that, according to Wigforss, the standard requisite for cabinet formation was majority support; a minority cabinet was acceptable only in exceptional cases and then only "as an information or agitation cabinet" of the Hornsrud variety. The third example of exceptional cases was completely bypassed. Approximately the same line of thought was followed by several other speakers (Molander, T. Nielsen, A. Ström, O. Hagman) who were critical of earlier policies on the cabinet question, and who insisted that Social Democratic cabinets conduct a more socialist policy and therefore should not—except for demonstration purposes—be formed without majority backing. Some speakers hinted at an idea that was prominent in discussions in the press. It implied the hope that a nonsocialist rally would take place and provide for the formation of a strong majority cabinet without the necessity of Social Democratic involvement. In the meantime, the party would consolidate, achieve greater perspicacity in regard to its own objectives, and conduct relatively radical propaganda. Then, possibly after quite a few years, the party would win a majority in both houses. (This might follow a period of conflict between socialist majorities in the two houses.) Finally, from the vantage of a new, stable position, the party would be able to implement essential socialist demands. This idea was a diluted version of an old Marxist dream (that had been particularly dear to German Social Democrats during the empire). In theory, after a period as the unfettered opposition, one would achieve power, the whole power, and a stable power. One of the speakers, M. Västberg, declared "that we Social Democrats must try to force the bourgeois parties together so that they will be capable of governing, not because we want a bourgeois rally that will oppose us, but to give us an opportunity to actualize questions that are vital to us and thereby also gradually mobilize a majority in support of the Social Democratic program of action and thus obtain the firm foundation we need for a Social Democratic cabinet that wishes to and can accomplish things."

The Social Democrats suffered defeat at the 1928 election; thus the question of a cabinet under the party's leadership did not become a pressing issue as quickly as had been supposed. However, the inconsequentiality of the general directives on this question that had been agreed upon at the 1928 congress came to the fore after the 1932 by-elections, when the party leader received a cabinet post. Although certain statements made during the 1928 congress were cited, the views then presented played a subordinate role in the discussion that unfolded in 1932. The party undertook the responsibility of forming a cabinet without assurance of a majority for "a positive if limited program" and without intending to restrict itself to a policy of demonstration. In other words, one of the cases considered at the congress had transpired. Through collaboration with the Farmers' party, the cabinet thereafter obtained the requisite parliamentary backing.

The debates on the cabinet question that took place after 1928 will not be further considered; they had little to do with party principles.

Lastly, we should note that the party's position on parliamentary cabinet formation parallels its over-all relation to democracy. At one time the Social Democrats reasoned that if they won power through democracy, then democracy was good—otherwise they would resort to other methods. When they despaired of success by democratic means, a revolutionary line was justified with Marxian phraseology. As the party grew, its attachment to democracy became increasingly based on principle. In regard to the question of cabinet formation, the party followed the same sequence of thought: the party could become involved if it was tactically suitable, otherwise not; the party did not have to heed parliamentary convention. The disinclination to assume responsibility that was not of tactical advantage was vindicated by referring to generally Marxist views but the party successively came to acknowledge that it had the same rights and obligations as other parties. The view of democracy and parliamentarianism as agencies to be used when suitable but that could be repudiated when not expedient has, for the most part, disappeared from Social Democratic debate—together with the Marxist devices that lent them the semblance of plausibility.

By and large the same viewpoints that entered into the debate on cabinet socialism had also been used as arguments in the earlier debate concerning the seating of Social Democrats on committees appointed by the king. Participation in such committees also implied an extension of parliamentary activity and could be said to lead to compromises and increased political responsibility. On the other hand, in view of the enormous legislative importance of committees, a positive contribution to committee work seemed to be almost a natural consequence of the policies otherwise pursued. The latter view was never seriously contested on principle.

To the author's knowledge, the question was first raised in October 1907. Prime Minister Lindman invited H. Lindqvist and Nils Persson to sit on the committee on work contracts that was to be appointed. The invitation was considered at a meeting of the executive committee of the party administration together with the Secretariat of the Confederation of Trade Unions (*Landssekretariat*). Some urged that the invitation be rejected, especially since a representative of the politically neutral Swedish Workers' Union (*Svenska arbetarförbundet*), a rival of the Confederation, would be a member of the same committee. Despite the clumsy wording of the minutes, Lindqvist's defense of a contrary standpoint well illustrates the general reformist line of thought.

> Shall we consent to sit among the infected or not? We meet them everywhere, in the riksdag, in the municipal council, on official boards and committees, in short, everywhere in public work. Our congresses have stated that we should participate

> in political life, that we should try to infiltrate all possible spheres. This had led us to this point. If we want to change this tactic, these resolutions, then we ought to go to the congresses and say that now we have arrived at the point you desired, but we cannot go further because we collide with people we cannot work with, [and] we want to withdraw from everything and resort to a large-scale strike if one devises anything against us that we don't like—yes, this would certainly be a breezy way of escaping from work and responsibility, but if anyone believes that the movement would gain thereby he sadly deceives himself, if he believed that because one acted more adroitly, that if one participates in the preparatory deliberations that it will be different—but if our opponents are permitted to work out the proposal themselves, then we know what it will amount to and we can be assured that the proposal will be passed by the riksdag without further ado.

It was then recommended, 6 to 1, that Lindqvist and Persson accept the appointment. It should be added that, after having participated in the committee's work (in opposition to the committee majority), Lindqvist and Persson, as members of the special committee on contract questions at the 1910 Riksdag subsequently helped defeat the bills that were founded on the deliberations of the royal committee of which they had been members.

In 1908 Thorsson was appointed a member of the civil commission that was to supervise national defense for a period that was at first estimated at five years. The members of the executive committee of the party administration had approved the appointment. The party's left wing, especially the youth federation, evinced keen dissatisfaction at Thorsson's appointment. In its annual report the administration justified Thorsson's decision by stressing that the party had supported the need for civil supervision of national defense. "Elementary political logic thus dictates that we not refuse to help supervise when this [opportunity], although with altogether too narrow restrictions, is actually offered." At the 1911 congress the (*dechargeutskott*) objected to the fact that Thorsson had acted without consulting the party administration; speakers in the attendant debate alleged that membership of a Social Democrat on the civil commission did not conform with the party's antimilitary stand. However, the congress resolved, 58 to 51, to approve Thorsson's conduct. It was then proposed that a party member who was offered membership on a royal committee or a similar appointment "the acceptance of which can be presumed to be politically binding on the party" confer with the party administration or, if the administration were not in session, with its executive committee; a Riksdag man should consult with the Riksdag group if the legislature was in session at the time.

In November 1911 Branting informed the executive committee that Staaff had queried Lindqvist and himself about their attitude toward possible committee appointments. The contemplated appointments concerned a temperance committee and an investigation of national defense. Branting held that an appointment to the temperance committee could hardly be refused. It would also be difficult to deny someone an appointment to the committee investigating national defense since it would entail "retrenchments and savings." A member of the executive committee was of the opinion that the party should not permit itself to become involved, at least not as long as it could not appoint representatives itself. Yet the appointments were recommended, 4 to 1. The executive committee concurrently agreed "to express the propriety [of the fact] that the appointees consulted with the committee before [reaching] their actual decisions." Radical criticism of participation in the defense investigation was rebutted in the press with the assertion that committee work was a consequence of parliamentarianism.

In May of 1914—after the Hammarskjöld cabinet had been formed and elections following dissolution of the lower house had been held—the question of committee membership was again broached, this time within the party administration itself. A proposal to the effect that committees should be appointed by the legislature was rejected, 11 to 7. A recommendation that Social Democrats consult with "party authorities" before being seated on committees was also turned down. The minutes taken do not indicate whether this decision implied a departure from the directives given at the 1911 congress or simply a refusal to give them strict enforcement. In any case, the question was again brought up at the party congress later that year. One motion then made insisted that Social Democrats be prohibited from sitting on any royal committees; another asserted that such debarment should apply if the parties themselves could not appoint committee members; a third motion would have a party vote decide whether party members could sit on committees. The party administration considered "that it follows as a consequence of the party's parliamentary activity that the party ought to participate through its representatives even in the investigation of questions by royal committees," and simply proposed that the resolution passed in 1911 be respected. Some members of the administration—Sandler, Vennerström, Ström, Månsson, Neuman—entered the reservation that important political committees be filled by members of the legislature. The proposal of the party administration was finally ratified.

Since then the question has not been the subject of any fundamental debate. Judging by the minutes of party meetings, Social Democrats have consulted with the party administration or with its executive committee before accepting committee appointments only in relatively few cases—and hardly ever in recent years.

THE FINAL CONCEPTION OF THE DEMOCRATIC PRINCIPLE

The Swedish Social Democratic party has never fully developed a detailed constitutional policy. The general demand for popular government—primarily civil liberty, universal suffrage, and a parliamentary system—has been predominant. Constitutional reforms per se have not been an important issue in party debates.

The demand for universal suffrage and increased civil liberty recurs in all documents on policy since the party's inception. Palm's program of 1882 called for the "unrestricted right to organize" and the "abrogation of all laws and ordinances that restrict the freedom of the printed word and the rights to assemble and organize. . . ." The section on the franchise reads as follows: "Universal, equal, and direct suffrage with secret ballots for each member of the state, male and female, who has reached the age of twenty-one, for all official posts in state and local governments. Sundays or holidays should be designated as election days." The reference to the right to vote for "all official posts in state and local governments" probably did not imply that such posts would be filled by elections. Here, as in several other instances, Palm seems to have given an incorrect rendition of the Danish Gimle program that referred to elections to "national and local institutions." Essentially the same theme occurs in subsequent Swedish Social Democratic programs adopted during the 1880s. The Gotha program mentioned the right to vote at twenty years of age and referred to the possibility of a compulsory franchise (the duty to vote), but these particular demands have not been espoused in Swedish programs. The demand for the franchise appears in the very beginning of the 1897 program: "Universal, equal, and direct suffrage at political and local elections for all citizens who have reached their maturity without any discrimination based on sex. Election day to be a Sunday or national holiday." The following sentence was added to the last article (XI): "Constitutional guarantee of complete freedom of organization, assembly, press, and speech."

Appeals for a unicameral system and for referendums are prominent in the party's early programs. Palm's program contained references to "the abolition of the two-chamber system" and "direct legislation by the people's deputies." The latter wording was evidently intended as a translation of the Danish wording in the Gimle program, "direct authorization of the people"—one of many examples of Palm's carelessness in rendition. The 1885 program of the Social Democratic Union called for a unicameral system and "direct legislation by the people, that is, the right of the people to be the ultimate arbiters of the acceptance or rejection of legislative changes passed by the Riksdag." The Gotha program also mentioned "direct legislation by the people" together with the people's right to decide war or peace. (The Gotha program did not refer to the need for a unicameral system since the German legislature was not divided into two chambers.) The 1897 program demanded "the abolition of the upper house" but did not mention the institution of the referendum. However, the article on national defense did state that "the Riksdag, and, ulitmately, a referendum shall decide war and peace." The points here reported were probably not featured in public agitation. The demand for a unicameral system was most likely implicit if not explicit in the frequent attacks on the upper house. The press does not seem to contain any references to referendums.

A few additional constitutional issues emerged. The program of the Social Democratic Union called for "the abrogation of the king's right to declare war." This statement is odd in view of the fact that the monarchy was not mentioned in other contexts, but it may be explained by the fear of a war with Norway. Many programs mentioned democratization of the judicial system. The Gotha program demanded "administration of justice by the people" and "free judicial custody." Article V in the 1897 program read as follows: "Trial by jury in criminal cases. The counsel for the defense to be appointed by the local government or by the state. Free legal counsel."

The question as to whether the polity should be a monarchy or a republic was not considered in early Social Democratic programs. The German and Danish models were undoubtedly decisive on this as well as other questions. References included in some programs can possibly be interpolated as indirect demands for a republican polity, as the mentions of "democracy" in the 1886 program of the Social Democratic Union, for instance. The question of a republic was not brought up at any of the party congresses prior to 1905. However, the party position was obviously republican on principle. Presumably, the question was not discussed because it was assigned secondary importance in relation to the franchise and could hardly be actualized before the franchise had been won.

The party's republican bias was constantly featured in the Social Democratic press and in public agitation. At a republican meeting held on January 25, 1889 pursuant to the homage paid to the king on the occasion of his sixtieth birthday, Branting summarized the arguments that were and are used to substantiate the demand for a republic. Palm, Sterky, and Janhekt also addressed the meeting, which adopted a resolution directed at the abolition of the monarchy. Branting described the monarchy as "a slap in the face to the ideal of equality," as a focal point of demoralization, servility, and corruption. Europe's kingdoms had been of popular genesis, they had emerged with the disintegration of the feudal system and had been supported by broad strata among the people "who no longer endured their many petty tyrants. But then the kings had themselves become the oppressors. With the rise of the bourgeoisie to the position of the ruling class, the monarchy had "become the agent of the bourgeoisie, its most aristocratic doll, which is led about and shown to the people on important occasions." Although the king had become "the doll of the upper class," he was not altogether insignificant in his own right.

> Power he still has—seldom or never to do good, his education, his whole environment and position protect him from this—but he can do harm; he can retard progress, obstruct freedom, and demoralize the people. . . . We Social Democrats must thus be the sworn enemies of all that concerns monarchy for two reasons: because it is obsolete and corresponds to stages of development that are long bygone, and because it is now nothing but the foremost representative of the dominion of the upper class and bourgeoisie which it is our purpose to put an end to for all time.

Propaganda for a republic was not a salient feature in the party press, but Social Democratic newspapers often emphasized their republican position and even more frequently printed personal attacks on the king. Displays of public curiosity about the king's person evoked irritable reproof. In a typical example, when a worker was said to have proposed three cheers for King Oscar II on the occasions of the monarch's visit to Gothenburg in August 1904, *Ny Tid* deplored the thought "that a regular worker takes the time to stand and wait at the harbor for an hour and raise a cheer for a plaything of beach society, a Marstrand fixture (Marstrand is a fashionable summer resort on Sweden's west coast)." Occasionally one acknowledged that, although a republic was preferable, there was not much difference between a monarchy and a republic. In an unusual editorial written during his "conservative" period, Danielsson claimed that under certain circumstances a monarchy could be better than a republic, but that this did not apply to the Bernadotte dynasty. On a few occasions—in particular during the Norwegian crisis of 1905—the king's behavior was even praised. One's over-all impression of the attitude of the Social Democratic press is that the vehemence of its criticism of the royal family and its attacks on the monarchist system gradually abated.

The period during which the question of the democratization of the polity was of immediate urgency (1905–1920) was also characterized by relatively lively discussion of special constitutional questions. The configuration of the democracy that was soon to be realized was the subject of deliberations both in the press and at congresses.

At the 1905 congress, the articles on constitutional policy in the party program were subject to additional amendments, some of which were largely of a formal nature. The formulation of the franchise demand was simplified. The demand for civil liberties was, for no particular reason, moved from Article XI to Article II and was given this wording: "Complete freedom of speech, press, and assembly"; the principle of constitutional establishment of such liberties was thereby discarded. A special clause (in Article IX) demanded "unrestricted right of organization" and the "abrogation of all class legislation (the Åkarps law and the employment law for example) that hamper the workers' freedom of movement." In conjunction with a general modification of the Article on national defense, the references to Riksdag decrees and referendums on questions of war and peace were deleted. More important—the republican and the unicameral problems were brought into the debate. Z. Höglund had moved that the demand for a republican constitution be inserted in the third clause. Branting opposed the motion, declaring that all members of the party "were republicans at heart and soul" but that the question was not of immediate concern. No one moved approval of the motion. Rydén wanted to strike the demand for a one-chamber system from the program: the performance of the French senate during the Dreyfus affair had shown that a democratic upper house that was relatively independent of fluctuations in public opinion could, indeed, be of value. In accordance with Rydén's proposal—which was approved, 71 to 70—the third clause was reworded as follows: "Constitutional revision that realizes a totally democratic form of government."

The demand for a republic that was brought at the 1908 congress won greater support. Z. Höglund, who now emerged as one of the leaders of the party's radical wing, justified changing the program in regard to this issue by reading out loud part of Branting's antimonarchist speech of 1889 (cited in the foregoing). Branting explained that his speech had been occasioned by the monarchist demonstration attendant upon King Oscar II's sixtieth birthday. The republican standpoint should be given emphasis when appropriate, but a program change on this subject was unnecessary at this time. A bourgeois conservative republic was scarcely better than a bourgeois conservative monarchy. The party administration shared Branting's view. Rydén called for a special pronouncement to the effect that "it is self-evident that the Swedish Social Democratic party, like the whole of international Social Democracy, is a republican party." However, he did not "want to see the first youth that came along thumb his nose at our program." Rydén's proposal was adopted as a resolution. The formulation of the program was to be decided by a roll call, which was indicative of the importance the delegates attached to it. The proposal of the party administration that the program be approved without changes won in the roll call, 164 to 124. The dissenting votes were cast for the formulation of a declaration affirming the party's prorepublicanism. Several prominent representatives of the youth movement—P. A. Hansson, G. Möller, R. Sandler, and F. Ström—were included in the minority.

At the congress of 1911 Höglund moved that the third clause in Article I include the words "One-chamber system. Republic." This time a majority in the party administration did not want to oppose the proposal demanding a republic, but did not think the party should bind itself to a unicameral system, especially since a demand for such a system had been dropped from the program at the congress of 1905. Branting urged that the old article be retained unchanged; he was of the opinion "that changes in the party program should be adopted only when a factual modification of an idea within the party or a circumstantial change in one of the questions considered in the program or the actualization of a question not considered at all for a program amendment." He described proposals for a program amendment based on the republican demand—which all were really agreed on in principle—as student politics. Höglund declared that the king had demonstrated that he sided with the employers at the time of the big strike and that the Conservatives tried to use royal power "as a buffer against the advancing Social Democratic party." A demand that the Riksdag group deal with the question arose through the proposed program amendment. When it came to a vote, Branting's proposal was defeated; the proposal of the party administration was then approved by 75 votes against 56 in favor of Höglund's demand. The third clause in Article I thus read: "Constitutional revision that implements a republican and democratic form of government." During this congress the unconditional stipulation for trial by jury in criminal cases was also eliminated and the statement affected was reworded in more general terms.

Constitutional issues were thoroughly discussed at the congress of 1914. Several delegates moved that the Riksdag group be charged with forcing through the demand for a republic. Others urged that a demand for a unicameral system be inserted in the program. The party administration rejected the motions, the first because the Riksdag group was not obligated to "unconditionally and immediately" introduce proposals on all demands that had been adopted in the program; to the contrary, its job was to determine the appropriate time for the presentation of a reform. "The time to introduce proposals for a republic in the Riksdag will have arrived when the inner logic of events will have supplied the necessary foundation so that such a demand will be interpreted in *all* quarters as what it is: a serious political *action*. The [nation's] outlook should accordingly have undergone a development that would make the establishment of a republic not only seem theoretically correct to the greater part of the nation but also seem to be just what the situation called for." Abolition of the monarchy would probably not be accomplished through proposals in the Riksdag but "through direct notice to the person concerned of the people's firm decision to put the constitutional amendment into effect." The question would mature with the party's growth to the point where it might be realized; the importance of a constitutional revision along republican lines should be accentuated in the party's informational activities. In respect to the unicameral proposal, the administration reiterated its previous finding that the party should primarily devote its efforts to a democratization of the system of representation. In the course of the debate, Z. Höglund urged that the Riksdag group be charged with emphasizing the demands for a republic and a unicameral system in constitutional proposals; he pointed out that the events of the past year illustrated how substantial the power of the monarch really was. The vote was taken by a roll call, and the party administration won with 79 votes against 53 for Höglund's proposals.

After a relatively short debate and without taking a vote, the 1917 congress rejected a motion that the program call for a unicameral system and that this demand, together with the demand for a republic, be pursued by the Riksdag group. However, the congress did decide on two program amendments of a constitutional nature. The party administration recommended approval of a motion that the program demand establishment of the institution of the referendum: even if its organization were democratic, the representative system could not always guarantee that the view of a popular plurality would be decisive, and the referendum was of value in attaining such a guarantee. "In the opinion of the party administration, this institution is a necessary complement to the representative system for a people who wish to live under complete self-government. Its application will be an important lever in making the people better informed politically, and it is a natural expression of the training for independent responsibility that is emphasized in the party's general principles." The administration particularly stressed that the right to call for a referendum should not be restricted to the government but also be available to "such a preponderance of those who are politically franchised that they could be regarded as expressing a more widespread wish within the nation." It further recommended that the referendum be complemented with the initiative. There was no opposition to the introduction of a fourth clause in Article I with the wording "Popular self-government was amplified by the introduction of the referendum," nor to an addition to Article VI demanding "the democratization of the civil service."

The amendments adopted in the 1920 program revision in articles pertaining to constitutional matters were essentially of a formal nature. In accordance with the proposal of the program commission, the first article was devoted to "general freedoms and rights"; it was enlarged to include the principles of freedom of speech, press, religion, organization, and assembly. Constitutional demands proper were transferred from Article I to Article II and were more rigorously formulated: "Popular self-government. Universal, equal, and direct suffrage for men and women who have reached their maturity. Republic. A Democratic system of representation. Referendum." The program commission had proposed a declaration in favor of a unicameral system. In justifying this proposal, Sandler argued that if both houses were to become completely democratic and therefore equal, as called for, the bicameral system would be superfluous. A series of speakers—Branting, Engberg, and Möller, for example—contested that a truly democratic two-chamber system did have a function; they questioned whether the upper house might not be converted into a body that represented economic interests. This standpoint, which was upheld by the party administration, won without a vote.

The congress further treated the application of democratic principles to administration and justice. Article III, which was to replace the first clause inserted in the former Article VI of 1917, passed without debate. Instead of "the democratization of the civil service" the article would read "administrative agencies of experts, recruited and controlled on a democratic basis." The program commission's rationale for this proposal contained statements of wide purport in regard to principle. "The bureaucratic career system must be destroyed to give free scope to individual ability. This presupposes an extension of the field of recruitment and the abolition of the artificial selection that the bald requirement of a university degree easily results in. It means that merit and competence alone will determine promotions and that the principle of seniority will be eliminated. It means the abrogation of the demarcation between lower and higher grades of civil servants and [the establishment of institutions that will provide genuinely qualified competence with an opportunity to attain all grades. But it consequently also means the end of security of tenure for civil servants as a sacred principle. In order that the most competent may advance, the less competent must step aside, all in the interests of society." These views, and the reference to the principle of security of tenure in particular, can be interpreted as an expression of the desire to depart from important aspects of Swedish administrative tradition.

On the recommendation of the program commission it was further decided that the demands for reform of the judicial system be grouped in Article IV. This article incorporated several demands formerly embodied in Articles

VI and IX. It thus demanded "popular influence on the judicial system," "laymen's participation in the administration of justice," "free legal assistance," humane penal legislation, and abolition of the death penalty. (The latter was legislated the following year.) The statement previously included in IX:1 regarding the abolition of class legislation that hampered the workers' freedom of movement (the Åkarp law, among others) was replaced by the more general statement "Legislation discriminatory to workers shall be repealed." The last clause in Article IX calling for enactment of workers' protective legislation—"where possible"—without discrimination in regard to sex was similarly replaced by a demand on principle for "equality between men and women in the eyes of the law." The program commission declared that it thereby simply wished to establish a viewpoint already shared by party members. Two completely new clauses were introduced that were connected with long-held party beliefs. The new additions concerned revocation of the special military penal code and "public trial of all court cases."

These articles did not stir up any notable debate at the congress, but a proposal made by the program commission did. It had the unanimous backing of the commission, which justified it in only a few words. The proposed clause was to read: "Judges shall be chosen through elections between [candidates] qualified for the post." This proposal did have a connection with the phrase previously in force regarding "increased popular influence . . . on the appointment of judges," but was far more definite. The party administration disapproved the proposal. Generally democratic viewpoints had been offered in its defense by P. A. Hansson, Linder, and Möller. K. Schlyter was the foremost antagonist of the proposal. He cited the often dubious consequences of the election of judges in the United States and stressed the inadvisability of binding the Social Democratic members of the acting legal commission to a congressional resolution. The congress subsequently rejected the proposal of the program commission, 141 to 35.

Of all the constitutional demands presented at the party congresses, those that had to do with the establishment of a republic and of a unicameral system received the most attention in the Riksdag and the press. Social Democratic papers often featured the demand for a republic, especially when the king used his constitutional authority to institute measures that were regarded as obstructions to the process of democratization. In May 1906 Staaff demanded that the king dissolve the lower house in order that more pressure for the franchise might be brought to bear on the upper house. *Social-Demokraten* commented that if this demand were refused, Sweden would find itself with "an *active* republican party"; "a monarchy that . . . selects our Swedish upper chamber for political support against a disfranchised people . . . chooses to become not a harmless decoration but a dangerous anachronism." Similar pronouncements were made during the constitutional conflict of 1914; elimination of "head" departmental budget requirements was recommended as a demonstration. Attempts to actualize the republican issue were particularly prevalent within the Youth Federation. The congress of 1909 resolved to put into effect "forceful agitation for a republican constitution." However, the party never did produce any concerted republican action. When Lindhagen presented the demand for a republic at the 1912 Riksdag, his action was discountenanced by both the confidential council and the Riksdag group; it was also criticized by a number of papers. Social Democrats underscored their republicanism in the Riksdag, but they repudiated Lindhagen's demand on the ground that it was not of current concern. However, the Social Democratic minority report of the constitutional committee contained an obvious threat; the report declared that the demand for a republic could become urgent "soon enough . . . if a monarch, obstinantly insisting upon his royal power, should create stubborn opposition to the demands of an unequivocal and determined popular will." Even after the constitutional conflict of 1914, the same line that prevailed in 1912 was still predominant. At the 1914 Riksdag the Riksdag group rejected, 43 to 11, a proposal for a party motion on the republican issue; when such a motion was nonetheless made, the Social Democrats on the constitutional committee registered their disapproval of it on approximately the same grounds given in 1912; when it came to a vote in the lower house the motion garnered only 19 votes, with 129 opposed. During the crisis in the autumn of 1918 it briefly seemed as though the republican demand would really become pressing. A considerable number of meetings gave rise to proclamations favoring a referendum on the question, a recommendation that was backed by several newspapers. Writing in *Arbetet,* Engberg offered a trenchant argument for the prompt establishment of a republic: "The Monarchy stands as a wall between the people and the state. . . . Therefore: may the demand for democratization take the form of a demand for the democratic republic!" At the Riksdags of 1919 and 1920—the years immediately following the victory of the fundamental demand for democratization—the republican line scored its greatest triumphs. Both in 1919 and 1920 the Social Democrats on the constitutional committee gave their support to a proposal initiated by the Left Socialists for a referendum on the republican question. In 1919 this proposal managed to win 56 votes, with 75 opposed; in 1920 it received only 47 votes, with 119 opposed. However, the Social Democrats did not waste much effort on this question; they did not insist that the demand for a republic be realized within the near future.

Proposals for a unicameral system were presented at the Riksdag not fewer than six times between 1912 and 1920. The constitutional committee disapproved them all, and they were all later rejected by the Riksdag, often without debate and usually without a vote. Only a handful of Social Democrats supported the line favoring a one-chamber system. At no time could a motion for such a system claim more than twenty-odd votes. Its treatment in committee and chamber indicates that the party minority that espoused it progressively dwindled in size, especially after the left wing, which had been most radical on this and the republican issue, broke away from the party. A fundamental vindication of the retention of a bicameral system was delivered by Möller in a 1915 *Tiden* article, "A Democratic Problem," which drew a great deal of attention. According to Möller, sympathies with a unicameral system were essentially nurtured by discontent with the undemocratic upper house under the existing system. In a socialist state, which would have a greater workload than the existing state, two chambers would be particularly necessary to deal with the facts of the matters under consideration. The upper house would satisfy the need for experts, whether selected by different corporate bodies (universities, the medical corps, and trade unions, for example) or elected by local representative bodies from certain categories of experts in specific fields. This house should, however, have only a suspensive veto on the lower house. These viewpoints were connected partly with Conservative proposals for elections by corporations or interest groups, partly with plans for special economic councils that were widely recommended in postwar years, and partly with the Russian council plan. The viewpoints did not go uncontested, but they nevertheless frequently reappeared in Social Democratic debate during the following years. At times it was even suggested that the "political" parliament be replaced in part by a representation of the "economic and social democracy." Apparently, however, no reform plans were made.

The least noticed of the important constitutional questions was without doubt the popular referendum. Everything indicates that this question was adopted in the party program without being subject to serious reflection. However, after the defeat of a couple of proposals on the issue, the 1920 Riksdag decided to call for an investigation into the question. This decision was supported by certain Conservatives as well as by representatives of the left. In the summer of 1920 the first Branting cabinet appointed a committee to carry out this investigation.

Since the democratization of the legislature 1918–1921, constitutional issues have remained in the background. The Social Democrats have helped bring about many reforms that they considered to be consequences of the democratic system or at least complements to it: the broadening of the power of the Riksdag in regard to foreign policy (1921); the introduction of the consultative referendum (1922); the introduction of the open vote in both houses of the Riksdag (1925); the rescinding of economic criteria for the franchise to the upper house (1929); lowering the minimum age requirement for the franchise at certain elections (1937); revocation or modification of certain qualifications for the franchise; minor modifications of regulations governing national and local elections. Yet neither these nor other constitutional issues have been a focal point of party activity. Before leaving this subject, however, we shall review the positions taken by the party in regard to constitutional issues that were formerly the subject of much discussion among Social Democrats, as well as various other questions that subsequently acquired a sense of urgency.

Only one party congress since 1920 has dealt with constitutional issues. Motions for adoption of the demands for a unicameral system and the decisive popular referendum in the program were made at the 1928 congress. The party administration did not wish to restrict the freedom of action of the Riksdag group and therefore disapproved the proposals without giving a specific reason. Both proposals were rejected after a debate; the cameral proposal, however, was not defeated before a vote was taken that gave it 108 votes to 135 opposed.

Proposals for the establishment of a republic have been made on five occasions in the Riksdag since 1920; the last of these was made in 1933. Social Democrats have never taken the initiative on these proposals. The constitutional committee has consistently and concisely recommended their rejection. Although Social Democrats have manifested no interest in promoting the issue, they have asserted their fundamental standpoint in various ways. In 1924 party representatives on the constitutional committee recommended that the question be submitted to a consultative referendum, but since the riksdagsman who introduced the proposal had not insisted on this they could not call for such action. However, a great number of Social Democrats in the lower house supported the proposal, which managed to win 53 votes to 94 opposed in this chamber. In 1925 Social Democratic dissentients on the constitutional committee declared that they favored a republic on principle but that they did not consider the question to be pressing and therefore disapproved the proposal. In 1928 and 1932, on the other hand, the dissentients called for an investigation into conditions in other countries and into the constitutional amendments that would be necessary for election of a chief of state. The dissentients did not advance any demands in 1933, but the houses presented the same proposal for an investigation that had been made previously. It is significant that a vote count has not been demanded on this question since 1924, and that the debates have usually been brief. Social Democrats have expressly emphasized that their demand is "based on principle" and does not have topical significance; at times they have hinted that they do not really take the question seriously. A study of the reports of the constitutional committee alone might convey the impression that the republican demand could be realized at any time. Nothing could be farther from the truth. However, the Social Democrats' firm adherence to their principles on this issue is not altogether without significance. Should a monarch attempt to overstep the bounds of parliamentarianism, the party could immediately advance these principles by citing its previous declarations.

A study of the Social Democratic press uncovers unequivocal testimony to a shift in the party's outlook during this period. Previously—and particularly during periods when Social Democrats were bound by cabinet responsibilities—party newspapers frequently published articles that underscored the party's republicanism with a certain asperity. The traditional arguments were reiterated: a republic is the consummation of formal democracy; the king is surrounded by an air of snobbism and servility; in crises the power of the monarch can be utilized by reactionary forces. At the same time, the papers admitted to the lack of urgency of the issue. Nonetheless, at least one suggestion was made to the effect that the party actively conduct propaganda for a republic. In recent years the economically worded statements have assumed another coloration. As a rule, republicanism is still sustained on principle, but it is so completely based on theoretical principle and is qualified by such strong emphasis on the absence of any intention to actualize this demand that the net result is support of monarchism with reservations. *Social-Demokraten* articles on the royal jubilees of 1928 and 1938 seem to earmark this trend. In 1928 Engberg wrote that the Social Democratic party must fight the hereditary monarchy. The monarchy is "doomed by progress itself. Sycophants and gadabouts can guild it. A vocal quasi-patriotism can cheer for it. A loyal clergy can pray for it. As democracy matures and becomes more purposeful, [the monarchy] must one day be eradicated as unsuitable for the task of popular self-government." Ten years later Z. Höglund declared that Swedish democracy, "in cooperation with a loyal monarchy," had probably withstood the stresses of the past decade better than a young Swedish republic could have done. The Swedish king, "who appears without pretensions of being a superman, without a dictator's manners," was preferable to modern dictators. "This does not mean to say that constitutional monarchy is the last word in the development of constitutional philosophy. We remain faithful to our republican ideal, but this question has lost all sense of urgency in a situation where the monarch himself functions as though he were the president of a republic." The reason for the more recent modulation of the party's attitude toward the republican question is probably threefold: the monarch has long refrained from any attempt to exercise his personal power; a feeling for decorum constrains the government party from making statements that even indirectly touch upon the person of the head of state; lastly, as Höglund suggested, modern dictatorships have made the monarchy seem but an insignificant deviation from a consummate democratic structure. The situation at present has made provocation of conflicts on this issue seem even more far-fetched than previously.

Proposals for the establishment of a unicameral system have also been introduced from time to time, most recently in 1932. Representatives of groups to the left of the Social Democrats have consistently taken the initiative in regard to this question as well. The constitutional committee has dismissed such proposals in a few words, and, as a rule, all Social Democrats have backed the committee's verdict. The brief debates on the subject that took place in both houses indicate that the Social Democrats have increasingly come to accept a bicameral system. On only one occasion, in 1924, did one of the houses take a vote count on this question; the lower house then rejected the proposal 113 to 37. In 1932 the constitutional committee expatiated more fully than usual against the proposal in question: "our two-chamber system . . . has been found serviceable for the task of securing circumspection, continuity, and self-control in the cognizance of the affairs [before it] on its present democratic foundation." Even the great majority of Social Democratic representatives accepted this justification for the rejection of the proposal.

The unicameral problem has otherwise not been the subject of much discussion. When the vote of the upper house occasioned the resignation of the second Social Democratic cabinet in the spring of 1923, it was maintained that the lower house ought to have a decisive influence on cabinet formation —a view that was later also advanced in the debate regarding the institution of the order of the day. However, this line has not been pursued with any determination and during recent years demands for a curtailment of the authority of the upper house have simply not arisen. The Social Democratic member (Leo) of the committee that made an investigation 1927–1928 of the composition of the upper house only called for the elimination of the eligibility census and thus did not support the proposals of various other committee members for the establishment of cooption and special eligibility categories. The idea of a radical reform of the composition of the upper house as previously espoused by Möller and others seems to have been abandoned.

One Social Democrat, Viktor Larsson, sat on the referendum committee appointed in the summer of 1920. The committee prepared a proposal for a constitutional provision to the consultative referendum that was definitively adopted in 1922. However, the committee's second report in 1923 disapproved the establishment of the decisive referendum; in both cases Larsson sided with the majority. Other motions for the establishment of the decisive referendum have subsequently been made in the Riksdag, but the Social Democrats have not initiated such proposals. Further, with a few possible exceptions, Social Democratic members have concurred with the constitutional committee's disapprobation of such proposals, and no Social Democrat has argued for these proposals in the Riksdag. One can therefore safely assume that the party has no interest in broadening the institution of the referendum beyond the narrow confines established by the constitutional amendment of 1922.

Among other problems of constitutional philosophy discussed during this period was the question of strengthening the executive power. This question was actualized during the minority parliamentarianism of the 1920s and early 1930s. Since the formation of the fourth Social Democratic cabinet in 1932, it has ceased to be a subject of discussion; instead, parties outside the coalition cabinet have criticized the growing power of the executive branch. Particularly during the six-year period (1926–1932) when Social Democrats were not in the cabinet, proposals were made within the party that were aimed at strengthening the executive power, primarily by the formation of stable majority governments. It was mainly from this point of view that several party leaders such as Engberg, Möller, and Åkerberg urged a return to the majority elections which, they thought, would considerably improve the possibilities for the formation of a solid majority in the lower house. However, this thinking did not seem to engage a majority in the party: prominent members—primarily P. A. Hansson—repudiated the idea. At the 1930 Riksdag several leading Social Democrats called for an investigation in regard to the strengthening of government power. To this end they recommended that cabinet members be admitted to committees, that the institution of the order of the day be introduced in the lower house, and that the four-year term of the lower house be reckoned from the time of the by-election, even if the election took place as a result of the dissolution of the house. The Social Democratic Hansson cabinet subsequently introduced a proposal containing the first of these recommendations, but without success. An investigation into the latter recommendations initiated by the same cabinet led to a negative result.

In this context we should finally consider the Social Democrats' stand on two issues that were intimately related to political democracy: the position of women and the school question. These issues have not played a vital role in ideological debate, and the party's stand on them does not reveal any important features. In regard to these issues and others, the Social Democrats have expanded on ideas once championed by the Liberals.

The position of the party during its first phase on issues related to women is to some degree an exception to the above. It was determined by the idea that complete equality between the sexes would accompany the victory of socialism. The question of the rights and position of women was therefore regarded as only a small part of The Social Question. This standpoint was most clearly expressed in Bebel's book on the subject, *Die Frau und der Sozialismus*. Subsequently, however, the Social Democrats espoused various demands for reform aimed at the repeal of laws that relegated women to a subordinate position vis-à-vis men. The first demand was the franchise for women. As indicated, this question was consistently included in the party programs. In practice, however, this demand was brushed aside during the franchise strifes of the early 1900s: at the time, realization of general male suffrage was considered the principal objective and all efforts were concentrated to this end. Both before and after the establishment of universal suffrage Social Democrats have taken part in reforms to attain legal and political equality for women. However, party programs have not included any stipulations for party participation in this cause, and it has never been considered by party congresses.

The demand for equality on principle has also been stressed in regard to the position of women engaged in gainful employment. However, disagreements on this issue have arisen within the trade union movement—a circumstance that does not fall within the scope of our study. Several Riksdag proposals for investigations into the possibility of circumscribing the position of married women in government service have been rejected with Social Democratic assistance. A motion was brought at the 1932 party congress, urging that in view of the then-current economic crisis married women be excluded from local and government service; it further called for an investigation into limiting the gainful employment of married women in industry. In its statement on the proposal the party administration asserted that the solution of unemployment problems must be found elsewhere. The congress rejected the proposal, but the attendant debate revealed sharp divisons of opinion.

Party agitation among women has been dealt with separately on several occasions. Resolutions enjoining such agitation were accepted by several of the early congresses. Special women's organizations were created. In 1904 the women's trade union began publication of the paper *Morning Breeze* (*Morgonbris*), which was primarily directed at female readers. In 1920 Sweden's Social Democratic Federation of Women was formed. The participation of working-class women in elections was at first negligible, but has progressively increased—although the difference in frequency of voting between men and women in this social group is still relatively big. In recent years successful moves have been made to increase female representation in political and local institutions.

The Gotha program included the following points in regard to schools: "Universal and equal popular education throughout the nation. Universal compulsory school attendance. Free instruction in all educational institutions." Other early Social Democratic programs contained similar references. The program of 1885 of the Social Democratic Union in Stockholm, for example, demanded "Obligatory, free, and common primary school instruction for all without regard to class or sex." The constituent congress adopted an unusual resolution that pronounced existing elementary schools unsuitable and urged that party organizations support the establishment of schools based on scientific principles and organize socialist schools. The following points were inserted in Article IV of the 1897 program: "Separation of school and church. Development of the primary school into an elementary school that is common to all and that fulfills cultural requirements." The term "elementary school," popularized by Fridtjuv Berg, was here adopted to designate the common primary school that the party called for. Party representatives in the Riksdag did not present any proposals to follow up the program during the next few years. The 1908 party congress resolved to request that the Riksdag group introduce a proposal on this issue and commissioned the party administration "to investigate which methods and pressure tactics the party might avail itself of in order to force through a primary school reform along the lines indicated by the party program and the resolutions adopted by the party congress." The words "the resolutions adopted by the party congress" referred to resolutions on instruction without the profession of faith. Various proposals on the elementary school (1909) and related issues subsequently introduced in the Riksdag did not yield any result. The Liberal-Socialist Edén's coalition cabinet in which Rydén was minister of public worship and education (until November 1919) did consider the question. In 1919 the so-called School Commission was appointed; one of its assignments was an investigation of the establishment of the elementary school system.

The program revision of 1920 called for amplification of the article on the school issue. This article, which became Article V after 1905, was worded as follows:

> Free instruction in public schools.
> A common primary school as the foundation for the education of the citizens.
> Specialized schools for the crafts, industry, commerce, agriculture, and the professions.
> Guaranteed admission to higher institutions of learning for those qualified. Economic obstacles to their education shall be eliminated.
> An educational system without the profession of faith.
> Promotion of free research and educational activities.

The amendment proposal had been presented by the program commission; it was adopted unchanged and without debate. Since the rationale given by the program commission can be regarded as an authoritative expression of the party's viewpoint, it deserves to be quoted in full (except for the references to instruction without the profession of faith).

> The main difference between the proposal and the present Article V is the extension of demands to apply not only to the primary school but to the school system as a whole and to free research and educational activities as well.
>
> Because of the great importance of the organization of the school system to the creation of the new society, the program article must embrace the entire educational system.
>
> The principle of free instruction in public institutions of learning is of primary importance. Such institutions shall serve society's need to provide all citizens with a good education and certain groups with a specialized education. They are not institutions for private investment of capital. Tuition should therefore be without charge.
>
> The principle of free instruction should, moreover, be broadened to the extent that the interests of society require and its resources suffice.
>
> The foundation of the entire educational system shall be the common primary school, which should be equipped so that it can serve as an elementary school. The first grades of the present secondary school should accordingly be eliminated. The primary school shall be the public school. Private schools shall be supported only in genuinely exceptional cases as, for example, when a private school carries on meritorious experiments with new educational methods.
>
> All higher education shall be founded on the primary school.
>
> In addition, arrangements shall be made for specialized schools for various practical occupations and for advanced specialized instruction through the university and other higher institutions of learning.
>
> Admission to higher institutions of learning at present excludes many who are genuinely qualified, partly because of inappropriate admission requirements (the present matriculation examination [*studentexamen*]), but above all because of the financial difficulties [encountered] by children of the lower income groups in continuing their education.

Because it is in the vital interests of society to utilize special aptitudes within just those spheres of work in society where such aptitudes are most valuable, such formal and substantial obstacles must be removed. In this connection special attention should be given to the unfavorable position of the rural population compared with the urban. To permit the cultivation of aptitudes to be entirely dependent upon private economic conditions, individual enterprise, and the vagaries of chance is mismanagement of society's most important natural resource: the individual's own capacities and disposition. The cost of utilizing this resource is a good capital investment for society.

A party whose principles establish the securing of nonmaterial as well as material culture as the purpose of party activity cannot limit its cultural endeavors to that which appears "expedient" at the moment. All free research that advances knowledge, all free educational activity that aims at the dissemination of the findings of research and at deepening the culture of the masses must be precious to the party that wishes to reform society. The school program should therefore be amplified with an article that expresses the party's desire to promote free research and educational work.

The 1927 school reform, passed with Social Democratic assistance, fulfilled the party's wishes in many respects. However, at the time of the presentation of the school bill in a joint proposal the party made a series of demands that were not realized—at least not to the extent desired. Among other changes, the party urged that the commercial or trade high schools (*realskolorna*) be uniformly connected with the sixth grade in the secondary schools. (According to the Riksdag decision they would be connected with the fourth or sixth grade.) The party also wanted successive repeal of semester fees, financial assistance during the school year to indigent but gifted students, and the abolition of the matriculation examination. In a statement concerning a motion on the school question made at the 1928 party congress, the party administration stressed that efforts for reform would be prosecuted. "Much obviously remains to be done before the idea of a unified school can be realized and a practical balance between the different functions of instruction in the schools can be effected. However, it is self-evident that our party will carry out its principles in its future school policy in the respects mentioned." No attempt to really carry out the elementary school principle has been made since, however. Foremost among recent school reforms initiated by Social Democrats is the 1936 decision to increase attendance at primary schools from six to seven years.

Summary

WHEN THE Social Democratic movement made its appearance, the Swedish nation was characterized by a severely restricted franchise and considerable civil liberty. The propaganda opportunities available to the new movement were practically unlimited from a legal standpoint, but its opportunities to gain influence through direct political activity were narrowly circumscribed. The party could set forth its ideology and program with less restraint than would have been possible in most other countries, but it could not envision their realization within the framework of the existing constitutional philosophy.

Under these conditions and with a view to the examples of other nations, the party began to debate which tactics should be called into use. Two lines were discernible—the revolutionary and the reformist—but this classification implies gross schematization. In fact, several different lines could be detected in the frequently vague and ambiguous statements that were made. Some optimists believed that democracy—meaning, primarily, universal suffrage—would be won through peaceful, democratic means. Yet they did not renounce the thought of winning the franchise by revolution—a political, democratic revolution—in order to subsequently use democracy to implement socialism without violence. Others regarded a revolution of this kind to be inevitable. A third line foresaw and worked for a social revolution that would mean the victory of socialism; the social revolution might be coextensive with or follow the democratic revolution. This third line frequently regarded political work as essentially a form of propaganda that would lay the groundwork for but could not itself result in the realization of socialism. Interpretation of the various declarations made entails considerable difficulties, not least because the word "revolution" was used at an early stage to designate not only a violent insurrection but also a gradual development, an evolution. Finally, the party subsumed an anarchist faction that was indifferent or hostile to all participation in elections and the legislature and campaigned for violence and other forms of direct action. This faction was, however, influential for only a short period.

Basic to early Swedish Social Democracy and common to all the factions it embraced is the view of socialism as a goal that overshadowed all others, and of revolution and lawful activity as tactics, together with the establishment of the seizure of power, a total and stable victory as the objective of all party activity. Marx's major perspective prevailed. A society was either capitalist or socialist; either the bourgeoisie or the proletariat was its ruler. Therefore, it did not occur to Social Democrats of that period that they might win only some power, or power for a limited time: in their view, when they did emerge victorious, the future would be theirs. In this sense the movement was totalitarian. In Marx's terms, the proletariat, having been nothing, would become all.

This outlook is based on historical and philosophical reasoning that is mixed with metaphysics, but under certain conditions it could conceivably have been translated into practice. If industrialization had proceeded with extraordinary speed for a couple of decades and if an undemocratic government, based on a very restricted franchise, had been maintained at the same time, constitutional changes—whether effected by peaceful or violent methods—might conceivably have led to a socialist majority government without any intervening period of transition. But developments in Sweden did not follow this pattern any more than developments in other nations.

Social Democratic debate in what was called the tactical question had a mark of unreality. The party was too insignificant to be able to look forward to any significant political success within the near future. Further, the proletariat, to which the party program was addressed, represented but a fraction of Sweden's population. Once the anarchist faction had been repudiated, party activity was of necessity directed toward winning universal suffrage. In the course of several years, Social Democracy became essentially a party that championed the franchise at the side of bourgeois liberalism—and in its shadow. The actual practice of working for democratic causes strengthened the democratic line within the party itself. It was impossible to demand the franchise and coincidently proclaim that a revolution would take place even if the franchise were granted. Various circumstances contributed to make Branting, who represented moderation and reformism from the start, the dominant figure at the turn of the century. His strength was mainly derived from the working masses that had come to the party via trade unions; they had no revolutionary ideology, and they regarded the Social Democratic party as a medium through which they might improve their position through sociopolitical measures. By the time the first comprehensive constitutional reform became law, 1907–1909, the party had accepted democracy as the basis of its activity.

The immediate objective now became the prosecution of complete democratization of the legislature, abetted by the increased action potential the party had gained. In the main it adhered to legality, but under the influence of revolutionary movements in other countries party members sometimes threatened extraparliamentary action. In any event, there was no further mention of a social revolution—only a democratic revolution. The constitutional reform of 1918–1921 realized this objective.

Enactment of the reform was followed by a purge of the remnants of revolutionary doctrine. Democracy was proclaimed a leading party principle. The party gradually became involved not only in securing democracy but also in extending democratic ideology. The policy of cooperation and compromise that democracy required banished the idea of capturing total power as if it had been a dream. Swedish popular government was characterized by a convergence toward an ideological center and by the negligible influence exerted by extremist groups. Favorable economic auspices provided the condition for steadily growing and more purposeful concord. Enervation or annihilation of workers' movements in other nations and the rise of dictatorships made the defense of Swedish democracy the chief object of the party. With each year the party's perspective shifted a little, until the idea of socialization finally receded into the background and the word "democracy" was accorded the sacred position once reserved for "socialism."

While Social Democrats were engaged in the fight for universal suffrage they had paid little heed to the composition of the cabinet or its authority. The idea of a total power takeover had obstructed realistic analysis of the state of affairs that would probably follow democratization. International congresses had condemned Social Democratic collaboration with other parties in the cabinet. The radical line that used Marx's major perspective as its point of departure considered a Social Democratic cabinet or Social Democratic participation in cabinet work an anomaly in a capitalist state: as far as they were concerned the cabinet was the chief organ of the bourgeois apparatus for impoverishment. However, Swedish Social Democrats were confronted with the same dilemma as their counterparts in other nations. Should they prevent the formation of cabinets that adopted some of the party's demands by disassociating themselves from such cabinets? In 1917 cabinet socialism was accepted in practice by virtue of the Social Democrats' entrance into the Edén cabinet. This was, however, considered only a provisional arrangement to implement democracy. But the inner logic of events forced the party onward. A genuinely Social Democratic cabinet was formed three times in the course of four years. During subsequent years when the party stood outside the cabinet because of defeats in the Riksdag and at elections, the idea of totality returned in diluted form: demands were made that the party form a cabinet only under special, carefully defined circumstances and that it thus should be assigned less responsibility for the goovernment than that ascribed to other parties. This notion lost all semblance of validity as soon as the party was again offered the power of government pursuant to its triumphs at the 1932 elections. The formation of a coalition cabinet under Social Democratic leadership after the 1936 elections signified the total victory of the democratic ideology of the pursuit of concerted settlement of differences as well as of unqualified cabinet socialism.

The exact configuration of the democracy that was first considered a tactical instrument and later a guiding principle has never been the main question in Social Democratic debate. The central institutions of popular government —universal suffrage and political liberty—have predominated. Yet the party formerly also called for reforms of secondary importance. Realization of these reforms—primarily the establishment of a republic, a unicameral system, and the referendum—would consummate the democratic order. Since the monarch's recognition of parliamentarianism and the reform of both houses on the basis of universal suffrage these demands have been retracted, or have, in any event, lost all immediate significance. The Social Democratic party has come to accept a polity that has evolved through the accommodation of the traditional Swedish order to the principle of popular government.

The Nation and Defense

The Discussion of the 1880s and 1890s and the Conflict over the Reorganization of the Military of 1901

THE SWEDISH SOCIAL DEMOCRATIC movement declared that it, like the socialist parties of other nations with which it was related, was an international movement with an internationalist orientation. Consonant with Marx's exhortation and prediction, the proletariat of all nations would unite to prepare for the subversion of the capitalist order and the establishment of the socialist society in accordance with jointly drafted plans. The victory of socialism would also mean the breakthrough of internationalism: the world would form one single socialist society or, in any case, a number of socialist societies that would work together in concert and in peace. War was dependent on the capitalist order, or rather, on the class structure, whose ultimate expression was the capitalist society. The only effective instrument for peace was therefore socialism itself. The military establishment was both an agency in the power struggle between capitalist states and a weapon that the upper class could use against the lower class. The victory of socialism would make all armed force superfluous. As a rule, however, this vision was combined with the view that the state as an entity did have some value insofar as it was founded on a national community, at least under the existing social order. The Social Democratic movement combined liberalism's appreciation of the right of nations to self-determination with its own faith in a world of peace, freedom, and progress. The essential difference between the two ideologies was that the Social Democrats considered a mighty upheaval necsssary to the achievement of their goals.

In its application as a point of departure for political action, this broad perspective could be viewed from different angles. As advocated by the International prior to World War I, Social Democrats were to refuse all participation in national armaments to the extent that this was feasible and would thus be instrumental in this sphere in furthering the fall of the capitalist system. On the other hand, it was also asserted that inasmuch as war and defense were allied to capitalism, and capitalism would not capitulate before the productive forces and means of production had reached a certain degree of development, Social Democrats should regard armament as a temporary necessity and adopt a standpoint friendly to national defense. This attitude of resignation had its counterpart in the economic sphere in the view that Social Democrats should work in behalf of big industry and the concentration of capital while awaiting the breakdown of capitalism.

Other lines of thinking have acquired relevance when Social Democrats have attained a position of some power in a country. Reformist lines have then emerged even in the area of national defense. They have partly been occasioned by the desire to safeguard national unit, a value that even Marx had recognized. They have also been prompted by the desire to pursue humanitarian and internationalist ideals fundamental to socialism, even though such endeavors would be made within the framework of the capitalist state. Attempts to secure peace, to limit military preparations, and to democratize the military organization have had Social Democratic support despite the fact that such attempts—according to the strictly Marxian viewpoint—could not lead to lasting results unless attended by the victory of the international proletariat. Thus, in this as in other spheres, ideological extremism has been replaced by short-term practical policies contingent upon concrete, closely related considerations.

Such discrepancies between ideology and practice were of secondary importance in the young Swedish Social Democratic movement. Sweden did not harbor nationalist aspirations of any note; in many ways it was one of the most homogeneous countries in Europe. The only question of foreign policy of the late nineteenth century that gave rise to debate and dissension was the shape that the Swedish-Norwegian union would take. Differences of opinion on this issue manifested themselves even among Social Democratic leaders, but they agreed in their sympathy with Norwegian claims to equality and on renunciation of war as a means of preserving the union. The radical element of the middle class concurred with the Social Democrats on this point. Problems that might have resulted from an aggressive foreign policy disposed toward expansionism and the formation of alliances simply did not arise.

Many programs have attested to the internationalism of the Social Democrats. The Palm program of 1882, which was based on the Danish Gimle program, proclaimed: "The efforts of the Social Democratic party are largely [expended] in a patriotic spirit, but, in its conviction that the workers' movement is international in character, [the party] is ready to sacrifice everything to help usher in Freedom, Equality, and Brotherhood among all nations." We cannot draw any conclusions from the phrase "in a patriotic spirit"; this was undoubtedly an erroneous translation of the Danish "in a national spirit" (*"i en national Stamme"*), which was, in turn, evidently derived from the Gotha program's "within the framework of the national state of today" (*"im Rahmen des heutigen nationalen Staates"*).

The program presented by the Social Democratic Union in Stockholm in 1885 contains these statements: "The workers' question is, however, neither local nor national, but international. Although its sphere of activity is mainly within Sweden, the Swedish Social Democratic Workers' party, mindful of the international character of the workers' movement, shall therefore strive to fulfill all the duties incumbent upon Swedish workers toward their brethren in other nations. The universal brotherhood of man is a goal of the future for us as well." Sections of the rest of the program indicate that one contemplated the introduction of international law even before the triumph of socialism. The Gotha program of 1889–1897, which was regarded as the program of the Social Democratic party, was substantially the same as Palm's program of 1882 (with the difference indicated). The following statements—which still stand—were introduced into the program of 1897: "The interests of the working class are the same in all countries with a capitalist system of production. With the development of world trade and production for world markets, the workers' position in each country will be dependent on their position in other countries. The liberation of the working class is therefore an undertaking in which all civilized people must take part. In recognition of this, Sweden's Social Democratic party declares itself to be *one* with Social Democracy in other countries."

The issue of national defense was by and large bypassed in Social Democratic debates of this period, which were dominated by questions of socialist principle and the franchise. This insignficant, Utopian-tinged movement did not consider the organization of the nation's defense in the prevailing capitalist society to be a pressing problem. Although pervaded by mistrust and criticism, this nonetheless relatively passive attitude toward national defense was understandable in view of the fact that Sweden became aware of the exigencies of modern armament at a rather late date. Of course, the defense issue was an important item on the agenda of the Riksdag. Since Sweden's defense was of old based on a system of quartering soldiers in private homes, this issue became a perpetual point of contention between the two chief factors in the Riksdag: the bureaucracy, with the concomitant upper class, and the propertied farmers. However, the individual's contribution as legislated by various reforms of the defense program was scarcely burdensome. In 1885 the period of conscription was increased from 30 to 42 days; in 1892 it was further extended to 90 days. The standing army that was based on the quartering system was retained. Social Democrats protested against both decisions, but the additional defense burdens did not become the main targets of the party's propaganda.

Typically, the defense issue was not touched upon in many of the declarations that the party incorporated into its programs during this period (for example, the program of the first congress of workers from southern Sweden of 1888). The declarations made were uniformly based on foreign prototypes and consequently contained only the usual Social Democratic demands for abolition of the standing army and establishment of a militia system. The idea of a militia—especially the plan to make rifle clubs a central component of the defense system—was, indeed, advanced by radical elements in Sweden's middle class, but the influence of international socialism was most certainly decisive to Social Democratic sponsorship of the idea. Palm's program of 1882 contained these items: "Abolition of the standing army, establishment of general popular armament." Again we evidently encounter a poor rendition of the Danish Gimle program, this time of the reference to establishment of "a national popular guard" (*"almindeligt folkevaern"*). A series of other statements made during the 1880s also contained the term "militia system" to designate the kind of military organization intended. The following demands were incorporated into the 1885 program of Stockholm's Social Democratic Union: "Abolition of the standing army and the establishment of general popular armament (*milisarmé*) as long as total disarmament is considered inadvisable. Martial law shall be suspended in peacetime." The general statements of principle that introduced the program maintained that Social Democrats must strive for "an ordered state of justice between nations" and, more immediately, for "the neutralization of the Scandinavian countries." Among the program items reported in *Social-Demokrate* between 1886 and 1907 were the demands for "international courts of arbitration" and "the abolition of the standing army." The official program of the newly organized Social Democratic party, the Gotha program, called for "Universal compulsory military service. A popular guard instead of a standing army."

At the four party congresses prior to 1900 the defense issue was not treated at all—or only in a peripheral article. Some vague questions were broached at the first congress regarding the conduct proper to a Swedish soldier under certain circumstances: should he obey if commanded "to murder his brethren and fellow men" or should he only "defend our native land against invasion by eternal violence"? The congress resolved without debate to exhort party members "to strive with all appropriate means in order that citizens in uniform under no pretexts lend themselves to violence against the freedom and rights of other citizens." The 1891 congress resolved to urge workers to form rifle clubs. This exhortation was included in a resolution on the franchise and was, in fact, mainly intended to make the workers combat-ready in view of the internal conflicts that might possibly develop within the nation. A motion was made at the 1894 congress demanding a clarification of the party's position "on militarism, or in the event of an outbreak of war." The congress "considered that it should not devote its time to a question of this kind which is of no current significance." The new party program adopted at the 1897 congress included a section (II) with this wording: "Popular armament instead of a standing army. Courts of arbitration for international disputes. The Riksdag and, ultimately, a popular referendum to decide on war and peace." There are no specific data on the origin of this section and it does not appear to have been discussed at the congress. Of final note is the fact that only one Scandinavian workers' congress of this period considered the defense issue. This was the congress of 1897, which unanimously adopted a resolution demanding reductions in military budgets, arbitration of international disputes, guarantees for the neutrality of the Scandinavian countries, and the referendum to decide on questions of war and peace.

Since the defense issue was not subject to more vital discussion it is generally impossible to delineate exactly the views of the party leaders. The data available on Branting alone suffice to indicate the evolution of his opinion on this issue.

Judging from the Branting quotations that are available, his stand on defense underwent a significant transformation between 1885 and 1900. In 1885 and 1892 he opposed the modest ramifications of the defense system then proposed. Later he urged an increase in defense preparations, if through channels other than those approved by the cabinet and Riksdag majority. This transformation is striking in the documents Branting wrote during this period; it is strange, therefore, that writers on the subject have chosen to deny it and insist that Branting held roughly the same views throughout his life.

Branting's first known remarks on the subject were made in April 1885 and pertained to a Riksdag proposal for extension of the period of compulsory military service. Branting's criticism of the proposal is indicative of his flatly negative stand at that time. "Peaceful development [in the direction] of justice and freedom, which will enable the mass of the people to come to love our land and its institutions, will give us far greater security than all our futile rattling of weapons has hitherto been able to provide." He amplified his thoughts in an article written in 1890 with the title "A Danger to the People" (*"En folkfara"*) that appeared in the tract *Light and Freedom* (*Ljus och frihet*) published by the utilitarian Lennstrand. Lennstrand was considered a nihilist in regard to defense. We cannot determine whether Branting was of the same persuasion at the time, but we can ascertain that his article in no way suggests a positive deposition toward defense. The article was introduced with a verse borrowed from a recently published collection of anticlerical and antimilitary poems. Freely translated, this is its message:

Look not to the east or south,
Nor to neighboring black clouds
For portents of peril and destruction
to our native land.
The enemy is in our midst!

Branting began his article with a reminder of the decision to take up questions regarding defense legislation and militarism as the main agenda of the International Social Democratic congress scheduled to convene in Brussels in 1891. This, said Branting, was natural in view of the central importance of these questions to the workers: the so-called national defense weighed upon the workers more heavily than any other state measures. Several factors had contributed to the recent upsurge of European militarism: Bismarck's aggressive policy, the anxiety of the bourgeoisie to protect its property, the appetite for colonial acquisitions, the aspirations of the upper class to secure remunerative employment for its sons. Yet militarism should not be regarded exclusively as an inevitable consequence of capitalism. The phrase "militarism exists *only* as a safeguard for the strong box of the upper class" is an oversimplification. A policy of violence was necessarily connected with capitalism, but even the existing system permitted gradations in such a policy. "This allows a broad margin for the return to more sound conditions without any real necessity of stepping too hard on the toes of the class state." The example of the United States, among others, demonstrated this. A different policy ought to be feasible, particularly in Scandinavia. "What good would it do if a sparsely populated country with inadequately exploited resources and in opposition to all kinds of geographic, national, political, and historical conditions were to assume a miniature copy of the stifling armament that is cursed by its bearers in Europe? Despite the preposterously high premium and unsuitability of method of paying for it, the *risk* of conflagration remained the same and . . . under unfavorable political conditions even the most costly defense would be insufficient." According to Swedish tradition the army was composed of professional soldiers, and this tradition had not been shaken by the institution of compulsory military service, "for a conscripted army is simply a militia, the popular call to arms that comes to the assistance of the professional army in times of danger. . . ." Commenting on the propaganda for a stronger defense system then circulating in Sweden, Branting wrote that it would have no prospects of success if the Swedish people were united and had self-government. "But today the bane of class dissention prevails, and the ruling class' pursuit of egoistic class interests *can* play us a foul trick even in regard to militarism's danger to the people." The farmers had previously constituted "a reliable bulwark against militarism," but the agreement reached in 1885 showed that they were no longer dependable. The question was, therefore, whether the working class would soon attain the strength necessary to thwart effectively the military plans that had been drawn up. Branting concluded his article with some flagrantly inflammatory remarks.

> How shall we prevent the victory of the enemy that lurks among us? There is only one possibility: *quickly* reinforce the power of the irreconcilable foe of militarism, the future conqueror of the vampire, the working class! You, whom these lines reach, you who did not think you had a direct interest in the rapid development of the workers' movement—the genuine, the *international* [workers' movement]—here is a focal point for your efforts: come to our aid, then the waves of 'the defense movement' will not be able to drown our cultural development! And you workers . . . whose red banner means fraternity, peace, and the union of people in brotherhood, shoulder your duty to do *all* you can to hold off as long as possible the enemy of today—militarism. When the time is ripe the capitalist class society will fall all the more easily if you can prevent one of its most important pillars from becoming implanted and ironbound in undisturbed peace.

This outlook differs on essential points from the view that Branting embraced a decade later and which is customarily alleged to be distinguishing for him. The article does not contain one positive word about defense. It does not suggest that a new military order based on a militia should be introduced; to the contrary, Branting almost seems to approve of the Swedish tradition of a standing army complemented by conscription; strangely, even the conscripted force is regarded as a militia—possibly because of the brief training period involved. The word "militarism" is used to designate strong defense in general, not just certain aspects of the defense organization. It is most extraordinary that Branting does not suggest that extension of the franchise would make the workers more willing to partake in the strengthening of their country's defenses; he instead assumes that such defense reinforcement would be trammeled if the workers attained a position of power within the immediate future. In this connection he further states that dissensions within the nation make augmentation of defense possible (some years later these same dissensions were said to make support of defense demands impossible), and urges those who stand outside of the Social Democratic party to back the workers for the express purpose of repelling militarism (he would later regard the Social Democrats' hostility to defense as a factor that threatened the movement with isolation).

About two years later, in October 1892, Branting introduced a discussion on the defense question in Uppsala. The extraordinary session of the Riksdag that would extend the period of compulsory military service to 90 days and institute other changes in the military organization was to convene within a few days. Using some of the arguments he had advanced in his article "A Danger to the People," Branting inveighed against the cabinet's defense bill. He branded it as "a concern of the upper classes" and alleged that some armament demands were not prompted by the fear of external foes but by the desire to secure upper-class dominion over the workers and particularly by the idea of using military force to suppress strikes.

Yet on several points Branting accentuated a different outlook—or, at least, different views—than he had emphasized before. He took definite exception to "the simple dictum, made familiar at many popular gatherings" stating that "the worker has no native land to defend." Even if most of the people did not receive their fair share of the gross national product they did not have "either the cause or the right to lessen their children's chances to come into their share of the inheritance in a better and more satisfactory fashion." National groupings were natural, at least for the time being. The true international ideal was "a brotherhood between freely self-grouping societies," not "absolute uniformity imposed by a national vote." Unmitigated nihilism toward defense was therefore misleading, even though it had "a relative legitimacy in view of upper-class clamour for sacrifices by the people, while the upper class itself does not wish to sacrifice anything."

Still more noteworthy is Branting's emphasis of a close correlation between the franchise and defense issues. Optimum effectiveness of the nation's defense could be achieved by granting full civil rights, not by increasing the burdens of defense. "Accomplish what it behooves you by this measure in order that the people may feel they have some share and interest in this native land, and be assured that . . . Sweden, after such a sacrificial feat, (will stand) infinitely stronger than it would become by the most extensive military training that you could hope to impose upon a refractory lower class stooped by [the weight of] its burdens." Franchise reform was not made a condition for worker participation in a new defense organization as later stipulated: it was thought that such reform per se would open up new defense possibilities. The motto was no longer "first the franchise, then defense," but "the franchise instead of defense." Social reforms were also recommended from this viewpoint. "Exert . . . all efforts to make the native land such that it *can* become dear to the people: this is not only the best domestic policy, it is, moreover, the *sole* defense policy that promises any prospect of continued national independent existence."

Albeit in vague terms, Branting propounded that direct improvements in defense could be made in ways other than those indicated by the government. The term "people's army," which occurred frequently in his speech, was evidently used to imply not only that the defense organization should be founded on a democratic, political order but also that it should be developed in accordance with new principles. Branting seemed well disposed toward military drills in schools and toward voluntary rifle clubs, but renounced "the parade exercise." Here we detect a hint of the idea of a militia—although the word itself is never used and Branting's exact intent is not clarified.

The extraordinary session of the Riksdag of 1892 passed the cabinet's defense bill (once certain groups of farmers and urban Liberals had switched to an assenting vote). Branting wrote a scathing criticism of the new legislation in *Social-Demokraten.* He contended that the legislation had come into existence "by virtue of a *corruption* long unequalled in the history of the Swedish Riksdag. . . . The people's cause is betrayed, it is sold, bound and surrendered to the beast (militarism) that will consume it to the marrow. . . . Sweden's civilization will be suppressed into a corner so that the distorted side of culture, systematized brutality, can, in the guise of militarism, alone dominate the seat of honor."

Branting's maiden speech in the lower house at the 1897 referral debate (preceding remittance of the proposal on the administration budget to committee) contained statements that follow the same line as his Uppsala address five years earlier. The state that cancelled a good part of its military appropriations in order to raise the country's material and cultural level would have a head start. "I am certain . . . that this could be a safeguard for independence and freedom that would be equal and perhaps considerably superior to numerous regiments of soldiers and numerous instruments of murder that we cannot procure in time for them to be completely inducted [and installed] before they are outdated and have to be replaced by new, expensive commodities of the same kind." He reiterated this view at the Riksdag of 1898.

Branting's address on "Militarism and Culture" at the Verdandi Union at Uppsala in March 1899 marks a new phase in his development. He first delivered an acid attack on militarism, by which he apparently meant massive contemporary armaments in general. His criticism followed a more "Marxist" line than before. He thus cited with approbation the resolution of the Social Democratic Congress in Brussels of 1891 that decried militarism as an inescapable consequence of exploitation and class conflict. Enlarging upon this resolution, he charged that the large contemporary armies were to a great extent "directed against profound social movements which one does not think one can handle without rifles and bayonets." Despite militarism's dependence on capitalism, it would be possible to ease militaristic pressure under existing societal conditions. In this context, Branting demanded with far greater firmness than before the abolition of the standing armies and conversion to a militia organization. His precise intent was, however, again not defined. He stressed shortening the period of service, cutting back on repetitious drills, and transferring instructional locales to areas other than the barracks; he repeated his conviction that barrack life had a destructive influence and tended to produce a military caste. If one approached "the ideal of a militia that keeps the people free from military tyranny and does not make the army a separate caste" one would "return, albeit at a higher level of development, to the time when free men in Greece gladly assisted in the defense of a native land that gave them so much because it made them participants in a highly [developed] culture."

The defense issue gained new urgency in 1900. It became known that the cabinet was preparing a proposal for a new defense organization to be presented at the 1901 Riksdag; the new order called for the total elimination of the quartering system and extension of the period of compulsory military service to about one year. The main impetus for these plans was most likely, on the one hand, Russia's aggressive policies in Finland (viewed in relation to the increased importance of the iron ore deposits in northern Sweden), and, on the other, the tensions between Sweden and Norway and the latter's military preparations in particular. In response to this situation, Branting wrote a remarkable article on "The Franchise and Conscription" for the May Day issue of *Social-Demokraten*. He began by affirming that the circumstances surrounding the franchise question had altered during recent years. The working class and its demand for universal suffrage had receded into the background; now only the Liberal franchise movement, with its predeliction for compromise, had any prospects of success. What position should one take toward the impending proposal for a new military organization under these circumstances? Branting postulated that the working class totally repudiated such a proposal, asserting "Militarism is the enemy! Fight him inch by inch, not one additional day of training, not one additional penny in appropriations." But Branting himself could not share this standpoint. He contended that not even those who most vehemently attacked militarism really accepted total nihilism in regard to defense, which was, moreover, inappropriate to a social class that was moving ahead. The Social Democratic party wanted to transfer Sweden's wealth from a few to the entire people. "But this entails the self-evident duty to guard this national wealth so that it will not be stolen by strangers while we wrangle among ourselves about the share of each." The party must "strive for an *armed populace,* an army that is not suited for aggression, external or internal, but which is all the stronger in defense, an army upheld by true civic spirit but equipped according to the requirements of military technology to the extent that our resources permit and sufficiently trained so that each man is on familiar terms with his weapon." Thus conversion to an army based entirely on conscription should not be automatically rejected. An army founded on this principle might be better and more popular than the present force. Certain reforms would, however, be necessary to its realization: elimination of parade drills, transfer of training exercises to the school and home community "so that the barracks, the hotbed of brutality and vice, will not have the opportunity to poison the youth that fulfills and completes military service within them." Branting did not mention the word "militia," but, in this as in other cases, he apparently based his reasoning on concepts related to the militia principle.

The queston then, Branting continued, was how to combine the franchise and defense questions. Social Democrats had customarily demanded that the franchise take priority. Both democratic and social reforms were needed to create a civic spirit that would support a defense organization. One must therefore constantly stress "that the franchise issue is our main defense issue." This did not mean that the workers were to "traffic with" their contribution to the solution of the defense question. "Is it fitting that a leading class of the future with idealistic purposes comments on such matters: "business is business!" Would it not be nobler to disdain "to mix two—say what you will—different questions, one social and one national, in political cunning. . . ." Those who had unwavering confidence in the progress of the working class should "have the conviction that the franchise question will be resolved . . . without the necessity of combining it with that which even a negative view would term refusal to participate in defense." A few remarks in a similar vein concluded the article. Its essential message could be summed up as "defense first, then the franchise."

We shall presently return to a consideration of Branting's performance at the party congress of 1900 and in the defense debate of 1901. Before continuing, however, let us once again remind ourselves that Branting's standpoint underwent considerable revision between 1890 and 1900. The last mentioned article reveals him as an unmitigated champion of augmenting the nation's defense. The Branting of some years earlier had repeatedly criticized existing defense arrangements as being altogether too comprehensive and costly. Yet approximately a decade later he was prepared to consent to an increase in defense without prior franchise reform. His change of mind can be partly attributed to but cannot be dismissed by the explanation that Branting had, in the interim, become an adherent of reform of the defense organization along the lines indicated by the principle of a militia.

Then what really caused this change? Only more or less probable suppositions can be made. Social Democratic developments in other countries most likely influenced Branting to some extent; this would be particularly true of the patently prodefense statements made by German Social Democrats. (The Jaurès influence would make itself felt at a much later date.) Branting's Riksdag work may have convinced him of the necessity for a strong defense. He reacted strongly to the Finnish Russianization policy, which may also have made him apprehensive about dangers to Sweden. Finally, it is evident that his position in the article "The Franchise and Conscription" was to some degree determined by political considerations. Since the movement for peoples' parliaments had lost its force because of conflicts between Liberals and Social Democrats, it was important to avoid total isolation of the workers' party. Elements of the bourgeoisie frequently pointed out that the workers' reluctance to assume the burdens of defense was a sign that they were not yet ready for the franchise. It was therefore assumed that substantiated assent to participate in defense would reduce opposition to the one democratic reform that the Social Democrats regarded as their essential goal at the time.

Palm's addresses do not bespeak much consideration of the defense issue or of international problems. His initial address presented the by then familiar idea that patriotism and internationalism could easily be combined. Drawing upon German and Danish examples, he sometimes referred to general popular armament as the only democratic form of defense, but never went on to clarify this thought. His pamphlet *Upper Class Politics and the People's Politics,* issued in 1889, contained the usual criticism of military training and called for "abolition of the standing army that now impoverishes the people." As far as is known, there are no extant statements by Palm on the defense question that date from the 1890s.

Judging by the scant data available, Sterky and Danielsson both started as nihilists in regard to defense but ended on a positive track. In the late 1880s, Danielsson's *Arbetet* articles were unmistakably antinational. He was sentenced to a prison term for the publication of a poem proclaiming that it did not matter to the people "which beast tore them apart, the Swedish lion or the Russian eagle." An unsigned *Arbetet* article spoke of the fatherland as a torture chamber for the workers. At a Malmö meeting early in 1891 Danielsson forced through a resolution charging that the defense movement intended "to strengthen the defense of the upper class against the lower class."

The more Sweden armed herself, the more difficult it would be to remain neutral in the event of war. In any case, he continued, the working class did not wish to participate in national defense until it obtained "civil rights and humane conditions of existence . . . and the army was replaced by an armament of the people in conformity with the principle: the rifle on the wall and the commander [chosen] from the ballot box." In the course of his general shift in position to the right, Danielsson also altered his stand on defense. Prior to the extraordinary session of the Riksdag of 1892, he made a speech recommending that the party support the defense proposal if the cabinet promised to grant universal suffrage. He cited the Russian threat as cause for the establishment of a strong but also democratic army. At approximately the same time he bitterly attacked the cabinet proposal per se in the event it was not combined with a promise to grant the franchise. In following years *Arbetet* published some articles that could be described as sympathetic to defenses. The Social Democratic "program is not disarmament but popular armament." "Under present conditions it would be lunacy for a nation to forswear its right and deny its duty to defend itself." Only a peace movement based on international socialism—not only on humanitarian considerations—could effectively work for a durable peace. Following publication of Branting's article "The Franchise and Conscription," *Arbetet,* no longer under Danielsson's editorship, declared itself along the same lines, but insisted that the question of the franchise be accorded a more prominent place than Branting thought necessary.

As indicated, Danielsson came to represent a national line in later years. Like Branting, he declared that the Social Democrats' patriotic sentiment was upheld by the idea of creating a people's Sweden, a socialist Sweden. He described this forward-looking patriotism in expressive, often quoted terms:

> Can a Social Democrat love "the rush of our streams" as long as the hydroelectric power of the waterfalls is private property, love "the leaping brooks" as long as only the owners of the banks may fish crayfish and well-paying Englishmen angle for trout, love "the melancholy sighs of the dark forest" where the . . . axe has driven away the wood nymph and other lyrical [creatures], love "the starlit night" under which the teeth of starving proletarian hordes chatter with cold, and "the light of summertime" that illuminates them as they sweat and toil day and night? Can he love all this? Yes, he can and should love it as the youth loves the maid of his dreams whom he must first conquer, or as the wanderer his goal, which he can reach only by a long and arduous path. In this sense I am a patriot.

Sterky's first known statements on the defense question date back to 1887 when he delivered an address with the characteristic title "The Sacrifice of the Lower Class for the Defense of the Upper Class." His attitude at this time was obviously negative. He claimed that "the great majority of people have no property to defend and that the native land in which they live is nothing but the property of their oppressor, the upper class." As Höglund pointed out, this was merely a rewording of part of the *Communist Manifesto:* "The workers have no fatherland. One cannot take away from them what they do not have." Sterky criticized the defense proposal of 1892 in *Ny Tid* on the ground that it was conceived solely in the interests of the upper class. On at least one other occasion, however, he expressed an attitude more sympathetic to defense. In 1897, pursuant to Tolstoy's assertion that workers should not serve their time in the army, he wrote: "We *are* not in a socialist society now. And although we consider war to be among the most loathsome, crudest, yes, most criminal manifestations of the class society, it cannot be denied that in view of current conditions there *are* circumstances under which one must defend one's country. If, for example, culturally backward Russia were to attack Sweden, we are certain that Sweden's workers, however meagre their reasons to 'love their fatherland,' would not hesitate to defend it." He added that defense should preferably be organized on a more popular basis.

A series of articles by the Christian Socialist, A. F. Åkerberg, entitled "The Cause of Peace and The Social Question" that appeared in *The New Society* (*Nya samhället*) in 1886 was one of the most fundamental expositions of the defense issue from a socialist viewpoint during this period. Without attempting a detailed examination of the state of Sweden's defense, Åkerberg tried to demonstrate that the abolition of armament would, in general, help solve The Social Question; in so doing, he offered a fresh viewpoint. The savings that could be made by doing away with defense could not *directly* benefit the working people because of the natural law—the ironclad wage law—which decreed that the salaries of workers uniformly tended to fall to the lowest possible level. But disarmament would channel additional capital into large-scale production, which would consequently greatly increase in capacity. The distorted reaction between production and consumption would then "assume such proportions that something would have to be done to remedy it and smooth it out," that is, the process of socialization would commence. Åkerberg thus applied Marxist teaching to the defense question in a unique fashion. According to his theory, the waste implicit in defense provided a safety valve for capitalist society; with the elimination of defense, the Marxist theory of catastrophe would become applicable.

The attacks on nationalism and the defense movement that appeared in the small, extremist papers *Folkets röst* and *Proletären* were particularly acrimonious. *Proletären,* for example, alleged that existing conditions in Sweden offered nothing that could persuade workers to defend the country. Were freedom won and socialization realized, however, the working class would have cause to esteem Sweden more highly than other nations and nihilism toward defense would accordingly disappear.

The above account has mainly been concerned with declarations made by party leaders on important occasions. We can therefore assume that they represent deliberate, carefully formulated statements and consequently do not provide an accurate picture of the popular attitude toward defense as rendered in propagandist speeches, articles, new items, or resolutions passed at various meetings. Popular propaganda was without doubt characterized by hostility toward defense and everything connected with it. Words such as "raw," "brutal," and "inhuman" echo in reports on military conditions: officers were presumed to be snobs and drill fanatics; the training of recruits was described as an exercise in murder or as a rehearsal for human slaughter. This mood of hate is as patent in *Social-Demokraten* as in other party newspapers. Speeches and resolutions dismissed defense as being but an instrument of the upper class in its fight against external, but perhaps, primarily internal foes; the Social Democratic party was hailed as a shield against "the slaughter mania of the upper class." Comments that were obviously antinational were customary if not predominant. Marx's allegation that workers did not have a native land was often used as a basis for speeches. One of the movement's most prominent agitators, C. Lundberg, termed the Swedish flag "a butcher's apron"; patriotism was called a suggestive device of the upper class.

During the 1890s and later, Knut Wicksell, who was not really a socialist but was often regarded as one because of his radicalism, tried to show that Sweden could best serve her own interests and those of world civilization by uniting with Russia. This would give Sweden security, and her people could contribute to Russia's cultural development. Wicksell's theory did not, however, win any adherents in Social Democratic ranks. *Social-Demokraten* asserted that Russia represented reactionism and despotism and that the Swedish working class would lose all its freedom if Sweden were to become "a Russian satrap." The party press similarly rejected Bengt Lidforss' later suggestion that merger with Germany would be a natural step for Sweden.

As this exposition indicates, it is difficult to give an over-all characteristic of the Social Democratic position on defense and related issues for this period. First of all, rifts between short-term and long-term views would tend to make themselves keenly felt in a movement with ambition but relatively distant future objectives and thus produce exceptional ambiguity on the defense question in particular. One view of defense regarded it from a broad socialist perspective, another restricted itself to consideration of concrete proposals that specifically pertained to Swedish conditions; one and the same person propounded different views at different times. Second, several party leaders evidently modified their views. Yet there is no doubt that by the late 1890s the over-all climate of opinion on defense was more positive and well disposed than it had been ten or fifteen years earlier.

A few general reflections are strongly indicated. The goal of the future was the international victory of socialism; war would then disappear and defense would be obsolete. Political and social reforms that would improve the conditions of Swedish workers were more immediate goals. Once the immediate goals had been attained, it was commonly supposed that Social Democrats would be prepared to defend their native land which, by virtue of their efforts, had become more worthy of sacrifice. But the actual question was what the party would do in the situation at hand—and this was not answered with the concurrence present of far-reaching questions.

With only a few exceptions, Social Democrats seemed to wish to sustain national solidarity per se. But were they willing to defend that solidarity under existing conditions? As a rule, party programs and other declarations can be interpolated to answer in the affirmative, but not with much conviction. Their response was cloaked in Marxist formulas: workers had no native land; defense was an instrument of the upper class, designed to serve against internal as well as external enemies. It was not unusual to encounter the idea that the true conflict was that which prevailed between classes, not between nations; this postulate was sometimes presented with such ardor that it implied absolute negation of the defense question. Although not many party members who were in the public light were defense nihilists—opposed to all defense—party agitation must have been designed to create such nihilism to a considerable extent. Even the first Branting articles discussed here cannot fail to give the impression that they are hostile to defense on a first, uncritical reading.

The frequent confusion between "defense as a whole" and defense as it then existed in Sweden contributed to the lack of clarity on this issue. The latter was consistently the object of especially caustic attacks by party spokesmen: it was expensive, undemocratic, and inefficient; they criticized the strict discipline, the drills, the social position and conduct of officers, the use of troops to suppress strikes. Like the throne and the church, national defense was simply both a symbol of and a fortification for the power of the upper class. The isolated training of recruits and conditions of barrack life implied a danger to the moral and physical health of youth and probably—though this was not articulated—to their social and political education as well. In barracks, as in schools and churches, the youth of the working class was to be drilled in the service of the upper class. Each extension of the period of conscription meant an extension of the dominion of the upper class.

Was the party majority that was not nihilistic toward defense eager to replace the existing defense organization they described as militaristic with another organization more to their liking? One would be led to believe that such would be the case according to the Gotha program and the program of 1897, as well as various program statements passed during the 1880s. Arming the populace or the establishment of a militia was, in theory, in conformity with Social Democratic thinking. Yet such concepts were of absolutely no importance in party agitation until the end of the period just discussed. The negative line ruled supreme; the programmatic references to a militia appear to be borrowed from other countries and acted only as a kind of camouflage for the regular propaganda of censure. The idea of drawing up a positive defense program did not assume concrete form until Branting offered his contribution to the question at the end of the 1890s. However, judging from Branting's statements at the Riksdag of 1901, even his proposal presupposed that the militia principle could be applied only in a democratic society. There was no attempt to define the exact usage of the terms "militia" or "popular armament," which illustrates better than anything else the passive attitude to the defense issue.

Basically, "militia" seemed to imply training outside of the barracks, primarily in voluntary rifle clubs. One stressed that soldiers were to store their rifles in their homes. However, both these suggestions were equivocal. The 1891 congress' approval of the organization of rifle clubs was, without doubt, motivated by the idea that these clubs might be of use in internal strifes, a speculation subsequently voiced by several representative party members. In all probability similar motives played an important role in demands for a militia. One apparently thought of the militia as a kind of army of the lower class that would serve in the event of internal conflicts and do battle against the standing army and garrison-trained conscripts, which represented a weapon of the upper class. Members of the Young Socialist movement expressly stated that a militia would be used against "the enemy within"; the idea of arming the populace was "just as good an idea as the general strike." The suspicions that the middle class entertained in regard to such ulterior motives were probably a contributing factor to its rejection of a militia organization.

The development toward increased interest in defense that can be detected, at least in statements made by Branting, Danielsson, and Sterky, became more clearly formulated with the advent of new defense demands in the beginning of the twentieth century. A skillfully handled, moderate policy on the franchise now seemed to have prospects of partial success, if not complete victory. Anxiety about the international situation had increased. Branting dominated the party to a greater extent than he had before or would later: Danielsson and Sterky had died; Palm had been compromised; the Young Socialists were weak and passive; the new opposition of youth had as yet not made its debut. Against this background and although largely motivated by tactics, the party offered a positive alternative to the defense program backed by the general's staff, the cabinet, and the Riksdag majority.

The fifth party congress convened in July 1900. Branting's introductory address on the political situation stressed the urgency of the defense issue and expressed the conviction that Swedish workers did not wish to shirk their obligations to their native land. A proposal by the party administration that the congress declare itself on the subject was remitted to a committee, which, in turn, prepared a resolution that was unanimously approved with the exception of some minor amendments. As the attendant debate suggests, the resolution was a compromise. It began by stating that the party was "absolutely opposed to all militarism but not to a defense system based on a popular and democratic foundation, as, for example, that in Switzerland, insofar as circumstances may summon such [a system] to the defense of national independence, freedom, and civilization." The questions of the franchise and compulsory military service were linked together. The first requisite for efficient national defense was a strong civic spirit, but such a spirit was inconceivable without civil rights. The congress therefore considered "Sweden's upper class responsible for systematic mistreatment of our country's foremost defense question and for thus jeopardizing our national independence because of its selfish and short-sighted franchise refusal." The proposal for one year's compulsory military service that had been presented "without a trace of serious justification" was said to be "an excellent example of how defense questions should *not* be treated."

The party administration was enjoined to obtain the party's opinion once the announced cabinet bill had been preferred. This resolution is especially noteworthy because of its favorable attitude to defense and because it did not stipulate solution of the franchise question as an unconditional requisite for participation in strengthening defense. Branting, who seems to have provided the mainspring for the resolution, introduced the accompanying debate by emphatically stressing that the party could not be indifferent to national values and that it ought to affirm its intention to defend Sweden. His speech suggests that the clause in the resolution requiring that party opinion be canvassed after the presentation of the military organization bill was intended to win over those who were sceptical about the saliently positive statements contained in the resolution.

Some speakers (Olaf Persson, Kata Dalström) were apparently in complete accord with Branting. On the whole, however, although no one moved rejection of the resolution, many differences of opinion were in evidence. Many (Ehnrooth, Chr. Nilsson, Thorsson) would have had any participation in strengthening defense conditional upon the granting of universal suffrage. Lindley represented a completely negative standpoint, viz., Sweden was in no immediate danger; the Swedish people had fewer rights than those of any other European country with the exception of Russia [sic]: "we thus really have nothing to defend." A. Björklund, who had earlier been recognized as the most adroit theorist of the revolutionary line, said he was a solid supporter of defense, but for reasons that were quite different from those of the other speakers. One year of military service was not too much, for, in reality, the workers' own defense movement was also involved. "Our fellows in the party need to train in order to defend Sweden against her enemies—and [to defend] us against the upper class. We need to drench the defending army with our own ideas, and the longer our fellow party members can operate in [the army], the more they will be able to accomplish by way of saturating it with our point of view." Björklund thus reversed the usual argumentation: even though it was not ascribed the character of a militia, the defense organization was regarded as a potential weapon of the working class, not as a protection for capitalism. The minutes of the congress do not indicate that his viewpoint evoked criticism—nor that it won any support. The debate as a whole demonstrated that the compromise resolution could embrace the most contrary views; in another address Branting had noted that the proposal had been formulated with a view to value of a unified stand. Here, as on other occasions, ambiguity was used to cover up dissension. Writing in his paper, however, Branting commended the resolution as indicative of the party's emancipation from phraseology. It was "the best testimonial that the Swedish working class *is maturing* [to become] *of influence* in the native land that it ultimately will bear in [its] strong arms."

The proposal of the general staff for a new military organization including one year of compulsory military service, was presented in November of 1900. It provoked lively discussion within the party. When the party administration met in Stockholm early in December, differences of opinion were clearly articulated. Branting's introductory remarks affirmed the existence of three different currents of thought: "one that was utterly nihilistic toward defense and did not want to have any part of additional defense, one that maintained that the franchise question ought to be solved before further defense expenditures could be contemplated, and lastly, the opinion that the speaker himself embraced, that both questions ought to be preferred at the same time but without combining them." Branting justified his stand on facts and political considerations. As Bebel had declared in the German parliament, under certain circumstances the Social Democratic party should "fight to the last drop of blood when in defense against a lower-ranked power." A totally negative standpoint would obstruct solution of the franchise question, for its opponents would thereby gain a new argument against extension of the franchise. Therefore, the best thing to do would be to vigorously contest the proposal of the general staff—which would probably also become the cabinet bill—and offer a counterproposal based on democratic principles. Branting answered the debaters who alleged that as a rule workers were opposed to any augmentation of defense by asserting that "the opinion of the masses" was not always "the only valid [opinion]."

Lindley propounded a view nihilistic to defense, as he had done at the party congress. He claimed "that the workers as a class have nothing to defend, no property, no right of representation. Even Russia is ahead of us in some questions, for example, in the question of accident insurance." Several other speakers (Tholin, Lindblad, Thorsson) aligned themselves with this outlook or criticized the idea of formulating a positive proposal without thereby explicitly articulating unadulterated nihilism vis-à-vis defense. They criticized the party leadership for its tendency "to fritter away our party program, article by article." The congress nevertheless decided to appoint an editorial committee to draft a proposal: the committee's efforts resulted in a proposal for a party manifesto that was unanimously adopted. The manifesto had patently been prepared by Branting; it signified another triumph of his ability to achieve unity through accommodation of differences. The manifesto denounced the general staff proposal for a new military organization as militaristic and recommended that it be replaced by a militia organization, including a manual of arms in schools and rifle clubs, a school for brief recruit training, which would possibly be followed by maneuvers, although the latter were considered of secondary importance in comparison with free rifle practice and shooting contests in home communities. As in Switzerland, the troops were to obtain their weapons from the state in order that they might continue their training without cost. Augmentations of defense should, under any conditions, be accompanied by certain reforms directed against militarism: the abolition or reform of court martials, suspension of martial law in peacetime, guaranteed right to redress of grievances and freedom of the press for conscripts. The cost of such an extension of defense should not "be slapped on the classes without private means": progressive taxation of large estates was therefore necessary to cover defense costs. Universal suffrage was not unconditionally linked to defense reform, but the manifesto concluded by pointing out the relation between the two. In the event that "the rulers, without regard to the workers' demand for full civil liberties, should try to force through the proposal of the general staff or an essentially similar [proposal]," the workers were exhorted to drive ahead the franchise question "especially by means of demonstrations during the decisive days." The franchise question had to be solved from the point of view of defense in particular, "because no mechanical defense apparatus can come to the rescue if the defenders lack the right spirit, because an army organization imposed by the upper class against the will of the majority and in which the people have had no say can never be pervaded by the willingness to sacrifice what alone can make for a successful defense, because, in a word, the franchise question is our most important defense question. . . ."

The party administration did not obtain the opinion of the membership before adopting and publishing the manifesto, thereby evidently bypassing the clause in the congressional resolution that had required that the members be heard. This omission did not literally conflict with the resolution, however, for the latter referred to canvassing the membership only after the cabinet bill had been presented. In any case, the results of such a canvass would have had little importance once the party administration had announced its unanimous opinion.

After the cabinet had presented its defense bill, which was in close agreement with the proposal of the general staff, party agitation concentrated on the defense issue. Party newspapers assailed the proposed solution as undemocratic and militaristic; their protest was in particular directed to the cabinet's omission of the franchise issue. At more than 100 meetings Social Democrats declared themselves against the cabinet bill and called for deferment of a decision on the question. Partly as a consequence of schism in the Liberal party, Social Democrats apparently played a more prominent role in the campaign connected with the defense bill than on any previous occasion. Without advancing a motion for a more positive proposal, Branting delineated his stand in a series of Riksdag speeches. The warm recommendation he gave to a proposal for military drills in secondary schools that had been considered prior to the comprehensive military organization bill is indicative of his attitude. The problem was, he declared, to obtain an organization capable of reinforcing the nation's defense force without in any way strengthening "the militaristic spirit which is rightly so odious to our people. . . ." Branting gave the longest speech in the main debate on defense. On the whole he followed the lines drawn up in the manifesto of the party administration. The cabinet bill, with its demands for a long period of military service, the barracking of troops, and a corps discipline elicited by training and drill was based on a militaristic spirit. A popular majority opposed the bill; the current eagerness to see it passed was connected with a reluctance to solve the franchise question. "Your tongues speak of danger to the native land while you are really thinking of something else," cried the Branting majority. "You do not arm yourselves against an external foe, but against the franchise." To be effective, a nation's defense must first of all have the people's support. Thus army organization should be "Swiss rather than Prussian." Branting touched upon the constitution of the militia that the party recommended. To the greatest extent possible, military training, and gunnery in particular, should be completed in voluntary organizations before recruits were sent to a special school, which they would therefore attend for a relatively short period (approximately five months). Branting apparently did not contemplate a standing army of any appreciable size. He did not give a precise description of the complete organization of the proposed militia; his allusions in this regard suggest that his plans were rather vague. Nor did he clarify in which specifics the militia organization would basically differ from the system of compulsory military service proposed by the general staff. He would, for example, claim that a militia organization could be developed only "in an atmosphere of freedom." "Full civil rights represent an indispensable condition for serious consideration of such a system of defense." Through this mode of argumentation Branting arrived at the conclusion that universal suffrage was a requisite for an efficient defense system.

Social Democratic defense policy in 1900 and 1901 signified a new orientation of considerable moment. The general statement on popular armament made in the party program previously had the character of an irrevocable declaration; it now served as a point of departure for a positive if not thoroughly formulated proposal. This development in party policy was a victory for Branting, who succeeded in reconciling dissident opinions in a unanimous decision, both at the party congress in July 1900 and at the meeting of the party administration in December of the same year.

This policy shift must not obscure the fact that criticism of the cabinet bill on military organization was the focus of party agitation. The party's main role was that of the opposition to extension of compulsory military service and of the defense organization in general, rather than that of the champion of a militia. As the debates reveal, the presentation of a positive line was largely determined by tactical reasons. The positive line obviously had no prospects of success; it is doubtful whether it would have been adopted if its prospects had been better. Its main function seems to have been to buttress attacks on army and cabinet plans. The possibility of pointing to a positive proposal, even if it did not correspond to existing realities, must have been of enormous help to Branting in his Riksdag appearances. However, the negative line probably had the greatest effect on the general public, both within and outside the party. The resolutions adopted at party meetings in the spring of 1901 did not include any declarations favoring a militia—only declarations opposing the cabinet bill and recommending deferment. The ensuing Social Democratic campaign established the party as the nation's foremost antimilitary or—according to the opposition—antidefense movement.

The obvious ambiguities and inconsistencies in Branting's statements during this period may in part be attributed to tactical considerations. Branting used *one* line of argumentation when he sought to persuade the party to prepare a declaration favoring defense, *another* when he attacked the cabinet and Riksdag majority. His May Day article of 1900 had maintained that the party should help strengthen the nation's defense, even if the franchise were not granted. In the course of the 1901 debate he tried to prove that the militia organization advocated by the party could be implemented only in a democratic society. Moreover, his conciliatory tone in the May Day article does not readily agree with his irascible criticism in the debate of the following year. The over-all impression of Branting's behavior is that whenever his conciliatory tactics did not succeed in persuading the bourgeois majority to make concessions in either the defense or franchise questions he reverted to a more aggressive, negative position that he had held earlier. His caustic assertions in the Riksdag may possibly have been provoked by the hesitancy within the party that greeted his positive proposal on defense. The lack of more complete data makes a conclusive appraisal of his reflections during this period impossible.

Toward the end of his account of the discussion on the military organization of 1901, Höglund writes: "Thus the defense question was 'solved' while the franchise question died. The psychological effects of this blind policy on the Swedish working class were immense. At this moment the view that was fundamentally hostile to defense caught wind in its sails." This description is undoubtedly valid insofar as the defense issue occupied a far more prominent place in party activity during the ensuing years than it had at the end of the 1880s, and antidefense propaganda gained considerably in significance. The extension of compulsory military service to eight months or a year made conscription a far more tangible burden than earlier—which, in turn, provided the conditions for the formation of a more widespread and vigorous reaction to military service. Yet the new defense act of 1901 did not convert the party from willingness to participate in defense to nihilism toward defense. The party's preponderant attitude toward defense was already negative, even though the issue had been of subordinate concern. The positive resolutions of 1900 constituted but a brief and problematic intermezzo. The youth movements that were the principal standard-bearers of antimilitary propaganda in the early 1900s had cause to believe that they had the support of party tradition.

The Controversy; Pro- and Anti-Defense, 1900–1914

A special kind of disarmament movement emerged during the period immediately following passage of the Military Organization Act in 1901. According to the terminology used by its adherents, the movement was defense-nihilistic. Its foothold in the Social Democratic party grew steadily firmer until the years just preceding World War I, and its agitation progressively gained in scope and effectiveness until it reached a par with prodemocratic propaganda in public debate. However, large groups within the Social Democratic party remained loyal to the fundamentally prodefense view that had prevailed at the 1901 congress, and defense therefore became the most controversial issue in intramural discussions. Time and again the conflicts between those friendly to defense and those nihilistic toward defense threatened party unity. Provisional compromises were reached with great difficulty, but they succeeded in delaying rupture of the party for a while. The gains that the faction friendly to defense made immediately before and during the world war were basically due to the international picture. At the same time, its opposition assumed positions that became progressively more extreme. The consequences of the dispute came to the fore at the 1917 congress, but when the so-called Left Socialists broke away from the Social Democrats a temporary relaxation of intraparty conflicts ensued. The basically prodefense line—which may have been described as antiarmament in relation to the attitude of nonsocialist parties (and the Conservatives in particular)—had won a victory.

More than any other party controversy the defense conflict represented a breach between generations, between older members, who occupied the party leadership, and younger members, who aspired to the leadership. The great majority in the party administration and in the Riksdag group consistently adhered to the line friendly to defense. On the other hand, defense nihilism dominated among the young socialists and in the movement that became of prime importance following the expulsion of the Young Socialists from the party, the Social Democratic Youth Federation, formed in 1903. The rift between generations was most pronounced around 1910. Several leading representatives of the new youth federation subsequently transferred to a course that was friendlier to defense and reinforced the Branting-led camp. During the latter part of the period the defense conflict became a focal issue in the power struggle between Branting, the leader of the Social Democratic party, and Z. Höglund, leader of the youth federation. As in 1900, the victory of the line that was friendly to defense meant that Branting again held a dominant position in the party.

Why did the movement nihilistic toward defense emerge in the beginning of the twentieth century? Why did its first support come from the youth organizations? One of the answers to the first question was that, as indicated, the military organization act of 1901—passed against vigorous Social Democratic opposition—entailed personal burdens of an entirely different kind than those imposed by previous defense arrangements and thus provided a basis for popular antidefense agitation. Because of the occasional use of troops to keep order during labor strifes, many workers regarded defense forces as the weapon of society's rulers in the class struggle. The only time that the risk of warlike conflict was imminent was in 1905 at the time of the dissolution of the union with Norway; the workers' strong reaction to the Swedish threat of war undoubtedly resulted in a critical attitude toward the military in general. International Social Democracy was alive to the mounting threat of war, but expected that an outbreak would be averted, not least through the solidarity of the working class. An immediate risk of war for Sweden seemed improbable, especially after dissolution of the union with Norway and in view of the unlikelihood that Russia would be capable of conducting aggressive action because of her inner turmoil and recent war with Japan. Yet all these viewpoints are of subordinate importance. Of most significance is the fact that the Swedish Social Democratic party was passing through certain stages of development as had their counterparts in the Social Democratic parties of other nations. Before the Social Democratic party of any country had gained such strength that it began to feel a real co-responsibility for the nation's government it exhibited markedly hostile tendencies toward defense; this was a common pattern. Swedish defense nihilism was influenced by views propounded in other countries—by German views (K. Liebnecht's *Militarism and Antimiltarism* was a principal source)—and by discussions in Norway and particularly in Denmark. As we shall see, Swedish propaganda was tailored to the views applicable to small nations according to the pattern of Danish radicalism and Social Democracy.

The position of youth organizations as the spearhead of anti-defense agitation also had its parallels in several other countries. On this as on other issues, youth organizations, which have been the group farthest removed from power, have evinced a predeliction for extreme, long-range standpoints that have been little concerned with the actual situation at hand.

The following will first give a synopsis of the phases in the debate on defense up to the party congress of 1917, then explore the underlying ideas of the controversy. Before embarking on this review, let us remind ourselves that, to all external appearances, the Social Democratic party seemed to set its sights on armament reduction, to be followed by gradual disarmament. The antimilitary and antiarmament offensive was uniformly a central feature in the party's election manifestos and its other public declarations.

Organized antidefense propaganda can be said to begin with the Congress of the Socialist Youth Union (the Young Socialists) of 1901, which convened shortly after passage of the defense act by the Riksdag. The Young Socialists had previously espoused the idea of a militia and had stressed the necessity of defending Sweden against external foes. The 1901 congress resolved that the youth union instead carry on antimilitary propaganda, which, as expressed in *Brand* and various pamphlets, bore an obviously nihilistic stamp in regard to defense. The Union's 1903 congress adopted a resolution that delineated the views and aims of the movement: "Whereas the Congress is of the opinion that the proletariat does not have a fatherland or anything else to defend and considers [the idea] that the subjects of a nation should, on command, go out and murder the subjects of another nation to be a barbaric legacy, the Congress accordingly declares that the Socialist Youth Union is defense nihilistic and therefore wishes to amend the program as follows: 'one of the most important tasks of the Union is to fight against the misery of war in whatever form—militarism or armament of the populace—and with all the means at its disposal.' " In ensuing years, antidefense activities became the main object of the union. It made special efforts to circulate propaganda among the armed forces, and sometimes union members would refuse to perform their military service. Young Socialists were frequently sentenced for unlawful agitation and anticonscription strikes. At the 1905 congress the union resolved to exhort local clubs to carry on propaganda for anticonscription strikes not only "among those who have been forced into the soldier's uniform but also among the proletarian youth that is subjected to the recruitment efforts of the modern schools for murder." The stand taken by the union at subsequent congresses is of no direct interest in this context since the Young Socialists cannot be regarded as a Social Democratic faction after their exclusion from the party in 1908.

The decisions reached on the military question at the 1903 congress is one of the main reasons why a number of local clubs deserted the union and why a new youth organization—the Social Democratic Youth Federation—was formed. The new federation appeared in reaction to the antipatriotism and fundamental defense nihilism of the young socialists. In the beginning, it followed the lines of the Social Democratic party. A conference held in 1903 approved the party program; the federation's organ *Forward* (*Fram*) did criticize the existing military organization but nonetheless presented a stand amenable to defense. The federation harbored a tendency to adopt the initial line of the Young Socialists, which regarded the military partly as a weapon against external enemies and partly as a protection for or even as an aggressive instrument of the working class. Federation members, who later became noted for their downright negativism toward defense, unfolded a similar line of reasoning. The signature "M—n" (Fabian Månsson) urged workers to join rifle clubs in order that they would be armed against both internal and external foes. "One thing is certain: we shall never surrender our national position—no more than our organizations [will]—as long as one bullet and one man remain to execute the avenger's bloody mission. One thing is sure, we shall save [our] honor even though we may not save lives, whether the fight be waged against external or internal foes." P. A. Hansson believed that the workers should perform their military service and even enlist in order to win over the military to the side of the workers in the struggle for the franchise. However, defense nihilism became progressively more pronounced in *Fram* articles, especially after 1905, and the youth movement as a whole concentrated on antimilitary agitation to an ever increasing degree. We shall return to the federation's congress of 1905, at which time its position was made more clear cut.

The defense nihilist movement developed independently of the Social Democratic party and became the cardinal cause of youth organizations. Since no regular party congress was held between 1900 and 1905, the movement was able to gain appreciable momentum before being subjected to official party judgment. After the military organization act of1901, the defense issue remained in the background at the Riksdag for a number of years; nor did Social Democratic riksdagsmen attempt to introduce either the militia principle or disarmament on the floor. At the 1903 Riksdag, in his capacity as a member of a provisional committee that was to examine a motion for an investigation into the defense question, Branting proposed that one explore the possibilities of closer cooperation between the main branches of defense and concomitantly try to obtain guarantees that defense expenditures would not be excessive. Neither this proposal nor his statements made in the ensuing debate advanced any general criticism of the military establishment. The foci of attention of both the party administration and the Riksdag group were the franchise and various sociopolitical questions. Not even the principal organs of the Social Democratic press printed any detailed discussions of the defense issue or of the antidefense movement. Some articles in these papers, however, definitely denounced the movement and criticized defense nihilism in the course of their attacks on the activities of the Young Socialists in general.

The antagonisms that had gradually developed within the party finally came into the open at the party congress that convened in February 1905. The congress was faced with a number of motions that called for more stringent, that is, more antimilitary phrasing of the defense article in the party program. The party administration suggested an emendation that satisfied this requirement to some degree. The section on defense clause would accordingly read: "A popular defense system. Fight against militarism. International courts of arbitration." The attendant debate produced a concession to the defense-hostile faction whereby the word "militarism" in the second item was replaced by "the military establishment." This amendment was challenged by demands for more radical changes. At the main vote it was contested by a countermotion for a proposal demanding "fight against the military establishment in all its forms." Branting defended the proposal of the party administration as an attempt to reconcile divergent party opinions. International disarmament was the ultimate goal, he affirmed, but the party should (as it had done previously) back popular armament as a transitional phase. Judging by a remonstration directed at him later in the debate, Branting seems to have implied that a militia would also constitute a protection against the upper class. The second item would spell the party's repudiation of the existing military establishment. However, Branting explicitly emphasized that the article as a whole did not intend to exclude absolute defense nihilists: "We must . . . even out our differences so that divergent opinions can be accommodated in the party. Those nihilistic as well as those friendly to defense should be accommodated." Branting was supported by most of the older leaders in the party and in the trade union movement—Lindqvist, Lindblad, Lindley, Thorsson, and Victor Larsson.

The radical line claimed not only the Young Socialists and some representatives of the Social Democratic Youth Federation but also a number of party men not included in these movements—Palm, among others. Men such as Christiernsson, Rydén, and Hinke Bergegren emphasized above all that Sweden under no conditions could establish an effective defense and that a militia or popular armament would be as bad or worse than the existing organization. Several speakers called themselves unconditional defense nihilists.

When a vote was taken the party administration won by a narrow majority, 93 to 75. Some representatives, such as Rydén and Z. Höglund, who were considered defense nihilists, nevertheless voted for the administration proposal because they could not wholly accept the alternative offered by the opposition.

Branting expressed his satisfaction with the decision of the congress. From a tactical viewpoint he thought it appropriate that a significant minority in the party followed a line nihilistic toward defense: this would increase possibilities of exerting pressure on nonsocialist parties. Yet this was a stand that Branting would not hold for long.

The first congress of the Social Democratic Youth Federation convened in June 1905, some months after the party congress. *Fram* offers only a summary review of its deliberations. It reports that some of the motions made at the congress were defense nihilistic, and that others called for antimilitary propaganda. A basic distinction was thus drawn between defense nihilism and antimilitarism—which was not always done thereafter. The federation board, whose spokesman was P. A. Hansson, proposed that the federation support the directives on defense of the party program—with the proviso that the federation assert its antimilitarism and the need for agitation among the armed forces. Such agitation was to make the army "unfit for use as a weapon against the workers by the ruling class." Hansson claimed that through class-biased legislation and economic oppression, the powers-that-be had given "the word native land a ring that is scornful [to our ears]" and that Sweden could in any event not defend itself against the major powers. He allegedly did not wish to recommend that the congress issue a statement nihilistic to defense, for this would also entail objection to military service, which only "results in imprisonment and saps our agitation of some of its strength." Other speakers (Fabian Månsson, Hj. Gustafsson, Ström) called for explicit defense nihilism; this, they said, need not entail objection to military service—which could only amount to a meaningless demonstration. The decisive argument against the military establishment was that Sweden was not able to defend herself against large-scale aggression. Ström pointed out the unreasonableness of demanding, in the fashion of the party program, "a popular defense system" and a "fight against the military establishment" at one and the same time. A resolution proposed by Månsson was finally unanimously accepted. It was worded as follows: "The Federation shall pursue vigorous antimilitary agitation aimed at creating a sentiment in the land *against* military expenditures and *for* instead turning such means to the benefit of small farmers, the enlightenment of the populace, and workers' pensions."

Social Democrats actively sought a peaceful solution to the crisis following dissoution of the union with Norway in 1905. The approaches of the party and the youth federation manifested characteristic disparities. The party administration published a petition calling for a conciliatory policy toward Norway but containing no threats of opposition to military action. A demand was made within the party administration for an examination of the possibilities of a work stoppage or of a refusal to take part in mobilization, but leaders such as Branting and Thorsson criticized this proposal, and it was subsequently defeated. On the other hand, the youth federation issued a proclamation with the title "Down with Weapons!" (*"Ned med vapen!"*) that called upon the workers to form a resistance movement to war, with violence, if necessary. Z. Höglund, who was legally responsible for the proclamation, was sentenced to prison.

During the next few years antidefense agitation was stepped up. It would not be an exaggeration to claim that it was the essential line in the activity of both the Young Socialists and the new youth federation. Several defense-nihilistic brochures were published and innumerable meetings came out in favor of the total abolition of defense. Special efforts were made to influence the military forces via speeches and pamphlets. The extraordinarily intensive propaganda campaign against defense that was carried on by the youth organizations gave many the impression that the Social Democratic party was primarily a defense-nihilist party. The 1906 Riksdag passed new regulations to limit antimilitary agitation, which were followed by additional restrictive legislation.

A number of defense resolutions were adopted at the 1907 congress of the youth federation. On the initiative of the party administration and pursuant to a corresponding resolution passed in 1905, the congress ruled that the federation should prosecute "vigorous antimilitary agitation with the aim of total abolition of the military establishment," and campaign for international courts of arbitration and for cooperation between workers' organizations on an international scale. An extensive round of debate ended with unanimous acceptance of the resolution. Speaking on behalf of the party board, P. A. Hansson explained that the resolution was intended to bring out the constructive factors in the antimilitary position: international courts of arbitration and international cooperation. He took it for granted that the federation was obviously "defense nihilistic," but in a different way than the Young Socialists. The latter believed that workers had no fatherland to defend; the federation based its stand on Sweden's inability to defend herself. The popular system of defense mentioned in the party program "is in reality nothing more than a democratized military establishment, in addition to which, it is inferior as a defense to the present [system]." Höglund, Möller, and Sandler, among others, largely followed suit. Möller declared that whether one called oneself defense nihilistic or antimilitary was simply a matter of taste, for there was no real difference between the two terms. It was even suggested (Hj. Larsson) that defense nihilism was justifiable in that Sweden was not worth defending: workers of other countries enjoyed a higher level of culture and civil rights, which made their situation quite different from that of the Swedish worker.

A motion brought up the question of a strike against military service, but the congress ruled against agitation for such a strike for the time being since the federation was still too weak to be effective in such action. The pros and cons of the movement for voluntary rifle clubs were thoroughly debated. P. A. Hansson and other speakers were of the opinion that this movement ought to be discouraged since there was no chance of turning the Swedish rifle clubs into a "red guard" in imitation of the Finnish model. Möller, in particular, countered that violence might have to be employed to abolish private capitalism and that the rifle clubs might be useful for this purpose. "It is . . . a very good idea to use the means of the existing state to assist us in its overthrow." The following resolution, prepared by Höglund, was unanimously approved: "Without at present passing any judgment on the possible usefulness of a radical rifle-club movement as a red guard of the working class, the Congress considers that the Federation ought to counteract the present voluntary rifle-club movement." There were additional statements favoring the neutralization of Sweden.

A number of motions for program amendments in an antimilitary vein were made at the party congress of 1908. Now that the Young Socialists were no longer recognized as a legitimate party faction, the youth federation became the nucleus of defense nihilism. Severe differences of opinion manifested themselves in the party administration's preliminary deliberations on the motions presented. Nils Persson, who declared himself to be an antimilitarist, questioned "whether it would moreover be so terrible if Sweden were conquered by another civilized state." Most of the other debaters protested against this thought; included in their number was Lindley, who had previously expressed the same idea as Persson. But now Lindley contended "it would be a reversal for socialism in this country if another country were to devour Sweden. It is therefore precisely the Social Democratic [party] that must combat such a conquest." Branting, Thorsson, and others definitively renounced defense nihilism. The administration finally agreed on a compromise proposal that would be submitted to the congress. Another proposal regarding the party position on the voluntary rifle-club movement was also prepared. The divergence of opinion present in the party administration was again revealed. Some regarded this movement as a useful weapon for "defense against the enemy within"; others condemned it as a militaristic organization; still others saw it as a valuable component of national defense. The proposal that was finally accepted was obviously intended as a kind of middle road between these diverse opinions.

The new program article on defense that was recommended by the party administration read as follows: "Fight against militarism. Gradual reduction of military burdens toward disarmament. Binding awards of arbitration, permanent neutrality for Scandinavia, vigorous international cooperation between workers' organizations against war." The significant part of the new formulation was the deletion of reference to a popular defense system. On the other hand, it contained no hint of a positive attitude to defense. Branting explained to the congress that the administration recommended this proposal on the condition that it win the support of the great majority of delegates; he believed it ought to be acceptable to both defense sympathizers and defense nihilist. P. A. Hansson announced that the youth movement would back the proposal, which might be combined with the view that Sweden lacked the capacity for defense against a major power. Nevertheless, a minority in the congress desired a more radical formulation: they wanted the first two items combined to read "fight against the military establishment for the purpose of disarmament." The proposal of the party administration finally won, 162 to 80.

The party's position on the voluntary rifle-club movement was treated in another context. The administration proposed a resolution whereby it would be left to the individual party member to decide whether or not to support the movement; nonetheless, workers who were members of rifle clubs were called upon to counteract any tendencies toward militarism and chauvinism that they might encounter in the clubs. The administration statement included a sentence vaguely suggestive of the possibility that rifle clubs might be of importance to the internal struggle. "Since . . . the peace and freedom of the people will never be truly secure as long as capitalism has the power to appeal to armed violence, the voluntary rifle-club movement cannot, for the time being, be considered objectionable under all conditions from the party's point of view." P. A. Hansson, who acted as the representative of the youth movement on this issue as well, spoke with obvious irony of this equivocal sentence which purported to show the administration's "revolutionary sentiment." He characterized the rifle-club movement as a form of militarism and proposed a declaration demanding that the movement be blocked and that the party's Riksdag group be requested to oppose granting state appropriations to the movement. This proposal passed "by a great majority" against the distinct objections of Branting and others.

In a *Social-Demokraten* article written after the 1908 party congress, Branting tried to give the resolution on defense then passed an interpretation that would not clash with his own stand. The congress wanted "to stress more clearly that the protection of our independence lies more [truly] in a high level of culture than in the ever inadequate military material of a small state." He added, however, that the congress had also established that "there is room within this common framework of opinion both for those who consider the premium for military insurance at present inescapable as well as for those who dare to trust that a more rapid rate of disarmament will not increase our risks, for each year the European working class gains ever-greater power to tip the scales against any peril of war." Answering criticism of the resolution that appeared in the nonsocialist press, he asserted that the demand for a reduction of the burden of supporting the armed forces, in the direction of disarmament, must be viewed in light of the item in the program article that referred to courts of arbitration and other agencies to avert war. He intimated that there would be no attempt to realize the first demand until such agencies had been put into effective operation. The entire article indicates that Branting considered a negative stand on the defense issue to be not only objectively unsound but also politically dangerous.

The congressional resolution seemed to bring about a relaxation of tensions within the party, but this respite would only be temporary. The following year the rifts widened; the program directives were shown to lend themselves to varied interpretations. Because of its successes at the 1908 election, the influence of the Riksdag group was much enhanced. This group now offered a standpoint that the youth federation (whose leaders still remained outside of the legislature) regarded as a deviation from the established party stand. In some cases this contention was incontrovertible; for example, at the 1909 Riksdag Social Democratic members supported appropriations to the voluntary rifle-club movement. In other cases the question was moot. The Riksdag group considered that the party program sanctioned its support of certain essential military expenditures; on the other hand, the opposition continued to demand systematic disarmament measures. One of the steps that the opposition criticized was Thorsson's seating on a civil commission formed on Liberal initiative; the commission was to superintend the military establishment and was thus considered authorized to assist in making it more efficient and democratic. The opposition considered that collaboration in this commission involved Social Democrats in an order that it should instead censure on principle.

The discontent that prevailed in the youth federation was expressed at the federation's congress of 1909. To be sure, this congress revealed a rift between a "right wing" that favored close cooperation with the Social Democratic leadership and a "left wing" that was usually critical of the leadership. But acute dissension did not arise on the defense question. After a long debate that "the Congress ruled to classify as secret," a resolution was passed regarding strikes against military service with a formulation that was somewhat more positive than the 1907 resolution: youth ought to discuss the question and familiarize itself with the use of strike as a weapon in various situations. The tactics of the Riksdag group on the military question was subjected to severe criticism in a resolution demanding, among other things, that the party's representatives vote against all military appropriations and assert the principles behind the party stand instead of devoting themselves to criticism of details. Special reproof was directed at Thorsson's seating on the civil commission and against the instrumentality of certain party Riksdag men in promoting appropriations for the rifle-club movement and the fleet.

The more radical tactics pursued by the Riksdag group at the 1910 session may have been partly occasioned by criticism from the youth federation. The group voted against appropriations to the rifle-club movement on the grounds that it was ineffectual and unnecessarily costly; the Riksdag group would adhere to this stand until 1937. Moreover, the group worked in behalf of a reduction of various appropriation requests—but without entirely rejecting them. In the debate on appropriations for the salaries of conscripts, Rydén gave a long speech that can correctly be termed defense nihilistic. Defense was first of all "a combat weapon of the upper class [for use] against the workers." He propounded "that when one tries to lull us Swedes, a small nation of 5 million people, into the idea that we, with our defense, can stand up to a major power that is twenty to thirty times stronger than we are, this constitutes an attempt to make us project from a self-deception which I, for my part, can under no circumstances accept." Branting and Thorsson's contributions to the debate were less radical, but they did not denounce Rydén's speech. When it was subsequently published in pamphlet form, however, Branting's foreword pointed out that Rydén's view was not predominant in the movement. It further suggested that disarmament was of international concern but could hardly be realized before the working class had won its victory in the large nations. Other nations would consider that a people that completely dismantled their defense organization placed little value on their independence, and they would be treated accordingly.

At the 1911 Riksdag both Liberals and Social Democrats presented proposals for an investigation into a reduction of military expenditures. The proposal put forward by Social Democrats offered a plan for reduction of the defense burden from 80 to 60 million crowns and for shortening the period of compulsory military service. In the course of the ensuing debate—which did not result in any concrete action by the Riksdag—Branting and Thorsson underscored the party's fundamentally positive disposition toward defense, and Rydén's speech was somewhat less extreme than that which he had given at the previous session. The cautious tactics of the Riksdag group were criticized by disarmament enthusiasts; Höglund, for example, termed them 25 percent antimilitaristic. Discord on the defense issue was further aggravated by the requests presented by the Lindman cabinet for additional appropriations—particularly for the fleet.

Under these conditions it was assumed that the 1911 congress, which would convene in the Riksdag's midsession, would result in a bitter contest between the party's several factions. The disarmament line dominated the Stockholm workers' commune. Branting feared that this line would prevail at the congress, and he evidently contemplated retiring from the party leadership if this occurred. The debate on the Riksdag records brought out criticism of the Riksdag group and party leadership at the opening of the congress. A motion on the defense issue exacted replacing the first two items in the program by a single phrase: "Total abolition of the military establishment." It was further moved that the Riksdag group be enjoined to present disarmament proposals on the floor of the Riksdag. The party administration disapproved both motions with a reminder that recent congresses had thoroughly considered the defense issue and that representatives of the youth federation had expressed their satisfaction with the program formulation decided upon in 1908. Making the article more rigid "along a line utterly nihilistic to defense would prevent fellow party members who cannot recommend immediate disarmament in the present state of foreign affairs from actively participating in party activities in this important sphere and would thus weaken rather than strengthen the party's contribution to the fight against ruinous militarism that we all seek to wage." Three of the twenty-three members who could be regarded as representatives of the youth federation—P. A. Hansson, Z. Höglund, and F. Ström—disagreed with this pronouncement.

In the main the debate at this congress produced the same views that had been voiced before. Both lines believed that they acted in complete accordance with the principles of international socialism; both cited proclamations issued at congresses held by the International and by the programs of various Social Democratic parties. The youth federation called attention to the fact that the Danish and Norwegian parties were more radical than the Swedish. Commenting on this comparison, Stauning, the Danish party leader, who had attended the congress, made it known that even the Danish socialists had decided to strive for successive reduction of the armament burden once it became obvious that their demands for disarmament had no prospects of success. Hansson, the chief speaker for the youth federation, emphasized that the federation was not indifferent to the cause of Sweden's independence and freedom. Having made this point, he asserted that the issue was replacement of armed defense by cultural defense: "binding awards of courts of arbitration, steadfast proclamation of neutrality, and vigorous promotion of the workers' international rebellion against war." Hansson concluded that the party's riksdagsmen should have proposed disarmament, not just a limitation of armament: the former would have been received with enthusiasm by the people.

When the vote was taken on the proposal for program amendment, the majority in the party administration won the decision, 84 to 48. The principal dividing line ran between the older party members and representatives of the youth federation. Most representatives of the leading circles in the party and in the trade union movement aligned themselves with the majority; their number included, in addition to Branting, Thorsson, Lindqvist, Lindblad, Victor Larsson, Källman, and Olaf Olsson. It is interesting to note that two of the most influential men in the youth federation, Fabian Månsson and Möller, also backed the party leadership. Palm, Lindhagen, and Kata Dalström were among those who sided with the minority. Once the vote had been taken some suggested that the majority had really been in favor of the antimilitaristic line but that many had voted as they did in order to avoid increasing intraparty dissension to a point where it would become critical.

However, a resolution proposal made by Vennerström that was closely allied to the stand of the youth federation was subsequently approved, 72 to 59. It read as follows: "Disarmament is the really vital [goal] that we must strive toward with all possible force, and although the gradual reduction of military burdens represents an active attempt to ease the economic pressure that weighs excessively upon the people, it only marks the road [leading] to attainment of the goal which can most conveniently be followed at present in conjunction with forceful assertion of positive guarantees of peace." In all likelihood several delegates supported the party administration on the program vote on the sole condition that their radical view would be expressed in this resolution. Branting and almost all of the older leaders in the party administration voted against the resolution. However, once the resolution had been passed and it was made clear that it did not constitute a vote of no-confidence in the Riksdag group nor a rescission of the previous ruling, Branting declared in writing that he would not dissent to it. Månsson and

Möller were among those who voted with the majority on both occasions. Finally, the congress adopted the same resolution on the voluntary rifle-club movement that was passed in 1908. But Branting took exception to this. Although he did not believe that the movement should be supported since it had developed into a link in the chain of militarism, he thought it inadvisable "to hurl oneself with exceptional force against just that part of the defense establishment that can, in any event, acquire the most popular character. . . ."

In the interim between the eighth and ninth party congresses, 1911–1914, the defense situation underwent considerable changes—as did the party's position on defense. Instead of the reduction in arms that the Social Democrats wanted, the 1911 Riksdag granted additional defense appropriations, the most controversial of which concerned the building of the so-called F-ship (a large cruiser). These appropriations were approved by a majority in the lower house in the face of Liberal and Social Democratic opposition. At the elections to the lower house that were held the same year, Social Democrats carried on vigorous agitation for armament reductions, and even the Liberals held out prospects of limiting the defense burden. The Staaff cabinet formed after the elections stopped work on the F-ship project. It ordered defense investigations to study the defense question in its entirety; four Social Democrats were named to this investigative body—Branting, Thorsson, Rydén, and Christiernsson.

For the next few years the defense question dominated the scene. The collection for the F-ship project that had been begun on private initiative won widespread support; the total amount collected was accepted by the Liberal cabinet on the conditions that had been drawn up. Social Democrats chastized the cabinet for this: they regarded the collection largely as a political maneuver, and Rydén described the F-ship "as a symbol of hostility toward the people's power, as upper-class insolence and hypocritical patriotism." At the 1912 Riksdag Branting proposed—without success—a study on the subject of eliminating the possibility of the use of military forces in labor conflicts; he emphasized that widespread support of defense was inconceivable as long as the armed forces could be used as a weapon against "the enemy within." The propaganda to augment armaments devised by Conservatives and various other groups between 1911 and 1914, which was combined with attacks on the cabinet, met with bitter Social Democratic opposition. Like the Liberals, the Social Democrats were inclined to regard this propaganda as a crafty and deliberate attempt to bring the cabinet to defeat and thwart the advance of parliamentarianism and democracy. Defense sympathizers called attention primarily to the increase in international tension and to the heightened threat of war that this implied. By the autumn of 1913 it was evident that even the cabinet had been won over to an extension of the period of military service and augmentation of defense in general. Yet the cabinet plans did not satisfy the Conservatives, and the Social Democrats that did take a positive stand on defense considered them altogether too far-reaching. At the referral debate preceding remittance of the proposal on the administration budget at the first Riksdag session of 1914, Branting could nevertheless affirm that the Social Democratic group was in complete concord that defense ought to be maintained. "We are all agreed that our land must not, cannot be left unprotected against possible encroachers. . . . I have wished . . . to make it clear that there is no question of refusal on the part of any faction to participate in national defense, but that the issue concerns setting the entire defense [system] on a course that really corresponds to the aspirations of *Swedish democracy*."

The conflict between the throne and the Staaff cabinet and the consequent formation of the Hammarskjöld cabinet resulted in the by-elections that were held at the end of March and beginning of April, 1914. In conjunction with the elections the Social Democratic party administration issued a manifesto that repudiated demands for increased armaments but also asserted a distinctly positive line. Ström and Vennerström opposed this assertion. According to the manifesto the party was striving for peace and brotherhood between all people and was therefore the irreconcilable foe of militarism. "But [since it is] operative at a time when the robber politics of the ruling classes and cliques demonstrate that they can still render international coexistence insecure, even Social Democracy must, in the interests of the working people, assume its share in the arrangements that may prove provisionally indispensable for the protection of the independence, freedom, and future of our people against possible attempts at aggression or violations of neutrality." The party administration considered that the current defense expenditures could be reduced from 80 to about 70 million crowns. It became apparent at this time and in the course of debates later in the year that many Social Democrats who had previously espoused disarmament had become convinced of the advisability of maintaining a military defense. This applied to Rydén, Fabian Månsson, Möller, and P. A. Hansson, among others. One party member—Christiernsson—agitated for an increase in armaments, but did not leave the party. At the same time, however, defense nihilistic propaganda was intensified, primarily by the youth federation, now under the leadership of Z. Höglund.

Three special proposals confronted the second session of the 1914 Riksdag. These can be roughly summed up as follows: the Conservatives demanded

100 million crowns in defense appropriations and one year of compulsory military service; the Liberals demanded 90 million and 280 days; the Social Democrats 70 million and six months' military service. The latter proposal also called for various organizational changes and for the concentration of naval defense on the submarine fleet. With the outbreak of World War I, the Liberals and Conservatives reached an agreement, largely as a result of Liberal concessions, but the Social Democrats clung to their original proposal. Branting adopted a unique position: he both worked in behalf of the party line and recommended a settlement between nonsocialist parties. It is therefore probable that, for practical reasons, he favored a stronger defense than that proposed in the party proposal. During the debate that preceded the final decision on September 12, Rydén acted as the party spokesman: "The party is ready to vote for a positive defense program. . . . Sweden shall be defended. In this respect we are in agreement with other parties. But the burden of defense should not be made so heavy that it stifles all constructive work for the nation's domestic development, which is essential not least in regard to the creation of a genuine disposition and capacity to protect security and independence in time of danger." Shortly before this the decisive regular elections to the lower house were held. Prior to these elections the executive committee of the party administration had issued a manifesto; although this manifesto sharply criticized settlements reached between the nonsocialist parties, it did refer to "the people of Sweden who are prepared to defend the nation's freedom and independence to the last. . . ."

The year before the outbreak of the war, the Swedish Social Democratic party had taken a stand on the question of working-class action to prevent war through the medium of the strike—a question that had been the subject of much discussion by the International. In 1913, at the request of the secretariat of the International, the party administration issued a report stating that only a defensive war was conceivable for Sweden and that the idea of using strikes to forestall war therefore did not apply to this country. It further requested that the International refrain from establishing regulations that would be binding upon the workers of different nations in regard to the strike question.

Relations between the youth federation and the party were the main issues at the federation congresses held in 1912 and 1914. Scant attention was therefore paid to programmatic questions, although the federation did explicitly underscore its radical stand on defense. The 1912 congress witnessed protests against the idea of arranging trial mobilization; each member was instructed to decide for himself whether or not to strike in the event of such mobilization. The 1914 congress went even further. It passed a resolution calling for intensification of disarmament agitation. It further stressed "the importance of extraparliamentary action against militarism, action directly aimed at rendering militarism inserviceable as the tool of the ruling classes against the proletariat and its struggle for liberation." Youth clubs should discuss the means—such as antimilitary and general strikes—that might conceivably be used in connection with extraparliamentary action.

The ninth party congress convened in the beginning of August 1914 but was adjourned after two days and met again at the end of November of the same year. The defense issue did not come up until the second convention. Reports of the proceedings and debates suggest that a majority at the congress were more positively disposed toward defense than previously. The prevailing sentiment at the congress was nevertheless more negative than that of the Riksdag group and party administration. A forceful minority evidently still supported the defense nihilistic line of the youth federation. The issue first came to the fore in conjunction with a review of the activities of the party administration during the preceding period. A motion was made for censure of the administration manifesto that had been issued prior to the autumn election on the ground that it was altogether too positive toward defense; this motion was rejected—but by a narrow majority—70 to 61. Several motions were presented in regard to the programmatic declaration on defense; some called for a more positive formulation, others for a more negative formulation. The majority in the party administration believed the article should be retained unchanged but added that "closer correlation between the party's program and politics" was desirable; the proposed program commission should thus be assigned the task of revising the program in time for the next congress. Two of the resolutions previously adopted—the one directed against the rifle-club movement and the one regarding interpretation of the program article on defense (the Vennerström-sponsored resolution of 1911)—ought to be revoked. Four members of the administration (Branting, Thorsson, Lindblad, and Palmstierna) urged that the second item in the article be given a less categorical formulation, viz.: "With better guarantees, gradual reduction of military burdens toward [the end of] disarmament." Ström alone opposed revising the article; Sandler, Ström, Vennerström, and Hansson opposed revoking the resolutions already passed. (The first three were concerned with the resolution of 1911, and Hansson with the resolution on the rifle-club movement.)

The protracted rounds of debate offer nothing new. The votes taken were indicative of the strength of the radicals. A vote of 75 to 65 ruled that the program article be retained unchanged. On this point Ström triumphed over the rest of the party administration. However, Branting subsequently remarked that this time the left-wing opposition had been on the defensive; there was no question of making the article more stringent along lines hostile to defense, as was the case in 1911. Nevertheless, the overruling of the nearly unanimous decision of the party administration and the relatively feeble support given to the proposal made by Branting and others were salient features of the congress. Vennerström's resolution was confirmed, 87 to 56. Retention of the resolution pertaining to the rifle-club movement also signified a distinct reversal for the party administration. The outcome of this issue may in part have been determined by the arguments advanced by Ström and Vennerström for revocation of the resolution, which suggested that the movement might be useful to the working class in domestic strifes: "the possible aggressive actions of bourgeois parties or groups may force the working class to fight for its liberation along other than purely parliamentary roads." It was said that some delegates who favored the voluntary rifle-club movement on other grounds considered this statement so precarious that they instead voted for the original resolution against the movement. Branting and Thorsson opposed the decision "with the explanation that it is completely contrary to our whole outlook on the defense question."

The 1914 congress also ruled on the question of possible collaboration with Liberals in the cabinet—as noted in a previous context. It was assumed that such collaboration would exclude all attempts to change the military organization decided on in 1914 for the duration of the war. The majority in the Social Democratic party adhered to this stand throughout the war.

Intraparty dissension persisted nonetheless. Technical differences, primarily on the defense issue, were linked to the dominant question of the youth federation's relation to the party. The fact that the party majority provisionally backed the existing defense organization necessarily made it representative of a more positive outlook on defense; on the other hand, under Höglund's leadership the youth federation progressively approached fundamental defense nihilism. The schism between the two was thus widened. Overt preparations were made for a split—and at times such a rupture was frankly advocated. Some federation members accused Branting and other party leaders of treason against socialism.

Conflicts that are illustrative of this situation came to the fore at the 1915 Riksdag. Höglund and numerous other representatives of the radical line had now won seats in the lower house. The Riksdag group decided that no proposals were to be made to abrogate or circumvent the 1914 defense act. In spite of this, Höglund—backed by several party members—took the floor as the opposition when the house deliberated on defense appropriations. He contended that implementation of the military organization decided upon in 1914 should be postponed. The great masses of the people regarded militarism more and more "as primarily a political and economic class interest of the ruling classes." Höglund affirmed that the Social Democratic party held to its demand "for gradual reduction of military expenditures toward [the end of] disarmament, a program article that also underscores that disarmament must be the essential demand which we must strive for with all our might." He added, however, that he did not think it would be possible to demobilize right now, immediately after the end of the world war. Branting alleged that Höglund misinterpreted the party standpoint: the party did not postulate instantaneous disarmament and was not nihilistic toward defense. "On the contrary, we have distinctly asserted that to us, as to other parties, this Swedish native land is precious and dear, and that it is by no means our intention to leave it undefended. . . ."

At the election campaign of 1914 the party had presented a positive program, and this stand had been approved by the party congress. The congress had also presupposed that rescission of the act of 1914 could not be considered within the near future. In response to Branting's remarks, Höglund retorted that it was an incontestable fact that the party embraced "two fundamentally different lines which can both, with reason, claim to stand wholly and completely within the party framework." Branting concluded his comments with the rejoinder that "when he (Höglund) wishes to impart the illusion that within the party there are two equally legitimate lines that are mutually and completely antithetical regarding the question of a positive defense, it is, of course, quite notorious that the party includes representatives of the line for which Herr Höglund is the deputy and standard-bearer, but it is equally notorious that this line has not succeeded in gaining leadership of the party nor a majority at our congresses."

This exchange is indicative of the intraparty polemics of the period. Both of the antagonistic lines claimed to represent the prevailing opinion. Reciprocal accusations and distortions of fact aggravated the friction between them. The desire for concord perceptible at the party congresses and aimed at constructing a common platform of action fell into obscurity in the course of the debates in the Riksdag, in the press, and at various meetings. In the case just discussed Branting obviously adopted an untenable position inasmuch as his version of the party's standpoint did not agree with the testimony of congressional rulings. In an attempt to prove that his own view was ascendant in the party he had stressed that the radical line had not captured a majority at any congress. He failed to point out the also notorious fact that this line had been the most powerful at several congresses but that it had been prevailed upon not to take advantage of its opportunities by virtue of the compromise proposals worked out by Branting and the party administration. At congressional debates Branting himself had declared that the party program could sustain the radical line on defense just as easily as it could those factions more friendly to defense. His performance in the Riksdag was apparently motivated by anxieties that the party's element of defense nihilism would hamper collaboration with the Liberals and possibly induce them to ally themselves with the Conservatives. Writing in his newspaper, Branting contended that Höglund's tactics would result in continued rule by the Right and thereby counteract the essential purposes of the party. When Branting, Palmstierna, and Steffen later in the session voted in favor of appropriations to the rifle-club movement, the youth federation vented its fury in enraged criticism.

The breach in the party manifested itself in the Riksdag in a far more obvious way than before on other issues as well. Lindhagen's motion for an investigation into disarmament in the Scandinavian countries was, for example, warmly endorsed by Höglund and others of his persuasion, but the majority of the party's representatives in the lower house voted against it, with explanation that such an undertaking lacked by any practical value. Because of such parliamentary skirmishes, the Riksdag group adopted a so-called disciplinary rule that provided the possibility in certain cases of intervening against party members who asserted individual opinions in the Riksdag that clashed with the decision of the party majority.

Disputes on the position to be taken in the event of war were closely related to the defense controversy. With only a few exceptions, Social Democrats were adamantly bent on preserving neutrality. During the war the party time and again proclaimed its desire for peace and its renunciation of the activist group that wanted Sweden to ally with Germany. Judging by statements in the press, the great majority in the party—with Branting at the head—really hoped for the victory of the Entente. They regarded Germany as a stronghold of the autocratic tendencies that had until recently prevailed in Sweden; England and France, on the other hand, were viewed as bastions of freedom and democracy. Only a few were pro-German, on the ground that this nation was the foremost exponent of well-developed social policies and Social Democracy. They regarded Russia with the same horror with which most people viewed Germany. Yet this division of opinion was of scant importance. In the autumn of 1915 the party expelled a few members—Järte, Yngve Larsson, and Steffen—for carrying on activist propaganda, but this did not lead to particularly violent controversy. Of greater importance was the fact that Höglund and his cohorts aligned themselves with the so-called Zimmerwald line. Influenced by Lenin and Russian Bolshevism in general, they regarded the war as a means of reaching a settlement between capitalist states that socialists should try to profit by: the capitalist war would be followed by the proletarian revolution. They also contended that Swedish Social Democrats should use all means to prevent Sweden from becoming implicated in the war. Extremist groups of nations actually at war used the war itself to spur on their revolutionary propaganda; in peaceful Sweden extremists used the risk of war as a goad. For the leaders of the circle connected with the youth federation, the war and the familiarity they gained of Russian Bolshevism, which had gained momentum because of the war, brought about the development and delineation of opinions already in existence. At the same time, they probably considered that an aggressive, if not an out-and-out revolutionary policy dedicated to peace might enable them to overcome the party leadership, which clamored for neutrality but was obviously committed only to lawful measures. They used the same tactic that the Russian Bolshevists would employ one and half years later: they surpassed the reformists in the zeal of their proclamations for peace.

The decisive collision of the two lines occurred in October 1915 when the youth federation proposed convoking "a national Swedish workers' congress, possibly to be enlarged into a peoples' parliament, for the purpose of organizing the most forceful possible pressure for peace. . . ." At a subsequent meeting in which the executive committees of both the party administration and the youth federation participated, Höglund spoke of general and antimobilization strikes as antiwar weapons. The party administration wished to plan measures to preserve neutrality, but criticized the notion of extraparliamentary action. It looked upon the proposal of the youth federation as a device to discredit the party. On February 1, 1916, this proposal was formally rejected. Beforehand, however, the youth federation had secretly invited various workers' organizations to a congress. When the administration's executive committee learned of this, it issued a warning against attending the congress. Thereafter the administration and the representative body of the Confederation of Trade Unions (*Landsorganisation*) met to consider the development: a large majority (18 to 3 in the party administration, 33 to 1 among the confederation representatives; agreed upon a statement renouncing the contemplated congress. The statement held that during the immediately preceding period the Swedish government had pursued a distinctly neutral policy and that the risk of war had apparently diminished. In the event of imminent war, a general strike would be transformed into an antimobilization strike on the one hand and into an armed rebellion on the other. It was impossible to fix rules that would apply to such a situation "for all depends on the mood that the course of events would create among the masses." The statement thus did not completely dismiss the idea of a general strike in the event of war, but rather the final decision on such a strike. The party leadership was to keep a watchful eye on events and actively strive to preserve neutrality. Most Social Democratic newspapers supported the stand taken by the administration and criticized the conduct of the youth federation.

Nonetheless, a considerable number of workers' organizations—which, however, constituted but a minority in the party—sent delegates to the congress convoked by the youth federation, which convened March 18 and 19, 1916. The congress decided to issue a manifesto entitled "Peace at Any Price" (*"Fred till varje pris"*) to Sweden's workers. It treated the possibility of Sweden's voluntary intervention in the war but it could be interpreted to imply a defensive war as well. The manifesto referred to the necessity of preparing "extraparliamentary mass action in answer to all warlike plans." The first such action would be a strike directed primarily against the branches of industry that would be vital to a war effort, for example, ammunition factories and communications. This measure might even include "obstruction"—which evidently meant sabotage. The congress added that such a strike was not sufficient in itself, and one might possibly be driven "to a battle of a more acute nature." If the government were to precipitate the people into a war "all obligations to such a government would naturally cease [to be in force]." The manifesto concluded with the words "Our slogan is *peace at any price."* These words could be interpreted to mean that the actions enjoined in the manifesto might even apply to a defensive war. After the congress had adjourned, some of its principal delegates—Höglund, Hedén, Oljelund—were sentenced to prison or hard labor for treason. (These sentences were subsequently reduced or repealed by a superior court.)

By the spring of 1916 the battle that formed around the congress and its proclamations took a turn that could be described as a true rupture of the party. Members of the party administration who were partsian toward the youth federation resigned from the administration; federation sympathizers within the Riksdag group formed a special left-wing faction and created their own organ, *Politiken*. The two lines did not prepare for the coming party congress of 1917 by trying to arrive at a compromise but by arming for a test of strength. The first test would be the defense question.

The 1917 congress, which convened in February, was faced with a number of motions for the substitution of the word "disarmament" in place of the first sentence in the article on defense. The special program committee that did the preliminary work on the agenda before the congress rejected these motions and took a stand that was patently prodefense. It was obvious that the prodefense faction was no longer inclined to yield to the youth federation. The committee maintained that the dedication of Social Democracy to disarmament as its ultimate goal was self-evident. The party was striving for an international community of justice in which the military system would be replaced by a police force that would be common to all nations. It was impossible to determine how quickly this goal would be reached; the present program article should in any case be retained until the situation became clearer. "Social Democracy, which asserts the right of nations to self-determination, cannot disclaim the responsibility of defending this right whenever it is attacked. A standpoint that is defense nihilistic per se must therefore be definitively rejected." In contrast to its actions a few years earlier, the party leadership—the administration was in complete agreement with the findings of the program committee—pursued the line that fundamental defense nihilism had no place in the party. However, the committee suggested an amendment to Article III, Paragraph 3, which would introduce the paragraph with the words "establishment of an international legal order." Two members of the committee, Lindhagen and Vennerström, agreed with the motions proposed in regard to the first sentence of the defense article. They did not base their opinions on pure defense nihilism. They claimed, among other things, that if the word "disarmament" alone were used it could even be interpreted to mean that Sweden would disarm only pursuant to an international agreement. Amendment of the paragraph was justified on the ground that a clarification was desirable inasmuch as the majority no longer wished to acknowledge "antimilitarism" within the party.

Treatment of the defense question at the plenary session of the congress clearly indicated that the positive line had gained ground within the party during the war years. Several speakers (Sandler, Möller, Rydén) admitted that they had once been opposed to defense because of the argument that Sweden was in any case unable to protect herself, but that they had since changed their minds in this regard. It was said that the attacks on defense made by the youth federation during recent years had acquired a stamp of fundamental defense nihilism, which was unacceptable under any conditions. Branting and Thorsson ardently advocated the standpoint that the majority in the Riksdag group had adopted. Among those who wished to amend the article along the lines suggested in the motions proposed were absolute pacifists (Spak), fundamental opponents of defense under the existing political and social conditions (Grimlund), and adherents of the view that defense was unnecessary as far as Sweden herself was concerned (Vennerström). The congress ruled, 134 to 41, to accept the findings of the program committee with regard to both the justifications and the recommendations that it advanced. The party thereby expressly repudiated defense nihilism for the first time since the defense question had become a subject of serious discussion.

After the congress of 1917 the faction that had formed around the core of the youth federation left the Social Democratic party and formed the Left Socialist party. It would be many years before defense would again play an important role in the Social Democrats' intramural debates.

This review has reported the arguments that were accented by the several factions in intraparty debates. These need to be complemented by an exposition that integrates the motives and ideas that appear conclusive to the outcome. Let us first examine the decidedly antimilitaristic—or, if one prefers—antidefense ideologies.

It is frequently alleged that the Young Socialists and the Social Democratic Youth Federation differed distinctly in their standpoints on defense. This allegation undoubtedly contains some truth, especially if one compares the positions of the two movements when rivalry between them was keenest (*c.* 1905–1910). Yet there was little difference in the practical consequences of their policies: although only the Young Socialists actively worked for a strike against conscription, both movements demanded total abolition of the defense establishment. Further, some of the views propounded by the Young Socialists recurred in the youth federation; in later years, after Höglund had succeeded Hansson as leader and *Stormklockan* had replaced *Fram* as the movement's organ, the youth federation to some extent actually reverted to the argumentation used by the Young Socialists. Both of the competing lines reveal an understandable tendency to accentuate the differences between them and ignore the similarities.

We shall consider the Young Socialists' view of defense only during the years preceding the congress of 1908 when the movement could be described as a faction within the Social Democratic party. This view is unfolded in *Brand* and *The New Will of the People* (*Nya folkviljan*) as well as in a few pamphlets and brochures. The movement brought its propaganda to the people primarily through the medium of small meetings and conferences, but there are no available detailed data on the proceedings at these gatherings. The Young Socialist movement can be designated as antinational and fundamentally nihilistic toward defense. It regarded patriotic ideas as suggestive devices that served the interests of the upper class, and therefore considered defense, no matter what its make-up, a link in the capitalist system of exploitation. It was frequently alleged that defense was mainly intended for use against "the enemy within." *Brand* charged that militarism was "the greatest curse inherent in our modern societies . . . the fatherland is synonymous with the life and property of the upper class . . . militarism is the same everywhere, whether it consists of a conscripted army or a militia, whether it is found in a so-called free republic or in a despotically governed state." The movement believed that it represented true Marxism, and perpetually cited Marx's dictum that workers had no native land. One pamphlet declared that patriotism is "a phrase, a prejudice . . . the most stupid of all prejudices"; another described patriotism as "this raw and antiquated emotion . . . which, clothed in a dressing gown and patched together by bits and pieces of history, shouts at [town] squares, rattles around in the barracks, sits turgidly in armchairs, and fortunately dies of stupidity." As a rule they assumed that war would become obsolete with the victory of socialism, but they also contemplated the possibility that the action of the international proletariat might render war impracticable even before the advent of this victory, primarily through the use of the general strike. At times a genuinely pacifist standpoint was proclaimed. It was better for a people to be subjugated than to fight. Resignation to foreign oppression might even have a constructive influence. "In oppressed Finland a [type of] art and poetry has emerged and a feeling of nostalgia and melancholy has grown which could never be replaced by the attributes that the character of the people would have acquired if the Finns had defended themselves with weapons in the old-fashioned way." Militarism —which usually meant defense in general—was also assailed on the ground that it had a brutalizing influence and was destructive to culture. Primitive Marxist thinking was apparently predominant in this view, but general pacifist and humanitarian attitudes were also important to this current of thought.

The line of distinction on defense that was drawn between the Young Socialists and the youth federation was not uniformly observed. From January 1905 to April 1907 clubs representative of both groups organized a joint committee for antimilitary agitation which arranged meetings and published brochures. In 1906 it issued a brochure entitled *Socialism and Militarism,* which advanced the customary ideas of the Young Socialists. It asked what benefit the poor could derive from the nation and the culture that they were called upon to defend. "We do not own a foot of our so-called fatherland and, as far as our share in its culture is concerned, it is negligible or nonexistent, for cultural values belong only to those who have money." "Defense," the brochure continued, "existed only to serve the economic interests of the ruling class in international rivalries and to suppress the [country's] own people." Some brochures on defense issued by the youth federation—for example, Höglund's pamphlet *Down with Weapons* of 1905—echo approximately the same ideas as those championed by the Young Socialists. The federation also distributed translations of foreign writers such as Tolstoy and de Maupassant that were generally antimilitary and pacifist but were not specifically Marxist.

A fairly distinct defense ideology gradually developed within the youth federation, which came to repudiate the argumentation employed by the Young Socialists as anarchist and non-Marxian. This standpoint was most current in *Fram,* but was also propagated in a number of brochures issued by the leading "young democrats." In contrast to the stand adopted by the Young Socialists, it implied recognition of the value of patriotism and of the composition of the national community. *Fram* repeatedly expressed this idea and criticized the antipatriotism of the Young Socialists. Patriotism, wrote P. A. Hansson, can readily be combined with internationalism. "The internationalism that is upheld by Social Democracy only wishes to bring nations together and prevent them from warring against one another." In another article Hansson castigated a Young Socialist, A. Jensen, for his interpretation of Marx's dictum that workers had no fatherland. Marx was right, said Hansson, but his statement referred solely to the fact that a worker's position in the class structure was not affected by attributes peculiar to any nation, because his position was determined by capitalism—which was international. Marx's statement could thus not be considered a basis for "shallow antinationalism." True Marxism was not indifferent to "the right of nations to independence, no more than it tolerates the oppression of a class or an individual." Articles written by Sandler and Ström claimed that the national spirit of the proletariat, which had been weak because of its [the proletariat's] class position, had grown with the breakthrough of socialism (socialism meant "the renascence of patriotism"), and that patriotic sentiment was already perceptible among Social Democratic youth.

This standpoint was hardly compatible with fundamental defense nihilism, which held that a Social Democratic party should under no conditions take a positive stand on defense. The demand for disarmament was primarily justified by the claim that Sweden could not defend herself. On this point the youth federation and those Social Democrats who were absolutely nihilistic toward defense drew upon the Danish line sponsored by radicals and Social Democrats in that country, whose attitude was summarized in Hörup's words "What good is it?" (*"Hvad kan det nytte?"*) This thinking was most ardently propounded in Fabian Månsson's brochure *Can Sweden Defend Herself?* (*Kan Sverige försvara sig?*) of 1907. Månsson tried to show that in order to be able to defend herself against a major power, Sweden would have to spend billions of crowns in one-time expenditures for naval stations, a fleet, and fortifications, and would thereafter have to carry an annual military budget of 800 million crowns. Although he passionately proclaimed his fundamentally friendly attitude toward defense, he nonetheless drew the conclusion that it would be meaningless "to ruin the nation's economy in order to pretend to play defense," especially since the facilities of the defense apparatus could be employed by the upper class to ensure suppression of the workers. This line of thinking served as the theme of the attacks on defense published in *Fram*. Such attempts at sham defense would not only be ineffective but would constitute a war risk by virtue of their very existence and could, in crises, become a shield for the few against the masses. This rationale affirmed on the one hand a certain kind of patriotism that emphatically repudiated the idea of surrendering Sweden to a foreign power, and on the other, a kind of practical nihilism toward defense. Popular armament was finally rejected on the ground that it was as unsatisfactory as the existing, more specifically "military" system.

The demand for a defense system that was not of a military character was a necessary complement to this theme from a theoretical viewpoint. This requirement was partly satisfied by the demand for cultural, political, and social reforms, in accordance with Branting's recommendations; these would of themselves give the country greater powers of resistance. It was also met by the demand for an amplification of "cultural defense," protective institutions, through the introduction of measures that would keep Sweden—and preferably other nations as well—out of war: awards by international courts of arbitration, the neutralization of Sweden and of Scandinavia as a whole, cooperation between the workers of all nations in war prevention. At times it was suggested that neutralization of Sweden would necessitate the establishment of a so-called neutrality defense: a military force would perform a type of guard duty in connection with armed conflicts and, if possible, bring violators of neutrality to justice or, in any case, confirm that violations had occurred in order that they might be dealt with through diplomatic channels. According to Hansson, such a neutrality defense would consist of "reinforced police control and inspection ships" and would entail only negligible expenditures.

This entire outlook was summarized in the second edition of P. A. Hansson's account of the purposes of the youth movement, published in 1909. ". . . we know that the nation's resources are not sufficient to provide it with an adequate defense. We ask then: why throw away the resources produced by the sweat and travail of the people on an inadequate defense? And we demand an end to this folly and that the means be used to further the culture of the nation. Yet we love the native land that we go forth to win, and we will not tolerate that its freedom be taken away. We therefore seek to cooperate with our brothers, the workers of other nations, who also fight against militarism in order that workers may jointly, by virtue of their organized might, by their refusal to perform military service and through [the use of] general strikes and blockades, prevent wars and force states to resolve their differences by peaceful means, through international courts of arbitration and similar [institutions]."

This line of argumentation was not the only one offered. It was developed gradually in the course of debates within the youth federation and in conflicts with both the Young Socialists and the Social Democratic party leadership. (It is indicative that in the first (1905) edition of the work just quoted, Hansson did not formulate his opinions with equal precision.) Moreover, a variety of arguments against military defense were offered in public agitation. In one article Hansson himself offered seven different arguments against militarism: the increased risk of war, the national ruin that it would lead to, the obstruction of progress due to the shortage of funds for cultural purposes, destruction of the race, the agony of the youth, its lack of value as a defense, the possibility that it might become a weapon against the working class. As the account of the congressional debates indicates, defense nihilism was at times even vindicated by the allegation that Sweden did not offer any significant advantages that were superior to those offered by other nations.

The variety of defense nihilism that was typical of the youth federation was based on practical reasons, not on principle. The idea underlying it did not evince any particularly Marxist characteristics. It acknowledged—at least indirectly—that it was understandable that some countries have a defense. Sweden's sparse population and unfavorable military situation were advanced as the decisive arguments against a Swedish defense. When representatives of the youth federation did cite Marx it was not just because they believed they were following Marx's example in regard to dispassionate, realistic, "Marxist" thinking. They also stressed that they considered collective, not individual action to be the essential agency, and that they believed the victory of socialism could provide the conditions for universal peace. Individual refusal to perform military service and humanitarian pacifism, which the Young Socialists propagated, was often said to prove that the message they promulgated did not conform to true Marxist philosophy.

When *Fram* ceased publication in 1912, *Stormklockan* became the main voice of the Social Democratic Youth Federation to a greater extent than previously. Antimilitary propaganda was heavily featured in *Stormklockan,* especially during the years around 1914. Yet the clearest exposition of the radical line on defense was that given in pamphlets prepared by Höglund and others. The pamphlet *The Fortified Poor House* (*Det befästa fattighuset*), published by Höglund, Ström, and H. Sköld in the autumn of 1913, offers the most lucid vindication of the defense nihilistic standpoint presented in Sweden. A brief review of this exposition follows, preceded by a reminder that it is representative of a great many contributions to brochures and newspapers.

The Fortified Poor House stresses views based on fundamental principles. As indicated in the Foreword, the writers thus do not explore the question, "whether Sweden, in her position as a small state, really can defend herself." They did not believe the answer to this question was decisive to arriving at their particular standpoint. Their underlying idea was that the Swedish working class had no reason to take part in defending a capitalist Sweden. Höglund developed this theme in other contexts as well, both before and after the outbreak of hostilities, in strings of catchy phrases. "In the capitalist state," he wrote in a brochure issued in 1913, "the worker almost finds himself in enemy territory. The state—is the upper ten thousand, the propertied classes. All their instruments of power are designed to subjugate him, to keep him subdued, to help capital strip him bare. It is like this everywhere, in Sweden as in Russia or America." In the summer of 1915 he wrote that it hardly made any difference to a worker's situation which capitalist system he happened to be living under and that his position, whether Sweden succeeded in defending herself or not, would inevitably be worse than before. The conclusion must be: "no war for the sake of this country."

Höglund attempted to vindicate this simplified Marxist approach in the pamphlet by providing a detailed rationale. The militarism of that day was "basically nothing more than a capitalist power and business interest." Capitalism had to find a way of disposing of a nation's surplus products and invest capital in colonies that would yield a good return; it had to assert itself in competition with capitalists of other nations. But above all the armed forces filled political and social functions. "The first aim of defense is to protect the capitalist class against the enemy *within,* it is the armed lifeguard of the capitalist masters [to be used] against the exploited masses who have begun to wake up to a realization of their situation and now demand their rights under the banner of socialism." With the advent of socialism the cause of war—class conflicts—would disappear, and thereby war itself. The pamphlet brought up the objection raised by those who thought state control of industry would increase friction between nations. The authors contended that this objection was of absolutely no consequence, for the victory of socialism also meant the liquidation of the state as such.

A special section of the pamphlet was devoted to "the Sweden of the class society." It brought into relief the unequal distribution of wealth, the absence of political democracy and the opposition of the upper house to social reforms, deficiences in the cultural life of the nation, the large share that military expenditures claimed in the budget, and the effect of defense on the nation's economy in general. Sweden was found to be a class society intent upon the oppression and exploitation of the working class. Sweden was even said to be one of the most backward countries in the world, "together with Prussia, Spain, Hungary, and Russia . . . the chief stronghold of reactionism in Europe . . . an eldorado for capitalist pillagers, ravagers, speculators, militarists, political reactionaries and compromisers." The authors thus returned to their fundamental standpoint, as specifically applied to Sweden. The objective of the Social Democrats could be reached only by

> fighting and vanquishing the social class that now rules, the bourgeoisie and its society, the present class state. But the ultimate weapon of power of the bourgeoisie and the ultimate protection of the class state . . . in Sweden as elsewhere is solely military might and the *coup d'état* that is backed by military might. . . . Military might is thus the last recourse of the bourgeoisie and the most dangerous enemy of Social Democracy. . . . Social Democracy's entire military policy must aim at undermining and liquidating the chief weapon of power of the class state. Its principle must be that not one man, not one penny be granted to a military establishment in a class state. There can be no question of expansion here, nor of tolerance, nor of reform, but only this one [objective]: raze."

Antimilitary policies were vindicated on the ground that they were the only true patriotic policies. For Social Democracy's "fight against capitalism and militarism, its struggle for the liberation of our people from economic and spiritual slavery is . . . the most noble patriotic deed." In contrast, the rich who exploit the masses so that they themselves may live in luxury are the ones who lack patriotism. Their slogan should be "Profit above all else."

It is true that the argumentation presented in *The Fortified Poor House* is related to views previously propounded in socialist agitation. But the theoretical extremism of the actual exposition of the problem departs to some extent from the varieties of defense nihilism hitherto discussed. In the main it does follow the line that was dominant in Young Socialist agitation: the theme of the pamphlet can be summed up in Marx's dictum that workers had no fatherland. But in contrast to the Young Socialists, the authors announced that they were friends of the country of their birth; indeed, they claimed that in comparison with defense zealots they were the only true friends of their native land. This inference was drawn by establishing the socialist goal as the major premise. The real task at hand was to create better conditions for the Swedish people: this was true patriotism. In this respect the authors used the same logic as that employed in *Fram* and by the early Social Democratic youth movement. On the other hand, they deliberately did not employ the argument that Sweden was unable to defend herself: it would have been impossible to fit this into the general scheme of reasoning. If defense of the nation was unreasonable from the standpoint of the workers, there was no point in examining the feasibleness of such a defense. In other words, this defense nihilistic line is more fundamental than that expounded in *Fram,* for example. This argumentation had to apply to every nonsocialist nation. The pamphlet did not touch upon the speculation that the advantages that accrued to the workers through capitalism as it existed in Sweden, compared with the capitalist systems in Russia or Germany, were sufficiently superior to warrant defending Sweden for this reason alone. However, it must be assumed that the authors would have responded to this thought in the negative: otherwise the entire structure of their reasoning would have rested on a most flimsy foundation. The exceedingly heavy emphasis given the role of the military as a protection for the upper class against the lower class—an argument that was especially stressed in discussions of Swedish conditions—was obviously necessary in order that the question of the value of defense to Sweden's workers under *existing* circumstances could be completely bypassed. In conclusion, it should be noted that Höglund and other party members that stood at his side concurrently availed themselves of entirely different lines of argumentation; for example, in the previously cited brochure of 1913, Höglund maintained at one and the same time that it would be hopeless to defend Sweden and that it was highly unlikely that anyone would want to attack Sweden.

Branting was without doubt the foremost representative of the party faction that was positively disposed toward defense even during this period. As a rule, Branting served as the Social Democratic spokesman in the Riksdag and as the leader of the majority at party congresses. By and large he expressed the same basic view that he had advanced around 1900. He presupposed that the workers had an interest in the preservation of Sweden's independence even under the conditions then prevalent in the nation; he further assumed that under certain circumstances a military defense for this purpose could prove to be of decisive importance, perhaps primarily through its deterrent effect. On the other hand, he conceded that the socially ascendant classes were inclined to strengthen the military establishment beyond the bounds of necessity for their own selfish reasons and that they thus overlooked the value of political and social reforms to national solidarity and thereby, indirectly, to defense. "When a people feel that they are masters in their own country, that something is being done about the wrongs they suffer, that they are governed according to and not contrary to their wishes, yes, then the desire for defense also flourishes." So proclaimed Branting at an address he gave in Uppsala in 1913.

In 1906 he had also launched a scathing attack on the use of armed troops in labor conflicts. Said he on the floor of the Riksdag: "That which contaminates the military question is that we cannot think of our army for use solely against external enemies, for it has regrettably also happened that [the army] or parts thereof have been commanded into service on occasions when it has seemed altogether too apparent that it has been used for the benefit of the special interests of the ruling classes, for the benefit of capitalist interests, as a weapon in our party conflicts, and not exclusively as a protection for our common country of birth."

From time to time Branting noted the risk that an increase of the defense burden would also increase the already widespread antipathy to defense. In other contexts, when answering charges that the Social Democrats were wanting in their will to defend the nation, Branting portrayed the party faction that was hostile to defense as being of no significance. On the whole, a review of Branting's comments on defense shows that his remarks were greatly influenced by tactical considerations and that they accordingly accented different subtleties on different occasions. However, since such a review would not reveal any basic modifications of Branting's opinion, there is no need for us to subject it to close scrutiny. Probably under the influence of Jaurès' work on the subject, which was published in 1911, Branting frequently returned to his old idea of converting to a people's defense, a militia, in his addresses at the 1914 Riksdag. Branting moreover often referred to Jaurès when treating the defense issue, for the latter's ideas closely paralleled Branting's opinions as previously expressed on many occasions.

Some of Branting's statements which directly or indirectly criticize antidefense propaganda within the party are especially important to an understanding of his fundamental views on defense. In a 1907 *Fram* article entitled "What Is the Aim of Antimilitarism?" (*"Vart syftar antimilitarismen?"*), Branting discussed the treatment of the military issue at the International Social Democratic congress held in Stuttgart earlier the same year. Referring to the proceedings at the congress, he directed a warning to the youth federation about its concentration on antimilitaristic propaganda. The proposal to call a general strike in response to an outbreak of hostilities as espoused by Hervé was criticized on the grounds that it was Utopian and would lead to anarchism. Even Jaurès' conciliatory standpoint was rejected. On the whole Branting aligned himself firmly with the German standpoint. One could not expect that the working class would be able to prevent the outbreak of war, whether it resorted to a general strike or to other measures. The success of the action of Sweden's workers in 1905 had no bearing on this point: the opportunity to prevent a Swedish war of aggression could not be expected to return. Moreover, the antimilitary stand of the International did not include directives to attempt to impede defense of the independence of one's own country nor to create agitation that would lower the resistance of the people or army to possible aggression. The Germans had definitively opposed such action, for they adhered to the principle "that in extreme cases free men and free peoples protect their rights and independence with weapons in their hands." Continued Branting: the presence of such a popular sentiment is "a safeguard against violent aggression and is a sign of mental health; should it vanish, it might seem as though the ideal of peace had scored a victory, but, in reality, we would be confronted only by a symptom of decadence and dissolution." The intent of a resolution passed by the Stuttgart International, which referred to educating working-class youth in the spirit of brotherhood among men, was "to strengthen the resistance of the civic, humane, and progressive spirit within the conscripted army against the adverse influences of the military traditions of drill and blind obedience." The purport of the resolution was not to demoralize the defense of one's native land. Branting added that he assumed the Social Democratic Youth Federation was pursuing a similar "sensible" theme in its antimilitary propaganda—an aside that was probably intended to influence the federation in the direction Branting desired.

In concluding his *Fram* article, Branting stressed that socialist agitation should not concentrate on certain special problems. Socialists had been inclined to restrict themselves exclusively to central economic problems and dismiss all others as bagatelles. There was now a tendency to go too far in the opposite direction; some factions within the party combined religion, temperance, and the military with the main problem—socialism's struggle against capitalism. Instead, one's attention and efforts ought to be directed on all Social Democratic demands as a whole; the means for the realization of these demands should be determined in this perspective. "I think it is clear that if this gauge is applied, the fight against militarism will be the more auspicious and promising the more definitely it makes known its intention to be inexorable toward military wrongs in its purging and supervisory activites, but to in no way compromise the nation's potential capacity to protect its neutrality and existence."

In his Uppsala address, "Patriotic Policies" (*"Fosterländsk politik"*) of 1913, Branting attacked both armament enthusiasts, whom he accused of forgetting the implications of social reforms to defense, and those who would demobilize. The idea of "an unarmed cultural defense"—long a favorite notion of the Social Democratic Youth Federation—was characterized as Utopian and said to derive "its main support in quarters where the phrases of syndicalism and anarchism rule supreme." A party that wishes to be taken seriously must "establish goals it would *want* to realize if it had power." In other words, he took it for granted that the program of the youth federation could not conceivably be intended as a foundation for practical policies. The phrase "the worker has no fatherland" conflicted with the spirit of the entire International and was, in reality, abandoned by Marx himself when he spoke of the danger that Russia represented to the peace and freedom of Europe."

Branting subjected *The Fortified Poor House* to a particularly virulent attack. He charged that the pamphlet used the word "militarism" "as a designation to cover not only the case spirit and brutality that so markedly characterizes an army that is kept isolated from the rest of the population as if it were a nation within a nation, but also as equivalent to all military complexes in general." This made it possible to inject defense nihilism into attacks on the deficiencies of the military establishment. The theses of the International had been completely misinterpreted; among other errors, the disarmament demand had been interpreted as signifying unilateral disarmament when it really meant gradual, joint disarmament of all nations. Swedish Social Democracy did not endorse the view promulgated in the pamphlet. Branting maintained that it had to be made absolutely clear that the pamphlet really provided a gold mine for armament zealots in their battle with the Social Democratic party. If the Swedish people were led to believe that the real core of socialism was "to cry with purblind fanaticism for instantaneous *razing* of every military safeguard for the existence of our nation, then one would indeed have accomplished much more to cripple and trammel our advance than the cries of warning of all our Conservative and Liberal adversaries have been able to accomplish."

Particularly in the beginning of the period under discussion it was sometimes suggested that an army built on universal conscription might prove of value from a socialist viewpoint as a protection against the upper class conspiracy to stamp out socialism, and that it might even become an agency for socialist action. This was a reversal of the usual train of thought: the military was here regarded as an asset of the working class, not of capitalism. Lidforss, who was generally friendly to defense, enunciated this theory in pregnant terms in a May Day speech he gave in 1905:

> Should the antimilitary sentiment unexpectantly lead to tangible results in our nation, the final outcome would be that, at the decisive moment, the reactionaries would be in command of absolutely trustworthy soldier material trained according to

> all the rules of [military] art, while the Social Democrats would stand virtually defenseless. I cannot imagine that this is a desirable [state of affairs]. I therefore believe that Social Democratic youth [evinces] sagacity when it accepts the free instruction in the use of weapons that the state is good enough to bestow upon it, for the day *can* come when it may have use for them against Russia, which lingers within Sweden's boundaries.

Lidforss also pointed out, however, that he was only referring to the self-defense of the working class. As our consideration of the entire subject reveals, this rationale for defense was never of much consequence. In later years it would only flicker fitfully in the debate on the rifle-club movement.

Gustaf Steffen's article "Militarism and Socialism," published in *Tiden* in 1911, is one of the most basically formulated vindications of a positive stand on defense. As did Branting in the article "What Is the Aim of Antimilitarism?" Steffen treated the ambiguities in the usage of the terms "militarism" and "antimilitarism." He declared that he was himself antimilitaristic in the sense that he wished to fight against everything pertaining to the military complex that conflicted with the spirit of democracy and socialism, but that he definitely opposed the variety of antimilitarism that wished to abolish the country's defense. The latter brand of antimilitarism did not at all constitute a means of combatting war, as its proponents claimed; generally speaking, it was not even a tool against militarism, no matter which interpretation was given this word. To the contrary: Sweden's disarmament would not mean the end of militarism in the nation, but would lead to "the incorporation through military force of the Swedish people into the military establishment of a foreign state . . . two years' compulsory military service and military slavery under foreign officers. . . ." No human being could foreswear the exercise of violence independently of his neighbor's designs. "If he wants to fight, I must fight him—or become his slave. And if I am his slave, a characteristic of slavery is that he can force me to fight for him." Another, special point of view also dictated that defense was imperative to a state that was developing toward democracy and socialism, as in a young Social Democratic society. A counterrevolution supported by foreign aid would be a real threat to such a state; it would "for centuries be an easy prey to socially reactionary foes within and without." Even if world peace were to be organized on an international scale, military might would be indispensable for many years thereafter: peace would be confronted with powerful enemies "not least because it is the social order that is based on socialism that ultimately determines peace." Each member of the peace-keeping compact must contribute to the armed might necessary to secure peace. Steffen concluded by pleading for rational and realistic thinking on the whole question. The extreme proposals of the "antimilitarists" were as meaningless as means to preserve peace "as Catholic processions and prayers used as remedies for cholera or earthquakes."

Other *Tiden* articles published in 1915 and written by two young Social Democrats attempted to demonstrate the untenability of defense nihilism from a pure Marxist view. Möller examined the slogan "the workers have no fatherland" which was derived from Marx. Möller ascertained that in the *Communist Manifesto* this assertion was immediately followed by "since the most immediate goals of the proletariat are to capture political power, elevate itself to [the status of] the national class, and form itself into a nation, it is nevertheless national, even if by no means in the same sense as the bourgeoisie." From a superficial point of view, Marx could thus be cited as the authority by both defense nihilists and by the nationalists in socialist ranks. In fact, however, Marx simply meant that the workers as a class did not have a fatherland, no more than did the bourgeoisie in its capacity as an international class. This did not prevent the individual worker from having a fatherland nor the working class of each country from concentrating its efforts within the confines of its national boundaries in order to become the ruling class in that country—that is, to identify itself with the nation. According to this interpretation, Marx's statement had nothing to do with the defense issue. It should rather be evaluated on the basis of the right of nations to self-determination, a principle that was universally recognized by socialists. In conformity with this principle, each nation had the right to defend its inviolability; socialism thus had to countenance defense on principle. The Social Democratic Youth Federation had previously acknowledged this; its expedient defense nihilism was determined only by the opinion that Sweden was unable to defend herself. A modification of their estimation of Sweden's defense potential had caused many older members of the youth federation—including Möller himself—to abandon their defense nihilism.

Engberg's analysis of the Marxist stand on defense started from a broad theoretical perspective. He based his conclusions on a specific interpretation of the import of the materialist theory of history. This interpretation postulated that an international legal order must faithfully correspond to the international economic order. The current international situation was connected with the capitalist order. "The way out of a legal order in which states stalk each other like wild animals with a brutality uninhibited by any bounds in the struggle for existence thus coincides, according to the other Marxist view, with the way out of the private capitalist system of production." According to what Engbert termed modified Marxism—which, in contrast to 'raw' Marxism was said to acknowledge the possibility that conscious human effort could affect the system of production—a purposeful economic policy could gradually pave the way for international peace: "the peace-oriented line coincides with the sociopolitical line." Yet it would be meaningless to try to achieve peace without changing the system of production. For this reason defense nihilism was incompatible with Marxism. The former was "a message from a bird's-eye view proclaiming that it would be possible to abolish international anarchy without first eliminating the system of production from which it stems of inexorable necessity." The Marxist position on peace was diametrically opposed to the defense nihilist position. "According to Marxism, disarmament is effected by eliminating the international anarchy of violence; according to defense nihilism, elimination of the international anarchy of violence is effected by disarmament." Armed defense must be regarded as a stern necessity as long as the dominion of capitalism prevailed. Dismantlement of defense was conceivable only after capitalism had been supplanted. To express this view and provide a bit of "applied science," Engbert proposed this formulation of the defense article in the party program: "Gradual reduction of defense burdens toward the goal of final universal disarmament to the extent that the international anarchy of violence is vanquished through the reformation of the private-capitalist system of production in a socialist direction and better guarantees of peace are thereby obtained."

Engberg's article is an interesting expression of a common variation of Marxist thinking. Fairly complicated reasoning is employed to establish that defense ought to stand in relation to the risk of war. The point of departure is that international conditions, like all else, are dependent on, or, rather, are a manifestation of the prevailing system of production. For the present it is assumed that this system entails war and a strong national defense, but this situation was expected to change in the future. Social Democracy should work in line with development, that is, for a reduction of defense burdens concomitant with the transformation of capitalism. According to the very same reasoning, socialism should apparently have worked to augment defense during an earlier period when capitalism was growing stronger instead of withering away. Similarly, in those nations and at those times when capitalism was flourishing socialism ought to have worked in behalf of the concentration of capital, for the impoverishment of the proletariat, and so on. This reasoning could obviously be employed only because it was combined with the concept of the imminent liquidation of capitalism.

Karleby, another socialist theorist, advanced a similar interpretation at a somewhat later date. He declared that defense nihilism "with all its radical mannerisms" was "a typical bourgeois phenomenon." Defense nihilists did not understand "the character of the military establishment as a necessary expression of the needs of the class society and class rule, which will not disappear until the class society itself [disappears]." According to true Marxism, disarmament could not be realized prior to the overthrow of the class society. "But during the period of transition between the modern capitalist [society] and the fully formed socialist society, which is called the dictatorship of the proletariat, military power, like official power in general, must become a weapon in the hands of socialist groups, a defense against an obstructionist middle class that thirsts for a *coup d'état*. . . ."

The Triumph of the Positive Line versus the Modified Rationale for Disarmament

UNQUALIFIED RECOGNITION of the value of national unity has increasingly become a purposive, consistently stressed basis for the activity of the Swedish Social Democratic party. In the early 1900s the party still harbored groups and factions that either refused or were reluctant to recognize this value. To be sure, the defense nihilistic propaganda of the youth federation was not rooted in unpatriotic sentiments; yet the sharp distinction that the federation sometimes drew between Sweden as she was—the promised land of capitalism and exploitation, in the federation's view—and the socialist Sweden of the future—made for a kind of qualified patriotism. However, after the rupture of the party in 1917 and the democratization of the Swedish body politic that followed shortly thereafter, expressions of patriotism uttered in the general debate were hardly ever qualified by reservations or doubts. To the contrary, patriotism became more and more pronounced during this period, which was distinguished by Social Democratic successes and by an improvement in the position of the working class. During the 1920s the Swedish flag was occasionally carried side by side with the red banner of the International in demonstration marches; by the 1930s this practice had become the rule. The patriotic speeches of leading Social Democrats have differed from the nationalistic proclamations of the representatives of nonsocialist parties in one important respect: they have more emphatically asserted that feelings of national solidarity must be demonstrated primarily in endeavors for social reform and cultural progress to ameliorate the situation of the needy sections of the populace and lessen economic inequalities. In a speech delivered on Sweden's National Flag Day, June 6, 1922, Branting stressed the oneness of national sentiment and social conscience. P. A. Hansson's speech on the National Flag Day twelve years later echoed the same idea: "Love of our native land is not and cannot be qualified. It is within us, it guides us and drives us, it is stronger than any other force. Just for this reason [the sentiments that] flow [from it] should be united into collective action on the part of Swedish manhood to build this Swedish native land of ours into a secure home for all

Swedes on the firm foundation of [national] solidarity." It has often been said that Swedish democracy and social welfare policies have given the working class of this country cause to experience a different kind of patriotic feeling than it could before these reforms were introduced.

Internationalist ideology has been able to exist side by side with patriotism. Social Democrats have frequently cited the saying that a little internationalism induces one away from the country of one's birth while a lot of internationalism leads one back to one's native land. It is hardly possible to delineate unequivocally exactly what was meant by this supposition or by the continuously stressed concept of internationalism in general. Marxist doctrine of an international class conflict on an international scale waged by the proletariat against the bourgeoisie has no doubt been a tenet vital to many, even though they may not have pursued this thinking to its logical conclusion. It has not been difficult to combine this view with the idea of national solidarity because no concrete problems that would demand exact definition of one's opinions have arisen in this area. Nonetheless, the general impression left by the Social Democratic debate is that internationalism, regarded in this rather vague manner, has become less and less important as an ideological factor. This decline in the significance of internationalism is connected with two developments: the demotion of the broad Marxist perspective to a subordinate role and the aftereffect of the victories won through national solidarity during the world war, which had also diminished the hopes once placed in an international workers' action. Cooperation between Social Democratic parties in different countries has continued, but the resolutions of the International have been substantially deflated in their importance as directives for the several parties.

Internationalism was supposedly often interpreted to mean simply the desire for and faith in an international peace that would be secure and durable. At the same time, resigned Social Democrats have been inclined to look upon the state of world peace that Marxism postulated could arrive only after the victory of the working class as possible even under existing conditions, before the triumph of socialism. As a norm for action, internationalism has thus implied disassociation from all nationalism and chauvinism—that is, from attempts at national self-assertion which have been considered incompatible with the accepted principles of international coexistence—and with the desire to apply such principles in foreign policy.

Inasmuch as no important political party in Sweden has represented an aggressive nationalism, the Social Democratic position has not been remarkable in this regard. In the only case of Swedish territorial expansion that has arisen—that pertaining to the island of Åland in the Baltic—it was natural that the Social Democrats follow an active policy, supported by the principle of a people's right to self-determination. Branting, then prime minister, was the only Swedish political figure to have his name intimately associated with the demand for Åland's unification with Sweden. It appeared to be equally far-fetched for nonsocialist parties and for the Social Democrats to use armed force to drive through this demand, which had been rejected by Finland and by the League of Nations. Despite criticism from the Right, the Liberal-Social Democratic cabinet maintained a policy of absolute neutrality during the Finnish war for independence in 1918. In this instance, party policy was to some degree determined by uncertainty toward the red-led rebellion in Finland, which some regarded as a class struggle in the real Marxian sense and others viewed as primarily a Russian Communist attempt to render Free Finland completely prostrate. Both parties of the Left forced through the decision to join the League of Nations, and after a while even the major nonsocialist parties were anxious to keep Sweden in the League. The position of the Social Democrats on the whole question of Sweden's membership in the League was characterized in the main by a relatively robust faith in the potential of the organization. Party members long entertained the hope that the League would bring about partial or universal disarmament and that it would lead to a revision of the peace treaties ratified at the close of the world war. These treaties were subject to considerable Social Democratic criticism, though it may not have been as bitter as that advanced by groups who had hoped for a German victory. There is reason to state that the Social Democratic party was long prone to the same exaggerated optimism regarding the League's ability to maintain peace as it had previously displayed toward the value of a workers' action on an international scale. The League now largely replaced the International as the buttress for optimistic views on foreign policy. This substitution of ideological props evidently came about as the Social Democratic party came to concentrate more and more on fortifying the inroads already made by democracy and on pursuing a reform policy that did not entail socialization measures or rapid, radical changes. The substitution was also determined by the new positions of power that workers' parties attained in several countries in postwar years, which would, in turn, enable these parties to participate in the League's leadership.

With the split in the party that took place in 1917, one line on the defense issue definitely disappeared from Social Democratic debate. This was the fundamentally defense nihilistic line. Within a few years the disarmament concept would again gain considerable momentum, but then it would not be based on the general Marxian viewpoints that had become so flagrant in the propaganda issued by the youth federation. The expression "defense nihilism" came to be used only as a term of disparagement; those who would champion the cause of unilateral national disarmament in the late 1920s were to renounce the designation "defense nihilists." The rancorous, brutal idiom that had often been invoked by defense abolitionists now appears but seldom. The phraseology that acquired currency became even more temperate than the actual opinions held.

During the eight-year span, 1917–1925, the party did not suffer any really drastic rifts on the question of defense. All agreed that the military act of 1914 should be preserved for the duration of the war; agreement on this was, indeed, a condition of the collaboration between Liberals and Social Democrats in the cabinet formed after the 1917 election. When the war came to an end, two currents of thought dominated the political scene. One looked with hope to the influence that the League of Nations, which had been planned during the war years, might exercise on defense policy. The League was to organize peace, possibly by placing the major military forces at its service. In view of the importance of the League, a reduction in defense ought to be able to take place immediately, and in time more complete disarmament would be realized under the leadership of the League. Instantaneous disarmament was out of the question: it was too early to judge the efficacy of the League, which might also need to employ the military forces of individual states. These speculations were complemented by the notion that, irrespective of the birth of the League of Nations, the international situation ruled out the likelihood of another war for a long time to come—or at least of a war that would threaten Sweden. The great military monarchies had been vanquished, a feat that itself discredited the very principle of militarism. Although many stipulations in the peace treaties were harsh, the treaties had expunged some of the causes of war, particularly by their broad application of the principle of the right of a people to self-determination. Democratic and socialist movements had won greater support and better chances to exert their influence: this was considered a victory for the forces of peace. It was thought that the new Russian regime had abandoned all plans of a world-wide revolution and was now committed to peaceful endeavors. And perhaps most important—the war had to be followed by a period of recovery. In the course of a debate on defense in 1920, Branting summarized the reasons for optimism about the prospects of peace. "It can . . . not be denied that the weariness of war that is spread throughout the world and which is very very strong in all nations, conquerors as well as conquered, must assert itself. . . . Now a relaxation of tensions has taken place. . . . And we have, moreover, created an institution, this League of Nations, which may initially suffer from shortcomings and imperfections, but nevertheless affords us new opportunities of immediately dealing with incipient conflicts as soon as they arise and of eliminating them so as to provide a settlement that the great majority on both sides [of the dispute] desire."

These lines of thought were the springboard for the defense policy of the Social Democrats. The party's Riksdag group often helped defeat motions for disarmament studies proposed by the Left Socialists. During the attendant debates Social Democratic representatives affirmed that the principle of national unity must be safeguarded, that unilateral disarmament would be impossible, and that abolition of the armed forces of individual states was conceivable only in conjunction with the establishment of a supernational system of justice that would transcend the law of individual states. In this postwar era all parties favored a cutback in armaments; in this respect, with the exception of some factions in the Liberal party, the Social Democrats went further than nonsocialist parties. In the 1919 session of the Riksdag the term of compulsory military service was provisionally reduced and the defense budget was pared down. Prior to the by-elections to the upper house in the autumn of 1919 the party pronounced its hopes for the abolition of the existing military system in conjunction with the establishment of a league of nations. "It is hardly conceivable that a civilized European people that has introduced a democratic order throughout and taken its fate into its own hands would ever revert to a policy which, with inexorable logic, must provoke new and worse catastrophes of the same kind that the world has now experienced." The defense burden should be substantially and immediately eased. In November of the same year the Liberal-Socialist cabinet appointed a committee to review the defense system. It was presumed that the committee (which took three years to complete the review) would propose a defense system that would be relatively limited in comparison with the military organization of 1918. Subsequent riksdags enacted additional provisional cutbacks in the military organization of 1914. Statements made by Social Democrats during the Riksdag debates followed the pattern just described. There were no appeals for unilateral Swedish disarmament. The party maintained its basic rejection of the voluntary rifle-club movement on the ground that the movement was unnecessarily expensive and of little military value.

The program commission that presented its recommendations for a revision of the Social Democratic program at the party congress of 1920 had worked on the assumption that changes in the international situation called for new directions on defense. The commission proposed that the program article on foreign policy and defense be placed as the last article, XVII, following all domestic questions, and that it contain first of all a statement repudiating secret diplomacy and espousing popular control of foreign policy. The commission was of the opinion that "secret diplomacy . . . stands unmercifully bared as one of the greatest threats to international understanding and a peaceful order." The party program should therefore call for a democratic union of all peoples. The peoples' federation that was being organized at the time of the presentation of the proposal might not completely meet this requirement, but it signified a step forward and should therefore receive Social Democratic support as representing a first essay in the right direction. The peoples' federation rendered meaningless or superfluous all existing demands for international law, awards of courts of arbitration, and the neutralization of the Scandinavian countries. Nor should the new program concern itself with the idea of international antiwar operations of workers' organizations; this question was not pertinent to the political program of the Swedish Social Democratic party but to the party's activities within the scope of the International. Finally, the program should include these words: "An international police force. Disarmament." For the time being, a standing military organization under the control of the peoples' federation would be necessary. Absolute defense nihilism was thus out of the question. However, the international agency that was to keep order would guarantee the right of nations to self-determination, which would, in turn, eliminate the need for each state to maintain a separate national military organization. "The logical final demand of the program article" must therefore be "disarmament." According to this reasoning, a Swedish military force that was part of an international police force could not be considered a component of national defense in the real sense. The commission also declared that disarmament had become a pressing issue and that the party should strive to carry out this demand nationally as well as internationally. Social Democracy must "work on the initiative of the parliaments and governments of different countries toward agreements on disarmament and, at the same time, demand substantial reductions in the national military establishment preparatory to general and total disarmament."

The only serious dispute on the commission's recommendations that arose at the congress concerned these last items. Pursuant to a recommendation made by Engberg to the commission, the party administration proposed that the article not refer to disarmament but to the abolition of all things military that were not required by the international police force. Hansson, Möller, and Sandler, who had formulated the commission report, dissented. During the debate, Engberg contended that it was impossible to place the word "disarmament" next to the demand for an international police force: he did not accept the commission's opinion that disarmament was in no way related to the international military organization. In his answer to Engberg, Hansson followed a line that cannot be inferred from the recommendation of the program commission: he alleged that disarmament even implied abolition of the international police force when this would be feasible. The entire question was remitted to an editorial committee; the committee's proposal, which was unanimously accepted, gave Article XVII the following wording:

> Popular control over foreign policy. Secret diplomacy shall be eliminated.
> A democratically organized federation of peoples.
> An international police force and disarmament.

When this wording had been approved, Karleby, one of the members of the editorial committee, delivered an account of the committee proceedings stating that he had favored introducing "a statement for a positive defense policy" in the program but had refrained from making this recommendation because the committee—whose membership included Branting and Hansson—was agreed that such a policy was incompatible with the program formulation that had already been accepted. This account indicates that differences of opinion could arise on the interpretation of the article. In fact, the formulation—which still stands—can embrace radically different interpretations. For example, disarmament can be regarded as a final objective that can only be reached by international cooperation; in this case, a positive defense policy, even a building-up of defense, would be in conformity with the party program. On the other hand, the word "disarmament" can also be taken to mean "unilateral disarmament," in which case steps toward immediate Swedish disarmament would be considered true to the program. It is also unclear whether disarmament necessarily entailed abolition of even the international police force that was to be organized, or whether disarmament would instead take place in conjunction with the establishment of such a police force. However, since the wording reads "An international police force and disarmament" it seems most natural to accept the latter alternative, that is, to agree with the interpretation of the program commission that a Swedish contribution to the international police force is something that falls outside the frame of military defense in the true sense.

In March 1923 the reviewing committee delivered its report. In accordance with a proposal of the standing majority of the middle-of-the-road parties, defense expenditures would total about 123 million crowns; the Conservative proposal entailed expenditures of 136 million, the Social Democratic proposal not quite 100 million crowns. It was estimated that the military organization of 1914 would now cost in excess of 180 million crowns. As a rule, the Social

Democrats recommended shorter terms of military service than the other groups in the reviewing committee; according to one Social Democratic proposal, for example, the regular term of service in the infantry would be 180 days, while the rest of the committee proposed a term of 255 days.

The Social Democratic demurrer—signed by Johan Nilsson, Wigforss, Victor Larsson, and Engberg—did not dwell on the possibility of total disarmament. It simply noted that the expectations for lasting peace and reconciliation between peoples that had been so marked early in the postwar period had not been fulfilled; for this reason the dissentients considered unilateral disarmament inconceivable. In their criticism of the position taken by the majority in the committee and as a vindication of their own proposal, the dissentients above all maintained that, politically, Sweden's defense situation was much improved in comparison with what it had been before the war and that substantial cutbacks in defense were therefore reasonable. More specific reasons, some of which concerned military technology, were also given. In regard to the possibility of greater risks of war in the future, the dissentients stated that it would be extremely difficult to evaluate such possibilities and that the defense system should therefore be made as flexible as possible—that is, it should be so constituted that augmenting such a system would not encounter serious difficulties and could be accomplished without too much delay. In the present situation Sweden did not have to fear direct attack by any power.

At the Riksdag of 1924 the Trygger cabinet introduced a bill for the organization of the defense system. As the cabinet emphasized, the bill was intended as a basis for a concerted solution to the question. It was estimated that the costs of the proposed organization would not exceed those entailed by the provisional arrangement then in force, 138 million crowns. An attempt was made to comply with the different opinions that had been proffered. The cabinet proposed, for example, a 195-day term of service in the infantry (in contrast to the 255 days suggested by the reviewing committee) and a 240-day term in the artillery, the same period that had been proposed by Social Democrats on the review committee (in contrast to the 350 days recommended by the majority). It became apparent already in the course of the debate preceding referral of the cabinet bill to committee that it would not be able to win measurable support. A motion made by the Social Democrats that was closely allied to the demurrer entered in the review committee became the basis of the work assigned to the special committee appointed to make a preliminary study of the defense question. When a vote was taken towards the end of May the upper house followed a demurrer entered by the Conservatives which was based on the cabinet proposal; the lower house accepted the committee's recommendation, which largely agreed with the Social Democrats' motion. Since an accommodation of opinions was thought impossible, the question was thereafter dropped.

The debates at the 1924 Riksdag are not really important from the viewpoint of their ideological content and will thus only be mentioned briefly. The main theme of the Social Democrats' arguments was that the international situation had improved to such an extent that substantial disarmament could be implemented without danger. In this connection it was said that Sweden's defense ought to be a defense of neutrality, designed exclusively for the purpose of dealing with violations of neutrality. The objection was raised that it would not be possible to distinguish between the defense of neutrality and national independence because a violation of neutrality that could not be repulsed would automatically become a threat to independence. The significant part of the debate is that the great majority of Social Democratic speakers—such as Olaf Olsson, Wigforss, and Möller in the upper house, and Branting, P. A. Hansson, Engberg, and Thorsson in the lower—did not bring up the question of total disarmament and apparently did not even consider this possibility. To the contrary, they presupposed that defense was necessary and that in the current situation the Social Democratic line was sufficiently secure from a military point of view. Following the cabinet example, they characterized their proposal as a concerted solution and urged other parties to cooperate in its implementation. Only a few party members appealed for unilateral disarmament. These members—Elof Lindberg, Lindhagen, Fabian Månsson—had for a time associated themselves with the Left Socialist line but had recently rejoined the party. Lindberg, who offered the most perspicuous explanation of his standpoint, asserted first of all that military defense did not constitute a safeguard for peace and that it should be replaced by other guarantees. At the time, this standpoint represented an exceptional and insignificant position, but in the future it would be provided with a far more complete argumentation in its defense.

At the party congress of 1924, which convened after the defense issue had been treated in the Riksdag, the question of defense did not arise except in the context of a debate on a party administration proposal for a manifesto to be issued in anticipation of the coming elections to the lower house. The proposal, which was in principle ratified by the congress and subsequently published without the introduction of any important amendments, justified the reduction in defense proposed at the Riksdag with by then familiar arguments. Direct risks of war were declared to be "so distant that no one wishes to hazard pointing them out." The Russian threat could not be used as an excuse for agitation now that Finland had gained her independence. Militaristic and reactionary elements had been repulsed on an international scale. Most recently, the English and French elections had increased the opportunities for a peaceful solution of international problems. If the Social Democrats were able to carry out their proposal for partial disarmament, "Sweden will again demonstrate her position as a leader among states that prove by their actions their steadfast love of and ardent desire for peace." It was noted that although the Social Democratic proposal implied a considerable saving it had also been worked out along lines that were most efficient in view of the existing military situation. The proposal for the manifesto was criticized at the congress by a series of speakers (E. Lindberg, Hellberg, Bärg, Fast) who wanted bolder emphasis on the ultimate goal of disarmament and a more pronounced reduction in armaments established as an immediate goal. However, most of the delegates in essence supported the proposal of the party administration.

The Social Democratic cabinet formed after the elections of 1924, which was led in turn by Branting and Sandler, prepared a new bill on the organization of the military that was introduced at the Riksdag in February 1925. Although the cabinet proposal had not been worked out in collaboration with the Independents, it did, in fact, represent a compromise between the standpoints held by the Independents and the Social Democrats in 1924. The bill stressed that it purported to attract broad and firm consensus among the people for the proposed organization. Concise arguments of principle were presented to support the cabinet bill. Sweden, it was maintained, was hardly confronted with any risk of direct aggression by another state; the only danger of war that might arise would be provoked by the nation's possible entanglement in conflicts between other states. "It is, however, in the nature of things that the military might be needed for the most immediate purpose of protecting ourselves against involvement in conflicts between others at the same time constitutes and must be able to be used as a defense of our independence in case we should be unsuccessful in keeping out of a conflict." The special committee appointed to prepare the question approved the bill with only some minor changes; this approval was backed by both Social Democrats and Independents. The Riksdag in turn also approved the compromise thus formulated, whereupon some Liberals also gave their support to the committee decision. The Conservatives, on the other hand, contested the new organization with an ardour that was reminiscent of the defense controversy of 1914.

It was estimated that the new defense organization would cost about 107 million crowns annually during the first decade. There would be additional conversion costs and other extra expenses that could not be directly ascribed to the organization itself. Substantial retrenchments were made, especially in regard to the army: seventeen army units were eliminated, including seven infantry and four cavalry regiments. The regular term of military service was fixed at 140 days for the infantry and 200 days for most other branches of the army.

By and large the same arguments that had been offered at the 1924 Riksdag were again brought up by Social Democrats in the debates of 1925. The significance of the fact that the new defense system was based on a popular consensus and was thus legitimate from a democratic point of view was heavily emphasized. As Sandler said, "When the defense establishment in a democratic society is so organized that it becomes society's servant in deed and spirit, the concept of defense also wins an ever greater place in the heart of democracy." "It [the defense establishment] feels in an entirely different way than before that it bears the responsibility for the fate and safety of the entire nation. . . ." Engberg expressed similar views: "Our desire to live as a free and independent nation is, I believe, deeper and more firmly rooted now than it has perhaps been for a long time. . . . We in the Social Democratic party no longer discuss defense or no defense, as we used to do. . . . With the political installation of the working class in the democratic society [has come] a vital feeling that we all stand jointly responsible for the fate of the nation in the present as well as in the future."

Once again, the idea of unilateral disarmament remained in obscurity and was not broached by any of the party's leading speakers. However, this idea was possibly more noticeable in the debates of 1925 than it had been one year earlier, as the comments of Lindberg, Hallén, and Luterkort, among others, reveal. Hallén represented himself as the interpreter of a pacifiist line of a Christian ideological coloration. According to this line, a noble policy constituted the best protection against enemies. "Besides our kindred peoples of the North, is there any country in the world that has been more conscientiously upright in its international policy, that can hold up a cleaner, more immaculate shield than ours? . . . The world will not do violence to such a culture, that would be a suicidal insult to rational living." Other speakers, such as Lindberg and Västberg, accented in particular the slim risk of war and the devastating effects that would result from a war with modern techniques of warfare.

Two distinct lines can be discerned in the treatment given the defense question by the Social Democratic press in the spring of 1925, especially in the newspapers' comments on the decision reached. Most party organs wholly supported the line pursued by the cabinet and the Riksdag majority. Armament limitation was described as a victory for democracy and for peace efforts, but the press also stressed that the great effectiveness of the nation's defense was due to its firm popular anchorage. "The greatest significance of the Riksdag decision can be ascribed to the circumstance that the workers of our land have for the first time committed themselves to a positive line on defense," wrote Vougt in *Arbetet*. "We should be able to assume that even parties that had previously boasted of their sympathies for defense realized this and saw therein a stronger guarantee for the country's independence than [that represented by] a number of regiments and naval units imposed upon the country. The anchoring of the reform in the will of the people signifies a breakthrough in our history." Engberg, writing in *Social-Demokraten,* alleged that the decision had brought about a reconciliation of democracy and defense and had thus laid a stable foundation for a durable defense system. The settlement reached on defense was also a settlement between the old narrow-minded patriotism of the right and the new patriotism of the workers that envisioned an international system of justice. Some party newspapers, however, regarded the new defense organization essentially as an initial but all too small step toward disarmament. They asserted that preparations for further arms reduction and eventually for total disarmament must be actively prosecuted. This faction of the party either denied or ignored the value of the new defense organization from the point of view of defense per se.

Following the arms reduction of 1925, the defense issue gradually again assumed the proportions of the main point of contention within the Social Democratic party. Disarmament sympathizers—that is, the faction that actively espoused unilateral Swedish disarmament and that had been represented only sporadically in previous debates—were now gaining such strength that they were expected to constitute a majority in the party by about 1930. The case decisive for this movement was presented in the Riksdag and at the party congresses between 1928 and 1932; it will be treated in the proper context. The general reasons for modifications of opinions and sentiments within the party are more difficult to establish. One was obviously the course of international events. Some had provisionally accepted the positive line on defense in the anticipation that the League of Nations would set up a stable judicial system that would assume protection of the League's member nations and concomitantly effect disarmament within these nations—possibly with the exception of the forces they would contribute to the League's own military organization. When these expectations were not met, the idea of unilateral disarmament again waxed important to those who did not anticipate a war in which Sweden might be involved or did not believe in the nation's capacity to defend herself in the event of such a war. The shift in opinion was also connected with improvements made in the international situation within a short period of time—apart from the relative failure of the League. Russia did not seem disposed toward an aggressive foreign policy. In Germany the nationalistic juntas were in retreat and the nation was flourishing under the consolidation of democracy. Economic settlements had ameliorated relations between former enemies, as had the Locarno Agreement of 1927 and the arrangements reached regarding the evacuation of the occupied German provinces. Armaments had been curtailed in both England and France. Italy, the only major European power with a predominant nationalistic junta, was prevented by domestic shortcomings and lack of alliances from converting her intentions into action other than isolated incidents that bore no threat to world peace (for example, the Corfu Affair). Repeated attempts to arrive at agreements on universal disarmament or on a limitation of armaments had proved fruitless. Moreover, because of Sweden's remote geographical position and the general sense of security that this imparted, Swedes could keep alive their optimism regarding the world situation longer than could the peoples in states closer to the world's political center. And by the late 1920s, the brief calm had already begun to give way to anxiety and tension.

Although the international situation gave cause for hope, developments in technological warfare and especially in offensive weaponry were thought to make it difficult or impossible for a small nation to defend herself. Prodisarmament sentiments among Social Democrats were stimulated by descriptions of the probable shape of a future war as outlined by military writers. The articles and books of a Major K. A. Bratt, in particular, had a marked effect on public opinion, as the debates of the time indicate. Aerial and gas warfare were thought to favor the aggressor and it was expected that their utilization would decide the outcome of an action. As in the early 1900s, statements that were intended to delineate problems associated with Sweden's defense were cited by some as reasons for disarmament and by others as reasons for augmenting defense.

Other circumstances that were linked to Sweden's domestic politics also helped promote the disarmament movement during this period. A number of political figures, some of which had allied themselves with the Left Socialists following the party split of 1917 but most of which had joined the Communist party, now reentered the Social Democratic party in stages. The former defense nihilists had modified their views, but as a rule they still represented extreme positions, especially on defense. Within a short time they had won influential posts in the party organization. This group constituted the nucleus of the disarmament movement and included, among others, Z. Höglund,

E. Lindberg, Vennerström, and F. Ström. The group also won support from prominent members who had remained within the party at the time of the rupture but now evinced a tendency toward radical opposition to the official leadership; foremost among these was Engberg, who had been editor of the chief party organ since 1924. We should also remember that P. A. Hansson, who succeeded Branting as party leader after the latter's death in 1931, required many years to attain a degree of authority comparable to that which Branting enjoyed during his last years. This hiatus in authoritative leadership was particularly meaningful in regard to the intramural disputes on defense. And finally, the party became generally more radical during the relatively long period 1926–1932 when it had no responsibility for the government. Its role as the opposition party afforded propaganda for radical and long-range demands a freer rein of expression.

There is no reason to closely examine the debate carried on by the press during the interval between the enactment of the new military organization of 1925 and the party congress of 1928. The arguments advanced by the press were rephrased in more specific, well-chosen terms in subsequent Riksdag and congressional discussions. A few remarks are, however, noteworthy. With only a few exceptions, Social Democratic organs in the northernmost province of Norrland were prodisarmament. The most ardent champions of disarmament in this group of papers were *The New Society* (*Nya samhället*), edited by M. Västberg, and *The Paper of the People of Västerbotten* (*Västerbottens folkblad*), edited by Lindberg. Once disarmament had been achieved, only a kind of sentinel to guard neutrality would be retained to determine when violations of neutrality had taken place. For a while, Engberg and others adopted a somewhat mediatory position; they could not accept the idea of total disarmament, but recommended a "defense of neutrality"—in contrast to what was termed "defense of independence." The former was interpreted as a defensive force designed to determine and prosecute breaches of neutrality. They assumed that there was no danger of a real attack on Sweden and that, in any event, such an attack could not be repulsed. P. A. Hansson and others asserted that defense increased the risks to national security and that it would be unreasonable for the party to scratch a defense organization that the party had recently helped establish. The classification of defense into defenses of neutrality and independence was contested on the ground that it would be illogical to conceive of a defense of neutrality that would not, if the act of aggression exceeded a certain limit, turn into a defense of national independence.

The party's internal discord assumed tangible form in the discussion of fleet replacements at the 1927 Riksdag. This question had not been resolved by the adoption of the new military organization but had been referred for further study to a committee in the autumn of 1925. The committee's report was delivered in December 1926; it recommended the building of new warships, including an aircraft carrier. P. A. Hansson and Eriksson (from Grängesberg), the two Social Democratic committee members, backed this recommendation, but many party newspapers attacked the proposal. On January 27, 1927, the workers' commune of Stockholm voted to enter a protest to the recommendation, an example subsequently followed by a number of other workers' and trade unions. The bill introduced by the Ekman cabinet followed the proposal, and was approved by the Committee of Supply against the objection of all Social Democratic members to the building of the aircraft carrier. Numerous Social Democrats supported this objection in the Riksdag and at times referred to arguments for disarmament in general as a basis for their dissent. By and large most party members evidently followed this line; only Sandler and Nothin, together with the members of the naval committee, Hansson and Eriksson, spoke in behalf of the larger appropriation.

A number of motions related to defense were brought up at the party congress of 1928; most of these called for program amendments along more radical lines or for program declarations sponsoring a more rigorous disarmament policy. The program commission rejected these motions. The program amendments in question—the inclusion of the words "complete and immediate national disarmament" or a similar phrase in Article XVII—were rejected on the ground that they conflicted with the principle accepted in 1920, which stated that the party program was to indicate objectives, not tactics. The commission gave most careful consideration to motions that party representatives in the Riksdag or cabinet be instructed to introduce bills for immediate arms reduction or for the replacement of the military organization with a neutrality guard to police the nation's boundaries and determine any violations of neutrality. This suggestion was contested on the ground that it implied a reversal of the policy that the party had been following, which required that the nation's military resources be maintained at a strength sufficient to repulse, not only "determine" violations of neutrality. "This policy best conforms with the whole view of Social Democracy toward the right of nations to independence and the duty to assert this [right]. It has also successfully served Social Democratic endeavors in behalf of a reduction in military armaments." Of course, all Social Democrats would, if possible, like to advance further on the road to disarmament, but the congress could not justly establish more specific directives on this point. One commission member, Engberg, was of the opinion that a new, drastic reduction in defense would be natural if one directed one's thinking to the neutrality problems that were presumably capable of solution. An official statement should therefore be issued supporting the prosecution of armament reduction. The defense organization of 1925 should not be regarded "as anything but the first result, moreover arrived at by compromise, of an endeavor the prosecution of which must not be deferred to a future date." The party administration agreed with the program commission; in addition, the administration presented a proposal for a statement that was obviously intended as a compromise formula. The objective was designated to be total disarmament. It was not necessary to determine the conditions for such disarmament. Many party members believed it would be feasible only after the establishment of an international police force; others advocated "immediate disarmament as well as a reduction of military establishments to [the status of] a neutrality watch without real defense duties." These words implied that even partisans of unilateral disarmament could be considered to operate in conformity with the party program. The party administration added that under certain circumstances a choice between these two standpoints might be inevitable, but that such was not the case at present because one was agreed on the practical objectives that could be won within the immediate future. "During the next few years the Social Democratic party can, without differences of opinion, direct its efforts to win a preponderant majority of the people to its point of view that the military burdens can be further and substantially reduced. But the questions of the right time for such a new step and the shape it should take are not sufficiently ripe to be decided at this moment. The Congress does not consider that it ought to give more specific directives in this regard. It is up to the party administration and the Riksdag group together to see to it that no opportunities for a reduction of military burdens go unnoticed and that the policy the party has hitherto followed in this sphere is pursued without hesitation."

P. A. Hansson introduced the extensive attendant debate in his capacity as spokesman for the party administration. In the main he enlarged upon the reasons given by the administration and program commission for rejecting the motions. The main risk for Sweden was that her neutrality might be violated through conflicts between other states, and it was up to the nation to be able to deal with such a violation. The navy was of particular importance from this viewpoint. Hansson did not recommend giving special attention to building up Sweden's air defense since he thought a direct attack on Sweden was improbable. In general, considerations of party tactics played an important part in Hansson's exposition. Popular opinion was not ripe for disarmament, and the party should probe the disarmament question more "from the viewpoint of what can be achieved than from the viewpoint of how far one should go in the event one had the possibility of carrying out one's wishes." Strategy that concentrated exclusively on demonstrations was prohibitive because of the party's position. A takeover of executive power would necessitate consideration of "how far the majority of the people had progressed in regard to their readiness for armament reduction." The introduction of overly radical proposals in the Riksdag would entail the risk that the groups with which collaboration was desirable might instead "compromise in the other direction," with the Right. It would be unwise for propaganda to assert that Sweden could not defend herself; this would make it difficult or impossible to arouse a sentiment for mobilization. It would be wiser to stress that no real threats to the nation's independence appeared to exist. Hansson's entire exposition seems to have been aimed at winning over the radical representatives by demonstrating that a comparatively positive standpoint not only was tactically advisable under existing conditions but also was the only standpoint that provided a possibility for further arms reduction. Some of his remarks can be interpreted as an acknowledgement of the fundamental factual validity of the demand for disarmament per se. The comments of other speakers also contain intimations to this effect. A. Törnkvist, for example, declared "our entire military policy is a question of how much we can tighten up and how much we can cut down. If we did not take this tack we would not exercise the slightest influence . . . on the number of crowns that shall be subtracted from the resources of the Swedish people and fixed on military objectives." A number of speakers (for example, Wigforss and Sandler) also asserted that although defense could be further reduced because of the unimportance of any existing threats to the nation, it nevertheless was of real value.

The clearest explanation of the reasons for the negative line was given by E. Lindberg. Said he, the Social Democratic party had, on principle, actually the same standpoint as the nonsocialist parties. The only difference lay in the parties' interpretations of the military and political situation, which led them to favor different measures of defense arrangements. Lindberg announced that he represented yet another basic standpoint. "We say it is not true that the existence of a military defense . . . yields less security than the absence of such [a defense]. But we also say that quite apart from any effect it might have on a feeling of security, a military defense could not fulfill its defensive function if our country were attacked." Lindberg thus arrived at a practical defense nihilism by following in part the same line of reasoning that had been propounded twenty years earlier within the youth federation. As the youth federation had tried to substantiate its arguments by referring to military science, so did Lindberg. In particular, he contended that developments in aerial science made defense impossible: there was no way of preventing devastating aerial attacks. Tactical considerations should not keep the party from propagating the ideal of disarmament. When two defense proposals came to a vote in the Riksdag one should, of course, vote for the least comprehensive of them. "But the party's acceptance of the disarmament line entails the declaration that we, when we attain power, will carry out disarmament. At present the standpoint is such that even if we had power we would not carry out disarmament." The speakers who generally followed the same line as Lindberg asserted with him that defense opportunities had been greatly reduced through developments in military technology, and even suggested that a considerable increase in armaments would be necessary to achieve a really effective defense. (Cf., for example, Höjer, Hallén, Wagnsson.) Disarmament or further arms reduction was justified by citing the need for applying state funds to social purposes. Västberg, among others, held that propaganda that was unmistakably prodisarmament would solidify the party's position with the electorate and influence the Liberal party in a radical direction. It was also maintained (Lindhagen) that if the party could not form a cabinet on the basis of a prodisarmament platform it ought to defer forming a cabinet until it could realize its true objectives. Apparently none of the speakers propounded a view fundamentally nihilistic toward defense.

At length, however, the divergent lines met in agreement. Motions for program amendments were rejected without a vote. By a vote of 158 to 128, the editorial committee was given the assignment of working out a proposal for a statement to be issued by the party. The minority, which, as a rule, evidently included those speakers who were more ardent defense sympathizers, voted for an immediate ruling on the question—which in practice would have meant acceptance of the resolution proposal of the party administration. The editorial committee prepared a resolution of basically the same import as that of the party administration, but which contained the following additional statement (inserted between the last two statements in the administration resolution proposal, as previously quoted): "The Congress finds, however, that the development in modern military technology in the shadow of aerial and gas warfare creates new problems with dreadful prospects that the whole world must be made aware of and which ought to give rise to prompt reexamination of the practicality of our entire military establishment." This addition satisfied the negative line, and the proposal was unanimously passed. According to the opinion of the editorial committee, as interpreted by Engberg, the additional sentence meant undertaking "an examination of military institutions in the light of the new terrible technology as well as an examination of the question as to whether military defense is of any use at all."

The congress of 1928 manifested a highly negative attitude to defense. It may be, however, that the statements made at this congress did not accurately reflect the party position. Those more favorably disposed toward defense, such as Branting and members of the party administration at the congresses of 1905, 1908, and 1911, ardently affirmed their basic desire for disarmament in order to achieve party unity. In their criticism of the idea of immediate disarmament in view of the party's political situation Hansson and others may have been partly motivated by tactical considerations, for arguments of this type were most likely to influence the opposition.

The congress was also to deal with a motion made by Richard Lindström to rescind the resolution regarding the party's position on the voluntary rifle club movement that had been ruled in 1908 and ratified in 1911 and 1914. The motion was justified on the ground that the rifle club movement was valuable to defense and that if supported by the workers it could even constitute a safeguard for democracy against enemies within the nation. Lindström also took up an argument that had been advanced many times in previous socialist debates. Lindström's proposal gave rise to a countermotion recommending that the congress underscore its previous rulings on the question. This move was held to be warranted by the fact that the rifle club movement was "an upper class movement," by the absence of any reason to arm the working class, and by the futility of trying to infiltrate the rifle club movement with socialist ideas. The party administration proposed that Lindström's motion (motion no. 1) be rejected and that the second motion (motion no. 2) not occasion any special action. The administration held that some Social Democrats were, in fact, members of rifle clubs and that no measures had been taken against these clubs; further, that revocation of the directives given to the Riksdag group in this question might therefore be in order. However, revoking these directives might be construed as a sign that the party had modified its fundamental standpoint, although there were no real reasons to make such a change. The rifle club movement was still very much subject to military influences and could be deemed unreceptive to democratic and socialist ideas. "Nor does there seem to be any necessity of urging the workers to become especially interested in instruction in the use of weapons in order to secure a tranquil development of society. Only one member of the party administration differed with this pronouncement, but his disagreement did not cause him to recommend approval of Lindström's motion.

The debates and rulings that took place at this congress evinced an exceedingly strong prejudice against the rifle club movement. Several branded the movement as reactionary and semifascist. Fabian Månsson alleged that its ulterior motive was "in extreme cases to paint the streets with the blood of the workers." Moderates such as P. A. Hansson and Engberg dismissed Lindström's motion on the ground that armament races in the class struggle should be avoided and that armed private clubs generally constituted a hazard to democracy. Lindström defended his proposal principally by pointing out that from the point of view of domestic politics, the rifle clubs could become a weapon of defense against antidemocratic movements. When the time came for the congress to render its verdict, Lindström's proposal was eliminated without a vote. Motion no. 2 ran against the proposal of the party administration, and the former won, 163 to 134. The congress thus further emphasized the party's disapproval of the rifle club movement.

In accordance with the ruling of the party congress, the Social Democratic group at the 1929 Riksdag brought a motion for the preparation of a written request for an investigation into the defense question; this inquiry was also to encompass the possibility of unilateral disarmament. The motion was rejected by the nonsocialist parties. At the 1930 session of the Riksdag, the Social Democrats again brought motions of the same purport; this time they gained the support of a great many Liberals as a part of the general rapprochement between Liberals and Social Democrats. The Riksdag voted to order a comprehensive investigation into the defense issue. According to the directives formulated by the majority in the Ways and Means Committee, the inquiry was "to examine the reasons cited on the one hand for strengthening military defense arrangements, on the other for demobilization of existing defense [arrangements] on the basis of international agreements, and on the third, for unilateral national disarmament." The investigation was said to be required because of the technological developments and changes in military policy that had taken place since the defense act of 1925 as well as by the necessity of examining all the alternatives to a solution of the problem. The investigation was obviously intended first of all to indicate ways to cut down defense expenditures. It was very expressly stated that the expenditures for the defense organization then in force could not be exceeded. The proposed directives were the reason why certain groups in the Riksdag—primarily the Conservatives—that were actually in favor of an investigation per se nevertheless opposed the proposal of the Committee of Supply. In their manifesto issued prior to the county council elections of 1930, the Social Democrats demanded "that the investigation into the military question called for by the Riksdag be carried out with all possible speed, in the course of which [investigation] the issue of Sweden's disarmament shall also be examined, and that in any event an additional, substantial curtailment of military appropriations be effected." The committee appointed by the Ekman cabinet subsequent to these elections included four Social Democrats who could be regarded as representatives of the different factions within the party: P. A. Hansson, Törnkvist, Vennerström, and Lindberg.

In similarity with the discussion at the party congress of 1928, the Riksdag debates of 1929 and 1930 on the defense question indicate that the party encompassed widely divergent opinions. The demand for a new investigation undeniably appeared to be an attempt to conceal the lack of a unified standpoint and postpone the conclusive struggle within the party to some future date. The following review of the main lines of argumentation will consider both the Riksdag debates and the treatment the subject received in the Social Democratic press, particularly in *Tiden*.

Advocates of unilateral disarmament or of drastic arms reduction, such as Lindberg, Engberg, Vennerström, Höglund, Wigforss, and Hallén, proceeded from the general assumption that, as a whole, the risk of war was negligible. In the main they advanced the same views given as justification for the arms reduction of 1925: The League of Nations, German disarmament, Russian repudiation of imperialist aims, the strong position of the peace-loving Western powers, the general postwar relaxation of tensions. They disputed the idea that the dictatorships might constitute a threat to peace by contesting that these states could not risk a war. Speaking in the lower house in 1930, Höglund declared that it was a historical fact "that dictators do not exactly thrive on their aggression toward foreign peoples either. . . . I, for my part, believe that civil war will more surely take place precisely in dictatorial states —as an inevitable consequence of dictatorship—than in democratic countries. Engberg stamped the Communist view that capitalism meant war as obsolete. "More careful reflection makes it plain to me that, in its pursuit of efficiency, capitalism must regard a war—which, of necessity, will be a world war—as a hindrance, an obstacle in its way. . . . It is totally erroneous to believe that capitalism needs war. There have been periods when it has needed it. Now we again face a period when capitalism itself best understands that war is not good business and that it pays to try to surmount the martial anarchy." Any war risk that might exist was attributed mainly to armaments. Swedish armaments were also pertinent in this respect, and Sweden could accordingly help alleviate the anxiety that was prevalent in the world by arms reduction. "Nor can we deny," said Wigforss in the lower house in 1929, "that if we show the courage to reduce armaments ourselves . . . even though we know that a disarmed or less armed state does run risks, then I believe that we will cast our weight on the right side of the scale as far as promoting peace in the world is concerned." On the whole, it was thought that disarmament of small nations might influence the major powers to follow suit.

To this argument about the inconsequentiality of the risk of war and Sweden's ability to further reduce this risk, some proponents of unilateral disarmament (such as Lindberg, writing in *Tiden*) appended direct criticism of the idea of a "solidarity defense," of participation in a kind of concerted military action against any state that violated the peace. As a rule, this idea was not subject to discussion. In all probability it was assumed that as long as no procedure for international military sanctions had been delineated, there was no reason to consider this eventuality in forming Sweden's defense policy. Emphasis was placed on the fact that, in any case, the League of Nations did not enjoin nations to maintain individual defenses.

The risk of war was believed to be particularly inconsequential as far as Sweden was concerned. Direct aggression against Sweden by one or more states was thought virtually inconceivable: there was no reason whatever for a nation to try to expand its territory at Sweden's expense. The sole risk of war for Sweden lay in a war involving several nations, in which case the warring nations might threaten or violate Swedish neutrality or otherwise try to involve Sweden in one of the warring power blocs. Yet even if this possibility were accorded paramount consideration, disarmament would still be needed as it would reduce the war risk in various ways. "The essential thing for the creation of a pacifist climate of public opinion is that war can break out as long as a military establishment exists. Pacifists believe that a country that has the courage to disarm does not run the risk of being attacked," declared Lindberg. In the course of the address just discussed, Höglund propounded that it was conceivable that attempts might be made to involve Sweden in a world war at a future date. But in fact, this demonstrated that armament did not constitute protection of neutrality. "To defend our neutrality in such a situation by the use of military might would be equivalent to the ruination of the country. If, on the other hand, we were to abandon neutrality and perhaps throw ourselves into a war on one side or the other because we otherwise had no chance to protect our neutrality we would, in any case, find ourselves in the same plight."

Further: If, contrary to all expectations, a disarmed Sweden should become the object of attack or of a violation of neutrality, the danger of full-scale war would still be fairly negligible in the long run. Höglund maintained that one could then in all certainty count on assistance from the League of Nations. "The League itself declares in its charter that it aspires to disarmament, and is it not then totally inconceivable that it would surrender an independent nation that takes the League's own statutes seriously to the aggression of a major power when this nation is moving toward a realization of the League's own program? It is all the more inconceivable since the League of Nations itself . . . has laid down the proposition that a state whose existence is threatened should refrain from military action and instead appeal to the League of Nations." From time to time it was also maintained that a violation of neutrality incurred through a war between other states could in any case not go further than the temporary occupation of part of Sweden. Wrote N. Anderson in *Tiden,* "If we did not have any military strength the worst thing that could happen would be the occurrence of fighting on our territory . . . and the temporary seizure of one site or another that would be suitable as a base for waging war."

Finally: To defend Sweden under the circumstances that might be anticipated would be just about futile and would in any case result in the devastation of the country because of the nature of modern warfare. When it came to defending national independence, moral factors were of far greater importance than military factors, especially in regard to small nations. This view, which was basic to disarmament sympathizers, was coupled by some with the assumption that in the event Sweden were attacked, a civil, passive resistance could prove effective. "A people as informed and freedom-loving as the Swedish people," wrote N. Andersson in *Tiden,* "would win and win without bloodshed by means of a well-disciplined, passive resistance." Writing in the same publication, G. Branting urged that Sweden disarm but also declare that she wished "to effect a strong, improvised defense built on spontaneous popular will and on all the resources that are always at our disposal." This article also seemed oriented toward mainly a "passive" defense, even though some comments indicate that the writer wished to combine disarmament and guerilla warfare. At times (e.g., K. Nilsson, writing in *Tiden*) it was hinted that hostile acts toward a disarmed country might be answered by a general strike in the nation under attack as an inducement to the workers in the aggressor nation to institute similar action. (Cf. Flodh's article in the same journal.)

Two views were ardently espoused by disarmament zealots in addition to the general arguments just discussed. They pointed to the community formed by the Scandinavian countries and regarded Danish and Norwegian plans for disarmament as giving Sweden special cause to disarm. Other arguments were reinforced by thus weaving them into a broader context. It was assumed that disarmament of the Scandinavian countries would be of considerable moral significance. "It would be strange," wrote Lindberg, "if the disarmament of Scandinavia, an example provided without external coercion which shows that safety and security are dependent on neither national military organizations nor defense alliances nor international armed force did not help break the hypnotic state in which the people of the major military powers now exist." The disarmament line was also thought to be of political value. Time and again proponents of disarmament contended that this line was calculated to win new votes for the party and cited the elections of 1924 to prove their point. They maintained that certain groups in addition to the working class, particularly those influenced by the sectarian church and temperance movements, stood to gain by a continued policy of arms reduction.

Sandler, Undén, Åkerberg, and Lindström were among the leading Social Democrats who were sceptical or completely negative toward the idea of disarmament. When speaking in Riksdag debates, the party chairman and Möller may have vehemently protested that they had not bound themselves to any definite standpoint, but their statements nonetheless reveal traces of strong doubt about the advisability of disarmament and give the impression that political considerations caused them to overemphasize their doubtfulness. This party faction, which was relatively prodefense, justified the demand for an investigation primarily on the ground that new conditions, such as developments in military technology, called for a renewed examination of the defense question in all its ramifications. Some thought that further limitation of armaments was conceivable, but several comments made in the debate (such as Sandler's remarks) disclose a scepticism toward not only plans for disarmament but toward plans for arms reduction as well.

This camp was not as optimistic about the risk of war as that which comprised partisans of disarmament. The sceptical group pointed out that endeavors toward international arms reduction had failed and that signs of increased political tension had appeared. The dictatorships in Germany and Italy were described as a potential menace to peace. It was not likely that the example of disarmament in Sweden or Scandinavia would be followed by other larger nations, in any case not by those that threatened to form expansionist policies. "I think we are fairly well agreed on the impression that Swedish disarmament might make on Mussolini's Italy or on Stalin's Russia," said Sandler in an upper house debate in 1929. "One might await a response from the democratic world, but if this were given what meaning would it have? It would mean that democracy in Europe stood disarmed and that all of Europe's military strength would be concentrated in the hands of dictators. Someone might say that this could nevertheless be described as a state of peace. Perhaps—war always presupposes two warring parties—but what would be the fate of freedom in Europe under such a 'pax Romana?' Disarmament of the small, noncontentious and peace-loving nations would, in fact, weaken the peace front in Europe and increase the risks of war. For the time being, the desire for peace would have to turn to a certain measure of military might for authority. From an international point of view, unilateral disarmament would therefore be meaningless or even dangerous. Wrote Åkerberg in *Tiden:* "A disarmed Scandinavia might possibly exercise moral pressure in behalf of disarmament within the League of Nations. But the indications are that a Scandinavia that retained a major or minor part of its military armaments but appeared in the League as a never-flagging preacher, indicating its own willingness to take the step to the kingdom of peace side by side with the other states in the world, would be a factor of far greater importance to disarmament."

An armed Sweden could thus be of some value to the preservation of peace and to international disarmament endeavors. This thinking was followed by the conjecture that under certain conditions Sweden might participate in actions against nations that violated the peace, and Sweden's defense could thus be regarded as a joint or "solidarity" defense. International disarmament was acknowledged to be the ultimate objective. Progress toward the attainment of this goal, however, postulated solidarity, possibly even military solidarity, between the nations that were working in the cause of peace. As a rule one assumed that the League of Nations would provide the framework for this united front; organized cooperation between the democracies was sometimes suggested. To leave the contingent responsibility of surveillance to certain major powers would be unwise and, in view of the position of the small nations, could also be dangerous. Speaking in the lower house in 1930, P. A. Hansson said that some might claim that small nations did not have to partake in the maintenance of an international police force. "Yet, that even a country such as Sweden should have obligations to secure peace and that we thus have a certain duty to examine without prejudice how we might best meet these obligations is completely in line with our Social Democratic outlook. I mean that one should also investigate how a small nation such as Sweden can contribute to the maintenance of the international armed force that even the most extreme pacifist considers essential to safeguard the world against violators of the peace." Sandler's comments on the subject in the address mentioned were even more definite. The democratic nations must find a way to reach concord and solidarity. They ought to banish the risks of war between one another and prepare an arms reduction "without making themselves defenseless against dictatorships that are founded on violence and might perchance act as transgressors of peace in the world." Small nations were duty-bound to partake in these efforts. "They should bear their fair share of the endeavors to guarantee a state of peace, they, themselves, should be prepared to stake something for their own freedom and for a good international order. They, themselves, should be prepared to wage war against war with the bold heart of a warrior."

Disarmament was also criticized from the Swedish point of view alone. A defenseless Sweden and, to a greater extent, a defenseless Scandinavia might represent a temptation to states that hungered to expand—even if this development did not seem probable at the moment. Sweden alone obviously had no chance of countering the aggression of a major power. However, the knowledge that such aggression could not be carried out without great losses should act as a deterrent to a potential aggressor. The nations involved in a struggle between major powers would hesitate to encroach upon Sweden's neutrality if they were assured that such encroachment would elicit a forceful reaction. In other words, the very existence of a national defense implied a guarantee of peace, however precarious. Furthermore, a country that defended itself had better prospects of obtaining outside help, possibly with the cooperation of the League of Nations, than a country that relied exclusively on the hope of outside assistance.

The investigation ordered in 1930 did not, as many anticipated, result in suspension of the defense debate within the party until the completion of the investigation. Disarmament sympathizers prepared a new offensive to be launched at the party congress of 1932. The disarmament campaign that Engberg conducted in *Social-Demokraten* aroused particular interest. He used both pacifist contentions and the argument that modern technological warfare rendered effective defense against aggression impossible. A sharp conflict of opinion could be detected between Engberg and the party chairman, who denounced the line favoring unilateral disarmament in a *Ny Tid* article. The economic crisis buttressed prodisarmament propaganda.

Under these circumstances many expected that the party congress of 1932 would lead to a deep party schism and possibly even to a complete rupture. However, it was again possible to avoid taking a definite stand and thereby reach a settlement that could muster a majority without rejecting the minority standpoint.

No less than fifteen motions at the congress concerned defense. Foremost among these were proposals that the Riksdag group be enjoined to work in behalf of unilaterial national disarmament. The party administration, citing the ruling of the 1928 congress and the defense investigation instituted in 1930, recommended the rejection of all these proposals.

> This investigation must obviously seek to clarify all questions related to international as well as national disarmament. This investigation should accordingly yield a clarification of the several lines, their prospects and the final concrete shape they would assume. The party would do well to postpone taking a position until such a clarification had been made. The party will, of course, without interruption continue its work for a reduction of Swedish armaments and for the propagation of the disarmament ideal and give its members complete freedom therewith to emphasize either national or international disarmament, as has hitherto been its wont.

This statement was the result of a compromise between the opponents and some of the proponents of unilateral disarmament. The pronouncement was backed not only by Hansson, Möller, and other members of the party administration who were relatively well disposed toward defense but also by Engberg and Höglund, who had appeared as opponents of the party leader. The congressional debate indicates that the settlement reached within the party administration was probably due, at least in part, to a general desire to avoid a contest for power that could lead to the resignation of the party leader and profound party schism. Only two members of the party administration dissented to the statement: Nils Andersson and Lindberg. The latter presented a proposal as an alternative to that offered by the party administration. Lindberg suggested that the sentences in the administration statement just quoted be replaced by the following:

> The reasons cited for national disarmament as a stage in the endeavors to speed international disarmament have been found to be so substantial by Social Democrats in Norway, Denmark, Holland, and Switzerland that they have accepted the line of national disarmament. These reasons are without doubt equally valid in Sweden. However, a prerequisite for a decision as to which forms and what pace the realization of national disarmament should assume is the clarification of a number of important questions, for example, the obligations entailed by our country as a consequence of its membership in the League of Nations and the Hague Convention, the employment of personnel [now] employed by the military establishment or defense industry if disarmament is realized, and whether or not some kind of police force should succeed the military establishment. The defense investigation now in progress should yield the clarifications that the party considers desirable in these respects.

Lindberg's proposal was thus a proclamation of unilateral disarmament as the party goal.

In accordance with this starting position, three main lines of thought came to the fore in the course of the exceptionally penetrating debate. The most positive line was advanced by those speakers, primarily Hansson and Möller, who declared that they did not have a definite opinion on unilateral disarmament or, in any case, did not give vent to such an opinion. The main theme of their argumentation was that the party ought to wait for the results of the defense investigation before committing itself to a specific standpoint. As far as their recommendation for approval of the administration proposal is concerned, Engberg, Höglund, and others—their declared partisanship to unilateral disarmament notwithstanding—also lent their support to this line. Sponsors of Lindberg's proposal constituted the third line. Most of the debaters said that they favored unilateral disarmament on principle, and hardly a voice was raised in explicit repudiation of this line.

The party leader first called attention to the investigation that was in progress. It would be illogical to first request an investigation, then take a definite stand before the investigation had been completed. "I, myself, place such importance on the investigation in progress that I openly declare that my final standpoint will depend on the results this investigation yields." To try to carry out unilateral disarmament immediately was inconceivable in view of the prevailing climate of popular opinion and the political situation. In his second statement, Hansson declared that he could not remain a member of the investigating body if Lindberg's proposal were accepted; he hinted that in this event he might not even remain in his capacity as the party leader. Although Hansson declared that he could not form a definite opinion before the completion of the investigation, some of his statements suggest that there was little likelihood that he would become convinced of the advisability of unilateral disarmament. Said he, the Social Democrats had based their work on the defense issue on the view "that what we need is not a defense of the nation's independence but resources to enable us to prevent our involvement in hostilities in the course of a war between other states. Why not adhere to this argumentation? Why permit oneself to be pushed toward argumentations that clash with the understanding of the value of freedom that is held by our entire people?" He also stressed that Sweden would be duty-bound to contribute to an international police force if one could be established. Möller brought up the possibility that National Socialism might become the ruling party in Germany and that all of western and southern Europe might fall under Bolshevik or Fascist dominion. The division of Europe into disarmed democracies and armed dictatorships would be a dangerous state of affairs; all cultural values would thereby be left at the mercy of barbarians. It was said that unilateral disarmament in Sweden would surely give rise to voluntary defense organizations recruited from the upper class and the farmers—but these could lead to dangers for democracy in the nation. Several speakers (for example, Vought) also maintained that the party must not give defense priority to other questions that were equally important, and that the demand for unilateral disarmament would disqualify Social Democracy from being the executive party.

The speakers who favored unilateral disarmament but nevertheless supported the administration proposal were evidently influenced by political and personal considerations. Engberg said that he did not wish to assert his fundamental view without regard to the other opinions in the party. "My view is clear, as is true of many others, but there are many who entertain vague ideas, and I have therefore asked myself whether the party ought to give a definite answer to the question that has been posed before we have reached greater clarity." He insisted that it was perfectly evident that the statement proposed by the party administration could encompass propaganda for unilateral disarmament. Höglund admitted even more openly that his support of the administration was influenced by other than purely factual considerations. "If it were not for the fact that a great many considerations other than those which applied to the matter concerned were involved, this congress would surely produce an overwhelming majority in favor of including the demand for Swedish disarmament in the party program and perhaps in its current policy as well. . . . In the hope that the next time there will be a forceful, resolute, and overwhelming majority for the inclusion of unilateral disarmament in the party's current program of action, I nevertheless beg, as the matter stands at present, to recommend approval of the proposal of the party administration."

The most painstaking justification for unilateral disarmament was again given by E. Lindberg. Said Lindberg, history showed that a military establishment did not provide a secure defense. The states that had been most highly mobilized had also had the greatest number of wars; wars therefore depended on armament, not vice versa. Sweden was not threatened by attack. "The new Russian menace, the so-called military Soviet imperialism, is a myth. . . . The Soviet Union . . . does not exist in order to bring about revolution in other countries; it is up to the workers of each country to carry out the revolution in their own countries according to Communist theory and tactics." The development of military technology had radically altered the military-political situation. Defensive weapons had not reached the same degree of efficiency as offensive weapons. The multitude of the people were, under all circumstances, unprotected against aerial attacks and gas warfare. An attempt at defense against a state that commanded greater resources would be futile; defense against a state with fewer means at its disposal might be successful but would entail unprecedented suffering for Sweden. Lindberg even took exception to the thought of Swedish contributions to an international police force. "I permit myself to hold to the belief that when a real decision on military sanctions must one day be made Sweden's workers and farmers will decline the invitation to send their sons as mercenaries to foreign soils." Lindberg believed that the existing defense organization ought to be replaced by a surveillant body both to prevent the emergence of domestic armed brigades that might imply a threat to democracy and to guard the nation's coasts and boundaries. Such a sentinel should not cost more than 25 million crowns, which would mean a budgetary saving of 100 million.

Proponents of Lindberg's proposal thought it quite natural that the party avow its standpoint before the completion of the defense investigation. One could take it for granted that the defense committee, whose membership was principally nonsocialist, would reject unilateral disarmament. Nor could one expect that the committee would produce any fresh arguments that could sway the Social Democrats in arriving at a stand. One also maintained that, in fact, a majority at the congress were for unilateral disarmament, and therewith sharply criticized delegates who were included in this category but nevertheless gave their support to the administration proposal. "The situation is very strange," said Ström. "If the party chairman should now win, it will be with the aid of two crutches. One crutch is called Arthur Engberg, the other Z. Höglund. . . . These two are both adherents on principle of unilateral disarmament, yet their overwhelming sense of loyalty causes the proposal for unilateral disarmament at this congress to be in the minority."

The final vote produced a victory for the administration proposal with 243 assenting and 165 dissenting votes. As this vote was taken by a roll call, we can examine the composition of the contending factions. A preponderance of the leading group in the party naturally belonged to the majority. With the exception of the dissentients, the party administration backed the party chairman; all of those voting who would become members of the Social Democratic cabinet one-half year later followed this line. A regional analysis discloses that most delegates from the northernmost province of Norrland voted with the minority. Southern Sweden on the other hand, and particularly the province of Skåne, largely voted with the majority. The workers' communes of Stockholm and Gothenburg had previously declared themselves in favor of unilateral disarmament; 22 of the delegates from Stockholm voted with the majority and 30 with the minority; of the delegates from radical Gothenburg, only 7 voted with the majority and 37 with the minority. The corresponding figures for the city of Malmö in Skåne province were 15 and 5. During the debate it had been suggested that women were particularly ardent supporters of unilateral disarmament, a supposition that proved true, as only 3 of the 11 female delegates voted for the administration proposal. The recognized fact that the new youth federation, unlike its predecessor twenty years before, did not oppose the party leadership was again confirmed when the vote was taken: a considerable number of the federation leaders aligned themselves with the majority.

Despite the victory of the administration's compromise proposal, the 1932 congress can be regarded as the culmination of the Social Democrats' negativism concerning defense policy during this period, or perhaps even during the party's operative period as a whole. To be sure, not a voice was now raised in behalf of defense nihilism, which had been of such importance prior to World War I. All acclaimed the value of national self-determination; no one suggested that defense of this principle was per se meaningless. Yet a positive line on defense was also absent. Speakers who favored the administration proposal on principle adopted a policy of watchful waiting pending completion of the defense investigation; they did not pledge their contribution to the maintenance of defense under all circumstances. They expressed their doubts, and some even intimated that they sympathized with the straight disarmament line. There is every reason to suppose that a majority at the congress were biased in favor of this line and that it was only tactical considerations as tendered by Engberg and Höglund that provided what might be called a technical victory for the party administration and party chairman's desire for postponement of a final decision on the matter. The rank and file of the membership was apparently of the opinion that defense in the proper sense of the term was valueless. The reasons given to substantiate this opinion varied: the negligible risk of war, the futility of trying to build an effective defense in view of new developments in military technology, the unprecedented devastation that would, under all circumstances, follow in the wake of war. The arguments might be summarized in one sentence: attack is improbable, but if it comes it will be more destructive and more difficult to resist than ever before.

Yet, as was true of the debate on the same subject in 1928, the congressional debate of 1932 very likely leaves an exaggerated impression of the party's negativism. We can assume that the spokesmen for Hansson's line overemphasized their dubiousness and wait-and-see attitude in order to win over the middle group that was willing to leave the question open but accepted unilateral disarmament on principle. One had to ensure party unity for yet another congressional term; now, as so often before, it was primarily the party leaders who were inclined to compromise and who expressed themselves with considerable delicacy in order to attain compromises. But even if we presuppose that the party chairman and the speakers who directly aligned themselves with him represented a more positive disposition toward defense than their statements indicate, the fact remains that 40 percent of the congressional delegates were prepared to demand unilateral disarmament on the spot; in all likelihood a majority at the congress identified in principle with this line.

After the adjournment of the 1932 congress, the newspapers that championed the adoption of unilateral disarmament in the party program of action predicted certain victory for this line at the next congress. They even alleged "that the party's old basic disarmament stand has been accentuated to the extent that a delay in collective international disarmament will result in the acceleration of Swedish unilateral disarmament as a step toward international [disarmament]."

In reality, events took an opposite turn. The essential requisites for disarmament propaganda were nullified by a rapid succession of developments. It will suffice to recall the power seizure of National Socialists in Germany, Japan's prosecution of expansionist policy in China without effective intervention by the League of Nations, and Italy's overt preparations for aggression against Ethiopia. Between the years 1932 and 1935, the majority of people in Sweden, as elsewhere in the world, lost hope in the League of Nations as an important factor for peace. The rise of nationalistic movements persuaded even those groups of a fundamentally international orientation to work "provisionally" in behalf of stronger defense to preserve national unity. The Swedish Social Democratic press quickly reacted to the triumph of National Socialism in Germany by stressing the necessity of stepping up military preparedness for the defense of Sweden, her democratic institutions and social organization.

The defense commission's report, which was delivered in November 1935, was prepared under the influence of changes in world politics. With one exception, the members of the commission were agreed on the necessity of strengthening or at least maintaining the nation's defense. Representatives of the Right proposed an annual defense appropriation in excess of 160 million crowns; the majority, consisting of the Liberal party (now called *Folkpartiet,* "The People's party") and the Farmers' party (*Bondeförbundet,* later known as *Centerpartiet* or "The Center party"), proposed an annual appropriation of approximately 148 million crowns. (Both figures represent average expenditures over a period of years.) Three of the Social Democrats seated on the commission, Törnkvist, Åkerberg, and Vought (the last two replaced Hansson and Vennerström) proposed a defense budget of approximately 114 million crowns. Lindberg offered two alternatives: one called for arms reduction which would cut the defense budget to 98 million crowns, the other for disarmament, that is, for a body to supersede the defense organization that would superintend order and the observance of neutrality, at an annual cost of 25 million crowns.

The protest entered against the commission proposal and signed by Vought and Åkerberg dwelt on the state of foreign affairs and on the thought of Swedish unilateral disarmament. On the one hand it stressed that the international situation had materially deteriorated in various respects; on the other, it directed a certain amount of criticism at the deeply pessimistic outlook expressed in the commission by the representatives of other parties. Unilateral disarmament was out of the question from a strictly national as well as international point of view. Democratic states had to work together for peace and democracy. "It would be to the advantage of neither democracy nor disarmament if the states that are the principal representatives of these ideals were to render themselves defenseless while the powers hostile to the same [ideals] armed to the teeth." A defenseless Scandinavia could easily lose political independence. "In a world in which rapacity stands on watch and in which weapons are regarded a decisive factor, weakness can easily become a temptation to violence." "The idea that was partly behind the Swedish arms reduction of 1925, namely, that by setting a courageous and good example Sweden would be able to give the cause of arms reduction a push forward, has unfortunately proved untenable." It would be superfluous to enter into the old discussion as to whether Sweden was able to defend herself. "The only answer that needs to be given to such a question is that Sweden will defend herself if attacked and that she should not lack the means for her defense if there is a risk that she will be attacked." Lindberg's objection repeated the arguments previously advanced at various times by proponents of unilateral disarmament.

By and large the Social Democratic press went along with the shift in party policy that the dissenting voices denoted. The party's goals were disarmament and an international peace organization, but these goals would have to be deferred to the future. "The present world situation, which is marked primarily by the threat the large Fascist powers pose to peace and freedom" have, wrote Pauli in *Social-Demokraten,* "forced adherents of these ideas into a situation that does not permit of the combination of further advances along the road of arms reduction with clear-sighted aspirations for better and more sensible conditions." Even some newspapers that had once been prodisarmament now endorsed this line and declared that the first order of business was the defense of democracy. However, there were those who held fast to their old standpoints and referred to the report delivered by the defense commission as "the triumph of the general's staff."

Even before the commission had submitted its report the prime minister (who was also party chairman) stated that a concerted solution to the defense question was desirable. Implicit in this statement was the intimation that the cabinet was prepared to sponsor the instructions given by the party's representatives on the commission. Events that took place in the interim between the formulation and publication of the commission's report—above all, Italy's attack on Ethiopia and the consequent deterioration of the general international picture—reinforced the arguments for an increase in armaments; this development was given full play in the Social Democratic press. A meeting of the party administration in October was virtually unanimously agreed that the cabinet ought to introduce a defense bill at the 1936 Riksdag; it was assumed that in so doing the government would seek a compromise with the parties that occupied a middle-of-the-road position. The cabinet bill that was subsequently introduced also signified an appreciable enlargement upon the proposal made by the Social Democratic dissentients: the defense budget was estimated to total approximately 130 million crowns. Of particular interest is the cabinet's affiliation with the Conservative dissentients on the defense commission in regard to fleet appropriations. The bill underscored the value of having defense receive the confidence of all strata of the population. This aim would necessarily entail a cautious approach to mobilization. "If increased defense expenditures should necessitate neglecting social and cultural aims, and should a manifest competition arise between defense and other needs, sentiments that would jeopardize the durability of a legislated defense system might easily arise." Negotiations with representatives of the Farmers' party and the Liberal party were instituted but unity proved impossible to achieve. Social Democrats discussed among themselves how the cabinet could contribute to a material increase of the appropriations proposed in the defense bill. The condition for this was that the moderate parties gave evidence of their intention to pursue a policy of social reform by accepting a cabinet bill for an increase in old age pensions—the content of which was principally the same as that in a proposal that had been rejected by the nonsocialist parties the previous year.

The 1936 congress convened after the cabinet bill had been introduced, but not before the defense committee had completed its assignment. The congress did not take up the defense question as a subject for separate treatment. The only motion introduced was of a more general tenor: it would have the congress declare itself for "unilateral Swedish disarmament" and have the Riksdag representatives refrain from voting for appropriations for military purposes that were in excess of the limit proposed by Lindberg, that is, 98 million crowns. The party administration disapproved the motion, declaring that the party program and party congress had "placed the disarmament question in an international context" and that there was no reason to abandon this standpoint. This mode of expression was strange in view of the fact that previous party congresses had not repudiated the idea of unilateral disarmament but had, to the contrary, embraced this idea as equivalent to the demand for disarmament solely in an international context. It was thus unreasonable to reject the motion on the ground that it conflicted with the pronouncements of earlier congresses. The party administration also maintained that in resolving the defense question the party should try to achieve "an accommodation that will not lessen the opportunities for continued improvement of conditions within the nation." Other points of view would also have to be taken into consideration in settling the matter, and it would therefore be impossible to set a ceiling on military expenditures. This argumentation made it clear that the defense question had to be viewed in the light of the prevailing political situation in a very special way. It was also decided that the motion would be discussed in a general debate which, according to the minutes of congress, would concern "the political situation and the defense question."

The parliamentary situation proved to be paramount at this debate. Should the cabinet try to remain in power by seeking a compromise with the moderate parties on the defense issue? Or should it maintain a firm stand on its bill (on the whole) and resign if the bill were defeated? Or should it in some way couple defense and social policy and make its position on the first dependent on the demonstrated good will of nonsocialist parties toward social reform, first of all, on their readiness to accept the proposed increase in old age pensions? By and large those who wanted to see the cabinet remain in power were willing to further raise the party's bid on defense expenditures in order to gain a majority through the assistance of the party.

Only those aspects of the debate that were directly concerned with defense are of interest in this context. The sweeping change in the party's position that had taken place since the congress of 1932 was a salient feature. Not one speaker considered the possibility of introducing unilateral disarmament as a vital issue. The only question was the extent to which practical and tactical considerations dictated that the party cooperate for an increase in military expenditures. The prime minister declared that the achievement of a more efficient defense system had become the party's basic standpoint, and thereafter dealt with considerations that were primarily of a political nature. He emphasized that a powerful sentiment in favor of strengthening defense, a "defense wind," had emerged both within the party and among the people as a whole. He apparently thought it advisable for the Social Democrats to grant sizeable concessions to the demands of the moderate parties in order that a solution to the problem might be reached under Social Democratic leadership: this would enhance the prestige of both the cabinet and the party. Sköld, the minister of agriculture, took a stand that was somewhat opposed to this declaration and made a proposal—which he later retracted—that the cabinet resign if the Riksdag did not evince "tangible compliance" with the cabinet bill in its solution of the defense question. Wigforss, the minister of finance, underlined the difficulties presented by a substantial augmentation of defense in conjunction with a material increase in social expenditures. Several speakers—Möller, Höglund, Lindström, Akerberg, Sandler—enlarged upon the general reasons that had led the party to a definitively positive stand on the issue. The democracies could not stand unprotected when dictatorships mobilized. A strong defense would deter the large powers from violating Sweden's neutrality even though it might not make the country secure under all conditions. Disarmament would have to be considered anew in less troubled times. Höglund asserted:

> We must remember that everywhere in Europe where a military vacuum exists it is immediately filled by Nazi troops. If not [by] German Nazi troops, then [by] private troops with a nazi spirit from within the country itself. . . . If a Social Democratic party, under the enormous pressure of world events or even because of domestic political conditions, must momentarily redirect itself along the course of retreat on the military question, it has not thereby forsaken its fundamental standpoint. We are most certainly all agreed that as soon as the external situation permits, the antimilitary fight and the fight for arms reduction will be taken up again with all possible force.

Lindberg, Nils Larsson, and L. Svedberg, among other delegates, nonetheless declared their support of the principle of unilateral disarmament. In Lindberg's opinion the sentiments in the party that favored a strong defense system had been reinforced primarily because the party leadership and the chief party newspapers had not vigorously countered the prodefense propaganda of the nonsocialist parties. In the main he repeated his earlier arguments. The war threat had apparently not become aggravated. "The situation is thus not so dangerous. . . . Why is it not so dangerous? Because the major European powers know that they may have means of aggression but that they are unable to defend themselves. They cannot protect their civilian populations, and therefore do not dare to risk a war." However, neither Lindberg nor anyone else requested that the Riksdag group strive for unilateral disarmament in the current situation.

At the close of the debate the party chairman proposed a resolution that contained the following statement on the defense question:

> Swedish Social Democracy partakes with unflagging interest in efforts to [bring about] a secure international system of justice and universal armament reduction. It considers that it has a self-evident duty to try to prevent our country from involvement in the whirlpool of the armament race. The fact that in the present situation and in order to provide for a concerted solution to the defense question the Government has introduced a proposal for the reinforcement of military preparations meets with the full approval of the Congress. The Congress wishes, however, to emphasize

that a condition for the party's cooperation in a concerted solution is tangible compliance on the part of other parties toward our party. There must be guarantees that expenditures for external defense will not be to the detriment of the maintenance and development of internal defense. The Financing of the increased public expenditures should be so arranged that the larger share falls upon the incomes with the greatest supporting capacity.

This proposal passed "by an overwhelming majority." A proposal for amendment introduced by Lindberg was defeated. According to Lindberg's proposal, the reference to approval of the government proposal would have been deleted and the reference to future endeavors in behalf of disarmament would have been worded in a more definite fashion. The statement of the party administration regarding the motion before the delegates was approved.

A motion brought by G. Branting called for democratization of the military "as the party's requisite for acceptance of a new defense organization." Officers and enlisted men should in principle have the same rights of association, assembly, and speech as other citizens; measures should be introduced to democratize recruitment of officers and permanent personnel; noncommissioned officers should have better opportunities to advance to the rank of officers. The congress referred the motion to the Riksdag group and government "with the approval of the demand of the motion for the democratization of the armed forces."

After this congress the cabinet could be said to enjoy the broad sanction of the party in its attempts to reach a settlement. It entered into new negotiations with the leaderships of the nonsocialist parties and at once began discussions on defense, old age pensions, and the financing of the new expenditures. However, these negotiations did not yield a positive result. The special committee that treated the defense question made the line followed by the moderate parties the basis of its work; the solution submitted was closely related to this line. The government declared its readiness to accept this solution if its proposal on old age pensions were approved: this would demonstrate that the nonsocialist parties in the Riksdag did not wish to ignore social welfare. Nonsocialists, on the other hand, thought that these questions should be solved separately and were agreed that no concessions should be made on old age pensions. The majority of Social Democrats seated on the special committee then recommended approval of the cabinet proposal. Lindberg followed a separate course by appealing for the rejection of all proposals for the organization of the military establishment and for a new investigation in accordance with given directives.

The defense question was treated in the Riksdag on June 10 and 11. The debate was largely concerned with the negotiations between the several parties: all concerned charged one another with a lack of genuine desire to reach agreement. The government moved that the bill be approved, but made it clear that it did not intend to expunge a defense decision dictated by the moderate parties. Of most interest from our point of view is the very considerable support that the search for a positive solution to the defense question received from Social Democratic quarters. Lindberg's proposal was not put to a vote in the upper house; the vote in the lower house on the countermotion gave it 31 votes. Similarly, the party faction that was prodefense dominated the debate. Several speakers who had formerly been active in the disarmament cause explained the reasons for their change. Höglund interpreted a view circulating within this group thusly: "It is the threat that tyrannical dictatorships pose to small nations that has forced Social Democrats to relinquish temporarily the disarmament line in order that a Nazi army shall not occupy a military vacuum." The committee proposal won in both houses. The cabinet did not resign, however, until some days later, after the Riksdag defeat of the proposed adjustment in old age pensions.

The Social Democrats did not attack the newly decreed defense reform in the election campaign of 1936, and the party's election manifesto did not touch upon future Social Democratic policies on defense. When Hansson's coalition cabinet took office it emphasized that the defense act would be implemented.

At the 1937 Riksdag Social Democrats displayed a change of opinion in regard to the voluntary rifle club movement as well. Only the year before the cabinet had refrained from proposing any grants to this movement pursuant to the judgment of the party congress, as pronounced on several occasions. As usual, such appropriations had nevertheless been granted by the Riksdag; some Social Democrats had voted with the majority on this legislation. In 1937 on the other hand, the cabinet included an appropriation to the rifle club movement in the main budget proposal. The main justification given for subsidizing the movement was the treatment accorded the question in the Riksdag the previous year. The Social Democrats on the Ways and Means Committee now gave their approval to this proposal, which met with only scattered Social Democratic opposition in the upper and lower house. The grant did receive 42 dissenting votes in the lower house, but these were for the most part cast by members of other parties (Liberals and Socialists). The prime minister gave the principal explanation of the change in the party's opinion. "What has happened here," he declared, "is that in the general rally that has developed around our defense problems during the latest—I can hardly say years, but must say months—there has existed a desire to remove even the source of irritation that appeared in the conflict on the rifle club movement. As far as I am concerned, this implies . . . another view of the rifle club movement. . . . Yet I do not stand here in order to apologize, I stand here to declare that we have arrived at a state where it has become a matter of course for us to end strifes that serve no purpose, even in regard to this issue." He pointed out that many Social Democratic workers had joined the movement despite the party's repudiation of rifle clubs, and that it had not developed into a party movement. The Communists had advanced the Social Democrats' old view of the rifle club movement as a safeguard for the working class. The prime minister responded to this idea by stating that the movement should not be "a special armed organ for a democratic order." Such protection was the duty of the police force. "The rifle club movement shall continue to be, as it has been, a movement to afford those interested in the sport of shooting the opportunity to practice this sport. Should it have to be placed in the employ of defense it should be exclusively as an instrument in the hands of the lawful order to protect the interests of the public against whomsoever might threaten these interests." Hansson called attention to the remarkable turn of events whereby "just when a majority against appropriations to rifle clubs could be rounded up in the Swedish Riksdag, perhaps for the first time, we grant this appropriation with a greater consensus than before."

In contrast to the situation prior to World War I, the Social Democratic youth movement in the main allied itself with the party's defense policies during the period just discussed. It is true that for a while radical trends aimed at unilateral disarmament were stronger within the youth federation than they were within the party itself. Yet the federation never adopted any ruling that was at variance with the party program. Furthermore, the development of the federation followed essentially the same course as that taken by the party as a whole.

The defense question was not treated in detail at the first congresses of the youth federation. At the 1922 congress a motion proposing that the federation work toward total disarmament was rejected, but a motion calling for socialist agitation among conscripts was passed. Rickard Lindström—who was voted chairman of the federation at the 1922 congress, a post he would hold until 1928—appeared on this, as on several later occasions, as the spokesman for the prodefense line; he underlined the importance of instilling the defense system with a democratic and socialist spirit. Debates at the 1925 congress evinced a schism between the proponents and opponents of unilateral disarmament. This controversy did not result in any definite decision, but particulars regarding endorsements of the arguments propounded in the course of the debate suggest that the line favoring absolute disarmament was in the majority. The congress also considered the question of the voluntary rifle club movement; it decided to declare its preference that federation members not join this movement. Several speakers called the movement reactionary, an organization of the upper class. The minority opinion was voiced by Lindström: he reminded his opponents that socialists at times regarded the movement as a potential combat organization and asserted that the movement per se was neither undemocratic nor antisocialist.

The defense question was subject to close scrutiny at the next two congresses: partisans of defense and champions of unilateral disarmament clashed in heated debates. The 1928 congress was confronted with motions proposing that the federation carry on pacifist propaganda toward the end of disarmament; these motions called attention to the opinion that had prevailed at the recent party congress. The youth congress unanimously passed a resolution, prepared and generally held by the federation administration, calling for agitation against nationalism and chauvinism and for peace and public welfare. Most of the debaters spoke in behalf of unilateral disarmament. The 1925 ruling on the voluntary rifle club movement was given more of an edge insofar as it was said to denote "definite disassociation" from this movement and the youth clubs were instructed to inform their members that they should not join rifle clubs. Proposals demanding that federation members be absolutely prohibited from joining the rifle club movement were, however, defeated. The prodisarmament sentiment in the federation reached its climax at the 1931 congress. A series of motions demanded the issuance of a statement for unilateral national disarmament. The federation administration, led by Wallentheim—like Lindberg, a defense sympathizer—presented a resolution proposal that was obviously a compromise. The federation said it was pleased with the new review of defense and that it was the duty of the federation to "assist with all vigour in the propagation of the ideals of freedom and disarmament through both the written and spoken word" and to "combat vehemently all militaristic and chauvinistic propaganda." The proposal lent itself to varied interpretations and could therefore be unanimously accepted, but the debate revealed sharp differences of opinion. There is every reason to believe that the great majority of delegates were adherents of unilateral disarmament. In order to summon support for the proposal of the federation administration, Wallentheim, Lindström, and other defense sympathizers accented political points of view; should the federation declare itself for unilateral disarmament it ran the risk of clashing with the party and, as was the case with the old youth federation in 1917, of creating a conflict that might weaken the workers' movement as a whole.

The complete scope of the defense issue has not been treated at the two most recent congresses of the youth federation, but debates on specific problems testify to a change of opinion in the youth federation. Demands for unilateral disarmament have simply not arisen, and a number of debaters have accented the increasingly favorable disposition of the federation toward defense. Perhaps the best proof of the federation's change in attitude is the solidly backed ruling, passed by the federation's 1937 congress, rescinding the federation's pronouncements of 1925 and 1928 exhorting members not to join the voluntary rifle club movement. The federation now expressly stated "that membership and active participation in the voluntary rifle club movement is congruous with membership in Sweden's Social Democratic Youth Federation." Torsten Nilsson (federation chairman since 1934), among many other speakers in the debate, maintained that developments during the preceding years had dissipated antidefense tendencies and that more and more federation members had come to realize that defense and the rifle club movement constituted an essential safeguard for democracy.

Summary

IN AGREEMENT with the liberal philosophy of enlightenment on which it was based, socialism worked toward peace and brotherhood among peoples as a condition for the welfare and free development of the individual. Like their liberal predecessors and contemporaries, socialists anticipated that their goal lay within reach: a few decades of social and economic change, together with a corresponding ideological reformation, would lead to the new society. This thinking was expressed in a distinct manner in Marx's broad perspective. The class struggle and the victory of the proletariat were the means; an international community liberated from the coercion of the state was the goal. From this point of departure, national self-assertion and national defense must be regarded as obstacles or, to the extent that the historical view prevailed, as ingredients in a societal form that was doomed to destruction. This outlook was wed to views of a simpler, more concrete nature in the socialist movements of various countries. One attacked the existing political regime, the economically and socially ascendant groups; the country of one's residence was identified with this regime and with these groups. Should socialism help defend its domestic enemies against external foes? Should the exploited classes permit themselves to be educated as the protectors of the exploiters?

A current of thought developed by Marx and other socialist theories on a short-range view led to other conclusions. The principle of freedom applied to the people as well as to the individual. As long as state organizations existed they ought to encompass individuals and nations that belong together. Among oppressed peoples such as the Czechs and Poles, patriotism and socialism might therefore fuse in certain parties: the ideals would be first, national unity, then a socialist society. This current of thought was not of immediate importance to socialist movements among peoples who did not suffer under foreign oppression, but it gradually gained in urgency and cognizance. As long as the division of peoples into states prevailed, socialism must provisionally protect the nation state. Further, the stronger the hold socialism gained in a state, the stronger the reason for the movement to maintain such a state: a threat to the state became a threat to socialism itself. Should socialism permit other states, which could be considered reactionary from a socialist viewpoint, to suppress the nation because socialism had disassociated itself from the nation?

Here, as on other points, we arrive at the paradoxical conclusion that Marx's broad perspective, founded on a synoptic view of history, was ideologically applicable only if Marx's predictions were fulfilled within a short period of time. A socialist movement that enjoyed a tradition of successful activity within a state had to be national—if not because of patriotic sentiments, then in order to protect socialism.

The ideological transformation of Swedish Social Democracy in regard to national defense can be divided into fairly clearly delimited periods, each of which lasted about 20 years. The hallmark of the first period was that the defense issue per se was accorded little attention in party debates. The defense burden was not particularly heavy; because of the brief training period involved, compulsory military service could scarcely provide material for agitation that could appeal to personal aversion to such service. The party had not yet gained sufficient strength to make the adoption of a stand on the issues of the day absolutely necessary. Universal suffrage was the paramount demand: the attainment of universal suffrage would continue to be a prerequisite for successful action in other areas for many years to come. This explains why the defense question was, as a rule, not treated at party congresses during this period and why Branting was the only party leader to give the question close consideration on several occasions.

The statements that touch upon this question, however, evince an overwhelmingly negative attitude. Capitalism is described as the cause of war, and the road to peace is said to be an international socialist reformation. Defense is frequently considered a protection for the upper class—not least against internal enemies. Yet expressions of antinational sentiments are rare; whenever they do appear, they are linked with expressions of potential patriotism: once the country has become socialist, socialism will, in turn, become national. Militarism is one of the most odious concepts to Social Democrats of this era. Militarism was understood to mean on the one hand the defense organization in general, on the other, certain conditions existing within the military establishment: drills, extreme subordination, arrogance and snobbishness on the part of officers. Following foreign examples, the party programs refer to the establishment of a militia which, in contrast to the prevailing system, would be incontestably democratic in character. However, this demand was never pressed with ardor, even though it gained currency during the debates prior to the military act of 1901; it seems probable that its authors had in mind the democratic, socialist state of the future. Every now and then the suggestion was made that the army conscripted by compulsory military service and the voluntary rifle club movement could be turned into combat forces to serve socialist causes; however, this notion—which would have entailed a reversal of the party's military policy if it had been successful—is and will continue to be an exceptional idea without much influence.

Branting's comments on defense during this period do not bespeak a firm, uniform standpoint; to the contrary: his shifts of opinion were frequent and significant. On vital questions, however, Branting did arrive at a point of view which he would thereafter steadily affirm and which would become an important ingredient in the Social Democratic debate on defense in general. He stressed the value of national unity and acknowledged the necessity of defense under existing conditions. But he added that the requisite for effective defense was democratic and sociopolitical reform. This was the only way the great mass of people could be won over to military preparations; this was the essential condition for the cultivation of civil and national sentiments, which were more valuable to defense than quantity or technology. In establishing this principle Branting anticipated future developments on the defense issue. He also formed a strategy that would be utilized on numerous occasions, the last of which was the defense reform of 1936: Social Democrats countered military and nonsocialist demands for an arms increase with their own demand for domestic reform. A compromise along these lines could not be achieved prior to World War I, but 25 years later Social Democrats were to achieve not only a compromise, but true concord.

Strangely enough, Branting took exception to the strategy indicated here in his well-known May Day article of 1900. He then contended that the party should not bargain with its disposition toward defense but rather assent to an unconditional strengthening of defense. Yet this side-step was more illusory than real. Branting evidently expected that by taking a positive stand on defense the party would persuade the ruling groups to offer concessions on other matters—principally universal suffrage. From a cynical viewpoint it might be said that Branting wished to increase the party's influence by modifying it along lines sympathetic toward defense—while he himself without doubt presupposed the necessity of a stronger defense. Insofar as the party lent its support to the new standpoint, Branting was successful. But the defense reform resulted in a military organization that Branting and the rest of the party forthwith attacked with extraordinary vehemence; in the last analysis, the new military organization helped make the stark negativism toward defense even more solidly entrenched in the party.

From the early 1900s until the severance of the Left Socialist group in 1917, defense was perhaps the most frequently and most hotly debated question in the Social Democratic party. Most of the party leaders—the majority in the party administration and the rapidly growing Riksdag group—adhered to what may be termed the Branting line: they insisted on the necessity of defense but attacked militarism as such; they combined demands for political and social reforms with the defense question; they were sceptical toward or critical of proposals for increments in arms but nevertheless examined such proposals on their factual merits. This line was faced with an antagonistic group whose stronghold was the youth organizations subsequent to the expulsion of the Young Socialists by the Social Democratic Youth Federation. This opposition demanded the unconditional incorporation of the principle of disarmament in the party program and that the Riksdag group in general refuse to grant appropriations for military purposes. This opposition grew stronger and more successful at the congresses of 1905, 1908, and 1911. Defense sympathizers within the party were repeatedly forced to make concessions. Indeed, the absolute disarmament line would probably have become the party's official standpoint had not Branting's authority constrained the left wing from taking full advantage of its strength. The antidefense trend reached a climax during the period just before the outbreak of World War I. The war ushered in a change that soon manifested itself at the 1914 congress. The party group that was positively disposed toward defense gained strength and a sense of purpose; at the same time the youth federation, led by Höglund, further emphasized its nihilism toward defense. The schism that occurred at the 1917 congress and which estranged the leftist faction was in large measure the result of differences of opinion on the defense issue.

Defense sympathizers were essentially motivated by reasons that were common to all political currents of any note. The increase in international tensions was clearly brought out at the congresses of the International as well as in the prodefense propaganda circulated by the Right in Sweden. Around the turn of the century there had still been hopes that Swedish policy could be conducted without regard to what was termed "modern imperialism," but these hopes had now dimmed. The Russian menace, which dominated debates on defense, necessarily also affected Social Democrats, who had long viewed Czardom as the stronghold of European reactionism. Although Social Democracy was still wholly the party of struggle and malcontent, it could ascertain that many political gains had been made and that some gains had been scored for Social Democracy itself. At the end of this period, Branting, Steffen, and others influenced by such considerations were able to give increasing weight to the assertion that socialism must lend its efforts to defense even in Swedish society as it then existed; they even claimed that a socialist viewpoint in particular dictated that defense be accepted as a necessity for the preservation of advances that had been made. Young Marxists in the party complemented this theoretical vindication of defense. On the one hand Marx had stood firm in regard to a nation's right to self-determination; on the other hand, according to the materialistic view of history, national defense was inextricably linked with a certain stage of the development of the means of production and of society.

A characteristic of the party's antidefense faction was that it frequently appeared under the brutally honest designation "defense nihilism." It did not try to hide behind the ambiguous term "antimilitarism," which was itself value-charged. Defense nihilism assumed several forms. That represented by the young Socialists signified, on the whole, negation of the value of national unity itself. Drawing upon Marx's broad perspective, the Young Socialists referred to the nation and defense as the idealistic and material side of the rule of the upper class; as far as combatants in the social revolution were concerned, all armed organizations that did not serve the spirit of the revolution were necessarily antagonistic. This brand of thinking was sometimes combined with themes derived from Tolstoy and other pacifist writers of a Christian bent. It was better to yield to violence with noble resignation than to destroy one's soul by resorting to violence. They thus wished to apply the theory of the value of patiently borne suffering in regard to oppression by a foreign state—the very same theory that was scorned in respect to domestic politics as being a protection for the upper class.

A form of fundamental defense nihilism emerged even within the Social Democratic Youth Federation, particularly during the critical period just before and during World War I. The value of national unity as such was acknowledged, but the existing state, which was characterized by the political and social dominion of capitalism, was declared unworthy of defense. Stretching the application of the idea of a relation between defense and reforms to the extreme led to a rejection of all defense pending the fulfillment of socialist demands. However, this line was not preemptive during the Youth Federation's period of growth and breakthrough. The federation leadership during those years (from which many of the party's present leaders were recruited) was neither antinational nor basically nihilistic to defense. Its pure negativism to defense was motivated by a special reason that was suited to small states. "What good is it?" was the leading theme featured in agitation. A small country such as Sweden could under no circumstances defend itself against any of the powers from which attack was conceivable. A military organization would be meaningless, for it could never serve the purpose for which it was designed with the resources at hand. This argumentation often included references to writers on military affairs who complained of the inadequacy of the nation's defense and sometimes advanced defense requirements that all parties considered exaggerated or, in any case, impossible to satisfy. The "practical" defense nihilists demanded that military defense be eliminated and replaced by a so-called cultural defense. Sweden would thereby become neutral and agreements regarding international awards of arbitration would be established to secure peace. In addition, they invested a great deal of hope in the idea of workers' action on an international scale, first of all in the form of a general strike, which was advanced at congresses held by the International as an instrument to prevent war; this idea never gained wide support in Sweden however.

The purpose of this over-all description has been to recall some of the main trends of argumentation propounded by the various factions; it is therefore schematic and one-sided. On the whole, the potent antidefense propaganda conducted during these years employed the most disparate arguments. Several variable and sometimes partly mutually contradictory ideas could be combined in one and the same pamphlet, in one and the same speech. War was horrible and meaningless. Sweden's defense was essentially a defense of the Swedish upper class. Because it made the introduction of cultural and sociopolitical reforms impossible, defense aggravated the lot of the workers economically and socially. Armaments involved the risk of war, yet in the event of war they would prove valueless. Concentration on military efforts undermined the nation morally and materially. Militarism, with its subordination, its isolation of soldiers, its spirit of brutality and snobbery, impeded the progress of socialism and of the working class. "If you want peace, then prepare yourself for peace." "Workers have no fatherland." "The working class has nothing to lose but its shackles." "Not one man, not one penny to militarism." All these notions and slogans were aimed at people who were dissatisfied with their social and economic position, who habitually regarded rulers as suppressors and foes, who were inclined to think that defense expenditures and compulsory military service involved unnecessary personal sacrifices. The long period of peace in Europe had led the masses to view war as something irrational and unreal. Aside from the preservation of peace, the people had no international aspirations that could unite them. Further, since no specific sources of international friction existed, aggression by a foreign power seemed a phantom threat conjured up by upper-class agitators as an excuse for their selfish armament demands.

We have already noted that a change in the climate of opinion took place after the outbreak of the war. Now the authority of defense sympathizers was enhanced. The very war many had said was inconceivable was a reality. Now one could scarcely dispute the value of Sweden's armed forces to the preservation of the nation's neutrality, partly by dealing with direct violations of neutrality, partly by their deterrent power. Fundamental defense nihilism could only be sustained by outright revolutionary elements—which had disappeared from Social Democracy with the severance of the Left Socialists. The experiences of the war years even discredited the practical brand of defense nihilism propagated previously. Its chief argument, "What good is it?" had proved untenable. Events themselves had provided the answer to this question, which had been posed at thousands of meetings. A number of leading young Social Democrats drew the logical inference from these events and abandoned the line that called for unconditional disarmament. At the congresses of 1917 and 1920, P. A. Hansson, Sandler, and Möller followed in main the same line as Branting. At the 1920 congress, the party's repudiation of defense nihilism met with no opposition, and after a few minutes of debate the congress rallied around a new program article on defense.

In several important respects the party's adoption of a position on defense in 1920 fixed the direction of its future course. Recognition of the value of national unity has become increasingly unconditional. Fundamental defense nihilism has not been espoused at all since 1920; to the extent that it has been of any significance, practical defense nihilism has been activated by motives different from those which previously served as its mainspring. As an indication of the over-all trend, "defense nihilism" has been used only as a deprecatory term. Even those who were active in the cause of national disarmament have since adamantly protested that they are not defense nihilists: the very term has come to stand for an antiquated idea that has long been renounced. In the following we shall therefore use other terms to designate groups representing the line of absolute disarmament. We should bear in mind, however, that the disarmament enthusiasts of recent years have had exactly the same objective as that set by defense nihilists thirty years previously: total abolition of Sweden's defense, independent of international disarmament.

The weight of this trend of opinion did not become more perceptible during the first postwar years. The concord that was so marked at the 1920 congress endured for a few years. This concord was founded on a clear understanding of the nature of the most immediate objectives—but also on uncertainty due to the international situation concerning possible long-range courses of action. Sweden ought to join the League of Nations, which could conceivably become the organ for a supranational judicial system, and reduce the armaments that had been ordered at the outbreak of the war but which were no longer needed in their entirety. As the member of another party (K. G. Westman) said, one was now "behind the cyclone." All parties affirmed that arms reduction was feasible; the only question was how far it should be carried. But the future was otherwise uncertain. Some Social Democrats expected that the League of Nations would gain sufficient strength to be able to rule on all disputes without resort to violence. Some also speculated that the League might organize an international military or police force and concomitantly interdict member nations from arming independently. As they anticipated that the League would become universal in scope, they also theorized that all intranational defense organizations would disappear. Should such an international judicial system be established Sweden would have to be prepared to contribute military assistance. One would have to watch the course of developments in this regard for the time being. Against this background, the party agreed on the program formulation, "an international police force and disarmament," a wording that was extremely obscure. In agreeing on this formulation the party in general most likely meant that disarmament would be implemented on an international level together with the establishment of a supernational police force. According to this interpretation, the wording contained no directives whatsoever regarding Swedish defense policy. Yet the very same formulation was interpreted as an allusion that Swedish arms would be reduced. What is more important, the words could also be construed as a demand for not only international disarmament but for unilateral Swedish disarmament as well.

At the Riksdag of 1919 the Liberal-Socialist Edén cabinet forced through a provisional reduction of the military establishment. A review of defense was ordered the same year; the review committee was assigned the task of working out proposals for a new defense organization which, it was assumed, would be most circumscribed in comparison to the organization of 1914. Hopes that the League would become a secure instrument for peace with an international police force were not fulfilled. In 1923 the review committee delivered its report: all members of the committee recommended that Sweden maintain her defense. The drastic arms reduction espoused by Social Democrats was, in the main, effected in 1925 in collaboration with the Independents. This decision is interesting from the point of view of party history because of the deep antagonism it created between the Right and the two parties to the Left. However, of primary significance from the viewpoint of the evolution of Social Democratic ideology on defense is the fact that an overwhelming majority in the party's Riksdag group followed the positive line tendered by the Social Democratic cabinet.

Nonetheless, at the party congress of 1924 and at the Riksdag debates of 1924 and 1925 adherents of unilateral Swedish disarmament stood out as an active group within the party. This line grew rapidly in strength during the next few years. Its most active representatives included former members of the Left Socialist and Communist parties who had returned to the Social Democratic fold when their parties had split or dissolved. Their number included Elof Lindberg, Vennerström, Lindhagen, Höglund, and Ström. A situation arose which was reminiscent of the state of affairs prior to World War I. The cast of players was essentially the same as then, but the roles had changed: many members of the old youth federation who had remained loyal to the party and had gradually come to form the nucleus of its leadership now subscribed to the line that was favorably disposed toward defense. As was the case at the congresses from 1905 to 1917, a majority of the party's leaders were sceptical toward or simply spurned the thought of disarmament while, judging by congressional rulings and the results of local meetings, the rank and file converted to the extreme standpoint to an ever increasing extent. At the 1928 congress the delegates succeeded in deferring a decision on the party program by uniting in a demand for a new investigation into the defense question; two years later a Riksdag paper to this effect was ordered with the support of the Independents. Yet this decree was combined with an acknowledgment that the struggle for unilateral disarmament fell within the framework of the program, as did the struggle for international disarmament. The conflict between the two factions became even more severe. As Branting did in 1911, so the party chairman, P. A. Hansson, now summoned all his power to prevent a pronouncement that would have meant victory for the disarmament cause. In all likelihood a majority of the congressional delegates subscribed to disarmament. Yet a compromise was reached through an agreement between the party leader and a faction of the opposition that voted for a colorless, equivocal pronouncement while adhering to its own standpoint. The congress represented the culmination of the efforts in the cause of disarmament during this period.

The ideology of the new disarmament movement contained no antinational or Marxist views. On the whole, this ideology did not assume a distinctively socialist coloration: the arguments it advanced could be and were adopted, in some cases, by nonsocialist parties. Nor did its followers ask

"What good is it?" with the connotation that had been so common twenty years earlier. Their main line of argumentation went as follows: From an international viewpoint, and especially from Sweden's viewpoint, the dangers of war were negligible; new military technology had rendered offensive weapons incomparably stronger than defensive weapons, and war on the whole had become more devastating; the only effective way to avert war was to make oneself incapable of carrying on a war; disarmament would not expose Sweden to risks other than occasional violations of neutrality and possibly limited, temporary occupation; in the long run Sweden was not confronted by dangers of any significance, for it could count on help from the League of Nations. The League of Nations had also played an important part in conjectures regarding the insignificance of the risk of war. To some extent it had replaced the belief in international action by the working class disseminated prior to World War I; during the period in question, however, party debates contained only sporadic allusions to this belief. Some used Christian-pacifist reasoning in justifying the demand for disarmament, but this reasoning was never employed alone; it was used as an idealistic complement to the views grounded in practical politics.

The strength of the disarmament trend around 1930 was probably to some extent related to the general political difficulties that the Social Democrats faced at this time. The party had been excluded from executive power for a number of years, a situation which alone tended to reinforce radical endeavors. The party suffered defeat at the election of 1928 under conditions that brought out its points of contention with the nonsocialist parties. The party's social and economic plans were extremely diffuse; socialization had not yet been retired in favor of social policy. Given this state of affairs, defense became the most frequently discussed and most pressing problem in regard to the course of action that the party should follow.

The triumph of National Socialism in Germany and the accentuation of international conflicts ushered in a new opinion revision among Social Democrats, a revision more complete than any of the previous changes party opinion had undergone. The 1935 report of the defense commission, the 1936 cabinet bill, and the debates at the party congress and at the Riksdag of the same year clarified the new orientation. Only three years after a party congress had advocated disarmament a vast majority in the party was prepared to vote in favor of substantial mobilization. During the following years prodefense sentiments were on the rise. Even before the outbreak of hostilities in 1939, party differences on defense had vanished and the debate concerned methods, to the exclusion of questions of principle. For the first time a strong national defense was acknowledged to be vital to the party.

Each of the three periods into which we have divided the evolution of Social Democratic defense policy culminated with the party's adoption of a positive stand. During the introductory and intermediate phases of these periods, a majority in the party endorsed defense nihilism or disarmament. It is not surprising that a party representing those who are dissatisfied with the structure of the social community is, for the most part, less interested in the defense of that community than other political parties. This is an obvious relation that is corroborated by all sociological studies. What is of interest is the argumentation advanced by the several factions, the interchange between unmistakably divergent views, the antitheses between different groups in the party. These points call for a few complementary comments.

First of all, we must bear in mind the problems peculiar to the defense issue. The over-all evaluations that could serve as a groundwork for the party in taking a position on the issue are comparatively simple. One either recognized or denied the value of national unity; one either accepted or rejected the use of violence in the defense of one's interests. With the exception of those attitudes colored by Marxist or pacifist ideology, which will not be considered in this context, Swedish Social Democracy has chosen the positive responses to these alternatives. It has chosen to preserve the national entity; it has not condemned violence per se. Given these standpoints, the party's position on defense is largely determined by speculations as to future developments. But the bases for these speculations are far more complicated and, necessarily, far more uncertain than those underlying other political conjectures. Are wars really likely to occur? Could a war conceivably affect Sweden? Is a direct attack on Sweden likely? Does Sweden run the risk of suppression if it is attacked in the course of a war between other states? Or are neutrality violations or temporary occupations the only conceivable dangers to Sweden? Can the existence of a defense system entail perils that would not arise in an unarmed country? These are just a few examples of the questions that immediately come up. Besides this category of questions there is the question of the effectiveness of various defensive forces in all the situations that might theoretically arise as well as the problem of weighing defense expenditures against appropriations for other purposes.

The upshot was that one reasoned on defense from objective bases insofar as suppositions regarding reality, not evaluations, supplied the main premises, but that the thinking applied to this question was all the same more dubious than that employed in other spheres. Although the validity of the answer to a certain question defied appraisal, the answer might decide the position that would be taken on an entire matter.

Yet another factor must be added to the above. Two of the primary questions asked were whether an appreciable risk of war did exist and whether it could be assumed that a defense would substantially reduce a possible risk of war. A negative answer to either question opened the door for the entrance of absolute defense nihilism. A positive response to both questions meant that it would seem self-evident that the nation arm to the limit of her capacity. To put it another way: it did not seem logical to confront a small risk with a small defense, for if that which is feared should occur, a strong, not a weak defense would be essential. It was impossible to use the same formulas as an insurance company and calculate that a small risk required only a small premium. The defense review of 1923 touched upon this line of thought in its reference to the value of a flexible defense that could be augmented or reduced according to need. It was nonetheless obvious that no real flexibility of defense could be achieved.

Reflections of this kind provide the basis for the saying that the defense question is the stumbling block of the democratic form of government. In situations where the risk of war is great and defense is manifestly a guarantee for peace, first, and for freedom, second, democracies that are not hampered by domestic conflicts of too great a magnitude have the possibility of persuading the electoral masses to reach decisions entailing great personal sacrifices. But when times are calm and tensions reduced, democracies encounter enormous difficulties in maintaining their defenses. Such nations need to spend sums and produce results that cannot be expected to have any direct significance; they need to prepare for actions that supposedly will not occur. In such situations large bodies of the electorate will naturally be indifferent to or reject defense. Thus defense policy tends to swing between extreme views. As suggested, the basic difficulty is obviously the impossibility of improvising a national defense. It would otherwise be possible to be proarmament one year, prodisarmament the next.

These views contribute to an understanding of the fluctuations of Social Democratic opinion on defense. The party majority has oscillated between absolute disarmament and marked prodefense sympathies. On the whole these oscillations have been connected to the international situation. When times were calm, the majority was for disarmament; in times of unrest the majority wanted to preserve or reinforce the nation's defense. The principal difference between the defense nihilism of 1910 and the disarmament crusade of 1930 was that the former answered the question as to whether Sweden could defend herself in the negative, and the latter denied that a true risk of war existed. But we should note that with each swing of the pendulum between the two extreme views, the positive stand became more marked and more generally accepted. During the last period, Social Democrats were ready to mobilize before war had broken out; in 1914 they had still been aloof toward the bourgeois rally to the nation's defense.

The opposition that has existed on the defense issue between the party's leading group and the party's members and representatives has not arisen on any other issue. The party administration, particularly its leaders, seems to have been more consistently prodefense than the Riksdag group. The attitude of both the administration and Riksdag group have, however, differed from the opinion that has prevailed at party congresses during critical periods. On two occasions, in 1911 and 1932, the authority of the party chairman apparently blocked attempts by the congressional majority to lay down a totally negative line for the party. This divergence in opinion can be partly explained by the greater influence on party leaders of views that traditionally prevailed in government and Riksdag circles, together with the fact that the leaders were more alive to that which was politically feasible than the rest of the party. Moreover, more intimate and permanent contact with defense problems seems to have tended to create a sceptical view of the classic disarmament line. Many were the political figures who converted to a view that was relatively prodefense after they had thoroughly studied these problems. There is no denying that there were those who were defense nihilists and disarmament advocates even after they had familiarized themselves with the defense question. But it appears likely that the convictions of many of the party representatives outside of the group active in national politics were founded on grounds wanting in subtlety and clarity. A review of the innumerable debates on the question inevitably leaves one with the impression that information and acumen were not particularly well represented in radical circles: reasoning that was obviously flaccid and illogical was not uncommon. Add to this the disposition prevalent among less prominent party representatives to favor demonstration politics that appealed to the electorate; this tendency has not been as pronounced in the leading phalanx, which has had a manifest interest in maintaining the party's qualifications to govern and form coalitions by taking moderate stands. Partly subconscious motivations of this kind have undoubtedly been operative, even though they have been alluded to in the debate but rarely. The extreme, impracticable line was more attractive to aspirants in the second rank than to those in the first rank who had already arrived.

In recent years it has often been said that the Social Democrats' improved attitude to defense is to some extent due to the improved position the working class has gained through social and political reforms and its concomitant change in outlook. The worker now feels that he has the same rights as his fellow citizens in a native land that is worth defending. A broad view of the party's transformation suggests that there is something basically sound about this interpretation. Many of the slogans used by defense nihilists thirty years ago have lost their persuasive force. The situation of the individual worker has improved and the power of the workers' movements has grown. The nation's defense now also stands for the defense of a popular government under Social Democratic leadership.

Christianity and the Church

Three Basic Views

IN SOCIALIST THOUGHT there have been two main positions toward Christianity. On the one hand it has been maintained that this religion—as with all or most religious systems—directed men's views outside the temporal world and has thereby created indifference, or even opposition, to attempts to change society. The hope for eternal happiness and the fear of eternal torment have made earthly life unimportant. Concentration on moralistic efforts and an intensive religious zeal have obscured the importance of external, earthly conditions. Sometimes Christianity, and especially the established and powerful institutions of the developed churches, have been regarded as a consciously used means for giving the lower class the necessary suggestions for its quiet submission. In Marxist socialism, Christianity, like other ideologies, has not been characterized as a falsely proclaimed myth but as an aggregate of necessarily progressing illusions at a certain stage of development. In any case, Christianity, whether so intended by its adherents and preachers or not, served as a source of support for the state and the ruling class. It has been unequalled as the foremost propaganda instrument of the rulers. This opinion, which has its roots in Enlightenment anticlericalism and shares with it the view of religion as one of the prejudices which has hindered enlightened interest from becoming man's guide, led to the conclusion that socialism must oppose or at least reject Christianity. The victory of socialism will be followed by the downfall of Christianity.

On the other hand, there is the position that the Christian religion and socialism are based on the same assumptions. Christianity's teachings on the value of the individual, on everyone's equality before God, on love of one's neighbor, have been asserted to lead to a social order, which in its practical consequences, is characterized by social equality and collective activity for the good of all. Economic differences are regarded as contrary to the principle of the equality of all, and the acquisitive drive was characterized as an unworthy incentive from a moral point of view. As a rule socialists have placed the original, militant Christianity, which was considered radical and even revolutionary in contrast to successful contemporary religious communities which have been accused of forsaking the essentials of Christianity on the way to power. A Christianity which returns to its original purity shall meet a socialism which, in the struggle for better social conditions, has preserved the feeling for transcendental conceptions. This Christian Socialism, which was represented by clergymen as well as by labor leaders, corresponded in conservative circles to Social Christianity, which combined social reform demands with a marked social conservatism and whose adherents have included the foremost defenders of the *status quo* and the maintenance of the social hierarchy in a number of countries.

A third, more moderate and indeterminate line has also appeared in socialism. It is related to liberalism's principles of tolerance and freedom. Religious belief was placed outside the realm of political discussion; it was neither criticized nor evaluated. Religion was characterized as a "private concern." In this connection it was generally demanded that the state be neutral in religious questions, that state institutions not conduct religious propaganda, and that no church be connected or receive privileges from the state. In its repudiation of the State Church and in its opposition to confessional education in schools, this point of view has generally coincided with that of the radical anti-Christians.

Still other combinations of views regarding the church and Christianity have been found in socialist movements. The antireligious position, under certain conditions, can be combined with at least a provisional approval of the State Church and other corresponding institutions. Christian Socialism can be combined with the demand for separation of State and Church. All of these attitudes have appeared among the Swedish Social Democrats; different lines have dominated the discussion, one after the other. The Party's official position, however, has undergone almost no change.

The Antireligious and Marxist Lines

RELIGIOUS MOTIVATIONS were an essential part of the impetus for a socialist movement that existed in the 1840s. Götrek was, however much influenced by Marx, primarily influenced on this point by the Christian or, in any case, the religiously inclined French authors such as St. Simon, Cabet, and Louis Blanc. Communism is, he explained, a new name for Christianity whose views are in full agreement with the original Christian teachings. The communists should, in accordance with Christ's message, achieve their aims without resorting to illegal means. G. D. Forssell, one of Götrek's followers, stated that communism meant "a realization of peaceful democracy, of Christianity in its original purity." This teaching had been corrupted "until only the name with a heavenly humbug remained and when this holy teaching had degenerated to a scourge and a new chain of slavery, then could the first tyrant call himself a Christian."

Among the Swedish Social Democrats, on the other hand, not only an anticlerical but an antireligious and atheistic opinion was emphasized from the beginning. Several reasons for this can be assumed. Hostility toward the Church and its influence, especially in education, was conditioned by the conservative propaganda put forth by the clergy of the State Church. This hostility also made for a critical attitude toward religious teachings. Socialism's repudiation of church and religion led in turn to a direct antisocialist agitation by the Church, and because of this socialist criticism was further sharpened. But to this must be added other factors, which in Sweden, as in other countries, tended to give socialism other orientations in the 1880s than thirty years earlier. Religious views held an important place in the social conservative propaganda and in the nonsocialist trade union movement and they were, consequently, obstacles to socialist propaganda. Philosophy, sociology, and natural science had undermined or weakened religious beliefs in intellectual circles; this was true not least of positivism and Darwinism, which played a central role in the cultural debate. At just this time during the 1880s, Swedish literature became colored by atheistic and antimetaphysical points of view.

But above all: The theories of Swedish socialism came from Marx—and in some degree from Lassalle, who on this point was almost Marxist—and saw religion, in agreement with certain ideas in the materialist conception of history, as a part of the ruling ideology, of the ruling class' ideology. The attack on Christianity was a consequence of the Marxist dialectical revolutionary doctrine. The class, whose victory socialism predicted and worked for, must necessarily break with the ideas of the class doomed to destruction, as well as with the system of production supported by this class.

Antireligious views did not appear in the statements adopted in the official programs of Social Democratic organizations. They only contained the demand that the State Church be abolished and that religion be regarded as a private concern. The latter point was taken from the German Gotha program of 1875 and the Danish Gimle program of 1876. These points reappeared as early as 1882 in Palm's program for the Swedish Social Democratic Workers' Union. The aim was obviously to give expression to the principle of complete religious freedom. In the program of the Social Democratic Union of Stockholm, which was adopted in 1885, the seventh article advocated: "Complete religious freedom, that is, the separation of the Church from state and school. Religion is to be regarded as a private concern." Similar points are to be found in the program of the Workers' Congress of Southern Sweden adopted in 1888 and in several other programs of Social Democratic organizations.

Evidence of how related questions were handled at the time in Social Democratic propaganda is provided by a motion presented by the Uppsala Typographers' Union at the constituent party congress in 1889. The motion presented two questions. Was it useful for the labor movement, "that these standard-bearers seek with all their efforts, by the spoken as well as by the written word (in the press), to oppose our religion and faith in all things transcendental in general, which since time immemorial have been considered to be of priceless value to poor and oppressed humanity?" Further: if all the workers had common interests and ought to conduct a common battle, although there were many "who either hold to a greater religiosity or, in any case, have a strong antipathy toward the materialistic world view, was it not necessary from a purely practical point of view to attempt to lessen the division between these and the politically aware workers?" Probably as a result of this motion the congress took up for debate the party's position on religion. The question was whether the party should make "a statement against religion," as Branting and Sterky, among others, wanted or whether it should simply refer to the program on this question as Palm and others urged. The latter view won with 18 votes against 16 and the congress referred to "the article in the party's program where religion was declared to be every man's private concern" (by "program" was meant the Gotha program). There was no mention of repudiating antireligious propaganda. The spirit of the congress was expressed by the recommendation that "rationalistic schools" be established. In the succeeding congresses the religion and church questions were not raised. In the new party program adopted in 1897 an article (IV) was inserted—without debate, judging by the report of the congress—with the following wording: "Religion is declared to be a private concern. Abolition of the State Church and the Church budget." In Article V regarding education the program demanded, among other items, "the separation of school and Church."

A survey of the press shows that an active antireligious line was dominant during the 1880s and 1890s. Palm repeatedly criticized the Church and religion, before as well as after the 1889 congress; however, he sometimes—as in his first address—held that religion as such should not be attacked. According to his opinion religion was used by the upper class to make the workers submissive and politically indifferent. Typical is his statement about "The gluttonous black hypocrites, the clergy, those carriers and spreaders of the spiritual plague which for centuries has hindered the progress of mankind." When a Rector Bring at a conference of the clergy of the State Church in Lund in 1884 spoke of the possibility of a Christian socialism, Palm declared that such a combination was unreasonable and added: "It seems, however, that the clergy of the State Church are beginning to take alarm and grope for a lifeline so that they won't be pulled away from their stew-pots by the strong currents of the times." At an early stage, however, Palm renounced collaboration between socialists and the organized free-thinkers, the utilitarians.

Branting's statements contain more subtle distinctions. They reveal both a Marxist line, according to which religion is by necessity linked with a certain stage in socioeconomic development, and elements of the general belief in progress and enlightenment, which was nurtured at this time by positivism and the discoveries of the natural sciences. According to the first line of thought, religion would disappear when society matured into socialism; according to the latter, religious beliefs would be transformed or lose their importance when knowledge and enlightenment became more widespread and stronger. Branting's thinking becomes to some extent unclear and contradictory when the two lines of thought diverge. In two articles dated 1888 dealing with relations with the free-thought movement or utilitarianism—to which we will return later—the Marxist point of view is dominant. Socialism is presented as a complete world view resting on materialist grounds. It was certainly tolerant of religion, but religious and socialist views were incompatible. A man who became a convinced socialist could not adhere to his religion; this "is in the nature of the thing, for in socialism's historical conception, even religion ultimately becomes but a consequence of determined material causes, a view which no person of religous faith can accept." Socialism in Sweden had also taken an antireligious position and had therefore "as a rule disdained the quite easily bought, but not very valuable successes which could have been won in certain circles by reducing scientific socialism into a kind of modernized Christian sermon." Utilitarianism was to be regarded as almost a part of socialism and ought to be supported in the battle against "the clerical reactionaries who want to lay their heavy and dirty hand on the both of us, hostile to the death as they are toward general social and political emancipation and especially toward religious emancipation." When Branting subsequently repudiated utilitarianism as a popular movement, he emphasized in his articles on the religious question that religion would necessarily disappear when the social reasons for its existence had disappeared; atheistic propaganda was therefore not necessary. In an article dated 1895 he wrote that religion was a result of social evils

> from which men are forced to flee, at least in fantasy, to a better, more just world than that surrounding them. To the degree that this abundantly flowing source of religiosity is blocked, will religion be overcome, more radically than through the generally correct, superficial, utilitarian biblical criticism. It will die away as an organ that has fallen into disuse; it will fall from *indifferentism,* apathy, not through disputation and discussion.

Even religious persons, according to Branting at this time, could be Social Democrats. In a debate in Uppsala in 1891 on the topic "Are Christianity and Culture in Conflict with Each Other?", Branting maintained that religion was incompatible with a high degree of knowledge and general enlightenment. With the progress of science, the area which was open to belief in supernatural powers would become smaller, and when knowledge of scientific findings became accessible to all, religion would lose its importance. From this point of view, Christianity, as with other religions, must be considered "to be in opposition to culture, because the predominance of religious influence was characteristic of a low level of culture." The Church was charged with extreme conservatism on this occasion, as in other contexts. "It was always the Church which led the way for the opposition to sound development, and one always sees the Church at the head of the group which strives to check progress as much as possible."

Also enlightening for Branting's views is his review of Selma Lagerlöf's *The Miracles of Antichrist* (1898). Here he declared it to be a fantastic dream . . . to reconcile the world powers, modern socialism and Christianity. The two belong to different historical epochs, they meet only on the border areas of the modern world, where part of the Middle Ages remains on the edge of the twentieth century. It is not far from the truth to say that the real force in such movements is of a social, not of a religious nature, that, in other words, Christianity, interpreted as the gospel of the poor, is nothing other than socialism concealed in medieval dress, while modern socialism has cast aside the cloak as a superfluous and out-of-fashion garment. The essential thing about Christianity as a popular force has always been its social tendencies, not the supernatural trappings. In this sense, modern socialism is the rightful heir and perfector of popular Christianity—be careful to distinguish this from the clerical Christianity of the ruling classes!—and therefore the individual Christian faith is reconcilable with socialist sentiments. But modern socialism as a world power is nevertheless totally devoid of religion, not because it is socialist but because it is modern. The increasing knowledge of nature, of ourselves, and of society diminishes religion's primitive attempts to explain the world, as the morning haze lifts from the beams of the sun. The great antireligious power is not called socialism, but scientific enlightenment.

Danielsson attempted, like Branting, to regard religion from a historical point of view, but used almost the same mode of expression as Palm in his critique of the Church and Christianity. However, he was never allied with the utilitarian movement. As early as the beginning of 1888, he stated that the free-thinker agitation aimed at showing the absurdities in the Bible and the like had little to do with socialism. According to socialism, Christianity was a stage of culture which had passed: in the form of the State Church it had supplied a valuable source of support to the upper class. Antireligious propaganda ought to be included in political propaganda.

What is religion? According to socialism it is nothing else than the reflection in man's consciousness of social and cosmic forces. To show constant invariable laws for governing both these influences on man is therefore to destroy religion. To pull out the belief in God by the roots from man is only possible by showing him that neither in nature nor in society is there to be found a trace of divine impulse or a manifestation of divine will. But this brings us to socialism, for the teaching of man's capacity to remold his social conditions is in the present society a signal for the proletariat to take possession of society's forces of production and make itself master over them.

In a number of articles during the spring and summer of the same year the Church and Christianity were scoffed at and attacked. Several of these articles were prosecuted, particularly one in the form of a prayer, "To the Creator of the Universe," which was a satire on the doctrine of the Trinity. Prosecution and sentencing led Danielsson to make furious utterances. For example, he wrote that they wanted to force the workers to bow down "before the lying priest, who poisons your soul in the interest of your Lord and keeps you in animal ignorance of yourself, nature, and its laws!" At the end of the year Danielsson returned, in a long series of articles, to the utilitarian propaganda which was criticized mainly from the same point of view as that presented earlier. Especially disapproved as a naive form of agitation was the utilitarians' method of showing contradictions and peculiarities in the Bible. Even a Christian could be a good socialist. One had to view the Church and Christianity as historically determined phenomena; to show the unreasonableness of Christian dogma was not an essential task. Danielsson's own position was, however, clear. In a pamphlet published in 1889, *The Flies and the Spiders,* which dealt with the exploitation of different societal groups, he wrote, for example:

> The flies, that is, all of us . . . who have bowed our heads under the priest's anathemas . . . we, who allowed our oppressors to enjoy the fruits which their injustice has procured for them, while we became spiritually crippled by the degenerative influence of religion. The spiders, that is, the black-coated ones with deceitful, spying gaze, who entrap the foolish mind of believers with their infamous teachings and cultivate a spirit of stupefaction and enslavement . . .

Some Social Democratic newspapers treated the religious question in less detail but, almost without exception, in the same anticlerical and antireligious vein as the articles mentioned above. It can, without any doubt, be asserted that Social Democrats at this time appeared to be clearly antireligious and to a certain extent carried on an active atheist propaganda; further, their attitude toward the Church was characterized by extreme hostility. On this last point, a few sentences from Heurlin's "Catechism," which was much used in propaganda, might be cited as typical of the agitating tone: "What is a clergyman? He is the highest paid civil servant in a community. He preaches self-denial. And how man shall work six days in the week and rest on the seventh. He himself rests six days in the week and speaks deliberate untruths on the seventh. A hypocrite dressed in a masquerade costume! Different wordings were but variations of the theme to the effect that the Church's men were "the mercenaries of capital."

The Social Democrat's antipathy to religion was directed in equal measure at the nonconformist dissenters and at the State Church. The former were even mentioned in an especially contemptuous tone. One seemed to make a distinction between the intellectually refined superstitions of the State Church and the disordered and uncultivated superstitions of the nonconformist churches.

It is necessary to look somewhat closer at the utilitarian movement and its relation to the Social Democrats. On the initiative of V. Lennstrand a utilitarian association was founded in the spring of 1888. Certain so-called positivist ideas served as the theoretical basis for its activity. The first objective was to eradicate superstition and prejudice—above all religous faith. When this had occurred mankind would be guided by the principle of "usefulness" (thereby the name utilitarianism) and establish a "good society." To the extent that Lennstrand developed other than antireligious views he showed close kinship with the Social Democrats. Branting and Sterky belonged to the utilitarian association. Before the association was founded Branting published an article by Lennstrand in *Social-Demokraten* (for which he was fined) and in the fall of 1888 in the previously mentioned articles explained his support of utilitarianism. As already noted, Danielsson took a position critical of the utilitarian movement, but printed Lennstrand's prosecuted article and criticized the sentencing of Branting in "To the Creator of the Universe." This and certain other articles were also prosecuted and Danielsson was sentenced to prison. Branting, in turn, published Danielsson's article—as did Rydgren, the editor of *Proletärens;* the result was new prison sentences. That one speaks of a period of prosecution in the history of Swedish socialism is to a large extent a result of this series of interrelated interventions by the authorities.

In 1890 even Branting repudiated utilitarianism as a special popular movement. Several reasons for this might be suggested: the utilitarian movement began to appear as a political rival to Social Democracy; socialism and utilitarianism were confused in public discussion; antireligious propaganda could not reasonably become a central issue for the Social Democrats, who also felt a need to underscore this point. A discussion meeting held in November 1890 at which Branting and Lennstrand were the main speakers adopted a resolution proposed by the former. According to this resolution, in agreement with the Social Democratic program, the state should not "favor or oppose" any particular religious view. The meeting considered "the dissemination of scientific knowledge" to be "the most certain weapon against both religious and other [forms of] superstition," but considered that "one-sided irreligious propaganda" should not be the foundation "for a political popular movement." Such a movement should regard "the social and economic demands of the masses" as most important. In his introductory statement Branting held that collaboration between socialists and utilitarians had become impossible since the latter had showed tendencies to build a separate party and as such threatened to compete with socialism. Many, who might otherwise have become Social Democrats, had been frightened away by utilitarianism. The masses would become indifferent to religion as a natural consequence of the socialist transformation of society. Against Branting's proposal was one presented by Lennstrand, according to which "a special movement of free thinkers" would be able to prepare the way for the Social Democratic movement.

Thus was collaboration between the socialist and utilitarian movements concluded. The latter movement quickly declined and within a few years lost all political importance. It should be strongly emphasized, however, that the repudiation of utilitarianism did not mean any repudiation of the criticism of religion. Such criticism was not given a leading place, but neither was it disapproved. On the contrary, Branting's proposed resolution suggested that "scientific knowledge" was necessary to combat religous superstition, and Branting, in effect, considered all religion scientifically untenable. That Branting, Danielsson, and the other socialist leaders attacked religion quite independently of their attitude to the utilitarian movement has been made clear by the foregoing. One can possibly note a tendency toward increasing moderation in statements critical of religion through the 1890s, especially in Branting's utterances. The "historical" point of view became more and more dominant.

In addition, some peculiar components in the Social Democrats' position on the religious question should be emphasized. The dominant opinion among the leading Social Democrats seems to have been that religion was natural at a certain stage of development, but would disappear at a later stage, which in different contexts was characterized in different ways—sometimes by increasing enlightenment, sometimes by the abolition of social injustices, and so forth. Under all conditions they held that religious conceptions would necessarily lose all importance along with the complete victory of socialism. The official statements in the party programs against the State Church and in favor of religious freedom were short-term demands directed against the state, which was still ruled by the middle class; it would be meaningless for a socialist society to propose such demands. Often these program points (subsequent to the 1889 statements) were interpreted as implying that the party as such should neither approve any religious standpoint nor declare itself as atheist—a view apparently determined by tactical considerations. Much antireligious and atheistic propaganda was included in the activities of the Social Democrats, but this was largely placed on a general historical-philosophical plane. They did not seek to show the unreasonableness or contradictory nature of religious teachings, but maintained that these would disappear by themselves with the transformation of society. Therefore, in the long run, the surest way of destroying religion was to work for this transformation. The materialist conception of history (in one of its forms) with the doctrine of ideologies as a superstructure of social and economic conditions is decisive here. Religion was regarded with a sort of fatalism: it will pass away as its structural support—the middle class society—is demolished. However, to apply fatalism to this special point involves an inconsistency, which the theoreticians of the time seem not to have observed. According to the variant of the materialist conception of history under discussion, social and economic conditions are in turn dependent on the development of productive capacity. One could therefore just as well have viewed these conditions from a fatalistic point of view and ceased all agitation while awaiting the development of productive capacity. To some degree the vagueness and lack of clarity in the statements of the socialist leaders on these questions is probably explained by a lack of well thought-out and precise hypotheses.

Christian socialism was not completely absent from the young Social Democratic movement. Its leading representative was A. K. Åkerberg, who had maintained the necessity of social reforms from a Christian point of view even before the appearance of socialism, particularly as the publisher of the magazine *Sanningssökaren (The Truth Seeker)*. Åkerberg joined the Social Democratic Club in Stockholm at an early date and was for a number of years one of the movement's more active and prominent members. According to Åkerberg Christianity really contained a kind of socialist teaching; the church had, however, deserted the original faith and had therefore become hostile to the demands for the remolding of society. At the end of the 1880s, however, he ceased to be active in the Social Democratic movement. He was forced out of the administration of the Social Democratic Union in October of 1888 because of articles he wrote on utilitarianism in the Gothenburg newspaper, *Handelstidning,* and thereafter directed sharp attacks against the movement's hostility toward religion. In a paper published in 1891 entitled "Contemporary Society and the Atheistic Social Democracy in Relation to Christianity," he pursued his theme of earlier articles that Christianity and socialism, correctly understood, were closely connected. Christianity should move closer to socialism, but socialism should also move closer to religion. Now the Social Democrats had undermined morality by placing all responsibility on society.

> By undermining moral concepts and extinguishing every trace of reverence for religion among the working people, Social Democratic agitation exerts an indescribably pernicious influence—as far as that influence extends. It is not counterbalanced by the services it renders in enlightening the workers about their interests and rights and about the deficiencies and terrible wrongs in contemporary society; for to lose faith in God, in mankind's higher nature and immortal destiny—this is a loss that nothing can replace.

Later Åkerberg also criticized "materialistic" socialism as contrary to just Christian socialism.

Åkerberg's Christian socialism seems to have won scant following. Only a single article has been found in the Social Democratic press which expresses a point of view of this type. In *Nya samhället* (*The New Society*), a newspaper which was published for only a few months and on which Åkerberg was a diligent collaborator, an article entitled "Christianity and Socialism" was published under the name "——n" which maintained a positive Christian stand. The socialists want, it said

> not to do away with religion, but only the unsound parts of it, nor do we want to do away either with the agents of religion, we want to cast away only those who have made religion a guise for humbug . . . In a word, we want to have a religion where the multitudes no longer cry for protection against hunger and cold, we want to have a Christendom where Christ is our ideal . . . the world's first real socialist.

It should be added that as far as is known no clergyman of the State Church or any person involved in the activities of the Church joined the party during this period. On the other hand, at least one member of the State Church clergy, J. Nylander, demonstrated his sympathies with the Social Democrats by, among other things, speaking at a May Day demonstration. Since Nylander was sentenced to suspension from the Church after some socialist-colored speeches, his political activity ceased. Up to the beginning of the 1900s the combination clergyman-socialist was probably regarded as unreasonable from the point of view of both socialism and the Church.

RESPECT FOR RELIGION, ATTACKS ON THE STATE CHURCH

The dominant line of the Social Democrats toward the religious questions becomes progressively modified during the first two decades of the twentieth century. Hostility toward religion declines until it almost disappears. Neutrality toward religion is emphasized with increasing vigor and Christians are welcomed into the party; a number of Christian socialists win influence and representative positions in the movement. The demand for the abolition of the State Church and all that was related to it is retained; in a number of points of secondary importance the ties between Church and State are weakened through the party's cooperation with the Liberals. However, tendencies appear to soften or remove even these points from the party program. It begins to seem doubtful whether the Social Democrats in a position of power would attempt to realize their principal demands.

Tactical viewpoints certainly contributed to this change, whether they were consciously formulated or only entered in the background that determined the formation of opinions. Even if there is cause to believe that a large part of the Swedish working class, to which the party primarily appealed, was irreligious, it is obvious that an atheistic propaganda placed certain limits on the party's development possibilities. With the party's expansion its hopes for popular support grew; in order to win this, the propagation of viewpoints which were not of central importance had to be given up. That the rank and file workers were not interested in the battle against the Church seems to be apparent from the fact that the increasing possibilities to disregard religious ceremonies (baptism, confirmation, church marriage) were utilized to only a limited extent. It is characteristic that the attempts to create a sort of secular substitute for confirmation received little encouragement. We should also bear in mind that the fight for democracy was carried on in collaboration with a party (the Liberals) which had the Nonconformist church movement as one of its central supports. Criticism of the State Church was not an obstacle here, but antireligious propaganda certainly was. The collaboration at elections, which occurred in many places before the victory of proportional representation, was especially inclined to emphasize this condition.

The cultural climate during the period of the party's fast development was very different from during the time of the movement's origins. In the 1880s, atheism, stimulated by sociology and natural science, was a young and forceful movement. Irreligiosity probably became more extensive later, but it lost its burning power; atheism turned to indifference or resignation. This development characterized middle class radicalism as well as Social Democracy. Aggressive and enthusiastic denials became old-fashioned; instead it became matter-of-course to emphasize one's metaphysical needs and to complain over the impossibility of satisfying them. The kind of pragmatic, general religiosity, which under the influence of William James, Bergson, and others began to serve as a surrogate for more precise beliefs had, however, little impact among the Social Democrats.

Certain changes within the party and its leadership were also of importance. Some of those who used the strongest language against the Church and religion—such as Danielsson and Palm—died or lost their positions. With the expulsion of the Young Socialists in 1908, the most active antireligious group disappeared from the party; and with the isolation of the Left Socialist opinion began a similar, even if not so obvious decline of the antireligious influence in the movement.

An essential factor in the increased moderation of the Social Democrats was a progressively new orientation within the Swedish State Church. It is idle to discuss whether the milder opinions of the Social Democrats determined the Church's attitude or whether the Church's conciliation influenced the Social Democrats. One can reasonably regard this as a case of interaction. Step by step hostility diminished on both sides; the sharp attacks became fewer, expressions in favor of a certain mutual acknowledgement (if with great reservations) more numerous. In this way, new ideological attitudes gradually developed. During the nineteenth century the Social Democrats had maintained that the Church and its doctrines were in necessary, and therefore irreconcilable, conflict with socialism; Church leaders had viewed the socialist goals on the whole as incompatible with Christianity. In the beginning of the 1900s, on the other hand, it frequently happened that each party blamed the other for the mutual hostility; the socialists said they had reacted to the Church's attacks, the Churchmen to the Social Democrats. Later it became usual for socialists to say they were critical of the Church basically or exclusively because of its lack of social radicalism; the Church, in turn, maintained that the socialists' indifference to religious values, not their social theory, constricted the Church's appreciation of socialism. In our day even this latter type of mutual attack has tended to disappear.

Only a few observations can be made here on the question of developments within the clergy. Above all it should be emphasized that the dominant opinion within the Church was and in all probability still is critical of Social Democracy. This condition seems obvious: socialism has won only very limited support in the upper class, to which the clergy in Sweden definitely belongs—in contrast to certain other countries. The majority of politically active State Church clergymen have belonged to the Conservative party; in public discussion the clergy's contributions have, as a rule, been conservatively colored, even when they have shown an interest in social reform. When we speak here of a change in the Church's position, we are referring to something else: basic assumptions, tone, interest in social problems, and especially the opinion about Social Democracy.

A survey of pastoral letters, records of clerical meetings, and the writings of clergymen on social problems of the period 1900-1920 gives a clear picture of this change. It is not infrequent that one finds utterances dating from the early part of this period in particular which directly or indirectly are aimed against the Social Democrats and which express or suggest a clearly conservative opinion. In his pastoral letter of 1901, Archbishop Ekman complained about the socialist agitation which incited the poor "to feel dissatisfied with their lot" and held out the promise "that they could find happiness by overthrowing society." The clergy ought to show sympathy with the poor, but also make clear the comparatively small worth of earthly goods. Authoritative statements of the same character were made at several clerical meetings. Also, pamphlets purely hostile to the Social Democrats were published by clerical propagandists. But the general impression is that the conservative line became less sharp, that the interest in social problems widened and deepened, and that tolerance toward the Social Democrats steadily won ground. In 1908 the National Swedish Clergyman's Association, founded in 1903, arranged Christian social work meetings in which the Church's duty to actively participate in welfare activities was consistently and strongly emphasized. At the National Swedish Clergymen's Conference held in 1912, following a lecture on "The Church and the World of the Worker," a resolution was passed that expressed "sympathy for the movement that is now developing in the workers' world, insofar as it is concerned with providing an opportunity for all to live worthy of human beings." Young clergymen and theologians sought to discuss and debate with the workers in an organization called The Crusaders for the Cross (*Korsfararrörelsen*).

The clergy discussed social problems in a number of tracts and declared themselves in favor of different forms of what was generally called Christian socialism. They maintained that the Church in the past had shown far too little interest in the earthly betterment of the poor, and that Christianity was obliged to take the lead even in this area. Not infrequently did the Christian socialists place themselves in opposition to the Marxists. At the same time, they preached tolerance toward Social Democracy, which, they hoped, would by degrees abandon its "one-sided materialist orientation" and show greater appreciation of the Church and religion. Sometimes the Church's interest in maintaining good relations with a powerful popular movement was emphasized. The Church should not, it was generally said, join its destiny with any specific political party. Bishop Personne, known as a marked conservative, wrote in his 1910 pastoral letter that the Church stood outside of the parties, but that a State Church clergyman could ally himself with socialism just as well as with other views. Certain clergymen—E. Klefbeck, H. Hallén—joined the Social Democratic party at this time.

With the naming of Nathan Söderblom as Archbishop in 1914, the strength of social interest and political tolerance in the Church was greatly enhanced. As Archbishop, Söderblom followed the orientation he had publicly advanced twenty years earlier, and he thus came to personify the new spirit within the Church. His positions on political and social problems were further clarified in his pastoral letters. The Church could not bind itself to any particular party or to any particular economic doctrine. But it was in the nature of the matter "that the sympathies [of the Church] rest with those in society who are burdened, and with those orientations, which seriously make the concerns [of the burdened] their own." The Archbishop repudiated the view that the Church should preach "submission and contentment . . . to the unfortunate and distressed," and that man should "retain poverty so that the tasted fruits of suffering may overflow." He repudiated "that kind of benevolence which the Church receives for political and social purposes from those who, because of their conservative political ideas, deign to regard themselves as her natural protectors without for a moment personally partaking of her message of judgment and salvation." The godlessness of the workers had nothing to do with the Christian duty of the Church; furthermore, one could hope that their feeling for religion would be awakened. The Archbishop also emphasized national values and the importance of national defense and his pastoral letters thus served to rally the nation.

A similar development occurred within the nonconformist church movement. The necessity of social reforms was emphasized and the contributions of the Social Democrats in this area were recognized. Early conservatism and *laissez faire* liberalism were replaced by a similarly religiously motivated social reformism.

Religion and questions regarding the Church were, as a rule, not thoroughly discussed at Social Democratic party congresses during this period; the changes that were made in the party programs do not manifest any change in the party's viewpoint on these questions. At the 1900 congress no proposal or exchange of opinion occurred on this or related subjects. At the 1905 congress, however, three motions were presented of which at least two came from Young Socialist quarters. The proposals were of the same import: they called for the inclusion of program points on the fight against religion, against "the stupefying effect of religion," and against religious expressions that conflict "with science and the development of society into a socialist order." The reporter for the party administration, Kata Dalström, stated that approval of the motions would cause religious strife within the party and cripple its activity. "Let us not force party workers to carry on atheistic propaganda in their activities, if they don't want to do so." A number of speakers withdrew their requests to enter the debate at the suggestion of Hinke Bergegren, who pointed out that a discussion would be meaningless, and Program Article IV was unanimously ratified as it stood. On the other hand, a resolution was adopted in connection with these motions after a short debate. It was directed against the influence of the Church in the administration of the schools.

> The Congress resolves to oppose clerical power over the school with all existing means, and declares that the complete freedom of schools from clerical control is an urgent cultural necessity. In relation to this, the Congress expresses itself in favor of nonreligious education at all levels in State-supported schools. In addition the Congress advocates that the party administration awaken interest and understanding for Social Democratic ideas through publications and lectures, including those especially intended for the young, and in this way oppose clerical influence and all manner of superstition.

The motions and debate make it clear that certain groups wanted to propagandize in favor of the workers' boycotting the Church, to the degree that it was allowed, for example, by not having their children baptised or confirmed.

At the following congress, in 1908, a number of motions on the religious question with clearly diverging purposes were proposed. On the one hand, it was proposed that the program include a provision on antireligious propaganda—on "the battle against religious humbug," the fight against "the stultifying religion," and the like. On the other hand, it was urged that a special statement be adopted to the effect that one should not scoff at or be blasphemous toward religious persons and that nothing prevented persons with religious views from entering the party. Nearly all the speakers in the debate urged that the Social Democrats attempt to win over even the religious workers and that for this and other reasons the party should not bind itself to an antireligious viewpoint. J. A. Henriksson, the reporter for the party administration, stated that religion would always exist, even if it took on new and higher forms with society's development. The motions favoring propaganda hostile to religion were apparently unanimously rejected without a vote. The program article was kept unchanged. In addition, with only minor differences of opinion, the congress passed a resolution proposed by the party leadership which was said to clarify the meaning of the program expression "religion as a private concern." It was emphasized that

> no one needs to desert his religious views in order to join the Social Democratic party; that this article obviously is not to be regarded as any restriction on the right of individual party members to discuss religious questions; but that it does mean an exhortation to all party members in such debates not to deride or insult religious persons because of their convictions . . . that, finally, the article demands that party members vigorously oppose all prevailing religious coercion now in society, in which connection the Congress wishes to emphasize the demand for the separation of school and Church as a growing exigency.

Thereby was it authoritatively established that the phrase "religion as a private concern," which originally had meant the demand for religious freedom and the elimination of all religious coercion, should be interpreted as including, among other points, prohibition of irreligious activity by the party itself.

In the three following congresses these questions were subject to little attention. In 1911 the program articles on the Church and school questions were ratified; a proposal for an article on "replacing dogma and catechism instruction with instruction in ethics and the history of religion" was rejected with reference to the on-going official investigation of the school question. At the 1914 congress a motion was proposed by the Stockholm party local, according to which the Riksdag group would be commissioned "to carry on vigorous activity for the secularization of the primary school . . . as well as for the separation of Church and state." This proposal was rejected at the insistence of the party administration, which declared its "eager hope and expectation" that the Riksdag group, independent of any statement from the Congress, would promote the points in the motion and the demands contained in the party program. The 1917 congress decided without debate, on the other hand—in support of the party administration's own pronouncement regarded a motion—to commission the administration to "take into consideration in what manner the party could diminish the influence of the State Church and prepare for its abolishment through special information activities and work in the communities."

The program commission appointed in 1919 proposed, on the one hand, that the words "freedom of religion" be introduced in the first article of the political program; on the other hand, that the article on the State Church (which should form Article VI instead of Article IV as before) have the following wording: "Abolition of the State Church. The properties administered by the Church to remain the possession of society." In consequence Article V should not demand "the separation of school and Church," but instead "a nonreligious educational system." The proposed amendments did not mean, stated the commission, to suggest any change in the party's stand. The purpose of the phrase "freedom of religion" was—as with the previously used formulation on religion as a private concern—to make clear "on the one hand, that the religious convictions of party members were their own private affair; on the other hand, that the society was not to exercise any coercion in the free observance of religion." The earlier formulation had overlooked religion's powerful role in solidifying community structure. From the demand for religious freedom, it directly followed "that the state shall not put a premium on a certain religious view through maintaining a State Church." In this connection it was important to establish that with the abolition of the State Church the Church properties must remain in society's possession. Concerning the liquidation of the State Church system, the committee further stated:

> Churches and chapels, which were built for religious purposes and are regarded by many citizens as the natural meeting place for religious observance, should be placed primarily at the disposal of the free church congregations. Upon liquidation it is naturally the obligation of society to do full justice in a human way to the interests of the corps of civil servants which is then separated from its employment in the service of society.

The program commission's proposal was recommended by the party administration and was approved at the 1920 party congress. A long debate ensued about Article VI. Rector Hallén appeared as its foremost opponent and urged the formulation: "The coercion of the State Church is to be abolished. Superfluous Church properties are to remain in the possession of Society." Hallén and other speakers (Ruth Gustafson, I. Englund) maintained that the party's rank and file, especially the women, were not prepared for a fight against the State Church, that nonconformist religion and obscurantism would increase if the Church were abolished, and that the Church showed increasing understanding of social questions. The spokesmen for the program commission—Engberg, Möller, O. Olsson—and others answered to this that above all the State Church system was incompatible with freedom of religion. One considered that what members of the nonconformist religious congregations believed could not be considered to be at a lower level than that of State Church members, and that moreover the cure for obscurantism lay in good popular education. Abolishing the State Church would, in reality, not appreciably increase the possibilities of sectarianism for dissenting religious propaganda was already allowed.

The Socialist Youth Union conducted fiercely antireligious propaganda, which was one of the causes that led to a split in the union in 1903. At the 1905 congress the union adopted a stringent resolution on the fight against "religious superstition in all its forms." The Social Democratic Youth Federation also evinced a more radical tendency than that which prevailed within the party. The 1907 congress of the federation accordingly ruled to let the federation board compose a pamphlet on "the means which could be used to avoid religious ceremonies." The 1909 Congress ruled to encourage the workers not to have their children baptised or confirmed, to keep them from getting instruction in the Christian religion, and not to obtain help from the clergy in entering marriage—"unless they consider that they should partake in such ceremonies because of their religious convictions." According to the 1914 congress the federation board should "to the greatest practicable extent direct the federation's agitation toward the separation of Church and State." In this connection the federation should conduct "intensive activities to propagate information on the lackey services rendered by both the State Church and the nonconformist churches in the pay of those in power against the people's freedom and rights." The decision was justified by the former Pastor Spak, who contended, among other things, that the fight against the State Church had been disregarded by the party and that it was therefore up to the youth to seek to carry it out. Liberal theology, represented by the new Archbishop, was especially dangerous from a socialist viewpoint.

In the Riksdag and—during the years 1917 to 1920—in the government, party representatives expressed themselves in favor of changes aimed at limiting the relations between state and Church and collaborated to execute such changes. Special attention was aroused by the decision originating through the initiative of Rydén, the Minister of Education, to cut down instruction in Christianity and, above all, in the catechism in the primary schools. A number of Riksdag debates dealt with the questions of nonreligious education, abolishing the clergy's special authority in the primary school, weeding out from the Constitution certain religious membership requirements for office, and instituting an inquiry into the possibility of abolishing the State Church. Several of the proposals were defeated by the opposition of the upper house, which was dominated by the Conservatives.

The question of the position of Social Democracy toward religion itself was, as a rule, not dealt with in these debates. On several occasions, however, leading Social Democrats maintained that the party was not hostile toward religion; at the same time the party's Conservative opponents sought to suggest that the criticism of the State Church and of confessional instruction was fundamentally motivated by antireligious views. An example is the debate in the 1906 Riksdag provoked by a Young Socialist leaflet, *The Yellow Peril,* in which Christianity was made the object of a fierce attack. Several speakers suggested that Social Democracy was at least partly responsible for the statements in the leaflet and for the propaganda hostile to religion in general. Branting sharply retorted, emphasizing the distinction between socialism and anarchism and explaining that Social Democracy had clearly shown its disapproval of the tendencies "to make the party into a party hostile to religion." Similar statements were expressed in several of the debates on concrete reform issues that we shall consider.

In the discussion of a proposal in the 1903 Riksdag which would excuse children from instruction in Christianity if their parents wished them to receive education of another kind, Branting stated that the question of religious instruction in the schools must be taken up in a larger context: "the demand for complete religious freedom in the schools, conceived in the sense of liberation from all that pertains to dogmatic religious instruction, is a demand which must be presented with increasing vigor, and which is in league with the future." Branting concurred with a proposal introduced at the 1911 Riksdag by a Liberal representative (Knut Kjellberg) that the study of religion replace Christianity as a subject of instruction. Either one must completely abolish religious education in the state schools or, preferably, give it the character of objective instruction in the content and development of religion. Another Social Democrat (Waldén) characterized confessional education as "an unwarranted and pernicious constraint of conscience." At the regular session of the 1918 Riksdag the lower house decided to support a proposal for an investigation into the introduction of nonreligious education in the state schools, among other items. The Social Democrats' leading spokesman for this demand was Engberg, chairman of the provisional house committee that treated the question. Engberg held that education which created idealism was necessary, but that it need not be given in religious dress. The upper house rejected the proposal. In a number of other contexts the principle of religious freedom was placed in antithesis to regulations applicable to the State Church system.

A proposal for an investigation concerning the dissolution of the relation between state and Church was presented at the regular session of the 1918 Riksdag through Social Democratic motions in both houses. In the upper house a provisional committee disapproved the proposal, which was subsequently defeated by an overwhelming majority. In the lower house the proposal was disapproved by a provisional committee against Social Democratic objections. Engberg, who was the Social Democrats' main speaker, made a long speech based on historical-philosophical viewpoints. The State Church system had come about "during and thanks to a certain order of production" and does not correspond to the prevailing social and economic conditions. "As the economic and social basis has shifted and broken down, so has the religious superstructure disintegrated as a natural consequence." The Church was a class institution just as much as the state. This was natural,

> for in the form of the State Church, the Church, in effect, represents the religiously organized state. As long as the state is ruled by the propertied and private capitalist class, one can expect that all Church action will also naturally express the interests of the private capitalist class. Such has also been the case in our country. In the beginning the Church worked openly with the bourgeoisie, and right up to the present we have heard voices from her clergy opposing the struggle for the freedom of the unpropertied classes.

In opposition to the abolition of the State Church some had argued that the Church at least served as a check on obscurantism. Even if this objection had a certain legitimacy and it was conceivable that the Church in an enlightened state might become a pioneer for a new view of life, the principle of religious freedom must nevertheless have priority over other considerations. Hallén said that he was certainly in favor of getting rid of all religious coercion, but considered it unwise from the Social Democratic standpoint to place religious life wholly outside of the sphere of the state. The idealistic goals that might sprout from within the Church must have state support. The democracy of the future "shall guarantee that no dark powers shall pursue their aims or in any way arrest the lifegiving current of freedom, the search for truth, and rightmindedness before the domains of religious life." The proposal for an investigation was passed with 54 votes to 48 opposed. Because of the very small number voting and the secret character of the vote, one is not able to draw precise conclusions from these figures. However, since it is certain that hardly any Conservatives and only a few Liberals voted for the proposal, it is probable that the great majority of Social Democrats supported it.

Of important fundamental significance was also the proposal for an investigation of the question of abolishing the Church Assembly's right of veto which was introduced by Engberg in the 1920 Riksdag. Both the proposed and the supportive report of the Constitutional Committee—prepared by Social Democrats and Liberals—stated that the Church was a branch of the organization of the state; it was an anomaly to give Church representatives the right of veto in certain questions in opposition to the state's regular organs, the cabinet and the Riksdag. The proposal for an investigation was passed by both houses. All of the Social Democrats who spoke favored the proposal, though the socialist clergy (Hallén and Klefbeck) gave somewhat different reasons for their support.

A study of the handling of the religious question in representative Social Democratic newspapers and pamphlets shows that the neutrality principle was generally adhered to. Attacks on religion occurred, but they were characterized by less hostility than during the breakthrough period and had become more and more rare. It was often emphasized that antireligious propaganda was not the party's concern, and that Christians could be good socialists. The Young Socialist press was an exception; it excelled in blasphemy and contempt for religion. After the expulsion of the Young Socialists in 1908, however, the party could no longer be regarded as responsible for this.

Particularly notable is Branting's transformation. After the turn of the century he never seems to have made derogatory statements about Christianity and religion of the sort which were usual during his utilitarian period and which even occurred in the beginning of the 1890s. A number of articles in *Social-Demokraten* from the first year of this century show a consciously wrought out change in policy of action. An editorial in *Social-Demokraten* in 1900 entitled "Workers of [Religious] Faith and Socialism" emphasized that socialism was not hostile to Christianity, that Socialism wanted to assemble all workers "for the rights of labor against capitalist oppression," and that in working for this goal "Christians and free-thinkers could readily stand side by side." An article published in 1903 treated the subject "Socialism and Christianity" from the same point of view. Social Democracy was open to Christians. Many of the clergy had been defenders of the existing order and therefore strife had arisen. "But this strife has nothing to do with everyone's right to form and follow his own convictions in religious matters." The main idea was that people should be free to take a position, whether this resulted in religion's triumph or in its downfall. The following year the religious question was discussed in the Stockholm party local with Branting as the introductory speaker and Bergegren as his main opponent. The local passed a resolution proposed by Branting which maintained that according to the party program the Church must be completely divorced from the school and the state, but that religion should be kept out of the discussion. "In opposition to the attempt to make religion a pretext for splitting the solidarity essential to the working class, the meeting urges all party members to avoid religious disagreements in their work within the party for a better society. Such disagreement can only serve to arrest the progress of the workers . . ." Bergegren's proposal, which was rejected, contained an admonition to the party to "oppose public religious manifestations that conflict with science and with society's development into a socialist order." The question came up a couple of years later through a proposal made by Algot Ruhe for agitation against certain religious ceremonies (especially the rites of baptism and confirmation). Branting disapproved this tactic, which he considered incompatible with the principle of religion as a private concern, and added to his criticism of the proposal a declaration of principle:

> He who has written this has himself drawn the consequences of his personal opinion on religious questions without ostentation. That not all free-thinkers are similarly inclined to do this may be regrettable, but they can often have fairly valid excuses of a purely private nature. But as editor of *Social-Demokraten* it is not, from my point of view, my task to propagandize for my personal non-Christian views. In this capacity I have to adhere to the party's program article regarding religion as a private concern, that is to say, to work for general enlightenment on a firm scientific basis, but not to make the party organ into a battlefield for one kind or another of anti-religious propaganda.

Erik Hedén, in addition to Lidforss, the party's leading culture critic during this time, held to the same line as Branting.

This rule formulated by Branting was not always followed. But the exceptions occurred in such contexts, they could rather be said to confirm they rule. Carleson sometimes placed religion in a Marxist schema: the middle class was realistic and antiauthoritarian in its fresh and victorious youth, but in later days it tended to turn from "a splenetic scepticism" to "the old pious faith." Ossian-Nilsson had published an article in *Arbetet* containing a number of remarks hostile to Christianity; this was reprinted in *Social-Demokraten,* but the editorial page of the latter paper also included a negative critique by Natanael Beskow. Engberg, who by the end of the 1910s had become the party's most energetic anticlericalists, inserted in some articles mainly dealing with the Church question—their fundamental ideas will be considered presently—a critical analysis of Christianity as a socially conditioned view. The paper subsequently published reactions to these articles from the Christian viewpoint and stated, in answer to a question, that Engberg's articles had not represented the viewpoint of the party and that nothing prevented Christians from belonging to the party.

At the same time that *Social-Demokraten,* in the first article cited, extended a welcome to religious persons to join the Social Democrats, *Arbetet* declared —in an editorial "The 'Believers' and the Organization"—that any hostility to Christianity was alien to the party. Social Democracy had, on the contrary, had a restraining, diversionary effect on hostility to religion, which had naturally developed as a result of the distorted relation between the Church and politics. Only when religion had been used as a shield for the protection of economic interests and the *status quo* had socialism intervened. The declaration of the party program that religion was a private concern, implied that dogmatic denial of religion was as alien to the party as dogmatic adherence to certain articles of faith. The principles developed here were in large measure adhered to. Two of the paper's most prominent contributors—Lidforss and Engberg—were to some degree exceptions to this. When Ruhe made the proposal previously mentioned, Lidforss concurred in most respects with Branting's article in *Social-Demokraten,* but maintained that Branting went too far in his opposition to antireligious propaganda. If the Social Democrats really wanted to realize their demand for the abolition of the State Church, "then it is imperative that we also throw a critical light upon the quality of the spiritual sustenance that the state offers its people through the Church and the clergy. And how shall this be accomplished to any appreciable extent if not through our party organs?" In accordance with this standpoint Lidforss often criticized theological works and sometimes also expressed general opinions on religion as a hindrance to socialism. "It may be true," he wrote in an article answering Paul Rosenius' criticism,

> that socialism has very little to do with Darwinism, and there is also some truth in the contention that it does not have anything in common with atheism, but nevertheless atheism is a better soil for socialism than Christianity. If one postpones the solution of The Social Question to a life after this, one cannot have a deeper interest in solving it now or in protesting violently against it. This has also been recognized by the wielders of power . . . But quite apart from the direct benefit the workers' movement might gain from the dissolution of Christian dogmas, do not we non-Christian freethinkers feel that it is our simple duty to truth to openly state our

opinion of Christian superstitions, which even today make the air oppressive in castle and cottage alike.

In articles in *Arbetet* as well as in *Social-Demokraten,* Engberg's religious views were influenced by Marx and were asserted to be the consequences of a materialist concept of history. Religion was an ideological result of a fixed order of production. "The extraordinary apparatus up in the sky reveals itself as the negative of the earthly sphere projected into the celestial vault . . . Man's heaven stands as a protest against his earth." The complete freedom which man will obtain in the socialist society eliminates every external norm, even of a religious nature.

"The ought" is then at the same time preserved and abolished. The norm has coalesced with that which it would regulate. Man has realized morality by abolishing it. So also with regard to religion. As long as man stands before the Divinity, he is still in the realm of necessity. For in his creation he is determined by the Divinity. Freely creating, man will have conquered the state of opposition between himself and the divine . . . Thereby it is at the same time preserved and abolished. Man has realized religion by abolishing it.

These ideological assumptions were used in the long view, it should be noted, as arguments in the ongoing debate on the Church and religion. Especially sharp attacks were directed at certain churchmen's attempts to establish closer relations between the Church and Social Democracy. Archbishop Söderblom and others were accused of deliberate efforts to achieve a certain conciliation in order to save the Church; the new protestantism was a means "to politically corrupt the nation." The Church was really the same, no matter what the guise in which she appeared. "It is the bulwark of reactionaries, evil men, and liars in the battle between light and darkness, between truth and falsehood among mankind's children." The thought put forth from Christian quarters that the creation of good men would bring about the good society was unreasonable: men were shaped by the system of production and it was therefore necessary to change this. Along with this Engberg, like Lidforss, emphasized his "metaphysical need" and his cultural idealism. Christianity's "vulgar happiness morality" made it "a pernicious hindrance to the growth of a culturally worthy idealism." Socialism opposed this morality. "The Kingdom of bliss and felicity is, in addition, an immoral chimera, a calamitous inheritance from the Christian happiness morality, which is one of culture's most dangerous enemies . . . It is to Karl Marx's everlasting credit that he rooted out the whole pernicious view of happiness morality from socialism's outlook." While Christian opinion criticized socialism as materialistic, Engberg attacked Christianity as a cheap happiness doctrine.

The point of departure here is a line of thinking in Hegelian-Marxist metaphysics.

The parting of the ways among different lines that these examples suggest appear throughout the Social Democratic press. The neutrality principle is, however, fundamental. No representative Social Democratic newspaper seems to have systematically conveyed antireligious propaganda.

Two debates between Social Democrats and churchmen in the beginning of the 1900s are of interest in this context. In April 1907 a discussion was arranged in the town of Vansäter between Kata Dalström and the curate D. Grankvist on the topic "Can a Christian be a Social Democrat?" The Social Democratic speaker maintained in her remarks and in her resolution proposal, adopted by the meeting, that original Christianity worked for the sharing of property and for brotherly love and accordingly was in close agreement with the views of Social Democracy. The Churches had corrupted this teaching and made it into a support for the capitalist system; as examples of antisocialist religious leaders she named Bishop Billing and Bishop Waldenström, among others. Religious instruction based on Church dogmas, "which is given in our schools must be replaced with Jesus of Nazareth's doctrine of love and righteousness, so that children from the beginning may learn to understand that brotherhood and love of one's fellow man, which are the driving forces in Social Democracy, are also the driving forces in the ethic of Jesus of Nazareth." The answer to the question put to the meeting "must be that a Christian not only can, but ought to be, a Social Democrat." The clergyman debater sought to show that Social Democracy was hostile to religion and criticized the class conflict theory and the materialist concept of history from a religious standpoint.

In 1908 there occurred an enlightening newspaper polemic between the curate A. Sandin and the young Social Democrat, Rickard Sandler. The former had stated in a sermon that the socialists wanted to de-Christianize the people and "implant the coarsest paganism, not the paganism that can be characterized as a groping and seeking after God, but a paganism that wants to feed on hate and wade in blood." In answer to a question by Sandler he went on to say that Social Democracy was a threat to Christianity. Sandler sought in detail to show the contrary.

> Social Democracy has abstained from taking a party position in religious questions, whether to the advantage or disadvantage of Christianity . . . it is calumnious to blame Social Democracy when Christians and their leaders not only chose not to join, but also to oppose in all ways the movement which is the first prominent, earnest, and powerful endeavor to realize the moral principles, which Christianity has the honor to lend its name to.

Like many other Social Democrats, Dalström and Sandler made a definite distinction between the fundamental principles of Christian teaching and the views held by the existing State Church. The former were declared to be not only compatible with, but even to provide the prototype for socialism; the latter were attacked as the antithesis of socialism. This line, which was close to Christian socialism, was sharply distinct from both the dominant line of absolute neutrality, best exemplified in Branting's formulation of this principle, and from the sociological-philosophical antireligious line propagated by Lidforss and Engberg. All of these viewpoints differed from the breakthrough period's direct and hard anti-Christian agitation.

In regard to their fundamental position on the State Church and related questions, the great majority of Social Democratic statements during this time are characterized by a unified opinion. The bond between the state and Church ought to be dissolved; above all, confessional education ought to be completely eliminated. This opinion appeared even among certain Social Democrats who evinced an appreciation of the Christian religion. The general justification for the latter demand was based on the belief that full religious freedom could not be considered to exist as long as the state favored a certain church, trained youth in the doctrines of this church, and in different ways was connected with the church. This originally liberal thought stood as a fundamental principle; freedom of religion—like freedom of speech, the press, and assembly—was characterized as a civil right and the abolition of the State Church was its obvious consequence. But hereto was added the thought that Church influence, especially in the schools, worked in a conservative direction; the Church could, to a certain degree, be regarded as one of the propaganda institutions supported by the State or allied with it which were in the service of the existing social order. Especially under the influence of the French debate, the fight against the State Church was often characterized as a culture struggle for civilization (*kulturkamp*).

In a pamphlet published in 1918, Engberg systematically developed his viewpoint on the problem of the State Church. During the feudal period a unified church had corresponded to the prevailing system of production. Religious division had occurred with the growth of the burgher class. Protestantism had sought to guarantee itself a certain unity through the state. This order was natural only so long as burgher rule was undisturbed; the Church had then embodied "the vital idea world of the ruling class." When the working class marched forth, the Church "was compelled to seek a *modus vivendi*." The Church had chosen to be a people's church, "a church that protected freedom and culture, progress, and the people as a nation." But "reality lacked the foundation for the realization of these fantasies"; the gulf between the classes must also be "a gulf in the idea world of the people's religion." When Social Democracy has "directed itself against the connection between Church and state and has demanded a free Church and freedom of religion, it has only stated what factual reality logically points to." When the ruling class defended the State Church system it really only did so in self-defense. The existing order ought to be degrading the Church "because it reduces her to a purely parasitic existence."

The primary demand was the abolition of confessional education. Pamphlets and newspaper articles attacked the existing system of education on this point. The form of pedagogy used (especially teaching of the catechism) was declared to be archaic and anachronistic, but the system itself was also criticized from a more fundamental viewpoint. The inculcation of certain dogmatic beliefs tended from the start to limit the possibilities for free intellectual activity and consequently resulted in dullness and shallowness. In any case many of the statements and views presented in this teaching as true were unreasonable and doubtful. The time which was devoted to the catechism and biblical history should be given to the natural sciences or languages to really increase the possibility for the acquisition of useful knowledge. It was often maintained that nonconfessional education must be introduced as soon as parliamentary strength would allow it, even if it became necessary to postpone the complete realization of other points regarding the State Church contained in the party program. "Delay not one day longer than necessary in the preparation of a religious instruction for our schools which is free of dogma," proclaimed a representative editorial in *Ny Tid* in 1919.

> Religiously inclined men and women have their place in every culture. But let us be spared dogmas, let us be spared all that is old, mouldering, mummified, which we have dragged with us through the centuries, and which is incompatible with modern culture . . . Social Democracy has perhaps more immediate tasks just now than to take up the fight for the separation of Church and state . . . But what can not be postponed is the creation of a religious instruction for children and youth that is free of dogma, and [action] to deprive the clergy of the influence over the schools, which it has and which it abuses all too often for it to remain uncensured.

As a rule one assumed that the instruction then current would be replaced by objective instruction about different religions, partly also by instruction in ethics. Sometimes it was urged that all instruction that was intended to impart fixed value norms be abolished.

In general the Social Democrats apparently assumed the dissolution of the relation between state and Church would be brought about through successive steps. Among the reforms—other than the introduction of nonreligious education—which were given particular consideration in the debate were burial without Church rites and the right to freely leave the State Church. After these and other preliminary changes had been accomplished, the question of the complete abolition of the State Church would be taken up.

Scattered opinions in the press show, however, that a good deal of uncertainty was associated with the question of principle involved in the abolition of the State Church. One of the viewpoints most often put forth in this context is suggested by Branting in a leading article on "Civil Burial" in 1910. The principle of religion as a private concern, he emphasized, was incompatible with the State Church system. But when the abolition of this system came about, one must see to it "that the civil state does not heedlessly release the ties by which it binds the Church." With such a reform, the state must

> be well armed against the power encroachments which will quite certainly be attempted by certain obscurantist groups. The increasingly frequent Waldenströmian paeans to the Catholic Church, which never submitted to state power but rules with power over millions of souls, show clearly enough where our Swedish sectarian popes look for their models.

In abolishing the State Church one would have to ensure that the state retained the instruments of power necessary to the preservation of cultural values. Similar points of view were put forth by Erik Hedén, especially in a *Tiden* article in 1909. The State Church ought to be abolished, but this could not suitably be brought about from a culture viewpoint until an up-to-date school reform had been accomplished and found to work. Another problem was whether the enormous property of the State Church should be turned over to one or more uncontrolled religious organizations. Other party newspapers emphasized the view that a number of religious sects existing outside of state supervision might present a greater danger than one State Church of a relatively high level and controlled by the State. In *Arbetarbladet* it was stated as early as 1913—probably by its editor, N. S. Norling—that the demand for the abolition of the State Church should be stricken from the party program; during recent years sympathy for the State Church had increased within the party, "maybe not least because certain forms of sectarian religious activity have been found to be so questionable that they called for a strong counterweight." On another occasion the paper proclaimed "that nothing has been able to convince us that it would be advantageous from the state's point of view to allow the Church to descend to [a level] to which conditions following a divorce might drive her down to the level of intolerance and ignorance where, from what one can gather, most of the contemporary nonconformist churches are already to be found." After the 1920 party congress it was stated that the majority at the congress certainly represented a majority of the party's membership. A view more friendly to the State Church, however, had emerged in certain circles. "When the question becomes an immediate political issue, it is far from certain that one can expect to find anything approaching a coherent and unified Social Democratic opinion." In another of the party's leading newspapers, *Örebro-Kuriren,* similar views were stated. Between two evils, in this case the State Church and the nonconformist churches, one ought to choose the lesser of the two, "a State Church which can be legislated into keeping itself within certain bounds." Hesitation was even expressed about the suitability of now attempting to obtain nonreligious education. After the reform of the plan of instruction for primary schools was accomplished in 1920, its author, Rydén, urged that the demand for such instruction should not be taken up immediately; the important thing was to defend what had already been gained through the reform.

Acceptance of the Existing Order

AFTER 1920 some of the reforms in the areas discussed here, which had long been aims of the Social Democratic party, were accomplished. Thus have provisions been made for civil burial, changes in legislation have lessened the influence of the clergy in the parish, the clergy's special authority has been abolished in the municipality's handling of school matters, and certain constitutional provisions regarding religious qualifications for office holding have been relaxed or abolished. Proposals made on other important points have come to nothing. A committee, which completed its work in 1928, proposed provisions for freedom to leave the State Church, but this proposal did not lead to any measures by the government. Nor did an investigation into the Church Assembly's right of veto lead to any proposal in the Riksdag.

On the other hand, in the main questions of the introduction of a nonreligious education and the severance of the bond between state and Church, the Social Democratic party did not carry through the activities initiated before the advent of complete democratization. Though the party program was not changed, debates at the party congresses, in the Riksdag, and in the press suggest that in recent times the party *has not wished* to work for these reforms. The program articles on these reforms generally seem to have been regarded as dead letters. The neutrality line on religion, which had been largely accepted in the first decade of the 1900s, also became dominant in later years in regard to the Church. If one considers recent years, it is not an exaggeration to speak of a benevolent neutrality. Of central importance, however, is the fact that a progressive change of opinion has led to a viewpoint that can be characterized as a general acceptance of the existing order. This new viewpoint has also manifested itself in increased Social Democratic participation in elections to various Church organizations and offices, such as the election of the Church Assembly, Church delegates, and clergy. Social Democratic influence on certain agencies of the Church has, in turn, affected party opinion in favor of the Church.

The new situation can be regarded as a consequence of foregoing developments together with the party's increasing strength and power. Though the party often attempted to make a rigorous distinction between its position toward religion and its position toward the Church, the close relation between these attitudes is obvious. When the attack on Christianity ceased, one of the basic motives for the attacks on the Church also disappeared. Social Democratic animosity toward the Church naturally abated for other reasons during the long succession of years when the party held executive power or was the permanent leading contender for it. References to the Church as the helpmate of the bourgeois state were no longer convincing. The Church as a conservative factor appeared less dangerous to the nation's largest party, which willingly assumed the responsibility of government, than to a small party which was hesitant before the demands of parliamentarianism. The view of freedom of religion underwent a similar modification. Above all: here as in other areas, there was a conflict between what the party propagated and what it really wanted to accomplish during the time when it was solely in the role of the opposition; but with increased power this conflict became obvious.

Social Democracy's increased appreciation of the Church during recent years is related to the changing political environment during this period. When the international situation changed, the defense of democracy and of national independence came to overshadow all other goals; controversial questions which earlier appeared central receded into the background. The National Socialist regime in Germany strengthened sympathies for the democratic order in Sweden within the Church and in religious congregations in general; it also led to a more positive evaluation of the advantages associated with this order. Interaction between Social Democracy's moderate and national policies, on the one hand, and the increased democratic consciousness of the Church and other religious organizations, on the other, has rapidly mollified the sense of fundamental antagonism. Ideologically the *rapprochement* has often appeared in the form of a strong emphasis on certain common assumptions, such as the esteem placed on the value of the individual and on intellectual freedom.

The nonsocialist Left underwent substantially the same development as the Social Democratic party. Even in this section of the population criticism of the Church has been silenced. Not even the nonconformist church groups have campaigned for the abolition of the State Church in recent years.

During the 1920s and 1930s, on the whole, the principles of political neutrality and social interest came increasingly to pervade the activities of the Church. Developments thus progressed further in the direction indicated. It is probably unnecessary to delve deeply into this well-known state of affairs. A recent investigation of the social content in sermons published by a clergyman maintained that clergymen still devote too little interest to The Social Question, but the investigation, nevertheless, shows that on the whole, social reformist attitudes are incomparably more pronounced in sermons of recent years than at the end of the nineteenth century. Authoritative statements made in pastoral letters and at meetings of clergymen emphasize the importance of The Social Question; attacks on socialism have hardly ever come from such quarters in recent years.

Of importance to Social Democracy's relation to the Church and religion has been the appearance of Christian socialism as an organized force within the party. In 1924 a Christian group within the Social Democratic party was founded in Örebro. After this a number of similar groups were established in different places, which united in 1929 to form the Swedish Union of Christian Socialists. (Since 1938 it has been called the Swedish Union of Christian Social Democrats (*Sveriges kristna social-demokraters förbund*).) In 1933 the organization, whose first chairman was Bertil Mogärd (who served as a rector in Stockholm from 1930 on), included 23 groups with around 700 members; by 1939 it comprised 140 groups with 3500 members. The large majority of the members belong to free church congregations. During recent years several riksdagsmen have been members of the union. A press owned by the union publishes a weekly paper *Broderskap* (*Brotherhood*) and a series of publications that put forth the union's aims. In some elections the Christian Socialists have drawn up separate lists under the name of the Social Democratic party.

The union laid down its general principles in a program. The development of the individual and of society toward freedom and righteousness is best achieved by making Christ's teaching a living thing; God is our Father and the conditions of society should thus rest on the brotherhood of all; all men should bear the same obligations toward one another and enjoy the same political, economic, and social rights; a social democracy is the form of society which agrees with the Gospel. The goals of the union are said to be the application of the principles of the Gospel in the life of society so that the fruits of work shall accrue to those who work, to create a society resting on Christian brotherhood, to prevent war by all permissible means, to work against the use of intoxicating beverages, and to obtain justice and economic security for all in its principal adherence to the program of the Social Democratic Workers' party. Every group in the union should collectively join the Social Democratic workers' commune in its district.

The views expressed in the union's publications imply, in the first place, that the Christian doctrine correctly interpreted in accordance with its original form leads to a political and social program in general agreement with that of Social Democracy. Yet implementation of this program does not satisfy man's spiritual needs; this can only be achieved through religion. A socialist order of society tends to give man greater possibilities to occupy himself with spiritual concerns and it will therefore work to the advantage of Christianity. The first issue of *Broderskap* explained, in agreement with an English socialist, that "socialism is Christianity applied to economic life." One of the union's brochures states that it considers

> that through its political contributions and in its entire policy Social Democracy best furthers the social ideals contained in the Gospels; that it thereby follows the right way from the Christian viewpoint: reform and organization rather than violence and revolution; and that Social Democratic policy is thus the most appropriate instrument for a Christian transformation of society.

The Christian Socialists, writes *Broderskap,* "do not enter into such foolhardy attempts as to politicize their faith. It is their Christian faith which made them socialists . . . [They have] been Christians first, politicians second." The Christian Socialists should make Christians socially active and create a religious revival in socialism. "It has been the Christians' . . . grave error to have promised that all social questions would solve themselves, if only men became Christians. It is, however, quite a banal truth that not a single social question can be solved without concrete proposals and planning." Before the 1936 election the union's journal maintained that "the obviously un-Christian act of overthrowing the welfare government must be redeemed on September 20th by the voters' providing a majority for the resumption of welfare policies and for Christian influence on these policies . . . Should we not support the party that creates peace and security for the people and thereby paves the way for Christian faith?"

The union's publications often appeal to Christians who disassociate themselves from politics, particularly to those who have doubts about the Social Democrats for religious reasons. It is the duty of Christians as Christians to form opinions on social problems and to actively assert such opinions. A Christian who "restricts himself to saving his own soul and then to winning a soul here and there, but who leaves society, impregnated with iniquity, to remain as it is . . . is not evangelical." It is through politics that one influences society and "Christianity and politics consequently belong together." The publications point out that Social Democracy was formerly hostile to religion, but that this is no longer the case. Yet they also, perhaps especially so earlier, maintained that Social Democracy should officially recognize the legitimacy of Christian interests. This would, it has been said, be advantageous to the party, which now loses a number of votes for religious reasons. *Broderskap* has in several articles, in opposition to the program, favored the preservation of the State Church and education. Proposals in accordance with these views have also been presented at party congresses—as we shall see shortly. Peace and temperance have been promoted with particular zeal in the union's agitation.

The socialist theories which have customarily been considered incompatible with a Chrstian view have been subject to lively debate within the union. As a rule Christian Socialists have repudiated, or at least criticized, important points in Marxist social doctrine, especially the materialist concept of history. But it has been stated that to a certain extent Marxism can be accepted by Christians, as long as it is not regarded as a philosophy of life. One article states: "As long as socialism finds an inheritance in Marxism worthy of cultivating, it is the task of the Christian Social Democrat to bring Marxism to humility and insight into its limitations by dialectically placing the life of the soul and the categories of eternity in opposition to it." The concept of class conflict was held to be natural under given conditions; at the same time, however, the Christian goal was said to be to mitigate and eliminate it."

In regard to the Christian Socialist movement, it should finally be emphasized that it showed almost no tendencies to support the more conservative faction in Social Democracy in economic and social questions, as one might possibly suppose. On several occasions the union's journal has favored the socialization of production or has otherwise taken the radical viewpoint in this area. Christian socialists have ardently espoused the thought that the principle of free competition can not be approved from a Christian point of view as the driving force of development because it stands in opposition to the basic Christian principles of brotherhood and solidarity.

Religion and Church questions were not dealt with at the 1924 congress. At the 1928 congress a motion was proposed for amendment of the program article on the State Church. This article was considered by the proposer, apparently incorrectly, liable to interpretation as a demand for the abolition of the State Church "as a sect" and was, therefore, not compatible with the demand for freedom of religion. On this ground an elucidation was demanded that would clearly spell out the abolition of the State Church would only mean that this collective would be placed on a par with other sects. The motion was defeated at the urging of the program commission and party administration. The report of the program commission made it clear what the abolition of the State Church would mean:

> the system of state religion will be transformed into an order in which the churches are equal before the state and in which the citizens themselves freely decide whether they want to belong to any church at all and if so, to which. Since religious freedom must be understood to mean just such an order, the abolition of the State Church, far

from being in conflict with religious freedom, seems, on the contrary, to be its prerequisite.

The 1932 congress dealt with a motion by the Stockholm party local which, among other items, requested an opinion on the position of party members and the election of Church delegates. The congress held, in agreement with the party administration, that there was nothing to prevent the party's representation in legal Church organs: "Concerning Church commissions of trust, it should be left to the party members to decide themselves to what degree they, in accepting such commissions, consider themselves able to protect the interests of their principals in the Church's domain." In agreement with the Stockholm party local, the congress considered it suitable in election campaigning in the parishes that one "strongly emphasize the important economic interests that are here involved and avoid all that can give the impression that the party represents a position hostile to religion." No differences of opinion on this point came forth at the congress.

Not until the party's 1936 congress was the State Church problem gone into in any detail. Not less than six motions, of which one was put forth by the Christian Socialist Union and several others came from the same quarters, urged that the article on the abolition of the State Church be removed from the program or substantially modified. One of the motions was recommended in the main by the Västerås party local; the Stockholm party local which had brought a motion itself, disapproved it. The motion proposed by the Christian Socialist organization put forth that Article VI in the program should read either "The assertion of societal life in Church institutions" or "Cultural and spiritual values in general are to be maintained and made fruitful in societal life." In favor of the proposal it was stated that the article on the abolition of the State Church had not been made an issue by the party, whether in the government or as the opposition. It could no longer be asserted that a majority of party members wanted to realize this demand. "The Church is no longer an institution which the labor movement must view as an enemy to its purposes. As [Church] organs have been filled with representatives of Social Democracy, the Church, on the contrary, has shown itself to have the capacity to attain a view of social righteousness that has been useful in the formation of socialist thought in societal life." Because of this and the fact that the program article was often interpreted as a manifestation of hostility to religion, it should be replaced by a general statement of the kind mentioned. Another motion added over and above these points that "there is reason for Social Democracy to test whether evangelical Christianity is not a temporal power to reckon with in the battle against the dangers that threaten democracy from the violent movements which are progressing. With all its frailty, it seems that a part of the German Church nevertheless offered the all-devouring Nazi State an active resistance."

The party commission and party administration urged the rejection of the motions. According to the former, "with the broad religious freedom that has already been won within the basic framework of the present order . . . the demand for the abolition of the State Church does not have any special urgency." However, the demand for religious freedom could not "logically be realized if the different professions of faith did not have freedom and equality in relation to the State." The commission wished to give this view "an expression consistent with principle" through the formulation of Article VI. This did not have "any tendencies hostile to the Church or religion," but only wished to state "a scarcely avoidable consequence of the full realization of religious freedom." The party administration agreed in this. It did not want to deny that this article of the party program "does not agree with the development which the party's practical policies have undergone in this area," but that because of the reasons advanced by the program commission the article ought not be considered until a general program revision was undertaken.

The congress decided without voting to reject the motions. Only one speaker, a member of the Christian Socialist Union (E. Gustafsson), spoke in defense of the view expressed in the motions; he recapitulated in the main the arguments given in the union's motion. The criticism of the motions—put forth by five speakers—is notable from the standpoint that they did not demand that the program article they defended be realized; as a rule they assumed this would not happen. All of the speakers opposed all antireligious propaganda. One speaker (Oskarsson) stated that he certainly favored the abolition of the State Church, but he appears here to have been motivated by regard for the Church; it should, he said, "to the greatest possible degree be independent of the state in order to be able to serve Christian ideas." Another speech (E. O. Wiklund) declared that it was doubtful whether "we must stand guard over it [the State Church] at any price." The motions were interpreted as expressions of the tendency to regard a certain religious persuasion as the only right one and they were criticized mainly on this basis. The three most prominent speakers, Engberg, Fast, and Höglund, did not demand either that the discussed program article be carried through. Fast stated that the present formulation of the article did not agree with actual developments. This lack of correlation, however, did not involve any misunderstanding. "Everyone knows very well the party's aims and precisely where we stand." Höglund stated

> that the question of the abolition of the State Church, sad to say, is not a contemporary issue and probably will not become one for a very long time. As long as we have such enlightened Church ministers as Arthur Engberg, probably none of us would even suggest actualizing it. It is better to have an enlightened state that rules over an unenlightened church than to have an uncontrolled, unenlightened clergy without any state control whatsoever.

It was suggested that the Christian Socialists wanted to run "a sort of mission in the party, and instead of campaigning to make Christians into socialists, work to make socialists into Christians . . ." Engberg, the party administration's reporter, considered that the demand for the abolition of the State Church could only be understood as a consequence of the demand for religious freedom. The question of the State Church system was a subordinate question; the main thing was religious freedom. But this was actually already very great. The suitability of drawing the ultimate consequence of the principle of religious freedom must "be dependent on the given context and the given circumstances." Other viewpoints were added to this reasoning. Engberg could not believe "that the public, for the time being and in the foreseeable future, has the right to disclaim concern with the question of how the religious culture is to be molded." State regulation of the education of the clergy would be advantageous. The speaker feared also that if the State Church were abolished, the reactionary, powerfully-equipped Catholic Church would become the strongest church. "I see therefore . . . in the preservation of the existing order a not unsuitable but rather a valuable guarantee against the danger that Roman Catholicism represents, which, if the present order did not exist, according to my way of thinking, could be quite serious for our people."

The decision and, above all, the debate at the 1936 party congress shows that at this time the program demand for the abolition of the State Church was no longer regarded as a directive for the party's activities, but as a historic relic, possibly as a declaration of "principle" without any "practical" meaning whatsoever. As elsewhere in corresponding contexts, it was stated that the demand was not a question of current importance, in other words, one would leave it to "circumstance" to lend it urgency. Two factors in the debate are especially worth mentioning. The opinion now was that the abolition of the State Church was really only a sort of formal consummation of religious freedom; since the latter already was substantial, the State Church question was of secondary importance. Earlier, the State Church had been criticized from very different, specifically Socialist points of view, but these were not mentioned at all at the congress. Further: when views based on religious freedom were put forth previously it was maintained that the very existence of the State Church system meant a negation of this freedom. The other notable line of thought is particularly emphasized in Fast's speech. According to this, the program did not agree with developments, but this was not serious because the party's real aims were generally known. The reason given for keeping the program article was that no one believed that the party would seek to realize it.

The handling of Church and school questions in the Riksdag made it clear that as early as the beginning of the 1920s the majority of the party had in practice ceased to try to implement the party program. When in the 1921 Riksdag proposals were made to increase the teaching of Christianity in the primary schools—in general implying that the reductions made on Rydén's initiative would disappear—the Social Democrats certainly opposed the proposals, but they did not oppose the principle of confessional education. Thus, Rydén stated that the rupturing of the school should be prevented "through retaining—at least for our generation—Christian instruction in the schools, but giving it a more universally Christian character." Engberg said that he recognized "fully the necessity of solid, good, objective, and historical Christian teaching . . . so designed that it does not imply any violation of freedom of religion and freedom of conscience for vast numbers of citizens in this country." The standpoint generally maintained in the 1920 program and in the press debate around it had consequently been abandoned. The strong support that the proposals for an increase in Christian instruction won in the other parties probably contributed to the Social Democrats' wholly giving up the thought of a nonreligious education or for any thoroughgoing reform of religious education in the schools. At the time of the 1927 school reform it was once again made clear that the party refrained from promoting its programmatic line.

In the 1923 Riksdag proposals were introduced in the lower house for an investigation into the abolition of the State Church by a nonconformist church Liberal and by three Communists. The provisional house committee that handled the proposals urged their rejection because, among other reasons, the question lacked all contemporary interest. The three Social Democrats on the committee had diverging viewpoints; one followed the majority, another urged the rejection of the proposals while declaring his basic sympathy with their goal, a third recommended an investigation pursuant to the representatives' proposals. In the house debate only one of the Social Democrats' more prominent members, Engberg, expressed himself. He proposed that the house request an investigation of a general nature dealing both with whether and how the State Church system ought to be liquidated. Engberg had now abandoned the definite opinion which he had advanced some years earlier. He emphasized the problem's complicated nature, spoke apprehensively of the possibility that the abolition of the State Church might lead to increased influence among anticultural religious groups, and showed a general doubtfulness. The committee's recommendation was approved, 88 to 65; the house ruled to reject the proposals. The committee's minority voted for Engberg's proposal. The lower number voting gives no definite clues as to how the Social Democrats voted. In all probability a good many members of the party abstained from voting.

In 1930 another proposal was introduced in the lower house by the Communists for an investigation into abolishing the State Church and confessional education. The provisional house committee appointed to deal with the proposal unanimously urged its rejection. The committee's justification contained only a few general opinions among which was one stating that Christian instruction ought to be retained. The proposal was defeated without voting in the lower house. The Social Democrats who entered the debate all spoke against the proposal. The party's leading spokesman, Engberg, stated—as on earlier occasions—that the Church was a part of the state, not an independent equal entity. In addition, he put forth some new viewpoints. A conceivable reform was the transformation of the Church into a civil service department of the usual type, with the clergy employed in the same manner as other civil servants. "But the Communists' thinking is old liberal thinking, which still had some currency at the time when we put through the dissenter legislation, but which totally lacks relevance at the present time, for the way of life points in a wholly different direction." If the State Church were abolished Catholicism could win ground; "an inflexible and consummate Swedish State Church system" was preferable to this. Other speakers (Thomson, Månsson, Lundstedt) to some extent developed the same thoughts. According to Månsson, the Church was capable of sufficient rejuvenation to become "at one and the same time the servant and leader of the people." With this debate the Social Democratic party made clear that in practice it no longer worked for the standpoint that was still included in the program.

The most recent proposal for an investigation into the possible abolition of the State Church was made at the 1932 Riksdag. Those who made the proposal were again Communists. This time the provisional committee unanimously urged rejection, and the proposal was defeated without any debate at all on the facts of the matter. The State Church question seems thereby to have fallen into a category of matters which the Riksdag considers it meaningless to debate.

It is in the press that opinion changes within the party are most clearly expressed. Opinions hostile to religion hardly ever occur any longer. The compatibility of Christianity and socialism is stressed with ever-increasing firmness. Even the Christian Socialist line, according to which socialism and Christianity belong together, is expressed in representative organs. Under all circumstances the historical value of religion as a "culture formative factor" is recognized. In response to certain statements of opinion made by the Church, especially at the time of the ecumenical council in 1925, it was declared that the social interest views within the Church had won ground and the Church was hailed as an ally in certain Social Democratic aims, above all in the peace cause. When the Christian Socialist organization was established, different views on its values were expressed, but in no quarters was the combination of socialism and Christianity itself criticized. Some papers, above all *Social-Demokraten,* feared that the establishment of a special union of Christians would lead to divisions within the party and to the attempt to press certain special issues at the expense of important questions. The party's leader, on the other hand, came forth in favor of the union in *Ny Tid,* and his opinion was apparently the view most strongly represented in the press. It was said that a Christian socialist organization was natural, considering the party's neutral standpoint on the religion question, and that such an organization would tend to erase the conception of the party's hostility to religion. The questions of the abolition of the State Church and of confessional education fell into the background. It was often stated or suggested that these questions lacked all contemporary interest or even that the party program's demands did not necessarily have to be realized. The Church's changed position and the value of regulation and control in this area were among the reasons cited. At times one glimpses the view that the demand for the abolition of the State Church conflicted with the socialist principle "that the power of society shall have influence and control over the different phenomena of societal life, including the exercise of religion." Sometimes it was stated that Social Democracy ought to assist in reforming the Church's dogmas and organization in order to bring the Church closer to the people.

Engberg, who from the beginning of his political career devoted far more interest to these questions than any of the other leading Social Democrats, in the middle of the 1920s still held fast to the demand for the abolition of the State Church, but no longer supported his view on the same antireligious grounds as earlier. As editor of *Social-Demokraten,* he proposed in 1925 that the Social Democratic program be carried out in the following steps:

(1) Unification of the municipal community and the parishes
(2) Granting of the right to freely leave the State Church

(3) Abolition of the veto right of the Church Assembly
(4) Deletion from the constitution (Instrument of Government: §28) of the provision on the confession of the pure evangelical doctrine
(5) Reorganization in principle of religious education in the schools on the same basis as other subjects
(6) Abolition of the State Church.

Point 5 probably meant—as in Engberg's speech in the debate on the education plan in the 1921 Riksdag—the introduction of "objective" as opposed to dogmatic Christian education. Engberg emphasized certain difficulties in connection with the proposal on the right to freely leave the State Church: the loss of certain rights in the Church, such as the right to participate in Church elections would necessarily follow. Did this not show

> that not until the downfall of the State Church system and its accompanying obligatory confession, both in the form of compulsory membership in the State Church and—what is most important—of compulsory nonreligious education in the schools, can the beautifully expressed principle of paragraph 16 of the Constitution (Instrument of Government) be realized.

In opposition to Church opinion it was maintained that the Church was a part of the state. The practical consequence of this considered to be that after a divorce the so-called Church properties could no longer be considered to belong to the Church. After Engberg in the 1930 Riksdag clearly went over to a defense of the State Church system, he developed further reasons in his paper for his change in position. Religious freedom in Sweden—with the exception of compulsion of conscience in the schools—could be considered in practice accomplished, and the State Church system in itself offered obvious advantages.

> The special system in our land, whereby the Church establishment is an element in the system of state organs in general and the state itself prescribes the content of the state religion as decreed in the Constitution, is actually, in the hands of an enlightened executive power, quite a useful instrument for the maintenance of tolerance and freedom of movement . . . Precisely through its sovereignty in deciding whether and to what degree freedom of thought and speech shall be unlimited in religious matters and because it is not obligated in this area by any sort of concordat to exercise control over the observance of any "doctrine" in behalf of any "church" or "religious community," but is itself the vehicle and the subject of "churchly" activities—in this way the Swedish state can be tolerant and give free scope to the spiritual.

In subsequent years Engberg, as minister of education and ecclesiastical affairs, has often expressed a sympathy with both religion and the Church. Representative of his present opinion—and probably also of a very large segment of Swedish Social Democracy—is a statement in his 1938 tract, *Democratic Cultural Policies* (*Demokratisk kulturpolitik*):

> In the domain of the Church establishment, the reform work under the leadership of the government over the past six years had as its aim the breaking of the isolation between religious and secular culture, to let them penetrate and enrich each other, to raise this purpose above all party dissension, and to regard and deal with the religious life powers as innate resources in and supporting a sound cultural democracy. The very principle of evangelical protestantism represents the respect for human dignity, the assertion of the right of the individual, of the personality to oppose oppression, the respect for the rights and freedom of conscience and research, which inextricably belong together with democratic principles and a democratic philosophy. This real, intrinsic affinity in principle, whose importance the world could witness in the heroically courageous opposition of the German Evangelical Protestant Church to the demands of the dictatorial and totalitarian state power has constituted a natural lodestar for the government in forming and dealing with Churcho-political concerns. The Protestant Swedish Church and the democratic Swedish state sail here in the same boat. The possibilities for protestantism to live with us in freedom and without power encroachments by the state stand and fall with the democratic order itself.

The statements of certain other leading Social Democrats reveal opinion changes of the same kind. In the beginning of the 1920s Rickard Lindström was one of the few in the party who criticized not only the State Church but religion as well. In an article in *Frihet* (*Freedom*) in 1923 he hailed Bengt Lidforss as one of the sharpest adversaries of Christianity in Sweden; Lindström characterized Christianity as "this low and irrational doctrine . . . this sorry spectacle." Some years later Lindström declared that a socialist view was certainly compatible with Christian faith. During recent years he has expressed strong sympathy with the Christian faith and has agreed with the Christian Socialist wish for a revision of the party program. "Within the common Swedish people there is an inexhaustible fund of warm religiosity," he states in an article in *Ny Tid* before the 1936 congress.

> From this emanate life and social values of great merit. These must be protected, cared for, and improved. Social Democracy must give assistance in this. Therefore the party should not say no to the wish of the Christian Socialists for a positive emphasis in the program article that concerns the religious aspect of the societal problem.

Lindström also has demanded a Church reform that would provide better expression of the nation's religious need; without confessing faith in a "personal God" he has assisted in High Mass as a lay preacher.

Summary

WHEN SOCIAL DEMOCRACY emerged in Sweden, Church doctrine was regarded as an essentially conservative ideology from a secular point of view and its promulgation as one of the most important elements in the propaganda for the preservation of the existing order. For this reason alone an anti-Church and antireligious tendency was natural in a movement aimed at transforming society. Other conditions sharpened this tendency and contributed to the ideological form which it took. The findings and theories of the natural sciences and sociology stimulated the intellectual radicalism of middle class as well as socialist coloring to criticize traditional religious conceptions, and to arrive at a point of view that was a blend of active atheism and a rationalistic faith in progress. The Marxist doctrine accepted by the socialists was, in its more philosophical form, a variant of this combination. According to socialist lines of thought, which in different ways were connected to the materialist concept of history, religion was regarded as an "opiate of the people," a method for making men indifferent to their temporal situation by directing their sights to another world or, according to a more subtle theory, as a necessary ideology during the existing period characterized by oppression and exploitation. With the downfall of the class society, it was held that religion would be succeeded by rational and realistic assumptions. For Social Democracy the demand for the abolition of the State Church was obvious as a short-range demand. Religion also was, by definition, an enemy —an ideological support of the ruling class—to the leaders schooled in Marxism. Yet antireligious propaganda was not to become a main theme; religion would disappear "by itself" with the victory of socialism. Termination of collaboration with utilitarianism, which was primarily concerned with pure free thought agitation, was not a demonstration of the party's religious neutrality, but only of its placing political and social goals in first place.

Antireligious propaganda continued for a long while in the party, but it soon became less apparent and less representative. The desire to win over religious workers, collaboration with the middle class radicalism supported by the free churches, changes in the cultural environment which made atheism less convincing as a philosophy, and greater understanding on the part of the Church and the religious community probably all worked to enhance the growing moderation in the handling of religious questions. Some of the clergy joined the party; the view that socialism and "true" Christianity belonged together was represented in public agitation, even if only by a few. However, some party theorists better trained in Marxist dialectics than their predecessors in the 1880s still sought to place Christianity and religion in general in a historical-philosophical schema, according to which all supernatural views of this kind belonged to an epoch that in a short while would go under. The demands in the program for the abolition of the State Church and thereby also of confessional education were kept without opposition, and in the Riksdag the party's representatives worked for its realization.

A third period in the party's development can be said to have set in at the time when complete democratization made it possible to realize or at least be seriously concerned with the proposed demands. It now became apparent that these were not regarded as essential or even as warranted. As early as the beginning of the 1920s a large proportion of the party's representatives in the Riksdag voted against proposals which were in agreement with the party program; some years later such proposals came to be regarded as eccentric. When these questions were finally taken up at the party congress, demands for changing or abrogating the pertinent program articles were defeated, but the justifications given for the rejection of these demands actually emphasized the irrelevance of the program. The change is related to and can be regarded as a consequence of the events previously mentioned. The Church's moderation has grown along with that of Social Democracy. Christian Socialism has been promulgated by a growing and increasingly respected minority. But also new factors have been added. Being in power, or sharing in power, has made reforms of this sort appear both more difficult and less desirable than during the opposition time. Religious freedom has been broadened and the influence of laymen in the institutions of the Church has increased through minor changes. Instead of avoiding religious ceremonies and demanding the right to freely leave the State Church, the Social Democrats have sought to win influence within this Church. Marxist ideas have lost their motivational force. In the work for the preservation of national democracy the religious community seemed to offer support. Developments in recent years have been accelerated by these circumstances. It is typical that certain of the party's prominent men were able to run through the party's three standpoints in these questions in the period of about a decade.

The gradual shift in Social Democracy's position regarding religion and the Church is perhaps the most concrete manifestation of the party's general transition to a new ideology and to new lines of action. The development can be made clear by recalling the positions taken at the 1889, 1908, and 1936 party congresses. At the 1889 congress only a majority of a couple of votes prevented the passage of a proposal approving the promulgation of systematic antireligious propaganda by the party; the demand for the abolition of the State Church at this time did not arouse opposition or even debate. In 1908 it was emphasized that the party should not conduct irreligious propaganda and that Christians as well as others could be members of the party. A departure from the original principles in the question of the Church and school program was still inconceivable. In 1936 proposals for a softening of the program on these points were defeated. But the debate proceeded from the assumption that the articles concerned were not of current interest and should not be actualized. Retention of the articles was mainly vindicated on two grounds: they were purely formal consequences of the principle of religious freedom; they could not mislead anyone, *i.e.,* they could be preserved because it was well known that the party did not intend to realize them. Remarkably enough, the whole development of the party's standpoint from the 1880s to the present has taken place without leaving a trace in the program's principal clauses.

The Temperance Question

Socialism and the Temperance Movement in Competition and Conflict

AT THE BEGINNING there was a definite antagonism between Social Democracy and the temperance movement. To a large extent the critical or indifferent position of Social Democracy toward the temperance movement can be seen as a consequence of the basic principles it held at this time. The idea of the social revolution, to be carried through with the help of universal suffrage, tended to drive sociopolitical and, even more, private moralistic demands into the background. The misuse of alcohol was regarded, like, for example, prostitution, as a consequence of the capitalist system and it was thought that it would automatically disappear with the liquidation of this system. It was held often, under the influence of the doctrine of the Iron Law of Wages of Lassalle and others that an improvement in the living standard of the workers could not be won through an increase in temperance; if the workers reduced their consumption, the employers would lower their wages. Similar viewpoints have been of importance probably everywhere in the Marxist-colored labor movement. As late as 1899 Bebel was able to repudiate the demand for a program point on the temperance question at the German party congress on the ground that such "bagatelles" should not be allowed to cause an ideological rupture within the party. Contemporary socialist literature very rarely dealt with the temperance question. Only English socialism with its social reformist orientation took a more positive position.

Closely related to this is the fact that the temperance demand was traditionally a component in the liberal self-help ideology, which was regarded as early socialism's most dangerous enemy. For decades sobriety, thrift, and moral rectitude had been preached in education groups and workers' associations. Temperance resolutions were passed at so-called liberal workers' meetings. Publications distributed or supported by anti-socialist businessmen and capitalists and directed at a working-class readership, such as *Svenska arbetaren* and *Arbetarens vän* featured temperance ideas. The spread of temperance was often regarded as the only way of improving the situation of the working class and, in addition, as an antidote to socialism. The problem was stated as "temperance or socialism."

In order to understand the conflicts between Social Democracy and the organized temperance movement it is necessary to further understand the latter movement's development in Sweden. The first wave of temperance agitation, directed toward moderation rather than absolutism, led to the founding of a large number of organizations in the 1830s and 1840s, but later declined. *Svenska nykterhetssällskapet* (The Swedish Temperance Society), which served as a central agency, was of scant importance in the 1870s. It has previously been emphasized that the head of the organization, Sigfrid Wieselgren, son of Peter Wieselgren, was an old school liberal and saw the solution of the worker question exclusively in terms of raising the morals of the working class. The modern temperance movement was introduced into Sweden with the founding of a lodge of the International Order of Good Templars in Gothenburg in 1879. After a short time, however, a split occurred in the order and it divided into two branches, the Hickmanite or American and the Malinite or English branches. In 1887 they were again united. The number of Good Templars was about 1,600 in 1880, nearly 48,000 in 1884, 60,000 in 1887, and 95,000 in 1900. Other temperance societies were also founded in the 1880's such as *Sveriges blåbandsförening* (The Swedish Blue Band Society) with 65,000 members in 1894; the splitting-up of the Order of Good Templars led to the formation of *Nationalgodtemplarorden* and *Templarorden*. All together these organizations are reckoned to have had over 200,000 members in 1895. Without doubt the temperance movement obtained its followers to a great extent from the working class, in the country as well as in the cities. Further data regarding the movement's social composition are not obtainable.

Characteristic of this temperance movement was the demand for absolute abstinence, the adoption of certain religious assumptions, and the repudiation in principle of all political activity not directly related to the temperance question. Because of their strong emphasis on religion alone, organization such as *Godtemplarorden* and *Blå bandet* came into a certain conflict with socialist doctrine. In addition, many temperance advocates at this time were inclined to regard the temperance question as the central social problem and its solution as a solution to The Social Question. "Whenever the Good Templar Order is established the earth becomes a paradise, for honor to the Father and peace on earth are the great goals of the Good Templars," a statement made by a prominent temperance advocate, was typical of the attitude of many. To be sure, this opinion of temperance as the only matter of importance was not accepted by all—even in the 1880's socialists and other advocates of social reform were to be found in the temperance movement—but it was without doubt the dominant opinion. It can even be said that the very interest in temperance was often characterized by slight social concern. The primary goal seemed to be not the creation of a higher living standard and better societal conditions, but saving persons who were or might become drinkers from moral degeneration. The agitation often followed the same line as that used by revivalists: "the liquor devil" appeared essentially as a devil, as a seducer to sin. Whereas the clergy and preachers spoke of "true freedom" as consisting in following God's commandments, the temperance people spoke of "true freedom" as being reached through the control of the desire for alcoholic beverages. Between this orientation with its appeal to feelings of personal guilt, and the socialist doctrine, with its optimistic faith in mankind, which saw evil only in societal conditions, lay the gap which separates religious moralism from rationalistic and hedonistic faith in progress.

But the temperance movement also represented more positive conservative tendencies. This was especially the case with the American branch of the Good Templars, the Hickmanites. In spite of the fact that the program of the order proscribed political activity, its leaders put forth a conservative and antisocialist propaganda in speeches and writings. As with many other movements, antipolitical in principle, such a prohibition against politics was interpreted as a prohibition against radical politics. The clearest demonstration of this is found in the movement's main organ *Reform* (1881–1887), which was edited for several years by Carl Hurtig, one of the leading temperance advocates of the 1880s and later a clergyman. Even the paper's official statement of purpose, which emphasizes respect for the existing order, indicates a conservative orientation. The newspaper wished "to build up sobriety, industriousness, and diligence. It wishes to promote freedom while protecting order, honesty, sobriety, and fear of God." The paper presented a detailed account of a speech on socialism and the aims of the Good Templars given by Hurtig in Gothenburg on January 15, 1882. Hurtig's thesis was that the workers were not free and were oppressed because and only because of drunkenness. Socialism was materialistic and wished to equalize everything; the Good Templars set up high ideals. Happiness and success could be achieved, not through agitation, but through meekness. The political impotence of the workers would cease if they became diligent and sober.

> Be sober. Be meek. Do your work conscientiously. Be frugal. Fear God. Any diligent and healthy worker who observes these rules in his life will soon feel free from the oppression of capital. Capital will help him, and he will find himself happy and satisfied with his lot. No one has a life more free from care than a well-situated worker. . . . Begin by being an abstainer, a complete abstainer; and you will soon find that all of the other things will follow of themselves.

Another meeting led by Hurtig passed a resolution stating that "the ideas of the Good Templars and socialism cannot have anything in common." In later articles Hurtig explained that the order's administration did everything to exclude "those socially dangerous elements," they were charged with wanting to divide up everything and were equated with thieves. Sometimes the onerous situation of the workers was emphasized, but the only solution was said to be different forms of workers' insurance. Characteristic of the newspaper's markedly socially conservative position was its enthusiasm for Bismarck's social policies. Bismarck was considered to have earned the title "Germany's first and most powerful friend of the workers." The workers should seek close relations with the wielders of power who could bring them substantial help.

> The workers in Germany have finally discovered that liberalism is a handsome shell without a core, and that Social Democracy, if consistently carried out, leads to slavery, loss of religion, and despotism, instead of to freedom and daily bread. Consequently, the workers have finally, and after many miscalculations, found that their rightful allies are society's most distinguished and highest classes, whose interests are more closely bound with the workers' own than are those of some screaming Liberals and Social Democrats, who are trying to climb up to the high honors of the state on the shoulders of the people. Not only on the temperance issue can the workers find their real allies among the richest, the highest nobility, and the most prominent, but this is true also of their political interests.

The Christian Social party in Germany—an anti-Semitic, antisocialist, and socially conservative party—was presented as the best party from the point of view of the workers. The same issue that contains these statements includes an article which declares that the Good Templars stand apart from all political activity. A later series of articles castigates socialism for aiming to establish free love, the separation of children from parents, and the like. It also stated that a consequence of socialism might be that the rulers, faced with the threat of a revolution, might bring about an open military and financial rule. Shortly before the demise of the paper (coterminous with the reuniting of the two Good Templar movements) a couple of articles published on the labor question affirmed that self-help and, above all, sobriety, were the only solution.

> No worker who gives one *öre* to the drunkard's slaughter block of intoxicating beverages, the bar, should be regarded as . . . entitled to claim the right to complain over a small daily wage. The worker's lot can never be satisfactorily improved as long as intoxicating beverages are manufactured, imported, and sold in our country, if he does not embrace absolute abstinence with complete earnestness. In this way he himself can create, to a greater or lesser degree, a better social position.

The paper published by the Hickmanite, Vestenius in Malmo, *Framåt* (*Onward*), also contained attacks on socialism and on several occasions entered into polemics with Palm's *Folkviljan*.

The political position of the Hickmanites became clearly marked in 1883 when C. O. Berg—consul-general, businessman, conservative member of the upper house, and publisher of *Arbetarens vän*—was chosen to be the order's foremost leader. The election seems to have been primarily dictated by the desire to raise the order's social prestige. Berg was one of the most prominent representatives of the combination of social concern and distinct political conservatism of that day. He accepted the invitation to leadership (as "Noble Great Templar") under the condition that "nothing contrary to the Christian religion or the constitutions of the Scandinavian nations or hostile to the reigning royal houses" would be tolerated within the order. In his first communication to the order's membership he enjoined intercession from God "for all mankind, for kings, and for all the authorities, so that we may lead a pleasant and calm life in all piety and uprightness." On a number of occasions Berg emphasized the conservative goals of the order which he led, and particularly its royalist character. In an article published January 3, 1886, he stated that a Good Templar could not be a socialist; the Good Templars wanted "the brotherhood of all through the self-denial of love and mercy, through self-discipline and self-sacrifice," while the socialists wanted to abolish "religion, marriage, the right of ownership," and advocated "the breakdown of all existing order." It was even decided on Berg's initiative that Social Democrats should not be allowed to belong to the order—a rule which was abolished when both organizations reunited. During Berg's leadership the American Good Templar order was looked on very favorably by the authorities. On repeated occasions Oscar II showed his approval of the order's activities through monetary gifts and good wishes. On the basis of these circumstances it has been suggested that persons in leading positions consciously aimed to shape the Hickmanites into a conservative workers' movement as a counterweight to socialism. In Berg's own organ, *Arbetarens vän,* the Good Templars were characterized as "one of the strongest defenses against the subversive tendencies of the socialist and anarchist movements."

In the Malinite branch of the Good Templar order, conservative and antisocialist tendencies did not appear with the same strentgh as among the Hickmanites. A liberal-democratic line was probably dominant. The movement's leading paper *Svenska Good Templar* (1880–1887)—for a while its official organ—held mainly to a politically neutral position. The paper emphasized its generally liberal and democratic viewpoint, but also its desire not to drag the temperance movement into party strife. On one occasion, however, it published a sharp criticism of the socialist movement in response to an attack on the Good Templars by Palm. The Good Templars and socialists were described as competitors for the workers' votes, and the socialist leaders were accused of hostility toward temperance efforts. On several occasions conflicts occurred within the order between the more extreme antisocialists and those who wanted to preserve the order's political neutrality. Among the latter were E. Wavrinsky who became the order's leader in 1886 and later was chosen to be the head of the United Good Templar order. It deserves to be pointed out that after a meeting in December 1885 had declared that it was the duty of the "friends of temperance" to support Social Democracy, some leading members of the Malinite order—among them Oskar Eklund—wrote articles maintaining that the order was to stand apart from politics on principle, and, consequently, according to its bylaws, was prevented from collaborating with socialism. On the other hand, it was stated that individual members of the order were free to choose any political view. These articles were not, as is sometimes intimated, expressions of hostility toward socialism, but comprised only a declaration of neutrality.

Strong political conflicts persisted within the united Good Templar order, but outwardly the order seemed to maintain a neutral line insofar as it did not generally come out for or against any party or any political view. At the great lodge meeting of 1888 it was proposed by a lodge that socialists should not be accepted into the order, but this proposal was quickly rejected by referring to the order's bylaws. The official organ of the order, *Reformatorn* (*The Reformer*) continually emphasized that Good Templar lodges as such could not take part in any political actions. On the whole, one gets the impression from this paper that growing worker membership in the order and radicalizing tendencies among the workers increased interest in social and political reforms. Thus the paper expressed itself in favor of universal suffrage and a standard work day. Articles which dealt with the temperance movement and socialism criticized the opinion that drunkenness was a consequence of social ills; the wealthy misused alcohol as well as the poor and drunkenness was greatest during good times. Temperance work was not, as many Social Democrats believed, a trick of the powerful classes "to make the workers forget the political and economic questions that are more important to them." If the workers became sober their interest in further betterment would be increased and their possibilities for realizing their demands would be enhanced.

> All of the objections which are now made about political immaturity and the like would then at once disappear. The capacity for solidarity would become greater, the

> prospects broadened. All developmental work would come to be stamped by sound judgment and moderation which, unfortunately, are now so often lacking.

Here we have the suggestion of an opinion that later became predominant; temperance is regarded not as a solution of The Social Question but as a prerequisite for its solution.

The political line of the various Good Templar organizations—the neutrality principle, colored by conservative tendencies—led necessarily in a number of cases to actions against lodges and persons who wanted to advocate socialist or other radical propaganda within the order. Conflict is known to have occurred among the Hickmanites in Gothenburg, between the majority led by Hurtig and a socialist group whose leader was D. M. Heurlin; the result was Heurlin's resignation from the order. Similar conflicts appeared in a number of other places. Members of the order, and, in some cases, whole lodges became objects for punishment stipulated in the order's bylaws or were expelled from the order for reasons of socialist agitation, participation in suffrage and May Day demonstrations, and the like. Particularly at the end of the 1880's one of the continually reappearing areas of strife in the Good Templar lodges was the question of taking a stand on socialism. The lodges thereby became centers of socialist agitation and the organizations were not infrequently accused of being socialist. The situation was almost the same as in the trade unions; lodges, which to a large extent consisted of workers, constituted a natural base for socialist activity as did the trade unions. As late as the beginning of the 1900's a lodge was deprived of its rights for a certain period because of participation in a May Day demonstration; similar cases have possibly occurred even later.

The antisocialist press that was trying to woo the working class naturally sought to foment this opposition between Good Templars and Social Democrats. *Den Svenska arbetaren* explained that drunkenness and socialism were the main causes for the unfortunate position of the workers and that these two causes were mutually interdependent. "What is it that makes men susceptible to socialism in the first place? Dissatisfaction. What calls forth dissatisfaction? Need. What is the principal cause of need? Drunkenness. Drunkenness is consequently the socialists' most natural ally, and every attempt to oppose this vice is the same as to oppose socialism." The socialists feared the activities of the Good Templars because "the Good Templar order protects the workers from socialism."

Only a couple of points will be made regarding the activities of the remaining temperance organizations during this period. The extent to which the agitators in these organizations conducted political propaganda cannot be established with certainty, but to judge by the leading organs of the movement the principle of political neutrality was adhered to. In *Blå bandet* (*The Blue Band*) no political opinions appeared. The regulations for the association's traveling speakers included a prohibition against discussing any political questions inasmuch as such discussion would not be directly related to the temperance cause. The National Good Templar order had been founded by relatively conservative temperance advocates and on one occasion became the recipient of a written eulogy from the crown, but the order's paper, *Nationalkuriren,* contained hardly any political articles. This was also generally true of the Templar order's paper, *Templaren,* but here a deprecating tone toward Social Democracy sometimes appeared. One article emphasized that there was nothing to hinder socialists from belonging to the order, even though the organization refused to be a "help-mate to socialism"; another article criticized a resolution passed by a lodge because it was considered to be socialistic, but at the same time the article emphasized the political indifference of the order.

The essential background of the position of the young Social Democracy regarding temperance and the temperance movement may be suggested here. Because of its general social revolutionary views, socialism was already predisposed to a critical or at least skeptical view of temperance work. The word "temperance"—like the words "morality," "thrift" and "industriousness"—had become symbolic of a patriarchal conservative and old liberal view. The early temperance movement was stamped to a great extent by this view; it claimed to be politically neutral, but often showed antisocialist tendencies. Personal and organizational dissension appeared when socialists joined the movement. In addition, the socialists and temperance advocates to a great extent appealed to the same working class audience, and the competition in agitation between them sharpened their ideological opposition. The practical political struggle between liberalism and socialism within the working class was fought out primarily in the trade unions, where the victory of socialism was complete. Secondarily it was fought out within the temperance organizations, where by degrees an equilibrium was reached, a *modus vivendi* which became one of the foundations of the collaboration of the Left during the first decade of the twentieth century.

It is consequently, as sometimes occurred, not correct to see the conflicts between the temperance movement and socialism as a question of personal antagonisms or as purely circumstantial. To discuss whether fault lay with one side or the other is as meaningless as discussing where the fault lay in the strife between liberalism and socialism. This certainly does not mean that personal circumstances lacked all importance. That a number of socialism's leading men—such as Palm, Branting, Danielsson, Sterky, and Carleson—

were far from abstainers and held a certain contempt for temperance and other kinds of puritanism without doubt helped sharpen the conflicts and give them a vehement and personal stamp. There was, also, particularly among the leaders, probably a psychological distinction between the moralism and guilt feelings of the Good Templars and the outwardly oriented and optimistic social activities of the socialist workers.

Palm's opinions were of the irritating kind which helped create bitter feelings from the beginning; they are similar in type to Hurtig's propaganda against socialism in the Hickmanite order. The first encounter between the socialists and the temperance advocates seems to have taken place in Gothenburg when Palm held an agitational speech the same day (January 15, 1882) that Hurtig leveled the previously mentioned attack against socialism. A lively polemic followed these speeches. Later Palm often stated his opinion in *Folkviljan* in attacks against *Reform* or *Framåt,* the Malmo paper friendly to temperance. Sometimes Palm suggested that the workers would become more temperate if they received a higher status, but he passionately defended the moderate use of alcohol. The drawing power of the Good Templars was said to rest on "that mysterious secretiveness there with its degrees, signs, trappings, and the rest. And it is not strange that a people like the Swedes, intellectually dulled by the clergy, join it." The Good Templars were attacked with extreme animosity as opponents of socialism and as morally deficient people. Among other things, it was suggested that they tippled on the sly. Palm did not express any more thoughtful opinions on the temperance question; to a great extent his statements are suggestive of his antitemperance activity thirty years later.

The opinions of other socialist leaders are more important from an ideological point of view. Branting dealt with related questions in the conclusion of his 1886 Gävle speech "Why the Workers' Movement Must be Socialist." According to the Iron Law of Wages thrift and temperance could not help the working class.

> Suppose . . . that the entire working class as a whole abstained from every little enjoyment, such as a drink with meals, to bring temperance into the example. Now what would be the consequences? Do you think the workers would get to keep the few coins thus saved to spend according to their own inclinations and tastes? No, certainly not, in spite of all that the temperance journals and apostles of temperance may say. The often cited economic law that wages strive to sink to the lowest possible level would not take long to make itself felt. In a very short time unemployment would force the workers to sell their labor at the same price as they had formerly [received] *minus* the discontinued and unneeded pennies for *brännvin.* In the end the profits from the whole affair thus accrues to the employers, who will get their labor cheaper. . . .

Branting apparently soon abandoned this opinion, but kept his critical position toward the temperance movement as worthless or a clear danger from the point of view of the working class. As a candidate in the 1893 lower house election, Branting rejected the idea of legislating "what we should eat and drink." Many general opinions appearing in *Social-Demokraten* admittedly favored increased temperance, but they expressed no sympathy with complete abstinence. Under Branting's editorship, however, the paper did not publish attacks on temperance work of the kind which were usual in *Folkviljan* except in isolated instances. On one occasion it stated that those who repudiated Social Democracy for not having temperance in its program could well be done without by the party. These "one-sided dreamers collaborated," wrote the paper, "with the worst reactionaries and most unenlightened rabble in the country, with all sorts of religious madmen, but they choose not to hear talk of socialism, which goes radically to the roots of poverty, because we do not take vows to the evangelism of absolutism." This statement has been attributed to Branting.

In attacks that Danielsson directed against the temperance movement, in *Arbetet* the ideological line is strongly in evidence. In response to the previously mentioned proposal in which the 1888 great lodge meeting of the Good Templars in Malmo raised the question of a prohibition on the acceptance of Social Democrats into the order, he wrote, under the heading "A Dying Power," a detailed justification of the opinion that temperance in general and Good Templarism in particular were reactionary movements.

> The Good Templar order is dying because it has built its program on false grounds. It is not temperance and thrift that will save society. In addition, the Good Templar order is a religious institution. . . . The Good Templar order has become an institution to occupy the workers to divert them from concern with other social urgencies. It has become a means of the upper class to the detriment of the people, particularly because religion has played such a leading role in it [the order]. The upper class is most content when it has such trifles as this to occupy the minds and hearts of the workers and they are thereby weaned away from working on reforming society. And it moreover deludes the workers that temperance will transform society; if all men become temperate there will be another kind of society, another state of affairs will come into being one says to them. And in order that sober minds shall not reflect too much over the ills in society, [the upper class] has so arranged it that the stupefying and deadening influence of religion can make itself felt to an extraordinarily high degree—and, in addition, the Good Templar order supposedly does not concern itself with political questions. For one knows instinctively that these sober workers would be formidable opponents of society, and that their thinking and freedom of action must consequently be fettered.

This statement is remarkable for its collection of quasi-Marxist and partly contradictory arguments. Note the confused argumentation: first it is claimed that the Good Templar movement is a means of the upper class to occupy the workers with trifles, and immediately afterwards it is stated that sober workers would be especially dangerous to the existing order, and that therefore the upper class found it necessary to counteract the movement's consequences through religious propaganda and a prohibition against political activity! The belief that "capitalism" is a conscious and cunning power is given classic expression here. Almost a year later Danielsson once again discussed the temperance question in response to the founding of a new and comparatively radical temperance paper called *Absolutisten.* While recognizing the value of greater temperance, he criticized:

> the absolutists' sensational presentation of intoxicating drink as the primary *social evil.* They must have a very circumscribed view of society in order to come to this lamentable inference, and they cannot have broad perspectives when they, although democratically minded in other respects, make prohibition the a to z of their program. That radicals . . . cling with life and soul to such propaganda may well be considered a phenomenon, a sort of sickness, for in general Good Templarism is a refuge for reactionary philanthropy which wants to prevent the revolutionary uniting of the masses and misdirect their view of social phenomena at any price. Absolutism is dealt with in this manner and repudiated by the Social Democrats, not only in Sweden but in *all countries.*

Similar, though less sharp opinions, are also encountered in *Folkets röst,* whose editor, Pehr Eriksson, had earlier been a Good Templar. The announcement for the paper explained that it wanted to work for temperance, but against "the charlatanism and humbug in this area." What was meant here was explained in a later article, according to which the Good Templar movement had completed its role if it did not concede "that the prevailing social and economic evils are the greatest cause of misery and drunkenness. Primarily through a better economic and social system will it be possible to arrest drunkenness."

At Social Democratic meetings, or at meetings arranged on Social Democratic initiative, the relation between socialism and the temperance movement was discussed. They passed resolutions which denied the capacity of the temperance movement to solve The Social Question, they blamed the Good Templars for political indifference or conservatism, and encouraged temperance advocates to collaborate with Social Democracy. At one meeting held in Stockholm around Christmas 1885, to which invitations were issued by Palm and which was even attended by many Good Templars, a debate culminated in the following resolution:

> Considering that the meeting recognizes that absolute temperance is *not* sufficient to abolish the social ills which the majority of the people are suffering from, and that

> Social Democracy is the only political party which proposes a radical transformation of society to the advantage of all, and since the great majority of those who join temperance organizations are workers, and, further, since the interests of the workers are the same, the assembled declare that it is the duty of the advocates of temperance to support Social Democratic policies and to regard any attempt to obstruct them, whaever form it should take, as a betrayal of the workers and of the most sacred cause common to the oppressed people.

This resolution led to the previously mentioned actions from certain Good Templar leaders and to declarations by some lodges in Stockholm that they were opposed to all attempts at socialist agitation within the order. About a year later a socialist meeting in Stockholm passed a resolution which branded the Good Templar organization as "pure humbug because it works in the service of reaction through opposing the purposeful workers' movement or socialism." A meeting for Good Templars and socialists in Malmo in October 1887 criticized the religious ceremonies and reactionary leadership of the Good Templar order, and called upon the members of the order to work for "the complete emancipation of the effort from every religious influence and from any political leadership in the service of the ruling class."

The temperance question was not dealt with as a rule in the programmatic declarations which were passed in the 1880s by a number of different Social Democratic organizations. At the first constituent congress in 1889, however, two proposals on this question were presented. One (The Social Democratic Union of Stockholm) recommended that there be a statement on the subject; the other (The General Laborers Association of Stockholm) proposed a statement in favor of the prohibition of alcoholic beverages. The congress included in its declaration of views a resolution which—to judge by the wording—(an account of the attendant debate is lacking)—had come about through a compromise. In a first article the congress declared that it recognized what temperance work had done for the advancement of the workers, but it also emphasized that drunkenness was caused "primarily by the existing economic conditions." The congress continued by deploring that temperance work in the absolutist organizations "had fallen into the hands of reactionaries, takes the time of the workers to such a large extent that no time is left for work on social-economic and political questions, and by many (absolutism) is overvalued in such high degree that it is regarded as having the power to cure social evils." It protested "against the deceit of the upper class which is concealed in the assumption that if the worker becomes sober he will also have sufficient means for existence." Lastly, the congress declared its sympathy for temperance work "as doing its part to contribute to preparing among the workers the conditions for vigorous and lively participation in the Social Democratic workers' movement," and to encouraging the workers to be temperate. Taken in its entirety, this statement, considering the conflicts between the socialists and Good Templars, is surprising in its recognition of the value of the temperance movement and in its comparatively moderate criticism of its conservative tendencies. This statement shows that in spite of everything, temperance advocates had already achieved a certain position within the Social Democratic movement. It can also be established that several active temperance advocates such as F. V. Thorsson, P. M. Landin, J. Kjellman, and C. L. Lundberg were among the congressional delegates. Here, as in many other cases, it would be of interest to establish precisely to what extent the Social Democratic delegates concerned were members of temperance organizations. An investigation of this, however, encounters too many difficulties.

In the congresses of the northern and central districts of 1890 and 1892 the temperance question assumed a prominent position. At the 1890 congress a discussion of the question—which was put forth by the Workers' Club of Sundsvall—was introduced by Hinke Bergegren, who urged that "in the Social Democratic agitation great attention should be given to the influence of intoxicating drink on people's health and intellectual development," without committing the party to an absolutist position. Bergegren held that they should pay attention to the temperance question in order to get women interested in the workers' movement and that it would be unwise to take a position repudiating the many Good Templars who had joined Social Democracy. Nevertheless, the congress decided by a vote of 27 to 24 only to accept the position of the 1889 party congress. The minutes from the 1892 congress do not make clear its opinion of the temperance question, but indicate that sympathies for protemperance agitation were even stronger than in 1890.

At the 1891 party congress the temperance question was not dealt with, but in 1894 it was brought up in the form of a proposal for a statement on local option, a demand propagated at this time by the temperance organizations. The committee appointed by the congress proposed a general declaration of neutrality. W. A. Fagerström, with the support of Thorsson and others, urged that the congress recommend total prohibition and that it should also state that intoxicating beverages were "a hindrance to the proletariats' march forward" and that closer relations ought to be brought about between Social Democrats and temperance advocates. Branting proposed a resolution according to which the party should declare itself "completely neutral in the conflict of opinion over the use and non-use of alcohol." In the question of local option the congress ought to emphasize that such exceptional circumstances could lead to a deep-going amelioration of drunkenness, but that prohibition legislation contained a well-meant, but, always in its consequences, very dangerous invasion of the individual's most personal right of self-determination, an invasion which Social Democracy, as a party of freedom, must in principle disapprove of and which by no means can in any way be regarded as analagous to the interference in defense of the weaker against the tyranny of other economically stronger individuals which Social Democracy demands of the state powers.

Finally, the congress should encourage the party's newspapers "to take a thoughtful and cautious course in their position on the temperance question so that the party's work for its great goals will not be made more difficult by difference of opinion on this secondary issue." In justification of his opinion—which is not completely reported either in the minutes of the congress or in *Social-Demokraten*—Branting sharply criticized the temperance movement. He characterized it as "a passing phenomenon" which ought not to give rise to concessions or compromises. Religion and absolutism in regard to the use of alcohol ought to be private concerns. Branting suggested that in both cases it was a question of certain socially conditioned illusions which would disappear with increasing enlightenment. The temperance movement led to spying and to drinking on the sly. Prohibition would mean an oppression of the majority "in the misused name of democracy." With the elimination of the poverty problem the temperance question would cease to be a social problem and drunkenness would then "at the most be regarded as a sickness." Branting's motion was passed by the congress, winning 29 votes to 15 cast for Fagerström's motion.

This resolution, which implied a sharp repudiation of the demands of the temperance movement, can be said to signify the close of the first period in the development of Social Democracy's temperance policy. At the 1897 and 1900 party congresses the temperance issue was not taken up. At the 1905 congress the party's position on the temperance question was wholly different from that in 1894.

Social Democracy's Development toward a Positive Position

IT IS NATURALLY not possible to give any definite date or even any definite period for the transition of Social Democracy to a more positive position on the temperance question. But very schematically it can be said that the change came about during the decade following the third party congress. As this account has shown, strong links between socialism and the temperance movement were to be found even earlier. A not inconsiderable proportion of the temperance people had joined or shown sympathy with Social Democracy; many of the party's supporters had worked for closer relations with the temperance movement. The ideological line that afterwards became dominant had been suggested on numerous occasions. In general, however, socialism had taken a position of skepticism or repudiation. During the time around the turn of the century the dominant sentiment turned. Statements favoring relaxation of tensions and collaboration became increasingly numerous and authoritative. At the 1905 party congress the change can be said to be complete. Conflicts and divisions between these popular movements occurred after 1905, but they did not have the same sharp, fundamental character as earlier. Statements of the kind which Branting and Danielsson aimed at the temperance movement would have appeared absurd a couple of decades later.

What are the most important causes of this transformation? An essential condition was that many workers, unconcerned with the disputes among the leading groups, joined socialism as well as the temperance movement. They did not find it impossible to unite faith in a thoroughgoing transformation of society with personal absolute abstinence and work for the immediate battle against the misuse of alcohol. But to this must be added the changes that gradually occurred in the general orientation of both movements. With the growth and stabilization of the temperance movement, the revivalist and salvationist elements became less apparent; the movement became a powerful apparatus for the advancement of collective goals. Even though religious connections were preserved, they were no longer central to the movement's activities. The socially conservative tendencies of the 1880's disappeared, and, on the whole, followed the general development of liberalism from *laissez faire* to social reformism. The special goal of the movement became legislation that would abolish alcoholic beverages: local option and prohibition. The means to reach this goal was democracy, primarily through universal suffrage, and the temperance movement therefore became—like the cultural radicals, the nonconformist religious groups, and the socialists—one of the forces that impelled the democratic breakthrough. At the same time Social Democracy appeared to be less and less utopian and revolutionary, and the day-to-day political work for the franchise and social reforms came to mark the whole movement's activities. Collaboration was established with middle-class radicalism, which to a great extent won its recruits among temperance advocates. A new generation of Social Democrats largely schooled within the temperance movement, began to assert itself in the party's work. The ideology on the temperance question of the first period had become antiquated.

The emergence of the new opinions is revealed with great clarity in the newspapers and political literature. In numerous newspaper articles and brochures it was maintained that opposition between socialism and temperance had harmed both movements, that increased temperance was of value both to the situation of the working class in the present and with regard to the future plans of socialism, and that the party must therefore pursue an active temperance program.

This line of thinking found its voice in the temperance order Verdandi, which was founded February 2, 1896. The immediate reason for the founding of this order was that a Good Templar lodge, which had long been known for radical tendencies, was expelled for refusing to drop an openly irreligious member. From this lodge came Verdandi, which for a long time was neutral in principle toward Social Democracy, but in practice often worked for collaboration with it. Thus the 1902 national meeting of lodges encouraged members to support Social Democratic candidates at that year's election, and in other contexts Verdandi representatives expressed sympathy with the workers' movement. In 1926, while adhering to political and religious neutrality on principle, the Verdandi movement adopted a program statement declaring that the use of alcohol hampered "the battle for freedom of the working class" and weakened class solidarity; for these reasons Verdandi wished to "bring together the working class and its sympathizers in an effective fight against liquor and the liquor interests. . . ." Verdandi has never belonged to the larger temperance organizations: in 1900 its estimated membership was 2,700, in 1910 about 20,000 (in the latter year there were more than 450,000 organized adult temperance advocates): and during the 1920's and 1930's its membership was, as a rule, under 10,000. The great majority of Social Democrats active in the temperance movement consequently have belonged to other organizations, primarily the Good Templar order. As a connecting link between the temperance movement and Social Democracy, the Verdandi order has played a certain role. Nevertheless, it is primarily the order's general philosophy as expressed in various publications, especially *Verdandisten,* and its typical attempt to fuse the efforts of both lines, that are of interest in this context.

Two lines dominate. On the one hand, it is emphasized that temperance legislation and the prohibition of liquor as well as social reforms demand the realization of universal suffrage. Temperance advocates and socialists consequently have a common goal, which per se should be a motive for collaboration. It is only

> through political activity that the working class will be able to obtain better conditions for itself and, by degrees, transform society. The same even applies to the realization of those changes in alcohol legislation which are the most important and special goals the temperance advocates strive for. The common watchword of the workers' for the time being ought therefore to be: win *universal* suffrage.

On the other hand, it was also said that these movements complemented each other even from a long-range point of view. The misuse of alcohol worsens the position of the worker and causes a stupefaction which renders political activity impossible. Therefore socialism has an interest in supporting temperance. But complete temperance cannot be attained without thoroughgoing social change and therefore temperance advocates ought to support socialism.

> Are not alcohol and religion the leading weapons of the upper class for keeping the masses in a state of ignorance and indifference, their best means for obtaining docile slaves and strike breakers? Should it not, on the other hand, be dear to the hearts of the true friends of temperance to see social conditions so transformed that people will not be driven by circumstances to take refuge in the bottle and the bar?

The temperance movement strives, it is maintained, to improve the individual, the trade union strives to improve the work group, the political organization is necessary to improve the working class in its entirety.

These viewpoints continually recur. They are concentrated in a kind of theory of interaction between capitalism and alcohol. The misuse of alcohol is due to capitalism, but it also strengthens capitalism by weakening the workers. The thought is clearly formulated in a lecture given by Kata Dalstrom on July 31, 1904: "The great social evils are the causes of mass drinking—and this, in turn, supports mass poverty through stupefying and degenerating the masses—which again, in turn, allows those in power to keep the people down at a low standard of living." Through the use of the old ideology's basic assumption, they had come to a conclusion which was its direct opposite: earlier it was maintained that the abolition of capitalism was a prerequisite for temperance; now it was maintained that temperance was a prerequisite for the abolition of capitalism. But other reasons were also put forth. The medical argument, which was emphasized at this time in temperance work, played a large role. Örne insisted that the working class should not be permitted to become incapable through the misuse of alcohol of fulfilling its historic mission: "a physically degenerated class cannot carry out any missions." Alcohol caused accidents at work and generally reduced the capacity for work. Sobriety increased the social prestige of the workers and thereby their possibilities of political success. The manufacture and sale of alcohol was a powerful capitalist interest; through temperance a direct assault on a branch of capitalism could be made. To many it was clear that the temperance question could not be solved through a social transformation according to the party's orientation. The opinion that alcoholism was only, or essentially, due to bad social conditions was characterized as erroneous. The misuse of alcohol would not disappear, wrote Vennerström.

> through obtaining for the so-called lower stratum of society an existence that is more secure and more commensurate with human dignity. The fight against alcoholism can therefore never have satisfactory results by conducting it exclusively as a struggle for better and more equitable social conditions. It must be directed right against the misuse of alcohol itself. And in this as in other social areas it falls to the Social Democrats to be in the lead. . . .

Similar views were put forth by socially oriented intellectuals, such as Natanael Beskow and Knut Kjellberg who were outside of Social Democratic circles; the association *Studenter och arbetare* and the periodical *Social tidskrift* appealed to the social demands and ambitions of the workers to convert them also to the cause of temperance.

By degrees there occurred a shift in the views of the leadership of the party which can be clarified through observing the changing views of Branting. During this period the sharp tone that had characterized the 1894 proposal and his justification of it disappeared completely. In September 1900 Branting wrote an editorial on "The Workers' Movement and the Temperance Movement." It gives an account of certain conservative attacks against Social Democracy as hostile to temperance, which Branting countered with an opposite opinion. He wrote that "it is impossible to speak of any *incompatibility* whatever between socialism and either moderate or ultra temperance movements"; to do so is "an atrocious falsehood." In April 1901 he explained in an editorial that "Social democracy" is "decidedly well-disposed toward the great popular movement working for temperance." Branting maintains that he is critical only of certain exaggerations in regard to encroachments on the freedom of the individual and of the opinion, "a one-sided view, which is now fortunately dying out . . . , that temperance can replace and obviate the need for great social reforms."

During the following period the paper reported strong unmitigated temperance propaganda with great sympathy. At the twenty-fifth aniversary of the Good Templar order, Branting delivered a pronouncement which contained a tribute to the temperance movement. Although this movement was politically neutral and even though it embraced reactionary groups, it was, however, "by and large a pioneer in the struggle for living conditions more worthy of human beings. Even those who were doubtful about absolutism as the only tenable view had therefore followed the progress of the movement with increasing sympathy, particularly as it "now seems to be in the process of building its foundation on the physical sciences and sociology rather than on dogmatic moralism. . . ." Branting further developed these ideas in a greeting delivered at the tenth anniversary of the Verdandi order.

> Since it is certain that a lost proletariat can never be the bearer of a higher social order, the fight against the misuse of alcohol as a popular custom must belong to the preparatory work for a socialist transformation. Closer relations between Social Democracy and the present temperance movement are thus bound to come about.

Branting now seems to have radically broken with his earlier quasi-Marxist view. The Social Democrats, he wrote, have something to learn from the temperance people, just as the latter have something to learn from the Social Democrats.

> The socialists, who are accustomed to seeing everywhere only the evil consequences of the class society—an all-too-facile and comfortable interpretation sometimes—would benefit from the lessons absolutism can often provide: that a reform of the individual's will can, nevertheless, accomplish great things. They should raise their demands on themselves and on their comrades-in-arms and protect more than before the idealistic component, which the struggle for higher wages and greater political power can so easily obscure in the long run.

It is not possible to establish how large a proportion of the party's membership was connected with various temperance organizations at different times. The observation that the temperance movement was successful throughout the country in rapidly winning members within the working class in the beginning of the 1900's, however, can be taken as implying that a very large part of the Social Democrats enrolled in the party were also organized absolutists. In the party's representation in the Riksdag, the proportion of temperance adherents was greater than during later years. Of the four Social Democrats elected to the lower house in 1902, three were temperance adherents—all except Branting. Nine of the thirteen elected in 1905 were temperance men. It can be considered probable, however, that the interest in temperance was somewhat overrepresented in this election. In certain places, in attempts to win support beyond the corps of purely Social Democratic voters, there was a tendency to nominate candidates who were well thought of in the temperance movement. It is notable that the Social Democratic youth, in particular, was the transmittor of temperance philosophy within the party. The 1905, 1907, and 1909 congresses of the youth union decided, for example, that liquor advertisements should not be accepted by the union's publications, that liquor was not to be served at affairs arranged by the youth clubs, and that the agitation of the union should "more than before put forth alcoholism as one of the greatest obstacles to our advancement." At the 1907 congress 132 of the 180 delegates were supposedly absolutists. The youth union consequently was avant-garde of the party on the temperance question. To a great extent it was members of this union who advocated the stronger temperance views at the 1908 and subsequent party congresses.

Even at the 1905 congress, however, the official transition of the party to a more positive standpoint on the temperance question was evident. In eleven motions it was urged that the congress make a statement on the question and/or include the question in the party program. All these motions were highly sympathetic to temperance and several contained a demand for a program article on the prohibition of alcohol. Because of these motions the party administration urged that the congress pass a resolution but not make an addition to the program; such an amendment could seem as inconsistent with the practice of the party's newspapers, which accepted liquor advertisements, and could lead to the judging of election candidates primarily by their position on the temperance article. The proposed resolution should state that the success of the party of the workers was essentially dependent on the soundness and battle-worthiness of the working class, that the use of alcohol had a degenerative effect on individuals and on a people, and that the effects of alcoholism led to "a social danger which cannot automatically be presumed to disappear with the class society." The congress should accordingly state that the party wished to support the temperance movement—without binding itself to any special approach to the solution of the problem—and that the party's representatives in the Riksdag should "support the practical proposals which can contribute to sound progress in this area and to the general good." In the attendant debate all the speakers recommended some kind of clarification of the party's positive attitude on temperance. Many held that a program article was necessary because a resolution would soon be forgotten. Others maintained that a program article could bring about unnecessary strife within the party. A vote on whether a statement on the subject should be included in the program resulted in a vote of 125 in favor of such action and 48 opposed; even strong temperance advocates, such as Thorsson, belonged to the opposition. Subsequently a program article of the following wording was passed: "Promotion of the cause of temperance through education on the nature of alcohol and its effects in all public schools and through the support of practicable temperance legislation." This article was adopted by a vote of 131 to 6; the 6 dissenting votes were cast in favor of a much longer proposal, drafted in the same spirit. Some members, among them A. C. Lindblad and Wickman —not Branting—objected to including the question in the program, but at the same time expressed sympathy for the temperance struggle.

The transition in the development of a Social Democratic temperance policy concluded with the 1905 decision. Before we begin the account of the following period, we should look for a moment at a question often debated along with the problem dealt with here. It can be formulated as follows: In what degree has Swedish Social Democracy, personally and organizationally, benefited from the earlier and much more successful activities of the temperance advocates?

As noted by Lindbom, some have maintained the view, "that the temperance movement was a pioneer for [both] the trade union and political worker movements." This and similar statements are extremely unclear. Some probably meant that followers of the temperance movement to a relatively great extent were also members of the workers' movement, particularly the trade union movement. Such a view does not appear tenable. Certainly a large number of workers were temperance advocates and members of political and trade union worker organizations at the same time. But the statistical data collected by Lindbom show that—to the extent that the percentage of workers in certain occupations and in certain places who belonged to temperance organizations and to trade unions, is known—no correlation between temperance interest and membership in trade unions can be established. In other words, in certain places there were many temperance adherents and few trade union members, but in other places just the opposite condition prevailed. Some have similarly regarded the organizational knowledge in the workers' movement to have come from the temperance organizations as well as from the Liberal workers' movement and the nonconformist sects; at times the implication clearly is that the workers' movement to a great extent obtained its recruits from these quarters. Theories of this kind, formulated with a certain emphasis, can easily give an appearance of deep significance to the obvious—that before going over to socialism or entering a trade union some older workers had participated in other organizations. But as a rule the theory seems to be that the temperance advocates—possibly followers of the other movements mentioned—formed a kind of core group within the workers' movement. It would hardly be possible to provide any evidence either for or against this view. It is easy to list a number of prominent socialists who began as temperance advocates, but it is equally easy to give examples of socialist leaders who have had no connection with the temperance movement. Further enlightenment on the question would require a study that perused the membership rolls of associations and made an investigation of the participation of individuals in such associations—a study that the problem is undoubtedly not worth and which probably would not provide unequivocal criteria.

The Culmination and Fall of the Prohibition Movement

IN THE PERIOD after 1905 the dominant line in Social Democracy has been definitely positive toward measures promoting temperance. Differences of opinion have essentially revolved about the degree of state intervention and especially about the question of prohibition versus restriction. During the period before the restriction system came into being the prohibition line grew continually stronger; thereafter there was an increase in sympathy for restriction and in reaction against the prohibition demand contained in the program; and, finally, after the 1922 consultive referendum made prohibition a dead issue, a relaxation occurred and the temperance question as a program issue receded completely into the background. In the Riksdag the party, or in every case its majority, has as a rule, supported the proposals which were more restrictive and thus gained the assistance of the organized temperance advocates. Generally over half of the party's representatives have belonged to the Riksdag's temperance group or to the Social Democratic temperance group organized in 1923. This latter group had 80 members in 1923, 88 in 1928, 88 in 1932, and 90 in 1938. An investigation of the handling of Riksdag questions in this context is not warranted.

This can also be seen as the complete subordination of the special socialist view which appeared as an application of Marxist doctrine. In general the reasons for the adoption of a stand on the issue of prohibition versus restriction put forth at the party congresses and in the press were the same as those given in discussions of the question in other situations. Therefore a more detailed account of the arguments in the socialist debate is of little interest in an investigation of the party's ideology. This also applies to the movement which was directed against prohibition and restriction, and which, with Palm's assistance, asserted itself especially during the 1910s. Even here only the contemporary antitemperance propaganda is generally found, sometimes embellished with arguments of the type which we are familiar with from the socialists' remarks in the 1880s.

At the 1908 congress a large number of motions were proposed, a majority of which were aimed at sharpening the program article on the temperance question. During the debate a recommendation signed by 172 of the representatives at the congress, a majority of all the members, was presented; it urged that the following formulation be adopted: "The combatting of alcoholism through education is all public schools on the nature and effects of alcohol on the individual and society together with legislative activity, which, through the so-called local option and other effective legislative measures, will lead to the solution of the alcohol problem." This proposal was explained as necessary because of the unclear formulation of the previous program article and because the introduction of local option had become the most important temperance demand of the day. The new article need not, it was said, "make the party's nonabsolutists apprehensive." The party administration urged that the old program article be retained, and several speakers criticized the far-reaching demands of the temperance advocates. Branting did not speak in the debate, but stated in his newspaper "that the absolutist majority of the congress had created a dangerous and indefensible precedent when it put forth demands which had beforehand secured an immovable majority of the congress"; because of this the debate became "only humbug." The proposal to strengthen the program was passed, however, by a vote of 190 to 79. The congress further declared that the party press should give coverage to and support temperance work; however, it was pointed out "that no single question, no matter how important it appears to many, should be allowed to become so prominent that the party's character is distorted or its inner solidarity disrupted." The party's occasional publications should not be permitted to contain advertisements for alcoholic beverages.

The 1911 party congress marks the culmination of the extreme temperance line in that the demand for prohibition was practically unanimously approved. This was certainly due in large measure to the positive results of the temporary liquor prohibition put into effect during the 1909 general strike, which were taken to indicate that an effective application of prohibition was possible. The 1909 private referendum, in which almost 1.9 million votes supported the prohibition of alcoholic beverages, was certainly also of importance for the decision. The party administration unanimously put forth a proposal of the following content: "The combatting of alcoholism through education in all public schools on the nature and effects of alcohol on the individual and society and through legislative activity which will lead to legal prohibition of alcoholic beverages." This proposal was passed with only two opposing votes, which supported Palm's recommendation that the program article be retained unchanged. Among the arguments in favor of the party administration's proposal were the contention that a democratic party could not oppose a demand that was supported by popular opinion, and that the fight against alcohol was a part of the class struggle. Branting stated that he had reservations about the proposal. The experiences of the prohibition enforced during the general strike ought not to be exaggerated; a temporary prohibition of alcoholic beverages under more normal conditions would be more instructive. Branting said that he had followed Dr. Bratt's proposal and that this plan might indicate a better way than prohibition. "But now when the congress had decided on the prohibition of alcoholic beverages as a goal, this signifies a most inspiring arousal of the working class itself against the terrible evil which the misuse of alcohol is now creating in our country."

At the 1914 congress signs of a reaction against the prohibition decision can be noted. Several of the motions proposed urged a softening of the program article. The party administration favored the retention of the article in unchanged form, but a reservation by Branting suggested that the last words "legal prohibition of alcoholic beverages" be replaced with "general popular temperance." This, like several other program questions, was submitted to a program commission and thus was not actually dealt with by the congress. Sixteen delegates nevertheless announced that they shared Branting's view, while 107 members stated that they favored the existing program article. It also ought to be noted that the August meeting of the congress came out in favor of temporary prohibition because of the war, and that the later conference in Novemeber demanded the return of restrictions passed by the Riksdag immediately after the outbreak of the war, but later abolished.

In 1917 the proposals referred to the program commission in 1914, together with some additional motions on the subject, were taken under consideration. The motions indicate that the demand for a softening of the prohibition standpoint had won ground. The party administration proposed, however, that the old program article remain in tact, except for one change of little importance. Branting and Möller dissented. Branting declared it to be "objectionable that a party which does not demand personal absolutism of its membership and which indeed includes among its members and voters many tens of thousands of nonabsolutists should be bound to an article requiring absolute national prohibition"; and he emphasized his doubts about the possibility of maintaining prohibition. Both dissidents presented Branting's 1914 proposal. The detailed debate hardly provided any new viewpoints. Some said that prohibition was a consequence of socialism, pointing to the importance of the liquor interests, and maintained that it was in the interest of the whole of capitalism to render the masses easily manageable through drunkenness (Spak). It was also asserted that the prohibition article conflicted with the program's demand for individual responsibility; Thorberg alleged that the prohibition idea was based on the opinion that man did not have enough character to be educated to be temperate and must therefore have a demoralizing effect. The majority of speakers, however, presented more commonplace and more reasonable points of view; all the usual views for and against both prohibition and restriction were cited. The result was that the congress defeated the minority proposal by a vote of 138 to 35, and kept the program article in unchanged form. In addition, a resolution was passed against the Association for Civil Freedom, an organization opposed to prohibition and tighter restrictions, and which some Social Democrats had joined. The resolution stated that "giving the Citizens' Association support and encouragement can no longer be tolerated among friends of the party."

The deliberations at the next congress in 1920 show that the more extreme temperance line had become substantially weakened, although the prohibition line had not entirely disappeared. It was significant that two of the largest party locals—those in Stockholm and Malmö—which on certain earlier occasions had expressed themselves in favor of prohibition, now proposed deletion of the whole temperance article. A number of motions (e.g., from the party locals in Gothenburg, Uppsala, and Örebro) proposed a softening of the article in accordance with Branting's earlier proposal. To some degree the change that could be ascertained was due to the fact that the Left Socialists—who were generally thoroughgoing advocates of temperance—had left the party. Opinions were divided within the program commission and in the party administration. The majority in the party administration, in agreement with the party commission's proposal, urged that nothing be stated about prohibition; as before, the temperance article should demand education on the alcohol problem about further "legislative measures, that would both remove the social causes of alcoholism and prevent its social damage." Furthermore, the congress should state that prohibition legislation should not be passed before at least two-thirds of the men and women eligible to vote declared themselves in favor of such legislation through a national referendum. Five dissidents in the party administration, supporting an alternative proposal of the program commission, wanted the idea of prohibition retained, although in somewhat modified form. According to their proposal the temperance article should read as follows: "The combatting of alcoholism. Education on the effects of alcohol on the individual and society. Measures for removal of the social causes of alcoholism. Restriction and prohibition legislation." Two other dissidents requested that the program article simply come out in favor of national prohibition of alcoholic beverages.

The debate dealt mainly with the proposal of the party administration and the alternative proposal of the five dissidents. It was notable that certain prominent party members who had been organized temperance advocates for a long time (Åkerberg, Engberg) took the side of the party administration, while emphasizing that the demand for prohibition split the party and that in all certainty the sentiment for prohibition among the workers was less strong now than earlier. It was also charged that temperance advocates had become overrepresented through skillful and ruthless tactics in elections of different kinds. The dissidents (such as Oscar Olsson, Viktor Larsson) criticized the administration proposal on the grounds that it was unclear and necessarily gave the impression that the party had shifted its position on the temperance question. The minority proposal won by a bare majority—118 votes to 105—over the proposal of the party administration.

After this the question of a referendum on prohibition was taken up. After several votes the proposal of the party administration was passed. In the last vote 98 supported this proposal and 85, a proposal which did not contain a provision for a two-thirds majority, but only a qualified majority. The congress consequently adopted a statement—not a program article—with the following wording:

> Because the maintenance of a national prohibition of alcoholic beverages presupposes that it has support in a firm and predominant popular concensus, the congress declares that the Riksdag should not pass prohibition legislation before the country's men and women who are eligible to vote in a national referendum express themselves in favor of such a prohibition on alcoholic beverages by a majority of at least two-thirds of those participating in the voting.

The rulings of the congress had a peculiar character. This was particularly true of the program article itself. The words "restriction and prohibition legislation" could be interpreted to mean that the article called for restrictions and, possibly, under certain conditions, even prohibition; but they could also —as the debate made evident—be taken to mean that restrictions little by little would lead to prohibition. It is not unlikely that this lack of clarity was intentional and was thought to facilitate the support of those favoring the restriction system. In addition, the congress in its special statement opposed prohibition legislation should it win less than two-thirds of a majority in a referendum. In a manner similar to that of several other organizations at this time, the congress also (if somewhat vaguely) programmatically favored prohibition, but maintained that it should satisfy more severe conditions than other kinds of legislation.

In the referendum on prohibition of alcoholic beverages held in August 1922, well-known Social Democrats spoke out in the press and elsewhere both for and against prohibition. A study of the press shows, however, that many newspapers, among them *Social-Demokraten,* did not systematically advocate its viewpoint, even where this can be gleaned from scattered statements. The desire not to emphasize conflicts within the party before the referendum is apparent. After the prohibition referendum the Social Democratic press, in line with the whole public discussion, put forth the view that the prohibition question would not be a pressing issue for a long time to come. When the newspapers were criticized by those friendly to prohibition for not working to accomplish it, *Social-Demokraten,* among others, answered that the prohibition referendum "was arranged precisely in order to free the political parties from agitation," and that belief in prohibition was not required by the Social Democratic program. Ny Tid maintained that the words "restriction and prohibition legislation" in the program meant freedom of choice on the question of restrictions or prohibition.

After the prohibition referendum the temperance question slipped into the background of Swedish politics in general as well as in Social Democratic party debate. At the party congresses held after 1922 it has been touched upon only fleetingly or not at all. At the 1924 congress only three motions were proposed on the subject, two of them originated in small party locals and one was put forth by a private individual; on the one hand, a softening of the prohibition article was desired, on the other, a sharpening of the article. The party administration declared that it was undesirable to arouse new strife over the formulation of the article. Changing the article was not necessary after the prohibition referendum, because a permanent prohibition of alcoholic beverages could not, in any case, be regarded as an issue until after a new referendum were held. The referendum recommendation of the party administration to reject the motions was approved without voting. Only a single motion, dealing with a question of a detail was brought before the 1928 congress and that motion was defeated. In 1932 the Uppsala Party local proposed deleting the words "restriction and prohibition legislation" from the program, but the party administration urged rejection of this motion which was defeated after a short debate. In addition, the congress passed a resolution against illegal traffic in alcoholic beverages in which the party membership was encouraged to support action against this trade. A motion on the prohibition of advertisements for alcoholic beverages in Social Democratic newspapers was declined without voting. At the 1936 congress the temperance question was not brought up in any form.

It has often been maintained that the temperance question, and particularly the issue of prohibition, played a greater role within Social Democracy—especially in the period of 1908–1922—than warranted by the support for this demand among the party's voters and those connected with the party. Some believe that the temperance advocates succeeded in securing a disproportionately large influence in the nomination of candidates for national as well as for intraparty elections by driving ahead their viewpoint while more or less ignoring other issues. It is not possible to make any well-grounded judgment on this point. In general, the handling of the temperance question within the party, as in the whole country, can probably be regarded as corresponding to the development of worker opinion and public opinion in general. During the decade prior to World War I, the temperance movement underwent a great growth and the demand for prohibition won a large following. This was made clear primarily through the large unofficial referendum of 1909. Little by little a reaction occurred; it was largely related to the emergence of the restriction system and was also stimulated by certain foreign experiences. After the 1922 referendum prohibition was no longer regarded as a realistic possibility. Nevertheless, it is conceivable that advocates of prohibition within the Social Democratic party during certain times succeeded in obtaining a more dominant position than their strength in the social democratically oriented working class would warrant. There are many examples of how a group that totally concentrates on a certain definite issue can assert itself within an organization where this issue is not of central importance to the other members. As far as the program article in question is concerned—if it is interpreted as a demand for prohibition—it obviously does not reflect the dominant opinion within the party. Its ambiguous character has, however, made possible its preservation without much dissension.

Summary

THE YOUNG Social Democracy regarded the misuse of alcohol—as it did war, crime, and immorality—essentially as a consequence of the capitalist system, or, expressed in more Marxist terms, as a social and moral evil that was necessarily related to this system. With the formation of the socialist society, the alcohol problem would disappear. The temperance movement was readily regarded as one of the means through which the existing order intended to perpetuate itself, as a method to remove or conceal one of the conditions that showed the shortcomings of this order, and as a part of the socially conservative and old-liberal ideology of self-help. In any event, temperance was regarded as being of little value. The idea that a working class could obtain tolerable living conditions through temperance and thrift contained in itself an attack on Marxist theory.

As soon as belief in collaboration with other movements to win limited goals gained acceptance, it became impossible to maintain these views. In the battle for democracy the socialists and temperance advocates found a common platform. The need of the masses of workers for an immediate improvement in that situation drove them to the temperance movement and forced socialism to accept it. The socialist leaders changed their position on the question while maintaining Marxist premises. The misuse of alcohol was characterized as a means of keeping the proletariat suppressed. Its abolition was one of the prerequisites for the formation of a class conscious and active working class. Alcohol was now assigned the role previously given to the earlier temperance movement—that of a tool of capitalism. The development that coincidently took place in the temperance movement gave support to this view. Within the movement socially conservative and old-liberal tendencies were succeeded by those favoring democracy and social reform; the individual moralistic view gave way to the social.

Along with the growth of Social Democracy and its shedding of the Marxist line, the temperance issue came to be regarded mainly in terms of suitability or advantage to the society from a short-range point of view. A general ideology was replaced by deliberations directly pertinent to the situation at hand. The specifically socialist viewpoint was abandoned. Utilitarian points of view, of the more general and vague kind which characterized day-to-day political discussion, became decisive. Socialism can thereby be considered to have moved close to the sentiments which, primarily for reasons other than the programmatic positions of the major political parties, prevailed among the majority of the people. The party has not sustained an independent line.

Consumer Cooperation

The Change from Criticism to Appreciation of the Cooperative Movement

COLLABORATION between private groups for the purchase and distribution of goods, unlike cooperation in the production of goods, has not played a central role in socialist theory. Such collaboration has been propagated by socialists, but it has not been regarded as a means of solving The Social Question. Lassalle saw it as an arrangement that was of no importance in improving the circumstances of the working class. Marxist-oriented socialism was for a long time indifferent or hostile to the consumer cooperative movement. The English workers' movement, on the other hand, entered into intimate collaboration with the cooperative movement at an early date. To judge from the relatively few statements which can be found, a large segment of Swedish Social Democrats rejected the movement, at least for about a decade. Like the temperance movement, consumer cooperation appeared to be an expression of petty bourgeois, undiluted liberal self-help ideology, supported by writers and workers who were outside the socialist camp. According to the theory of the Iron Law of Wages, a lowering of the price of consumer goods could lead only to a corresponding decline in wages. Even when this view was abandoned, Social Democrats often remained critical of cooperation as a means of diverting the interest of the working class away from the essential goal: the conquest of political power. A particularly important reason for the lack of faith in consumer cooperation was the Smith Circle Movement, which, for various reasons, was fought by Palm and other Social Democrats. When this movement failed, consumer cooperation in general was also discredited. For many years thereafter, they were inclined to equate this kind of cooperation with the Circle Movement and to repudiate it on this ground alone. The subject was otherwise of little importance because only a few consumer cooperatives were in operation at this time.

Consumer cooperation was not dealt with in the programmatic statements of the 1880s and 1890s. Nor does it seem to have been a subject of discussion in this context. At the constituent party congress a motion from the painters' union of Gothenburg was presented which did, in fact, raise the question of whether consumer associations "consisting of class-conscious workers' corporations" ought to be established, but no statement was made on this. Information on the position of the Social Democrats during this time, therefore, can only be obtained from newpapers and brochures. During the years 1883–1885 *Folkviljan* published a large number of attacks on the ideology of self-help in general and on consumer cooperation as a manifestation of it. The sharp edge of these attacks was often directed against the Circle Movement, but the writers explicitly and repeatedly stated that all cooperative enterprises of the Schultze-Delitzsch variety were worthless to the workers, for if the cost of living declined the workers' wages would also decline. The argumentation is taken from Lassalle. The first time *Social-Demokraten* dealt with consumer cooperation seems to be in an article appearing in 1886 on consumer associations in Belgium. It declared that the opinion that there were no benefits to be gained through similar organizations represented an obsolete theory, yet it criticized consumer cooperation as tending to train the workers to be petty bourgeois. Several years later, in 1894, Branting discussed cooperation in an article entitled "An Antiquated Quack Remedy." The cooperative associations provided, he wrote, no solution whatever to The Social Question; they offered only superficial changes. Nonetheless, it was possible for socialism to support them since it did not wish to neglect contemporary problems because of visions of the future. He explains further,

> that we socialists certainly do not overlook or disdain the advantages of cooperation for the workers where it can suitably be used. In contrast to the blind admirers of this system, however, we are also aware of its disadvantages, of which incomparably the most important is the persistent temptation it contains to *weaken class consciousness* among the workers, to replace the feelings of solidarity, which ought to unite *all* parts of the unpropertied class, with a business interest that unites only a pack of privileged businessmen.

Cooperative associations, which by their very nature cannot be fully public in the present society, entail the danger of dividing the workers. "But if this danger can be avoided anywhere, it is precisely in the socialist cooperative enterprise, whose members are brought together not only by an economic interest in cheap goods, but by a common insight into the great mission shared by the working class." The article, written in a somewhat hesitant tone, apparently concludes by recommending purely socialist consumer associations along the Belgian model; cooperatives, if they are encouraged at all, should be closely connected to the party, in the manner of the trade union movement. In *Arbetet* critical statements about cooperatives also appear from the beginning of the movement. An unsigned editorial from 1891 speaks of

> the myth of Rochdale's paradisical consumers' association. . . . To organize workers for the purpose of obtaining somewhat cheaper provisions for them by doing away with dealers and small shopkeepers is neither anything remarkable nor anything that will transform society. It is *liberal capitalism.* We wish to call it Smithism because it was L. O. Smith, big businessman and *brännvin* distiller, who conducted the great unsuccessful experiment with this idea in Sweden.

Other statements appear to indicate that, at least during the 1880s, a critical opinion of consumer cooperation prevailed.

During the 1890s another ideological line gradually came into prominence. This should be viewed essentially as a result of the spontaneous action of the workers themselves. Just as the workers formed trade unions to obtain higher wages without any socialist motivation and entered temperance associations for private reasons in spite of the negative stand of socialism, so they also began to form consumer associations in order to obtain cheaper goods—again acting independently of socialist doctrine. Here, as in other cases, the socialist leaders in their attempt to bring together the workers approved these attitudes and gave them a formal justification. Without doubt they became convinced of the value of the cooperative movement from a socialist point of view. Socialist philosophy showed itself capable of creating a theoretical support for consumer cooperation just as readily as it lent itself to demonstrating the meaninglessness or unsuitability of such cooperation.

During the 1880s and 1890s consumer cooperation was discussed in a growing number of trade unions and locally established groups of workers; in several cases positive results were obtained. In Stockholm a Social Democratic worker, A. Rylander, was the most active in organizational work and agitation for the cooperative idea. Some months after Branting's previously mentioned skeptical editorial, Rylander wrote a series of articles in *Social-Demokraten* where he maintained the value of cooperation from a socialist standpoint. He emphasized its importance in moral training and its capacity to serve as a support to the party.

> The Social Democratic party in an economically backward country ought not to neglect to use this important source of power, and neither has it any reason of principle for doing so. A party which demands common production and distribution in all or most areas certainly should, from a reasonable point of view, encourage with all of its energies even the weakest attempts which can now be made as a step in the right direction. . . . Let us then create something which can give the unbelieving something to ponder over. . . . Let us begin by unifying our economy as far as we can. The time has passed when men believed they could create or change its economic foundations by a few strokes of the pen. Why not then go forward step by step in the economic sector as in the political—deliberately and boldly, yet carefully—advancing our positions.

At the same time, in November 1894, The Workers' Cooperative Consumer Association was founded under Rylander's leadership. Everyone had the right to acquire shares and in this way become a member, but it appealed primarily to workers. Not until 1897 was the necessary minimum capital—6,000 crowns—subscribed in full and the enterprise able to begin operation.

In Gothenburg, A. C. Lindblad, who became editor of *Ny Tid* in 1898, assumed the leadership in the cooperative organization work. In the winter of 1895–1896 Lindblad proposed that a consumer association be established within the Gothenburg party local. A committee was appointed, which in April 1896 presented a report recommending consumer associations as providing "support in the class struggle."

The committee was agreed that the old form of consumer associations, based only on profit-sharing, did not correspond to the view of the working class on the matter. The consumer association must become a tool in the class struggle, a support in the struggle of the working class to obtain a more tolerable standard of living for itself. . . . In other words, it should furnish the workers with ammunition in the social war they wage for a better society.

Several statements made around this time pointed out that the workers were impoverished not only by the factory owners at their place of work, but also by the businessmen in the stores. Consumer associations were a weapon against the enemy, the organized capitalist class, and should be "a transitional stage in the new society." They cited Bebel and Charles Gide, the special theorist of cooperation. In addition, they cited the Belgian party associations as models. In 1898 the cooperative association *Fram* (*Forward*) began operation in accordance with these views. The association was the property of the party local—with certain rights for private individuals to purchase shares—and only members of the party local were entitled to a share of the profits, which would be proportionate to their outlay in purchases. By February 1899 it was decided, however, that all purchasers should be participants in the profit sharing.

In Malmo, where cooperative ideas had been practiced to some extent since the late 1880s, Danielsson began an energetic agitation for them in the spring of 1897. In a number of articles he broke away from the earlier negative line and placed consumer cooperation in an ideological context. The Iron Law of Wages was explained to be incorrect in its general form. Socialist theory had the capacity to abandon untenable viewpoints and showed its truth and practical utility in that it does not exhaust its power in futile attempts to do violence to reality, but allies itself naturally and without constraint to all the diverse popular movements in different countries with the aim of leading the working classes forward along historically opened and safe paths to a higher degree of culture and to a social position of greater freedom.

Consumer cooperation, when taken charge of not by liberal manufacturers but by the workers and primarily by the Social Democratic party, should also prove advantageous from this point of view.

Nothing that is of practical advantage to the workers, as long as it is not unworthy of their principles as a struggling lower class, no practical activity aimed at mitigating need or at making poverty more tolerable ought to be disdained by Social Democrats. They should, on the contrary, be in the vanguard, assume the initiative, and take over the leadership.

In Sweden the time was ripe for cooperative activity on a greater scale. The groundwork has been well prepared by the trade unions, and since the drive to action in the political arena is virtually paralysed among the working class, its numerous dormant forces could be put to use here instead. Through the rapid development of consumer associations we would also provide ourselves with the very best rearguard support in the event of an attempt to force through a suffrage reform by means of a general strike.

In a pamphlet published later Danielsson asserted the same viewpoint. In January 1898 the question of consumer associations was taken up by the Social Democratic association in Malmo. After several deliberations it was decided in March at a meeting between the collaborating trade unions and a committee appointed to investigate the question, of which Danielsson was a member, to form the consumer association *Pan*. Contrary to the plan in Gothenburg, it was decided from the beginning that profits were to be distributed according to purchases. Everyone had the right to subscribe to shares. The leader of the enterprise was a worker, O. Persson.

In the country's three largest cities cooperative associations thus came into existence in the years 1897–1898 under the leadership of Social Democrats and with the support of socialist-oriented organizations. They apparently thought —in accordance with Branting's statement of 1894—that these associations would remain in a close relationship to Social Democracy; it was not uncommon to regard them as counterparts to the trade unions in the area of goods distribution. However, membership in these associations was usually not limited to persons who were members of the corresponding trade unions or party locals, although a couple of smaller associations did enact such restrictions. The great majority of the associations established by workers at this time did not approve the principle of membership restrictions, and enacted a policy of membership open to all.

In 1898 the cooperative movement was noted for the first time in a report of the Social Democratic party administration. The reference was characterized by a somewhat hesitant sympathy. It was stated that the consumer association founded in Stockholm in 1898 had obtained a number of successors—in Gothenburg, Malmo, Gävle, Hellefors, and Bofors. The administration states that it does not want to go into "an exposition of reasons for and against the cooperative system." However, it adds later the fact that it is obvious that cooperative efforts assert themselves along with the growth of the working class, since they make possible a lower price for food and thus mitigate the subsistence struggle of the workers.

The cooperative organizations, brought along as auxiliaries, so to speak, in the forward march of the working class, can also serve as a valuable material support in the ever-extending conflicts, which, as the events of the day plainly show, will determine the character of developments in the immediate future.

In June 1899 the leaders of the cooperative associations in Stockholm, Gothenburg, and Malmo met at a conference to prepare for the establishment of a union of consumer associations. They decided to turn to the Social Democratic party administration and request an opinion on the party's position regarding the movement. The question was taken up by the executive committee on June 12th. Lindblad, with the concurrence of Rylander, declared that the party should utilize the cooperative movement "as a social backbone." Branting considered the question to be a peculiar kind, since the party program had nothing to say about cooperation, but he did not want to state an opinion in opposition to it. It was decided "that the party administration strongly support the cooperative enterprises and influence the party press to work more actively for this institution as one of the party's own concerns." The three cooperative associations which arranged the conference then invited the consumer associations throughout the country to a cooperative congress in Stockholm. This conference, which was held September 4–6, 1899, brought together representatives from 41 associations with a combined membership of nearly 9000. A large proportion of the organizations regarded themselves as workers' associations and the participants at the congress were for the most part workers.

In conjunction with the congress several Social Democratic newspapers stated opinions which showed very considerable appreciation of cooperation and a tendency to want to join the movement to the Social Democratic camp. In *Social-Demokraten* F. Nilsson wrote that cooperation ought to be "of the greatest importance for the whole economic liberation effort of the Swedish workers"; foreign experience also showed "that the workers' organizations could gain good economic support from strong cooperative enterprises at critical times." Other newspapers quoted Jaurès' words to the effect that cooperation would be able to create "communistic crystallization centers in the capitalist disorder." From the scant information about the congress which is available it appears evident that any attachment to the Social Democratic party had not been considered and that during the proceedings of the congress a politically neutral line became more and more distinctly manifest. The initiators proposed and the congress decided to establish a cooperative union consisting of consumer associations. In the proposal for bylaws sent out before the congress convened, the initiators had included a regulation according to which the union's central office, among other things, should "keep a watchful eye on the development of the cooperative movement to see that it becomes an important factor in the struggle of the working class for existence and for a worthy place in society." An organization committee appointed by the congress changed the proposal by inserting the phrase "in raising [the level of] the common people in moral as well as in an economic respect" after the word "factor." The congress finally decided on a formulation that was wholly free from class emphasis; the previously cited words were replaced with "to disseminate general training in citizenship and to raise the level of the people in moral as well as in economic respects." The principle of political neutrality, which the cooperative movement has subsequently upheld, was thereby established. As far as is known no criticism of the position taken by the congress, was presented by the Social Democrats.

THE DEBATE OVER THE NEUTRALITY AND INDEPENDENCE OF THE COOPERATIVE MOVEMENT

At the 1900 party congress the question of cooperation was taken up for the first time. Pursuant to a motion, a resolution was unanimously passed after a few comments not reported in the protocol; its wording was as follows:

> With reference to the party program regarding the takeover by society of the means of production, before which no essential betterment of the working class with regard to its position in society can be expected, the congress states its sympathy with the cooperative movement as an educational transitional form toward the goal of Social Democracy and an important means in the class struggle. The congress, therefore, issues a strong appeal to the organized workers throughout the country to actively participate in it.

The statement seems to take a middle line between the critical position of earlier years and the enthusiastic faith in the value of cooperation which appeared in certain discussions at the end of the 1890s. It sympathizes with cooperation and recognizes its importance as a weapon in the class struggle, but maintains that cooperatives cannot essentially improve the position of the working class. The impression is that of a tired old Marxist opinion of the kind expressed in earlier statements on the temperance movement and certain other sociopolitical efforts. At the 1905 congress a similar, perhaps somewhat more positive resolution was adopted.

The question was more thoroughly dealt with at the 1908 congress. Pursuant to a motion the party administration proposed a statement characterizing the cooperative movement "as an important means in the liberation struggle of the working class, whose goals are the eradication of poverty and creation of a social order based on socialist principles through the conquest of political and economic power in society." Cooperative enterprises in the area of production as well as distribution ought to develop the capacity of the working class to take over these functions. The workers were therefore encouraged to support the cooperative associations through membership and the purchase of goods and to assist in the founding of new associations. During the debate a speaker (Lindley) contended that cooperation was not specifically socialist and that the cooperative movement was not so solidly based that one could predict what value it would have. "We want to support cooperation that paves the way for socialism, but it is unwise to bid the workers support all cooperative enterprises." It was emphasized that The Cooperative Union (*Kooperativa förbundet* or *KF*) had indicated its political neutrality. In spite of these reservations, the speaker urged approval of the party administration's proposal. Palm, on the other hand, criticized the proposal. The cooperative movement had demands which had to be combatted. "We want to have a cooperative socialist society, but want to have nothing to do with the present petty bourgeois cooperative movement." The party administration's proposal, however, was approved without a vote. It signifies yet another step toward the recognition of cooperation, which was now regarded as one of the roads to socialism.

The question of cooperation was also brought up at the Scandinavian workers' Conferences. In 1901 as well as in 1907 resolutions were passed which in general had essentially the same content as those of the Swedish party congresses of 1900 and 1908.

Enthusiastic recognition of the value of cooperation from a socialist viewpoint is often found in the press in the early 1900s. In answer to the contention voiced by bourgeois elements that there was a certain contradiction between the cooperative movement and the idea of "revolution through class conflict," *Social-Demokraten* and *Arbetet* explained in the summer of 1901 that cooperation could be regarded as a stage in the revolutionary class conflict, if only one recognized that revolution was a slow transformation, not a bloody upheaval. It was even conceivable that the cooperative associations would gradually displace the capitalist system by building up socialism within the capitalist framework. Another newspaper alleged that there was no conflict present "between the cooperative idea of self-help and the theory of the class struggle," for the returns the cooperative movement made were not a decisive influence on the workers. "They know that they lay the basis for the new building of society that is to come, at the same time that they, as a class, seek to get a foothold in the society that has cast them out." Some years later *Social-Demokraten* wrote that cooperation was nothing but

> an abolition of the right of private ownership, an expropriation of the capitalist and the private usurper, whose profits in cooperation return to those he formerly lived off and taxed. It begins with the displacement of the retailer, continues with the wholesaler, and proceeds by degrees so as to make even the private capitalist superfluous.

It is suggested that even in a socialist society cooperation, as a flexible form of organization, would have a function to fulfill. *Ny Tid* from 1909 contains a couple of characteristic articles. The *Gothenburg Morgonpost* had declared that cooperation ran errands for socialism. No person, answered *Ny Tid,* wants to deny "this crystal-clear fact." In all contemporary societies a socializing process is, in fact, taking place which functions "far less with the help of the state than through the voluntary activity of individuals in their different economic groupings. The cooperative movement takes a leading place among these." This movement was admittedly less conspicuous than political work "but is nevertheless of extraordinary importance for the socialization of society, just as its activity is of a far more *revolutionary* nature than it appears to be at first glance." Through the organization of the consumers, influence over production would also gradually be gained.

The articles just cited were written in connection with the debate that was occasioned by the tenth anniversary of KF in June of 1909. The great appreciation of cooperation within Social Democracy was expressed in different ways. *Social-Demokraten* published a special issue on the cooperative movement. In this issue Järte supplied an overview of "Socialism and Cooperation" in which he established that socialism had moved from indifference or hostility toward the consumer cooperative movement to a recognition of its great value. With the revisionist currents, which had learned from the experiences in England and Belgium, cooperation had gained a secure place in socialist theory and practice. "All Social Democrats are probably also beginning to agree on the truth in Bernstein's words that the problem of socialism's realization essentially coincides with the question of the economic potency of the cooperative organizations." Järte favored stronger economic collaboration between the small landowner and the industrial worker. In this way one would be able to obtain not only lower prices, but "an increasingly greater regulation over the whole grocery business." Branting sent a greeting to the KF congress in a telegram which, in a rather sensational way, hailed cooperation as a socialist weapon and moreover suggested that its activity ought to be systematically directed to this end.

> Cooperation silently builds up the social system of socialism in the midst of capitalism, completes through direct action the takeover of centralized production by the state and commune, and becomes, when permeated by the socialist spirit, an indispensable part of continually increased importance in the forward movement of the working class. If we also can soon have in Sweden a cooperative organization equal to our proud trade union [organization] then will the movement's material stability be secure.

Here it appears Branting wants to regard cooperation as the third main weapon of the Social Democratic movement, along with the party and the trade unions. The impression the message conveys is that it is referring not to a politically neutral, but a purely socialist organization.

As our account has shown, the Social Democrats' appreciation of cooperation applied not only to the principle itself, but also to Swedish cooperation as it actually took shape, in other words, primarily to the activities of KF. To distinguish between the opinions of cooperation as a principle and as an actual reality is, as a rule, not possible. However, in regard to the conduct of KF and especially its political neutrality, certain divergencies can be ascertained. Sometimes this neutrality was simply recognized as natural and correct from the point of view that the cooperative associations wanted to reach as large an audience as possible. Cooperation is, maintained an article in *Arbetet,* "not a class movement, but a general societal movement, for the benefit of every member of society who enters it, be he a worker, a white-collar worker, or a capitalist. For cooperation is only a form of organization for the great purchasing public." But it also occurred that Swedish cooperation was attacked as being insufficiently allied with the workers and stamped as "social liberal quackery." After the 1909 congress the paper *Smålands Folkblad* contained an article significantly entitled "Cooperation and the Other Labor Movement" in which cooperation was accused of wanting to appear as a movement in itself that had no more in common with Social Democracy than with the Conservative party. The Social Democrats ought to see to it, the article contended, that persons sent to the cooperative congress "desire honest collaboration and consensus with the trade union and political worker movements and their organs." The newspaper also pointed out that cooperation could not carry out "more than a limited part of the liberation efforts of the people."

A review of KF's political activity during this period is necessary in order to understand the Social Democratic discussion. The neutrality line was expressed at the annual congresses held by the union. In 1900 two motions were presented which represented other opinions. According to one motion, the previously cited regulations on the duties of KF should refer to raising the level of "the working class" rather than "the people;" according to the other, KF should include only associations "whose members all belong to the Social Democratic Workers' Party." The former motion was rejected without voting; only two members—out of 36—opposed the decision. During the debate the speaker who represented the majority stated that political and religious views should not be allowed to split the cooperators. "All should be included, Catholics as well as Lutherans, liberals or socialists as well as conservatives." The other more far-reaching motion was subsequently withdrawn. At the 1901 congress G. von Koch, KF's secretary from 1899 to 1905, spoke on cooperation. In this, as in other statements of the time, one finds the beginnings of an independent cooperative ideology. Cooperation is of itself a powerful instrument for bringing about peace between and within peoples, for raising the position of the weaker, and for obtaining a more just distribution of property; the idea of cooperation is, "more than any other, suited to pave the way for a new order of things, where the social contrasts of our times will be abolished, where life will be worth living for all, and where mother love will triumph over tyranny and class hate." Here we encounter the self-help ideology of old liberalism in a new, more socially radical, form. In order to reach their goal, the followers of cooperation must avoid dissension. "Therefore all that can act to obstruct and divide, such as political questions and religious disagreements, should be set aside as being private concerns." Only the central goal of "building up a more beautiful, a more ideal society" must be maintained. As self-help through cooperation was regarded as the essential, the struggle to re-structure society cooperatively became something that had nothing to do with politics: cooperation became a theory of society outside of party politics.

The principle of political neutrality certainly did not prevent Social Democrats from taking a prominent position in KF as well as in the individual consumer associations, nor did it preclude clearly political statements in the latter. However, hardly any partisan political statements were made in the name of KF during the early years. This applies to the congresses as well as to the union's organ, first *Social Tidskrift* (edited by von Koch) and after 1904 *Kooperatören*. Democratic and social reformist tendencies are unmistakable, but more specific taking of positions is avoided. A certain change, especially in *Kooperätoren,* can be detected during the period when M. Sundell was the editor of the Journal and KF secretary (1905–1910). This change can simply be attributed to the fact that von Koch was a liberal and Sundell a socialist with radical leanings. A contributing reason may also have been the organized attacks by private business that cooperation was subjected to under Sundell's editorship. In any case, *Kooperatören* during this time printed several articles that expressed distinctly political views, most notably declarations of solidarity with the labor movement. On one occasion it was stated, for example, that cooperation was just as much a means to reach socialism as the political and trade union worker movements were. Sharp declamations against capitalists, employers, and businessmen were common. Sometimes KF took a position in worker-management conflicts. The 1905 congress decided to send out subscription lists for the benefit of workers during a lockout. In relation to this the administration sent out a manifesto to the followers of cooperation throughout the country which declared

> that the sympathies of the followers of cooperation in economic conflicts are on the side of the workers. . . . It is indeed part of the cooperative idea to take over not only distribution but also production. Thus when a conflict between the producers and the middlemen arises, the position to be taken is consequently very clear to anyone who understands the cooperative idea.

On the other hand, cooperatives counted on and received help from the Social Democratic party and the trade unions in certain cases. It has been established that many party locals intervened in behalf of the cooperative organizations in the conflict with the margarine trust. However, after the 1909 general strike, in which *Kooperatören* took the side of the workers, the paper deplored the fact that certain trade unions had dealt with the cooperatives in the same way as with the capitalist enterprises. "In the art of waging war the workers have not developed beyond shooting down their own troops." A lesson to be learned from the general strike was that the mass of the workers must enter the cooperative movement. In 1908 KF had requested from the Social Democratic party a loan of 50,000 crowns from the general strike fund. The request was not granted, but it appears that this was not for any reason of principle.

On the whole KF's politics during this time give the impression of a—very understandable—lack of clarity. It did not explicitly depart from the neutrality principle, but it often expressed its sympathies with that orientation which was, in fact, most strongly represented in the organization. This situation corresponds to that of the temperance movement in the 1880s, which in a similar way adhered to a neutrality principle but did not hide its antisocialist tendencies. When cooperation was attacked from conservative quarters as socialist, it noted its neutrality; when it was characterized by socialist quarters as lacking zeal, it emphasized its friendliness to the workers. This line was preserved in large measure until the cooperative movement had gained such strength that a stricter neutrality policy appeared possible.

Branting's telegram on the occasion of KF's tenth anniversary resulted in an exchange of opinions in *Social Tidskrift* which sheds further light on this question. Von Koch, who was no longer active in KF, wrote in an article in the journal that a confluence of the socialist and cooperative movements appeared to be occurring. He did not offer a general criticism of the movement, but warned against a development along the lines of the Belgian pattern, in which consumer associations were limited to party members. Sundell answered that the understanding between the cooperative and the workers' movements was now better than before, but that the followers of cooperation adhered to the neutrality principle. There was no question of bringing cooperation into politics, although it must obviously take an interest in certain tariff and tax questions. During von Koch's time it sometimes happened that associations became members of KF even though they limited their membership to persons who were enrolled in a trade union or worker commune; now such associations could not gain entrance. "They must now be *politically neutral,* i.e., take members of different political persuasions . . . in order to gain admission to KF or to purchase from its warehouses." In a final article von Koch declared that in judging the political position of cooperation one must not place chief stress on whether one or another association was bound to the Social Democratic party, but consider the general tendencies that characterized the movement. That Branting's telegram—the reading of which was followed by cheers for understanding between the trade union and cooperative movements—aroused certain doubts in cooperative quarters seems evident from an article by Sundell on "Cooperation and Other Popular Movements." The telegram and its reception would in all likelihood, wrote Sundell, be used to scare conservative people away from cooperation. However, this possibility should not cause alarm. "But we are also prepared to defend the neutrality of cooperation to the extent that it will not be entangled with any particular party, [nor] establish any particular dogma as infallible and demand that homage be paid to it." In the remainder of the article Sundell emphasized that cooperation in England had demonstrated its ability to bring together conservatives and Social Democrats, and that cooperation was also related to popular movements other than the workers' movement, especially the temperance movement. The tenor of the whole article was that

Social Democratic recognition was accepted with pleasure, but that cooperation must not ally itself with the workers' party to the extent that it lose its chances outside of this party.

The congress of the Second International, held in Copenhagen in 1910, made a statement on cooperation for the first time which dealt with the line on production as well as consumption. Cooperation was beneficial "in that it increased the power of the proletariat through the suppression of the middleman and through the creation of forms of production which are dependent on the organized consumers" and because it raised the position of the workers and through training prepared the way for socialization. Although cooperation itself could not lead to the goal of socialism, socialists should nevertheless participate in cooperation. The wording of the resolution was not clear on the question of the political line cooperation itself ought to follow. The resolution was commented on in some Swedish newspapers. Karl Eriksson wrote in *Örebro-Kuriren* that, in the main, Swedish cooperation had the character referred to by the International. It stood, partly due to Sundell, "alongside the trade union and political workers' movements as a third, equally valuable big brother." The tone in *Arbetet* was more doubtful. The Social Democratic party should have nothing to do with bourgeois cooperation. Cooperation must be made to serve as a weapon in the class struggle.

> Therefore cooperation cannot remain neutral in the struggles of the trade unions against the employers, but ought to support to the best of its ability striking or locked-out comrades. . . . A socialist cooperation of this kind has been awaited for a long time: now in our time it has begun to emerge victorious.

The newspaper summarized in four points the advantages of cooperation to socialism: it lowered prices, trained party members to be merchants and industrial leaders, could and should be a model employer, and, finally, could through "expanding to control the whole market become a direct road of transition to the socialist state" at the same time that, under the existing conditions, it supported the trade union movement.

At the 1911 party congress statements on cooperation were inserted in two parts of the party program. This was probably due to some degree to encouragement from circles interested in cooperation. The specific issue was, however, the agricultural question: the proposals were formulated by the agricultural committee appointed by the congress. In the special program article devoted to the agricultural question the importance of cooperation from various points of view was stressed as a solution to this question. Furthermore, the section of the preamble which dealt with the "counter force" which was released in the working class by the concentration and proletarization tendencies of capitalism was changed. Along with the organization of the workers in the trade unions for the purpose of raising wages, their organization "as consumers cooperating to bring down living costs" was now pointed out. In addition to the struggle between the workers and the purchasers of work on the labor market it is further pointed out that "on the commodity market . . . a corresponding struggle between the different interest groups is beginning to appear." Pursuant to this, the paragraph concluded: "This whole class struggle will never cease before society becomes so transformed that the fruits of labor accrue to those who work." With this program change cooperation was placed alongside of the trade union movement as a part of the class struggle and was thus fitted into the Marxist schema of the preamble.

The Social Democratic Youth Federation held a more extreme opinion than the party on the question of cooperation as well. This was particularly apparent at the 1912 congress, where the Federation unanimously passed a proposal which, among other items, exhorted the Social Democratic youth to work toward these ends:

> working class affiliation with the cooperative movement, the spread of a socialist spirit throughout the movement, and, above all, the exclusion of the bourgeois element, as far as possible, from influence in the leadership of the cooperative enterprises.

Not even the youth movement demanded that purely socialist cooperative associations be established, but it surely wished that the associations, consisting partially of bourgeois elements, be led by socialists and work in a socialist direction.

At this time, however, there appeared within KF a mounting effort to completely realize the neutrality principle in practice. Örne, who after Sundell's death in 1910 became editor of *Kooperatören,* was an authoritative representative of this view. After the ruling of the 1911 party congress, he wrote weeks after the congress an article addressed "To the Organized Workers of Sweden." The article urged the workers to support cooperation as never before. But he emphasized at the same time the neutrality view.

> Cooperation is without political and religious color in its activities. It is concerned only with purely economic questions and accepts as members persons of all persuasions and from all walks of life, as long as they look after consumer interests.

In practice it was wholly natural that the two largest societal groups, the industrial workers and the small farmers, gave the movement its main support. Time after time Örne returned to this point. In a later article, written in response to the 1912 ruling of the Youth Federation, he declared that "it is simply a necessity for the survival of consumer organizations that political conflicts be kept outside of the work." One must learn to see this and also to understand

> that in its aims cooperation is such that it should, within its limited sphere, be able to satisfy even the most radical demands for the reorganization of society, although the political party terminology cannot be directly transferred to it.

During the autumn of 1912 the position of cooperation was debated in an effort to clarify the question. At the congress of the Swedish Confederation of Trade Unions (*Landsorganisationen,* or LO) held in September, the secretariat, pursuant to a motion, proposed a statement of essentially this wording:

> Whereas cooperation has its principal support among organized workers, and, further, since it is, in the main, a movement in the class struggle, which the developments of each day intensify, the congress holds that persons who are employed in cooperative enterprises . . . ought to belong to their respective trade unions, and the congress holds that it is the duty of the administrations of the cooperative organizations to employ only organized workers.

According to this proposal LO should establish certain rules for the activities of cooperation. When the proposal was introduced, KF's invited representative, K. Eriksson—editor of *Örebro-Kuriren*—asked to speak. He maintained that it was debatable whether cooperation was a movement in the class struggle. Judging from the very incomplete account, he also appears to have made certain objections to the proposal. Another speaker urged that the resolution be made milder, that the words regarding the duty of cooperation to employ only organized workers be deleted. This amendment proposal was approved by a margin of 3 votes; the 57 dissenting votes were cast for the secretariat's proposal in its original wording. In dealing with another motion of somewhat similar content, the question of the independence of cooperation was again brought up.

Some weeks later *Kooperatören* contained an article by Örne on "Cooperation's Independence" which definitely turned against the forces wanting to direct cooperation's behavior in certain areas, which came from the LO congress. Certain statements indicate, wrote Örne, that many "still want to regard the cooperative movement as a sort of appendix to the trade union and political movements of the working class, a phenomenon for which the other organizations are able to write laws." This misconception must be done away with. Cooperation's independence must be recognized. Certainly the industrial workers needed cooperation for the regulation of prices, and cooperation, in turn, could not reach its goal without the collaboration of the working class. As an employer, cooperation could, among other things, render services of the trade union movement, and the latter could benefit cooperation through agitation. But collaboration would be at its best if one party abstained from attempting "to decree laws" for the other.

Subsequent to the appearance of this article a discussion unfolded between P. A. Hansson in *Social-Demokraten* on one side, and Örne in *Kooperatören* and K. Eriksson in *Örebro-Kuriren* on the other, which brought to a head the question of cooperation's relation to the workers' movement. According to Hansson, the KF representatives at the LO congress had made an uncalled-for and exaggerated declaration of independence. As a defender of the interests of consumers, cooperation wished to be open to all and had therefore committed itself to political neutrality, i.e., neutrality in class conflicts. "Swedish cooperation is also formally established on this principle." But it would be a mistake to see in this the reason for the success of cooperation. "This should be sought instead in the progressively clearer insight of the workers into the value of cooperation to them as a class, particularly as a weapon in their struggle for liberation in the class struggle." The middle class should also be able to enter the movement, "but an exaggerated regard for such participants should not cripple its real character as a movement for the protection and progress of the working class." References to the independence of cooperation made at international conferences implied essentially only the same kind of independence which the trade union movement had vis-à-vis the political movement.

> One regards the political party, the trade union movement, and cooperation as three equally important branches in the great struggle for the liberation of the workers, [all of] which ought to maintain the most intimate collaboration, but without being organizationally joined in a way obstructive to any one of them.

In a later article Hansson emphasized that the words about cooperation as a movement in the class struggle were not an empty phrase. On extraordinary occasions cooperation could "be called upon to assist directly in the class struggle of the workers." Once again it was declared that the middle class were welcome to join the cooperative movement. "But this must not occur at the expense of the clear task of worker cooperation to be a means in the class struggle. Should this be a consequence, it would certainly be better if the middle class formed its own cooperation." But there was no danger of this, for the middle class really had no interest in cooperation.

In their replies Örne and Eriksson dealt with the question of what was meant by cooperation as a weapon in the class struggle. "What is really meant by the phrase about cooperation as a class-struggle movement?" wrote Eriksson in *Örebro-Kuriren*.

> Presumably it implies that under certain conditions cooperation should in a particularly effective way support the working class as a *consumer class*. In what way can it, then, most effectively do this? By making it into a movement only for workers (Implied: the socialist workers?) or by permitting it to comprehend all consumers who want to be cooperators? The answer should be easy to give. The more far reaching cooperation becomes, the stronger and more powerful it becomes. . . . In the last analysis the interest of the working class is served—and in these respects it obviously completely coincides with the interests of consumers in general—*best by a unitary cooperative movement,* which thus, from a socialist point of view, must be preferred and supported.

Örne stated that if by the class struggle one meant the striving to obtain a society without profit for capital or the striving of the workers to organize society's economic relations, cooperation could, in a way, be said to be a part of this battle. But the phrase about cooperation as a class-struggle movement was "most unclear and ambiguous; it is, in other words, a phrase that does more harm than good." It would be as meaningless to speak in a general way of cooperation as a class struggle as to apply this term to the trust system.

> We have emphasized with great energy that cooperation is willing . . . to negotiate with the trade union movement about the mutual exchange of services, but at the same time we have insisted that cooperation not be under the command of other movements.

The 1912 debate marks the end of a critical period in the relations between socialism and cooperation. It is characterized from the socialist position above all by a recognition in principle of cooperation as a part of socialist action. Appreciation also dominated the socialist view of the actual functioning cooperative movement, but certain differences of opinion appeared regarding the orientation of this movement. Socialists did not hold that cooperation should be transformed into a purely socialist movement on the Belgian pattern, but they wanted to consider cooperation "a weapon in the class struggle" and insisted that the movement more or less explicitly accept this opinion, i.e., recognize socialist principles and, in certain cases, lend practical support to the labor movement proper, above all the trade union movement. We will return to the significance of this opinion. In cooperative quarters the principles of independence and neutrality became increasingly secure and precise. A cooperative ideology which could possibly be called socialist, but under no conditions Marxist, began to be formed. Friction between the movements obtained its special character from the fact that a number of the leaders within cooperation were prominent members of the Social Democratic party. It shows a conflict between different orientations within the party over tactics and, to a certain degree, over goals.

Benevolent Neutrality

THE QUESTION of the relation between cooperation and Social Democracy has not been dealt with in detail since 1912, neither at the party congresses, nor at congresses of the youth movement or LO. To be sure, the 1920 party congress decided to add a program statement on cooperation: "Society encourages cooperation." This article was, however, a part of the program revision put through at that time and was of very modest significance in the debates on the revision. The spokesman for the party administration, G. Möller, stated only that society very naturally ought to promote cooperation: "cooperation will play a large role in the socialization process, but cooperation will never be able to replace society as an entrepreneur." It is notable that in the program article, which has been kept unchanged, nothing is said of the position of cooperation with regard to socialist theory. In its justification of the proposal, however, the program commission emphasized cooperation's "important role in the great socializing process."

Discussion on cooperation within the Social Democratic party has by degrees changed character. Above all the position on the neutrality principle has changed. In the immense number of newspaper articles and pamphlets on cooperation published during the 1920s and 1930s there are hardly any examples of pronouncements that cooperation must function as a weapon in the class struggle and regard itself as a part of the socialist workers' movement—pronouncements that had been common at an earlier date. On the contrary, they emphasized time after time that cooperation must remain outside of all party politics, that it would become split and lose its value if it had a more accentuated political color. The cooperative movement's independence has been recognized, and Social Democracy's position toward the movement has concomitantly become stamped by benevolent neutrality.

Within the cooperative movement itself the neutrality line became continually more matter of course and undisputed. In an article in *Kooperatören* in 1927, Örne declared that cooperation in Sweden began to progress in earnest once it was realized that its "only purpose is to organize the procuring of goods for the member families through joint business activity." There were members who were of the opinion that

> cooperation must clearly indicate as its goal the transformation of society and declare its willingness to collaborate with others who are guided by the same aims. . . . For my part I will never tire of repeating that these are following a fundamentally mistaken way of thinking. Cooperation can never accomplish anything of value through declarations or phrases borrowed from other areas of activity. . . . No, cooperation is in itself a new economic system of revolutionary importance.

In other presentations Örne expounded in detail on the necessity of a neutral cooperative movement. By the 1930s the need to assert this view appeared to have completely disappeared; declarations of neutrality were no longer necessary.

The reasons for this development ought to be easy to establish, at least partially. The vigorous growth of the cooperative movement—to a certain degree also including expansion into the area of production—has represented a confirmation of the suitability of the neutrality line. There was an easily perceived contradiction in the view that cooperation should be open to all and appeal to all citizens independent of their class and party but, in addition, act as an auxiliary in the class struggle. Ruptures within the workers' movement have perhaps contributed to Social Democracy's acceptance of the neutrality principle; the Communists as well as the Left Socialists have followed another line. The weakening of the entire class struggle ideology within Social Democracy has obviously also been of importance. The labor contracts of the workers employed by cooperation have been drawn up in such a way that friction between the trade union and cooperative movements has been obliterated.

Recognition of the neutrality principle naturally does not mean that Social Democracy is indifferent toward cooperation. During recent years leading politicians of different parties have marked their respect for the activities of cooperation, but Social Democratic pronouncements have been characterized by special cordiality. The statements that invited Social Democratic ministers have made at the cooperative congresses are indicative. Branting, as prime minister, paid homage to cooperation at the 1920 and 1922 congresses, though his wording was not as strong as in 1909. In 1922 he stated, among other things, that

> the government wants to be a popular national government, and one of the most important bridges to other social classes probably is the consumer cooperative movement, which is not built on class lines. I keenly hope that Swedish cooperation may be expanded to reach increasingly larger segments of the population, indeed, that the time may not be far off when it will comprise a majority of the people. Here is an

> opportunity for the working population to transform society along secure and peaceful lines.

In the late 1930s Möller and P. A. Hansson made similar pronouncements. At the 1937 congress the latter stated:

> What naturally interests me as the representative of the public, as a socialist, is that here within our industrial production there appears a force which eliminates the private profit motive and concretely illustrates the capacity to collectively carry on production with success.

At the 1939 congress the prime minister dealt especially with the contributions of cooperation to democracy and declared that "the prime minister and party chairman" joined in wishing the movement well.

In more theoretical discussions today consumer cooperation seems to be generally regarded as a form of socialization. The doubt which appeared earlier in the emphasis on cooperation's incapacity to replace true socialization is no longer discernible in authoritative statements. Sandler's exposition in "The Problem of Socialization" is typical. It characaterized consumer cooperation as a type of socialization. When it has been built up into an ideological system or has become, on the whole, a vigorous movement, it strives

> to expand its area of activity via the distribution apparatus back to the field of production. Its most important purpose then becomes the distribution as well as the production of goods the consumers need on behalf of the organized consumers. There is no reason in this line of thought to stop before even the raw material sources themselves are also taken over by the cooperative organization. We shall then have arrived at a system characterized by the consumers' common ownership of the means of production and distribution, and by the operation of the productive apparatus as the consumers' common enterprise for the direct satisfaction of their needs.

The distinction between state socialization and cooperative socialization is essentially that the latter is carried through by a special method, through the consumers' own cooperation. Sandler evidently intended to emphasize that total socialization will follow from the natural development of cooperation. Even more limited cooperative activity could be considered a kind of socialization. A number of leading Social Democrats have given expression to the same line of thought. This viewpoint naturally does not mean that one might not consider other forms of socialization—primarily the direct takeover by the state—to be preferable. Sometimes, however, there is a hint that the cooperative line, freely developed, would be the best, or that certain forms of cooperation ought to be able to exist even after the state had taken over the means of production. It has even been said that socialism did not seek to wholly eliminate private initiative, for cooperation would be permitted in a socialist state.

Like the neutrality issue, this question of the position of cooperation according to socialist theory has not been prominent in Social Democratic debate in recent years. This is connected with the fact that the entire problem of socialization has been pushed aside. The recognition of cooperation as a form of socialism is not the result of a greater propensity toward socialization. Rather, it appears, at least in certain cases, to be an indication of a tendency to establish the progress of socialism in spite of the fact that the socialization previously envisioned had not come about nor was it energetically propagated.

There is no reason to go into greater detail concerning the cooperative ideology which developed with the growth of cooperation in Sweden and other countries. It ought to be emphasized, however, that this ideology placed strong emphasis not only on cooperation's neutrality principle, but also on its independence. It held that cooperation should not receive special privileges from the state; the cooperative movement both wished to and ought to show its viability under the same conditions as other forms of enterprise. Because of this attitude as well as its concern for free trade, cooperation has frequently evinced pronounced liberal characteristics. This cooperative liberalism has been made evident time after time in the movement's criticism of proposals for state intervention in economic life. Cooperation's theorists are not wont to characterize the societal form they seek as socialist, even though they may regard cooperation as a means of transforming the economic order. By defining socialism primarily as an economy directed and planned by officialdom, one rather differentiates this kind of system from cooperation, whose principle is voluntary cooperation. On the whole, however, cooperative propaganda has been primarily devoted to more immediate and concrete concerns. The union of families on a democratic basis to obtain satisfactory and cheap goods has been the immediate goal that has remained in the foreground.

Summary

CONSUMER COOPERATION had certainly been propagated by earlier socialist thinkers, but at the time of the appearance of Social Democracy it was chiefly found in liberal self-help ideology. It was regarded by leading Social Democrats with indifference or suspicion. Cooperation, it was held in certain quarters, was without importance in raising the position of the working class because lowering the prices of the necessities of life must lead to a lowering of wages. In other quarters it was thought possible that certain results might be obtained through cooperation, but this was declared, in any case, to be only a palliative of little value. If the working class became involved in cooperative activities, it could be split and its zeal for conquering political power and totally transforming society could be weakened.

However, cooperative organizations developed, frequently under the leadership of Social Democratic workers who were theoretically unschooled. The desire to obtain economic benefits through collaboration was decisive. This aim led to a fundamental change in official socialist doctrine. Even if the socialist goal had to be won mainly through other means, the cooperative movement could be of immediate value from the viewpoint of the workers and could establish a line of action in the social struggle. The cooperators should, like the trade union members and party voters, be troops in the army of the class struggle. Cooperation would prepare for socialization from below. As a rule, however, it was not demanded that cooperative associations include only party members. Any one should be able to join these associations, but every member should be conscious of his higher political and social duties and serve as a base of support for the workers' movement and primarily for the trade union movement. In reaction to this line of thought a cooperative ideology came into being which proclaimed independence and neutrality, but at the same time saw in cooperation a means to transform society.

This, the socialist ideology of the second period, contained an internal contradition. This was manifest practically in that it appeared absurd to invite the bourgeois-minded to participate in cooperatve activity and at the same time ask that cooperation engage in the class struggle, i.e., in partisan social and political actions. The theoretical weakness lay in that a historical-philosophical view obscured social reality. Using one of Marx's general lines of thought as a premise, a reasonable argument could undoubtedly be made for viewing cooperation as one of the forces which undermined capitalist society. Yet this did not mean that cooperation should necessarily be considered an intentionally socialist organization. In reality, one demanded that cooperation not be socialist in a party sense, but rather in a different, undefined sense—inasmuch as it was, in fact, a part of society's development toward socialism.

The cooperative ideology corresponding to this also showed some strange characteristics. Cooperation was said to have nothing to do with politics, but was nonetheless described as a movement devoted to transforming society. In order to reach its goal cooperation must be apolitical, in other words, its aims must not be presented as political but as social and economic. Behind these ideas lay the thought that cooperation should not operate through political means—by forming a party or joining any already existing party. Voluntary cooperation, which is the essence of cooperation, made it possible to characterize the movement as apolitical in spite of the fact that its theorists proposed goals which, according to conventional usage, were political to an eminent degree.

During recent decades the neutrality principle has been unconditionally recognized. There is no longer any discussion as to whether one should ask the cooperative movement to support the party or trade unions. But at the same time cooperation has become even more appreciated from a theoretical socialist viewpoint than earlier. It is described now as a form of socialization, not as a means in the social struggle. This change is related to the continual attenuation of the socialization concept and the waning of interest in socialization in the older sense. This is the explanation of how a movement which was characterized as typically liberal half a century ago is now regarded as typically socialist.

Recapitulation and Summary

EARLY SWEDISH SOCIAL DEMOCRACY was almost totally dependent on German, especially Marxist, influences. It signified a break with the older Swedish workers' movement, and it represented only a small part of the relatively unimportant Swedish working class. These facts must be strongly emphasized. It is all too common to regard the Social Democracy of the 1880s and 1890s in the light of the movement's later development, and to find traces in the statements of the young men who were then the leaders of opinions and programs of action which would not become decisive until much later. It has almost become a dogma that around 1885 Branting put forth the fundamentals which have since provided firm guidelines, while as a matter of fact Branting himself abandoned his original views on essential points. It is also usual to regard Social Democracy as identical with the working class and, consequently, to view changes in the movement's programmatic activity as indicators of changes of opinion within the working class. Not until the beginning of this century—though subsequently to an increasing extent—can Social Democracy be said to be representative of the workers. The larger the Swedish working class became, the greater the influence of Social Democracy over it. For decades the party constituted a minority in a societal class of small importance; now it is supported—except for scattered groups in other segments of the population—by an overwhelming majority of the largest social class in the country.

In agreement with Marx's doctrine, the young Social Democracy believed itself called upon to educate the Swedish working class to take over political power and to socialize, which were considered necessary consequences of the development of liberal and capitalist society. Since industrial capitalism, which was the basic postulate of the ideological schema, was only slightly developed in Sweden, this whole position can be understood only if we remember that the leaders were wholly dominated by international socialist doctrine and paid comparatively scant attention to Swedish conditions. They counted on a rapid industrialization of Sweden, not because it could be anticipated on objective grounds at this time, but because Marx's general prognoses pointed in this direction. With industrial capitalism would come concentration of ownership of the means of production, the disappearance of the middle class, and an increase in the size and poverty of the proletariat. An analogous development would unfold in agriculture at the same time as a decline in the importance of agriculture in relation to industry. At a certain point the conflicts within capitalist society would lead to the—peaceful or violent—revolution out of which the new socialist system would arise.

Capitalism and socialism were thus considered to be two clearly distinct systems. According to Marxist dialectics the one system would be superseded by the other; in other words, when capitalism reached its culmination, socialism would come. It is true that this idea was, as a rule, not applied as rigorously as the Marxist catastrophe theory postulated it should be. One conceived of the possibility of gradual socialization. The dialectical conception was nonetheless decisive for political opinion in the stricter sense. Socialism's conquest of power would be total; the proletariat would for a time take the place of the bourgeoisie as the wielders of the power of the state, and it would then—with greater or lesser speed—carry on the activity that would bring about socialism and which, according to true Marxists would not be completed before the abolition of the state itself. In order to win political power the working class would have to be enlightened and organized. It must, in addition, possess the means necessary for the conquest of power. Revolutionary possibilities were discussed, but they could not readily appear as fundamental to a party of a few thousand members. The struggle for universal suffrage became the clear tactical line. Through this battle the workers could be won and organized at the same time as one wrested control over the political instrument which would lead to the conquest of power. Through its practical work, the Social Democratic party became primarily a suffrage party.

This rapid change of the party's goal was supported by the view derived from Marx that the Socialist theorists should not ponder over the precise nature of the socialist order. This view can be explained by Marx's major perspective: socialism would not prevail until the forces of production reached such a level of development that the problem of distribution no longer presented great difficulties. This part of Marxist doctrine was naturally eagerly accepted by the party's ideologists, who lacked all practical and theoretical knowledge of business leadership and industrial organization. It became not only possible but intellectually correct to speak of socialism without going into the actual make-up of the socialist society. It was sufficient to know that this society would satisfy mankind's unfulfilled desires, that it would bring social equality, general material well-being, and a high level of culture. Few questions have been so little discussed within Social Democracy as socialism.

Faith in the total victory of socialism and in the incomparable value of the society of the future, however, colored the whole ideological debate. Capitalist society—as even Swedish society of the 1880s was inconsistently characterized—was continually seen from the perspective of the imagined future. To be sure, in principle one held that capitalism represented an advance over earlier systems of production, and, at the stage development had reached, that capitalism was the most effective, the best conceivable form of society. But this did not preclude the charge that all the wrongs, misfortunes, and vices—which, it was assumed, would disappear with socialism—were the fault of capitalism. The existing society was blamed for everything. War, international conflicts, armaments, poverty and social distress, class strife, woman's dependent position, crime, prostitution, drunkenness, superstition, and ignorance were all characterized as consequences of capitalism. With socialism war would disappear; nations and men would live in freedom, equality, and brotherhood; women would become men's comrades; sexual relations would be characterized both by freedom and mutual consideration; drunkenness would give way to the moderate, cultivated enjoyment of alcohol; crimes would be rare and socially unimportant; knowledge and culture would enrich men and make them happy.

This faith in socialism as a salvation and all-transforming power necessarily created a certain indifference or distrust both toward orientations that were zealously striving to better conditions within the framework of the existing society and toward doctrines which taught that social conditions in general were of little importance to human welfare. Swedish Social Democracy was certainly not critical or opposed to social reforms of limited scope; at the party's constituent congress a number of reforms of this kind were put forth. But it is characteristic of the early debate that all improvements of this kind were regarded as comparatively unimportant. Even after Social Democrats gave up the view that nothing could stop the progressive impoverishment of the working class, social welfare measures were regarded as palliatives whose greatest value was often said to be that they spurred the workers on to new and more fruitful efforts. The dominating role of the great socialist utopia appears even clearer in other areas. Cooperation, which was designed to reduce the cost of living through the common purchase and distribution of goods, and temperance, which wanted to elevate the morals and material situation of the workers through abstinence, were opposed as methods of checking or escaping socialism. Religious conceptions were regarded as a consequence of the deficiencies of the social order, as a flight from reality, and also as a defense for conservative groups in their opposition to the inevitable transformation. With socialism the need for religion and for illusions in general would disappear. On these points the Social Democrats were at marked variance with the earlier workers' movement.

The young socialism was often accused of being materialist or materialistically oriented. There obviously was a certain truth in this accusation. It concerned neither materialism in the philosophical sense—which was hardly touched upon in the Swedish socialist debate—nor the materialist conception of history: simply the fact that Social Democracy regarded as essential only that which can be called an external transformation, a change in the order of production and thereby of society. Spiritual and moral phenomena, which were highly respected elements in the cultural tradition, often appeared as dubious or dangerous from the standpoint of socialist ideology. A virtue carried to the point of asceticism or at least of severe self-discipline, an aesthetic sense independent of social zeal, an inner life which revolved around religious, philosophical, or moral problems, sacrifice and suffering, patiently endured—these things were not valued or, in any case, only with great reservation. Every conception, every emotion which might distract from the social struggle was suspected of being a product of capitalist propaganda or a psychological consequence of the capitalist system. To a certain degree this was because the church, the official representative of the spiritual world, had quickly and energetically come to the defense of the existing order against socialism during this early period.

This naturally does not mean to suggest that the Social Democrats themselves did not possess what are conventionally called idealistic motives. On the contrary, it can be assumed that the men who, in the face of overwhelming external difficulties and often at a personal sacrifice took on the task of preaching the coming of the new society, possessed an uncommon measure of unselfish compassion and an unusual capacity to become enthusiastic about distant goals which they never believed that they themselves would reach. In this regard they were similar to the original representatives of the evangelical movements whom they considered it their duty to oppose. And in their preaching were interwoven ideas of untiring battle against an evil opponent, of salvation and human perfectibility, which had been and were vital in the religious movements. They worked, as they defiantly emphasized, only for an earthly goal, but their new earth was like the old heaven.

Certain parts of Marxist ideology were abandoned fairly quickly, either by being explicitly repudiated or by simply not being mentioned. The theory of surplus value and related conceptions disappeared from the debate at an early stage, although they did leave a residue of ideas that were used in vague, varying senses (impoverishment). Marxist social theories, which originally had been central to the whole socialist prognosis, were given up or reinterpreted under the influence of German revisionism and the experiences in various countries. As early as the late 1890s the opinions of Branting, Danielsson, and the other leaders were wholly different from those they had proclaimed when Social Democracy first appeared. What remained of Marxism was mainly the more general lines of thought, which were not so dependent as the special theories and predictions on what actually came to pass: belief in the victory of the socialist "system" over capitalism, in the classes as exponents of different orders of production and, consequently, in the necessity of the class struggle, and belief in the materialist conception of history and historical determinism.

The concentration of Social Democracy on obtaining universal suffrage and the successes it won here were successively accompanied by a revision of the ideological lines. In the beginning of the 1900s the mass of the working class flocked to the party through the cadres established by the trade unions, and the desire to satisfy the immediate interests of the workers forced large-scale goals into the background. In the struggle for the complete realization of democracy, Social Democracy collaborated with Liberalism; with this collaboration, which as early as 1914 was regarded as capable of leading to a coalition government, came an attenuation of the belief in the irreconcilable conflict between the middle class and the socialists and thereby also of the idea of a conquest of total power. Through parliamentary activity in the increasingly democratized state, democracy itself came to be considered not only as a means but as a fundamental principle. Social Democrats demanded a number of social reforms without justifying them on specifically socialist grounds, and, with the help of the Liberals, they achieved success on certain points; the tendency to devaluate such reforms disappeared in the process of working for their realization. The party's theorists had showed little interest in agriculture at the beginning, and to the extent that they paid any attention to it, had regarded it from the same perspective as they did industry. Now, however, they concentrated on winning over small farmers and agricultural laborers through a policy aimed at widening and safeguarding private ownership in certain areas, and which was consequently in clear opposition to the Marxist doctrine originally accepted. The 1911 program revision signified confirmation of a shift in the social perspective of Social Democracy.

On questions of a more peripheral nature the gradual transformations in the party were even more marked. Antireligious propaganda, which prevailed during the movement's first stage, was replaced by explicit religious neutrality; certain groups even used the teachings of Christianity as an argument for Social Democracy. The demands for the abolition of the state church and the introduction of nonreligious education were retained, but were stressed only by the party's radical youth organizations. Consumer cooperation and temperance, which Social Democrats had originally opposed, now enjoyed party support—partly as a means of immediately improving the position of the workers, partly because they were thought conducive to the material and moral preparation for socialism. An attempt was made to monopolize cooperation in the same way as the trade unions had been taken over, but after a short period of uncertainty and discord a line triumphed which was friendly to the cooperative movement without insisting on its transformation into a tactical instrument for Social Democracy.

The changes Social Democracy underwent corresponded to changes in other lines and organizations. The Liberal party of the first decade of this century represented a brand of democracy, a cultural radicalism, a social reformism, which, during the latter decades of the nineteenth century, had not gained a foothold in any larger party. Even the Conservative party, established in different stages at the beginning of this century, harbored an interest in and a favorable attitude toward reform, in contrast to the older conservatism. Social Democracy's interest in agricultural questions was partially the result of the dissatisfactions called forth by the increased appropriation and exploitation of land by private companies in Norrland. The nonconformist churches as well as the state church showed ever-growing interest in social questions and did not appear as the antisocialist propaganda institutions they had earlier. Modern consumer cooperation was organized mainly by Social Democratic workers and did not proclaim, in the manner of earlier cooperative movements, a generally liberal ideology of self-help. The temperance movement went from an individualistic temperance line to a democratic and social reformist orientation and therefore did not come into the same conflict with socialism as earlier.

Although Social Democracy developed from doctrinaire Marxism to revisionism, and in conjunction with this moved closer to other political lines and popular movements, the general feeling of social and political antagonism was probably stronger during the decade before World War I than during either the preceding or subsequent decades. Rapid industrialization created an enormous working class whose critical position toward society had not yet been checked or dissipated by democracy, by a considerable improvement in living conditions, and by a system of social reforms. Social Democracy, which previously had been an unimportant sectarian movement, became the great party of the dissatisfied; its task was to represent, exploit, and foment criticism of society. The idea of the class struggle was transformed from theory to an emotionally charged attitude. Perhaps the most significant manifestations of this attitude may have occurred in areas other than those dealt with here. It affected the activities of the trade unions and the labor strife that culminated in the general strike of 1909. In a more limited political sense this condition was especially apparent in the conflict on defense policy. Even though a large segment of the party was favorable to the defense view, it can probably be argued without exaggeration that the Social Democrats' primary issue of agitation for a number of years was the demand for a cutback in or elimination of military defense. In justification of this demand, which basically had little to do with the achievement of socialism, certain elements in Marx's major perspective were fused in a peculiar way with conceptions of the stability of the political situation abroad and the meaninglessness of defense; in addition, appeals were made to personal disinclinations to accept new burdens and duties. The party was more effective in this than in any other area in rallying the discontented. The extreme line, which came to dominate the party's youth movement in the years just prior to World War I even saw the abolition of defense as the central goal for socialist activity that was to address itself to the issues of the day.

The defense question was coupled with the other big source of political controversy—the question of extending democracy through representational reform and parliamentarianism. The position on defense of the Left, and especially of Social Democracy, was a principal reason for the opposition of the Conservatives to a further democratizing over and above that put through in 1907–1909. Leading Social Democratic circles often maintained that only complete recognition of the principle of popular government could create a broad basis of support for defense within the Swedish working class. The severe political ruptures of 1914 essentially reflected this opposition. The peaceful development of the Swedish social order appeared to be squarely in danger.

The war led to a general relaxation of tensions. The defense question was resolved through an accommodation of opinions, which a large proportion of Social Democrats supported in reality, if not formally. In 1917 the factional, defense-nihilist line, which had become dominant in the youth organization, was ejected from the party. In order to make democratization possible the party entered into a coalition government with the Liberals the same year. The Conservatives yielded under the pressure of world events and the barely veiled threat of revolution from the Social Democrats; in 1918 the essential decision in the complete realization of popular government was obtained.

With the end of the war the defense question lost the character of a burning issue. Social Democracy was able, at one and the same time, to take a position basically favorable to defense and to demand an important reduction in the size of the army organization decided in 1914.

In this situation, when democracy had been achieved, the defense question had moved to the background, and everywhere in Europe ideas of a thoroughgoing transformation of society became the order of the day, the question of the realization of socialist goals came to be seriously considered for a while in the Swedish party. The principle of socialization, which for many years had represented only an ideological background to day-to-day political demands and debates, was presented now, when Social Democracy appeared close to attaining a majority and political power, as a short-range programmatic demand. Its import had certainly changed since the party's beginnings. The concentration of wealth, the elimination of the social middle classes, and the increase in the misery of the working class, all parts of Marx's prophesy, had failed to come about. Socialization could not occur through the expropriation of a few expropriators. It was explained to mean instead, on the one hand, the successive transfer of the more important natural resources and industries into society's possession, on the other hand, the planning of production on a national scale. The socialization demand in this sense was presented as a topical question through the 1920 program revision. One generally accepted the plans put forward some years earlier by English guild socialism, regarding the socialist organization of production. At the same time the party program's general preamble was revised; in essential points it gave up the Marxist schema while preserving a number of Marxist modes of expression.

A few weeks after the adoption of the program revision, which aimed at updating the socialization issue, the first Social Democratic cabinet was formed. It was an inevitable consequence of the party's commitment to the democratic and parliamentary system. Social Democracy was regarded as one party among other parties and as obliged by the conventions of the new order to undertake responsibility for the administration of the state. When the majority-supported government of the Left was split and no new coalition was able to be formed, the largest party, even though a minority party, had to form a foundation for the government. But the new government cabinet also signified a confirmation that the Social Democrats had abandoned an important ideological line. Notions of the conquest of total power, of the absolute opposition between a ruling and a ruled class, and of the victory of the socialist "system" over capitalism were definitely given up when the Social Democratic leaders became the governors of the land—without proposing any action of a socialist character in the original meaning.

The first Social Democratic government, however, dealt with one point wholly in agreement with the views of the new program. It appointed a socialization committee which was to issue reports and proposals regarding socialization. The committee, which functioned for almost fifteen years, became extraordinarily important in the ideological discussion. Not because it made any comprehensive, guiding proposals regarding the implementation of socialism; in practice its activity would not extend this far. Its importance lay in that it served as a symbol of the party's great fundamental goals, as evidence that these goals were still living realities, but also as an excuse to postpone their realization to the future. Year after year Social Democrats insisted that the party could not reasonably put forth a socialization proposal until the socialization committee had concluded its works, which was of necessity extensive and time-consuming. The existence of the ideals of socialist principles was made secure at the same time as their realization was avoided.

As it had once progressed under the auspices of Marxian thought, the ideological transformation of the party now continued under the auspices of the socialization committee. Appreciation of democracy as a value in and of itself became ever more conscious. A democratic ideology was formed; tolerance, collaboration with other groups, mutual concessions came to be regarded as necessities in successful popular government. Social Democrats regretted that Swedish parliamentarianism had become minority parliamentarianism, and when forming cabinets, the Social Democrats attempted to achieve a firm collaboration with the party or parties traditionally considered to belong to the Left. Especially P. A. Hansson, Branting's successor as party leader, gave voice to the idea of mutual collaboration. Social Democracy followed the same line which has generally been decisive in Swedish politics in recent years; divergencies have been reduced, all of the larger parties have unreservedly accepted democracy, and the extremes of both right and left have not been of any importance. The Social Democratic governments concentrated their activities on achieving sociopolitical reforms and decisions believed to be to the immediate benefit of the poorer groups in the population, primarily the industrial working class.

The vague proposals advocating industrial democracy, which had been energetically propagated for several years were given up. A radical proposal to increase inheritance and property taxes with the aim of attaining a more equal distribution of property was not renewed, for it was assumed to have contributed to the party's setback in the 1928 election. On this, as on a number of other points, the influences of English liberalism and socialism have been decisive. The foremost intermediary of these influences has been Wigforss; he and Myrdal have been the party's most creative theorists during recent years. Several radical demands in other areas which were strongly emphasized as late as the period around 1920—such as the demands for a republic and the abolition of the state church—were written off without any program changes or great debates.

In his last welcome address to a Social Democratic party congress Branting emphasized the change which the conception of the socialist society had undergone since the party had come into existence.

> We then had a rather simple and schematic conception of it, which can best be expressed [by saying we thought] that once we obtained political power, we had only to step into society and make ourselves at home in order to bring about its regeneration. Now we understand that political power is not enough, and that there is much else to do besides conquering [such power]; that the transformation of society only begins when this power is attained and that this transformation will take a long time.

He added that the choice of the reformist line by the Swedish working class must be seen against the background of the development of Swedish society on the whole. "We point this out not to commend ourselves for any special wisdom, for it is our old Swedish culture, the structure of our country now, and our whole history which has shown us the way." In several ways these statements are representative of the debate during this period. Social Democracy began to be regarded as part of Sweden's political history, not primarily as an international phenomenon. The idea of a transformation gradually occurring within the democratic framework was accepted by Social Democrats without reservation. But at the same time they preserved conceptions of a thorough-going change, of the building-up of a new socialist society.

Some years after the First World War, as before it, the defense question became the issue that caused the most serious ruptures both within the Social Democratic party and in Swedish politics in general. It is true that Social Democracy no longer included a line basically nihilistic toward defense as it had earlier. Feelings for the value of national unity had become increasingly clear and were unconditionally emphasized even in Social Democratic quarters. But, on the one hand, the party as a whole held an optimistic view of the world situation and therefore wanted to go a long way in the curtailment of military defense, and on the other hand, a large segment of the party considered all armaments meaningless and thus demanded unilateral Swedish disarmament. In all probability this line was adhered to by a majority at the 1928 and 1932 party congresses, and only the determined opposition of the party leaders prevented the passage of resolutions which would have established the disarmament line.

In the beginning of the 1930s the economic crisis and the tense international situation brought about a further shift in Social Democracy's lines of action and ideology. Two possibilities were discussed in the face of the crisis: either the party should regard the crisis as a death crisis of capitalism and work for immediate socialization measures, or else it should try to put through measures within the framework of the existing "system" which would immediately improve the situation and which could be expected to win support within large groups outside of the party. The clash between the major socialist perspective and short-term viewpoints was now clearer than it had ever been before. While phraseological concessions were made to the party's left wing, the 1932 congress decided that the party should work for an active crisis policy without thrusting socialization to the foreground. The Social Democratic cabinet which was established after the election victory of the same year expanded the framework of crisis policies in collaboration with elements outside the party and achieved great parliamentary successes on this basis. The crisis quickly passed and a new period of growing prosperity began; in conjunction with this the new welfare policies acquired extraordinary prestige and in the 1936 election Social Democracy won yet another election under their banner.

Welfare policies also meant a liberation from the problems that had previously colored Social Democracy's appearance. When the crisis broke out, the work of the socialization committee had gone on for so long that it seemed necessary to choose between realization or abandonment of the idea of socialization. The crisis policies brought about a respite in the pressure to make such a choice, and would eventually, because of their scope and success, push the whole question of socialization into the background. Welfare policies meant a tremendous expansion of reform work, built on sociopolitical motives, and such policies were of great dimension without socialization. The activities of the committee on socialization could be terminated in 1935 even though the committee had not worked out any program for socialization; to be sure, a member of the committee did subsequently publish treatises on the subject, but neither did these contain the proposals envisioned when the committee had been appointed. This disappearance of the whole problem complex whose solution was formerly considered to be the main task of the party could occur without difficulty under the aegis of welfare policies. The socialization principle, which from the beginning had followed Social Democracy like a shadow in regard to policies oriented toward immediate goals, now disappeared from the debate and propaganda. It was replaced by the welfare ideology. Socialization measures were certainly not foreign to this ideology, but were regarded as only one means among others to obtain for society in its entirety the best possible results. Social Democracy's distinct ideology, originally of Marxist derivation, thus disintegrated. Occasional references to welfare policies as a form of socialization showed only the strength of the traditional terminology.

The economic crisis consequently led to an acknowledgment and confirmation of an ideological shift which had gradually occurred. Increasing tensions in the international situation led to a similar result in regard to the party's position on military defense. When the possibility of war became apparent the overwhelming majority in the party came out strongly in favor of defense. The 1936 army organization was decided upon without the formal collaboration of the Social Democrats, but the party had declared its support of it and it was passed by a government led by Social Democrats and supported by a lower house with a Social Democratic majority.

The foregoing chapters have not dealt with the developments over recent years for a number of reasons. It is, however, well known that the ideological line which made a breakthrough with crisis policies in the early 1930s and obtained especially pregnant expression in debate and practical application in 1936 has since been further amplified and accentuated. Accommodation and welfare ideology have ever more systematically and deliberately been declared to be decisive for the party's actions. Socialism is no longer regarded as a "system" which in time will defeat and replace the capitalist "system." The existing order has become the foundation for the activities of the party and Social Democracy has thereby taken on the character of a conservative party in the true meaning of the term. International tensions, which culminated in World War II, resulted in actions which symbolized the new position. Defense of the nation's freedom and democracy became the goal above all others. The coalition government formed in December 1939 only crowned a consensus, a levelling, which already existed. The principle of unity was a reality long before the war prompted the parties to formally manifest it.

The Social Democratic congress held in the beginning of June 1940 can, from the point of view presented here, be said to mark the end of a period in the history of the party. The congress unanimously and without debate commissioned the party administration to arrange for a review of the party program. Sandler, the spokesman for the party administration on this matter, emphasized that it was vitally important to ensure "agreement between the party's program and the party's policies." This signified a complete break with the opinion often presented earlier, according to which the party program, and especially its preamble, could be preserved as a historic document that was not binding upon the party in practice. Of all the motions which laid the foundation for the decision to revise the program, only one contained a detailed proposal for a new program. The contents of this motion are, however, revealing. According to this proposal the principle of class conflict should be abolished, the article on socialization drastically modified, the article on the constitution reduced to a demand for a democratic form of government, and several other demands, such as free trade and the abolition of the state church, should be deleted. The last paragraph of the preamble should contain a statement declaring Social Democracy to be "one with the Swedish nation"—not "with Social Democracy in other countries," as the program then read. A new article should demand "national defense on a democratic basis." A decade earlier a proposal with these contents would have seemed preposterous; by 1940 it signified simply a confirmation on all points of the party's actual policies.

Also significant is the statement on the political situation made by the party chairman-prime minister. After giving an account of Social Democracy's position on the forming of governments during different periods, Hansson dealt with the origins and activities of the national coalition government. He proposed here that cooperation between the major parties in the government would be possible even under normal political conditions. Parliamentarianism in the usual meaning is based, maintained Hansson, on a system whereby there is a majority and an opposition, which could be transformed into a majority. If the majority became a permanent one, the parliamentary system would not be able to function in the established way. With an eye to the future, one could therefore discuss whether "democracy's natural order should [not] be collaboration on the broadest possible base right up to the cabinet level"; within the collaborating parties an objective, active opposition—but not one bound by party politics—could assert itself. Even if the prime minister did not consider this idea to be of immediate concern, his statement made clear the softening of political antagonisms which the previous years had brought and the attendant change in Social Democracy's general attitude.

It is unnecessary to deal further with the transformation which Swedish Social Democracy underwent during its first sixty years. In the ideological debate socialization has been replaced by the general welfare, class conflict by "the people's home", democracy as a tactical means by democracy as the highest principle, the total conquest of power by compromise, agreement, and collaboration among others, internationalism by the national viewpoint, indifference and suspicion toward various religious and humanitarian popular movements by appreciation and a desire for mutual understanding. Modern Social Democracy in important ways is closer to the old liberal workers' movement than to its own original views.

This certainly does not mean to imply that the fundamental conceptions and goals which were the premises of old Social Democracy have been relinquished. Remaining are the faith in progress and enlightenment and the belief that the concern of political activity is the well-being and freedom of the individual, the desire to work for an equality which will limit socially determined differences among men, the faith that a wider framework for human freedom can be created through greater prosperity and culture, and the desire for peace and closer relations among peoples. But these ideas, which are usually regarded as liberal, are held by all of the major political parties in modern Sweden. There was thus no distinctive Social Democratic ideology. Distinctions among the major political orientations in Sweden lay essentially in that they emphasized different viewpoints, that each party was particularly zealous in pressing certain demands that were less actively represented by the other parties. Schematically it can be said that at present Social Democracy is distinguished from the other parties through its special concentration on social reforms and state intervention on the whole.

The development of Social Democracy in Sweden and in other countries has been interpreted and explained in different ways. We will deal here with some of the main points in the debate.

Why has Social Democracy's ideology undergone such thoroughgoing changes? This frequently posed question ought to be preceded by another: Why did a Marxist labor movement arise in the 1880s?

This question clearly coincides to a great extent with the question of the reasons for the international influence of Marxism. This question has in turn been answered in different ways. For Marxist believers the answer is comparatively easy. Marx's doctrine had appeal because social conditions made possible an understanding of the truths of this doctrine. This line of thought certainly invites difficulties. Sometimes it is assumed that the success of the doctrine is essentially dependent on its truth, and the word truth is used here to mean that the doctrine corresponds to reality. At other times, proceeding from a relativist line of thought in Marx, it is emphasized that the success of an ideology is dependent on its satisfying definite needs or interests; that such is the case is presumed to be demonstrated (through circular reasoning) by the success of the doctrine. When Marx's doctrine is declared to be true from this point of view, one is using a pragmatic social concept: truth is equivalent to success. At the same time, however, the concept of truth is used in its usual meaning, because the assertion that Marxism satisfies certain needs and is therefore successful is assumed to be true in the sense that it agrees with reality. But the conclusion must be that if Marxism is no longer believed, it is no longer valid. For many scholars who are not Marxists the success of Marxism has appeared difficult to explain. Marxist socialism must, writes Keynes, remain a problem to all historians of ideas—"how a doctrine so illogical and so dull can have exercised so powerful and enduring an influence over the minds of men, and, through them, on the course of history." Nonetheless, many attempts have been made to give reason, in general formulas, for the influence of Marxism. A common view is that Marx's doctrine, in an unusually suggestive way, combines reality and utopia; the industrial working class, to which Marx primarily addressed himself, saw its own situation described in broad outline in Marx's writings and obtained from them certainty about the rapid and complete social transformation, which would appear so desirable to a class living under difficult conditions. Marx formulated, it has been said, in an extraordinarily emphatic and effective way the social protest which marked the outlook of the proletariat at the time of the emergence of industrialism. The boldness and scholarly claims characteristic of Marx have been regarded as tending to strengthen his authority. The more formal qualities of Marx's writings have been considered to have the same effect. One speaks here of the brilliance and power evoked by the dialectical method. It has often been maintained that Marx became a great propagandist through his simplifications and his ability to summarize his views in a few easily understood phrases, but it has also been claimed that Marx's heavy and inaccessible language instilled respect and confidence in the poorly educated people it aimed at influencing. It is obviously easy for different social-psychological lines to give "explanations" for Marx's success according to their conceptual systems.

There is no reason to explore related questions in greater detail; their examination would require a special investigation. However, a few indisputable facts, which have received too little attention in the debate on this point, ought to be mentioned. Most important is that Marx's views have not been the foundation for all modern labor parties or even for all Social Democratic parties. In England and America his philosophy has played a comparatively subordinate role. Especially notable is the fact that in England, the country whose society formed the foundation for Marx's sweeping generalizations, his theories have not been accepted by the Labour party. This shows that there is no necessary relationship between modern workers' movements and Marxism. Marx won his great victories primarily in Germany and in countries where German influence has been important. The question of the reasons for the success of Marxism should therefore be answered in the first place through a detailed historical investigation of the development of early German Social Democracy, and especially of the conflicts between the supporters of Marx and Lassalle within this movement. It should further be noted that the very assertion that Marx had a dominating influence on the workers is arbitrary. To what degree Marxist doctrine or the work of Social Democrats to obtain immediate improvements in social and economic conditions was decisive for the support of the workers cannot be determined with any certainty. We only know that the leading groups within Social Democracy in certain countries were Marxists. The probability is that Marx's theories had little effect on the mass of workers; the softening or abandoning of these theories, which took place everywhere, did not meet much opposition from the workers. A parallel with two more recent political movements can be enlightening here. In 1917 Russian Communism won the support of a large proportion of farmers and workers, as the election to the constituent congress showed, but probably no one would maintain that this was the product of communism's general ideology; the demand for peace and other current issues is considered to have been decisive. The support that German National Socialism rapidly won among the voters in 1930–1932 can similarly be assumed to have depended on the immediate demands the party put forth, not on its long-term political ideas, which were little in evidence in the propaganda.

The groups within the Social Democratic parties that primarily represented Marxism can, on the whole, be assumed to have consisted of persons who were interested in intellectual matters but lacking in liberal educations. A study of the congressional debates of the different parties strikingly reveals that, with few exceptions, the leading delegates held to an assortment of concepts and expressions derived from a handful of socialist theorists, but showed little familiarity with scholarly and political literature as a whole. The English debate on the "Fabian Society," with its orientation toward concrete social research and its openness to non-doctrinaire viewpoints was on an incomparably higher plane. It is characteristic that Bernstein, whose main work is so superior to the Marxist literature of the time, was strongly influenced by the English environment in which he was active for many years. In regarding the leading Marxist groups one is inevitably reminded of Macaulay's words about the followers of the English utilitarians; these were

> persons who, having read little or nothing, are delighted to be rescued from their own sense of inferiority by some teacher who assures them that the studies which they have neglected are of no value, puts five or six phrases into their mouths, lends

them an odd number of the Westminster Review, and in a month transforms them into philosophers.

That young Swedish Social Democracy became doctrinaire Marxist must be understood from these viewpoints. German influence on Swedish political and cultural debate was extraordinarily important. Marxism, just as well as social conservatism, appeared as a result of this influence. The young men who were in the vanguard of Swedish socialism obtained their political ideas predominantly from Germany, and their theoretical contributions were hardly more than paraphrases of the proclamations of the German authorities. Moreover, the ideological studies of the older leaders were considerably circumscribed. Discussions on anarchism and syndicalism in Sweden, for example, indicate that the principal body of literature of these movements was unknown to the Swedish leaders. The position of the Swedish working class toward Marxism before the turn of the century need not be discussed; the great mass of the working class was, of course, not Social Democratic. When Social Democracy later came to represent the majority of Swedish workers, its Marxism had already become attenuated. Still, a number of concepts fundamental to Marx were accepted at that time, and it can, with reason, be maintained that the movement continued to have a predominately Marxist color for another couple of decades.

When the question is raised of the reasons for Swedish Social Democracy's departure from Marxism and, more generally, its transition from radical social protest to welfare policies, these factors must be kept in mind. The development of Social Democracy cannot be wholly identified with that of the working class; early Social Democracy did not represent the working class.

Concerning this central question, it should be strongly emphasized that the history of Social Democracy can be treated from wholly different points of view. The ideological changes of the Swedish party can be seen as a part of an international process. In all of the countries where Social Democracy has obtained a significant position of power, it has undergone generally the same development as in Sweden. This was brought out in our observations on international Social Democracy earlier in this work; it is made even more evident by a study of the Social Democratic parties in different countries. The International, where men were able to talk and pass resolutions with a certain irresponsibility, consistently shows a greater measure of Marxist and radical ideology than the individual parties which constituted it. What is notable about the Swedish movement is not its ideological development, but its extraordinarily great success—which has, in turn, resulted in a greater ideological development in some areas than in others, even though the general direction has been the same. To judge from a summary investigation, it would be possible to draw fairly complete parallels to the present work in a number of other countries. It is consequently incorrect, as not infrequently occurs, to view modern Swedish Social Democracy as the result only of conditions peculiar to Sweden. It ought to be pointed out in this context that the Swedish movement has more recently received its most important influences from a different source than earlier. In the 1880s and 1890s influences from Germany were decisive; during the latest decades contact with the English debate has been the most fruitful.

Social Democracy's development ought further to be seen against the Swedish environment in which it occurred. The movement's early adoption of a moderate and reformist character was due to the strong traditions of freedom and justice which prevailed in Swedish society. No special legislation directed against Social Democracy was enacted; the opportunity to propagandize had few limitations; the state made no systematic attempts to prevent the growth of the movement through the use of existing legislation. Universal suffrage in elections to the lower house, which became the party's first concrete goal, could be won without serious conflicts, and the same applied to the later achievement of complete democracy. In response to Social Democracy's increased moderation came heightened interest in social reforms on the part of other political parties. Modern Swedish industrialization has developed side by side with social legislation through which consequences of industrialization, which in certain other countries threatened social stability, were by and large wholly avoided. The relatively distant and secure international situation and the absence of economic crises of the magnitude which rocked other nations were the conditions that enabled Swedish Social Democracy to make the transition to moderate reformism so steadily and free from friction. During recent decades increased social equality, the higher living standard of the working class, and the significant degree of economic differentiation that has come about within this class have probably worked in the same direction. The impoverishment theory, with its radical consequences, has not only shown itself to be untenable in its original interpretation; even the attenuated psychological interpretation given to this theory by certain theorists has lost all significance in the face of advancing economic improvement. To what degree this improvement is related to the activities carried on by trade unions allied to Social Democracy will not be discussed here.

One can also naturally attempt in greater detail to place Social Democracy's ideological changes in relation to fluctuations in the business cycle. It is obvious that the party's policies have been dependent to some extent on the economic situation at any given time. But it ought to be emphasized that its ideological development has been determined by many factors and that a more complete connection with the business cycle therefore cannot be established. Some examples from a more recent period will make this clear. The 1920 socialization program was shaped during a period of prosperity and rising wages. A retreat from this program was already noticeable after the election setback in the fall of the same year, and during the difficult crises of the following years the socialization question was relegated to the background. The liberalizing process, which can be said to characterize the party during the 1920s, has been related to the industrial expansion during this period, but this process had already begun during the crisis years. The radical tendencies in evidence around 1928 were obviously not the result of any worsening in the workers' situation, but were the outcome of a number of other circumstances, such as influences from England and opposition to the government in power. On the other hand, the proposals which were presented in the 1928 Riksdag were marked by the prevailing economic situation; the rapid increase in prosperity naturally gave rise to thoughts of raising property taxes, not to thoughts of socialization. The crisis in the beginning of the 1930s led to a resumption of socialization agitation within certain groups, but on the whole the crisis became one of the reasons why the question of socialization was deliberately and definitely shunted aside. The frequently presented schema, according to which Social Democracy becomes more radical during times of crisis and more conservative during prosperity, can not be applied to Swedish Social Democracy without modifications and interpretations which render it meaningless.

The presentation which has been given in the foregoing chapters has attempted—with due consideration of the conditions mentioned—to put forth a viewpoint which seems to be particularly important to the analysis of the history of ideas. Marxist doctrine, which was of overriding importance to early Social Democracy, contained a number of predictions which were refuted by the course of events and which suffered from internal contradictions on decisive points. This necessarily led to the dissolution or re-interpretation of Marxist theories as the party developed. During the first decades, changes in the ideology of the party essentially meant that one after another of the concepts that had once been uncritically accepted were jettisoned upon continued confrontation with reality. What remained were only the most general lines of thought in Marx's major perspective—of which the belief in socialization, the materialist conception of history, and the doctrine of the class struggle were of greatest importance. Thereafter the party's theoretical transformation continued as a consequence of practical political work within the democratic framework. Our intent has been primarily to show the character of Social Democratic development, from the given assumptions, as an inevitable process of ideological dissolution. This viewpoint, which also applies to Social Democracy in other countries—even if the process in Sweden has, for a number of reasons, been particularly marked and complete—has been presented as the central theme, even though it can and should be complemented in various respects with other viewpoints.

In Sweden as in other countries differences of opinion have arisen over the question of whether the development of the labor movement toward new and less radical viewpoints was mainly the work of the leaders or the rank-and-file, of the intellectuals or of the workers themselves.

On the one hand, it is maintained that political work, and especially political power, softened the radicalism of the leaders and led to a concern with short-term goals, to compromises and collaboration. The leaders became corrupted by the positions they gradually gained in the bourgeois state and lost their original idealism and militant zeal. Their example and their agitation among the masses then seduced the latter to seek moderation and self-effacement. This opinion has been most clearly developed in syndicalist theory, above all by Sorel: parliamentary activity itself was repudiated as destructive; the spirit of class conflict should be kept alive through strikes; a moral elite of workers should be trained to assume the leadership of their class; intellectuals were characterized as beguilers and traitors. This distrust of parliamentary activity within a democratic framework is shared by communism, whose doctrine, like that of syndicalism, with particular sharpness asserts Marx's theory that the liberation of the working class should be the work of that class alone.

On the other hand, it is alleged that it is precisely the masses of workers, who are most exposed to economic and social hardships, who are interested in immediate improvements and have little understanding of ideological systems and goals assigned to the distant future. It is these masses who have worked in a reformist and socially pacifist direction. This line of thought affirms that within different labor movements it has been the intellectuals who have been the radicals and doctrinaires, while the trade unionists have worked for moderation and successive reforms. It is pointed out that syndicalist theory was formed by theorists who took little part in practical politics and who had little knowledge of the attitudes of the workers. In respect to communism, one maintained that its basic writings were authored by a group of exiled intellectuals who lacked contact with the Russian working class, and that there was no reason to believe that the great support that the workers gave to the Communist revolutionaries in 1917 indicated that the workers accepted the movement's theoretical system.

The question under discussion has been partially answered in regard to Swedish Social Democracy in our previous discussion. However, some remarks ought to be added.

When, around the turn of the century, a preponderance of the Swedish working class joined the Social Democratic party, it was led by a group of intellectuals who espoused a modified Marxist theory, but, in addition, worked energetically for the realization of short-term demands, above all, universal suffrage. It is, as previously noted, impossible to judge whether Marxist ideas or immediate political and economic demands played the larger role in winning the support of the workers. Considering, however, that the party won its great support primarily through the trade unions, and that the suffrage question was at this time far and away the party's leading program point, it is probable that the workers at first were attracted by the short perspective. This is also indicated by the turn-about in position toward popular movements working to raise the moral and economic condition of the workers which took place at this time and which was clearly dependent on the initiative of the workers themselves. The cooperative and the temperance movements had been regarded by the leaders with a distrust that was partially attributable to Marxist dogmatism; when the workers began to establish cooperative associations and enter the temperance orders, the leaders changed their views. It is probable that the vision of the future society, which was a part of the Marxist perspective, was also valuable as propaganda, but nothing indicates that it was decisive. On the whole, one gets the impression that the views expressed by the men in the ranks were more concretely oriented, less ideologically colored. It was primarily the leading intellectuals who put forth the more abstract and Marxist lines of thought.

During the subsequent period the question is complicated by the fact that the workers, or more correctly the trade union leaders, to an increasing extent began to be included in the leading groups within the party; it becomes less possible than earlier to equate leaders and intellectuals. It is nevertheless clear that no special radicalism or Marxism can be detected among the workers who participated at administration meetings and congresses. The main conflict occurred in the early 1900s between the party leadership and both of the youth associations, and, after the expulsion of the Young Socialists, with the Social Democratic Youth Federation. These youth associations, however, cannot be considered to have represented the ordinary worker to any great extent; it can, on the contrary, be asserted that persons who had never been workers and who possessed formal education were dominant within the Young Socialists and within the Social Democratic Youth Federation, in any case during its later period. Branting and the party administration probably held a secure majority among the trade unionists. When it came to extraparliamentary actions—as in 1902, 1907, and 1917—it appears that the workers consistently displayed the greatest hesitation. During recent decades there have been no persistent conflicts within the party. There is nothing to indicate that the party leadership, the intellectuals, or the party functionaries have generally been more moderate than the rank-and-file, or than the workers who voted for the party as a whole. The question of socialization was brought up around 1920 and in the beginning of the 1930s mainly by party men in the intellectual group; the same was true of the question of industrial democracy in the beginning of the 1920s. In neither case did the workers show any special interest; the trade unionists were largely critical or indifferent toward the latter question. The radical advances of 1920 and 1928 led to setbacks for the party, which in any case makes it probable that they were not especially popular among the workers. More important than anything else, however, is the simple fact that the more radical labor parties which were established—whether through breaking away from Social Democracy or otherwise—won comparatively little support. Time after time the leaders of these parties, obviously because their attempts to win popular support were unsuccessful, were forced to return to the Social Democrats.

It can with a certain amount of truth be said that power weakened the radicalism of Social Democracy. But this must not be taken to mean that the leaders became more conservative because of the positions they won as representatives of the movement. The statement is true only to the extent that it is self-evident: the whole party changed its program and its ideology on the road to power for reasons which were sufficiently emphasized in the foregoing. The enormous simplification which characterized the debate during the first period was a result of the gap that separated the party from practical activity. The softening of ideology occurred successively, half unconsciously, in the same measure as real political accomplishments became possible. Problems and social reality itself assumed a different character in the eyes of the doers.

The above discussion does not imply a denial that on certain occasions conflict occurred between the party leadership and the majority of the membership. Judging from the party congresses, it is probable that such was the case on the defense question during certain periods—before World War I and around 1930—and here and there tendencies of similar conflicts can be found in respect to other issues (e.g., socialization in 1932). Conflict has occurred between the leading group, in the narrow sense of the term, and an opposition led by party men of the second echelon; the radical opposition has assembled a majority of the party's congressional representatives, or, in any case, has won comparatively large support among them. The reasons for conflicts of this kind must be determined from the accounts of the individual cases. It can be stated very generally that the stronger sense of immediate responsibility of the party leaders, their insight into the objective shortcomings and political dangers of the radical proposals, and their inclination to choose standpoints that would not place the party outside of the real decision-making in the Riksdag have been decisive in such cases. As in other parties, prominent members of the party outside of the real leadership have shown greater understanding of extreme views than the leaders. Conflicts of this character have been of moment only in regard to the defense question, when the mass of the party has uniformly shown a bias toward radical stands which in an unreflective and emotional way appeared most attractive.

Neither is it to be denied that in particular cases the social advancement that attended successful political activity directly influenced views. This relationship, however—as the foregoing account indicates—certainly has not played any role worth mentioning. Among the reasons for this is the fact that, in Sweden, a seat in the Riksdag or a cabinet post does not lead to the estrangement from the rank-and-file that it does in several of the large democracies.

In this context we also ought to deal with the frequently discussed question of the importance of historical determinism to the activities of Social Democracy. According to some authors the idea that socialism must necessarily triumph has weakened the workers' desire to battle; according to others, it has reinforced their zeal. The former view is a central argument in syndicalist criticism of Social Democracy, but it has also been put forth in other quarters. Determinism, wrote Kelsen, carries with it the risk "that a certain confident fatalism may replace the highest [level of] activity." The elder Liebknecht, on the other hand, compared socialists with Islamic warriors; they were invincible as long as they believed in victory. And the Swedish philosopher Hägerström wrote that the feeling that development demands certain actions enhances the intensity of the striving; "in this way Marxism, precisely by virtue of its view that the realization of the moral task *must* occur, actually becomes a moral power of the highest potency in the consciousness of the masses." Like Liebknecht, Hägerström compared socialist and religious faith; a proletariat that believes it is realizing society's imperative feels in the same way as religious believers who feel themselves called on to perform "God's work."

Two diametrically opposed views are maintained here, without any more thorough attempt at substantiation, a situation that of itself engenders suspicion. As a matter of fact both opinions appear to be capricious—quite apart from the dubiousness of the basic assumption, namely that the Social Democratic workers act out of a belief in historical determinism. There is nothing to indicate that a belief in victory works in a definite direction. On the contrary, it seems probable that such a belief can have an enervating effect on some temperaments and a stimulating one on others. And it ought to be clear that under different circumstances a belief can have very different effects. Certainty of an immediate victory can call forth a desire for personal sacrifice that will not arise when it is believed—with the same certainty—that the victory will belong to a later generation. A lesser sacrifice might seem natural on the basis of absolute faith in victory, but a greater sacrifice, for example of life itself, could appear unreasonable on the same basis. The opinions of the authors cited are so generally held that a detailed critique is not possible or necessary. Similar assertions, however, are continually to be found in the literature on socialism and Marxism.

Liebknecht and Hägerström, like many other authors, attempted to make their viewpoints plausible by comparing Marxism's historical determinism with religious faith. The error in this comparison in this context is that the religious conceptions, which must be assumed are intended, contain the promise of personal compensation for the sacrifices made in the service of God; a believer who carries out "God's work" and thereby loses his life receives a heavenly reward in a new existence. Such a belief is not provided by Marxism, and the substitute which it gives—the idea that other men, possibly future generations, will obtain happiness—cannot play a similar role as a personal incentive. In Hägerström the view of a primitive certainty of belief on the part of the proletariat is obvious; it is reminiscent of the earlier idea, commonly expressed by "enlightened" people with a blending of sympathy and mild contempt, that "the people" needed and blindly accepted religious ideas. Corresponding lines of thought in Liebknecht and other doctrinaire Marxists are even stranger inasmuch as they are combined with a personal faith in the inevitability of socialism; from this point of view, however, either the proletariat's certainty of belief ought to be considered unnecessary for the victory of socialism or else such a certainty of belief should necessarily be assumed to appear at a certain stage of development and thus propaganda for its value consequently be regarded as superfluous. Liebknecht's view is one of many examples of the thoughtless coupling of the materialist conception of history and historical determinism with the conviction of the decisive importance of ideological conceptions.

Closely related to this subject is the question to what degree historical determinism has influenced political activities. In the statement cited, Kelsen probably means not only that determinism tends to weaken the moral force of the workers, but also that it leads to a curtailment of the party's positive and practical work. When Steffen on different occasions in Sweden spoke of developmental fatalism, he also evidently proceeded from the assumption that belief in the "coming" of socialism led to a certain passivity in regard to positive reform work. This opinion probably has some legitimacy as far as early Swedish Social Democracy is concerned. This helps explain the relatively scant interest in practical activity manifested by Social Democrats in the beginning. It is obvious that the disinclination to formulate concrete plans for the socialist society is related to Marx's doctrine that socialism must come, but that its structure could not be predicted. To further clarify the role of determinism is not possible: it is woven into the whole of early Social Democratic ideology. In general it can probably be said that determinism has been more of an ideological embellishment used in argumentation than an independently operative motive. This has been especially obvious during recent times. When a measure is proposed, it is said that society is ripe for it, that life demands it, that it falls in the line of development; when a proposal is repudiated, its rejection is justified in like manner. There is hardly anything left of historical determinism apart from references of this kind to "life," "development," "change." These expressions have taken on some of the same magical character ascribed to, for example, "God," "natural rights," and "Reason" in the debates of bygone days.